D0004274

Human Biology and Behavior / An Anthropological Perspective

Mark L. Weiss
Wayne State University

Alan E. Mann
University of Pennsylvania

SCOTT, FORESMAN/LITTLE, BROWN HIGHER EDUCATION
A Division of Scott, Foresman and Company
Glenview, Illinois   London, England

To Sandy and Michelle

Though Pedantry denies,
It's plain the Bible means
That Solomon grew wise
While talking with his Queens
— W. B. Yeats

Credits are listed at the back of the book beginning on page 655, which constitutes a legal extension of the copyright page.

Front cover, Background, Chris Sorensen/The Stock Market; top, Robert P. Carr/Bruce Coleman Inc.; bottom, F. Jackson/Bruce Coleman Inc.; line art, Norm Frisch

Back cover (top), Robert P. Carr/Bruce Coleman Inc. left, line art, Norm Frisch

Library of Congress Cataloging-in-Publication Data
Weiss, Mark L.
    Human biology and behavior : an anthropological perspective / Mark
  L. Weiss, Alan E. Mann.—5th ed.
      p.   cm.
  Bibliography: p.
  Includes index.
  ISBN 0–673–39880–3
  1. Physical anthropology.   2. Human evolution.   I. Mann, Alan E.
II. Title.
GN60.W44   1989
573--dc20   89–10267
                                              CIP

3   4   5   6 — KPF — 94 93 92 91 90

Preface to the Fifth Edition

Human Biology and Behavior is intended to introduce students to physical anthropology. The book begins with a description of the modern fields of anthropology and their integration with the social, biological, and medical sciences, followed by a discussion of general evolutionary thought. With evolution as a framework, we then deal with the long-term biological and behavioral trends in primate and human evolution, ending with the hows and whys of modern human variation.

An introductory text should emphasize two major themes, adaptation and evolution, and their interrelationships with successful behavior. We have tried to present the basic data of modern physical anthropology within a framework of these themes, concentrating on being intelligible and on using a minimum of jargon, but not oversimplifying. We have not given neat conclusions to problems to make it easy for students. If a question, such as the origin of anatomically modern humans, is currently unresolved, we list the alternative hypotheses, summarize the data, and then allow students to draw their own conclusions. We have also made every effort to integrate material from branches of anthropology, such as archaeology and ethnology.

Since many introductory students may not encounter another anthropology course, we have tried to convey how anthropological thinking can be applied to help answer significant questions: Why do people differ at every level, from molecules to behaviors? How much of our behavior, if any, is built into us? How does culture affect the path of evolution today? How is the aging process we all pass through related to our evolutionary legacy? What is a proper diet? Why do we have back problems? What does anthropology tell us about the spread of epidemic disease in past and present societies? The uniqueness of anthropology lies not so much in its data—which often come from other disciplines—as in its way of analyzing and interrelating the data. We hope that the comparative, evolutionary view of human existence comes through in the book and that students will use the perspective in analyzing current and future issues.

The fifth edition is marked by significant updating as well as attempts at increased clarity where necessary. Chapter 2 contains a detailed discussion of molecular genetics, as well as the more usual treatments of Mendelian and population genetics. This provides the groundwork for an expanded coverage of the use of molecular techniques in investigating phylogeny, modern human variability, and even forensic applications. We also continue the tradition of discussing genetics prior to any detailed investigation of evolutionary forces. We feel that the latter can best be appreciated after achieving a firm grasp of genetic concepts. The introduction to evolution has expanded coverage of classic Neo-Darwinian thought and of recent challenges to traditional ideas about the rates and modes of evolution (Chapter 3). The vertebrate evolution section (Chapter 4) provides a discussion of the suggested events that marked the Mesozoic/Cenozoic boundary, as well as additional comparative illustrations. The coverage of the primates is now organized into three chapters (5, 6, and 7), with an introductory overview of taxonomy and distribution followed by chapters on behavior and evolution. The primate evolution chapter (Chapter 7), like those devoted to human evolution (Chapters 8, 9, and 10), reflects the reevaluation of primate and human evolution necessitated by recent fossil discoveries.

One particularly noteworthy change in this edition is our decision to modify hominoid taxonomy to conform to the increasing amounts of comparative evidence which closely links chimps, gorillas, and humans. The text now describes the family Hominidae as being composed of two subfamilies, Paninae and Homininae. All discussions of human evolution refer to the hominines. We realize that this may create some initial confusion in the classroom, but in our judgment the importance of students understanding and recognizing our close relationships with the African apes overshadows the difficulties. An introduction to the study of hominine evolution (Chapter 8) has been completely rewritten, incorporating discussions of current interest, including taphonomy and dietary reconstructions. Chapters 9 and 10, which describe the hominine fossil record, have been revised to reflect recent debates concerning the nature of the evidence for culture in human evolution.

The section on modern human variation continues to be updated in light of new developments in molecular biology, such as linkage relationships in genetic disease. The chapters on human variability have been reorganized. Chapter 11 deals with variability as the outcome of genetic and nongenetic factors and discusses a number of ways in which to assess variation in human populations. Chapter 12 considers human polymorphisms, with an expanded coverage of the molecular and evolutionary aspects of variability, especially restriction fragment length polymorphisms. The chapter on the biological history of human populations (Chapter 14) still investigates the concept of "race," but greater emphasis is placed upon the use of genetic markers to trace population history, and population structure of modern groups is now included.

Throughout this edition we have tried to improve clarity of passages deemed difficult by students. The glossary too has been significantly modified, and the first text mention of a listed word is presented in italics. A complimentary instructor's manual is available to instructors requesting it from the publisher on school letterhead.

Students are often justifiably awed by the coverage of physical anthropology; it covers virtually everything about people and evolution. As might be imagined, no one person can be an expert on all the relevant areas; hence our coauthorship. Although each of us concentrated on his own area of specialization, we cooperated throughout the book's development. Being trained at the same institution helped provide the necessary commonality of background.

We would like to thank the many students and colleagues who provided much sound advice during the preparation of all five editions. We extend our gratitude to the reviewers of the fifth edition: Robert Halberstein, University of Miami; John Lukacs, University of Oregon; Joseph Mannino, University of Wisconsin–Green Bay; Jeffrey H. Schwartz, University of Pittsburgh; Robert Sussman, Washington University. In addition, one of us (MLW) would particularly like to thank Alec Jeffreys for his aid in pursuing the applications of molecular biology to physical anthropology, and one of us (AEM) would especially like to thank Janet Monge for her help in all phases of preparation of this edition. We would like to thank Peggy Gordon for the thoroughly professional manner in which she dealt with all aspects of the production of this edition. We also thank editors Harriet Prentiss and Julie Howell of our publisher Scott, Foresman/Little, Brown. We express our appreciation to Linda Darga and Karen Davis for preparing the Instructor's Manual. We especially thank Professor S. L. Washburn for his encouragement and help during our apprenticeship at Berkeley and for his contributions to anthropology.

Finally, thanks to Emily, David, Evan, and Laura, and to our wives Sandy and Michelle.

Contents

1

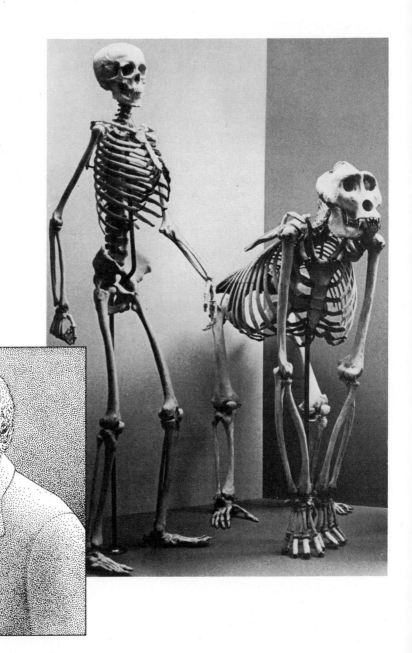

Anthropologists apply a holistic approach to the study of our species to discover ties among aspects of human functions and activities.

The Perspective of Physical Anthropology

The world is not as simple a place as people used to think it was. Five hundred years ago, a European man could look around his world and believe he truly understood much of what he saw; what he could not see was not meant to be understood. Animals and plants, it was supposed, looked as they always had and always would. The rivers and oceans, mountains and deserts, were just where they always had been. European man was the highest creature, created to rule the planet; woman was made to be his helpmate, remaining in the background, raising his children, and always providing solace and a hot meal. It was a comfortable world to believe in, but by the end of the seventeenth century, this narrow, limited image began to crumble. Brought about by industrial development and the decay of the old social and economic orders, people increasingly questioned the nature of the world, asking why things were as they were and how they got to be that way.

It took more than a century for natural historians and scientists to break through the established ideas of European thought. In the early nineteenth century, Charles Lyell, a British geologist, showed that even the earth's appearance is not fixed for all time, for its topography is slowly but constantly changing. Charles Darwin and Alfred Russel Wallace proposed a theory of organic evolution that not only accounted for the diversity of life but also suggested that life changes over time in response to the demands of the environment. Nowhere was the change in thinking more drastic than in the way humans viewed themselves. An important consequence of the Age of Discovery in the sixteenth century was that returning explorers brought reports about the great variety of other human societies and races. Europeans, however, believed that their way of life was the ideal, their ideological and social systems were the best, and they alone had been created in God's image. It was understandably unsettling to hear that human existence was as diverse as wildflowers in the fields. The idea that humans, like other animals, had descended from more primitive forms was anathema to many nineteenth-century minds.

FIGURE 1.1. Columbus being received at the court of Barcelona in February 1493.
In addition to bringing back six Native Americans, Columbus brought many items,
including their mineral products, food, and clothing.

People in Europe were fascinated by the tales the travelers brought
back of peoples living in strange lands with even stranger ways of life.
Many individuals from Africa and the Americas were exhibited to incred-
ulous Europeans (Figure 1.1). The strangers were regarded as imperfect
copies of their European counterparts in social organization, religious
thought, and physical appearance. The French natural historian Georges
de Buffon (1707–1788) described the Native American:

> Although the savage of the New World is about the same height as man
> in our world, this does not suffice for him to constitute an exception to
> the general fact that all living nature has become smaller on that continent.
> The savage is feeble, he has neither hair nor beard, and no ardor whatever
> for his female; although swifter than the European because he is better
> accustomed to running, he is, on the other hand, less strong in body; he is
> also less sensitive. . . .[1]*

*See page 613 for notes to Chapter 1.

Buffon's inaccurate knowledge of Native American populations did not discourage him from describing them in derogatory terms. Fortunately, other European and American writers were not so biased, and they compiled accurate data on the living patterns of non-Europeans. Information, both biased and unbiased, on the variation among human populations around the world was gathered throughout the eighteenth and nineteenth centuries. The modern science of anthropology began with the attempts to understand and relate these accumulated data.

Anthropology

The word *anthropology* is a compound of two ancient Greek words (*anthropos = man; logia = study of*) that was first used in the sixteenth century, although humans were studied long before the subject had a name. The ancient Greeks and Romans wrote vast accounts of the habits, manners, and appearance of their neighbors. Like those of later Europeans, these comparisons were most often flattering to the writer's group. While such early studies were generally self-serving, modern anthropology has come far in helping people understand each other. In its current form the field is generally divided into four subfields: cultural anthropology, linguistic anthropology, archaeological anthropology, and physical anthropology. Although each focuses on different aspects of being human, they all share certain interests and perspectives that define both the field and its borders with other social and natural sciences. Anthropologists try to look at problems on a broad scale to discover the interconnectedness of human activities and functioning. Professionals in other disciplines tend to concentrate on one aspect of human activity, for example, political scientists on politics, economists on the economy, and psychologists on the behavior of individuals. By contrast, an anthropologist with a primary interest in economic systems will look at the way in which subsistence patterns affect and are affected by a group's religious beliefs, art, politics, social networks, and the like. As we shall see in later chapters, there are often very important ties between various aspects of a group's behavior. The anthropologist's attempt to take a broad view of the human situation and the interrelationship of its parts is called *holism.*

One aspect of holism in anthropology is its biocultural perspective. Anthropologists often look beyond social activities themselves. They may study the ways the social behaviors and culture of a group interplay with the members' biology (Figure 1.2). For example, how do technological changes affect the health of a population? In what ways did human behavior mold the evolution of our ancestors? Because anthropologists must often contend with less than complete information, holism is usually more a goal than a reality. Yet the approach is a distinguishing characteristic of the discipline.

In part because of its holistic perspective, anthropology lends itself to *cultural relativism,* or the attempt not to judge people's behavior by the standards of the anthropologist's own society. It is not up to the scientist to say that one group is better than another or that a group's approach to a problem is either good or bad. Within a culture's *own context* we can identify the causes and consequences of behavior, alternatives that other

groups use, the historical development of activities, and possible future paths, but it is generally not the scientist's role to make value judgments about the society. This is not to say, however, that cultural relativism can serve to justify ethical horrors such as genocide.

Often behaviors that appear peculiar or abnormal to an American make sense in the context of another culture. Many Americans, used to eating beef and other meats, have looked at pictures of undernourished people in India and remarked about the "silliness" of those who suffer hunger when all they need do is slaughter and eat their sacred cows. Yet anthropologists who, in keeping with cultural relativism, have considered this interplay of religion and nutrition, suggest that there is a definite logic to such practices. Marvin Harris, an anthropologist at the University of Florida, notes that because much of India is deforested, the dung of these sacred cows serves as a prime source of cooking fuel. The manure is also a major source of fertilizer, and the cows themselves produce oxen for farming. Perhaps the people are actually better off letting the animals survive to provide a constant source of energy than killing them for a short-term supply of protein followed by a long-term future without cows, fuel, or fertilizer.

Human behavior may be logical even though the logic may not be immediately apparent to a casual observer. By putting behaviors in the broader framework of the total culture, the anthropologist can demonstrate the logic.

Members of a culture do, however, tend to view their own behaviors as the "right" ones. This cultural self-centeredness is referred to as *ethnocentrism*. By showing that other cultures with different histories and different environments operate under different constraints, anthropologists help to dispel ethnocentric views that have long been the basis for discrimination and exploitation. There are many cases too where cultures with similar backgrounds meet a similar need with alternative solutions, with neither necessarily being better. This does not mean that everything that people do is logical or beneficial. Anthropology, however, is illuminating when it points out certain inconsistencies in our own actions, such as the self-destructive behaviors of drinking and smoking that are widely practiced and accepted in our culture (Figure 1.3). Anthropology can thus be a liberating science.

Ethnocentrism is by no means unique to our culture. Throughout time many groups have belittled the appearance and behavior of others. Nineteenth-century Japanese found the "hairy and smelly" Europeans repugnant. Africans who covet the land of the Pygmies of central Africa use the physical and cultural differences of this group as an excuse for their exploitation. Ethnocentrism is found more often than we would like to admit.

Lastly, anthropology is a comparative science that describes and compares cultural behaviors, language structure, and physical attributes. By looking at variations in behavior and biology, we can attempt to understand the association between specific features. For example, does the color of a people's skin relate to variations in climate or nutrition? Are there any commonalities in family structure among groups in which mobility is of major importance? Questions of this sort can be answered through the use of comparative data.

Appreciation of the ways others function can be of practical importance. Humans evolved for millions of years as members of small groups in which everyone knew everyone else. This is quite different from modern society, where we interact daily with many people whom we neither know nor can predict. Doctors, social workers, teachers, government agents, and businesspeople must interact with those they do

FIGURE 1.3
Not all of our activities are either logical or healthy.

not understand. With the increasing internationalization of business and the marked cultural heterogeneity of Western countries, this situation is becoming more common. By being sensitized to the functioning of other peoples, we can begin to improve the operations of both the people and the society. As described later, this is a goal of applied anthropology.

Cultural Anthropology

Cultural anthropology tends to be popularly associated with study of exotic, "primitive" peoples. Although most early anthropologists did record and analyze non-Western cultures, the field has expanded. Today the perspectives and techniques of cultural anthropology are applied to all peoples, whether salvaging information about disappearing cultures or focusing on a modern Western society. In part, earlier anthropologists sought to record non-Western cultures before they disappeared under the impact of colonialism. In some cases disease, genocide, and the helplessness created by cultural collapse eliminated not only the culture but also the people themselves. The description of a culture—the traditional crafts, languages, social relations, religious beliefs, and the like—is known as *ethnography*.

Ethnology

Once anthropologists have amassed a large body of descriptions about a culture, they can go a step beyond and try to explain some of the diversity. A comparative, cross-cultural analysis of societies is called *ethnology*. While ethnography is a description of a culture, ethnology is more theoretical. Using the basic data of ethnography, the ethnologist looks for recurring patterns of behavior and explanations for them.

The basic data of the ethnographer are obtained by carefully recording observed behavior over an extended period. Whereas most social scientists use a statistical, quantitative approach to data, the cultural anthropologist's technique is more qualitative. Sociologists who are interested in residence patterns, for instance, may utilize census and questionnaire data to plot population movement, to note the percentage of adults who live near their birthplace, and so on. Cultural anthropologists traditionally do not gather information this way but rather use the ethnographic or participant observation approach (Figure 1.4). The anthropologist becomes a member of the group while observing its activities and interviewing individuals who are knowledgeable about their culture, asking questions such as: Who changes residence? Under what conditions? To what extent do people follow the stated norms? To what extent are the ideals ignored? How do individual preferences and idiosyncrasies affect such decisions?

Recording Cultural Behavior

Recording cultural behavior is not always a straightforward task. The biases and mind-set of both the observer and informant can influence the observations. The wording used in describing an event can subtly influence the interpretations. While the anthropologist's description

FIGURE 1.4
The cultural anthropologist lives with and observes people to gain insight into the functioning of their society.

of a culture is fuller than that of other social scientists, it is less easily manipulated and analyzed with statistics and may be more subjective.

Over the years, many field anthropologists have documented the cultures and societies of a wide variety of groups, often at different points in time. This research enables us to compare patterns of activity among groups as well as to trace changes in behaviors within a group. Once patterns are detected, various models or theories about the working of a culture can be used in forming an explanation. Anthropologists do not all agree about how cultures are structured, how they function, how they have changed, or even what aspects of culture are worthy of study. Some focus on the material aspects of a culture, while others look at the symbolism present in all cultures. Others look at the ways cultural activities help a group adapt to a particular environment or ecological setting, whereas some are more interested in the ways culture affects the development of people's personalities.

One lesson that has been learned is that people are human no matter where they are born or how they are raised. Non-Western cultures are not the products of less intelligent or savage people, nor are they "primitive." Cultures are the outcome of many historical, ecological, and psychological factors, and they are a mechanism of coping with life's opportunities and problems. Some groups may be more technologically developed than others, but this is by no means an indication of superiority or inferiority. Given the natural resources available to Eskimos and their need for mobility, for example, they created a rich and innovative hunting technology.

Applied Anthropology

Decades ago, it was apparent to a small number of cultural anthropologists that the same approach used to study nonindustrialized societies could be effectively applied to the study of Westernized cultures or subcultures. Additionally, some felt that this research could be practically applied to helping various social interactions run more smoothly and effectively. This branch of cultural anthropology is known as *applied anthropology*. Some applied anthropologists are involved in formulating public policy, such as the distribution of scarce resources. These professionals will often work in a bureaucracy to try to channel goods, funds, and services in a manner that is harmonious with the needs and goals of both the bureaucracy and the people. In addition to their use in Third World countries, major American government agencies and corporations employ applied anthropologists as mediators. They also use them to smooth social interactions within their organization, to explore alternative solutions to problems, and to understand the beliefs and practices of the organization itself.

Medical anthropology is a growing sphere of applied anthropology. Anthropologists in this field work with the medical system in an effort to mesh available medical services with the client's cultural beliefs and values regarding health and disease. Members of different cultures or even subcultures may have widely varying beliefs about health and disease. The medical model of the dominant American culture ascribes problems to physical causes such as microbes or aging, although many people still attribute disease to supernatural causes. We also have many folk beliefs that may or may not have some validity, such as getting your feet wet causes colds, chicken soup cures colds, and toads cause warts. Such beliefs are an important part of a culture. Knowing these beliefs may be important in obtaining patient cooperation. If a person does not appreciate that diet can ease or worsen an illness, efforts to change diet may be wasted. Medical anthropologists may also look at the interconnections between health or medical systems and other parts of a culture. In the West, we expect ill people to "act the part" and thus we confine and isolate them. Not all societies see illness this way. In some societies family members and religious systems are much more involved in care and curing than in the West. Illness may have direct ramifications on economics and other aspects of life. In keeping with this holistic approach, medical anthropologists also look at the biological side of disease. How, for instance, do certain cultural practices affect disease patterns? How do people adapt biologically to disease?

Linguistic Anthropology

Linguistic anthropology specializes in the examination of language, another form of human behavior. All normal human beings can learn to use language, that is, a spoken, open-ended communication system. Because it is open-ended, language can communicate any concrete or abstract thought, even if the thought has never been expressed before. All human languages are capable of communicating any thought or feeling within the culture; "primitive" groups do not have "simple" languages.

Humans possess unique biological structures in the vocal cords and muscles and the soft anatomy of the throat that make spoken language possible. There also seems to be a number of unique developments in the brain that permit the production of speech sounds and their organization into meaningful strings of words as well as the understanding of the speech of others. At about the age of eighteen to twenty-eight months, a child will spontaneously begin to learn the language he or she hears, without parental guidance or encouragement. Greater understanding of the nature of language and its biological basis may come from observations of the way children learn to produce these speech sounds and to incorporate the rules that govern correct language usage into their brain. By examining the communication systems that our close living primate relatives, like chimpanzees, employ in the wild and by attempting to teach human language to these apes, we may also be able to identify those language-related biological features that are central to speech production in humans.

Given the crucial importance of language in human development, scholars from a number of fields, including psychology, biology, anthropology, and linguistics, are all involved in its study. Anthropologists are interested in examining the range of modern human languages and in understanding the structural elements common to all. Identification of these common patterns provides not only insight into the nature of modern languages but also clues for the reconstruction of language origins. The evolution of language is one of the most important events in human history. By looking at the fossil bones, stone tools, and other evidence of our evolutionary past as well as the data from the study of modern languages, anthropologists seek to understand how and why language developed. Certainly, language is crucial to the development and maintenance of human societies (Figure 1.5). Without the abilities language offers for organizing and communicating complex thoughts, subtle emotions, and abstract concepts, human behavior and culture as we know it would not be possible.

FIGURE 1.5
Not all language is spoken. Much of what we communicate is conveyed by nonverbal means.

Archaeological Anthropology

The discovery, excavation, and reconstruction of the fragmentary remains of past human cultural activity are the responsibility of archaeologists. Anthropological archaeologists are usually concerned with the remains of prehistoric societies, those early human cultures that did not leave written records. The investigations of the relics of the great civilizations of the Mediterranean and Middle East are normally performed by archaeologists of another sort: classical archaeologists. Because prehistoric sites often represent the most ancient of our ancestors, those peoples who lived long before the discovery of agriculture, animal domestication, and the use of metals, the work of the anthropological archaeologist usually involves the analysis of those materials that will be preserved, such as stone and bone tools, broken animal bones, fire-blackened rock, and burials. Highly perishable materials like plant remains and insects are only rarely discovered. The scarcity and poor quality of the remains found at many locations have increasingly forced archaeologists to turn to sophisticated methods to wring every bit of detail possible about an ancient culture from available evidence. Ideally, these bits and pieces of the past provide the clues that allow archaeologists to reconstruct the lives of the peoples who once occupied the site, living on the local resources and passing on their cultural traditions and their genes to their children (Figure 1.6). Archaeologists want to learn how this human group established a long-term, successful adaptation to their environment and why their society disappeared. Realistically, they seldom achieve this goal. They can do little to reconstruct social systems, religious beliefs, and marriage practices from the few scraps left in the ground after a culture disappears. Sometimes the archaeologists must draw conclusions from what is not present, gaining insight, for example, from the absence of burials, fire, and other signs of complex behavior.

The details archaeologists painstakingly piece together can also yield important information about the general pattern of human cultural history. Perhaps the most basic of these questions concerns the very nature and origins of human existence. Just how does one identify uniquely human behaviors in the archaeological record? If chipped stone tools, campsites, fire, and broken animal bones are discovered, does this mean these ancestors were able to think and behave as we do? Just how far back in time do humanlike qualities extend?

Other general questions archaeologists examine are the following: Has human evolution involved a slow, gradual increase in complexity

and sophistication of tools, weapons, and other artifacts? Are certain specialized patterns of adaptation characteristic of particular environments? What are the circumstances surrounding the invention of agriculture, which seems to have occurred almost simultaneously in several parts of the world around 10,000 years ago? Why did some extremely successful cultures in seemingly rich environments completely break down? Answers to these and other questions can help us to understand the nature of human adaptation and the role of such factors as migration patterns, population density, diseases, and subsistence patterns in the molding of modern human societies.

Physical anthropology is the subdiscipline of the field that deals with the biology of past and present humans (Figure 1.7). In keeping with the holistic approach, however, the physical anthropologist looks beyond purely biological phenomena to discover how biology and behavior interact with each other and with the environment. Generally the field is recognized as having three branches which often overlap: *paleoanthropology (paleo = old)*, or the study of fossil humans and near relatives; primatology, or the study of primates; and the study of modern human variability and adaptability.

Paleoanthropology, which documents the biological history of humans, can also help the archaeologist to reconstruct past human behavior. Examining the fossil evidence of human evolution, paleoanthropologists have begun to understand the intimate relationship between biology and behavior. They have found a biological basis for culture in the size and complexity of the brain, in upright posture, and in other anatomical evidence. When these facts are described and documented by the paleoanthropologist, they help archaeologists with their reconstructions.

Primatologists study primates, the group of mammals that includes humans, apes, monkeys, and some less well-known forms called prosimians. In addition to being an important discipline in its own right, primatology offers the study of human evolution a sense of continuity and valuable means of comparison. Some primatologists focus on the behavior of our relatives in part for the insights it can offer into our own behavior and that of our ancestors (Figure 1.8). Others look at the physiology, anatomy, genetics, and biochemistry of living primates for help in clarifying our own biology. Sometimes it is even possible to construct ties between the biology and behavior of nonhuman primates. Medical researchers are particularly interested in using primates for research because they are so similar to humans.

Specialists in modern human genetics and physiology document the limits of human variability. We know there are many ways in which people vary. Some of these differences are unique to each person; others characterize whole groups. Anthropologists have devised many means to document the ways in which people can vary and have gathered much data to plot the distribution of human variations. Beyond the descriptive level, human biologists have demonstrated the environmental and

Physical Anthropology

FIGURE 1.7
This famous drawing of man by Leonardo da Vinci (1452–1519) illustrates an early concern with the biology of our species.

FIGURE 1.8
Some primatologists are interested in behavior observation.

cultural factors that influenced these characteristics. They attempt to document how variations help humans to adapt biologically to their environment.

The Meaning of Variation

Physical anthropology gained much from the mass of information about non-Europeans gathered earlier, especially in the seventeenth century, when skilled anatomists like Edward Tyson (1650–1708) dissected the bodies of human beings and apes and described the similarities between them. Modern physical anthropology derives directly from Charles Darwin's *The Origin of Species,* published in 1859.

Darwin's work on evolution changed the discipline's emphasis and point of view markedly, although not as rapidly as one might like. Before and even for a long time after Darwin, physical anthropologists studied people by classifying them according to racial stereotypes, invariant pictures of human populations that assigned everyone to one of the categories. Physical anthropologists measured living people to find the height of a typical European, the size of a typical Asian's brain, and the color of a typical sub-Saharan African's skin. The fossil evidence was categorized in the same way: If a fossil excavated in China did not look exactly like one found in Java from the same period, the two fossils were assigned to different species. Behavior patterns, too, were handled inflexibly: Sub-Saharan Africans were lazy, Jews greedy, Asians inscrutable, but contemporary northern Europeans beyond reproach. Variability within a group was disregarded; differences between groups were considered all important and ancient. Thus were a series of stereotypes, or typologies, established.

Colonialism fed this typological view of humans and spread it abroad. Europeans eased their consciences when they exploited others by proving "scientifically" that the subjugated people were, and always had been, less human than they. It was easier to think of people as unchanging.

Our understanding of past and present human variability has changed radically in the last few decades, partly because of advances in genetics, paleontology, and ethology (the study of animal behavior), and partly because of changes in social values. We now appreciate past and present human variability, and we no longer search for stereotypes because we recognize that they do not allow for that variability. Physical anthropologists today study real populations, not imagined ideals. In both living and extinct populations, variation *within* a group interests us as much as variation *between* groups. Looking at both kinds of variation seems the best way to reconstruct the path along which we evolved and to recognize how we are changing today. The direction of evolution is to produce adaptation to an environment, to make the search for food easier, and to give protection against climate, predators, diseases, and anything else in the environment that affects our ability to survive and reproduce. From an evolutionary point of view, it is fortunate that all people are different, for variability ensures the ability of our species to survive in a constantly changing environment. Some people have bigger teeth, some resist diseases more effectively, and some are taller. If people did not vary, groups could not adapt to changes in their environment.

We adapt to changing conditions in ways similar to those of other animals. We can adapt biologically via biological evolution or culturally by changing our behavior. The two means are not unrelated, for our biological makeup greatly affects our cultural abilities. Our ancestors 3 million years ago may have been biologically incapable of controlling fire, burying their dead, or communicating as we do today. Alternatively, the highly technological, urban environment most of us live in may be placing demands on us that we are biologically ill equipped to handle. Thus we see that the interaction between our biology and our culture is complicated and that physical anthropology has relevance to some of our present problems.

Anthropology as a Holistic Science

Westerners treat nature as something that can and should be dominated. In this, we view ourselves as just a step below the gods; the world and all things in it are to be exploited. Lately, however, we have begun to see what many non-Western people knew long ago: Humans are part of nature, not apart from it; to survive we must learn to live within the restrictions imposed by the environment. The fact that our culturally determined uses of the environment must mesh with our biology is at last gaining acceptance in our society. The world is not infinitely plentiful, and the human body is not infinitely adaptable. If we are to endure, our biology and our behavior must complement each other.

As a holistic science, anthropology can offer a unique perspective on many human situations and problems. This perspective can lead to innovative solutions or at least new lines of investigation. If we want to feed the undernourished peoples in Africa, it is not enough to send boats of grain. We must know that the infrastructure of the country (the roads, transport systems, government agencies) can handle the task. We must also make sure that the political climate does not preclude equitable distribution and that the influx of food will not simply create a situation that allows exploitation by those who own trucks. Will the donated food drive down the price of locally produced commodities, thus leading to lowered production? Is the food appropriate to the recipients: Do they have the fuel to prepare it? Will they accept it as a reasonable source of nutrition? Do they know how to prepare it? Too often solutions are proposed without full appreciation of their ramifications.

Similarly, a large-scale view can be helpful in understanding medical problems. How do new diseases develop? How do they spread? What cultural factors affect epidemics? Such questions are of obvious significance to situations like the global spread of AIDS, yet it has not always been obvious that such questions must be asked.

Anthropology can offer ways of tackling many important questions. For generations, there has been discussion of the roles of biology and culture in our propensity for warfare. Is it a purely learned behavior dictated by our culture, or did we evolve as predators? Are our awesome weapons merely cultural substitutes for large teeth and long claws? To prevent future holocausts we must know more about the causes of human aggression, a subject much studied by physical anthropologists. Has evolution built aggression into our brain structure, as some have suggested? Or, as is more likely, is a behavior such as aggression learned during socialization? Our brain allows for a tremendous amount of variation; physical anthropologists must seek the limits of this variability.

What are our cultural and biological limits? To find an answer we must look at what we are today and how we came to be that way. The physical anthropologist's three major specialties—the fossil evidence of human evolution (paleoanthropology), primate biology and behavior, and modern human variability—all help answer this question, and we can add information from the other divisions of anthropology and from the life sciences and the social sciences.

By studying hominine (our "human" ancestors) fossils we can try to reconstruct our ancestors' appearance. Were they large brained? Could they walk on two legs? With the answers to these basic questions, physical anthropologists can attempt to answer more intriguing questions:

How was our ancestors' anatomy related to their behavior? If they were bipedal (walking upright on two feet), what does this reveal about how they lived? Does it imply that they needed to use their hands for things other than getting around? Did they use their hands for carrying food and tools? What does the ability to make tools tell us about their social organization? How might using tools have affected our ancestors' biological evolution? Why are all humans able to make tools and speak languages?

We can find some answers to these questions by looking at the biology and behavior of our close relatives, the monkeys and apes, particularly our closest relatives, the chimpanzees. What does their behavior reveal to us about human evolution? Do chimps ever walk upright? If so, why and when are they bipedal?

We know that people are variable today, but how and why do they differ? How have the evolutionary processes molded the genetic differences between groups? To what extent have people adapted to environmental problems by nongenetic means?

These questions can be of pragmatic as well as academic interest. Not all people can digest the sugar in milk; drinking it makes them ill. In fact, this is true of most of the world's adolescents and adults. What sense does it make, politically or biologically, to send milk to people suffering from malnutrition? Knowledge of normal human variation can aid in the diagnosis and treatment of disease, the assessment of a child's growth and development, the investigation of nutritional adequacy, and the formation of public policy.

The remainder of this book focuses on physical anthropology, which, it has been noted, depends upon a knowledge of evolution. Modern evolutionary theory possesses great explanatory abilities. With an awareness of what evolution is and is not, we will be better able to understand the depth and dimensions of questions such as those asked above. It is only with a fuller understanding that we can ever hope for workable solutions.

The Emergence of Evolutionary Theory

Clearly, few ideas have changed our thinking about ourselves and the world around us more than the theory of evolution. It is the foundation on which physical anthropology and indeed all the life sciences are built and the framework within which information about any living entity can be organized and made understandable. It is hard to imagine how scientists studied humans and other forms of life without knowing anything about evolution. Although some still claim that evolution remains only a theory, we have more than enough evidence to demonstrate that evolution is a fact and that it has affected, and continues to affect, every living thing. All animals and plants, including the living, dead, and extinct, are ultimately related by having descended from the first life forms on the planet. Evolution is a fact, but the mechanisms that underlie its operation continue to be investigated and debated. The study of evolution, like evolution itself, is a dynamic process, with new patterns of understanding emerging all the time. In the past several decades, molecular geneticists have refined our knowledge of evolution from the level of the species and the individual to the level of the individual cells and further still to the chemicals within those cells that specify how hereditary material is transmitted from one generation to the next.

Before we go from full-size people down to molecular structure, however, which will be the subject of Chapters 2 and 3, it will help to see how a viable theory of evolution was developed. Only with such an understanding will we be prepared to look at the molecular, cellular, individual, and populational basis for evolutionary change.

Pre-Darwinian Theorists

Theories of evolution preceded Charles Darwin by about a hundred years. Until the mid-eighteenth century, natural history was a gentleman's pastime. Studying all the things around us—the plants, animals, soil, and water—was a fascinating hobby, but these studies only raised new questions. Europeans who had set out in the Age of Discovery to almost every part of the earth returned with precious metals, gems, spices, and silks. They also brought back samples of the flora and fauna (plants and animals) and sometimes "strange-looking" human beings as well.

By 1700, natural historians knew about staggering numbers of plants and animals from Africa, the Americas, and Asia; in fact, it was becoming almost impossible to keep track of them. Some new items that became known to the general population kept their native names: The words *potato, yam, tobacco, orangutan,* and *gorilla* were adopted into European languages. But most native names, if known at all, were unpronounceable for European tongues. One solution was to give animals and plants names that could be understood by all educated Europeans. These would have to come from the "universal" languages, Greek and Latin.

Linnaeus   One eighteenth-century naturalist assumed the enormous task of classifying and naming all living things (Figure 1.9). Carolus Linnaeus (1707–1778), a Swedish botanist, noticed similarities in the structures of many kinds of plants and animals. He believed these might reflect "ideal ground plans" that were followed when the plants or animals were created. Finding only a few kinds of structural organization among many types of plants or animals, Linnaeus attempted to group all living things by placing them in categories based on their common ground plans. He thought of these categories of plants and animals with similar physical features as fixed, permanent groupings. As he set up his taxonomy (system of classification), Linnaeus did not think of plants and animals with similar structures as being closely related by descent; all they shared was the same general plan.

Linnaeus published his most complete taxonomy in 1758 as the *Systema naturae* (System of Nature), a hierarchic arrangement of all known animals and plants, in descending categories assigned by common physical features (see Table 4.1 for an example of the Linnaean tax-

**FIGURE 1.9
Carolus Linnaeus in 1775
(engraving after the
portrait by Alexander
Roslin).**

onomy). Linnaeus felt his classification reflected the creator's use of numerous ground plans, but others saw in the groupings some sort of evolutionary association. They thought these physical resemblances might indicate actual biological relationships. Later natural historians incorporated his taxonomy into evolutionary structure.

Cuvier A few decades later, another scientist was spending his years carefully comparing the structures of one animal with those of another. Baron Georges Cuvier (1769–1832) contributed much to our growing understanding of the living world. Under this French naturalist's direction one of the major biological sciences, comparative anatomy, came into being. Mineralized animal bones and teeth found in local limestone quarries were given to Cuvier to identify. He demonstrated that the bones did not belong to any known *living* animals. Bones of extinct animals had been turning up for centuries, and people had debated whether animals could become extinct, a reasonable question given the traditional belief that all the animals ever created were still alive.

Cuvier was convinced by the bones that some animals had become extinct. But how? Religious faith worsened his dilemma. To resolve this problem he proposed an intriguing theory, *catastrophism*. According to this theory, in the past the planet had gone through a series of worldwide catastrophes, in which all living things were destroyed. A new creation followed each catastrophe, and the newly created animals and plants survived, fixed and unchanging, until the next catastrophe wiped them out. This ingenious idea protected Cuvier's religious faith yet made certain that the evidence of extinct life would no longer be denied. Recently, the idea of worldwide animal catastrophes has been revived as a way to explain the sudden disappearance of the dinosaurs about 65 million years ago (see Chapter 4).

Lamarck Cuvier was not the only Frenchman interested in the relationships between living and extinct animals. Baron Jean Baptiste de Lamarck (1744–1829) saw that animals were not fixed in appearance but changed in response to the needs of life in that environment. He asked himself what caused these changes and how they were continued. His answer was that acquired characteristics are inherited. If an animal changes its appearance in response to the demands of its environment, the change will be passed on to the offspring, which will be better suited to life in this environment. The most famous example, although one that Lamarck himself did not use, is the giraffe's long neck. At one time, according to this theory, giraffes had necks like other animals. When the leaves on which they fed became harder and harder to reach, the giraffes stretched their necks, making them longer, to reach the food. This length of neck was passed on to the next generation, and bit by bit the elongated neck of today's giraffe was attained.

Lamarck was only one of the thinkers of his time who saw that the environment could have an important influence on animals and plants,

FIGURE 1.10
Charles Darwin in 1840, at the age of 31, four years after returning from his voyage aboard the *Beagle*.

and that living things can survive because they possess biological features that permit them to exploit a particular set of resources in their environment—in short, because they are adapted to that way of life. Although Lamarck's ideas gained some support, most scientists of the day remained unconvinced.

Lyell　While Lamarck was presenting his theories, a Scotsman whose main interest was the planet itself was developing different lines of evidence. Charles Lyell (1797–1875) traveled widely in Europe and parts of the United States, tracing the stratigraphic (rock strata) history of nations. He amplified the ideas of another British scientist, James Hutton (1726–1797), who had studied many of the geological formations in England and concluded that the earth's physical features were the result of natural forces operating in a uniform manner. Lyell also observed the effects of nature on the earth's surface, noting the weathering action of wind, rain, and temperature and the meanderings of rivers slowly wearing away their beds, forming terraces as they gouged deeper and deeper. Lyell believed these natural forces had made the planet look the way it does, slowly but constantly altering the world's topography.

Lyell called his theory *uniformitarianism,* suggesting that most environments are exposed to slow change. If these forces of change, working at their incredibly slow pace, made the plains and valleys, the hills and mountains, they must have been at work for a very long time. Lyell's hypothesis broke away from the ideas of early nineteenth-century Europe, which accepted the world, like the animals and plants, as forever fixed and unchanging. Europeans were shaken by the idea of the earth being extremely old. Many continued to hold with Archbishop James Ussher, a seventeenth-century prelate who counted back through the genealogies in Genesis and determined that the world had been created in 4004 B.C. Lyell did not specify how long it had taken to carve the earth into its present appearance, but if natural forces were responsible, many millions of years would have been required. In 1830, Lyell published all his evidence in his *Principles of Geology.* In 1831 a copy of this book found its way into the cabin of a young naturalist, Charles Darwin (1809–1882), as he was about to sail from England on a five-year, round-the-world scientific voyage on H.M.S. *Beagle* (Figure 1.10).

Charles Darwin　As an amateur naturalist, Charles Darwin had read some of the important books on zoology. Although he probably knew about Lamarck's views, he did not doubt the prevailing view of the fixity of animal species. His observations on the voyage of the *Beagle* were what led Darwin to develop a workable theory of evolution (Figure 1.11). Tracing those observations and the speculations they inspired will give us greater insight into the genius of Darwin and how the idea of natural selection grew and took shape in his mind.

On his voyage across the Atlantic, Darwin read Lyell's book. Uniformitarianism and the view of a constantly changing, ancient earth im-

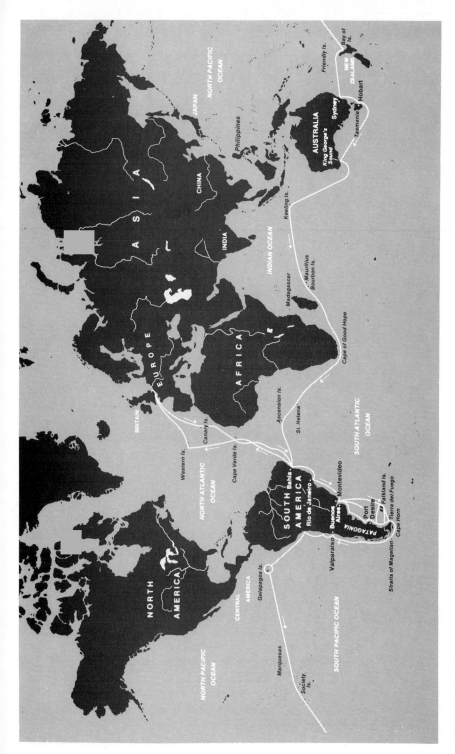

FIGURE 1.11. The voyage of the *Beagle*.

pressed him. The observations he made during the voyage increasingly modified his ideas about the traditional interpretations of life.

South America The *Beagle* was to chart the lands and sea along the coast of South America, giving Darwin a chance to visit much of the southern part of that continent. On the coast of Argentina he discovered fossil bones of extinct animals in a cliff. Although the animals no longer lived in any part of the world, Darwin was sure that the fossil bones of the giant ground sloth he had found belonged to a creature much like the living, although smaller, tree sloths in South America. He found forms of other extinct animals that were like living animals in many ways. These discoveries raised doubts that species are fixed and that all animals ever created were still alive. Darwin found horse bones in geological contexts that left no doubt about their great age. Although the horse was not known to have existed in the New World until the Spanish introduced it early in the sixteenth century, it obviously had been in South America earlier but had become extinct. (We now know that the horse actually evolved in North America, eventually spread to Asia, and became part of the animal life of Eurasia and Europe. It became extinct in the New World about 10,000 years ago, only to be reintroduced by Spanish explorers seeking the "City of Gold.") Darwin wondered why the horse and the other animals were no longer to be found in these areas.

After visiting the very tip of the continent, Tierra del Fuego, the *Beagle* rounded Cape Horn and sailed up the Pacific coast, making more surveys while Darwin examined the geology of the Andes. Darwin's exploration of the mountains coincided with a tremendous earthquake that caused great damage and loss of life. The profound modifications to the land the earthquake produced reinforced in his mind the notion of change brought about by natural forces.

The Galapagos The ship's first landfall after leaving South America on its trip home was the Galapagos Islands, fifteen volcanic islands 600 miles west of Ecuador. The life forms here gave Darwin one of the indispensable keys for his theory. The islands contained one of the earth's most exotic animal populations. Reptiles abounded, including iguanas (dragonlike lizards) and large tortoises. There were many shore birds but only a few land birds, among them many finches. Darwin spent as much time as possible collecting specimens and making observations.

Just before the *Beagle* set sail, Darwin had dinner with the governor of one of the islands, who said he could identify which island a tortoise came from simply by looking at the color and design on the shell. On his long voyage across the Pacific to Tahiti, Darwin thought about this remark, and began examining more closely the animal specimens he had taken from the different islands. He had been cataloging these specimens without regard to which island they were from. Now he realized that tortoises and especially finches from the different islands looked different.[2]

The Galapagos have fourteen species of finches, now called Darwin's finches (see Figure 3.5 for an illustration of the diversity of the species). Although they are different species, they do not have markedly distinct physical features. Their plumage is rather dull, varying from gray to black to green. The only definite differences among the species are the size and development of their beaks; some are short and stout, others are long and slender. Finches identify members of their own species for breeding and territorial purposes by differences in beak shape and size. Their plumage and all other features are so similar that, unlike other birds, they might have trouble finding mates (the selection process is called *mating preference*). Thus, differentiation in the beak has sustained reproductive isolation among species.

Darwin had seen that diversity in beak shape permitted the various species of finches to adapt to different environmental niches. It seemed reasonable to think also that the finches had such diversity because the islands did not have a normal complement of other kinds of land birds with which they would have had to compete. If the islands had had woodpeckers, for example, the woodpecker finch probably would not have appeared (Figure 1.12). Because this finch does not have the woodpecker's strong, hard beak, it uses a twig, held in its beak, to pry up bits of tree bark and reach the insects underneath. The finches (including a ground-feeding, seed-eating finch) seemed to have developed adaptations to ways of life led by other kinds of birds on the South American mainland that were not present on the islands. These finches appeared only on the Galapagos, and they differed in slight but meaningful ways from the mainland finches. Darwin was convinced that the environment

FIGURE 1.12
The woodpecker finch of the Galapagos, using a cactus spine to extract an insect from a tree branch.

shaped the physical features of animal species. The finches also showed that species can modify their appearance over time, because all must have been descended from a common ancestor.[3]

After visits to Tahiti, Australia, and South Africa, the *Beagle* reached England in October 1836; Darwin never left England again.

Evolution by Natural Selection   Although Darwin had learned on the voyage that animal species apparently adapt to their environment, he still could not say how the environment can influence the development of physical features in a species. He began to study domesticated animals, and soon confirmed his earlier observations that individuals in virtually all animal populations are not identical. The differences in appearance may be very slight, but they do exist. Could this variability be connected to the ways by which animals adapt to their environment? The answer to this crucial question came to him from reading Thomas Malthus's essay on population.

Malthus (1766–1834), an economist, writing about how population sizes are kept stable in animal groups, observed that many more individuals are born into an animal species than ever reach maturity: the number of adult animals remains more or less constant. High infant mortality must prevent most of the young individuals from reaching adulthood. This was the key Darwin had been seeking. Could the choice of which young individuals reached adulthood depend on their ability to survive? Could their ability to survive be related to their physical features? If all animals in a species varied in physical features, perhaps some variations permitted a better adaptation to the environment. The environment, then, would select those individuals whose variations made them better able to survive. These animals would stand a better chance of surviving to maturity and thus of reproducing. The variations that permitted these animals to survive would be passed on to the next generation. In contrast, variations that were not as adaptive would be weeded out by the environment. Darwin's name for this weeding out process was *natural selection*, but he also thought of it as the survival and reproduction of the fittest, a process that could account for the changes in appearance of animal species.

Darwin and Alfred Russel Wallace   Darwin had the outlines of natural selection in mind by the late 1830s, and he began accumulating data to support his hypothesis. He was aware of the controversy such a theory would engender in scientific and theological circles, and he was not eager to be in the center of the battle.

Alfred Russel Wallace (1823–1913), like Darwin, was a natural historian. He had traveled widely to study animal and plant life and to collect specimens for European zoos and museums. According to his autobiography, while on such a trip to the Malay archipelago in southeast Asia, Wallace contracted malaria, and during a fever delirium, a theory of evolution almost exactly like Darwin's had come to him. Wallace communicated his ideas on evolution to scientists in England.

Darwin's friends, aware that he was working in much the same direction, persuaded him to announce his theory publicly, and in 1858, Darwin and Wallace jointly announced their findings. A year later, Darwin published his book, *The Origin of Species*. He avoided referring to human evolution in this work, except for a cryptic sentence at the end: "Much light will be thrown on the origin of man and his history."

The storm Darwin had expected soon broke. Refusing to be drawn into the controversy, he retired to his home and left the fighting to such men as Thomas Henry Huxley (1825-1895), an anatomist superbly qualified to carry on the battle (Figure 1.13). Huxley himself published *On Man's Place in Nature* in 1863, carefully analyzing the anatomical similarities between humans and the apes, and describing the remains of a primitive, extinct human found at Neandertal in Germany as evidence for human evolution. In 1871 Darwin's *Descent of Man* confirmed Huxley's views and presented a strong case for considering humans and all other life as subject to evolutionary change (see Figures 1.14 and 1.15).

Examination and explanation of evolutionary theory and its application to humans in particular will form the heart of this book. Before looking at modern ideas about evolution we will first set the stage by looking at some of the information Darwin did not have, specifically that of the science of heredity, or genetics.

FIGURE 1.13
Thomas Henry Huxley.

FIGURE 1.14
Caricatures of Charles Darwin (left) and Thomas Huxley which appeared during the controversy over evolution.

FIGURE 1.15. Another caricature of Darwin, by W. H. Beard. Titled "The Young Darwin," it suggests a scene in which the details concerning modern humans' relationship to the apes are told to Darwin by two very intelligent and human-looking apes.

Summary

Anthropology is a comparative science divided into four major subdisciplines: cultural, linguistic, archaeological, and physical anthropology. Its chief characteristic is its holistic approach to human problems, which seeks to illuminate the ties among various aspects of human functions and activities. This is often accomplished by the comparison of different cultures or even species. In this book we will concentrate on the three branches of physical anthropology—studies of fossils, studies of modern human variation, and studies of our closest living relatives—to try to answer questions about human evolution.

Humans are animals whose biology is like that of other animals, but we alone have immeasurable potential for the learned modification of behavior. This ability to learn and the specific things we learn depend on and can affect our biology.

In all cases physical anthropology is an evolutionary science focusing on the process of adaptation. To appreciate the processes that affect human populations and have influenced their development over time, an understanding of evolution is essential.

Although there were earlier evolutionists, the climate of the mid-1800s and the genius of Darwin and Wallace resulted in the flowering of an evolutionary view of life. Darwin and Wallace proposed a theory of evolution based on differential reproduction, or natural selection. According to this theory all populations in nature show variability in physical features that determines who survives and reproduces and who does not.

The individuals whose variations let them adapt more fully to the environment have a better chance to survive, mature, and reproduce. Their hereditary material may in time characterize the entire population.

Although this concept has formed the foundation for our understanding of evolution, discoveries in the twentieth century—especially the mechanisms that govern the transmission of hereditary materials from one generation to the next—have provided a much more detailed picture of the way evolution operates. These mechanisms and how they affect the process of evolution will be described in the next two chapters.

2

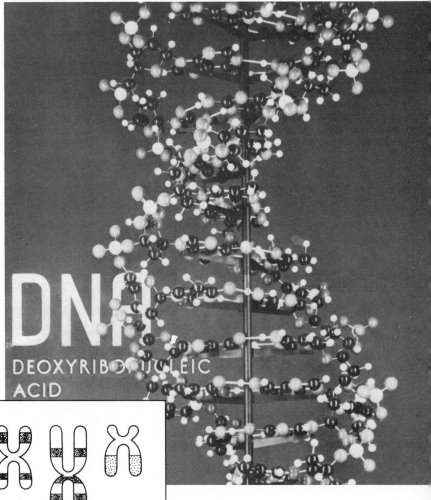

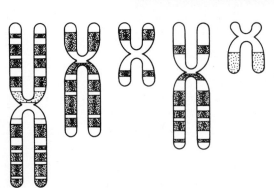

Understanding evolution demands a knowledge of genetics, for evolution is genetic change over time.

Genetics: The Study of Heredity

We have all noted, either consciously or unconsciously, similarities in appearance among members of a family; children look like their parents, siblings, and cousins. This concept of family resemblance is neither new nor surprising, for it has been noted for millenniums. We are likewise not surprised to find that organisms give birth to the next generation of the same species—cows have calves and humans have children. These statements may seem obvious, yet it was not until this century that scientists widely appreciated why these phenomena occur. A major biological discipline has developed to study heredity—the science of genetics. Physical anthropologists and biologists have used the discoveries in this field to understand more fully the mechanisms of evolution, at the base of which is genetic or hereditary change.

Evolution itself means change, or more specifically, change in the genetic makeup of a group. George Gaylord Simpson (1902–1984), an eminent evolutionary theorist, has referred to the process of evolution as "the stream of heredity"[1]* that flows from generation to generation.

A clear appreciation of the flow of our evolution and all it implies about us comes only with an understanding of the behavior and functioning of the hereditary material, known as genes, and the processes of evolution. Genetics helps us understand modern human variation. Many physical anthropologists investigate similarities and differences between living peoples, asking questions such as: Which of these variations are inherited? What are their causes? Explanations can be provided at several levels. The proximate, or immediate, cause may be that people have inherited different genes. At another level, however, one can ask why and how different genes came into existence, why certain populations are characterized by different genes, and why similar genes are found in different groups but at different frequencies. All these evolutionary ques-

*See page 613 for notes to Chapter 2.

tions relate to the history of genes in populations. As we shall see, the answers are not just of academic interest but can carry social, practical, and medical importance.

Some anthropologists are more interested in the large-scale changes seen in the fossil record. The microscopic events that intrigue geneticists seem far removed from the impressive alterations most associate with the word *evolution,* from water to land animals, from reptiles to mammals, from apelike to human organisms. Yet these massive reorganizations in body form (morphology) are the visible evidence of small alterations accumulated over millions of years. Thus, here too, understanding the relationship of genes and evolution is important, although we do not have the ability to study past genetic events with the same precision as those occurring today. We can try to deduce an explanation for certain events or trends, such as the variations among groups in different times or places and the commonalities in language skills, tool making, and the like across the whole species.

Levels of Analysis

Genetics has three ways of analyzing the material that gives living things the power to reproduce themselves: biochemical, chromosomal, and populational. At each level of analysis we are looking at the behavior of genes, the hereditary units, at a different stage of magnification. Biochemistry tells us what the genes are, what they do, and how they change or mutate. Aggregates of genes form structures called chromosomes, and it is in these larger units that genes pass from one generation to the next. Chromosomal genetics helps explain why we all resemble our relatives in one or another way, yet why nobody looks exactly like someone else. This area focuses on the mechanisms that allow the stream of heredity to flow across the generations. Population genetics shows us how evolutionary forces can change a gene's frequency. Physical anthropology is an evolutionary science, and it is the population, not the individual, that evolves. We take to the grave the same genes we were born with—we, as individuals, do not evolve. The makeup of our group, however, can change over time; population genetics helps demonstrate the hows and whys of this alteration. The following discussion will present a number of new terms and concepts. While learning these words, it is easy to forget the larger issue. Keep in mind that the biochemical, chromosomal, and populational processes are not unrelated. At each level we seek to understand different aspects of the complex system whereby genes and the information they carry pass through time (Figure 2.1).

Genetics: The Transmission of Information

Before discussing biochemical genetics, let us consider exactly what is transmitted from generation to generation in Simpson's stream of heredity.

During the eighteenth and into the nineteenth century, the theory of preformation was widely accepted. This theory stated that either the sperm or the egg held within it a preformed *homunculus,* a microscopic version of the person yet to be (Figure 2.2). Upon fertilization, this homunculus was somehow stimulated to start growing, ultimately to be-

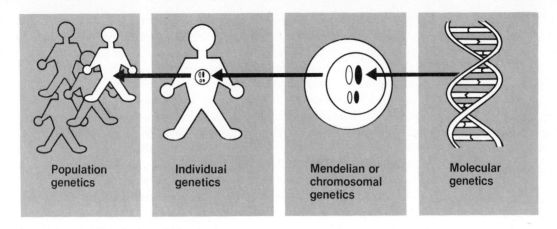

FIGURE 2.1. Geneticists study the transmission of information from generation to generation of cells, individuals, and populations.

Population genetics · **Individual genetics** · **Mendelian or chromosomal genetics** · **Molecular genetics**

come an adult. The theory of preformation owed much of its favor to vivid imaginations and to optically poor microscopes.

The knowledge that has since been uncovered through the work of many scientists has, of course, discredited the preformation theory. We now know that the material passed via sperm and egg is a coded set of instructions, much like a written language. Chemical counterparts of letters are put together to make words, words are cast into sentences, and

FIGURE 2.2. Three homunculi. In earlier centuries it was thought that sex cells carried a minute, preformed person within.

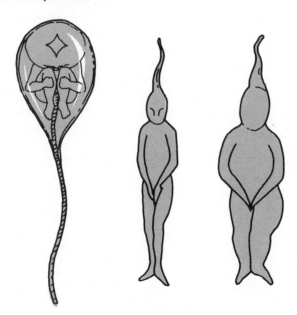

sentences are organized into paragraphs. Just as paragraphs can constitute a set of directions, the chemicals of the hereditary material can also be strung together in an almost infinite number of arrangements to form directions. The sperm and egg, when united, form a book of directions for the development and functioning of an organism. These "blueprints" are read and interpreted by biological machinery, thus assembling the chemical "building blocks" into new individuals. A book with one general pattern of directions may make a person, and one with another pattern, a butterfly. Variation among people in part depends on relatively small differences in the chemical words. Additionally, while these genetic instructions are quite specific and usually followed faithfully, environmental forces can enhance or interfere with the assembly scheme, thus making the final organism the outcome of both hereditary and environmental factors.

Biochemical Genetics: The Genetic Material, DNA

The average animal cell is composed of a variety of microscopic structures that perform different roles (Figure 2.3). Among these are the cell membrane, which controls the passage of materials into and out of the cell; the mitochondria, where biochemical reactions generate energy for the cell; and the nucleus, which houses the genes. Other cellular structures carry out other roles. For the moment it is the nucleus that interests us, for, with the exception of mature red blood cells and reproductive cells, each of the trillions of cells in the human body has exactly the same amount of genetic material: deoxyribonucleic acid, or DNA. This material fulfills three irreplaceable roles. As the *genetic* (originating) material, it transmits directions on how to build a new individual. This transfer occurs on two levels: from parents to offspring and from the single original cell, the fertilized egg, to each of the billions of descendant cells in an individual. These two operations, passing information from generation to generation of individuals and from generation to generation of cells within the individual, are very similar. DNA's third function lies in the content of the information it transmits, for it instructs the cells about which proteins to make and how and when to make them. Proteins are molecules with special chemical properties that are involved in the body's construction, development, and functioning. Because the genes direct the production of proteins, all of the significant anatomical changes throughout human evolution ultimately result from changes in genes.

In structure, DNA is a double helix; it looks like a ladder twisted into a spiral. Like a ladder, DNA has two important elements: the supports (or backbone) and the rungs (Figure 2.4). The DNA supports are made of sugar and phosphate molecules, while the rungs are made of four chemicals called *bases:* adenine (A), thymine (T), guanine (G), and cytosine (C).

The sugars of the backbone are linked via chemical bonds in a highly regular fashion. Without going into the details of organic chemistry, we can simply say that the sugars are not symmetrical, which means that the backbone has a directionality, as shown in Figure 2.5a. At the left of

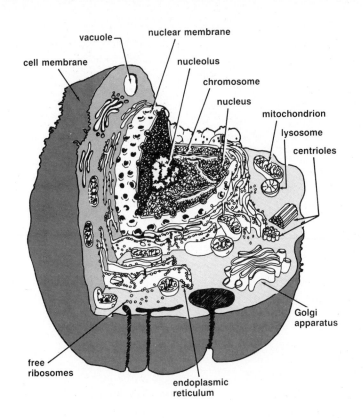

vacuole — nuclear membrane
cell membrane
nucleolus
chromosome
nucleus
mitochondrion
lysosome
centrioles
free ribosomes
endoplasmic reticulum
Golgi apparatus

FIGURE 2.3
A schematic view of a cell and a transmission electron micrograph showing some of these structures in a bat's pancreatic glandular cell. The plasma membrane is the boundary of the cell and selectively allows substances to enter and leave. The mitochondria produce energy for the cell, while proteins are actually constructed at the ribosomes. The nucleus contains the chromosomes, which are made of DNA— the genetic material. Symbols in micrograph: N = nucleus; M = mitochondria; G = Golgi complex; ER = rough endoplasmic reticulum.

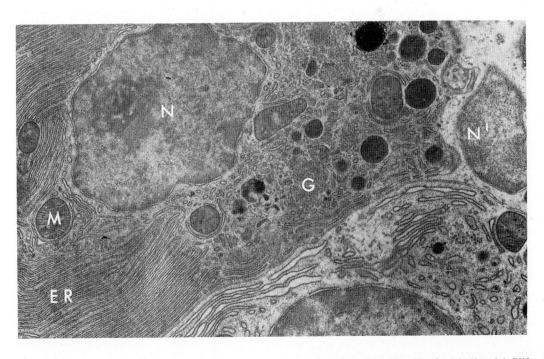

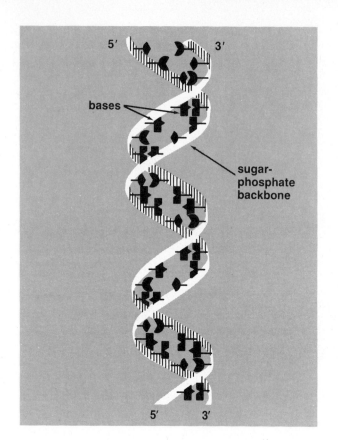

FIGURE 2.4
The double helix of DNA.
The backbone is composed
of sugar and phosphate.
The cross links are
chemicals called bases.
Each backbone has a 5' end
and a 3' end.

the backbone is the flat side of a schematic sugar; at the other side is a pointed end. In the language of genetics the flat end is called the 5' (read as "five prime") end. The pointed end is called the 3' end. Since DNA is a *double* helix, it has two strands of sugars, or two backbone molecules. While one strand has its 5' end on the left, the other strand will have 5' to the right (Fig. 2.5b). The two strands are linked by the rungs, or bases.

While the backbone fulfills a structural role, all of DNA's informational activities rest on the rungs or bases. Because of specific physical-chemical factors, A normally pairs, or bonds with, T and G with C to form a rung (Figure 2.6). Once the sequence of bases making up one side of the helix is known, it is easy to figure out the base sequence in the complementary strand (Figure 2.7).

To summarize, DNA's structure is a double helix with a backbone of alternating sugar and phosphate molecules. The backbone has a polarity—one end is called 5', the other 3'. Links between the backbone are formed by pairs of bases, either A with T or G with C.

New Copies of Genes

As noted, one capability of DNA is replication; it can make copies of itself. These copies are then either passed on to new cells within a person or to a new generation of individuals via the sex cells. Replication

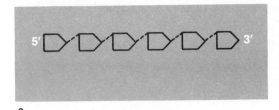

a

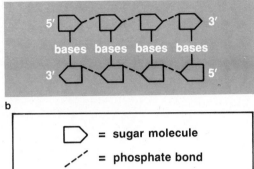

b

FIGURE 2.5. (a) The backbone of the DNA, made of alternating sugars and phosphate bonds, has a directionality. (b) The double helix has two backbones running in opposite directions and linked via bases.

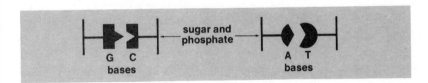

FIGURE 2.6
The DNA bases pair in a very specific fashion: A with T and G with C.

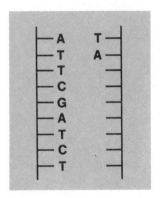

FIGURE 2.7. With the sequence of one strand of the DNA known, the sequence of its complement can easily be determined. As an exercise, fill in the letters for the empty rungs on the right.

is carried out prior to the production of new cells, including the sex cells (Figure 2.8). This is accomplished by "unzipping" segments of the DNA helix. That is, the double helix opens along its long axis by splitting the bonds that normally unite the members of a pair of bases— As separate from Ts and Gs from Cs, exposing the ends of the bases that can form bonds. Bases on each of the now single strands of DNA can attract new, complementary bases (for instance, A attracts T) along with the sugar and phosphate supports, thus building new, second strands of DNA.

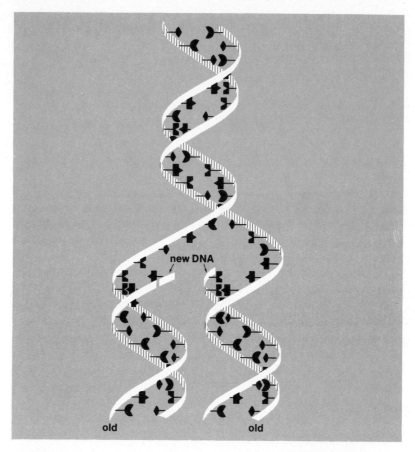

FIGURE 2.8. When new cells are formed by cell division, copies of the DNA are produced as a result of the base complementarity. The original helix opens and the bases of each strand attract new complementary bases: A attracts T, T attracts A, C attracts G, and G attracts C. Thus, from one double helix of DNA, two double helices are produced.

The new DNA bases that are chemically attracted to their complements during DNA replication come from a constantly replenished pool within the cell. Thus, one helix, through DNA replication, can form two helices: Each strand directs the production of a new copy of its complementary strand. Now having doubled the gene copies, the cell can divide in two, apportioning to each new cell an identical copy of the genetic material via a process called *mitosis.* Mitosis thus produces two cells from one.

A somewhat different chain of events follows DNA replication in the formation of sex cells. This process, *meiosis,* yields cells that pass instructions to offspring.

Almost always the replication of DNA proceeds smoothly; on rare occasions, however, something goes wrong so that the sequence of bases in the new DNA is altered. This altered sequence is a *mutation.*

Functionally defined in general terms, the gene is the unit of DNA that produces a functional chain of chemicals; the chain is either a functioning protein or a subunit that combines with other such chains to form a functioning protein. Proteins are a large group of complex molecules that regulate and promote the body's development and functioning. Among other roles they work as enzymes, accelerating biochemical reactions; as transporting agents, carrying iron, oxygen, and hormones to the tissues; as structural supports, as in bones; as antibodies, fighting off disease organisms; and as regulators of gene action, turning genes on and off during development.

Almost every cell in the human body carries a full complement of genes, with more than a yard of DNA squeezed into the nucleus. Depending on the cell's location in the body, some of its genes are "turned on" and others are "turned off": Only some of the genes actively direct the production of proteins; the rest are inactive. This is why, for example, the red blood cells contain hemoglobin (the oxygen carrying protein) and the stomach cells produce digestive proteins. Much remains to be known about the processes controlling and regulating this functional differentiation, but gene regulation will clearly prove to be a key to understanding proper development and health. When regulatory mechanisms go awry, diseases such as various cancers can occur.

All proteins are molecules constructed from twenty "building blocks" called *amino acids* (Table 2.1 and Figure 2.9). A gene specifies the order, number, and kinds of amino acids that are to be hooked together to build a protein. In rough outline, the production of proteins is relatively simple, although one has to pay attention to the terminology. The

TABLE 2.1
Amino Acids and Their Abbreviations
Proteins are constructed from building blocks called amino acids. All amino acids share certain properties that allow them to bond to form long chains. A chain that can perform some function is called a protein. The essential amino acids (boxed) are those that must be present in our diet; we cannot manufacture them from other substances.

Amino Acid	Abbreviation	Amino Acid	Abbreviation
Alanine	Ala	Leucine	Leu
Arginine	Arg	Lysine	Lys
Asparagine	Asn	Methionine	Met
Aspartic acid	Asp	Phenylalanine	Phe
Cysteine	Cys	Proline	Pro
Glutamic acid	Glu	Serine	Ser
Glutamine	Gln	Threonine	Thr
Glycine	Gly	Tryptophan	Trp
Histidine[a]	His	Tyrosine	Tyr
Isoleucine	Ile	Valine	Val

[a]Histidine is essential for children.

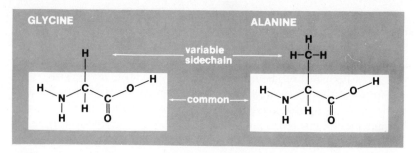

FIGURE 2.9. Diagrams of two amino acids. Notice that, while all amino acids share a common part, the distinctive nature of each amino acid is determined by the part of the molecule called the variable sidechain. C = carbon, O = oxygen, H = hydrogen, N = nitrogen.

sequence of bases in DNA guides the construction of a related molecule called *messenger RNA* (or mRNA), which carries the DNA's coded instructions to the region in the cell where the protein is actually constructed. At the production site the protein is fabricated out of the amino acids.

The processes collectively referred to as *protein synthesis* are constantly going on inside us. However, the determination of which protein is being made at what moment and in which cell is the outcome of many complex regulatory mechanisms. Although they are beyond the scope of this book, these mechanisms are intensely studied by molecular biologists, who have demonstrated that many enzymes are involved in the processes summarized below (Figure 2.10). Again, not only is the form of the protein product of importance in normal development and functioning, but the regulation of amounts of protein made and their timing can also be of great evolutionary significance.

How Proteins Are Made

During protein synthesis a portion of the DNA helix opens to expose the bases in each strand. One of the strands (it is always the same strand) attracts free-floating bases, as in DNA replication. But there are two major differences between protein production and DNA replication.

mRNA Is an Intermediate

For one, now DNA base A does not attract T but pairs with the base *uracil* (U) instead. Also, the sugar molecule in the single strand is slightly different from that in DNA, so that the substance produced is ribonucleic acid (RNA). (The prefixes *ribo* and *deoxyribo* refer to the kind of sugar in the backbone.) Because this RNA carries the genetic message, it is called specifically *messenger* RNA, or mRNA. The mRNA is a complement of its DNA. Wherever DNA strand has A, the mRNA has U; wherever the DNA has T, the mRNA has A; and so on.

Reading the Code

When the mRNA strand is completed, it detaches from the DNA. The two DNA strands reunite to reform the double helix, and the single strand of mRNA moves to where protein is manufactured (the ribosomes in Figure 2.3). Upon its arrival, the information in the sequence of mRNA bases directs the gathering and joining of amino acids to form the protein. The process is accomplished by "reading" the bases of the mRNA in "words" of three "letters" (bases). The word UUU, for example, specifies the amino acid phenylalanine; CAA specifies the amino acid glutamine (see Table 2.2). These three-letter words of the mRNA are often called *codons*. They are always three letters long and are read without overlapping: the cell reads bases 1, 2, and 3 as one word and bases 4, 5, and 6 as another; the second word is never composed of bases 2, 3, and 4.

The message in the RNA is translated into a protein by the pairing of mRNA bases and those of a molecule called *transfer* RNA (tRNA). The tRNA can be visualized as a short molecule with three bases jutting off one side and with an amino acid on the opposite side. If the mRNA contains the word UUU, it will attract the tRNA with the bases AAA, which always carries the amino acid phenylalanine. After the tRNA pairs with the mRNA, the amino acid is bonded to its neighboring amino acid, and this process continues until a whole string of amino acids is formed. At this point the amino acid chain, either a functioning protein or a subunit of a protein, separates from the mRNA. We can now for-

Assembling the Protein: tRNA, Another Intermediate

TABLE 2.2
The Genetic Code
Each three-letter word in the mRNA either specifies a particular amino acid or tells the cell's machinery to end the chain of amino acids (here called punctuation words, or *pun*). To convert this table of mRNA words into its complementary DNA sequence, substitute A for U, G for C, T for A, and C for G. However, the normal convention is simply to convert to the DNA sequence of the inactive strand by substituting T for U. Thus, the mRNA word UUC, coding for phenylalanine, is said to correspond to a DNA sequence of TTC.

First Position	Second Position				Third Position
	U	C	A	G	
U	Phe	Ser	Tyr	Cys	U
	Phe	Ser	Tyr	Cys	C
	Leu	Ser	Pun	Pun	A
	Leu	Ser	Pun	Trp	G
C	Leu	Pro	His	Arg	U
	Leu	Pro	His	Arg	C
	Leu	Pro	Gln	Arg	A
	Leu	Pro	Gln	Arg	G
A	Ile	Thr	Asn	Ser	U
	Ile	Thr	Asn	Ser	C
	Ile	Thr	Lys	Arg	A
	Met	Thr	Lys	Arg	G
G	Val	Ala	Asp	Gly	U
	Val	Ala	Asp	Gly	C
	Val	Ala	Glu	Gly	A
	Val	Ala	Glu	Gly	G

mulate a more specific functional definition of a gene: A gene is the series of codons that constitutes a sentence of directions for the production of a protein. The events involved in making a protein are shown in Figure 2.10.

More on the Code

We have discussed two aspects of protein synthesis: what happens and how it happens. The "what" involves the transfer of information from DNA to mRNA, the subsequent pairing of mRNA with specific tRNA's carrying specific amino acids, and the final coupling of amino acids to form the protein. "How" revolves around the ability of Gs to bond only with Cs, As with Ts or Us. The genetic code, as Table 2.2 shows, is redundant: More than one word can specify the same amino acid. This results from the need to code for twenty amino acids. If the words were only one base long, the language would have only four

FIGURE 2.10
Diagrammatic
representation of the
construction of a protein.

PROTEIN SYNTHESIS

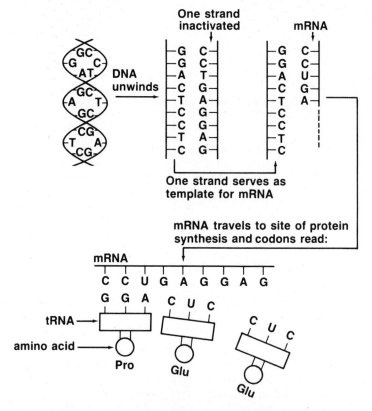

Amino acids unhook from tRNA and zip together to form a polypeptide chain that is either a functioning protein or part of a protein. These are 3 of the 146 amino acids of the β chain of normal hemoglobin:

Pro   Glu   Glu

words (A, U, C, and G) and could code for only four amino acids. If the words were two bases long (AA, AU, AG, AC, etc.), there would be words for only sixteen. Three-letter words provide sixty-four possibilities, with the result that many triplet words may specify the same amino acid: UCU, UCC, UCA, UCG, AGU, and AGC all code for serine, for instance.

The code also has multiple "punctuation" words, or codons that do not specify any amino acid; they provide the period at the end of the sentence. When one of these codons is reached, an amino acid is not plugged into the chain, and the sequence is terminated. Likewise, an *initiation codon* (AUG) starts the formation of all mRNAs, although the amino acid methionine may be cut from the final protein.

In sum, DNA directs the assembly of mRNA, which in turn attracts its complementary tRNA. Each tRNA carries a specific amino acid, and the amino acids, ultimately under the direction of the DNA, are bonded together to make a protein.

Gene Structure

With the advent of more sophisticated techniques for studying and manipulating genes, it has become apparent that in many forms of life the structure of genes is more complex than what we have described here.

We have pictured a gene as a continuous stretch of bases that specifies the structure of a protein. This is true for procaryotes (organisms without a cell nucleus, such as bacteria). Genes in eucaryotes (nucleated organisms, such as humans) often have an interrupted sequence. From one end of a gene to the other, there may be a sequence of bases that codes for part of a protein, then a series of bases that does not, and then another sequence that encodes part of the protein (Figure 2.11). The parts of the gene that direct the construction of the protein are called *exons* (for

FIGURE 2.11.   The DNA for some proteins of eucaryotes is split into segments that are translated into protein (exon) and segments that are not (intron). When first made, the mRNA has parts corresponding to the introns. These are then cut out to produce the processed mRNA.

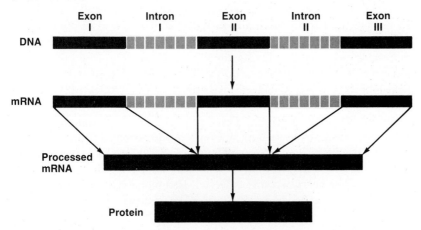

expressed), while those that are not reflected in the final protein are referred to as *introns* or *intervening sequences* (IVS). Not all eucaryotic genes have this alternating structure of exons and introns, but many do.

Very briefly, the whole sequence of an interrupted gene—exons and introns—is transcribed into mRNA; however, again with the aid of enzymes, the mRNA corresponding to the introns is spliced out. Prior to being read, the mRNA counterparts of the exons are bonded together and then the amino acid chain is constructed as described.

One implication of this discovery is that there is much DNA that does not direct the structure of protein. A typical hemoglobin gene is interrupted by 2 introns, the first being roughly 125 bases long and the second being 800 to 900 bases long. Some genes have dozens of introns.

Surrounding the genes are immense stretches of DNA with no known function. These *intergenic* (between the genes) sequences might be significant to the regulation of gene action. Regardless, to the degree that we can judge from well-studied areas of DNA, it appears that only about 10 percent of DNA actually codes for protein, about another 10 percent is found in introns, and the remaining 80 percent is intergenic.

This knowledge of DNA has many implications for understanding the hows and whys of evolution, for as mentioned, evolution is the accumulation of changes in DNA through time.

DNA and Mutation

The evolutionary process that can generate new genes is called *mutation,* or an alteration in the sequence of bases in a gene. Such alterations can come about in a number of ways, including the insertion of new bases into the sequence or the deletion of bases. Bases can also be interchanged between the two DNA strands.

One well-documented example of a human mutation deals with the base sequence of a small part of the DNA coding for part of the hemoglobin protein, the molecule that carries oxygen through the blood. The contrast between the normal form and the altered version that produces sickle-cell hemoglobin illustrates not only mutational events but also the ramifications of mutations for individual development and functioning. As we shall see, there are also major effects on the person's population.

The only difference between the normal and sickle-cell versions of the proteins is that the sixth amino acid is glutamic acid in the normal form but valine in the sickle-cell variant (Figure 2.12). Such a change in the protein occurred by altering the DNA. The difference is created by mutating the normal genetic word CTC to CAC. The altered base sequence in the mRNA (GAG→GUG) attracts a different tRNA, one that carries valine rather than glutamic acid. An apparently minor change in the initial sequence, affecting a base less than a hundred-millionth of an inch long, causes many secondary effects in the people who have sickle-cell disease. Because this form of hemoglobin does not carry oxygen well, the heart has to work harder than normal to get enough oxygen to the tissues. The heart becomes enlarged. Red blood cells with sickle-cell hemoglobin are shaped like sickles instead of the usual circular forms and

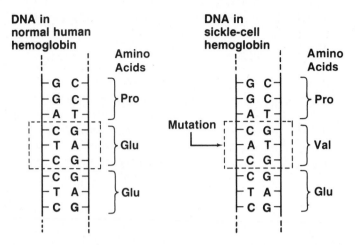

DNA in normal human hemoglobin | DNA in sickle-cell hemoglobin

Amino Acids

```
— G  C —
— G  C — } Pro
— A  T —
— C  G —
— T  A — } Glu
— C  G —
— C  G —
— T  A — } Glu
— C  G —
```

```
— G  C —
— G  C — } Pro
— A  T —
— C  G —
— A  T — } Val
— C  G —
— C  G —
— T  A — } Glu
— C  G —
```

Mutation

FIGURE 2.12. Comparison of the DNA sections for normal human hemoglobin and sickle-cell hemoglobin. These sequences show the only difference between the genes for these two hemoglobins. This base pair difference results in a difference in the amino acid sequence, which in turn causes functional differences. The left-hand strand of the DNA in each diagram directs the production of the protein. To use the genetic code table, it is necessary to convert the DNA triplets into mRNA words.

thus clog the small blood vessels (Figure 2.13). The clogging in turn causes bleeding into some joints; abdominal pain; underdevelopment and deformation of the bones; damage to the brain, liver, and kidneys; and ultimately death. These secondary effects result from the close relationships of all the body's parts; if one structure, such as hemoglobin, is changed, development or functioning in other parts can also be altered.

Genes may also be mutated by the deletion or insertion of genetic material. These processes, depicted in Figure 2.14, may drastically alter the structure and functioning of an amino acid chain.

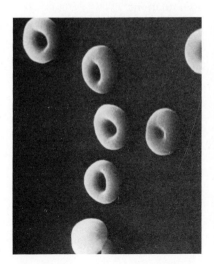

FIGURE 2.13
Micrographs of normal (left) and sickled red blood cells.
It is apparent how the sickle-cell disease got its name. (Normal cells magnified × 5,100; sickled cells × 4,800.)

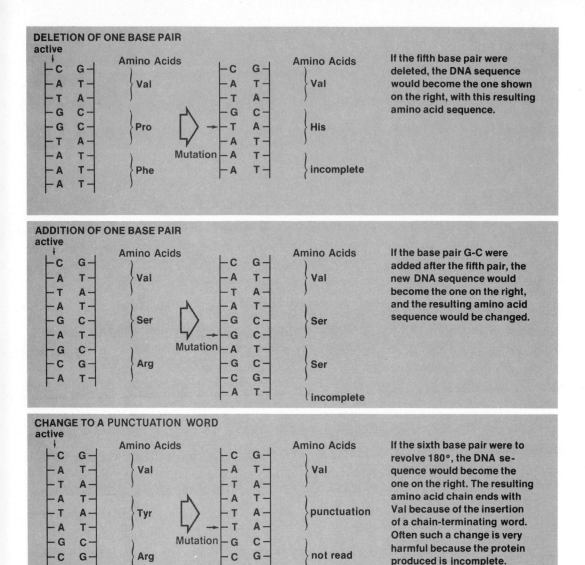

FIGURE 2.14. Three possible types of mutations. On the left are hypothetical pieces of DNA and the amino acid chains that the left strand would produce; on the right are mutated forms of these strands and the amino acid sequences that the mutant forms would produce. In using the genetic code table, it is necessary to convert the DNA triplets into mRNA words. These diagrams do not illustrate all possible mutations; for instance, more than one base pair could be lost or gained at one time.

Mutations are caused by a *mutagen,* any agent that can break the DNA and allow pieces to drop out, change position, or be inserted. The best-known mutagen is high-energy radiation, such as X-rays and ultraviolet light, but almost any source of energy, even high temperature and visible light, can break the genetic material. (It has even been suggested that wearing briefs instead of boxer shorts increases testicular temperature and therefore mutations.) Many chemicals and some foods can also produce mutations. Mustard gas, a nerve gas used during World War I and more recently in the Iran–Iraq conflict, is a powerful mutagen. Even caffeine can cause mutations under some conditions.

Mutations are evolutionarily important only if they can be passed from one generation to the next; they must be present in the sex cells. A mutation in any cell other than a sperm or an egg cannot affect one's children. Shielding of the gonads (the sexual organs, the testis and ovary) from X-rays is important, for children are derived from these cells.

Spontaneous mutations, which probably are produced by some unidentified mutagen, occur at a rate of about 1 in 100,000 to 1 in 1,000,000; a specific new mutation appears in approximately 1 out of every 100,000 to 1,000,000 sex cells.

Because of the vast number of genes (estimated to be several tens of thousands per cell) with which we are endowed, roughly one out of every twenty sex cells carries a newly mutated gene; a sizable proportion of the world's people have a mutant gene. Taking a broad view of mutation as any change in the DNA, intronic and intergenic as well as exonic, an even greater number of mutations could be said to exist. *Back mutations,* or reversions from a mutant back to the original type, do occur, although rarely. As mutations occur more or less at random and there are millions of bases, it is easy to see that the likelihood of exactly reversing a previous mutation and thereby reverting to the original form is quite low.

A rudimentary knowledge of biochemical genetics helps dispel misconceptions about mutants. Most noticeable mutations are simply a change in one amino acid in a protein. Such a change can result in deformities, but rarely would a person carrying a mutant gene show the abnormalities dreamed up for late-night horror movies, and even more rarely would one so malformed survive for any length of time. When we also realize that several of the people we encounter during a day have a new mutation, it becomes clear that mutations do not generally cause horrifying physical deformities. More often they make very minor changes in the visible anatomy, and these come from developmental modifications caused by altered formation and function of a protein. The resultant disorder may vary all the way from unnoticeable to lethal. An extreme example of a "silent," or harmless, mutation in an exon is the case in which a base change does not result in an amino acid substitution. For example, mutation of the codon UUU to UUC still results in the incorporation of phenylalanine into the protein.

In the last fifteen years we have witnessed a revolution in molecular biology with the advent of recombinant DNA technology. Although a full understanding of the techniques and theories of this burgeoning field is far beyond the scope of this text, it is worth sketching some of the major points of the process, for molecular biology has much to contribute to an understanding of human evolution. In the last chapter, we will also consider some of the ethical ramifications and medical potentials of this field.

A clone is a population of cells derived from a single ancestral cell. Biologists have studied and worked with clones for many years, but molecular cloning techniques in conjunction with recombinant DNA have greatly expanded the capabilities of researchers. Consider the potential of techniques that could allow people to grow and harvest millions of copies of a particular piece of DNA. On the medical front, these copies could be used to produce proteins that are lacking in people with various diseases, such as diabetes. There have been attempts at gene replacement therapy—to "infect" a person with a normal gene he or she lacks. DNA copies might also be inserted into important plants to provide them with disease-resistance genes or genes that increase their yield. The potential benefits, humanitarian and economic, are tremendous. The availability of millions of copies of a specific piece of DNA would be of great value for molecular studies.

How then to accomplish the goal of making millions of copies of a specific, desired piece of DNA? Geneticists considering this question used viruses and several techniques developed since the late 1960s. Viruses are little more than small pieces of DNA or RNA inside a protein coat (Figure 2.15). Whether a virus contains DNA or RNA, a virus infection involves the injection into a host of the viral nucleic acid. Once inside, the nucleic acid replicates itself many times over and directs the production of new virus shells. Each new shell takes in one copy of the viral nucleic acid, and, when many new viruses have been produced, the

FIGURE 2.15. This diagram depicts a virus as a protein casing enclosing a piece of genetic material—either DNA or RNA. About 250 million angstroms (Å) equal an inch. On the right is an electron micrograph of a virus that infects bacteria (× 110,000).

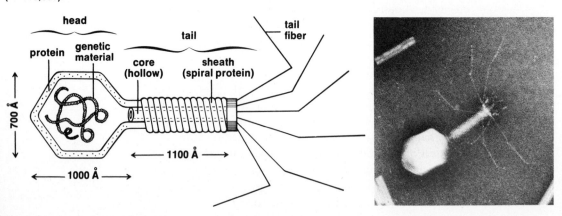

host cell bursts, spewing forth the new, genetically identical viruses. Here then was a possible "factory" system. If one could attach the DNA of a species of interest to the viral nucleic acid, a molecular factory could be developed. When the virus reproduced, the attached DNA of interest would be produced too.

How then to manufacture DNA that is a hybrid of virus DNA and that of a species of interest? This was accomplished by using a class of enzymes called *restriction endonucleases* or *restriction enzymes*. These enzymes recognize specific sequences of bases in DNA and break or cut the DNA wherever that sequence appears. Hundreds of such enzymes are now known. The enzyme Eco RI cuts DNA wherever it sees the sequence 5'GAATTC3', and it cuts between the G and A. Now picture the complementary strand to this. Remembering that the 5' end of the complement will be to the right, it reads 3'CTTAAG5'—the exact same sequence! It too will be cut between the G and A. Thus, the double helix is broken by Eco RI as shown in Figure 2.16. This leaves what are called *sticky ends*—short stretches of bases able to attract their complements.

The DNA of a virus is rather short, and in many viruses a particular enzyme site may be present only once or twice, possibly not at all. The DNA of a human, being much longer, may be broken into thousands and thousands of pieces of different lengths. All of the pieces, though, will have these sticky ends. If the viral and human DNAs are mixed, some of the viruses will attach to a piece of human DNA to form recombinant DNA.

By appropriately adjusting reaction conditions these hybrid molecules can not only be formed but also packaged into virus protein coats. These new, recombinant viruses are functional and able to infect and grow in bacterial hosts. The growing virus makes myriad copies not only of itself but also of the attached piece of human DNA. By relatively simple techniques, it is possible to identify which virus has been attached to a particular gene of the species of interest and thereby to study the gene and its protein product in great detail.

We have seen that the ability to form recombinant molecules can be used in medical settings. The physical anthropologist too can use the technology to clarify evolutionary relationships. Chapter 5 discusses the ways similar molecules in different species can be compared to determine degrees of evolutionary relatedness. We will also see how similar studies on human populations can shed light on the evolution of the groups.

Biochemical genetics shows us how information is transmitted in an orderly, highly reliable way from one generation to the next, how this information can be altered, and how it serves to direct protein synthesis. If we keep in mind the manner in which DNA is replicated, we will see in the next level of analysis how genes pass from parent to offspring and how the one-cell egg results in the adult with trillions of cells.

In this discussion of biochemical genetics, we have seen how genes can replicate, change, and direct the manufacture of proteins. In the next section, on Mendelian genetics, we shall see how the genes are packaged inside our cells and how they are passed on through time.

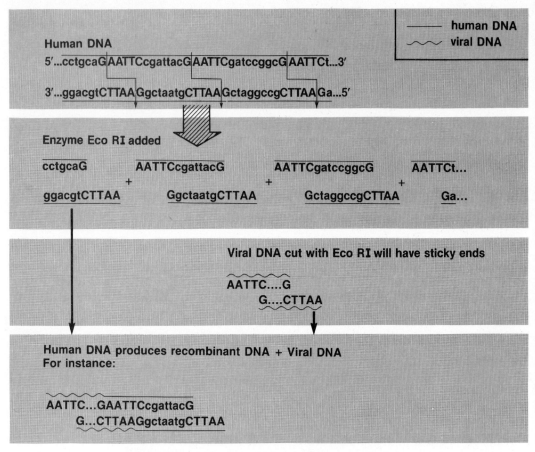

Human DNA

5'...cctgca**G**|**AATTC**cgattac**G**|**AATTC**gatccggc**G**|**AATTC**t...3'

3'...ggacgt**CTTAA**|**G**gctaatg**CTTAA**|**G**ctaggccg**CTTAA**|**G**a...5'

---- human DNA
～～ viral DNA

Enzyme Eco RI added

cctgca**G**   **AATTC**cgattac**G**   **AATTC**gatccggc**G**   **AATTC**t...
    +   +   +
ggacgt**CTTAA**   **G**gctaatg**CTTAA**   **G**ctaggccg**CTTAA**   **G**a...

Viral DNA cut with Eco RI will have sticky ends

～～～～
AATTC....G
       G....CTTAA
          ～～～～

Human DNA produces recombinant DNA + Viral DNA
For instance:

～～～～
AATTC...GAATTCcgattacG
   G...CTTAAGgctaatgCTTAA
～～～～

FIGURE 2.16. Restriction enzymes cut DNA wherever they see a specific sequence of bases. Eco RI cuts the sequence GAATTC at the spot indicated by the arrow. Upper case letters are used to show where Eco RI will cut this sequence. Any sequence of DNA is indicated by ellipses. After being cut, the unpaired bases can attract and stick to a complementary "sticky end" from the other species.

Mendelian, or Chromosomal, Genetics

In 1856 a Moravian priest, Gregor Mendel (1822–1889), failed his examinations at the University of Vienna for the second time. Although he suffered severe depression because of his failure, science benefited from it. Giving up all hope of receiving a diploma, Mendel decided to indulge his interest in natural history by conducting plant breeding experiments in his monastery garden. It was Mendel who initially described how biological information is transmitted from one generation to the next (Figure 2.17).

Mendel's Unit of Inheritance

Until Mendel's work was published in 1866 and for some time afterward, it was generally thought that we inherit a blend of traits from both parents. Darwin believed that each part of the body produced a germ that passed through the bloodstream to be concentrated into one unit in the sex cells; when the sperm and egg united, the parental hereditary units blended like different colors of paint in a bucket, producing a new individual. Even today this is a widely held but incorrect assumption; we all know of cases in which a child seems to be an intermediate between the parents. Skin color in particular would seem to follow this blending pattern. But although outward appearances may seem to hint at blending, the genes are chemical molecules that retain their individuality.

From his experiments with pea plants, Mendel learned that blending does not occur, that the sex cells carry a combination of genes that are inherited as discrete units and keep their individuality. Mendel noticed that mating a line of peas that always had yellow seeds with a line that always had green seeds invariably produced second-generation offspring with yellow seeds: The yellow character dominated over the green (Figure 2.18). Mating plants from a line that had only smooth seeds with plants that came from a wrinkled seed line produced only smooth-seeded offspring. In all, Mendel made observations for seven traits; luckily, these were traits that are inherited in a simple way. Many other traits, such as height in humans, are affected by more than one gene and also by the environment.

After he made these initial crosses (cross-matings), Mendel, a very patient observer, crossed the offspring with themselves. As other naturalists had noticed, this crossing produced plants with both seed colors and forms. Whatever was producing green seed color or wrinkled seed shape in the initial parental plants had not been lost or blended out of existence in their offspring; it had simply been hidden. Besides noticing that the parental traits did not blend in the offspring, Mendel also saw the arithmetical ratios in the third-generation plants and from these ratios deduced what was actually happening genetically. In the experiment involving seed color, a cross of second-generation, yellow-seeded plants produced 6,022 yellow-seeded and 2,011 green-seeded offspring. Mendel realized that this was a close approximation to a 3 : 1 ratio, the small

FIGURE 2.17
Gregor Mendel, the father of modern genetics.

FIGURE 2.18
The inheritance of seed color in peas, one of Mendel's classic experiments.

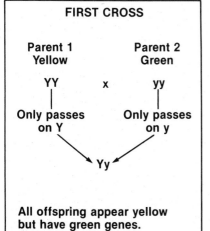

FIRST CROSS	
Parent 1 Yellow	Parent 2 Green
YY x	yy
Only passes on Y	Only passes on y
	Yy
All offspring appear yellow but have green genes.	

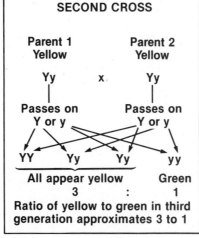

SECOND CROSS	
Parent 1 Yellow	Parent 2 Yellow
Yy x	Yy
Passes on Y or y	Passes on Y or y
YY Yy Yy	yy
All appear yellow	Green
3 :	1
Ratio of yellow to green in third generation approximates 3 to 1	

Body cell

Sex cell

Fertilized egg

Y = yellow
y = green

departure being due only to chance. In fact, for all seven traits that he studied, crossings of members of the second generation produced a third generation in the 3 : 1 ratio; three members showed one form of the trait for every one showing the alternative form. So close was the approximation to the 3 : 1 ratio that some have suspected that Mendel or one of his aides fudged the results to fit the observed to the expected outcomes more convincingly to help prove his case to an unbelieving scientific community. Several investigators prior to Mendel had conducted similar experiments, but finding that the results were not always exactly the same and lacking Mendel's insight, decided that inheritance had no general explanation.

How can one explain this approximation to a 3 : 1 ratio in the third generation? Certainly not by blending. Mendel hypothesized that each plant must contain two units (now called genes) for each of the seven traits, with one gene inherited from each parent.

Suppose two Yy pea plants are mated (Figure 2.18), where Y signifies the gene for a yellow seed coat and y that for a green. What, Mendel asked, might be expected in the offspring? If, as he thought, each parent contributes only one gene, there is a 50 percent chance that parent 1 will pass on Y and a 50 percent chance that parent 2 will contribute Y to the offspring. This results in a 25 percent chance (50 percent × 50 percent) of producing a YY offspring. The likelihood of a yy offspring is also 50 percent × 50 percent, or 25 percent. Yy offspring can come about in two ways: Y can come from either parent 1 or parent 2; thus, the total chance that these two parents will yield a Yy offspring is 50 percent. The YY and Yy offspring look the same (both have yellow seed coats), and there are three plants with yellow seed coats for every plant with a green seed coat. The postulated mechanism agrees with the observed results; the old idea of blending does not, for there are no yellowish-green seed coats.

Good examples of the absence of blending can also be found in our own species, for as Mendel hypothesized, each of us has two genes for each simple trait (see exception, page 61), having inherited one copy from each parent. The gene that determines the shape of the earlobe, for instance, has two alternative forms (Figure 2.19): One produces a protein that ultimately results in attached earlobes and the other causes unattached earlobes. Each of us has either two attached-earlobe genes, two unattached-earlobe genes, or one of each. If you inherit the attached earlobe gene from one parent and the unattached gene from the other, you will not have half-attached lobes, or one attached and the other unattached; nor will you pass on an intermediate, blended, "half-attached" gene. Because of gene dominance, you will have both earlobes unattached (see page 58), and you will pass on either the attached-earlobe gene or the unattached-earlobe gene; chance determines which one it will be.

As the biochemical geneticist defines a gene in terms of its DNA, the cellular geneticist defines it in terms of its inheritance as a discrete unit. In Mendel's first law, the *law of segregation,* he stated that genes keep

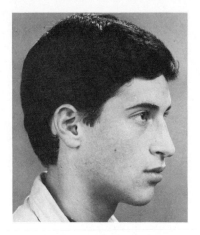

FIGURE 2.19. The boy on the left has two genes for attached earlobes. The boy on the right has unattached earlobes; he has at least one gene for this form of the trait.

their individuality and pass on to the next generation unaltered. The effects of some genes may be undetectable in some individuals because their presence is masked, but they are there nevertheless.

Chromosomes

The DNA sequences, or genes, are not found in a cell as thousands of structurally independent units. They are strung together to form *chromosomes (chroma = color; soma = body)*. We pictured a gene as a string of bases, and we can think of a chromosome as a string of genes contained within the cell's nucleus. Figure 2.20 sets out the physical hierarchy that has been discussed in reference to genes. Each of the trillions of cells in the body, except the sex cells, has a full complement of these chromosomes. In humans, the full complement is forty-six (Figure 2.21); chimps and gorillas have forty-eight, while another ape, the gibbon, has forty-four. The numbers do not necessarily mean that chimps are more advanced than we are or that gibbons are less advanced. Chromosome number alone is a very poor indicator of structural or genetic complexity; some plants have well over a thousand chromosomes. The full complement of chromosomes is very important because it guarantees that development will be properly regulated. The loss or addition of a chromosome in human cells usually results in gross malformation, if not death.

Earlier we discussed at the molecular level the ability of DNA to transfer information from one generation to the next. We saw how the DNA can be replicated so that parent and offspring can each have a copy. Here at the chromosomal level, we see the process by which the copies of DNA are parcelled out to the next generation of individuals in a sexually reproducing organism. As noted earlier too, a fertilized egg, once formed, must be able to duplicate its DNA and pass copies on to each new generation of cells, a second process to be discussed.

(Text continues on page 53)

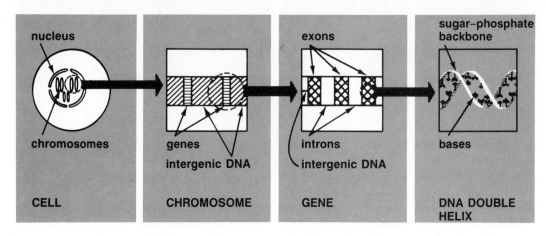

FIGURE 2.20. Schematic, exploded views of the physical structure of genetic material.

FIGURE 2.21. Karyotypes, or pictures of chromosomes. (a) A photo is taken through the microscope of a person's chromosomes. (b) The photo is cut up and the chromosomes lined up in pairs to make a karyotype, here of a normal female. Note the two X chromosomes (see next pages). (c) The 46 chromosomes in a normal male. (d) The chromosomes of a person with Down's syndrome. Notice the extra copy of the twenty-first chromosome. (e) The chromosomes of a child with *cri du chat* syndrome. Notice that part of the fifth chromosome is lacking. (f) The abnormal appearance of a person with Down's syndrome results from the extra chromosome. (g) The abnormal appearance of the child with *cri du chat* syndrome, characterized by low-set ears, a saddle nose, and epicanthic folds (page 54), results from the lacking chromosome part.

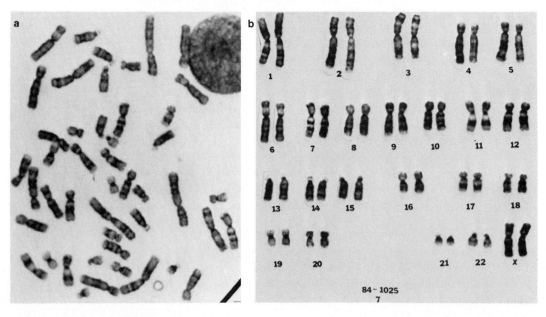

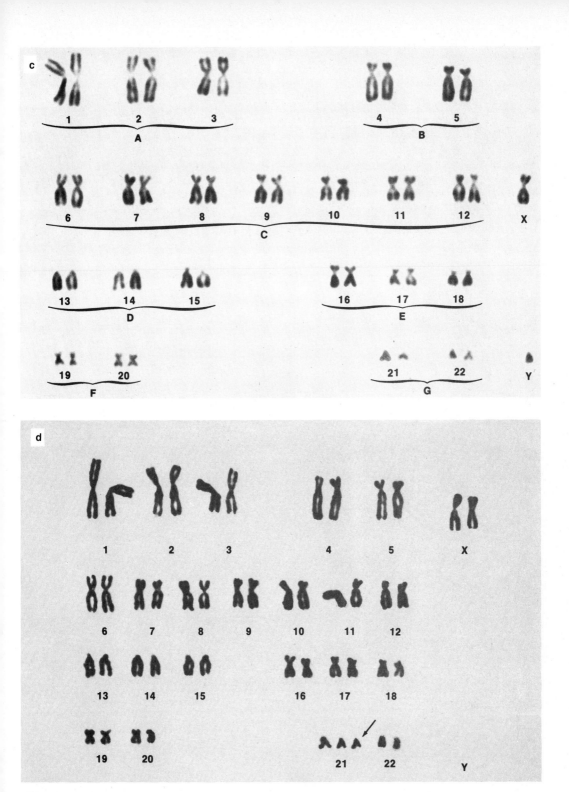

FIGURE 2.21, *continued*

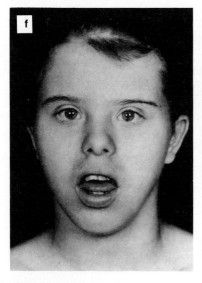

e

1 2 3 4 5 X
6 7 8 9 10 11 12
13 14 15 16 17 18
19 20 21 22 Y

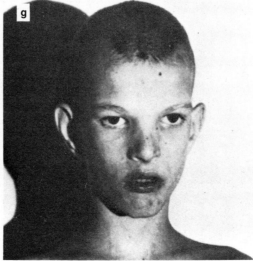

f g

FIGURE 2.21, *continued*

The fact that sexually reproducing organisms such as humans have two copies of every gene presents a problem. If each parent contributed a full set of genes to the offspring, the child would have twice as many genes as either parent—an impossibility simply because the nucleus does not have room. Most higher animals have solved this problem by forming sex cells with half the normal chromosomal complement. When a fertilized egg is formed by the union of egg and sperm, the full number is restored.

But not just any twenty-three chromosomes enter a human sperm or egg. The chromosomes in all but our sex cells occur in pairs, each member of the pair carrying genes that control the same traits. As the two chromosomes of a pair have the same linear arrangement of genes, they are said to be *homologous chromosomes,* or *homologs* (*homo* = *same; logos* = *proportion*), for they are similar in structure and function. Note that they are *similar*—not *identical*. One member is paternally derived, the other maternally. Mendel's peas each had two genes controlling seed color, with one gene on each of a pair of chromosomes; two other genes controlled seed form, and so on. Each sex cell must have one and only one member of each chromosome pair so that when two sex cells unite, the fertilized egg will contain the chromosomes in pairs. The sex cells are formed by *meiosis.* A consequence of this process is stated in Mendel's second law, *independent assortment.* The member of one pair of chromosomes that enters a sex cell is unrelated to which member of any other pair of chromosomes enters that cell. For instance, you have one member of chromosome pair 1 from your mother and one from your father. Likewise, one member of pair 2 is maternal and one is paternal in origin, and so on for the other pairs. When you form sex cells, the law of independent assortment states that your chromosome pairs sort into *gametes* (the sex cells) without regard to their origin. The members of the chromosome pairs you received from your mother need not stay associated when you make sex cells. Thus, considering only two chromosome pairs, some sex cells will have chromosomes 1 and 2 of maternal origin, some will have both of paternal origin, and some will have one from the father and one from the mother (see Figure 2.22).

Although we each have twenty-three pairs of chromosomes, for simplicity Figure 2.23 follows only two sets of chromosomes (four chromosomes) through meiosis, ending with four sperm, each with two chromosomes. Before meiosis begins, the chromosomes are not visible as distinct units. After they appear, the chromosome pairs line up along the middle of the nucleus; then the members of each pair separate, or segregate, moving to opposite poles of the nucleus. The cell then divides, producing two daughter cells, each with half the original genetic complement. The chromosomes have meanwhile duplicated themselves, and the cells split again, yielding four sperm, each with one member of every pair of chromosomes. In the female the procedure is the same, except that of the four sex cells produced, only one forms a functioning egg. When the sperm and egg unite, the full chromosomal complement is restored.

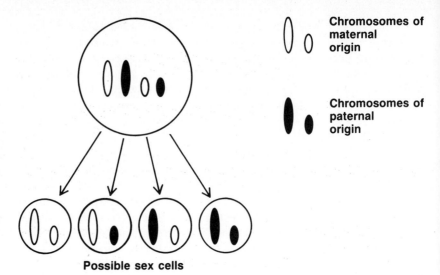

FIGURE 2.22
Mendel's law of independent assortment. The maternally and paternally derived members of different chromosome pairs sort independently when entering sex cells during meiosis. With two pairs of chromosomes four different combinations are equally possible.

Chromosomes of maternal origin

Chromosomes of paternal origin

Possible sex cells

On occasion, sex cells are formed with either too many or two few chromosomes. Down's syndrome is caused by an extra copy of the twenty-first chromosome and results in mental retardation and other defects. Down's syndrome can occur if during meiosis the members of the twenty-first pair of chromosomes do not enter separate cells but end up in the same sex cell in one of the parents. If the sex cell with two copies of the twenty-first chromosome fertilizes a normal sex cell, the resultant fertilized egg has three copies (one and one-half pairs) of this chromosome and develops into a person with the disorder.

Cri du chat (cat's cry) syndrome, named for the catlike sound an afflicted infant makes, results from the lack of part of the fifth chromosome. This too can result from a mistake during meiosis. Parts (f) and (g) of Figure 2.21 illustrate the morphological, or visible, changes that these anomalies produce, along with a picture of the chromosomal make-up (karyotype).

The larger chromosomes carry so much genetic information that too many or too few of them is incompatible with life. Abnormal chromosomes are not unusual in human fertilized eggs, but most of these are spontaneously aborted. It appears that as many as 20 percent of all pregnancies are spontaneously aborted, and half of these fetal losses are chromosomally abnormal. The fact that only 5 percent of chromosomally abnormal fetuses survive to birth shows that selection is actively eliminating most with a defective complement of chromosomes.

Mitosis:
Duplicating Cells

After the normal fertilized egg is formed, another process must allow this one cell to divide and thereby produce the trillions of cells in the adult; this is accomplished by *mitosis,* or cell duplication. During mitosis all the chromosomes line up along the equatorial plane of the nucleus and duplicate themselves (by DNA replication); the cell then splits into two cells, each with the full number of chromosomes (Figure 2.24).

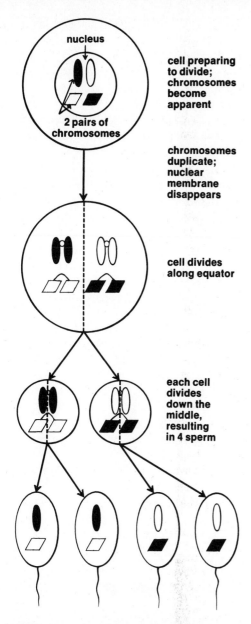

FIGURE 2.23. An abbreviated view of the process of meiosis in a sperm cell line. This process results in the formation of sex cells that contain one member of each pair of chromosomes. Eggs are produced in a similar fashion except that only one of the four final cells is a functional egg. Each pair of ovals and parallelograms stands for a pair of chromosomes. A dark oval or parallelogram represents the member of the pair inherited from the father.

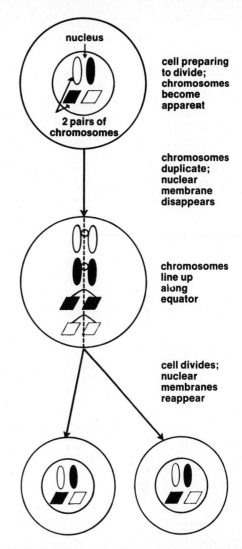

FIGURE 2.24. Mitosis is the process that results in the complete duplication of a cell. In humans, mitosis of a cell with 46 chromosomes (23 pairs) produces two cells, each with 46 chromosomes. This process is constantly occurring in all human body cells (except the sex cells). Thus, mitosis does not pass genetic information from parent to child but from one generation of cells to the next within one person.

As a result, the preponderance of cells in an adult have the identical, complete complement of chromosomes. As with meiosis, mistakes in mitosis do occasionally happen. Sometimes, for instance, the mechanism that controls mitosis goes awry, with one group of cells dividing much too often. This is a cancerous, uncontrolled growth. At other times, a cell does not divide properly, producing one daughter cell with an extra chromosome and the other with one too few, as a pair of chromosomes "sticks" together (Figure 2.25). Because of this mistake, called nondisjunction, some of the cells will not contain the proper forty-six chromosomes. If this happens very early in the development of an embryo, ultimately a large percentage of the cells will be abnormal. If the cell shown in Figure 2.25 represents the fertilized egg, it is apparent that all the subsequent cells will be aberrant and that the embryo will probably not survive.

Mitosis, then, is cell duplication; it does not normally change the number of chromosomes. It ensures that each cell will have all the genetic material present in every other cell except the sex cells. Sex cells undergo meiosis and incorporate only one member of each pair of chromosomes into each sperm or egg.

FIGURE 2.25. A malfunction during mitosis that results in some of a person's cells having too many chromosomes and some too few. Cells undergoing normal mitosis continue to yield normal cells.

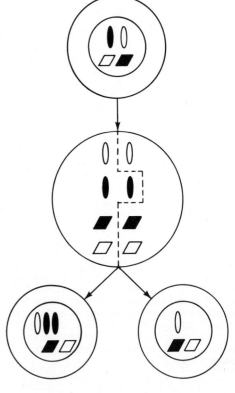

We have been discussing members of pairs of chromosomes as if they were identical. In a way they are, because both carry genes affecting the same traits. As Mendel noticed, however, the form of these genes can vary. Mendel studied the inheritance of alternative forms of the genes affecting seed form, seed color, and other traits. We noted the alternative normal and sickle-cell forms of a gene affecting human hemoglobin. The variant, or alternative, forms of a gene are called *alleles*. Alleles for a genetic trait are related in that they affect the same characteristic (such as seed color), but they have different effects on that trait (yellow or green seed color). Because each individual has two genes for every genetic trait, one inherited from each parent, the person can have two identical alleles (two yellow or two green) or two different alleles (one yellow and one green). Individuals with identical alleles are called *homozygotes* (either homozygous yellow or homozygous green [*homo = same; zygote = fertilized egg*]; those with both kinds of alleles are called *heterozygotes* (*hetero = different*). All allelic variation can ultimately be traced, at least in theory, to mutation. Alleles are important in evolution because they provide the genetic alternatives that natural selection can "choose" between. One of the central questions of physical anthropology is why some alleles are very common in certain populations; African populations, for example, have substantial frequencies of the sickle-cell hemoglobin allele, which is virtually absent in many other populations of the world. The answer lies in the evolutionary history of human populations. Before considering such examples of human differentiation, however, we must discuss several other genetic factors and terms.

We are now in a position to predict the proportions of various types of offspring resulting from matings that involve simply inherited traits. Meiosis (Figure 2.23) ensures that the sex cells will carry one gene for each trait. If a person is a heterozygote for hemoglobin, carrying one normal and one sickle-cell allele, half the sex cells will contain the member of the chromosome pair carrying the normal allele, and half will have the sickle-cell allele. Homozygotes for a trait can produce only one type of sex cell for that trait.

If two homozygotes for normal hemoglobin mate (A = normal allele; AA = normal homozygote; AA × AA describes the mating), both parents can contribute only a normal hemoglobin allele; therefore, assuming no mutation, 100 percent of the offspring will be AA. If the mating is between an AA parent and a heterozygous AS (S = sickle-cell allele) parent, the AA parent again produces A-carrying sex cells, while 50 percent of the time the other's sex cells will contain A and 50 percent of the time, S. The offspring can then be either AA or AS, and they will occur in a 1 : 1 ratio. The mating of two heterozygotes will yield 25 percent AA, 50 percent AS, and 25 percent SS. The most helpful way of showing these matings is in the matrices, as in Table 2.3. It is important to remember that these ratios refer to genetic constitution. Mendel's 3 : 1

TABLE 2.3
Computing Distribution of Genotypes
The table on the left shows the distribution of offspring of two heterozygous parents. In the table on the right, compute the distribution of the mating AA (father) × AS (mother).[a]

		Alleles in egg	
		A	S
Alleles in sperm	A	AA	AS
	S	AS	SS

Percentage equals
25% AA; 50% AS; 25% SS

		Alleles in egg	
Alleles in sperm			

[a]50% AA, 50% AS

---

ratio (75 : 25 percent) referred to appearance; as we shall see in the next section, because of dominance, appearance does not always reflect genetic makeup.

Dominance:
Masking Alleles

Mendel realized that genetic makeup is not always discernible from outward appearance. Often two individuals may seem to have the same form of a trait but are genetically different (Figure 2.26). This happens most often when one allele is dominant over the other. *Dominance* is the ability of one allele to mask the presence of the other when both are present in the heterozygote. Mendel could not actually see the difference between a pea plant that had two alleles for yellow seed color (the homozygote) and a plant that had one yellow and one green seed allele (the heterozygote). The action of the yellow allele in the heterozygote covered up the presence of the green allele; he had no way of telling the difference between the heterozygote and the homozygote for the dominant yellow allele. Homozygosity for the recessive (nondominant) green allele, however, is easily spotted: The seeds are green.

Our techniques for detecting the sickle-cell and normal hemoglobin alleles are refined enough to distinguish the heterozygote for sickle-cell hemoglobin from both homozygotes. These two alleles are said to be codominant: Neither masks the presence of the other. Dominance, then, affects our ability to detect the differences in the structure and function of proteins produced by alleles. At the molecular level, a dominant allele produces a protein we can detect directly or indirectly; recessive alleles do not.

Organisms with different genetic makeups may look the same because of dominance. The visible, measurable, or otherwise detectable appearance, known as the *phenotype,* is the same in the heterozygote and in the homozygote for the dominant allele. The dominant allele is by definition expressed and the recessive is not. Hence, when faced with an organism displaying a dominant trait, we cannot specify its genetic constitution, or *genotype.* The only way to distinguish heterozygotes and

FIGURE 2.26. An albino from Melanesia. The lack of skin pigmentation is caused by homozygosity for a recessive allele. The relatives of this person who carry one dominant and one recessive allele are normally pigmented, as are those who carry two dominant alleles; that is, these two groups look the same but are genotypically different.

homozygotes for the dominant allele is to look at close relatives to try to infer the genotype. Because the homozygous recessive has a distinctive phenotype, we immediately know its genotype. The genotype is also directly perceptible for traits that do not display dominance, such as the hemoglobin variation in humans.

Deduction of a person's genotype from information about relatives can be particularly important in medical counseling. Geneticists often must compile genetic genealogies in attempting to inform clients of their risks of bearing a child with a particular disorder. Cystic fibrosis is a hereditary disorder that interferes with proper digestion and respiration and leads to an early death. It is caused by homozygosity for a recessive allele (ff), while nonsufferers are either homozygous dominant (FF) or heterozygous (Ff). The genotype of normal individuals is impossible to decide in the absence of further information. However, if two apparently normal individuals give birth to an affected child, each parent must be heterozygous: Each passed an f allele to the offspring and, since the parents are not diseased, each must also have an F allele.

Many human characteristics nicely illustrate the consequences of dominance and recessiveness on the phenotype. Some result in phenotypes often described as inherited disorders like cystic fibrosis, while other dominant-recessive situations have no known benefit or detriment attached to the phenotypes. One such is produced by a dominant allele (W) that results in a white forelock: The hair just above the center of the forehead is white, while the rest of the hair is normally pigmented. The alternative recessive allele (w) does not produce this pattern. Here, then, there are three genotypes: WW (homozygous dominant), Ww (heterozygous), and ww (homozygous recessive). Because of the presence of the dominant W allele in the first two genotypes, the appearance, or phenotype, of these people is the same: Both have a white forelock. Because of the similar appearance of these two people, it is impossible to identify their genotype simply by looking at them.

Most of us fall into the third genotypic class: lacking the allele W, we do not have a white forelock and yield a second phenotype, normal hair pigmentation. People with the recessive genotype reveal it in their phenotype.

Dominance and recessiveness have to do with the expression of the alleles. Dominance does not mean that the dominant allele is the most common; the w allele for hair pigmentation is the most common even though its effect is recessive. In other cases, the dominant allele is most common. To reiterate, genotypes with one or two dominant alleles will express the dominant trait and thus be indistinguishable. Those lacking a dominant allele, the homozygous recessives, exhibit a second phenotype.

That environment can complicate the expression of genotype is illustrated by people who use hair bleach, cosmetic surgery, or a toupee. Their phenotypes have been drastically altered, but their genotypes are unchanged. For many traits, such as hair color, the phenotype is the product of both the genes and environment. The hair color specified by a set of genes can be greatly modified by dyes, sun exposure, and other environmental factors. We shall see that many traits are quite complex in their determination; often several sets of alleles and environmental features interact to produce the phenotype.

Linkage: Connected Inheritance

Mendel was lucky to study traits controlled by only one set of alleles. He was also fortunate in choosing traits controlled by genes on different pairs of chromosomes, for they are inherited independently of each other. The sex cells of a heterozygote for both seed color and form could therefore be of four types: a yellow and a round allele, a yellow and a wrinkled allele, a green and a round allele, or a green and a wrinkled allele. In other words, the sex cell's alleles for one trait had nothing to do with its alleles for the other trait.

If, on the other hand, the genes for seed color and form were linked, that is, if the alleles for both traits were on the same pair of chromosomes, the traits would not be inherited independently. If the green and round alleles were on the same chromosome and the yellow and wrinkled alleles were on the other member of the chromosome pair, the plant could not produce a sex cell with yellow and round or green and wrinkled alleles (Figure 2.27).

At times the sequential relationship between linked genes may be altered by crossing-over and recombination. During meiosis, when the

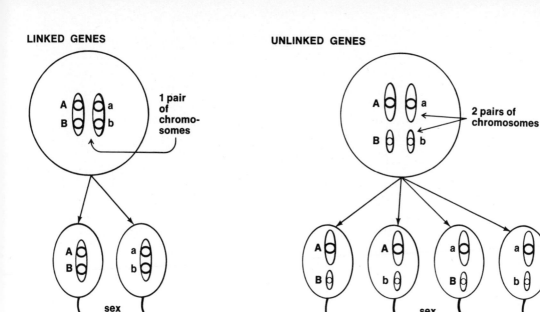

LINKED GENES

1 pair of chromo- somes

UNLINKED GENES

2 pairs of chromosomes

sex cells

sex cells

FIGURE 2.27. Linked and unlinked genes. If genes controlling two traits are on the same chromosome the genes are said to be "linked." A and a and B and b are two sets of genes controlling two genetic traits. Because both sets are on the same chromosome pair, there are only two probable sex cells produced during meiosis. Genes controlling two traits appearing on separate chromosomes are inherited independently and are "unlinked." Again, A and a are alleles controlling one genetic trait, while B and b control a second. When a cell like this divides during meiosis, 4 different sex cells can be produced.

members of a pair of chromosomes, or *homologs,* come together, they often break and cross-exchange genetic material (Figure 2.28). This results in new combinations of the genes on a chromosome, but the genes themselves have not been altered.

Another important function of chromosomes is determining an individual's sex. In fact, one pair of chromosomes, the X and Y, or sex chromosomes, regulate sexual development. Figure 2.21c shows the chromosomes in a normal male, one X and one Y. The normal female also shown has two X chromosomes. Because females have only X chromosomes, the eggs they produce must contain an X. Of the millions of sperm in the normal ejaculation, half carry an X and half carry a Y. If an egg is fertilized by an X-carrying sperm, the child will be a girl (XX); a Y-bearing sperm will produce a boy (XY).

As Figure 2.21c shows, the sex chromosomes are unlike members of other pairs of chromosomes, for they are not of equal size, and most genetic traits represented on the X chromosome are absent from the much smaller Y. This has major implications for the association of cer-

Sex Determination and Sex Linkage

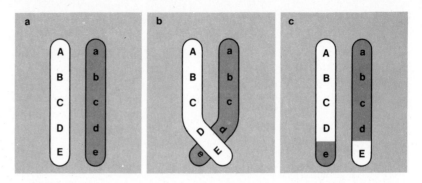

FIGURE 2.28. Crossing-over (b) and recombination (c) between members of a pair of homologous chromosomes (a). (a) Members of a pair of chromosomes line up in a cell dividing by meiosis; A and a, B and b, C and c, and so on signify pairs of alleles. (b) A cross-over occurs when both members of the pair break and cross-reunite. (c) The sex cell will contain one of these chromosomes, either of which has a new combination of alleles.

tain genetic disorders with sex. Hemophilia, the inability to form blood clots properly, results from a rare recessive allele found on the X chromosome. Because this allele is quite rare, a female is very unlikely to inherit two copies, one on each of her X chromosomes, so that female hemophiliacs are very uncommon. The Y chromosome is blank for this trait; it cannot have either the dominant, normal allele or the recessive, hemophilia allele. Males are much more likely to be bleeders than females, for the male has to receive only one hemophilia allele (on the X from his mother) to display the disorder.

Geneticists have traced the passage of an allele for hemophilia from Queen Victoria through subsequent generations of European monarchs (Figures 2.29 and 2.30). Since Victoria's ancestry was devoid of hemophilia, it is likely that a mutation occurred in either the sperm or egg from which she developed. Possibly it was the sperm, because her father was in his fifties when she was born, and mutations occur more often in older men. Three of Victoria's six daughters carried the trait; they were phenotypically normal and did not have trouble with clotting, but genotypically one of their X chromosomes carried the recessive allele. They could give birth to hemophiliac sons. One of Victoria's three sons, Leopold, inherited the harmful allele and therefore exhibited the disease. One daughter of Victoria, by marrying into the Hessian nobility, spread the allele to the German royal line and from there on to Russia. Another daughter married into another noble German line; from her offspring the gene eventually entered the Spanish royalty.

In addition to the few people who have too many or two few copies of a nonsex chromosome, some do not have a normal complement of sex chromosomes. Some females have only one sex chromosome. These XO (read it "X, Oh," but it means "X, Zero") individuals with what is known as Turner's syndrome have small breasts, no pubic hair, and partial development of the external genitalia, do not ovulate, and are sterile.

Anatomically they are obviously female, however. "Superfemales," XXX, are also known to occur. Generally, they too have small breasts and infantile external genitalia, and reach menopause very early in life.

Genetically defective males also occur, usually either XXY (Klinefelter's syndrome; Figure 2.31) or XYY. Klinefelter males usually have subnormal intelligence and a dysfunctional genital system. Much research has also been done on the XYY males. Because one or more Y chromosomes dictates "male," and because some claim that males are generally more aggressive than females, it was proposed that XYY men might be superaggressive. It is doubtful, however, that XYY men are more likely to be antisocial than normal men. Humans are far too complex for a simplistic tie between social behavior and a series of genes to exist. There is no doubt, however, that the sex chromosomes are in a delicate balance: an extra nonsex chromosome produces gross aberrations, and a deviation from the normal complement of sex chromosomes is highly deleterious.

FIGURE 2.29.   Queen Victoria with some of her descendents.

FIGURE 2.30. Queen Victoria's genealogy traces the passage of the sex-linked gene for hemophilia through her line. Women are carriers but seldom suffer from the effects of the disease.

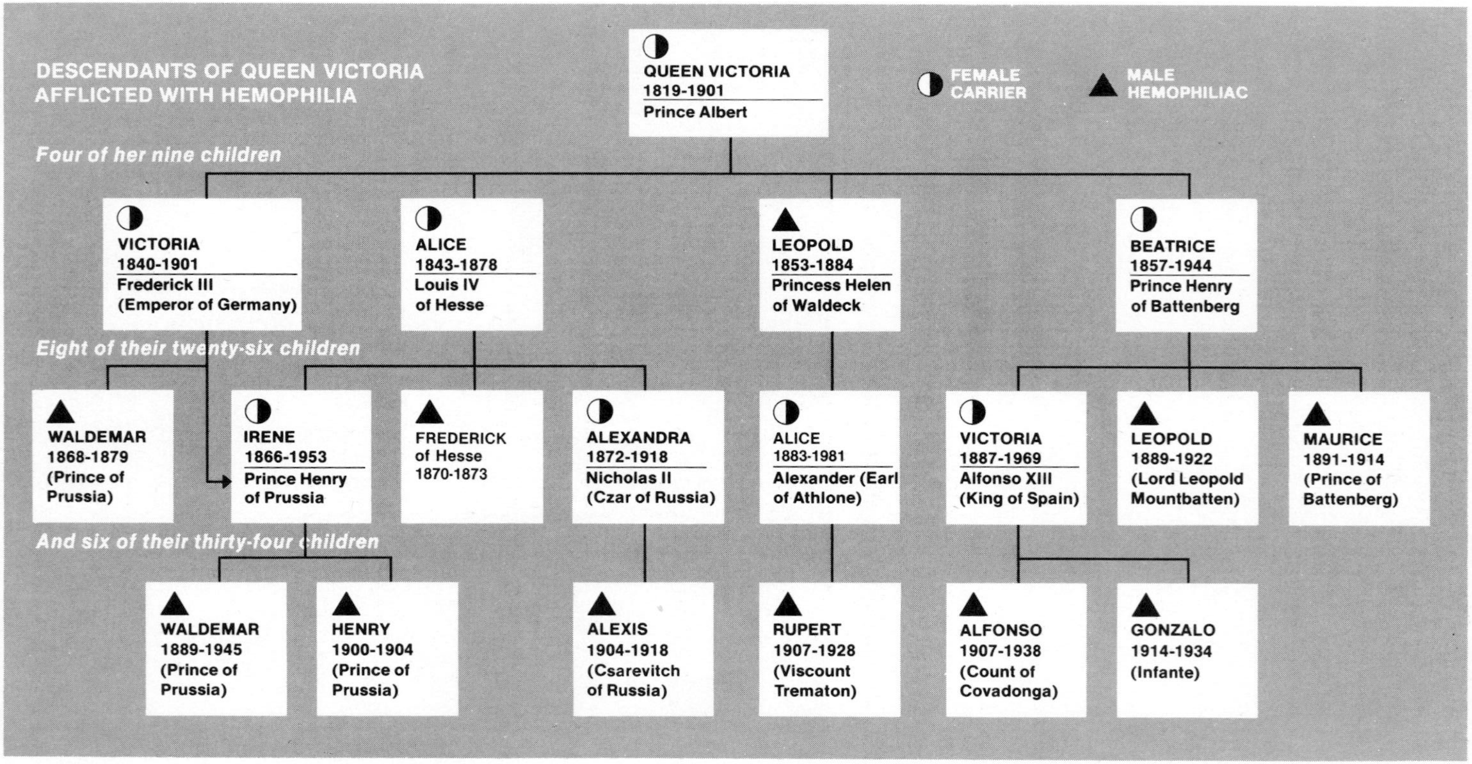

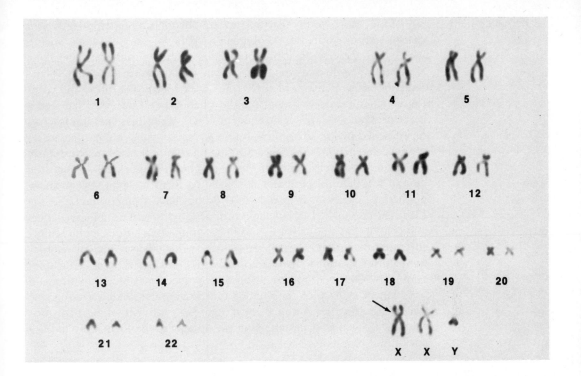

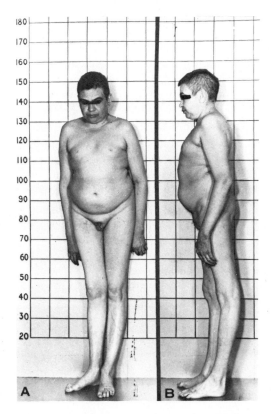

FIGURE 2.31. A typical karyotype of Klinefelter's syndrome. Men with this chromosomal abnormality (XXY) have long limbs and broad pelves. They also show some feminization; they have sparse body hair and femalelike breast development.

Polygenic Traits

One more term that relates to Mendelian genetics—*polygenic traits*—warrants attention. Polygenesis (*poly* = *many; genic* = *origin*), which is very common, is the control over a trait by more than one gene. Skin color, height, and weight are among these plurally determined characteristics. The genetics of these traits is extremely complex, and environmental influences also affect the phenotype. Knowing that genes make proteins, we can see how the products of several genes can interact to influence major anatomical traits. Many of the proteins that genes produce are enzymes that speed up the biochemical reactions constantly going on in our cells. The simplified diagram in Figure 2.32 depicts the human biochemical pathway necessary to form melanin, the primary pigment in our skin. In people who do not have a functioning enzyme 1, the path is blocked and melanin production drops. Also, phenylalanine builds up in the bloodstream, and the accumulating amino acid is shunted to produce more phenylpyruvic acid, which causes mental retardation, a disorder called phenylketonuria (PKU). The lack of enzyme 2, by a somewhat different means, also causes reduced melanin formation and variation in skin color. Skin color can thus be considered a polygenic trait, for both genes A and B must be present for normal pigment production, as well as genes affecting other steps in the formation and deposition of pigment.

Genetics and Individual Development

As we have seen, the genetic functions pass on the information on how to build a new body from simpler molecules. Basically, the division and reunion of the pairs of chromosomes in sexual reproduction provide for the perpetuation of the species and also constantly reshuffle the genes. When we consider also the modifying factors such as dominance, linkage, and allelic variation, we see that *ontogeny,* the development of the individual, is an intricate and delicately balanced process.

Timing of developmental operations is clearly of major significance. Not only must the proper molecules be produced in the correct amounts, they must be made at the correct time. Studies on hemoglobin, for instance, have demonstrated that humans and other higher primates make different forms at different stages in development. There are embryonic and fetal forms as well as the adult form we have discussed. Data gathered by M. Goodman at Wayne State University indicate that the different versions are adapted to functioning optimally under varying

FIGURE 2.32
A simplified biochemical pathway for the synthesis of melanin (skin pigment).

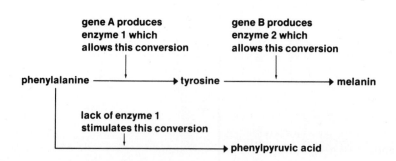

circumstances.[2] The fetal hemoglobin has certain characteristics that make it better able to transport oxygen *in utero*. At birth the individual has to extract oxygen from the air, not its mother's blood, for which a different, adult form of hemoglobin is better suited.

In the next chapters we will consider another aspect of the importance of timing. Major changes in adult appearance and function may come about by altering the timing of development. Changing the structure—the amino acid sequence of proteins—may not be the only or even most important way to change the anatomy of an animal. Indeed, changing the timing of development may be more significant in turning an apelike animal into a human.

The last subfield we must consider before applying genetics to evolutionary theory is population genetics. We need both Mendelian and biochemical genetics to understand how genes work and how they are transmitted from one generation to the next. But it is also very important to know about how genes behave within the population, because populations of human beings, not the individuals, do the evolving. In fact, evolution is best studied as changes in allele frequencies. Is the allele becoming more or less common and why? If its frequency is not changing, we are also interested in finding out why and how it is kept from changing.

The basic construct of population genetics is the *population*. This group has been classically defined as "the community of potentially interbreeding individuals at a given locality."[3] In nonhuman animals this group is relatively easy to delimit. Humans, however, because of their great mobility and cultural biases, confound attempts to outline their populations.

The boundaries dividing our species into populations are of two sorts, geographic or social. In Franklin County, Pennsylvania, a small religious isolate of 350 people known as Dunkers, an old German Baptist Brethren community, has kept itself in rather strict isolation from the surrounding peoples since the early 1700s. Since 1850, most of their marriages have been with other members of this group, for this is the socially preferred pattern. Thus, the maintenance of a cultural practice qualifies the Dunkers as an *isolate,* or a population.

Other boundary lines are not quite so clear, however. American Jews, for example, are not a breeding population to the extent that the Dunkers are, because interreligious marriages involving non-Jews are not rare. In fact, part of the problem in trying to outline breeding populations and determine the boundaries between them is that people do not necessarily mate in a specific group, at least in Western societies. Any American Jew has a reasonably high probability of mating with a non-Jew and vice versa.

Along with cultural factors, geography often determines the likelihood of matings: People living in Africa, at least before the Age of Exploration, were not likely to encounter an Asian. However, geographic and social barriers are not really so cleanly divided from each other. In many metropolitan areas in the United States, social values have produced a definite geographic division between predominantly white suburbs and minority-populated inner cities. The distance separating the two may be small, but the barrier to interbreeding is great. On the other hand, some earlier geographic barriers may now be eliminated by technological advances.

We are interested in the *breeding population,* which is sometimes called the *Mendelian population:* the group within which most matings will take place for geographic or social reasons.

We know the theoretical unit we want to study. Yet for the reasons referred to above it is often difficult to outline the boundaries of this group. In fact there may be various levels of "potentially interbreeding individuals." Are sub-Saharan Africans a population? They are when contrasted with Europeans or Asians. On the other hand, no one denies that a San Bushman in South Africa is much more likely to mate with another San Bushman than with an Ibo, who lives in West Africa. Generally the solution to such complexities will simply depend on the research project at hand and such practical matters as the availability of subjects, money, and time as well as biological considerations. This question will be reconsidered in Chapter 14.

Gene Pools, and Gene and Genotype Frequencies

For now, let us consider the idea that usually defines a population, which is the *gene pool,* or all the genes present in a population, and the relative frequency of each type of gene. Strictly speaking, we are talking in circles: The population is defined as the members of a gene pool, and the gene pool is defined as the sum of a population's genes. Another complication is the fact that one person can belong, at least potentially, to several pools. For simplicity, let us assume that we can define our population; this usually makes it very easy to describe at least part of the group's gene pool. The simplest case is a two-allele codominant trait. All we have to do is test a large enough sample of the people and express each allele as a proportion of the whole. The MN blood group system is a good example of such a trait. The MN alleles result in the attachment of molecules to the surface of red blood cells.

The two alleles for MN are M and N. The three genotypes, MM, MN, and NN, are distinguishable; there is no dominance and there are three phenotypes. Because there is no dominance, the number of phenotypes is equal to the number of genotypes. A person with two M alleles makes only the M-type molecules, which can be detected in a laboratory. The NN homozygote has detectable N-type molecules on the red blood cells, while both the M and N molecules can be detected on the red blood cells of the heterozygote. To describe the population's gene pool, all we need do is count the number of M alleles in the sample and divide by the sample's total copies of the alleles in the system (Table 2.4). We can find the frequency of N in a similar manner. Using an alternative method, we know that the frequency of M plus the frequency of N must equal one; therefore N equals one minus the frequency of M. Allele frequencies are the way a population's gene pool is described.

When dominance is present or if there are more than two alleles, computing allele frequencies is slightly more complex, but these problems can be handled, as will be seen below; given the time, desire, patience, and money, one can describe the gene pool for many genetic characteristics. Related but distinct parameters of a population's genetic makeup are genotype frequencies. These are simply statements of the frequency of occurrence of each genotype; how common is each homozygote and the heterozygote? Two populations could have identical allele frequencies, but the alleles could be put together to form different frequencies of the genotypes.

TABLE 2.4
Computing Allele Frequencies
When dealing with a simple two-allele, codominant trait, such as MN blood types, computing allele frequencies is simple arithmetic, as this example shows.

Number = 200				Suppose 200 people in a population were tested for their MN blood type.
Phenotypes and genotypes	MM	MN	NN	As there is no dominance, the genotypes are the same as a person's phenotype.
Number in each category	98	84	18	Suppose that in this particular case the people fell into the phenotypes as listed.
	Each person has 2 M alleles	Each person has 1 M allele and 1 N allele	Each person has 2 N alleles	To get the number of M alleles, count the number of M alleles in MM and MN people. Count the N alleles in NN and MN people.
		M = 98 people × 2 M alleles per person = 196 + 84 people × 1 M allele per person = 84 280 N = 18 people × 2 N alleles per person = 36 + 84 people × 1 N allele per person = 84 120		
Total number of alleles			280 M + 120 N 400	As each person has two genes for this trait, 200 people have a total of 400 alleles.
Frequency of M	280/400 = .70			The frequency of M alleles is the number of M alleles divided by the total number of alleles. As the frequency of M plus the frequency of N must total 1.0, N equals 1.0 minus the frequency of M. The frequency of N can be computed in the same way as for M.
Frequency of N	1 − .70 = .30 or 120/400 = .30			

We have said that evolution can be looked at as changes in gene frequency. Without evolution, the allele frequencies do not change. This idea was formalized by two early researchers in the mathematics of genetics, G. H. Hardy (1877–1947), an English mathematician, and W. Weinberg (1862–1937), a German physician; it is called the *Hardy-Weinberg equilibrium*. It says that allele and genotype frequencies will remain constant in an infinitely large, randomly mating population in which selection, mutation, and mixture with other groups are not occurring; an infinite population means that chance fluctuations in allele frequencies, known as genetic drift (see Chapter 3), are so rare that they can be disregarded. In this ideal, nonevolving population, how often members of two particular genotypes will mate is a function of probability.

In turn, the genotypes of offspring conform to the rules of probability and Mendelian genetics. Thus, the Hardy-Weinberg equilibrium is a probability statement; given allele frequencies and assuming that the group is not subject to any evolutionary forces, it predicts the genotype frequencies in a population. The prediction is that if in a randomly mating population selection, mutation, migration, and genetic drift are not occurring, the genotype distribution in the next generation will be unchanged. As the genotype distribution is unchanged, the allele frequencies will also be unaltered.

To understand these ideas better requires a look at probability. Suppose that two unweighted (honest) coins are flipped 100 times. The single most likely outcome is that 25 times both would land heads up, 50 times one would land head up and one would land tail up, and 25 times both would land tails up. The probability of getting two heads is the chance of the first one coming up heads (.5) times the probability that the second also lands heads up (also .5); .5 times .5 is .25 or 25 percent. The probability of two tails is likewise 25 percent. The probability of having the first coin land on heads and the second on tails is .5 times .5. However, one can have a head and a tail combination by having the first land on tails and the second on heads. Therefore, the total probability of a head and a tail is two times .5 times .5, or 50 percent. Extending these percentages to 100 repetitions, we arrive at the 25 : 50 : 25 distribution mentioned above.

Although this distribution is the most likely outcome with unweighted coins, if one allows for chance, it would not be particularly surprising to have results such as 24 head-head combinations, 52 head-tail combinations, and 24 tail-tail combinations. This small deviation from expectation is not significant and should not make one suspect the reliability of the results. If the results were significantly different from expectation, say 90 : 10 : 0, the honesty of the coins would be very doubtful.

Thus, we can state a hypothesis about the coins (they are honest), predict a distribution of head-tail combinations (25 : 50 : 25), carry out an experiment (flip them), and compare the actual with the expected results to see how well they agree. Last, we can state how well the initial hypothesis predicts the actual outcome and, based on this comparison, accept or reject the hypothesis. Hardy-Weinberg does the same thing in respect to the ways alleles come together to form offspring. It yields expected genotype distributions of the offspring in a given population assuming no evolution, which can then be compared to the real, observed distribution (Chapter 3).

Hardy-Weinberg states that given the allele frequencies of a population, the genotype frequencies in the next generation will conform to the rules of probability. These expectations are the probability of two identical alleles forming one type of homozygote, the probability of two different alleles uniting to form a heterozygote, and so on. The actual probabilities will depend on the actual frequency of the alleles. If the M allele of the MN blood type is very common, then MM people will be formed quite often; if M is rare, it will be very unlikely to form homozygotes.

We have used a matrix to predict the offspring of a mating. By modifying it slightly, we can use the same technique to predict the genotype distribution for a population of offspring, if we know the allele frequencies in their parents. If an infinite population has an M-allele frequency of 70 percent and an N frequency of 30 percent, and if it fits the other Hardy-Weinberg stipulations, the frequencies of the three MN genotypes in the children can be computed as in Table 2.5. In this hypothetical population all matings are occurring at random; thus, the frequency with which children obtain an M allele from the father is equal to the frequency of M alleles in males (.7). The chance of receiving an M from the mother is here also .7; the probability of a particular child being MM is .49. Put another way, 49 percent of all the children in this group are expected to be MM. Similar reasoning shows that 9 percent should be NN. The frequency of heterozygous children should be the frequency of the M allele multiplied by that of the N, *times two*, because the heterozygote can be formed in two ways. The M could come from the mother and the N from the father, or vice versa. As demonstrated above, these genotype frequencies in the children can be shown to correspond to allele frequencies of M = .7 and N = .3 just as in the parents. If evolution is ignored, we see that the allele and genotype frequencies do not change from one generation to the next. This is true by definition, as evolution means change: no evolution, no change.

Usually the Hardy-Weinberg rule is stated more generally. If the frequency of one allele, let us say M, is p and that of the other allele (N) is q, under Hardy-Weinberg conditions the genotypes occur in the following proportion:

$$p^2 MM : 2pq MN : q^2 NN$$

This ratio is the expected distribution of genotypes given allele frequencies of p and q, if evolution is not operating.

TABLE 2.5
Predicting Genotype Distribution
Assuming that the conditions of the Hardy-Weinberg equilibrium are met, allele frequency and genotype distribution do not change from the parental generation to the offspring.

AN EXAMPLE OF GENOTYPE PREDICTION:

Genotype distribution in parental generation
.49MM   .42MN   .09NN

Parents allele frequency: .7M, .3N

	Females	
	.7M	.3N
Males .7M	.49MM	.21MN
.3N	.21MN	.09NN

Genotype distribution in offspring
.49MM   .42MN   .09NN

A GENERALIZATION OF THE EXAMPLE:

Genotype distribution in parental generation
p^2MM $2pq$MN q^2NN

Where: p = the frequency of M; q = the frequency of N

	Females	
	pM	qN
Males pM	p^2MM	pqMN
qN	pqMN	q^2NN

Genotype distribution in offspring
p^2MM $2pq$MN q^2NN

A NUMERICAL EXAMPLE:

Population size: 100[a]

Observed genotypes: 49MM   42MN   9NN

Genotype frequencies: .49MM   .42MN   .09NN

Total number of M alleles:
    49 people × 2 M alleles per person = 98
  + 42 people × 1 M allele per person = 42
                                        ――――――
                                        140 M alleles

Total number of genes:
  100 people × 2 alleles per person = 200

Frequency of M allele (allele frequency of M):
    $140/200 = .70 = p$

Frequency of N allele (allele frequency of N):
    $1 - .70 = .30 = q$

Predicted frequency of MM offspring:[b]
    $.70$ M × $.70$ M = $.49$ MM = p^2

Predicted frequency of MN offspring:[b]
    $2 × .70$ M × $.30$ N = $.42$ MN = $2pq$

Predicted frequency of NN offspring:[b]
    $.30$ N × $.30$ N = $.09$ NN = q^2

---

[a]Although this population is not infinite in size, to simplify we will assume that genetic drift is not occurring.
[b]Because the predicted frequencies are the same as the observed distribution, we would conclude that there is no evidence for the operation of evolutionary forces.

Using Hardy-Weinberg to Estimate Allele Frequencies   The Hardy-Weinberg law can be used to estimate allele frequencies when dominance is present. Counting alleles (Table 2.4) is not possible because there is no way to distinguish the homozygotes for the dominant allele from the heterozygotes. Using the earlobe example (U = unattached; u = attached), while we do not know the genotypes of those with the dominant unattached phenotype, we do know that all of those with attached earlobes are genotypically uu. Assuming that the population is in Hardy-Weinberg equilibrium, we can reason that the frequency of u equals the square root of the frequency of uu. That is, for a population in equilibrium, if the frequency of the homozygous recessive genotype is the gene frequency squared, the reverse holds true too. Thus we obtain the recessive allele's frequency by taking the square root of the frequency of the homozygous recessive. Because the frequencies of the two alleles must add up to 1.0, the dominant allele's frequency is obtained by subtracting the recessive's frequency from 1.0 (Table 2.6).

A key concept linking genetics and evolution is *genetic fitness,* or the average reproductive success of each genotype. Fitness in the genetic sense does not correspond to "healthy"; a sterile person in the pink of health is nevertheless an evolutionary failure. Fitness is a measure of the average worth of each genotype in reproductive terms, caused by differences among people either in ability to survive or in fertility. As such, fitness is a function of both the environment and the genes, for a combination of alleles might be very helpful at one time or place, but harmful at another. There are no alleles that are "good" under all circumstances.

The basis of fitness, or reproductive success, can be judged in two ways. Taking a simple, two-allele codominant situation with its three genotypes, one can compute the average absolute reproductive success of each alternative. If AA individuals average 1.1 offspring, AA' average 1.2, and A'A' average .9, these absolute figures can be taken as measures of fitness.

We can also set the most prolific genotype equal to 1; it is the optimal in these conditions. We can then compute relative fitness. If 1.2 offspring is equivalent to 100 percent success, the relative fitness of AA (1.1 offspring) is .92 and that of A'A' is .75. Although absolute fitnesses are more accurate reflections of reality, the relative fitness values are much easier to deal with mathematically, and therefore are more commonly used. The average fitness of a population is, simply, equal to the

TABLE 2.6
A Numerical Example for Computing Allele Frequencies When Dominance Is Present

Number = 200			Suppose 200 people in a population were observed for earlobe type.
Phenotypes: Genotypes:	Unattached UU; Uu	Attached uu	Because there is dominance, there are two phenotypes corresponding to the three genotypes.
Number in each category	150	50	Suppose the observed numbers were as noted.
Percentages	.75	.25	Then these are the percentages.
Frequency of recessive allele	uu = .25 u = $\sqrt{.25}$ u = .5		To obtain the frequency of the recessive allele, take the square root of the frequency of homozygous recessives.
Frequency of dominant allele	U = 1.0 − frequency of u = 1.0 − .5 = .5		Because the allele frequencies must add up to one, the frequency of the dominant allele is obtained by subtraction.

fitness of each genotype weighted according to how often it occurs within the population. A population with equal numbers of AA, AA′, and A′A′ people would have an average relative fitness of

$$\frac{1.0 + .92 + .75}{3} \text{ or } .89.$$

Summary

An understanding of evolution, or the change in the frequency of genes in a population, demands a knowledge of genetics. Although we cannot reduce anatomical and behavioral factors to the level of genetic analysis except by inference, we can study the current evolution of modern human populations by their alterations in gene frequency.

We can analyze the behavior of genes at three levels: biochemical, chromosomal, and populational. From biochemical genetics we learn that DNA, the genetic material, directs the production of proteins, which are the basis of many functional requirements of life. The synthesis of proteins occurs through a series of biochemical steps: The inherited blueprint, the DNA, is "read," and its directions translated into a string of amino acids, a protein.

The evolutionary phenomenon known as mutation is the change in the structure of a piece of DNA, which can in turn alter the structure and function of a protein. Most mutations involve only a small rearrangement of the DNA, but because of the interconnectedness of the systems of the body, a small chemical change can have wide-ranging effects on survival and reproduction, as can changes in the timing of genetic events. The constantly and randomly occurring changes in the genetic material provide for genetic alternatives from which natural selection can choose the better adapted and discard the poorly adapted forms. The gene's degree of adaptation depends on the environment in which it is present.

Chromosomal or Mendelian genetics involves several indispensable terms: alleles, genotype, phenotype, dominance, linkage, and meiosis. All deal with how DNA is passed from parent to offspring or with how the genes function. We find that for many traits the genotype and environment interact to produce the individual's phenotype. Genes set certain limits on the degree of skin pigmentation, but the phenotype is affected also by environmental factors, such as exposure to sunlight, diet, and state of health.

In sexually reproducing organisms, such as humans, meiosis maintains the correct number of genes in every generation by producing sex cells with one gene for every trait. The union of sperm and egg creates a normal individual with two genes for each trait. Proper development depends on having neither too many nor too few copies of the genes. Because sexual reproduction has major effects on evolution (see Chapter 3), a knowledge of Mendelian genetics is important.

Population geneticists analyze the changes in gene frequencies that result from evolutionary processes. The basic concept of population genetics, the gene pool, describes the population's genetic makeup by means of allele frequencies and genotype frequencies.

The Hardy-Weinberg equilibrium uses information about the gene pool to predict how the genotypes would be distributed in a population that is not undergoing evolution. This distribution is based on probabilities, and in this ideal population, allele and genotype frequencies do not change. The Hardy-Weinberg rule can also be used to compute allele frequencies for traits showing dominance.

In the next chapter we will consider genetics, especially population genetics, and the evolutionary processes in some detail.

3

Evolution is an unending process guided by the forces of natural selection, mutation, genetic drift, and gene flow.

Evolution in Action

An analysis of human history in an evolutionary framework assumes that we accept evolution as an appropriate model for interpreting the data. Certainly, not everyone accepts this view, and several times in this century, the United States has been the home of anti-evolution movements. Although the reasons why this country should foster such movements are intriguing, the crucial question is whether there is any truth to the claim that evolutionary biology is not scientific. To respond, first we will review what makes a methodology a science and then see whether evolution fits with this definition.

As a first approximation, we can say that the scientific method is a structured way of solving problems. The structuring involves the formulation of a hypothesis—a statement of the problem—that is subject to testing and is potentially falsifiable. Data are generated by various forms of experiment, and the hypothesis is examined in light of the data. At this point, the hypothesis is viewed as either: (1) supported by the data, (2) disproven, or (3) requiring modification.

Mendel's work with inheritance in pea plants is a good example of this process. Mendel formulated rules about the integrity of genes and their ability to segregate (see Chapter 2). He performed experiments by breeding thousands of plants, then looking at the results and concluding that his initial hypothesis was supported. Unfortunately for Mendel, no one else paid any attention to his work at the time. Later, others did rediscover his publication, checked his results, and started to ask questions that extended and modified his conclusions. Some of the phenomena they discovered, such as linked genes, did not accord with Mendel's initial statements. In a treelike fashion, one question led to others, and the answers and more questions formed the field of modern genetics.

This rather sketchy and simplistic view of one scientist's work does illustrate a few key features of science in general.

1. Scientific hypotheses are fertile. They generate many new questions and areas to be investigated.

2. It must be possible for a hypothesis to fail tests to be considered scientific. If a statement cannot be tested and potentially disproven, it is not scientific.
3. The validity of a hypothesis is judged by how well it predicts solutions to new questions.
4. Scientific hypotheses, even when supported by testing, are tentative. They are not immutable but subject to refinement. We must always be open to modifying the hypothesis to fit future information.

Granted, this is a brief and admittedly "Alice in Wonderland" view of the way science and scientists operate. Scientists are people too, with egos and ambitions as well as ethics. The methodology sometimes goes awry in real life, but another feature is that it is self-correcting. Scientists are always checking each other's work, and inaccuracies are sooner or later corrected.

How well does evolution fit these criteria? How well have its conclusions been supported? It has been argued that evolutionary hypotheses cannot be tested for they deal with past events and therefore cannot be predictive. This is inaccurate for several reasons. For one, evolution is constantly going on, and in fact experiments can be designed to test the predictive success of evolutionary hypotheses. When dealing with an organism with a short generation, we can actually see evolutionary changes and check how well predictions fit observations.

Secondly, when dealing with past happenings, evolutionary studies can be retrodictive; that is, hypotheses can be generated about past events and tested against new data as they are uncovered. For a long time, physical anthropologists felt that human evolution was characterized by the early appearance of a large brain followed by the later development of the ability to walk on two legs. Fossils unearthed over several decades have clearly shown this to be false, in fact, 180 degrees off. The big brain developed late in our evolution. This revelation has in turn led to many other questions, which form large segments of this book. Evolution is a very fertile discipline. As new hypotheses are generated, they are also subject to testing by the criterion of predictive (or retrodictive) success and are eminently scientific.

A criticism often made of evolution is that, "after all, it's only a theory." Such comments indicate a prominent misunderstanding of the qualities of a scientific theory. In science, a theory is not simply someone's off-the-top-of-the-head thoughts. It is a set of general principles that have developed out of massive amounts of hypothesis testing and, as such, has the great weight of supporting evidence. We all have "theories" about why our favorite baseball team will win the pennant next year or why the government is pursuing a particular course of action. Such usage of the word *theory* should not be equated with the much more rigorous usage in the phrase *theory of evolution*. The latter is not just educated guesswork but has been developed, tested, and refined through millions of hours of human intellectual endeavor.

Keeping the scientific nature of evolutionary theory in mind, let us consider the processes that lead to evolutionary change. We shall outline the concepts put forward by Darwin and subsequently modified by new data and synthesized with the concepts of genetics: the Neo-Darwinian (*neo* = *new*), or synthetic, theory.

Generally there are said to be four forces that cause evolution: natural selection, mutation, genetic drift, and gene flow. Some theorists have postulated additional forces as well. In his original formulations, Darwin gave primacy to natural selection as the driving force of evolution, and he was largely correct. Natural selection is not synonymous with evolution, however. It is but one of the processes that can cause changes in the gene pool of a population and can produce evolution. The term *natural selection* consequently implies a choice, and choice implies variation. The variation that Darwin observed in natural populations had to have an origin, and the second evolutionary process, the one that produces variation, is mutation.

As seen in Chapter 2, mutations can alter the structure and functioning of the individual. Variation, once having arisen by the process of mutation, can then be affected by natural selection. Some mutations are adaptive; they help the individual survive and reproduce in a particular environment. Natural selection results in an increase in the frequency of this new, beneficial mutant gene. As noted, this is simply a consequence of the fact that those individuals with genes well suited for survival and reproduction in a particular environment will, on the average, outreproduce those with less well-suited genes. The better adapted genes become more common as time goes by. The flip side of this process is that selection can work to rid a gene pool of harmful genes. This differential reproduction of genotypes is natural selection. This is quite different from Darwin's view of selection as "survival of the fittest," for it is not whether you survive that is important but rather the number of offspring you produce relative to the number produced by other members of your population. Living to be one hundred years old without ever mating and reproducing not only would be less fun but also would be an evolutionary failure compared to having five or six offspring during a life span of fifty years. Certainly survival is an important consideration, but reproduction is the key to selection.

Viewed in modern terms, we see that much although not all evolution is the result of the interactions of these two forces—selection and mutation. Several important implications follow from this fact.

To reiterate, evolution's direction is to produce organisms that possess genes that are well-suited to survive in a particular environment. The force pushing in this direction is selection. It is the only evolutionary process to be said to have a direction. From this, it follows that humans are not the goal of evolution, nor are other animals working their way up a "ladder of life" to become like us. Chimpanzees are not going to become people someday. Each organism is evolving to survive in its own niche, in its own life-style, whether it is in the trees or underground, eating this food or that, active at night or day. Life forms are dispersing into different environments and ways of living, and the only goal is for each to be able to deal with its own problems. People are evolving to survive and reproduce in a very broad range of environments, but all require the ability to use a language, live in a cultural setting, make tools and so forth. Apes and monkeys have quite different requirements and are evolving constantly to live in their own spheres.

As adaptation to an environment is the goal, and as environments are always changing, evolution has no end. What is beneficial at one time and place will become obsolete as the environment changes. As we cannot predict how environments will change, we cannot predict what course evolution will take. Will future humans be bald and large brained, as some science fiction stories picture them? Only if those with less hair and bigger brains are better adapted for survival and reproduction in future human environments. Even if we could state with certainty that these two human traits would be highly advantageous in the future, there is still no guarantee we would evolve along this route. Mutations occur at random, not because they are needed. The organism cannot sense a need and order up the requisite mutation. Should an appropriate mutation simply not happen, natural selection would not have the raw material with which to work: no variation, no selection.

Mutations, as we saw in Chapter 2, do not generally yield the bizarre creations so popular in fiction. Those grossly abnormal individuals who do occur have multiple mutations or chromosomal defects and usually do not survive. In fact, as noted, it appears that many mutations are neutral. These neither harm nor benefit the individual and thus do not affect the chances of surviving and reproducing (Figure 3.1). The neutral mutation classification also includes those mutations that only affect fitness to a very limited degree. In other words, a mutation that increases (or decreases) an individual's fitness only minutely is effectively neutral. The fate of these genes is determined not by selection but by a third process called *genetic drift*.

Genetic drift refers to random fluctuations in the frequency of a gene from generation to generation. Initially a new mutation exists only within one individual (remember Queen Victoria). The odds that this mutant gene will be passed on from generation to generation are very small. The odds that it will increase in frequency are even slimmer. Nevertheless, the possibility exists, and, given the appearance of a large number of neutral or nearly neutral mutations, one can mathematically predict that a percentage of them will, just by chance, achieve 100 percent frequency in a population.

As you might expect, the smaller the population, the more likely it is that genetic drift will be effective. Using an example of drift that involves the loss of a fairly common allele via chance, imagine a small population of fifty people in which 10 percent have one form of a genetic trait (blue eyes) and the other 90 percent have the alternative (brown eyes). If an earthquake swallows up ten of the members, including all those with blue eyes, the frequency of the trait will have been markedly altered: The population has evolved, or changed genetically. If the pop-

FIGURE 3.1
Many mutations have invisible effects and do not significantly affect a person's ability to survive and reproduce. Some have visible effects but still do not noticeably affect normal functioning. This child has a rare dominant gene that causes polydactyly, more than five digits per hand and foot.

ulation is larger, say 1 million people, and 10 percent (100,000) are blue-eyed, the death by accident of five of these blue-eyed people will not significantly alter the genetic composition of the group; its evolution will not be affected. These are not examples of natural selection, for eye color has nothing to do with the chance of surviving the accident. Thus drift, too, can change the genetic composition of a group; its general tendency is to reduce the variation within the group.

A fourth case of evolutionary change is *gene flow,* or *admixture,* achieved through migration and interbreeding as individuals from one breeding population leave and join another. The movement and mating of people are often related to social values, to conflicts within or outside groups that result in fragmentation, to mating patterns, and to other aspects of social organization as well as to geography.

The effect of immigration on the genetic makeup of a population is directly related to the size of that population. In a small population, the frequency of many genes may be significantly altered, whereas a large population can absorb a sizable number of immigrants before showing a noticeable change. Emigration (outward migration) may also change the gene frequencies in the original population; in small populations, emigration may ultimately cause the total loss of certain genes.

Gene flow can not only alter the frequency of genes previously present in the receiving population but also, like mutation, introduce totally new genes into the group. Genes flowing between groups will act to reduce the differences between them.

These four forces are those known to produce changes in a population's gene pool. We have outlined the traditional view of their operation and relative levels of importance; natural selection and mutation are given primacy for changing the gene pool over time. Mutation provides the variation, and selection increases the frequency of beneficial new genes and decreases the frequency of harmful genes. For some time this view of change as being gradual, with small alterations building up to the major ones seen in the fossil record, has been challenged by an alternative hypothesis—punctuated equilibria. The debate, which will be outlined below, focuses on the rate of change involved in the appearance of new sorts of animals and the nature and relative importance of the evolutionary forces that produce the change. The debate does not question the documented fact that evolution occurs, however.

Evidence for Evolution

What then is the evidence that has been generated in support of the contention that these processes cause evolution? This is a very broad question that could take several lifetimes to answer. Fortunately the evidence falls into several categories, which we can briefly review.

Comparative Sciences

The popularity of a zoo's ape house indicates that we all recognize marked similarities between the inhabitants and ourselves; the behavior of chimps often reflects our own, and they certainly bear anatomical resemblances to us. We also recognize that other mammals share fewer similarities with us, while the reptiles are quite unlike us in anatomy and behavior. These observations are essentially evolutionary ones. Chimps are so much like us because until very recently (5 to 10 million years ago; the exact number is debated in Chapter 7), we and they were the same animal. Because chimps and humans on the one hand and, say, tigers, have not shared a common ancestor for upwards of 75 million years, we and tigers have diverged more completely. Reptiles and mammals last had a common ancestor over 150 million years ago, and so are even less alike in anatomy and behavior. By and large, the more similar organisms are, the more recently they shared a common ancestor.

Comparative sciences can thus provide evidence of evolution. Comparative anatomy was one of the earliest to do so; Darwin and his contemporaries drew heavily on it. Comparative embryology, the study of embryos and their development, was also used quite early. Recently, comparative biochemistry and immunology have provided information on evolutionary relationships; we now know, for example, that humans and chimps have very similar molecular makeups. Behavioral comparisons are also very informative.

A direct line of evidence for major evolutionary changes is the fossil record. Fossils are mineralized remains of past life forms. Most fossils are parts of the skeletal anatomy or teeth, but lately even fossilized footprints have been uncovered. Fossils record the changes in the anatomy of our ancestors. By understanding our anatomical evolution, we can try to deduce the alterations in behavior. Evolution is adaptive, and "form follows function." Organisms may begin a new behavior for which they are not particularly well suited. Over time the fossils show how the anatomy was modified so that the organism could better perform the behavior. Increasing dependence on the manufacture and use of tools, for example, created selection pressure for finer manipulative skills, and the hand anatomy was thus modified; selection also altered our pelvis and legs to accommodate better upright walking.

Fossil Evidence

We also have firsthand evidence of evolution: We have seen it happen. Many observational accounts deal with insects or microorganisms that have short generations and can change rapidly.

Observational Studies

Over the last fifty years we have seen the development of many antibiotics, chemicals like penicillin and streptomycin that can kill or retard the growth of certain microbes. Although miraculous, these drugs are self-defeating to a degree, for the widespread use of an antibiotic leads to the evolution of a strain resistant to that drug. Ingenious experimental designs have demonstrated that the initial microbial resistance to a drug is not induced by exposure to the antibiotic; rather, the antibiotic results in the increased frequency of this resistance by operating as a selective force.

Bacteria, like all living things, are biochemically variable. Some bacteria contain mutant genes that, among other effects, allow them to survive in an environment containing a particular antibiotic. These variants have undoubtedly arisen time and again for eons. They were of little use, however, until antibiotics were invented, at which time the mutation becomes highly beneficial to the survival of the microbe. Those containing the mutation can infect a person, survive the antibiotic treatment, reproduce, and spread to other people. This form of the organism becomes very common; the bacteria without this mutation are killed and do not spread.

Over the years of exposure to penicillin the organisms that cause syphilis, for instance, have evolved strains that not only survive penicillin but actually flourish on it. Again, this results from the random appearance of mutations, some of which alter the microbe's functioning and provide it with the ability to break down the antibiotic. With the evolution of microbial strains resistant to antibiotics, it becomes necessary to discover new antibiotics capable of checking the evolved organism. Physicians' reluctance to prescribe an antibiotic every time we have an infection is based on knowledge of this evolutionary process; if they blunt the usefulness of an antibiotic by using it to treat minor infections, they are only leading to the appearance of a microbe for which they may have no treatment.

A similar process has resulted in the appearance of insects resistant to the effects of DDT and other insecticides. DDT has been used to control populations of many insects, including houseflies, lice, and malaria-carrying mosquitoes. Mutations within an insect population may produce genetic variants that can tolerate DDT. As the insecticide is used, the resistant insects survive to reproduce, while the susceptible die off. This has led to the evolution of strains capable of surviving in environments with the insecticide.

An even more intriguing example, with a moral for our present ecological problems, comes from the attempt by Australian farmers to rid their continent of rabbits (Figure 3.2). Before European contact, Australia had no rabbits; very few placental mammals were found there. In the 1800s a variety of rabbits was accidentally introduced and, having rabbits' habits, rapidly spread through much of Australia, eating crops as they went. By 1928 there were 500 million rabbits on the continent. Farmers and shepherds, much perturbed by their economic losses, asked the government how they could reduce the rabbit population. Scientists came up with the apparently brilliant idea of introducing a disease, myxomatosis, which was lethal to almost 100 percent of these rabbits. The release of rabbit-biting mosquitoes carrying the myxoma virus almost eliminated the natural population. However, a few Australian rabbits had a mutation that made them resistant to the disease, and from these few survivors the population started to rebuild. The virus, too, was evolving. The disease organism's evolutionary strategy is not to kill its host but to coexist with it. The viruses that could infect a rabbit without killing it were also selected for. In a fairly short time, the rabbits' gene pool was modified for increased resistance, and the virus's genetic struc-

FIGURE 3.2
A view of the destructive capabilities of rabbits in Australia.
Running down the center of the photograph is a rabbit-proof fence. On the left, rabbits have eaten all the plants they could reach. In the process they destroyed land otherwise suitable for cattle and sheep grazing.

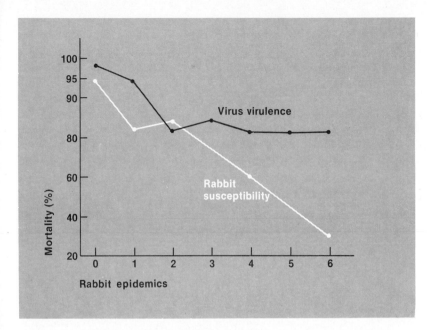

FIGURE 3.3. The decreasing susceptibility of Australian rabbits is illustrated by the rapid decrease in the percentage of rabbits that died upon exposure to a standard, highly virulent (disease-causing) myxoma virus. As the Australian strain of the virus underwent natural selection, its ability to kill laboratory rabbits declined noticeably. The time scale refers to the number of epidemics to which the population was exposed.

ture was selected for decreased virulence. Very soon after the epidemic, the rabbit population recovered (Figure 3.3)[1]*

Traditionally, theorists have held that these sorts of small-scale evolutionary changes are the stuff from which major alterations are made. The classic Neo-Darwinian view is that many little changes build up over immense periods of time to produce the changes seen in the fossil record; the little changes provide for the origin of the species.

Two Definitions of *Species*

To understand the evolution of species we must first define a *species* (plural: *species*). The definition of a biological species appears to be straightforward: Animals are members of the same species if normal males and females are actively or potentially capable of mating and producing fertile offspring.[2] All humans are members of one species, for fertile offspring result from matings between members of any populations. The horse and donkey are not classified as members of one species, for although they can produce offspring, these offspring (mules) are sterile; they are evolutionary dead ends. It is not possible for the genes of a horse to flow into the donkey's pool of genes or vice versa. It is at least potentially possible for genes from any human population to enter the pool of any other human population. Hence all living humans are of one species.

*See page 614 for notes to Chapter 3.

In theory it is easy to decide whether two living animals are members of the same species (although even this involves some difficulties). But this definition of a biological species cannot be applied when at least one of the animals is represented only by fossilized remains. We cannot know if the people living 2 million years ago could have interbred with us. We do know that they looked quite different from us, particularly from the neck up, and had a different technology and diet. Because of these differences we somewhat arbitrarily agree to call them a different species.

It appears that 2 million years ago there was more than one kind of human (Chapter 9). Again from anatomy, tools, and inferences about diet and behavior (but not breeding patterns, for these do not fossilize), we must decide how many species of humans coexisted. A definition of species based primarily on anatomy is called an *evolutionary, paleo-* (old) or *chrono-* (*time*) species concept. One expert defines an evolutionary species as a group of ancestor-descendant populations with its own evolutionary trends and tendencies.[3]

Origins of Species

Although new ideas have been put forward to account for the origin of species, Neo-Darwinian theory holds that there are two routes by which new life forms appear; both are forms of the process called *speciation* (Figure 3.4). Straight-line evolution, or *anagenesis* (*ana* = *upward; genesis* = *origination*) is the change of one form of animal into another form: One species replaces another. In anagenesis the number of species is not altered; one simply changes into the other through time due to the gradual accumulation of genetic change.

The fossil record supports the contention that at least for some time our evolution occurred by anagenesis. One-half million years ago our ancestors were different enough from us to be called a different (*chrono*) species. Over time this species evolved enough—mainly in respect to cranial features—to warrant being called by a different species name. The

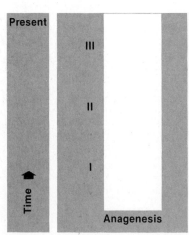

FIGURE 3.4
Through anagenesis, a chronospecies can evolve into another species: I→II→III. Through cladogenesis, a chronospecies can evolve into several more chronospecies and/or biological species:

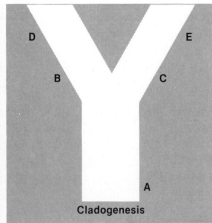

changes came about largely as a result of selection favoring mutations that increased brain size, the ability to use a language, and so forth. One species evolved into one, new species; this is anagenesis.

The second pathway is called *cladogenesis* (*clado* = *sprouting*), or branching evolution; one life form yields two or more new ones (Figure 3.4). One species is subdivided into two or more genetically isolated populations by the appearance of some geographic barrier. Depending on the kind of animal under consideration, isolation might follow a change in the course of a river, the appearance of a mountain or desert, the building of a city, or simply distance—anything that will effectively prevent mating between members of the populations. Because no two places on the earth are exactly the same, the inhabitants of the two (or more) areas will be subject to more or less different selection forces. They may have different food sources, be affected by different diseases, be exposed to different amounts of rainfall, or be preyed upon by predators with different habits. We can expect members of the groups to become more and more different as time passes. It is also unlikely that the mutations that occur in one area will be exactly duplicated in the other; hence more difference will result. Either at the time of or subsequent to isolation, drift also may cause the groups to differ genetically. Because interbreeding is not occurring, there is nothing to counteract these dispersive forces. Genes, or gene combinations, appearing in one of the isolated groups cannot spread to the other isolates. Differences accumulate over time, and ultimately the groups become so different that even if the geographic barrier were removed, the animals could no longer produce fertile offspring. When this condition is achieved, speciation is said to have occurred.

Geographic isolation is a prerequisite for branching evolution; nothing else that we know of can begin cladogenesis. Once geographic isolation and the ensuing divergent evolutionary changes have established two distinct species, other isolating mechanisms maintain the reproductive isolation even if the initial geographic barrier has been removed. Isolating mechanisms operate in two main ways to separate species. In the first, interbreeding never occurs. Such premating barriers include different courtship procedures or habitat differences that preclude the two from meeting. Second, if interbreeding does occur, postmating barriers come into play: The sperm of one does not fertilize the other's egg; the egg does not develop; or hybrid animals (offspring that come from interbreeding) are not able to compete with individuals of the parental groups or are biologically weak or even infertile, like the mule.

Thus, over time a variety of mechanisms develop to maintain the separation of two distinct species. In this way evolution, once having produced an array of genes that adapts an animal to its way of life, prevents disruption of the adaptive combination, which could follow breeding with other forms.

Very early in the evolution of our species, cladogenesis occurred. Several millions of years ago a group of humanlike animals became subdivided into geographically isolated populations. Each pursued separate evolutionary paths, adapting to somewhat different ways of life and, as will be seen, evolving into separate, contemporaneous species. Only one of these has continued through time, ultimately to become us.

Semispecies   Just as there are difficulties in applying our apparently straightforward definition of a biological species to long-dead animals, there are difficulties in defining species that are in the process of becoming reproductively isolated, for although members of the diverging groups may not be very successful at interbreeding, fertile offspring are occasionally produced.

There are many known examples of the inability of classification to reflect totally the complexities of speciation. Among our close relatives, the monkeys of Southeast Asia, are the rhesus monkey and the crab-eating monkey. The rhesus is found primarily in the Indian subcontinent, but outlying populations are found in Thailand. Crab-eating monkeys are common throughout the Malay Archipelago and Malaysia but also have outlyers in Thailand. In this small area of overlap, human disturbance of the environment results in occasional contact between the species, and interbreeding and fertile young are known. With how many species, then, are we dealing? Although the uncritical application of the biological species concept would define these animals as one species, most researchers regard them as two very closely related species, or *semispecies*. They reason that the interbreeding is so rare as to have virtually no effect on the vast majority of the animals in the central areas of the species' range. The interbreeding does not result in significant gene flow between the groups.

Rates and Patterns of Evolutionary Divergence   The aftermath of speciation is divergence. Once two animals have split and evolved isolating mechanisms, there is no way for them to evolve back into the same species, for the differences that have come into being are so complex that it is impossible to relive all the changes in reverse sequence. Greater and greater differences build up with the passage of time. This is known as *divergent evolution;* all cladogenesis is divergent.

Adaptive Radiation   Evolution does not happen at a constant rate (but see page 177); sometimes the rate of divergence can be quite rapid and the number of new species formed quite large. When an animal enters an environment that offers a number of unused new ways of life, or unoccupied *niches,* it may quickly diverge into many newly formed, geographically isolated populations and evolve biological features that adapt it for each of these ways of life, resulting in a lot of cladogenesis. This evolutionary pattern is called an *adaptive radiation*.

The finches Darwin observed in the Galapagos Islands gave him one of his clearest leads for formulating a theory of evolution. Today about fourteen species seem to have evolved from one ancestral species, which was derived from a mainland South America species. The first finches probably began their life on the Galapagos when a few mainland birds reached the islands by chance. They then spread to all the islands, and because finches do not normally fly great distances, each island's populations remained isolated from the others. The Galapagos have few other species of land birds and thus provided the finches with many vacant adaptive niches. In time, the finches underwent an adaptive radiation, a lot of cladogenesis, evolving to lead many new ways of life. The ground finches of the *Geospiza* group evolved heavy beaks suited for cracking seeds. Generally, the larger beaked birds are those that chose larger seeds for the preponderance of their diet. The tree finches are vegetarians with shorter, thick beaks, while the warblerlike finch (*Certhidea*) is insectivorous with a slender beak. The woodpeckerlike finch (Figure 1.12) evolved a behavioral adaptation for feeding. In each case, the finches specialized through the interplay of mutations and selection so as to use the available foods. When a mutation that slightly increased the robustness of the beak appeared in a bird that had to crack large seeds for its supper, for instance, it was increased in frequency through selection. Thus evolved the rather specialized beaks seen in Figure 3.5, as well as other features. Once the birds are no longer capable of interbreeding, even when living in the same area, we say they have speciated. This large amount of rapid speciation to take advantage of new ways of life is an adaptive radiation.

Convergent Evolution   Although all cladogenesis is divergent when investigated carefully, occasionally two animals superficially come to resemble each other more and more. The porpoise is a mammal whose ancestors lived on land. Over millions of years, after going back into the seas, the porpoise has come to resemble the shark in several ways; it has *converged* on the evolution of the shark. The porpoise has evolved streamlining for speed, strong tail fins for locomotion, and large teeth for predation. Yet internally the porpoise is nothing like a shark: It gets its oxygen from the air, not the water; it has internal fertilization and a uterus for incubating the embryo; its fins contain modified forms of the same bones in our limbs; and its skeleton's cellular structure is quite different from that of the shark. The porpoise's superficial similarities to a shark reflect only the facts that, as marine predators, both animals face some similar requirements and that natural selection has produced some common answers in both groups. Similar effects are seen in an aquatic reptile. *Convergent evolution* refers to the appearance of superficial similarities in unrelated species as both adapt to deal with similar environments (Figure 3.6).

Microevolution

Maintaining Variation

Variation among species is a result of the process of speciation as different mutations, coupled with different selection pressures and genetic drift, accumulate genetic differences in geographically isolated groups. Within a species variation is also of prime interest, and the ways in which the evolutionary forces increase or decrease the level of genetic variation is an important concern of the synthetic theory. The changing of gene frequencies in populations is called *microevolution*.

FIGURE 3.5. After inhabiting the Galapagos Islands, the finches underwent an adaptive radiation—a lot of divergent evolution. Among other features, the modern finches have come to differ in beak shape as the species specialized to eat different foods. Today there are four main groups (genera; see Chapter 4) and fourteen species.

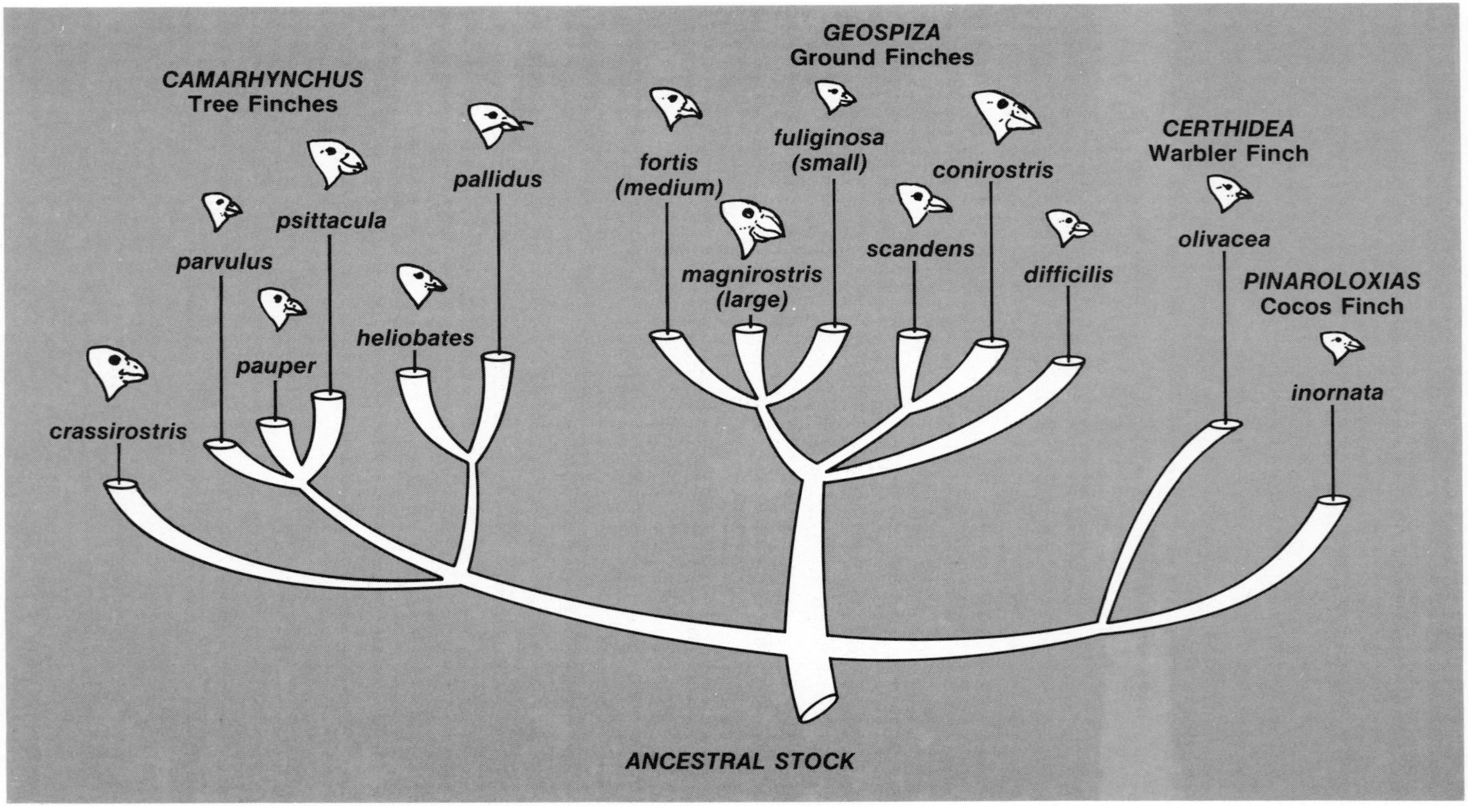

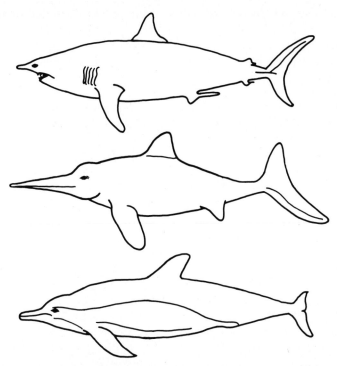

FIGURE 3.6. Convergent evolution can be seen by comparing three animals that, although only very distantly related, look very similar. All three evolved superficial features as a common adaptation to life as fast-swimming predators. From top to bottom, these are a fish (shark), a reptile (*Ichthyosaurus*), and a mammal (porpoise).

A species with little variation is in a very precarious evolutionary position. Should the environment of such a group alter rapidly, extinction will likely occur. The presence of variants, even those with no obvious value, provides a valuable defense against future disaster.

Theodosius Dobzhansky (1900–1975), among others, has shown that much variability is hidden in the gene pool.[4] He demonstrated this using fruit flies (*Drosophilia*) in selective breeding experiments designed to bring out hidden variation. The genetic trait Dobzhansky decided to study was the flies' preference for light or dark passageways. He started with flies from one population that he randomly divided into two groups. Initially, the two subgroups showed similar numbers of flies preferring light or dark passages. Then, in one strain, Dobzhansky selected only flies that preferred the light routes as parents for the next generation. In the other strain, only those preferring the dark were allowed to reproduce. As this pattern was kept up for several generations, there appeared a very marked difference in the preferences of the two strains. One chose the light the vast majority of the time, and the other principally chose the dark. This indicates that the original population had a large amount of hidden variation that could provide the basis for and be made apparent by selection. Such large amounts of concealed variability can offer the necessary paths to new adaptations. In part, this hidden variability was the result of recessive genes being brought to light. Recombination, by physically associating the genes in new arrangement, can also produce new variants.

Because of the significance of variation, it is important to understand the evolutionary processes that increase or decrease variation in populations. The examples we will use are on a small scale, involving slight shifts in the frequency of an allele controlling one or another blood protein. This is not to say that there were no variants for brain organization, pelvis structure, or hand dexterity; it is just that knowledge of genetic variations in complex anatomical and behavioral features is very rudimentary. The much simpler protein variants are better, although by no means perfectly, understood. It should be possible to imagine that the forces to be described were important in the evolution of a large brain size, upright posture, and other major trends discussed in the next several chapters.

Polymorphisms   Traits that show genetic variability are described as *polymorphic* (*poly* = *many; morph* = *shape*). For a trait to be called a genetic polymorphism it should meet two criteria. First, each form of the trait must be more common in a population (greater than 1 percent) than would be likely just from recurrent mutations. If one expression of the trait occurs in 99.99 percent of the people and the other is found in 1 out of every 10,000 people, the trait is not considered a genetic polymorphism. Second, the two (or more) forms of the trait must be *discontinuous;* that is, the expressions of the alleles must fall into discrete categories. There can be type M, N, or MN blood but nothing else. Hence, the MN system is a genetic polymorphism when both alleles are found in a gene pool. Stature is a polymorphism, but it is not a genetic polymorphism because the differences in height in a population do not fall into discrete classes: There is a range between 5'1" and 5'1.1". In addition, a person's height is determined by very complex interactions among many sets of alleles (stature is polygenic) and many environmental factors. The discrete, discontinuously distributed genetic polymorphisms are not subject to much environmental modification. However, the genes involved in producing both continuous and discontinuous variation are probably maintained in a population by the same sorts of evolutionary processes.

Polymorphisms can be preserved in several ways. The first and least realistic way of preserving variability is to have no evolution. Allelic frequencies will not change from one generation to the next in a randomly mating group in which natural selection, mutation, drift, and migration are not active, that is, when the population is meeting the rules of the Hardy-Weinberg equilibrium. But we know that the Hardy-Weinberg law's criteria make it an idealization. There is no infinitely large population that practices random breeding, lacks migration, and is not subject to selection and mutation. The rule is useful, though, because it allows us to compare observed data with an expectation (see page 70).

In the real world, if we do find a deviation from an expectation based on the Hardy-Weinberg model, we can go on to try to identify the factor(s) causing the departure. These factors may be of two sorts, caused either by chance due to errors in sampling or by one or more of the four evolutionary factors (Table 3.1). The chance referred to is not the same as those chance forces underlying genetic drift; here the chance is that the sample we draw does not accurately reflect the gene frequencies in the whole population. In drift, chance factors at the time of fertilization are changing the population's genetic makeup all the time.

Small departures of observed genotype frequencies from what we expect are more likely to come from errors in sampling, but large deviations lead us to think some evolutionary force is operating. To be more objective, we use statistical tests to help decide whether any deviation is likely to be due to chance. A statistical test cannot tell us that the difference definitely comes from one or the other alternative; it does tell us the odds that a departure from the expected result is caused by chance. The deviations have to be rather large before the statistics "tell" us that evolutionary forces are the most likely explanation; it is hard to detect evolutionary effects (Table 3.2).

Selection   Given that variation will not be maintained in the real world because of the absence of evolution, how can evolutionary processes account for variability in real, natural populations? There appear to be many traits for which the heterozygote is better adapted than the homozygote, at least under certain environmental conditions; of course,

TABLE 3.1
A Numerical Example for Predicting Genotype Frequency

Suppose that you tested a population sample of 100 people for MN and found the phenotype and genotype distribution to be:

$$MM = 14 \qquad MN = 52 \qquad NN = 34$$

a. What are the allele frequencies? (M = .4, N = .6)

b. What is the expected genotype distribution according to Hardy-Weinberg? (MM = .16, MN = .48, NN = .36)

c. How might you explain the difference between observed and expected genotype frequencies? (The most likely reason is chance. Other possibilities include selection for the heterozygote or nonrandom mating.)

Answer a, b, and c, given this observed genotype distribution:

$$MM = 50 \qquad MN = 0 \qquad NN = 50$$

Answers:
   a. M = .5, N = .5
   b. MM = .25, MN = .50, NN = .25
   c. Likely answer: selection against the heterozygote. Less likely: nonrandom mating or chance.

TABLE 3.2
An Actual Example of the Application of the Hardy-Weinberg Equilibrium

Dr. D. F. Roberts and colleagues gathered data on the MN blood group system for several groups in northwest India. The sample of Brahmins from Rajasthan state comprise 94 people distributed as follows:

$$M = 38 \qquad MN = 42 \qquad N = 14$$

The gene frequencies are thus:

$$M = \frac{2(38) + 42}{2(94)} = .627$$

$$N = 1.0 - .627 = .373$$

The expected genotype frequencies, assuming Hardy-Weinberg is met, are:

$$MM = (.627)^2 \qquad = .393$$
$$MN = 2(.63)(.37) = .468$$
$$NN = (.373)^2 \qquad = .139$$

As there are 94 people, these percentages translate into *expected genotype numbers* of:

Expected: MN = (.393)(94) = 36.9
Observed: 38

Expected: MN = (.468)(94) = 44.0
Observed: 42

Expected: NN = (.139)(94) = 13.1
Observed: 14

We can conclude that the agreement of observed and expected is so close that there is no evidence of evolution.

Data from S.S. Papiha et al. (1982), *Annals of Human Biology*, 9(3), 235–251.

to have heterozygotes, you must have variation. The situation in which each homozygote is less genetically fit than the heterozygote is known as a *balanced polymorphism*. Here selection is performing a balancing act by favoring the alleles in the heterozygotes and working against them in the homozygotes. In this situation, a point of balance, or equilibrium, is reached just as when a partially filled bathtub has the water turned on and the drain opened to balance water input and outflow. (Do not try this at home, as Murphy's Law states that you will flood your bathroom.)

As you might imagine, this aspect of population genetics can be dealt with mathematically, and Table 3.3 steps through an example related to sickle-cell hemoglobin. The effects of the sickle-cell hemoglobin allele(s) and the reasons why sickle-cell disease kills have already been mentioned (page 40). For some time it was not clear why the frequency of this allele was rather high, up to 20 percent, in certain African populations. If the allele is deadly, why hadn't selection reduced its frequency? The rate is high because those with normal hemoglobin are subject to severe cases of malaria; those who are heterozygotes (AS) are largely re-

TABLE 3.3
Allele Frequencies and Selection in a Balanced Polymorphism: The Sickle-Cell Case

---

BEFORE SELECTION

Fitnesses: Observation reveals that in malarial areas, AA people have about 90 percent as many children as AS individuals. SS individuals rarely survive and reproduce. If the fitness of AS, the optimum, is set at 1.0, then the fitness of AA = 0.9 and SS = 0.0.

Let us *assume:*
Population size: 121

Gene frequency: $A = \dfrac{10}{11} \quad S = \dfrac{1}{11}$

Then genotype frequency according to Hardy-Weinberg: $AA = \left(\dfrac{10}{11}\right)^2 = \dfrac{100}{121} \quad AS = 2\left(\dfrac{10}{11}\right)\left(\dfrac{1}{11}\right) = \dfrac{20}{121} \quad SS = \left(\dfrac{1}{11}\right)^2 = \dfrac{1}{121}$

These conditions represent an equilibrium point. Below we show that selection will operate so that the allele frequencies are not changed.

DURING SELECTION

Number of people before selection (assuming N = 121):	AA = 100	AS = 20	SS = 1
Selection:	0.1	0	1.0
People lost due to selection:	10 (malaria)	0	1 (sickle cell)
Number of alleles lost:	20 A	0 A or S	2 S
Survivors after selection:	90 AA	20 AS	0 SS

AFTER SELECTION

New gene frequency:

$$A = \frac{\text{number of A alleles}}{\text{total number of alleles}}$$

$$= \frac{2 \text{ A alleles} \times 90 \text{ people} + 1 \text{ A allele} \times 20 \text{ people}}{2 \text{ alleles} \times 90 \text{ people} + 2 \text{ alleles} \times 20 \text{ people}}$$

$$= \frac{2 \times 90 + 1 \times 20}{2 \times 90 + 2 \times 20} = \frac{200}{220} = \frac{10}{11}$$

$$S = \frac{\text{number of S alleles}}{\text{total number of alleles}}$$

$$= \frac{1 \text{ S allele} \times 20 \text{ people}}{2 \text{ alleles} \times 90 \text{ people} + 2 \text{ alleles} \times 20 \text{ people}}$$

$$= \frac{1 \times 20}{2 \times 90 + 2 \times 20} = \frac{20}{220} = \frac{1}{11}$$

---

sistant to severe malaria infection and, unlike the SS homozygotes, do not die of sickle-cell anemia. The point of balance that is achieved is determined by the relative disadvantage of each homozygote. If one homozygote is ten times better off than the other, its allele will be maintained at a ten times higher frequency. This is not a magic trick; it simply follows from the fact that the homozygote with the higher fitness will be better able to reproduce, and as a result, that allele will have a higher frequency. Certainly the balance is not ideal: People still die from malaria, and an unfortunate few succumb to sickle-cell anemia. But, all in all, the populations of malarial areas are better off with than without the polymorphism.

As might be predicted, when the environment changes, either by eradication of malaria or by migration into nonmalarial areas, the frequency of S drops. The black population in the United States was originally drawn from African populations in which the S frequency was between 8 and 15 percent. Today the frequency of S in the American black population has declined to between 2 and 6 percent. Part of this decline was due to the infusion of A alleles from whites, particularly in northern areas, but some of the change comes from changing selective pressures.

Much to the chagrin of physical anthropologists, sickle cell is the only balanced polymorphism they can talk about with great assurance. Scientists have hints and hunches about the causes of variation in some of the blood groups, blood proteins, and gross morphological traits, but they are not entirely convinced that those explanations are correct (Chapter 12).

Several other polymorphisms are thought to be maintained in equilibrium by malaria, including hemoglobin variants like Hb^C and thalassemia (a complex anemia), and a red cell enzyme variant known as G-6-PD deficiency. If true, this indicates that there is often more than one evolutionary answer to a problem. Malaria's role as a selective agent is more impressive when we realize that even today more than a million people die from this disease each year. Before something was done to control it, the mortality rate was much higher.

Mutation   All these polymorphic conditions, whether they come from balancing selection pressures, can be traced to mutation, the ultimate source of all new alleles. Even in traits generally not considered polymorphic, there is some variation by mutation. Many of the genetically caused disorders, such as PKU, alkaptonuria, and hemophilia, are as frequent as rates of mutation would lead us to expect them to be. Many of these deleterious mutations are recessive, which increases their variability by shielding the mutants from natural selection.

While mutation is responsible for the appearance of new genes, we have seen (page 53) that meiosis can also account for much variability in phenotypes. Combining already existing alleles in new arrangements provides a large store of variation.

Admixture The last mechanism preserving variation in a population that we will consider is admixture, or the mixture of genes from two or more gene pools. A flow of genes from one pool into another may not only change the frequencies of alleles in the recipient population but also introduce previously absent alleles. Mutation ultimately accounts for the appearance of new alleles, but migration and subsequent interbreeding can spread a new allele from one population to another.

The fate of a newly introduced allele generally is determined by selection. It seems fair to assume that an allele that reaches a noticeable frequency in a population has done so because it was selectively advantageous in the environmental conditions. Transplanting that same allele into a new population with a different genetic environment and possibly a different external environment may or may not be selectively beneficial.

Mixing genes from two or more parental populations may also form a new population, as it has with the American blacks. If we look at the frequencies of several genetic traits in American whites and blacks and in West Africans, it is clear that the allele frequencies in the American blacks fall between those of the ancestral populations (Table 3.4). Because American blacks are somewhat isolated from West Africans and American whites for geographic and social reasons, their gene pool, formed by admixture, reflects the formation of a new population, different from both ancestral populations.

Reducing Variation

To complete our theoretical picture of variation, we must consider the several ways in which it can be reduced. Natural selection, a primary force in evolution, is the most obvious.

TABLE 3.4
Approximate Frequencies of Certain Alleles in West Africans, American Blacks, and American Whites

Allele	West African Blacks	American Blacks	American Whites
A	.15	.17	.26
B	.15	.12	.07
O	.70	.71	.67
G-6-PD deficiency	.19	.11	.00
Hb^s	.11	.04	.00
cDe	.59	.44	.03
CDe	.07	.16	.41
cde	.21	.26	.39
Hp^1	.69	.53	.43
S	.13	.17	.35

Adapted from P. L. Workman, B. S. Blumberg, and A. J. Cooper, "Selection, Gene Migration, and Polymorphic Stability in a U.S. White and Negro Population," *American Journal of Human Genetics* 15(4): 430. Used by permission of the University of Chicago Press. © 1963 by The American Society of Human Genetics. All rights reserved.

Selection Complete selection against a dominant allele will completely obliterate that allele in one generation. All who have the allele are prevented from reproducing. If selection is not this severe, elimination will take longer. Much more common is selection against a recessive allele, which reduces variability in a population. Selection can decrease the frequency of a recessive allele at a much slower rate than it can work against a dominant. Suppose a population has two alleles controlling a trait. G is the dominant allele and its frequency at some time in the past was .8; the frequency of the recessive allele (g) was .2. Then some shift in the environment made the homozygous recessive (gg) a lethal genotype; selection did not operate against GG or Gg. Under the new conditions we can obtain the proportional contribution of each genotype to the next generation by multiplying the frequency of each genotype by its fitness (Table 3.5).

The new g frequency (after selection) is equal to the contribution of the g alleles from the heterozygotes because the gg people do not reproduce. As the frequency of the g allele drops, the probability of forming a gg homozygote decreases in accordance with the Hardy-Weinberg rule, reducing the rate at which selection can rid the population of the allele. As the frequency of the g allele drops, most of the g alleles will be found in heterozygotes, where they cannot be selected out. At a g frequency of .01, only 1 in 10,000 people would die, and all other copies of the gene would be in genetically fit heterozygotes. If, however, g were more common, say .1, 1 in every 100 people would be open to selection.

Mathematical analysis shows that the initial drop in the frequency of g is quite rapid and then starts to tail off. After one generation of selection against only the gg homozygotes, the gene frequency drops from .2 to .16; in the second it drops to .1344; from the twentieth to the fiftieth generation it drops only from .04 to .018. In humans the intervening thirty generations would take several hundred years to realize only a 2.2 percent drop in gene frequency.

After long selection, the frequency will eventually reach an equilibrium at which the rate of loss of the g allele is balanced by the production of new g alleles by mutation. Then every g allele lost because of natural selection against the homozygous gg will be replaced by the creation of new g alleles by random mutations. Such an equilibrium seems to have

TABLE 3.5
Selection Against a Recessive Allele

Gene frequency	$G = p$		$g = q$
Genotype frequency before selection	$GG = p^2$	$Gg = 2pq$	$gg = q^2$
Fitness	1	1	$1 - x$ (x = deaths due to homozygosity)
Genotype frequencies after selection. (That is, genotype distribution of those who will produce the next generation.)	p^2	$2pq$	$q^2(1 - x)$

been reached for genes causing metabolic disorders such as PKU. Eugenicists (those who want to improve our species genetically) have never been able to solve this problem satisfactorily when they try to explain how they propose to accomplish their goals.

When selection or drift causes a relatively common gene to become scarce, the variation does not disappear immediately. While diminishing, it illustrates a *transient* polymorphism. The variation is still there, but it is approaching the 1 percent level at which it ceases to be a polymorphism. Transient polymorphisms, such as the sickle-cell allele in American blacks, tell us that a population is in the midst of significant evolutionary change.

In the example we have considered, selection operates directly by biological means: A person with sickle-cell anemia rarely lives long enough to reproduce. Society, too, applies selective pressures against traits it cannot or will not tolerate. Many non-Western groups practice infanticide, often on those born with obvious congenital defects; a group leading a marginal existence cannot tolerate the economic drain of non-productive members. It is difficult to judge how such practices affect evolution, but they certainly would reduce the frequency of genetically caused disorders.

Genetic Drift Genetic drift, or the random fluctuation in gene frequencies in a small population caused by chance phenomena, also causes loss of variation. Drift will decrease variability in any population, but it will increase the variability *among* populations. Because drift is effective in small populations (page 80), it probably was of greater significance in our gatherer/hunter past.

While drift eventually fixes alleles at either 0 or 100 percent in a population, it maintains variability among populations. Consider 100 small populations, each with two alleles, A and A′, at frequencies of .8 and .2. After a long period of drift, the most likely outcome would be 80 populations with A at 100 percent and 20 populations fixed at 100 percent A′. After drift has rid all the populations of internal variability, drift is no longer possible. Variation among groups, however, would still exist. Although it is hard to prove that drift has occurred, it is difficult to imagine that it has not. Illustrating drift with data on humans essentially involves proving the negative, showing that differences among populations are not caused by selection. Evidence that closely related populations have little variation *within* groups but marked variation *among* groups certainly does imply drift. It is impossible, however, to demonstrate conclusively that the variation is not caused instead by undetected selection pressures.

A subtype of drift known to have affected human beings is referred to as the *founder's effect,* or the *Sewall Wright effect.* Here, variability is reduced in newly founded, isolated populations by sampling error; that is, the founding population, which could be as small as one pregnant woman, does not carry all the alleles at exactly their frequency in the original large population.

Several island populations today have limited variability because they are the descendants of a few stranded sailors. The nine mutinous crew members of the H.M.S. *Bounty,* six Tahitian men, and eight or nine Tahitian women founded a population on Pitcairn Island in 1790 (Figure 3.7). After a falling-out between the Tahitian men and the English, the population was reduced to Alexander Smith, the women, and some children. With such a small founding group, the genetic variability today is quite limited. It would be impossible for nine English men to carry all the alleles present in England or for fourteen or fifteen Tahitians to represent truly the Tahitian population. Even if the population had rapidly expanded, the genetic bottleneck that it passed through greatly limits

FIGURE 3.7. A family of Pitcairn islanders.

variability in later generations. Harry L. Shapiro vividly describes the history and biology of this new human population in *The Pitcairn Islanders.*[5]

Inbreeding and Homozygosity   Another phenomenon that may diminish variability in populations is inbreeding, or mating between ancestrally related individuals. If we go back far enough genealogically, any pair of individuals shares at least one ancestor; to measure inbreeding, then, we have to specify a base population, such as the original inhabitants of Pitcairn Island, as a starting point.

All homozygotes for a trait have two functionally identical alleles, that is, two pieces of DNA that synthesize a protein with the same amino acid sequence. The likelihood of being homozygous for any particular allele is related to the frequency of that allele. A person whose parents are genetic relatives represents a special case wherein the chance of homozygosity is somewhat greater; the amount by which it is greater is related to the closeness of the parents' genetic ties. Here the alleles can be identical because they are descended from one allele in the parents' recent common ancestor. This is homozygosity by descent. The smaller the group from which mates can be drawn, the greater the amount of inbreeding.

Figure 3.8 diagrams a case of inbreeding between first cousins. Child A may be homozygous because a gene in one of the great-grandparents was passed to both grandparents and both parents, as the hypothetical example illustrates for the X' allele; the child could be homozygous X'X' by descent. Thus, a child born to genetic relatives has a greater probability of homozygosity than does a child born to two unrelated individuals. Inbreeding therefore reduces genotypic variability and increases the chance of homozygosity.

In a population comprised of inbred lines, the genetic variation in the population as a whole may be maintained, but the variability within family lines is decreased. If one inbreeding lineage within a population contains only the X allele and one only X', variation is still present in

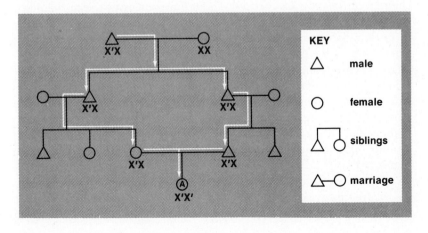

FIGURE 3.8
A genealogy showing how homozygosity for the allele X' in person A results from inbreeding. A's parents are first cousins.

the population's gene frequencies, but there is none within lines. Also there are no heterozygotes. Socially preferred mating patterns may subdivide a population into many inbred lines, further reducing genotypic variability.

Sharing ancestors, as do the parents in Figure 3.8, can be important socially as well as biologically. Almost all human societies have incest taboos that limit choice of mates, although the matings considered incestuous often vary. On the other hand, common ancestry can confer social importance, as it does for those who trace their heritage back to the Pilgrims. Socially, ancestors can be recognized for hundreds of years into the past and may even involve descent from an imaginary common ancestor, as in Australian Aborigine clans. But a common ancestor more than four or five generations back has little genetic effect; a mating between individuals who share a great-great-great-great-great-grandparent probably will not cause homozygosity by descent.

The layperson may think that inbreeding always results in retarded or otherwise defective children. Inbreeding can indeed result in mental retardation and other disorders by bringing together in one individual two copies of a harmful gene. But if such a gene either is not present in the lineage or has not been passed on in it, inbreeding does no harm. If homozygosity for a gene is advantageous, inbreeding will be beneficial.

As far as we know, inbreeding does not seem to have had any great effects on human populations. Some of the most extensive inbreeding is recorded in rural Japanese villages. Consanguineous ("blood"-related) marriages are encouraged, perhaps partly because in the small villages the choice of a mate may be limited to a relative. In some villages more than 25 percent of the marriages involved related individuals, and often more than half of these involved first cousins. Even so, the overall risk of deleterious disorders in the children of first-cousin marriages is not tremendously greater than in the children of unrelated parents. Obvious congenital defects appear in about 1.02 percent of the children of unrelated mates; they appear in 1.69 percent of the offspring of first cousins. The latter group shows about a 60 percent greater risk of congenital defects, but the traits still are not very common. The mortality rate for the children of first cousins increases about 3 percent over that for children of unrelated parents. Also in Japan, inbred individuals have slightly lower birth weights, are shorter as adults, and have lower IQs. William Schull, one of the preeminent researchers in this area, says that the emphasis on first-cousin marriages produces small but pervasive effects.[6] Schull also says that the number of live births for the consanguineous marriages is greater than that for the unrelated marriage group. The number of children who eventually reach the age of twenty-one, though, is about the same for both groups, meaning that the related individuals produce "extra" children to compensate for those who will die because of inbreeding.

The Japanese example is one of the most extreme cases of inbreeding, yet on the average the amount of inbreeding is roughly comparable to what one would expect if everyone were marrying third or fourth cousins. Very high levels of inbreeding occur in several small isolates. Among the Juruna Indians of Brazil about 73 percent of the marriages have both partners coming from the group. Because there are now only fifty-eight Jurunas, many of them are, to no one's surprise, related by descent. Mathematical computations show that their inbreeding is roughly equivalent to everyone marrying a second cousin. In fact, half of the twenty-two marriages studied involved people who are related through more than one line of descent, and one couple is related through eight lines.

Another inbred group is the people of Tristan da Cunha, a small island in the middle of the South Atlantic Ocean. It was first settled in the early nineteenth century by several English seamen. The population was increased both by importing wives and by saving several shipwrecked sailors. The population was about three hundred prior to its evacuation in the 1960s. Luckily one of the founders liked and encouraged accurate record keeping, so that today it is possible to trace, via birth and marriage records, almost everyone's ancestry. With the records in hand, Derek Roberts of England was able to compute not only the amount of inbreeding but also what brought it about.[7] Figure 3.9 shows that for the first three decades after its founding no inbreeding occurred. By then, however, inbreeding was almost inevitable. One man, age twenty-two, had to pick a wife, and of the eight eligible women, only three were not related to him. Choosing one of his first cousins, he started the inbreeding on Tristan. In later years often one had no alternative but to marry a relative. Although Tristanians preferred to marry nonrelatives, the closed population and its small size voided this alternative. In fact, the only cases of outbreeding since 1930 have been illegitimate births after a male came visiting. Again, as in Japan, full medical surveys indicate that congenital abnormalities are somewhat more common than in outbreeding communities. Inbreeding does not, however, guarantee that a medical problem will arise.

Like drift, inbreeding probably was more significant in the population structure of our ancestors. Given that the size of a population was very small for much of our history, probably ranging between twenty-five and one hundred persons, the number of potential nonrelated mates

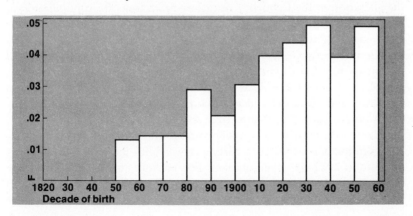

FIGURE 3.9
The degree of inbreeding in the Tristan population, by the decade of birth. The gradual increase in inbreeding reflects the gradual decrease in unrelated possible mates in this small population. F is a measure of the amount of inbreeding.

would have been very small, making inbreeding very likely. The practice of village exogamy, or marrying a person from outside one's own village, is quite common among modern gatherer/hunter peoples, possibly as a mechanism to retard the effect of inbreeding.

Admixture: Reducing Differences   We have seen that admixture can increase variation within a population; it can also decrease the differences among populations. Native Americans today have much higher frequencies of some blood types than they are thought to have had in pre-Columbian times, mostly because of interbreeding with whites. The Native American gene pool now is more similar to that of American whites. Gene flow among populations can be an extremely important evolutionary phenomenon, for it can spread new genes from population to population, thus reducing the differences between the populations.

Evolution in the Real World

We have seen how some evolutionary movements affect the genetic structure of populations. We have considered most of them as separate, each having specific effects on a population's evolution. In the real world, all the factors are more or less busily working. The most obvious interaction is that between selection and mutation. Mutation creates new alleles, which are then selected for or against in a specific environment.

Through drift, a newly arisen, beneficial mutation may disappear simply by chance; a newly hatched, extremely fit, mutant bug, for example, may be unintentionally stepped on. By this chance occurrence, the rare but highly advantageous allele has ceased to exist and so cannot be selected for. Alternatively, drift can override selection against a harmful allele and cause its frequency to rise to high levels in a small population.

Selection and admixture also are intertwined. The forced migration and subsequent admixture of Africans in the New World and the altered selective pressures have resulted in a greater decrease in the frequency of the sickle-cell allele than selection or admixture alone would have accomplished.

Mutation, selection, and gene flow can also operate to produce *clinal* variation. A cline is gradual variation in a trait over space, shown by the alteration in the frequency of one or more traits from population to neighboring population. A new, beneficial mutation (Q) may arise in one population. Because Q is advantageous, it is increased in frequency by selection. Meanwhile, gene flow carries Q to neighboring groups, and eventually to more distant populations where it also gradually increases in frequency. As a result, Q is highest in frequency in its group of origin and lower and lower in frequency in further and further removed groups. Selection pressures that change over space may also cause clines.

Selection may, in fact, operate on combinations of genes. If a certain combination of genes is particularly helpful, natural selection may operate on a whole gene complex. For instance, in malarial areas, the sickle-cell hemoglobin allele works especially well in people who also have the allele that reduces the amount of an enzyme called G-6-PD. The sickle-cell allele and the enzyme-deficiency allele are *coadapted:* They mix well with each other in a population's gene pool. In a malarial area, the combination of 15 percent sickle-cell alleles and 30 to 60 percent G-6-PD deficiency alleles produces a very high state of adaptation, as many people are protected against malaria. Selection works to maintain this combination.

Dogma, it was pointed out, is a word that does not apply to science. Although the previous sections present a rather standard and traditional view of genetic and evolutionary processes (the Neo-Darwinian view), not all such phenomena are fully understood and agreed upon. Now we will touch on a few of the current topics of debate on evolutionary significance. We will start out with questions initially raised decades ago but recently revived: Is the appearance of new species really as gradual as traditional treatments would have it? Can the processes discussed in reference to microevolution account for the divergence of species (macroevolution)? If not, there are many interrelated implications as to:

Questioning the Theory

1. the role of adaptation in macroevolutionary trends,
2. the ways in which new species appear, and
3. the relationship of microevolutionary forces to those of macroevolution.

The ways in which these modern questions are resolved will then affect how one views other aspects of evolution, for instance, how and why sex evolved and the degree to which macroevolution is a result of structural changes in proteins as opposed to changes in the timing of gene action.

Punctuated Equilibria

Charles Darwin based his ideas of evolution on the mechanism of natural selection. He visualized this process as operating on each generation, slowly and gradually perfecting the adaptation of the population by selecting the most fit individuals and weeding out those that were not as well adapted. In the Darwinian view of evolution, a population gradually changed over time, constantly accumulating modifications that altered its biology; eventually enough changes occurred so that a new species could be said to have appeared.

Although this view has come to represent the dominant theme in evolutionary thought, it has not been accepted without serious criticism. In the years prior to the publication of *The Origin of Species* in 1859, Darwin spent considerable time amassing evidence in support of evolution and discussing the basic concepts with scientific friends. One of these was the geologist Charles Lyell, who was introduced in Chapter 1 in the context of uniformitarianism. Lyell's contributions to the study of geology also included the construction of a relative chronology of earth history (Figure 3.10). Lyell wished to identify rock strata from various parts of the world and place them in a time-ordered sequence, from the earliest to the latest. It was already an established observation that if a geologist wished to distinguish one rock formation from another, the identity of the rock itself—limestone, sandstone, or whatever—was of limited value, since the same kind of rocks have been laid down at very different times. The most effective way for Lyell to accomplish his goal was to use the fossilized remains of extinct animals that were found embedded in the rocks. So although the earth was formed about 4.5 billion years ago, the chronology shown in Figure 3.10 only presents subdivisions of earth history covering the last 600 million years. Earlier fossilized remains become rarer and finally disappear, so that they cannot be used to distinguish one rock strata from another.

Lyell's examination of many rock strata had convinced him that the fossil species found in one rock deposit could be easily distinguished from those in deposits above and below. He also found that there was virtually no change in the biology of the fossil animals from their first to their final appearance. Animals seemed to appear abruptly, remain unchanged throughout their presence in the record, and then disappear just as suddenly, to be replaced by a new series of animals in the next higher strata.

Lyell pointed out to Darwin that these observations did not support his proposed notion of gradual change, but rather showed sudden appearance, relatively no change, and then sudden disappearance. Darwin remained unconvinced, arguing that the fossil record was incomplete, that strata that showed the transitions between different animal species had been destroyed, and that eventually the transitional animal forms linking animals from one rock strata to those above and below would be found.

Over one hundred years after the exchange between Lyell and Darwin, biologists including Nils Eldredge and Steven Gould have suggested that perhaps Lyell was right after all. These writers have emphasized that a considerable amount of investigation has failed to bring to light the transitional forms Darwin was sure would be found, and that even now the fossil record continues to show animal species that abruptly appear, remain relatively unchanged, and then disappear. Fossil evidence of gradual change of one species into another is exceedingly rare, leading Eldredge and Gould to propose that the Darwinian model of gradualism over time should be modified. In its place, they suggest a different pattern, one they have termed *punctuated equilibria*.

In contrast to Darwin's notions of the gradual change of one species into another, Eldredge and Gould argue that most species evolve very quickly, changing dramatically in a very short period often via mechanisms other than selection, so swiftly that it is unlikely that fossil evidence will be found (Figure 3.11). They further propose that once a species has evolved and has reached a state of equilibrium with its environment, selection will then operate to maintain the species in that form and to prevent the accumulation of the gradual changes that in the Darwinian model lead to the appearance of a new species. The punctuated equilibria model visualizes a species appearing abruptly and then entering a phase of minimal change or stasis. The species may disappear

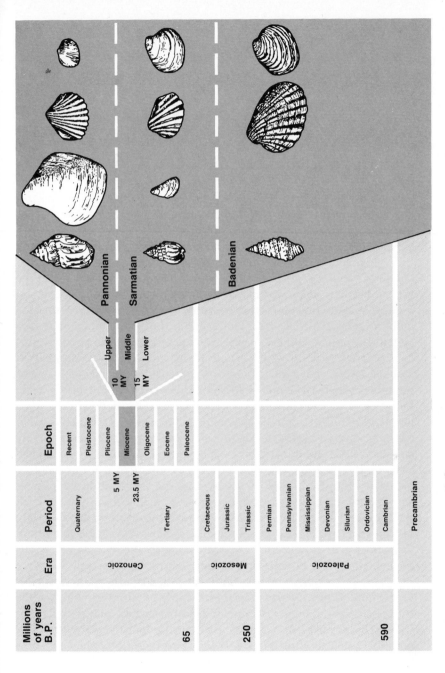

Millions of years B.P.	Era	Period	Epoch
	Cenozoic	Quaternary	Recent
			Pleistocene
		5 MY	Pliocene
		23.5 MY	Miocene
		Tertiary	Oligocene
			Eocene
			Paleocene
65	Mesozoic	Cretaceous	
		Jurassic	
		Triassic	
250	Paleozoic	Permian	
		Pennsylvanian	
		Mississippian	
		Devonian	
		Silurian	
		Ordovician	
		Cambrian	
590		Precambrian	

Pannonian

Sarmatian

Badenian

Upper
Middle
Lower

10 MY
15 MY

FIGURE 3.10. Example of the development of a relative time scale of earth history. Pictured are three distinct time-ordered groupings of fossil mollusk species found in geological deposits representing an extension of the Mediterranean Sea that covered parts of central Europe between 5 and 15 million years ago. Identification of the species of shellfish present also identifies the deposit and places it in the overall sequence of earth history. Here, the three groupings are called Badenian, Sarmatian, and Pannonian. Based on their relative position to other fossil-bearing rock strata that are found above and below them, these groups are placed in the Middle to Upper Miocene, which in turn is placed in the Cenozoic. The major divisions of earth history noted on the left are thus the result of placing hundreds of rock strata in their correct, time-ordered sequence. Table 4.2 presents a more complete listing of the dates of these divisions and relates them to the evolutionary appearance of major animal groups.

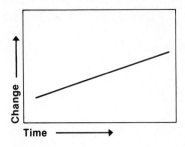 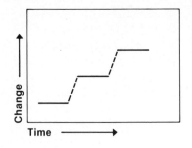

FIGURE 3.11. The classic idea of evolution by gradual change (left) is now being challenged by a view involving abrupt changes.

just as quickly as it arose, possibly due to replacement by a new species. Thus, the original species will rapidly appear in the fossil record, remain (relatively) unchanged for some period, and then suddenly disappear.

How and why would new species appear and disappear with such rapidity? Varying explanations have been offered. Several times over the years it has been suggested that a new species could come about due to a single, major mutation. Most recently, this idea has been associated with the geneticist Richard B. Goldschmidt. In 1940, Goldschmidt suggested that unique changes in the structure of chromosomes could produce a new species.[8] While admitting that most such *macromutations* would be very debilitating, once in a great while the alteration would produce a beneficial result. Goldschmidt's concept is probably extreme for a new species is not likely to arise from one genetic change. One problem would be for the mutant to find a mate. Yet mutations that rearrange chromosomes and/or alter development may be more important than Goldschmidt's critics have suggested. Hampton Carson studied a type of fly that had evolved into twenty-six different species inhabiting one Hawaiian island in the 700,000 years since the island had appeared. The species differ due to rearrangements in their chromosomes. Each species was founded by a very small number of ancestors, possibly only one pregnant female. To paleontologists this is a very rapid evolution. Tangentially, if we subscribe to Goldschmidt's view, we can finally answer that the chicken came first, having hatched from a reptile's egg.

Another explanation for the sudden appearance of new species looks more to the opportunities presented by populations living on the fringes of a species range. Because of their marginality, these populations will likely be small. As we have seen, small populations are most susceptible to genetic drift wherein chance factors can produce new combinations of genes that can come to characterize the whole of the small group. Drift of regulatory genes, or those that change the timing of developmental events, might be especially important in the appearance of markedly altered species. Once having arisen the new species might be able to replace its parental stock.

Besides drift, selection might also have a role. These small, isolated, marginal populations are likely to be placed under severe selection.

By definition, life in marginal areas will be difficult, and only the most fit will survive. Again, small alterations in development might be of major significance in the hunt for limited resources. Under these conditions, selection could rapidly produce new species. The punctuated equilibria model does not necessarily require evolutionary mechanisms other than those described in reference to microevolution.

Regardless of the mechanisms involved, the fossil record does offer evidence of rapid change centered on speciation events. One well-documented example involves East African snails from the Cenozoic era. A fossil bed 400 meters (1,300 feet) thick yields a particularly rich history of the changes experienced by thirteen species of these snails that shows a punctuational pattern—long periods of stasis and brief periods of rapid change. Just how common this pattern is remains to be seen, for few fossil lineages are as rich.

The notion of punctuated change is a reflection of the difficulties of studying the fossil evidence for the evolution of life. The fossils are often times extremely difficult to arrange into a reasonable sequence of evolutionary change. In the study of human evolution, for example, there are sites where several rock strata contain the fossil bones of our ancestors. The bones from one strata differ in a number of details from the bones deposited above and below them. Just how much change is sufficient to demonstrate the action of gradualism? How little change permits us to conclude that stasis is the pattern? How much time is required to document a gradual or punctuated change from one species to another? These are questions that are most difficult to answer by looking at the issue of punctuation from the perspective of the fossil record, and other difficult questions arise when we attempt to utilize this concept in the study of living populations. A geneticist studying a living population would consider 50,000 years to be an exceedingly long time, but a paleontologist studying the evolution of the mammals would consider 50,000 years merely an instant.

Whether microevolutionary phenomena can account for macroevolutionary change is a serious modern concern. The basic unit of microevolution is the gene, while that of macroevolution is morphology or form. As yet, we really do not know the relationship between the two in any detail. Studies of growth and development can give some clues as to how genes affect form, but as yet we cannot generalize as to how much or what kinds of genetic change account for the changes seen in the fossil record. Keep in mind too that these options—gradualism and punctuationism—are not mutually exclusive. Both may be happening in different times, places, and lineages.

The Evolution of Sexual Reproduction

Having looked at the generalities of the punctuationism-gradualism debate, let us consider an example dealing with a subject near to the hearts of most: sex, and why it ever evolved.

At face value, an observer might predict that sex should never have evolved. We have seen that the winner in the evolutionary race is the individual who passes on more genes to the next generation than others. For a species such as our own, which reproduces sexually each time an offspring is conceived, this is a particularly "expensive" proposition, especially for the female. Female mammals (and especially primates) invest a tremendous amount of time and energy to ensure the survival of their offspring, yet half the genes they are protecting are not even theirs! Even in a species whose maternal investment is not so great, the parents still have to devote some limited resources toward the production of sex cells that are only of value after union with those of the other sex. Wouldn't it be a tremendous evolutionary advantage if an individual could simply reproduce asexually? Every offspring would be a 100 percent return on the parent's "investment," not 50 percent. It certainly seems that the answer to this question is yes. Sexual reproduction does exist, however, and we must thus try to understand its function.

Asexual reproduction is common in many microorganisms. Essentially, it is reproduction by mitosis: The individual replicates its genes and then divides. One individual spawns two genetically identical offspring—or clones—and each cell line is separate and unique. Again, why did our ancestors abandon this seemingly efficient method of reproduction more than a half billion years ago? To date, there have been a variety of answers to this question, but none has received unanimous acceptance, and each would appear to have potential pitfalls.

An early explanation for the evolution of sexual reproduction was proposed in the 1930s by Sir R. A. Fisher (1890–1962), a famed evolutionary theorist, and H. J. Muller (1890–1967), a Nobel Prize–winning geneticist. Basically, Fisher and Muller argued that sexual reproduction allowed for quicker and more adaptive evolutionary change. Imagine, for instance, a situation in which mutations A, B, and C would promote survival in a particular environment. An asexual organism would have to have these mutations appear in succession in one cell line. As asexuality does not allow for the mixing of genes between individuals or lines, all three would have to appear in one line as a unit, a very unlikely event.

One result of sexual reproduction is the constant shuffling of genes every generation. Thus, even if mutation A happens in one individual, B in a second, and C in a third, the recombination of genes can relatively rapidly bring all three together in one individual. Put in other terms, sexual reproduction permits each new mutation to be tested for its worth in many different combinations, while asexuality tests it in only one array of genes.

This view has not gone without criticism, although there are certainly those who still stand by it. Some say that this advantage of sexuality only holds true under very limited conditions. For instance, computer simulations seem to show that sex would work this way only in very small populations. A theoretical criticism of the Fisher-Muller view is based on group selection; that is, its benefit is not to the individual but to the group. The Neo-Darwinian theory holds that selection will not favor traits that benefit the group but harm the individual. Fisher himself had great difficulty on this point and ultimately concluded that sexual reproduction was the only legitimate example of group selection; sex conferred no advantage on the individual, just the group.

One alternative relates to the flip side of the Fisher–Muller hypothesis. Not only does sexual reproduction put new gene combinations together, it is also constantly breaking them up via meiosis. This too can be viewed as beneficial since the environment is always undergoing change. If an asexual organism hit upon a very beneficial array of genes and its descendants became very common by outcompeting other cell lines, a change in environment could quickly result in extinction if this one genotype ceased to be adaptive. Determining whether sex is really beneficial here depends in part on how radically environments are likely to change and how rapidly the organism can reproduce in the new situation.

The explanations of sexual reproduction are generally gradualist in nature. Taking a punctuated view of macroevolution suggests other possibilities. Steven Stanley has proposed that the advantage of sexual reproduction is not to the individual or species but to whole groups of species.[9] How would this work?

We know that environments constantly change and that groups poorly adapted to the new conditions become extinct. How can sufficient diversity be generated to ensure that one or another group will survive in one or another changed condition? For asexual organisms, variation must result from different mutations in different cell lines. This process is not likely to yield tremendous diversity between related "species" (as the species definition relates to interbreeding, which is of course impossible in asexual organisms, the word is in quotes; the determination of species in bacteria is based on other criteria). Remember that in the punctuated view most diversification and evolution come about at the "instant" of speciation. As only sexual organisms can speciate and thereby generate a lot of diversity within the group of related species, it is the sexual organism that is likely to have sufficient variability (not within one species but between related species) to survive through time (Figure 3.12).

Today we are still asking the question, "Is sex necessary?" And if so, "Why?" We do see that the different models of evolution yield conflicting answers.

Given their viewpoint, it is not surprising that gradualists look to explain morphological and behavioral trends in terms of adaptation. In future chapters, you will see comments that primates evolved stereoscopic vision as an adaptation to life in the trees or that bipedalism evolved in our ancestors as an adaptation to life on open grasslands. Yet many punctuationists view these sorts of statements as "just so" stories. They say that the gradualists see a trait in a living species and then put together a tale to explain how it came to be. Certainly, there are times when these stories are accurate reflections of past events, but punctuationists assert that many times they are at best unproven and often wrong. The mere existence of a feature is not sufficient reason to state

Adaptation

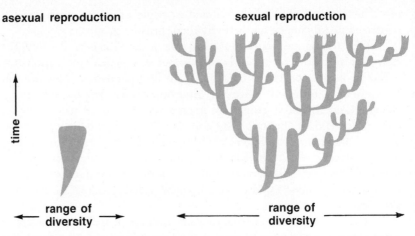

asexual reproduction   sexual reproduction

time

range of   range of
diversity   diversity

FIGURE 3.12. Sexual reproduction leads to much speciation and thus much interspecies diversity, according to Steven Stanley.

that the feature therefore *must* somehow be adaptive. The ability to form a plausible story that can account for the evolution of a trait does not prove that the scenario is a true reflection of history.

Sometimes, the punctuationists say, features come into existence as a by-product of development or past evolutionary directions. Stephen Gould and Richard Lewontin of Harvard University use an architectural analogy.[10] Spandrels are the triangular spaces formed by the right-angle intersection of two rounded arches (Figure 3.13). Many Renaissance churches have spandrels that are elaborately decorated with religious art. These areas were not purposefully designed into the cathedral. The basic architecture, however, called for intersecting arches, and the spandrels were an unavoidable by-product that was a likely spot for decoration. Alterations seen in the fossil record may likewise reflect biological "by-products." In direct analogy to the spandrels, architectural changes in one part of the body may cause structural changes elsewhere. In human evolution, as the brain enlarged and the head became rounder, the forehead appeared as a by-product.

Many have considered why the human canine tooth has diminished in size relative to that of most other primates. Most explanations try to uncover a positive advantage of the smaller tooth size, such as its greater rotary grinding ability or its need for less energy to grow. Ralph Holloway has put forward a model more in line with Gould and Lewontin's thinking, however.[11] It has been experimentally shown that the levels of male hormones in a developing primate affect the growth of its canine tooth; the more male hormone, the bigger the canine. We also know that one important aspect of human evolution was the increasing ability to live peacefully within a social group. Holloway put these two pieces together with a rather speculative assumption: The amount of male hormone in a primate affects that individual's aggressiveness. Assuming that this point is reasonable, Holloway said that natural selection would favor the survival and reproduction of those males with lower levels of aggression and lower levels of male hormones. A side effect would then occur, for as the average male hormone level dropped from generation to generation, the canines would get smaller. Selection thus would not be responsible directly for decreasing canine size. There was no advantage to small canines; they just came about as a by-product of other changes.

Gradualists do not say that such by-products never occur. They do maintain that adaptation is a key feature of large-scale changes and that major changes (from an ape to a human, for instance) are largely due to the accumulation of many smaller changes over long periods of time.

How much change is involved in going from an apelike animal to a human? This is another sort of question bearing on this debate that presently has no definitive answer. It is possible, however, to offer some educated guesses. In Chapters 6 and 7, we will describe some of the numerous anatomical and behavioral differences between apes and humans. As will be seen, they range literally from the top of the head to

FIGURE 3.13
Not everything is adaptive. Spandrels are a necessary byproduct of the intersection of two rounded arches.

the bottom of the feet. A list of traits pages long could be compiled to document all the fine details by which humans differ from an ape such as a chimp. Yet in contrast to these dissimilarities are molecular studies comparing human and chimp proteins that conclude that the two are more than 99 percent identical (the methods for determining this are dealt with in Chapter 7). M. C. King and A. Wilson proposed an intriguing solution to this apparent paradox.[12]

Proteins are the products of genes that control the structure of a molecule. There also appears to be a class of regulatory genes that act as on and off switches to control the timing of structural gene activity. The tremendous similarity between gorilla or chimp and human proteins reflects high levels of structural gene similarity but does not necessarily imply anything about the timing of gene function. Experimental evidence indicates that a small alteration in the timing of gene function can produce significant alterations in morphology, even when structural genes might not be mutated.

It has long been recognized that the development of a modern human exhibits *paedomorphism*. This rather impressive word refers to the retention of juvenile features (*paedo = child; morph = shape*) into adulthood. In many primates, during early life the head is quite large relative to body size (see Figure 3.14). As nonhuman primates grow and develop, their body proportions change quite noticeably as the growth of the head tapers off while other body parts grow at a great rate. The result is a relatively small head on a large body. In modern humans the newborn's head is also large, but it continues to grow and to maintain a relatively large size into adulthood. Thus, the human adult maintains something of the body proportions seen only in juveniles of other primate species.

Other examples of paedomorphism abound. As adults our heads are not only large but also quite round compared to that of a gorilla (Figure 3.15). Yet the head of a juvenile gorilla is also quite round. Humans maintain into adulthood the juvenile form found in the gorilla. It is certainly reasonable to consider that the paedomorphism results from alterations in the timing of gene operations rather than from changes in the products of the gene. Some genes that come into play at the time of sexual maturity in the gorilla may never be turned on in us, thus affecting the rates at which different body parts grow and hence their final shape.

King and Wilson suggest that the seemingly contradictory situation they describe can be understood by maintaining that much of the difference between us and apes comes about due to changes in regulatory genes.

Regarding the punctuationism-gradualism debate, one could maintain that a relatively small number of alterations in regulatory DNA could rapidly come to characterize a population. These alterations, which could greatly affect morphology, could contribute to the rapid appearance of a new species in accord with Eldredge and Gould's model. Nevertheless, one could also argue that such a process does not contradict more traditional views of evolution: It is simply a case of rapid evolution brought about by the processes (selection, etc.) that Neo-Darwin-

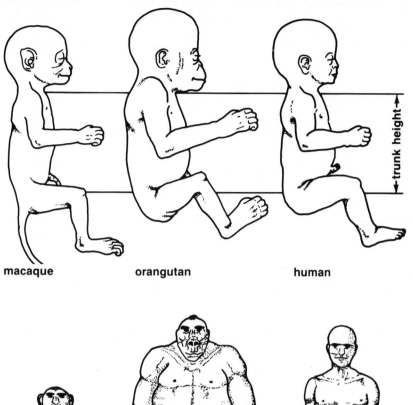

macaque   orangutan   human

trunk height

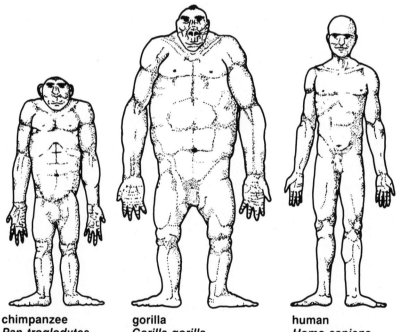

chimpanzee
Pan troglodytes

gorilla
Gorilla gorilla

human
Homo sapiens

FIGURE 3.14. Compared to other primates, the relative size of the head is not particularly great in newborn humans. The size of the head relative to body size is maintained to a greater extent in developing humans than in nonhuman primates, however. Here the three newborn primates are drawn such that their trunk lengths are equal; the adults are drawn to scale.

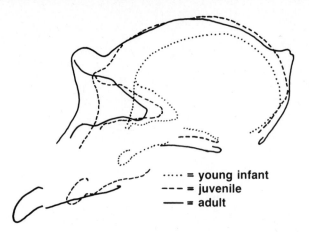

····· = young infant
--- = juvenile
— = adult

FIGURE 3.15. Superimposed sketches of the outline of the skull of an infant and an adult female gorilla. As the gorilla grows, much of the skull's roundness disappears.

ians have generally called upon as explanatory. Again, the so-called gradualists never said that all changes are equally slow or that all evolutionary change chugs along at some constant, slow rate.

Summary
We started this chapter with a consideration of the scientific method for solving problems. Several features characterize a scientific statement:

1. It generates new questions.
2. It can be tested.
3. It is predictive.
4. It is subject to change.

In all features, evolutionary statements are scientific. The original statements of Darwin and other early evolutionists have generated many new questions; some have since been firmly answered (and the answers produced new questions), others are still open to debate. In any case, there is much evidence from the fossil record, comparative sciences, and observed cases that evolution actually does happen.

The forces of evolution (natural selection, mutation, genetic drift, and gene flow) are discussed both in terms of what they are and what they are not. Selection is a directed force that produces adaptation, but it is not technically "survival of the fittest." Mutations are random in occurrence, and they do not appear as they are needed. Mutation is particularly important as it creates much of the variability upon which selection can act. Drift is also random; it is the fluctuation in allele frequency brought about by chance. Gene flow is the result of interbreeding between groups.

Macroevolution refers to large evolutionary changes, such as the appearance of new species. The definition of a biological species applies to animals actively or potentially interbreeding and producing fertile offspring. Extinct animals, on the other hand, must be defined by a concept of evolutionary species, based largely on anatomical similarities. New species appear by either straight-line evolution, or anagenesis, or by branching evolution, or cladogenesis. It is cladogenesis that has resulted in the diversity of life forms. For branching evolution to occur, a species must be subdivided by a geographic barrier into two or more isolated populations. Each evolves along its own lines until they become so different as to preclude interbreeding even if the geographic barrier were removed. The inability to mate successfully may be due to one or more isolating mechanisms, which may be behavioral, anatomical, or physiological. When a lot of speciation occurs quickly, it is referred to as an adaptive radiation. Although virtually all evolution is divergent, causing greater differences to accumulate between species, it sometimes appears that two are becoming more alike (convergent). These similarities, which come about as species try to adapt to similar environmental problems, are only superficial.

The unending process of evolution has only one directional force, natural selection, which produces adaptation. Because alternatives are basic to the operation of selection, the analysis of the effects of evolution on genetic variation deserves much attention. Selection can maintain variation in a population by favoring the heterozygote; this mechanism is known as balanced polymorphism. While the lack of evolution would also preserve variation, all groups are evolving. Although evolution is always occurring, we can identify those traits that are obviously undergoing change by knowing what the genotype frequencies should be in the absence of evolution (Hardy-Weinberg expectations). Mutation, admixture, and the shuffling of genes by recombination also serve to increase a population's variability. Selection, when it favors one homozygote, works to reduce a population's store of variation, as does drift. Within family lines, inbreeding also reduces genotypic variability. In the real world these forces are all interacting constantly and in very complex ways. As human population size and structure have changed, so has the impact of the forces.

Although many decades of investigation have gone into the attempt to understand evolutionary mechanisms and patterns, the answers are not engraved in stone. As with science in general, we must constantly reanalyze our present knowledge as new insights and information become available. Such is the case with regard to the punctuated equilibria model, which holds that macroevolutionary changes occur in jumps, interspersed with long periods of quiescence. Most of the changes are said to be tied to speciation events; the processes responsible for at least some of them are not those that account for microevolution. Many of the ramifications of both the punctuationist and the gradualist views affect how one then looks at particular questions such as the evolution of sexual reproduction or the role of adaptation in evolution. As time passes, some of the apparent contradictions between the two models are being resolved. In any case, the clash of the two approaches by no means reflects scientists' doubts as to the reality of evolution. On the contrary, the two models attest to the operation of the scientific method.

An understanding of vertebrate evolution provides essential background for the study of human biological and behavioral systems.

The Evolution of the Vertebrates

In earlier chapters we introduced the mechanisms of evolution, the ways in which animal species modify their physical features over time in response to the demands of the environment. Numerous examples illustrate how these mechanisms have operated to lead to the diversity of living forms that we see today. One group of animals, the vertebrates, offers especially good evidence of evolution; humans, along with many other animals, are classified as vertebrates. Because all vertebrates possess an internal skeleton and most have hard, distinctively shaped teeth, both structures that fossilize well, we have a very good fossil record of their biological history. Many of our biological systems were elaborated during vertebrate evolution: the general proportions of the limbs, the number of digits on the hands and feet, the internal bony skeleton, the eyes, the skin, the teeth, the brain, and most of the internal organs, as well as the basic plan of body organization. It is difficult, for example, to understand the evolution of the uniquely human mode of movement, bipedalism, without an appreciation of the development of the vertebrate bony skeleton and its adaptation to the requirements of life on land.

Evolution works on what is present, and rarely in the history of life do we find the evolutionary introduction of radically new features. Rather, evolution modifies the physical structures that are already a part of an animal's system. The skeletal elements and muscles that controlled movement in our early vertebrate ancestors permitted them to be successfully adapted to their environment. These elements existed because the animal needed them to interact successfully with its environment, not because they were going to evolve into human bipedalism. All its organs and systems had specific functions as parts of an interrelated complex that helped the living organism adapt to its environment. In the context of this book, an understanding of vertebrate evolution patterns provides an essential background for examining human biological and behavioral systems, like bipedalism.

Vertebrate Taxonomy

A *taxonomy* (*taxis = arrangement; nomia = distribution*), or classification, is a hierarchic arrangement of animals and plants into various groups that show how they are all related (a taxon—plural, taxa—is a taxonomic category). The Swedish natural historian Carolus Linnaeus made the first systematic attempt to classify all living things (see page 16). He anticipated no changes in his classification because he thought that all animal and plant species were immutable; once formed, they would not change. The organization, although not the specific groupings, of the taxonomic system in Table 4.1 is generally the same as the one Linnaeus devised two hundred years ago.

Linnaeus grouped the animals according to a number of shared biological characteristics. As we work our way down the hierarchic categories, we see that the common biological characteristics become more

TABLE 4.1
A Taxonomy of Modern Humans

Taxonomic Category	Category to Which Humans Belong	Main Biological Features Used to Categorize Humans
Kingdom	Animalia	Humans are animals (as distinguished from plants).
Phylum	Chordata	Humans are chordates; that is, they have concentrated nerve fibers running along the midline of the back.
Subphylum	Vertebrata	Humans are vertebrates, with internal, segmented spinal columns and bilateral symmetry.
Infraphylum	Gnathostomata (animals with jaws)	Humans are vertebrates with jaws.
Superclass	Tetrapoda	Humans are jawed vertebrates who live on land.
Class	Mammalia	Humans are mammals with hair and mammary glands; they are warm-blooded and nurture their young after birth.
Order	Primates	Humans are primates, sharing with other primates specialized structures in the ear region and enhanced blood supply to the brain.
Suborder	Anthropoidea	Humans are anthropoids, along with the monkeys and the apes. They are social-living, daylight-active primates.
Superfamily	Hominoidea	Humans are hominoids, sharing characteristics of the other living hominoids (the apes), with similar back teeth, shoulder muscles, and bones; they lack tails.
Family	Hominidae	Humans are hominids, along with our very close living African ape relatives, the chimpanzee and the gorilla.
Subfamily	Homininae	Humans are hominines with the anatomical equipment permitting habitual bipedalism.
Genus Species	*Homo* *sapiens*	Placement in this genus and species is based on details of brain and tooth size.

and more specific, from the most general category (kingdom), where humans are classified with all other animals, down to the genus level *Homo,* which humans share with only one or two extinct ancestors.

The subphylum Vertebrata includes all animals that possess these features, among others: *bilateral symmetry* (the right half of the animal is more or less a mirror image of the left half); an internal skeletal system with a segmented vertebral column, with nerve tissue shielded inside the column; and an enlargement of this nerve tissue (a brain) at the anterior (front) end.

The vertebrates are often divided into two major groupings, the jawless fishes, or *Agnatha,* of which the lamprey eel is one of the few living examples, and all the rest, which have jaws, or Gnathostomata (*gnatho = jaw*) (Figure 4.1). The *gnathostomes* are then further subdivided into the jawed fishes and the land-adapted vertebrates, or *tetrapods.* Among the jawed fishes are the *Placodermi,* or armored fishes, all of which became extinct several hundred million years ago; the *Chondrichthyes,* or cartilaginous fishes, so-called because their skeletons lack rigid bony tissue, whose main living representatives are the sharks and rays; and the *Osteichthyes,* or bony fishes, an extremely successful group made up of most of the living ocean and freshwater fishes. The Tetrapoda su-

FIGURE 4.1. Representatives of the major vertebrate groups.

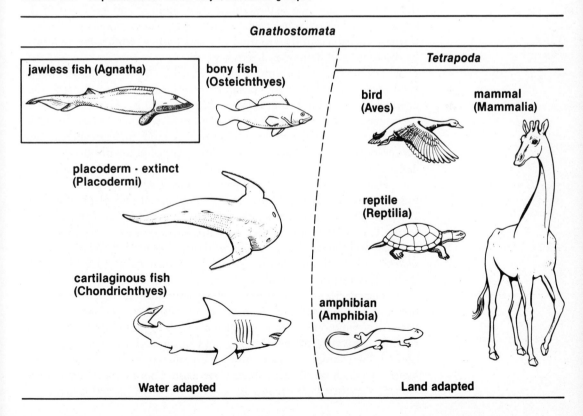

perclass is composed of four land or partly land-adapted vertebrate classes: Amphibia (frogs, toads, and salamanders), Reptilia, Aves (birds), and Mammalia. Animals in each of these classes are distinguished by biological features that are common to virtually all animals in their group.

Most mammals have a constant internal body temperature, a four-chambered heart, and fur. All mammals have mammary glands to nurture their dependent young after birth; the young also undergo a postnatal (after birth) period during which they depend on adults for food. Some mammals, grouped together as the placental mammals, have a placenta, which attaches the developing young to the mother's uterus, providing a system for nourishing and disposing of the fetus's metabolic wastes. Other mammals, the *marsupials,* such as the kangaroo, have no placenta but instead nurse their young in a pouch from a very early stage in their development. Finally, some mammals, the *monotremes,* have continued the earlier vertebrate pattern of egg laying.

The taxon below class is order. The class Mammalia contains over twenty orders, some of them extinct. Rodentia, the rodents, including squirrels, rats, mice, and beavers, is one order. Carnivora, the carnivores, including dogs, cats, weasels, badgers, foxes, bears, seals, and wolves, is another. Each order of mammals is distinguished by shared biological characteristics. Another of the mammalian orders is the Primates, in which humans are placed. The biological features that primates have evolved to suit them to their adaptive niche have made them very difficult to define. We will examine their biology and behavior in the next chapter before trying to define primates. The human suborder Anthropoidea, superfamily Hominoidea and family Hominidae, will also be discussed and defined in later chapters.

The human taxonomic subfamily is the *Homininae;* its members, who normally include humans and their immediate ancestors, are called *hominines.* The main distinguishing biological feature of hominines is our specialized mode of locomotion; *bipedalism,* or walking on two feet. The study of hominine or human evolution is a central focus of physical anthropologists; several later chapters will be concerned with the fossil evidence documenting the evolutionary development of our subfamily.

Below the subfamily level are the most specific categories, the genus and species. Every living and extinct animal and plant is given a *binomial,* or two-part name, that exactly identifies that particular life form. The binomial of modern humans is the genus name *Homo* (Latin for *man*) and the species name *sapiens* (Latin for *wise*), or together: *Homo sapiens.* All taxonomic binomials are written in italics to indicate that they refer to specific animals.

The species is the smallest working unit generally employed in the taxonomy of animals and plants. A smaller category, the subspecies, or variety, is sometimes used in detailed analyses of particular animals; it is roughly equivalent to the breeding population, and it is written as a trinomial. For example, modern humans are often classified as *Homo sapiens sapiens,* to distinguish them from close extinct hominine ancestors who are also classified as *Homo sapiens,* as in *Homo sapiens neanderthalensis.*

A number of major changes have occurred since Linnaeus proposed his taxonomic system. Many living animals have been discovered, identified, and incorporated into the system; extinct animals, too, have been added. Linnaeus considered the animal world as fixed and unchanging: He believed that all animals that had been created were still alive. Although Linnaeus did not recognize evolutionary relationships, we recognize today that animals' features are the result of the operation of evolutionary mechanisms and that similarity in biological characteristics often indicates a close past relationship. Animal species in the same genus have a closer evolutionary relationship than animals outside that genus; animals in the same family are closer in descent than those not in that family; and so on through the hierarchy.

Taxonomy and Evolution

Scientists have yet to identify the ancestors of the vertebrates. They certainly came from the large group of animals in the phylum Chordata. We believe the earliest true vertebrates evolved in the early part of the Paleozoic era, for there is fossil evidence of them by the Cambrian period, over 500 million years ago (Table 4.2).

In the Paleozoic era, as now, the planet was composed of seas and land, but their arrangement was very different. During the past twenty-five years a great deal of evidence has been amassed by geologists and other scientists to show that the continents and other major land masses are subject to movement, termed plate tectonics, or more commonly *continental drift*.[1*] Apparently the earth's land masses have always drifted very slowly in relation to one another, so the distances between continents today are merely their positions at this time. We know, for example, that the plate on which much of the North American continent sits is slowly drifting westward toward Asia and away from Europe, thereby increasing the size of the North Atlantic Ocean and reducing the size of the Pacific. At one time North America and Europe were joined into one large continental land mass that finally broke apart some 50 million years ago.

Knowledge of continental drift has helped us understand some of the geologic forces that have shaped and continue to shape the surfaces of the continents. The earthquake zone along the California coast results from the pressures that build up where the westward-moving North American plate is in contact with another, smaller plate that is moving northward. The geologic origin of many mountain chains can be attributed to the forces unleashed when two continental plates collided. Geologic studies tell us that during the latter part of the Paleozoic era, at the end of the Pennsylvanian and the beginning of the Permian periods, all the continents were gathered into two "supercontinents" (Figure 4.2). The southern land mass was *Gondwanaland,* and the continent to the north was *Laurasia*. During the Mesozoic era, these pieces moved to the north, separated, and gradually formed the configuration we know today.

The Water Vertebrates

*See page 615 for notes to Chapter 4.

TABLE 4.2
Geological Chart of the Last One-half Billion Years of Earth's History, Showing the
Times of First Appearance of Major Vertebrate Groups

Era	Period	Epoch	First Appearance	Millions of Years Ago
Cenozoic	Quaternary	Holocene		
				0.01
		Pleistocene		
				1.6
	Tertiary	Pliocene	• Homininae	
				5.0
		Miocene		
				23.5
		Oligocene	• Anthropoidea	
				37.0
		Eocene		
				56.5
		Paleocene		
				65
Mesozoic	Cretaceous		• Primates	
				135
	Jurassic		• Aves	
				205
	Triassic		• Mammalia	
				250
Paleozoic	Permian			
				290
	Pennsylvanian		• Reptilia	
				325
	Mississippian			
				365
	Devonian		• Amphibia • Chondricthyes • Osteichthyes • Placodermi	
				410
	Silurian			
				440
	Ordovician			
				500
	Cambrian		• Agnatha	
				590
Pre-Cambrian				

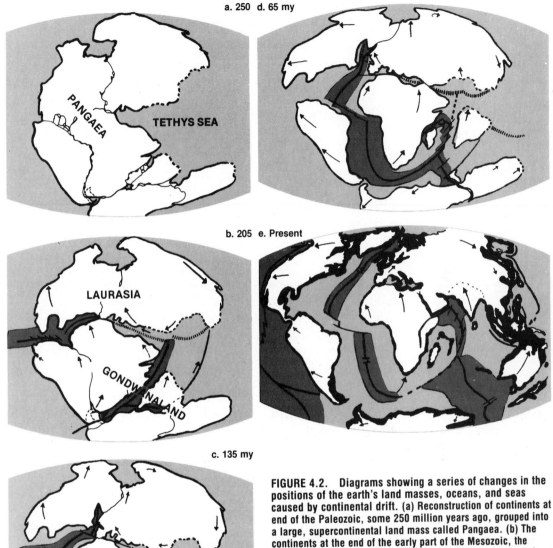

a. 250 d. 65 my

PANGAEA TETHYS SEA

b. 205 e. Present

LAURASIA

GONDWANALAND

c. 135 my

FIGURE 4.2. Diagrams showing a series of changes in the positions of the earth's land masses, oceans, and seas caused by continental drift. (a) Reconstruction of continents at end of the Paleozoic, some 250 million years ago, grouped into a large, supercontinental land mass called Pangaea. (b) The continents at the end of the early part of the Mesozoic, the Triassic, some 205 million years ago, when the formation of Laurasia and Gondwanaland seems to have begun (darker gray regions are opening ocean basins; arrows show drift directions). (c) Position of continents at the end of the Jurassic, some 135 million years ago. (d) Position of continents at the end of the Mesozoic and the beginning of the age of mammals, the Cenozoic, some 65 million years ago. (e) Position of the continents today. (Here and in later chapters *my* refers to millions of years ago.)

Geologists believe that during the Cambrian period, when vertebrates first appear in the fossil record, the planet's land masses were in a still different arrangement, although the exact configuration has yet to be worked out. The topographic features of the continents were very different from those we see today, which were formed much later. At that time, no plant or animal life had yet developed on the land, but there was life to be found in the waters, where plants along with some non-vertebrate animals had evolved.

The Jawless Fishes

The first vertebrate known to have joined this assemblage was fish-like, probably fairly slow at swimming, and perhaps lived in the ocean shallows along the shore. These early vertebrates have been grouped in a major vertebrate subdivision called Agnatha (meaning jawless). Most of these animals are extinct; the best known of the few living agnathans are the very specialized lamprey eel and the hagfish. These animals may seem completely unrelated to humans, but they possess some features that are a part of our biology, although now highly modified. Generally few radically new characteristics were introduced in the evolution of the vertebrates, including humans. Evolution operates by modifying existing structures. The gills of these early fish are controlled by muscles that, in the evolutionary continuum leading to humans, have moved up the neck, along the face, and now control facial expression. The nerves that supply these areas in humans are like those found in the early vertebrates; the structures remain, but they serve different functions.

In many features the Agnatha are very different from us (Figure 4.3). They have neither jaws nor teeth. Like all vertebrates, however, they possess an internal, segmented vertebral column and are differentiated from their prevertebrate ancestors by an enlarged area of the nerve cord at the front of their bodies. The brain in the lamprey eel's larva shows three enlarged areas on the nerve cord, specialized to deal with different sensory data. These in turn are divided into a forebrain (or forelobe), a midbrain, and a hindbrain, which control smell, sight, and co-ordination and hearing, respectively. Later in the evolution of the vertebrates, this basic plan was modified and enlarged. When vertebrates evolved for life on land, one of the most important areas that changed was the front of the forebrain, which controls the sense of smell. Eventually, in the mammals, this became the grossly enlarged cerebral cortex and completely covered the rest of the brain.

FIGURE 4.3.   Lamprey. Members of the Agnatha, the lampreys are specialized descendants of the early jawless fishes. The living animals are about 28 cm (11½ in.) long.

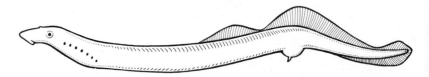

There is a break in the fossil evidence between the agnathans from the Cambrian and Ordovician periods and the middle and latter parts of the next period, the Silurian. Fishlike members of the Agnatha became much more numerous and varied in the Silurian, suggesting that they had undergone an adaptive radiation.

Fishes with Jaws

The fishes continued their expansion in the Devonian period, but we know little about the evolutionary relationships between the newly evolved forms and the continuing agnathans. Four groups of vertebrates existed then, all adapted to the water but with some different biological traits. The Placodermi, or armored fish, had a bony shield covering the head region like that found in many agnathans (Figure 4.4). The placoderms differed from the jawless fish in having movable jaws, formed from the first gill arch bones, that lay flat instead of in the normal vertical position. The dermal (skin) armor, hard plates covering the placoderm (and agnathan) head, was made of a substance called *dentin,* which forms the major part of vertebrate teeth. In many vertebrates, such as the mammals, the dentin in the teeth is covered with a thin layer of *enamel,* a harder, denser material. Vertebrate teeth appear to have had their origin in an inward folding of the dermal armor in the mouths of these early vertebrates. The first teeth were nothing more than small spikes sticking up from the inner surface of the mouth. Later in the evolution of the vertebrates, the teeth were restricted to the sides of the mouth and became firmly anchored in the jawbones.

The placoderms became extinct just after the Devonian period closed. The other two vertebrate classes that had evolved in the Devonian had better fortune. By the early part of this period, the class Osteichthyes, the bony fishes that came to dominate the lakes and seas, had appeared. Toward the middle of the period, members of the class Chon-

FIGURE 4.4.   Reconstruction of a placoderm from the Devonian period (actual size about 45 cm, or 1.5 ft). Notice the armor plating and the lower jaws.

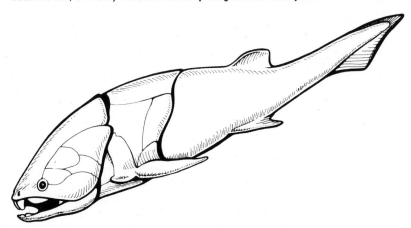

drichthyes turn up in the fossil record. These two classes differ in, among other things, the materials composing their internal skeleton.

The bony fishes have skeletal elements of hard, rigid bone; the Chondrichthyes, of which the sharks and rays have survived to our time, have a skeleton of more flexible cartilage. Because cartilage is laid down first in the embryonic development of many vertebrates, later being replaced by bone, scientists used to think that the bony fishes evolved from the cartilaginous fishes. Many now reject this idea, arguing that the bony fishes may be more representative of the ancestral condition and that the cartilaginous fishes keep the infantile condition into adulthood.

These two vertebrate classes are very successful animals. They underwent a series of adaptive radiations early in their evolutionary development, filling many marine and freshwater niches. The first land vertebrate seems to have evolved from the bony fishes. By the end of the Devonian, there is fossil evidence of a vertebrate at least partially adapted to life on land.

Transition from Water to Land

The vertebrates' evolutionary transition from existence in the water to existence in the air was an incomparably important event in the history of life. It set in motion the evolution of the reptiles, birds, and mammals. But a number of vital changes had to occur for animals adapted to water to evolve into land dwellers.

Evolution of Terrestrial Physical Features

Air Breathing First, the vertebrates had to evolve a structure that could take oxygen directly out of the air. It would replace the gills, which work like filters, absorbing oxygen from the water. As it happened, some primitive fish had lunglike structures, and thus a complex had already evolved that could give land vertebrates one of the basic necessities of life.

Body Fluids Another important condition had to be met. Body cells must have a watery environment or they will die. For a vertebrate living in the water this is not a problem, but a vertebrate that lives on land, surrounded by air, must keep its body moisture from escaping through the skin. Terrestrial adaptation, then, demanded waterproof skin to retain body liquids and an efficient kidney system to recirculate and purify the fluids. Most water vertebrates had such a system, but it became highly developed in the land forms. The kidney continually filters metabolic waste out of the blood, converts it into uric acid or urea, and stores it in the bladder for later excretion.

Reproduction Vertebrates living on land also had to evolve a new system for reproduction. The water-dwelling vertebrates, with several specialized exceptions, reproduce outside the body, using the water as an integral part of the process. A female fish deposits her eggs on the sea floor or in the water, and the male passes over them releasing sperm, which is transported by the water to fertilize the eggs. The eggs also need water all around them to dispose of metabolic wastes. They are not sealed capsules, but are open to the environment. The soft, gelatinous eggs develop into miniature versions of the adult. The eggs and young fish far outnumber the adult fish, but because the adults do not take care of their young, the mortality rate is extremely high, and only a very few of the young reach sexual maturity. (This point was recognized by Malthus, as we noted on page 22, and Darwin later used it in formulating his theory of natural selection.)

Locomotion   Water-dwelling vertebrates move in a highly specialized way. Fishes have body fins on their top, bottom, and sides as well as strong tail fins. The body fins are used for stability and turning, but not for locomotion. The body itself, undulating from side to side, snaps the tail fins back and forth and propels the fish through the water. Some of the earliest land vertebrates may have moved over the land by swishing their tail back and forth and using their side appendages to keep their bodies stable, but not to move or to lift them off the ground; these vertebrates moved with their bellies resting directly on the ground. A more efficient method of locomotion on land called for keeping the body off the ground and developing the fins into limbs strong enough to support and move the body's weight. The body fins of most fish are too weak to support that weight; normally the skeletal elements inside the lateral (side) fins are made of cartilage, too flexible to carry weight. One order of bony fish, the lobe-fins (order *Crossopterygii*), have lateral fins of a different sort, which they apparently use for locomotion. Because of this, they have robust and strongly developed fin skeletons, which is unusual for a fish. The lobe-fins first appear in freshwater deposits of the Devonian age, and were thought to have become extinct by the end of the Mesozoic. Fifty years ago, however, a living lobe-fin was caught off the coast of South Africa. A number of others have now been caught and studied.

The first land vertebrates may have evolved from the lobe-fins, for the bony elements of their lateral fins have the outlines of the terrestrial vertebrate limb system (Figure 4.5). The pattern, much modified, is still found in many modern mammals, including humans (Figure 4.6). A large supporting bone at the upper end of the fin became associated later in vertebrate evolution with the vertebral column and evolved into the shoulder blade (*scapula*) of the front limbs and the pelvic bone (*innominate*) of the rear limbs. The limb system itself consists of one upper-limb bone (*humerus* in the front limb, *femur* in the rear limb); two lower-limb bones (*radius* and *ulna* in the front limb, *fibula* and *tibia* in the rear limb); a wrist and ankle complex; and a hand and foot of five digits each. (See Figure 5.2 for a primate with all these elements in place.) The major elements of this design, common to all terrestrial vertebrates, can be seen in the ancient lobe-fins of the Devonian seas.

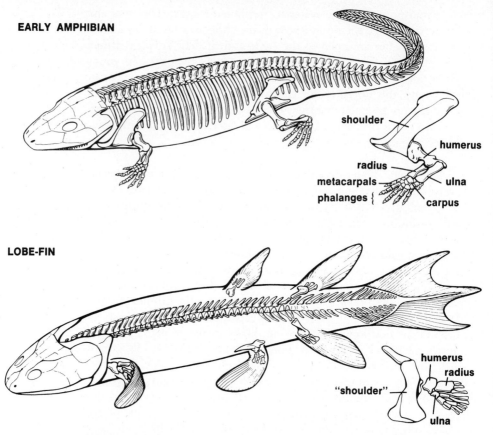

EARLY AMPHIBIAN

shoulder

humerus

radius

metacarpals

phalanges {

ulna

carpus

LOBE-FIN

humerus

radius

"shoulder"

ulna

FIGURE 4.5. Skeletons of an early amphibian and a lobe-fin showing the similarities in structure, particularly between the amphibian's front limb and the lobe-fin's lateral fin.

Early Land Vertebrates

The first terrestrial, or tetrapod, vertebrates appeared in the latter part of the Devonian period. They were primitive members of the class Amphibia, the amphibians. Their familiar and very specialized descendants are the frogs, newts, and salamanders, but the earliest of their kind were far more primitive. Like their relatives living today, these primitive amphibians had not completely evolved the necessary equipment that would fully adapt them to life on the land. Their skins were not watertight, their reproduction was still external, and their eggs had not developed a tough shell. Virtually all amphibians, both then and now, reproduce in the water, where their eggs develop.

In many ways, the amphibians are thus a transitional form, different from both the wholly water-adapted vertebrate classes that preceded them and the completely terrestrial reptiles, birds, and mammals that came after them. However, the amphibians should not be viewed as unsuccessful animals, dozing in late Paleozoic ponds waiting to evolve into a fully terrestrial vertebrate. The amphibians are well adapted to the en-

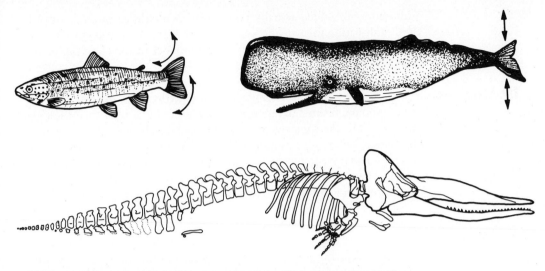

FIGURE 4.6. Whales are mammals that have adapted to a life in the sea. As a result, their terrestrial vertebrate skeletal system has modified to permit these creatures to move effectively in the water. Note the land vertebrate front limb bones with the typical number of bony elements in this sperm whale (who, like all whales, has lost its rear limbs).

Like the fishes, whales move in the water by powerful strokes of their tail fins, but while fish undulate their vertically oriented tail fins from side to side, whales, descendent from land vertebrates, possess muscles and bones that move their horizontally oriented tail fins up and down. (Not to scale.)

vironmental niches they exploit. Seen in the overall context of vertebrate evolution, these animals represent the continuum between the water and land forms.

The Reptiles

The reptiles evolved in the Pennsylvanian period from one of the early groups of amphibians. They were the first well-adapted land vertebrates, with waterproof skins, four limbs sturdily supporting their body, and profound changes in their reproductive system. Their fertilization was internal, with the male placing the sperm in contact with the eggs inside the female. When the female laid fertilized eggs, they were encased in a tough shell, which protected the developing embryo. Inside, along with the yolk for nourishment, was an extremely important membrane, the *allantois,* that collected metabolic wastes. The growing reptile's tough-shelled egg sealed it from the outside world, unlike earlier vertebrate eggs, which needed the water outside to flush away wastes. This self-contained incubator could be laid on land; this change, with the other reptilian evolutionary developments, provided the biological bases for a land vertebrate.

With a whole planet of empty terrestrial adaptive niches, the early reptiles quickly evolved a wide array of forms to exploit the diverse land adaptations open to them. Through the next 150 million years, they were the dominant terrestrial animal life, numbering among them the incredible and highly diverse group of reptiles we lump together as the dinosaurs but which actually represented many different kinds of plant- and flesh-eating forms. The living reptiles—snakes, lizards, turtles, croc- odiles, and alligators—are only a pale reminder of the large numbers of their ancestors that once roamed the planet.

The Mammals

One of the earliest reptile groups to evolve was the order Therap- sida, who are termed the mammallike reptiles because of their biological features. The *therapsids* were primitive, lacking the specializations found in living reptiles; yet a number of their traits so clearly foreshadow mam- mal traits that we may conclude that they were the ancestors of the mam- mals. There is ample fossil evidence that true mammals had evolved from the therapsids by the latter stages of the Triassic period.

The Cenozoic: Age of the Mammals

Some 65 million years ago, at the end of the Cretaceous period, the last period of the Mesozoic era, the dinosaurs, including such successful Cretaceous forms as the horned dinosaurs and the truly terrifying meat- eater *Tyrannosaurus rex,* suddenly and completely disappeared. Recent discoveries have suggested a possible explanation for this apparently in- stantaneous mass extinction.[2] Geologic deposits in various parts of the world from the very end of the Cretaceous period have been found to contain a very high percentage of the rare element iridium. Meteors and other extraterrestrial rocks also possess relatively large amounts of this mineral. It has been suggested that a large object (4 to 10 km in diameter) struck the earth and, along with hundreds of millions of tons of earth rocks, was vaporized at the point of impact. This resulted in the forma- tion of a temporary worldwide dust cloud, reducing the amount of solar radiation reaching the earth and significantly lowering atmospheric tem- peratures. The cold-blooded reptiles would have had great difficulty sur- viving even a short period of lowered temperatures, while the warm- blooded mammals could live through it more successfully. Along with the disappearance of the ruling great reptiles, the end of the Cretaceous also marks major extinctions of microscopic plant and animal life in the oceans, lending further support to the theory of a planetwide catastro- phe. Many paleontologists, however, remain unconvinced that an extra- terrestrial event was the reason the dinosaurs disappeared. They cite as evidence fossil studies that indicate that the dinosaurs may have been decreasing in numbers well before the end of the Cretaceous. Recently, there have been suggestions that some of these creatures may have lived on into the early part of the Cenozoic.

Whatever theory is ultimately shown to fit the data best, the dis- appearance of the dinosaurs was crucial to the development of the mam- mals. Mammals had been an inconspicuous part of the Mesozoic animal world, many most probably adapted to a *nocturnal* (active at night), *ar- boreal* (living in trees), and *insectivorous* (a diet of insects) niche. At the beginning of the Cenozoic, the mammals begin a series of adaptive ra- diations, expanding into the now-vacant niches left by the dinosaurs. Early in the Cenozoic, the bones of large, terrestrially adapted mammals begin appearing in the fossil record, and the stage is thus set for the evolutionary developments that will create the familiar modern mammal world. Among the most primitive mammalian orders still living are the insectivores, such as the shrew; at some time in the Cretaceous period the primates may have branched off from this group. Unlike most other mammal groups, however, the primates apparently maintained many of the primitive mammalian insectivore adaptations and as a result maintained the general vertebrate biological features that were lost or modified in other, more specialized mammal groups.

In discussing the biology of the mammals we will concentrate on the attributes that are most important in understanding the biology and evolution of humans. Like all living organisms, a mammal is a complex of interrelated anatomical systems, each influencing the others. We will discuss individual systems, such as reproduction or locomotion, because it is more effective to look at them one at a time, but no system works independently of the others.

The hard palate, the bony roof of the human mouth, is a good example of this interrelationship. It separates the breathing opening of the nasal cavity from the mouth. Many reptiles have no hard palate and cannot breathe effectively when they eat and swallow; their intake of oxygen is interrupted by a mouthful of food. Mammals, though, are more active, maintain a constant body temperature and a high metabolic rate, and have a larger, more complex brain. The constant supply of oxygen that these systems need has led to the hard palate and to other anatomical structures that permit continuous breathing even while the animal is eating. By itself the hard palate may not seem significant, but as part of a complex, interrelated system it is indispensable. It is also representative of an animal, the mammal, whose biology is significantly different from that of most reptiles. This difference is fundamental to the mammalian pattern and essential to the subsequent evolution of humans. Distinctive mammalian characteristics involve many other areas, such as growth and development, locomotion, reproduction, activity, behavior, and dentition.

Dentition From its origin as a folding in of the placoderm's armor, vertebrate dentition evolved to the condition seen in living reptiles, amphibians, and fish: a long row of pointed or sharp-sided, undifferentiated teeth (*homodont*) that are completely replaceable. Most reptiles have this kind of teeth (Figure 4.7). The mammalian pattern, which begins to evolve in the therapsids, shows significant differences. One of the most important is the close relationship of the teeth in the mammal's upper and lower jaws, which have evolved to fit and operate as a unit. They *occlude*, that is, their chewing surfaces are so constructed that the upper and lower teeth are able to fit precisely together, cutting, crushing, grinding, or shearing the food caught between. The reptile's homodont teeth in the upper and lower jaws usually operate independently, preventing most of them from chewing their food; they have to swallow it whole.

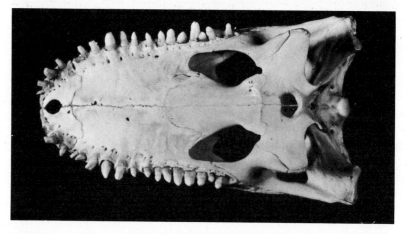

FIGURE 4.7. Two views of the homodont teeth of a reptile (alligator). Notice in the top photo that, with the upper and lower jaws together, the teeth do not occlude.

In nonmammal vertebrates, if one tooth falls out, another will take its place. In some reptiles the teeth are replaced periodically throughout the animal's life, with new teeth replacing the old in a wavelike progression starting in the front and working backward. Mammalian teeth are replaced only once; as a young mammal develops, the milk, or *deciduous* (shedding), teeth erupt from the jawbones. Later the milk teeth are replaced by the permanent dentition. If a permanent tooth is lost or broken, no new one will take its place.

The mammals also evolved differentiated teeth (*heterodont*). The therapsids, like the mammals, had four kinds of teeth—incisors, canines, premolars, and molars—each with distinctive shapes and functions in chewing (Figure 4.8). The incisors occupy the front of the tooth row in the upper and lower jaws. They are normally flat, chisel-shaped teeth that meet in an edge-to-edge bite; their function is to cut, slice, or gnaw food pieces into manageable bits to fit into the mouth for further chewing. Directly behind the incisors are the canines. In many mammals the canines are pointed, tusk-shaped teeth, projecting beyond the level of the other teeth. In the carnivores they are primarily an offensive weapon for bringing down prey. In other mammals, such as some of the monkeys and apes, they are used to split open bamboo shoots or other hard-surfaced food.

At the back of the tooth row are the premolars and molars. Depending on the particular mammal and its diet, these two kinds of teeth prepare pieces of food for swallowing by grinding, shearing, or crushing. In herbivorous mammals (Figure 4.9), whose diet is coarse, fibrous foods like grass, fruit, and leaves, the premolars and molars have ridged, corrugated surfaces that grind foods much as a millstone would. Carnivores, whose diet is primarily meat, have pointed-cusped premolars and molars with sharp sides (Figure 4.9). When the upper and lower premolars and molars are brought together as the jaws close, the sides of the upper and lower teeth slide past each other, and meat that is caught between them is cut or sheared as though by scissors. Primates, along with a number of other mammals, have bulbous projections called *cusps* on the chewing surfaces of their teeth. These cusps, which were part of the dentitions of the earliest placental mammals, originated as part of an insect crushing complex and have evolved in the primates to permit a wide variety of dietary adaptations (Figure 4.10).

These specialized teeth are found in the same order in every mammal. Furthermore, every mammalian species has a specific number of each kind of tooth, whereas in most reptiles the number can vary among

FIGURE 4.8. The heterodont dentition of a hypothetical early placental mammal, showing the kinds of mammalian teeth, their number, and their position (i = incisors, c = canines, pm = premolar, m = molar).

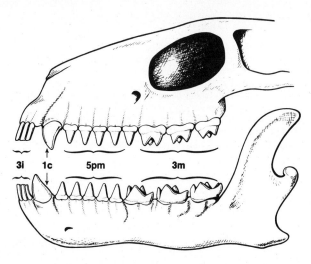

3i 1c 5pm 3m

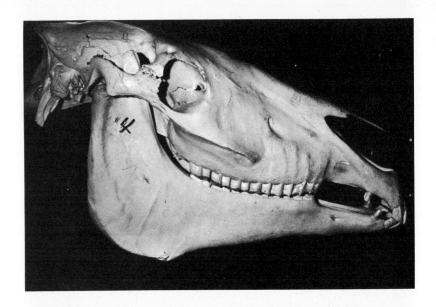

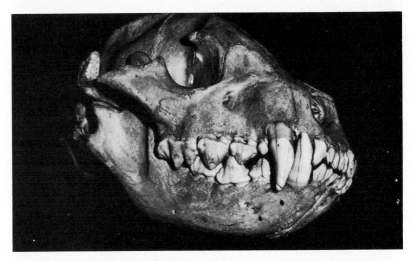

FIGURE 4.9. Occlusion in two mammal skulls. (Top) The skull of an herbivorous mammal, a horse, shows occlusion in mammals who use their back teeth to grind food between the flattened, millstonelike, chewing surfaces. The canines in the horse are much smaller than those in the carnivore, reflecting their relative lack of importance. In fact, many herbivore species no longer possess canines. (Bottom) In a carnivore, a hyena, the back teeth, the sharp-edged premolars and molars, occlude by sliding past each other, slicing or shearing meat between them much as scissor blades cut. The large, pointed canines also slide past each other, permitting the jaws to close. The incisors in the two mammals are also different, reflecting the different uses these teeth have in the adaptation of these animals.

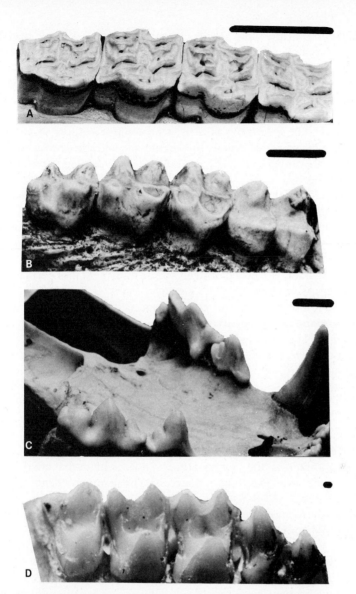

FIGURE 4.10.   From top to bottom, the upper molars of a horse, a gorilla (a primate), a lynx, and a tarsier (a primitive primate), illustrating the variation on the cusps of mammalian molars.

(a) Horse molars have a flat, corrugated surface that is effective in grinding coarse vegetable foods. (b) Like many primates, gorillas (apes closely related to modern humans) have molars with large, rounded, relatively pointed cusps capable of chewing a wide variety of foods. Note the "hollows" where cusps should be; these are pits worn in the enamel from hard usage, exposing the underlying dentin. (c) The lynx, a carnivore, has sharp edges on the sides of its molars that are efficient in cutting meat. (d) The tarsier, although a generalized feeder, possesses molars much like those of the earliest insectivorous mammals, with high-pointed cusps accompanied by sharp side edges and deep "basins" in the middle of the tooth. Pointed cusps from the lower teeth fit into the basins, crushing and, with the sharp edges, cutting food caught between.

(Photos not to scale; the black lines indicate the true size of one molar.)

individuals of the same species. Recent discoveries indicate that the earliest placental mammals may have had a total of forty-eight teeth; no living placental mammal has this many. To identify the number and kind of teeth in species of mammals, we use a simple formula: separate the upper and lower jaws and divide each jaw down the middle; count the number and kind of teeth from the incisors in the front to the molars in the back. The ancestral mammals' dentition (total of forty-eight) is stated as three incisors, one canine, five premolars, and three molars (see Figure 4.8), representing one quadrant of the total of upper and lower jaws. The dental formula is often abbreviated as 3i, 1c, 5pm, 3m, or even shorter: 3.1.5.3. This is the greatest number of teeth found in any known placental mammal. All living mammalian groups have lost one or more teeth from this maximum. The human dental formula is 2.1.2.3, meaning that in the evolution of our ancestors, one incisor has been lost from each quadrant, for a total of four; and three premolars have been lost from each quadrant, for a total of twelve. The human total of permanent teeth is thirty-two.

Because mammalian teeth are specialized for different functions, many mammal groups have lost types of teeth not needed in their adaptation. The form of the teeth, too, has undergone evolutionary modification in response to the needs of specialized feeding or other adaptations. Over time, different mammal groups have evolved distinctive dental features, both in the number and type of teeth and in the shape and size of the chewing surface.

The evolution of a differentiated occluding dentition has enabled the mammals to adapt to a wide variety of niches and to process efficiently the large amounts of food necessary to fuel the high activity levels, constant internal body temperature, and large brain that are the essential bases for mammalian adaptive success. The mammal's dental complex is also related to the other unique traits, and one reason for the mammal's limited number of teeth, fixed for each species, is the mammal's pattern of growth and development.

Growth and Development   Mammals and reptiles differ fundamentally in their growth patterns. Reptiles are born as miniature adults and continue growing until their death. This is one explanation for the continuous eruption of new teeth in reptiles; as they get larger, their jaws have room for additional teeth. The mammals' growth period, on the other hand, has definite stages: In infancy the young mammal depends on adults for care and nourishment; in childhood it begins to develop independence; in adolescence strong growth occurs; and in adulthood all growth stops. This distinctive system applies to many other biological complexes in mammals.

Bone growth, for example, is very different in reptiles and mammals (Figure 4.11). As a reptile grows, the bones of its skeleton become longer as new bone tissue is laid down at the ends of each bone; this method hinders the development of an efficient *articulation,* or joint, with the adjacent bone, because growth takes place at the joint. Mammal bones develop the articular ends early in life, and the ends grow little after that; growth occurs in an area just behind the articulation, where it connects with the shaft of the bone. As a mammal develops, the skeletal bone lengthens by the addition of bone tissue in these areas, not at the ends. As adulthood nears, the growth centers become smaller and smaller, disappearing altogether when the articular end of the bone fuses to the shaft. At this adult stage, the bone can lengthen no further.

Locomotion Growth and development of the long bones have much effect on locomotion (Figure 4.12). Reptilian locomotion, except in specialized snakes and the bipedal dinosaurs, depends on support and propulsion by the four limbs. In most reptiles these limbs are not directly beneath the animal but extend straight out from the shoulder and hip joints, the elbow joint and knee joint making a 90° angle to put the front

FIGURE 4.11. Comparison of bone growth in a reptile and a mammal. Long bone growth in a reptile: (a) bone in an early embryo, composed entirely of cartilage; (b–e) stages of growth, with cartilage being replaced by bone. Bone growth occurs at the ends of the bone and can continue throughout the animal's lifetime. Long bone growth in a mammal: (a) bone in an embryo, composed entirely of cartilage; (b–c) stages of growth, with cartilage being replaced by bone; (d) stage at which most longitudinal growth occurs, with new bone being laid down between the ends and the shaft of the bone; (e) adult stage, when ends and shaft have fused and little further longitudinal growth is possible.

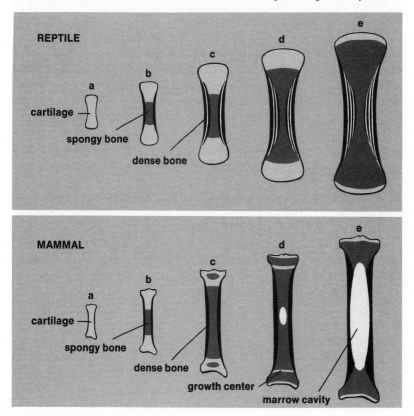

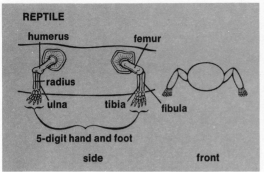 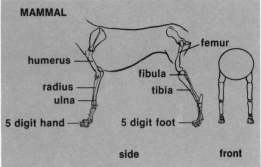

FIGURE 4.12. Comparison of reptilian and mammalian stances. The transition from a reptilian stance to a mammalian one meant that the limb bones were repositioned to elevate the body, which changed the limbs' function from merely propelling the body to supporting it as well. The bones were remodeled and their articulation was changed; their coordinated movement was gained by changes in musculature. See Figure 5.2 for the primate limb pattern.

and rear limbs in a supporting position. Most mammals, too, rely on four limbs, but their limbs are underneath their trunk, and their elbow and knee joints are tucked in under their body rather than out to the side. One of the anatomical changes that made this possible was the angulation of the ball of the upper bone of the front (humerus) and rear (femur) limbs, making a bend that permits the limbs to be placed in an efficient position to support and move body weight.

Reproduction and Childhood Development   Profound evolutionary changes have affected mammalian reproduction. As in the reptiles, fertilization takes place inside the female. The developing embryo remains inside the mother's womb, attached by the placenta, which gives nourishment and takes care of the embryo's wastes. Almost all mammals have this system, except the marsupials, whose young are transferred to a pouch at a very early stage of development, and the duck-billed platypus (a monotreme), which still lays eggs. The monotreme's ancestors indirectly illustrate the transition from the egg-laying reptiles to the placental mammals. Like other mammals, the platypus cares for its young after they are born.

Placental mammals give birth to live young that are relatively helpless at birth. Every mammal goes through a dependent stage, requiring food and care from adult animals. Female mammals possess mammary glands, which begin producing milk after their offspring are born. The dependency period gives the young mammal time to learn many of the behaviors it will need for survival. Reptilian females generally lay their eggs and then leave them, never to return. A young reptile must be equipped to deal with its environment from the moment it leaves the comparative safety of the shell. It must know what to eat and what to avoid, in short, everything it needs to survive in a hostile world. This necessity limits its possible actions, leaving little room for developing learned behavior. Having a reproductive biology conducive to learned behavior is one triumph in the mammals' evolution, for they can modify learned behavior rather quickly to respond to the environment's demands. Reptiles, relying more on biologically programed or instinctive behaviors, must do without this flexibility. The mammals' reproductive biology and the dependency of their offspring were basic to the subsequent appearance of humans, to whom a complex of learned behaviors is essential for survival.

Brain and Behavior Crucial to the ability of a young mammal to learn adaptive behaviors during its dependency period was the evolution of the mammalian brain. One of the greatest differences between the reptiles and the mammals is the size and complexity of their brains. All vertebrate brains perform a number of functions, including the regulation of the animal's internal systems, such as respiration, digestion, and heart rate. In addition, the vertebrate brain is the centralized location where information from all the animal's sensory systems—the eyes, ears, nose, and touch receptors—is received, sorted, and analyzed and where signals to the muscles originate in response (Figure 4.13). The brain acts

FIGURE 4.13. A generalized mammal, illustrating the relationships between sensory input and motor responses, and the mediating function of the brain.

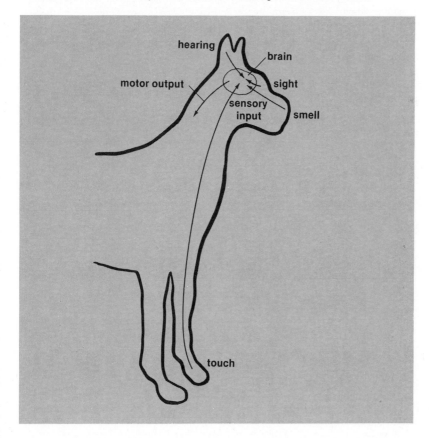

as a link between sensory input and the motor output to the muscles, the result of which is behavior. As the brain became more complex in vertebrate evolution, its ability to initiate more flexible responses to sensory data increased. What this amounts to is the evolution of *intelligence* in contrast to instinctive or biologically programed behavior. H. J. Jerison, a biologist who has studied the evolution of the vertebrate brain, defines intelligence as *the ability of an animal to construct a perceptual model of reality.*[3]

To understand the significance of this definition, let us briefly review the findings of the noted animal behaviorist Niko Tinbergen, who in his 1951 book, *The Study of Instinct,* reported his observations of the mating behavior of a small European fish, the stickleback (Figure 4.14). Tinbergen discovered that during the spring mating period, the female stickleback's belly became swollen with eggs, creating a distinctive bulging appearance. The sight of this swollen appearance promoted a male

FIGURE 4.14.   Stickleback mating behavior.

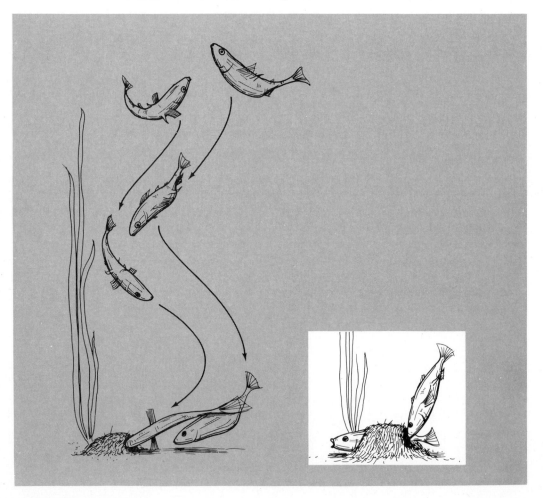

to perform a specific behavior, a zigzag "dance." The response of the female to this dance in turn triggered an appropriate response from the male, all culminating in the female's depositing of her eggs in a nest the male had prepared, which in turn resulted in the male's passing over the eggs to fertilize them. Tinbergen suggested that this series of behaviors was a fixed pattern, with each action directly triggering the next. He described the sequence thus: each behavior acts as a *sign stimulus* that serves as an *innate releasing mechanism* in the brain of the other animal and produces the next behavior in the series, a *fixed action pattern*. This fixed action pattern in turn acts as a sign stimulus to the other animal, which as a result produces that next fixed action pattern in the series, and so on. All of this suggests that these behaviors are biologically programed in the brain so that the receipt of sensory information (in this case by the eyes) of a particular behavior leads directly to a specific motor response or behavior. These are not learned behaviors; Tinbergen found that even sticklebacks raised in an aquarium away from other fish were capable of performing these actions successfully and in proper sequence. Thus, there seems to be a direct link in the brain between specific stimuli and particular responses. Since Tinbergen made his observations, we have found that the relationships between what an animal senses and what it does are sometimes more complex than those in this example. It seems clear, however, that this sort of biologically programed behavior is characteristic of many nonmammal vertebrates.

In mammals there appear to be far fewer direct links between sensory input and behavioral response. During the childhood dependency period, a young mammal, not having to survive on its own, can learn how to react appropriately to stimuli in the environment. As Jerison noted, the young mammal develops a concept of its environment and learns to deal with it successfully by observing the actions of its mother and other adult members of its species. Thus, the mammalian brain has taken on an increasingly important role in mediating between sensory perceptions and behavior. Instead of responding in accordance with genetically fixed patterns, the mammalian brain receives the sensory input, compares it to the model of reality constructed on the basis of previous experiences, and then initiates patterns of behavior it has learned will be appropriate in that particular context.

The biological basis for flexible patterns of behavior is the evolutionary development of the mammalian brain, especially the *cerebrum* (Figure 4.15). In the early vertebrates, three specialized areas developed to deal with varied sensory information: a *forebrain* for smell, a *midbrain* for vision, and a *hindbrain* for hearing and balance. In most early vertebrates, this sensory information was passed to the midbrain, where motor responses were initiated; in these animals, the midbrain was in control. In the mammalian brain a number of major changes have occurred; the most important is the elaboration and expansion of the forebrain into the cerebrum, or cerebral cortex. In the mammals all sensory information now terminates in the cerebrum, bypassing the hindbrain and midbrain, and it is there also that behavioral responses are initiated. Figure

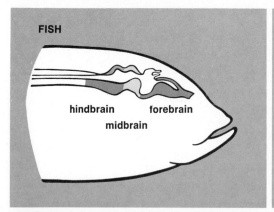

FISH

hindbrain   forebrain
        midbrain

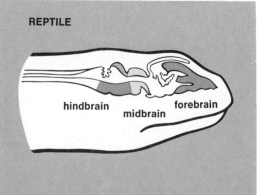

REPTILE

hindbrain   forebrain
        midbrain

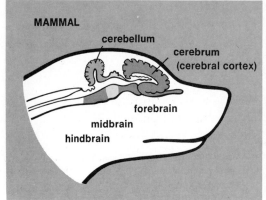

MAMMAL

cerebellum
            cerebrum
            (cerebral cortex)

            forebrain
    midbrain
hindbrain

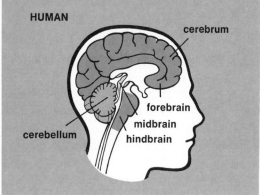

HUMAN

cerebrum

            forebrain
            midbrain
cerebellum
            hindbrain

FIGURE 4.15.   Evolution of the human brain. The complex and highly refined sensory apparatus that is the human brain has been built on the structure shown in the fish: a relatively large forebrain to deal with the sense of smell so important to fish, a midbrain with vision, and a hindbrain with balance and hearing.

The reptile's brain is more complex; because hearing and vision have become more important, the midbrain and hindbrain have enlarged, with the midbrain coordinating the reptile's greater sensory activities.

The mammal's brain is of still greater complexity. Sense coordination has shifted to the forebrain, which has developed a folded cerebrum on top that deals with memory and learning. The hindbrain has developed a marked cerebellum to coordinate the mammal's more varied actions.

The human midbrain and hindbrain have not increased in size in proportion to the forebrain. The large cerebrum dominates the brain and handles the functions that are unique to humans, including abstract thought.

4.16 is an illustration of the human brain, the most complex mammalian brain yet to evolve. The large cerebrum is convoluted to permit a greater number of nerve cells to be packed into a given volume; the other parts of the brain, especially the midbrain, have decreased in size, although the *cerebellum* continues to be an enlarged area because of its role in the co-ordination of muscular activities. The human cerebral cortex, like that of other mammals, possesses specialized areas that are responsible for the receipt of specific sensory information, the storage of memory data, the association of sensory data, the analysis of sensory information, and the issuing of motor commands to the muscles.

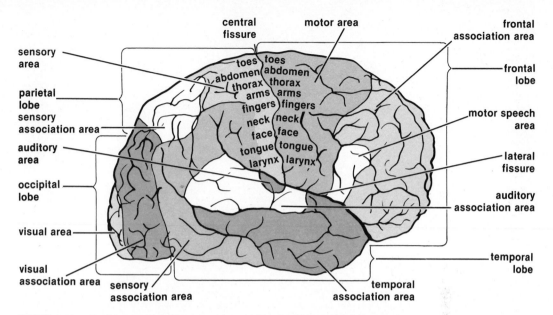

FIGURE 4.16. Human cerebral cortex (cerebrum), illustrating specialized areas.

In the evolution of the human brain, certain areas of the cerebrum have become elaborated as part of the human emphasis on complex learned behavior and tool making. The areas that have become especially developed are the frontal lobes, where deliberate, rational thought is controlled and "choice" decisions are made; the lower parietal lobe, where complex associations of sensory and other data occur; the temporal lobe, where memory is stored; and the lower frontal lobe, where the motor speech area is located. The motor control area in the back of the frontal lobe has undergone differential enlargement of an interesting sort. The nerve tissue controlling the muscles in various parts of the body is arranged in what would seem to be reverse order: The nerves controlling muscles of the toes and feet are on top of the cortex, whereas those controlling head and facial muscles are at the bottom (Figure 4.17). In most cases, the areas of the human motor cortex that control muscles in various parts of the body are comparable in size to those of our nearest primate relatives, the great apes. The two areas of the motor cortex that have elaborated control hand and finger movements and the tongue and lips. The reason for these particular expansions is clear: An important part of human adaptation is based on our ability to make and use tools, which requires fine muscular dexterity of the hands. Another of the unique attributes of modern humans, as we saw in the first chapter, is articulate language, which necessitates the highly developed control of tongue and lip movements. An enlarged cerebellum is also a part of this complex. Apparently the motor cortex of the cerebrum issues raw command signals, which are then translated by the cerebellum into a definite sequence of orders for the activity of specific muscles at specific times.

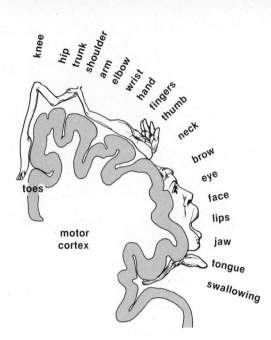

FIGURE 4.17. Human motor cortex, illustrating the areas devoted to various parts of the body.

The cerebellum is thus responsible for a thousand everyday habitual motor movement patterns (behaviors), such as brushing teeth, eating with utensils, and driving a car. When we realize how many muscles are working and in what extremely complicated sequences for even the simplest routine behaviors, it is clear why the human cerebellum is a large, complex organ.

The Mammalian Biological Complex

Mammalian growth and development of high levels of activity, high metabolic rates, and a constant internal body temperature are intimately related to the reproductive system and the enlarged brain. So, too, are the teeth that enable the animal to chew its food and the hard palate. Because its complex brain requires a constant supply of oxygen and nutrients, a mammal must be able to obtain nourishment on a regular basis and to breathe continuously; thus the high activity levels of most mammals. Conversely, the complex mammalian brain provides the basis for a flexible, responsive adaptation permitting mammals to exploit a wider variety of environmental niches. It is clear that without the evolution of the mammalian pattern of reproduction, with a period of childhood dependency, the development of the complex brain and intelligence would not have been possible. These traits, however, are biologically expensive, for they require an additional investment of parental time and energy. Because of this, mammals have also evolved a distinctive reproductive strategy. In most earlier vertebrates, adult population size is maintained by the production of large numbers of sex cells and immature individuals, the vast majority of which never reach adulthood because of the very high mortality rates (see Malthus's observations in Chapter 1). The mammals' strategy is to produce far fewer offspring, whose better chance of reaching reproductive maturity in turn ensures maintenance of the adult population.

These new, interrelated traits evolved on the foundation of previous vertebrate biology, but not at the same time or at the same rate. The therapsids, or mammallike reptiles, had some mammalian traits, and other traits and animals developed eventually; we cannot isolate one characteristic, instant, or individual as the origin of the mammals. The evolutionary transition from the therapsids to the mammals took millions of years, and even when mammals had evolved, they remained less important than the reptiles for many millions more. All these mammalian biological features were crucial to the subsequent evolution and successful adaptation of the primates and humans.

Summary

We have briefly reviewed the biological history of vertebrates. The vertebrates give us an excellent perspective on humans because many modern human biological features were first elaborated in earlier vertebrates.

The first fossil evidence of vertebrates is found in rocks of Ordovician age; by the Devonian period, all the known water-dwelling vertebrate classes had appeared. Primitive land vertebrates are known from the upper Devonian, but well-adapted terrestrial forms did not evolve until the Pennsylvanian period.

The vertebrate class to which humans belong, the mammals, developed from primitive, mammallike reptiles, and are known from geologic deposits of the upper Triassic age. At first they were subordinate to the reptiles, but by the beginning of the Cenozoic era they had become the dominant terrestrial vertebrate group.

The mammals differ from the reptiles in dental, skeletal, reproductive, neurological, and other traits. This biological complex forms the foundation for the evolution of mammalian intelligence, which has permitted mammals to learn appropriate ways of dealing with the environment in contrast to the more fixed behavioral pattern of other vertebrates.

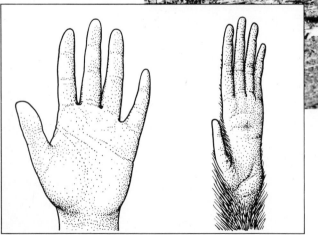

The molecular, biological, behavioral, anatomical, and fossil evidence tells us much about the order Primates, of which humans are a member.

An Introduction to the Primates

Fossil evidence, along with comparative anatomical and genetic studies, makes it clear that the primates appeared early in placental mammal evolution. Our place within the order Primates has been recognized for a long time; when Linnaeus classified mammals in the tenth edition of his *Systema naturae* in 1758, he listed the order Primates first (*Primate* means "first"), including within it four genera: *Homo* (humans), *Simia* (monkeys and the few apes identified at the time), *Lemur* (for the then-known lemur and loris prosimians), and *Vespertilio* (bats). Over the years some animals, like the bats, have been moved into their own order, while many newly recognized primates, including the many extinct primates whose fossil remains have been discovered, have been incorporated into the classification. For example, chimpanzees were not named until 1816 (genus *Pan*), and the gorilla did not get its scientific name (genus *Gorilla*) until 1847. It is intriguing to realize that this largest of the living primates had escaped the notice of scholars and was not officially recognized by science until almost the middle of the nineteenth century. However, by the time Thomas Huxley wrote his 1863 book, *On Man's Place in Nature*, enough was known about this animal for Huxley to write in some detail about the strong anatomical similarities between humans and the African apes, concluding that these creatures were our closest living relatives; Darwin agreed with that notion. A hundred years of biological research, including comparative biochemical and genetic studies, have reinforced Huxley's ideas about our close relationship with the other primates.

This chapter will introduce the members of the mammalian order Primates and will briefly describe the biological, including molecular, features that characterize a mammal within this order. Subsequent chapters will deal with their naturalistic behavior and the fossil evidence for primate evolution.

Defining the Order Primates

The order Primates is a good example of the difficulties involved in attempting to define groupings of animals on the basis of specific morphological traits. Despite the problems in establishing precise criteria, however, and the numerous alternative taxonomic schemes proposed to categorize primates, there is a good deal of agreement on which living animals can be considered primates (Table 5.1).

The general agreement on which living mammals belong in the primate order, however, does not extend to fossil animals; debate continues over those features that can be used to separate *all* primates from all other mammals. This is especially true of the animals considered to be the earliest primates. Placed in a separate category, the Plesiadapiformes, these very primitive mammals show few characteristic primate traits.

One rather general but not exclusive definition applies after a fashion: Primates are mammals that climb by grasping. One of the most important characteristics of the primates is the manipulative hand and foot. Also, most primates have the ability to oppose the thumb with the other fingers in a grasp; this facility is enhanced in most primates by the possession of nails instead of the claws found in many other mammalian orders. These features enable primates to climb and move in trees by grasping tree limbs. This ability is based on the retention in the primates of many of the elements of the primitive vertebrate limb bone system. Most other mammals have developed specialized limb systems based on the elaboration of only some of the limb bones, with the rest being lost or reduced in size. It has been suggested that climbing by grasping was important to the primates because very early in their evolutionary history they apparently evolved as *arboreal* (tree-dwelling) animals.

Recent attempts at using morphological traits to define the primate order have focused on the base of the skull in the region of the ear; here primates appear to possess several distinctive features, including a bulbous, inflated, bony chamber of the middle ear that is composed of bone derived from one part of the skull (Figure 5.1). In addition, several of the arteries in this region have become enlarged, and one has been lost. These changes appear to reflect distinctive adaptive requirements of the primates in hearing, vision, and increased brain size as they began to exploit new niches.[1*] These shared traits of the skull base would appear to provide objective criteria for defining animals as primates.

There are a series of features that seem to develop in the evolution of the primates and thus do not characterize all primates. Others are not unique to the order. These limitations preclude using these features to define the order. However, the late Sir W. E. Le Gros Clark, a leading comparative primate anatomist, suggested that the primates could not be defined on the basis of any specializations that they possessed as a group but rather by a lack of specialization. In Clark's opinion a number of evolutionary trends, many of which he believed were related to the primates' primary adaptation to life in the trees, distinguished these animals

*See page 616 for notes to Chapter 5.

TABLE 5.1
Classification of Living Order Primates

Suborder	Infraorder	Family/Subfamily	Genus	Common Name	Location
Prosimii (lower primates)	Lemuriformes	Lemuridae	*Lemur*	lemur	Malagasy Republic
			Lepilemur	sportive lemur	
			Hapalemur	gentle lemur	
		Indriidae	*Indri*	indri	Malagasy Republic
			Propithecus	sifaka	
			Avahi	avahi	
		Daubentoniidae	*Daubentonia*	aye-aye	Malagasy Republic
	Lorisiformes	Lorisidae	*Galago*	galago, bush baby	Africa
			Loris	loris	Asia
			Nycticebus	slow loris	Asia
			Perodicticus	potto	Africa
			Arctocebus	golden potto, angwantibo	Africa
		Cheirogaleidae	*Microcebus*	mouse lemur	Malagasy Republic
			Cheirogaleus	dwarf lemur	
			Phaner	fork-marked dwarf lemur	
		Tarsiidae	*Tarsius*	tarsier	Asia
Anthropoidea (higher primates)	Platyrrhini	Superfamily Ceboidea (New World monkeys)			
		Cebidae	*Cebus*	capuchin	tropical New World
			Saimiri	squirrel monkey	
			Ateles	spider monkey	
			Brachyteles	woolly spider monkey	
			Lagothrix	woolly monkey	
			Alouatta	howler monkey	
			Callicebus	titi	
			Aotus	night monkey, douroucouli	
			Pithecia	saki	
			Chiropotes	bearded saki	
			Cacajao	uakari	
		Callithricidae	*Callithrix*	marmoset	tropical New World
			Cebuella	pygmy marmoset	
			Saguinus	tamarin	
			Leontopithecus	golden lion tamarin	
			Callimico	Goeldi's monkey, callimico	

(continued)

TABLE 5.1 *(continued)*

Suborder	Infraorder	Family/Subfamily	Genus	Common Name	Location
Anthropoidea *(cont.)*	Catarrhini	**Superfamily Cercopithecoidea (Old World monkeys)**			
		Cercopithecidae			
		Cercopithecinae (subfamily)	*Cercopithecus*	vervet, guenon	Africa
			Erythrocebus	patas	
			Cercocebus	mangabey	
			Papio	baboon, hama-dryas baboon (into Asia)	Asia
			Mandrillus	drill, mandrill	
			Theropithecus	gelada	
			Macaca	macaques	Asia, Africa
		Colobinae (subfamily)	*Colobus*	guereza, colobus	Africa
			Presbytis	langurs, leaf monkey	Asia
			Pygathrix	douc langur	
			Rhinopithecus	golden snub-nosed langur	
			Simias	pig-tailed langur	
			Nasalis	proboscis monkey	
		Superfamily Hominoidea (apes and humans)			
		Hylobatidae	*Hylobates*	gibbon	Asia
			Symphalangus	siamang	
		Pongidae	*Pongo*	orangutan	Asia
		Hominidae			
		Paninae (subfamily)	*Pan*	chimpanzee	Africa
			Gorilla	gorilla	Africa
		Homininae (subfamily)	*Homo*	humans	worldwide

Adapted from W. G. Osman Hill, *Evolutionary Biology of the Primates* (1974). Copyright by Academic Press Inc., Orlando. Used by permission of the author, the publisher, and The Royal College of Surgeons of England.

from other orders of mammals.[2] Few primatologists today would accept Clark's view that these traits constitute a definition of the primates. They are useful, however, in providing a generalized view of the course of primate evolution. These trends are:

1. A generalized limb structure (Figure 5.2)
2. Mobile digits, especially the thumb and big toe (Figure 5.3)
3. Flattened nails and sensitive pads on the fingertips, instead of claws
4. Sharper vision, color vision, and depth perception (Figure 5.4)
5. A foreshortened snout (Figure 5.4)
6. Less dependence on the sense of smell

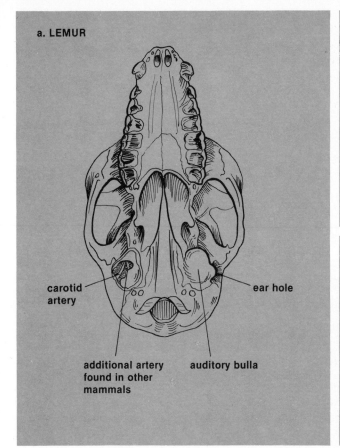

a. LEMUR

carotid artery

ear hole

additional artery found in other mammals

auditory bulla

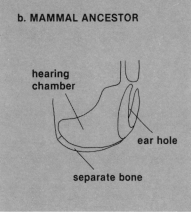

b. MAMMAL ANCESTOR

hearing chamber

ear hole

separate bone

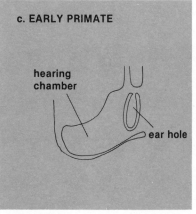

c. EARLY PRIMATE

hearing chamber

ear hole

FIGURE 5.1. (a) The base of the skull of a prosimian primate, a lemur, illustrating two major features often used in defining the order primates. On the right is the bulbous hearing chamber, the *auditory bulla,* where sounds are received and passed on to the brain. On the left, this bony bulla has been cut away, showing some detail on the inside of the chamber. The auditory bulla in all primates is made up of the same bone that forms the roof of the hearing chamber. (b) A cross-section view of the hearing chamber, which illustrates the structure most probably found in the early mammal ancestor of the primates. Note that the auditory bulla is a separate bone. (c) The condition seen in early primates. The significance of this change is not clear.

On the left side of (a) is the internal carotid artery, which is an important blood supplier to the brain. In other mammals, there is another branch of this artery (see dotted lines) that also passes through the auditory bulla on its way to the brain. Primates have lost this artery. The reasons for the difference are debatable, but it seems likely that a single large artery can supply more blood to the brain than two smaller ones. This change may reflect the evolutionary development of larger brains in the primate line.

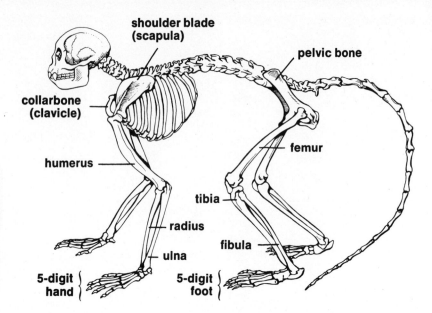

7. Fewer teeth than ancestral mammals
8. An expanded and elaborated brain, particularly the cerebral cortex

These trends are progressive in that they have continued to develop in the primate order, all living primates do not have every one of them, and the farther back we look through the primates' biological history, the fewer of these features we see shared by the early primates.

Methods of Taxonomic Classification

Linnaeus's taxonomic system was based on the idea that animals with many similar or identical biological features should be grouped more closely than those with fewer common biological features. This method of grouping animals is still employed for most taxonomic levels in the biological classification system. This is a subjective system, however, for it is up to the scientist to determine which of the thousands of biological features that make up an animal should be used in comparing it to another animal. Once the features that are to be compared are chosen, there follows the need to interpret these features on the different animals; how similar do features on different animals have to be to relate animal populations closely in a taxonomic system? Because of this subjectivity, scientists debate taxonomic orderings and often propose alternative classifications.

Only at the species level is there an objective criterion for defining members. As noted in Chapter 3, the classification of living animal populations into species is based on the recognition of mutual interbreeding. That is, if members of two different populations are able to interbreed and produce fertile offspring, they are considered the same species. For a variety of practical reasons, however, it is often not possible to determine fertile interbreeding. The two populations may live on different

marmoset

macaque

chimpanzee

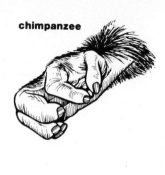

FIGURE 5.3. The hands of three different primates, showing the importance of nails to manipulative ability. The marmoset, a New World monkey, is one of the few higher primates having claws, which limit fingertip to fingertip touching, an ability both the macaque and chimpanzee possess.

continents, for example. And, of course, interbreeding cannot be judged on extinct animals whose only remaining records are fossils. In these cases and for all higher order categories in a taxonomy, relationship is based on comparisons of biological features.

In the more than two hundred years since Linnaeus published his classification, many scholars have proposed techniques for selecting features for comparison and outlined ways by which these comparisons are

Cladism

FIGURE 5.4. Clockwise from upper left: skulls of a prosimian, a tarsier; an ape, a gibbon; a New World monkey, a night monkey *(Aotus)*; and an Old World monkey, a baboon. Note the reduced size of the snout on these primates (the large snouts of the baboon and the gibbon are more related to their large canine teeth than to any enhanced sense of smell). The orientation of the eye orbits on the front of the skull permits overlapping visual fields and thus perception of depth. The large orbits of *Aotus,* the only nocturnal higher primate, and the tarsier, also nocturnal, are apparent.

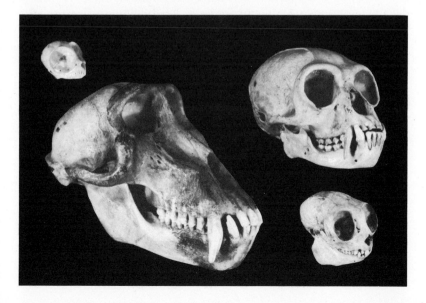

to be undertaken. Over the past twenty years, a technique, termed *cladistics*, initially proposed by the German biologist W. Hennig, has become an increasingly important method of taxonomic ordering and determining evolutionary relationships.

The goal of *cladism* is to order living and extinct animals to reflect ancestor or descendent relationships. Biological features are chosen for examination and comparison that can provide useful information in this area. The focus of cladistics, the method itself, is to determine the state of resemblance that the same biological feature has in different animal groups. By examining fossil or living animals, a feature can be characterized as either (1) ancestral (also called primitive), that is, the biological trait is found in this way in an ancestral group; or (2) derived (also called advanced), that is, the trait has developed in this way in the evolution of the animal group and is not found in an ancestor. Evolutionary relationships are determined based on the shared presence of primitive or derived features.

A *cladogram* is a graphic portrayal of a cladistic analysis. In Figure 5.5, five species are organized into an evolutionary model. Examination of the same features in the five groupings reveals that one (A) possesses an ancestral condition of the feature and that the other four possess a derived state. Thus A is placed as the ancestor. Further analysis reveals that B, C, and D possess a shared set of derived characteristics, and that while E also exhibits a character state derived from A, it is a different state. Groups B, C, and D thus share a closer evolutionary history than any does with E. Analysis of B, C, and D indicates that the derived state of the features in C and D places them both as descendents of B.

Cladistic analysis is thus founded on the analysis of a feature to determine qualities of shared derived or primitive states. Note that a cladistic analysis compares features and that the resulting cladogram is an expression of evolutionary relatedness. The time dimension—whether the animal groups are contemporaries or lived millions of years apart—plays no role. Often, however, a cladogram will also contain a time dimension, as in Figure 5.23, which describes the evolutionary relationships of the apes and humans, based on the shared derived states of their

FIGURE 5.5. The construction of a cladogram.

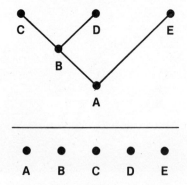

DNA. When times of divergence are included, a cladogram becomes a *phylogeny,* or a depiction of the evolutionary relationships of the animals in a time dimension.

Cladistic analysis has become a common technique for reconstructing relationships among animals, and the derived or ancestral state of a particular feature will be often noted in the following discussions.

The order Primates, including living and extinct forms, can be divided taxonomically in a number of ways, depending on how different primatologists view its evolutionary history. The traditional division is into two suborders, the Prosimii and the Anthropoidea, also called the lower and higher primates, respectively (presented for living primates in Table 5.1). This approach, however, has a number of limitations. It places the tarsiers with the lorises, galagos, and Madagascar primates into the prosimian category, and, as we will see, there is evidence the tarsiers should be considered evolutionarily intermediate between the other prosimians and the anthropoids, or even more closely aligned with the higher primates.[3] The prosimian/anthropoid division of the primates also does not take into account the extinct, very primitive, earliest members of the order, who share few biological features with later primates. In a recent encyclopedic survey of primate evolution, E. Delson and F. Szalay argued for a third suborder, the Plesiadapiformes, to accommodate these early primates and indicate the major difference between these early forms and later primates.[4]

The problems associated with this traditional primate taxonomy have led many primatologists to abandon it in favor of a division into the suborders Plesiadapiformes, Strepsirhini (prosimians without the tarsiers), and Haplorhini (tarsiers and higher primates; see Table 5.2). Although most working primatologists today prefer the Strepsirhini/Haplorhini taxonomy listed in Table 5.2, employing the terms *prosimian* and *anthropoid* or *higher primate* in discussions of evolution and behavior in this text makes it more convenient and understandable for us to use the traditional classification presented in Table 5.1.

The name prosimian (*pro = before; simian = ape*) suggests how the lower primates were viewed when they were first examined; the German word for them is *Halbaffe (half-ape).* The prosimians have a number of living representatives and a great deal of fossil material representing extinct members of the suborder. Living prosimians are limited to parts of Africa, Asia, and the Malagasy Republic on the island of Madagascar, although fossil finds in North America and Europe show that they were once much more widely distributed (Figure 5.6).

Prosimians as a group are small mammals, ranging in size from less than 100 grams (¼ pound) to more than 10 kilograms (22 pounds). They are, like all nonhuman primates, covered with fur, and many possess tails, which are occasionally longer than their body. They characteristically have large, mobile ears and large eyes in orbits that tend to be very large for the size of their skull. The orbits of prosimians (except the tar-

Living Primates: Taxonomy and Distribution

Prosimian Primates

TABLE 5.2
Strepsirhine/Haplorhine Classification of Living Primates

Suborder	Infraorder	Superfamily	Family	Subfamily
Plesiadapiformes*				
Strepsirhini	Lemuriformes	Lemuroidea (lemurs) Indrioidea (indriids)		
	Lorisiformes	Lorisoidea (loris)		
Haplorhini	Tarsiiformes (tarsiers)			
	Platyrrhini (New World monkeys)	Ceboidea	Callithricidae (marmosets) Cebidae (spider, howlers, etc.)	
	Catarrhini	Cercopithecoidea (Old World monkeys)	Cercopithecidae	Cercopithecinae (baboons, macaques, etc.) Colobinae (langurs, colobus)
		Hominoidea	Hylobatidae (gibbon, siamang) Pongidae (orangutan) Hominidae	Paninae (chimpanzees, gorillas) Homininae (humans)

*Included here for comparison is the suborder Plesiadapiformes, an entirely extinct group of primates.

sier) differ from those of higher primates in having a bar (the *postorbital bar*) across the outside. Higher primates have orbits totally enclosed in bone (Figure 5.7). Lining the back of the eye is the *tapetum*, a reflective surface found in many nocturnal mammals, which maximizes the low light intensity at night. Prosimians generally have large, projecting snouts, and they tend to rely on the sense of smell to a greater extent than the higher primates. Many have scent glands in the anogenital region or on the arms, which they rub against objects in their environment to scent-mark territory. Some use their hands or use urine rubbed on their hands or feet to mark the scent. Many prosimian primates possess rather sharply pointed, three-cusped molar teeth similar to the insectivorous teeth of early ancestral mammals. Many also have developed a "*tooth comb*"; that is, their lower front teeth have become horizontal and are used by the animal to comb through its fur or to get at tree gums or other food (Figure 5.8).

The rear limbs of many prosimians are markedly longer than their front limbs. This may be related to a particular form of arboreal movement termed *vertical clinging and leaping,* whereby the animal rests on a vertical tree limb with its rear limbs tightly flexed and its shorter front limbs holding on to the support. By a muscular "unwinding" of its rear limbs, the animal can leap across considerable distances. Although not

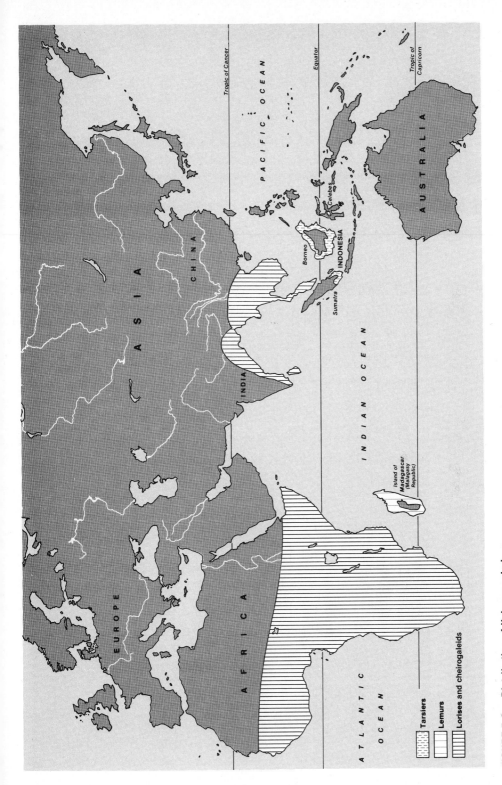

FIGURE 5.6. Distribution of living prosimians.

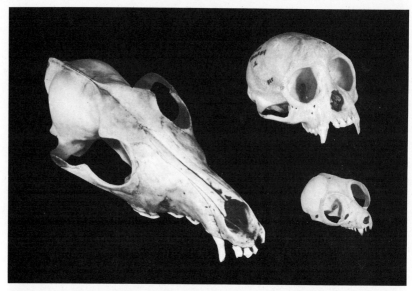

FIGURE 5.7.   Skulls of a dog (left); a higher primate, a New World monkey, *Cebus* (upper right); and a prosimian, a loris (lower right). The eye orbits of the dog are open across the top and back, a pattern common in many mammals. The loris's orbits have a completed postorbital bar across the top, but they are open in the back. The monkey, like the other higher primates, possesses an orbit entirely enclosed by bone.

FIGURE 5.8.   The skull of an indriid, one of the lemurlike prosimians from the Malagasy Republic. Note the horizontal placement of the lower front teeth into a dental comb. The inset shows the comb when the jaw is closed. In most lemurs and indriids there is a large gap between the two middle upper incisors into which the tooth comb fits; this allows the jaw to close fully.

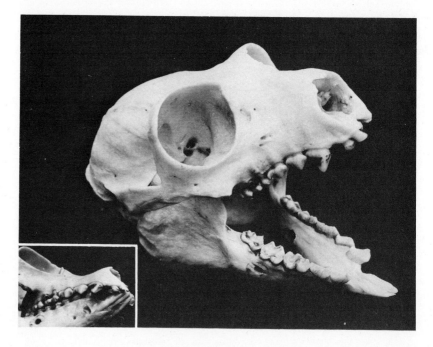

all prosimians move by vertical clinging and leaping, many possess its biology (Figure 5.9). All prosimians possess nails on their hands and feet, but some also have a claw on the index toe, which is used in combing through the fur and is therefore termed a *grooming claw*.

This general description applies to all the prosimians of mainland Africa and Asia: the lorisiformes, including the lorises of Asia and the pottos of Africa and the galagos or bushbabies of Africa; and in the main to the tarsiers of East Asia and to the lemuriformes: the lemurs, indriids, and aye-ayes of the Malagasy Republic (Table 5.3).

Lorises and Galagos   The loris group is composed of the slow and slender loris of southeast and southern Asia and the pottos and angwan-tibo of sub-Saharan Africa. The galagos, or bushbabies, are divided into four genera, all limited to sub-Saharan Africa. There may also be Madagascar members of this group.

All of these prosimians are nocturnal, and all, with one exception, are completely arboreal, inhabiting various layers of the Old World tropical forest. The one exception, an African bushbaby, spends some time feeding on the ground.

All of these prosimians are also small: The largest of the group weighs about 1.8 kg (4 lb), the smallest about 60 g (2 oz). Even with the long bushy tails some possess, the longest is only about 77 cm (29 in.) and the shortest less than 27 cm (10 in.).

The diets of the lorises and galagos range from completely insec-tivorous (including ants, caterpillars, slugs, and beetles) to those in

FIGURE 5.9.   Two living prosimians. The galago (left), limited to sub-Saharan Africa, is nocturnal, arboreal, and mainly insectivorous. The ring-tailed lemur (right), like all lemurs, is limited to the island of the Malagasy Republic. The diversity of prosimian life may reflect its relative isolation in the southern Indian Ocean. This lemur lives in social groups and spends considerable time on the ground foraging for the vegetable material that is its basic dietary food.

TABLE 5.3
Ecological Chart of Prosimians in the Malagasy Republic (Formerly Madagascar), with the Range of Adaptive Niches They Occupy

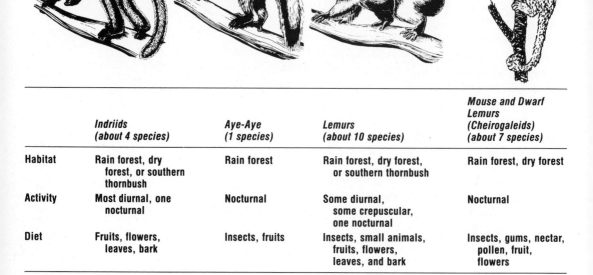

	Indriids (about 4 species)	Aye-Aye (1 species)	Lemurs (about 10 species)	Mouse and Dwarf Lemurs (Cheirogaleids) (about 7 species)
Habitat	Rain forest, dry forest, or southern thornbush	Rain forest	Rain forest, dry forest, or southern thornbush	Rain forest, dry forest
Activity	Most diurnal, one nocturnal	Nocturnal	Some diurnal, some crepuscular, one nocturnal	Nocturnal
Diet	Fruits, flowers, leaves, bark	Insects, fruits	Insects, small animals, fruits, flowers, leaves, and bark	Insects, gums, nectar, pollen, fruit, flowers

which insects are only a small portion, the rest composed of fruit, leaves, tree gums, and the occasional bird or other small vertebrate.

It appears likely that most lorises and galagos have a social organization in which the ranges of several solitary females are overlapped by a single male, who apparently will interact with the female only during the time of her reproductive cycle when conception is possible.

Based on a number of dental, genetic, and biological traits, a number of primatologists have suggested that a family of small Madagascar prosimians, the Cheirogaleidae, may in fact be more closely related to the African galagos than to the other Madagascar primates. In this group are the smallest living primates, the mouse lemur (*Microcebus*), with a body size of about 14 cm (about 5 in.) (Figure 5.10). A nocturnal insectivore, the mouse lemur lives in small groups, with as many as a dozen or more females sometimes nesting together during the day; males nest apart.

Another cheirogaleid, the dwarf lemur (*Cheirogaleus*), consumes plant materials (pollen, nectar, flowers, and fruit) that become scarce during the dry season. These prosimians store fat in the base of their tails, which permits them to hibernate during the food-poor dry months.

FIGURE 5.10. The mouse lemur, *Microcebus*, the smallest living primate. Mouse and dwarf lemurs may be more closely related evolutionarily to the galagoes of mainland Africa than to the other Madagascar prosimians.

Lemurs and Indriids Living isolated on the large island of Madagascar in the Indian Ocean off the coast of southern Africa, with few other mammals to compete with, the Malagasy (as the island is now officially known) prosimians underwent an evolutionary radiation into a diversity of forms. Discoveries on the island of an array of skeletal materials testify that as recently as two to three thousand years ago, there was an even more diverse assembly of prosimians, including a gorilla-sized lemur. Living Malagasy prosimians, not including the cheirogaleids just described, are divided into three major groupings, totaling fifteen species placed into three families (Table 5.3).

The lemurs (family Lemuridae) are small to medium-sized primates, ranging in size from about 500 g (little more than a pound) to 3.75 kg (8¼ lb). They differ in their adaptation from the loris group, with many of them following daylight (diurnal) or crepuscular (twilight) activity cycles and living mainly on vegetable foods like bamboo leaves and shoots.

The best studied of the lemurs is the *Lemur catta,* or the ring–tailed lemur (see page 148). Unusual among prosimians but very much like higher primates, this lemur lives in social groups of adult males and females and young. Its diet consists of fruits, seeds, and other vegetation. It also spends much time on the ground.

Indriids are the largest of the living prosimians, with the indri weighing as much as 10 kg (22 lb). Both the indri and sifaka (*Propithecus*) are diurnal, with the latter forming small social groups of adult males and females. The avahi, the only nocturnal indriid, is also the smallest (600–1,200 g, or 1½–2¾ lb). Like the others, it is a vegetarian, eating leaves, seeds, and bark.

The nocturnal aye-aye, the only living representative of the family Daubentoniidae (see Tables 5.1 and 5.3), is perhaps the most specialized living primate. Long, curved, continuously growing rodentlike incisor teeth are used to gnaw holes in the bark of trees as well as to open holes in coconuts. Equipped with claws on all digits except the big toe, it also has a very elongated, thin, middle finger, which is inserted into the gnawed holes in the coconuts to capture insects. This wirelike finger is also inserted into the holes to scoop out the pulp.

Tarsiers   Although considered here a prosimian, the tarsiers (Figure 5.11) possess many features that link them to the higher primates, and their precise taxonomic position continues to be a matter of some debate. With their large eyes; large, movable ears; and sharply pointed molar teeth, they appear prosimianlike. However, they lack the dental comb of the front teeth, and genetically and biochemically they share many anthropoid characteristics.

Tarsiers have a limited distribution, being found in the forests of the Philippines, Borneo, Sumatra, and several other additional islands of southeast Asia (see Figure 5.6).

Small in size (160 g, or 5½ oz) and nocturnal in activity cycle, tarsiers apparently form stable pair bonds, which, with their dependent young, form the social group.

Tarsiers are insectivorous, eating mainly crickets, cockroaches, moths, termites, and beetles, which they snare by perching just above the forest floor and pouncing when a prey insect happens along.

Anthropoid Primates   The suborder Anthropoidea, meaning manlike (*anthropos* = *man;* *oidea* = *like*), can be grossly divided into two major categories that correspond to the worldwide higher primate distribution: the Platyrrhini, or New World higher primates, and the Catarrhini, or Old World higher primates. *Platyrrhine* means flat (*platy*) nose (*rhine*); New World monkeys have flat noses whose nostrils face outward. *Catarrhine* or Old World higher primates have noses whose nostrils, like ours, are next to each other and point downward. Platyrrhine monkeys are placed in the superfamily Ceboidea, while the catarrhine primates are divided into the superfamilies Cercopithecoidea (the Old World monkeys), and Homi-

FIGURE 5.11. A tarsier. Note the huge eyes in comparison to the small body size in this nocturnal prosimian.

noidea (the apes and humans) (Figure 5.12 and Table 5.1). The living members of Anthropoidea are the higher primates; with one or two notable exceptions, they are social, diurnal animals. Many are arboreal, but others have evolved to fill terrestrial niches.

Biologically, living higher primates can be distinguished from the prosimians in a variety of ways. Among the most obvious are the following:

1. The dentition: Higher primates normally have much lower, more rounded molar cusps; no dental comb; and spatulate, chisel-shaped incisors rather than the more rounded prosimian incisors.

2. The brain: Higher primates tend to have a larger brain in comparison to body size.

3. The skull: Higher primates tend to have shorter snouts and eye orbits that are positioned close together on the front of the skull and directed forward; the orbits are entirely enclosed in bone.

4. Locomotion: Higher primates lack the limb proportions of most prosimians, with their short front and relatively longer rear limbs. (An obvious exception is humans, because of our bipedalism.)

FIGURE 5.12. Distribution of living anthropoids.

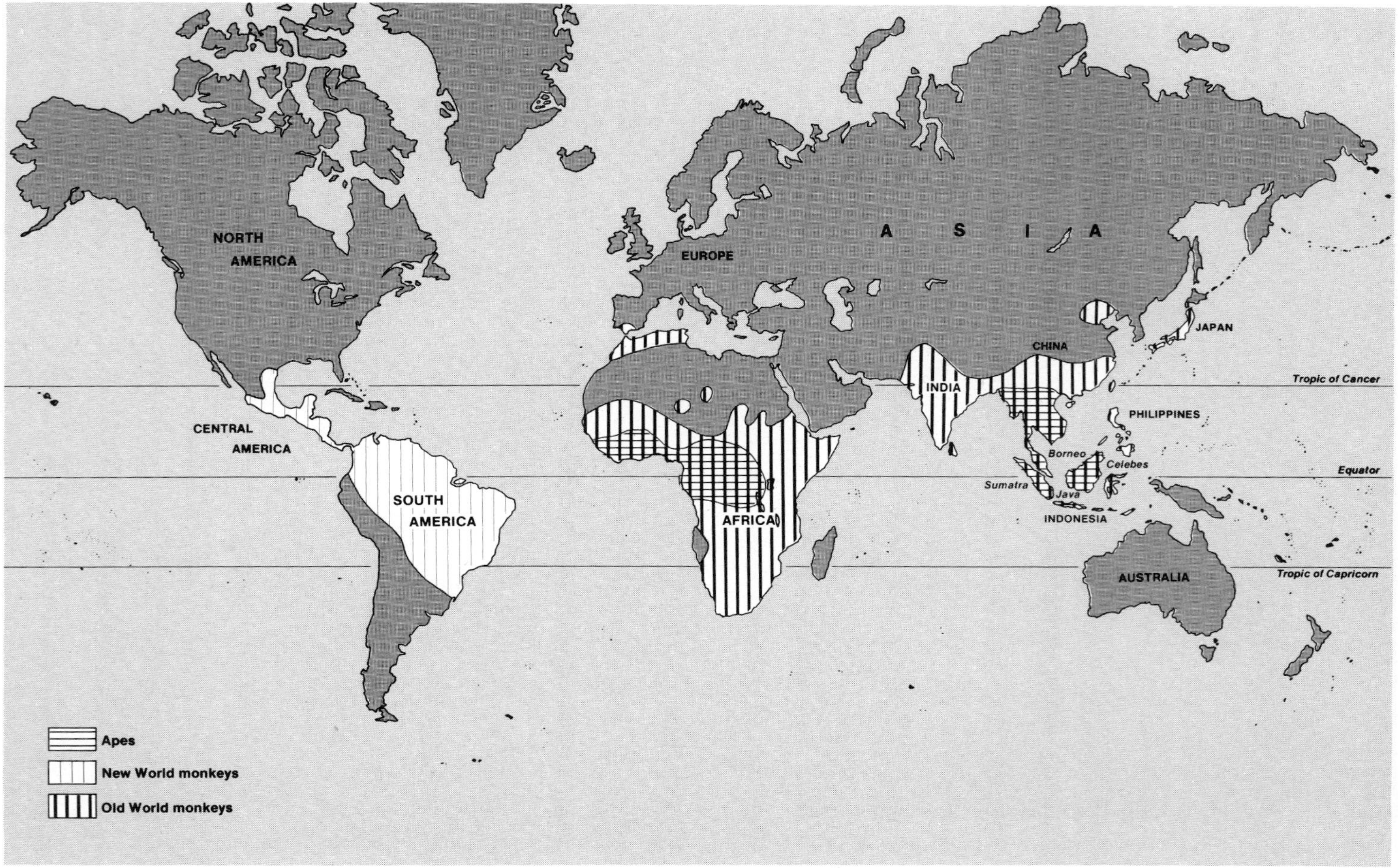

Apes

New World monkeys

Old World monkeys

The New World Monkeys   The New World monkeys, or Ceboidea, are widely distributed from southern Mexico through Central and South America to northern Argentina. All New World monkeys are arboreal. They are adapted to life in the trees of the tropical forest, and none have developed a terrestrial way of life. All New World monkeys are social, some living in groups as small as a single family unit. All are active during the day except the night monkey (genus *Aotus*), the only nocturnal higher primate (Figures 5.4 and 5.13).

FIGURE 5.13.   **The night monkey (*Aotus*). Notice the large size of the orbits for vision at night.**

The New World monkeys are separated into two families: the Callithricidae, which include the marmosets (Figure 5.14) and tamarins, and the Cebidae, which include the other New World monkeys (Figure 5.15).

Marmosets and tamarins are small monkeys (0.14–0.5 kg, or 0.3–1.1 lb) that are unique among primates in having only two molars in each quadrant, and unique among higher primates in possessing claws. Divided into four genera and more than a dozen species, these monkeys have a diversity of diets, several being insectivorous and others eating fruit or tree gums as well as insects. Socially, they appear to be organized into family groups of males and females and dependent young. Unusual among higher primates, twinning is common in these monkeys; unusual too, the fathers often carry the infants in the trees.

The majority of New World monkeys belong to the family Cebidae, representing a more diversified array of forms than do the Calli-

FIGURE 5.14. A marmoset. Marmosets, like all New World monkeys, can be identified by nostrils that are directed toward the side. Marmosets and other members of the Callitrichidae family are the only higher primates that possess claws on their digits.

FIGURE 5.15.   A New World monkey, the spider monkey.

thricidae. They range in size from squirrel monkeys (*Siamiri*) of less than 1 kg (2.2 lb) and about 32 cm (1 ft) long (a little more than double this length with the tail) to the howler monkeys (*Alouatta*), who can weigh as much as 7 kg (15.5 lb) and are 57 cm (2.2 ft) long, with tails at least as great as body length.

Biologically, some cebids are the only primates to possess a prehensile tail (Figure 5.15). Those cebids who have evolved this tail, like squirrel monkeys, howlers, and spider monkeys, use it for a variety of activities. Many hang by their tails while feeding; others use it in locomotion. The tail has fine muscular coordination and on its underside is a naked (furless) area, which like a finger pad is sensitive and has whorls or ridges.

Because of their great diversity in adaptation, different species of cebid monkeys often occupy the same trees, exploiting different resources. This is not the case among the Callithricidae, whose greater biological similarity has led to a virtual nonoverlap of species ranges.

Cebid monkeys are basically frugivorous, with various species preferring fruits of various kinds and degrees of ripeness. Many species supplement this basic diet with a variety of insects and occasionally small vertebrates, like tree frogs. In some species, like howlers, leaves can be an important dietary resource. Seeds and nectar are also eaten by some species.

Socially, the cebids are organized into groups that reflect their different adaptations. Family groupings to larger social aggregations of many males, females, and young can be found.

Although the biological history of the New World monkeys remains unclear, and although they superficially look like the Old World variety, a number of anatomical, biochemical, and genetic studies indicate that the Old and New World primates have been evolving independently for a long time—more than 35 million years.

The Old World Monkeys The Old World has two groups of higher primates: the Old World monkeys, or the Cercopithecoidea, and the apes and humans, or the Hominoidea. They differ from the New World higher primates in a number of ways, in particular the dental formula; all Old World higher primates have a formula of 2.1.2.3, while the New World variety have either 2.1.3.3 or 2.1.3.2 (marmosets).

Old World monkeys are an exceedingly diverse group whose adaptations, unlike those of the completely arboreal and forest-limited New World varieties, have expanded to include environments like open savanna and woodland; arid, high-altitude grassland, and even temperate regions like Japan, where cold, harsh winters are common. They are widely scattered throughout Africa; they are also found on the Indian subcontinent and eastward into Asia and the islands of southeast Asia.

Biologically, all Old World monkeys have a very distinctive set of upper and lower molars, called bilophodont molars. All but one possess tails, although not the prehensile variety. Like all catarrhine primates, all digits are equipped with nails. Old World monkeys are quadrupedal walkers, moving with the soles of the feet and the palms of the hand in contact with the surface. Front and rear limbs are usually equal in length (Figure 5.16).

Cercopithecoid monkeys possess a very distinctive pad on their buttocks. Called an *ischial callosity,* this region is covered with connective tissue and is relatively insensitive. It enables Old World monkeys to sit (or sleep) in trees for long periods without the discomfort we would experience.

The Old World monkeys are divided into two groups, the Cercopithecinae and the Colobinae. The colobine monkeys, the langurs of India and Sri Lanka and the colobus monkeys of Africa (Figure 5.17), have

FIGURE 5.16. An Old World monkey, the pigtail macaque (*Macaca nemestrina*).
Macaques are widely distributed through Asia, North Africa, and the tip of southern Europe
(Gibraltar). Like many other Old World monkeys but unlike New World forms, macaques
spend much of their active period on the ground.

been called the leaf-eating monkeys, for they possess specialized adaptations of the stomach and teeth permitting them to chew, digest, and derive moisture from large quantities of leaves. These traits permit them to live in areas that lack standing water, places closed to exploitation by the cercopithecine monkeys. There are also several species of colobines in east Asia whose diet is more diverse.

African colobus monkeys are mainly arboreal, while their Asian counterparts, the langurs, spend considerable time on the ground. Like colobine monkeys, the other major group of Old World monkeys, the cercopithecines, are also distributed through Africa and from Afghani-

FIGURE 5.17.   A group of Old World monkeys, the langurs (genus *Presbytis*). These Asian members of the leaf-eating Old World monkey subfamily, the colobines, are widely distributed through parts of south Asia. Like many other Old World monkeys, langurs are adapted to an arboreal existence but spend considerable time on the ground.

stan eastward through much of Asia, including the islands of southeast Asia. Biologically, cercopithecine monkeys possess expandable cheek pouches where they can stuff food, later to be pushed out of the pouch and chewed at leisure.

Baboons (*Papio*) and their near relatives, the drills and mandrills (*Mandrillus*) and the gelada (*Theropithecus*) are large African terrestrial monkeys (males can be 35 kg, females usually half the male size) who have evolved to occupy virtually every habitat in sub-Saharan Africa from the forests of West Africa to the savannas and woodlands of east and southern Africa to the semiarid highlands of Ethiopia. Flexible in their diet, baboons eat grasses, seeds, leaves, fruit, and insects, and have been observed killing and eating small vertebrates. Meat is, however, a very small part of their diet.

These African monkeys have a variety of social organizations, with their size and composition depending upon local environmental conditions. Most baboons live in large groups of males and females; some are organized into single male, multiple female groups.

Like their African counterparts the baboons, whom they resemble in many ways, the macaques (*Macaca*) are an exceedingly successful group. Sixteen species are recognized, distributed from North Africa on the west and then continuously eastward from Afghanistan to China and the southeast Asian islands. Included in this array are the rhesus macaques of India and the Japanese macaques, who are able to survive the rather harsh winters of Japan by eating tree buds and tender bark. Elsewhere, like baboons, macaques have developed various dietary strategies. Socially, macaques are organized mainly into groupings of adult males and females and young.

Mangabeys (*Cercocebus*) are a limited group of basically arboreal African fruit-eating monkeys organized chiefly into one male, multiple female groups.

The final cercopithecines to be described is the most common and diverse group of African monkeys, members of the genus *Cercopithecus* (about 20 species) and allied genera.

Cercopithecus monkeys, as a group known as the guenons (Figure 5.18), are found throughout sub-Saharan Africa. Primarily arboreal, they

FIGURE 5.18.   A *Cercopithecus* monkey, or guenon. Guenons are found in many environmental settings throughout sub-Saharan Africa and are the most common monkeys of that continent. This animal, one of about twenty species of *Cercopithecus* monkey, is the lesser spot-nosed guenon (*Cercopithecus petaurista*).

are mainly omnivorous, eating leaves, blossoms, and fruit as well as insects and small vertebrates. They are not large monkeys, ranging from 50 to 57 cm, or 18 to 24 in. in body length, with their tail always longer than their body; in some species there are significant differences between male and female size. One species of these monkeys, *Cercopithecus aethiops,* known as the vervet, is perhaps the most widely distributed, and also spends considerable time on the ground.

Socially, *Cercopithecus* monkeys are usually found in single male, multiple female groups, but multimale, multifemale groups are known.

The Apes and Humans   Placement in the Hominoidea superfamily group is based on a number of biological features. Among the most distinctive are that hominoids lack tails, possess characteristic upper and lower molar teeth, and share a set of anatomical features in the upper trunk, shoulder, and arms inherited from a common ancestor who used them to climb or hang in the trees.

Fossil evidence, especially dated to the Miocene epoch (from 23.5 million years ago), demonstrates that the hominoids were once a far-ranging group with numerous members living throughout southern Eurasia and east Africa. Today, apart from modern humans, who are the most widely distributed animal species ever to appear on the planet, the hominoids have a much more limited distribution. Divided into three families, they are currently found only in limited parts of the African and east Asian tropics (see Figure 5.12).

The family Hylobatidae is composed of the lesser or small-bodied apes, the gibbon and the siamang. Both of these animals are adapted to the forests of southeast Asia. Habitually arboreal, their small size (6–11 kg, or 13–25 lb) and upper trunk adaptations permit them to move through the trees in an under-the-branch swinging motion termed *brachiation*. The lesser apes are organized into pair-bonded family groups with dependent young.

The orangutan (*Pongo*) is the single member of the family Pongidae (Figure 5.19). Orangs are very large animals (males weigh 75–80 kg, 165–175 lb; females 35–40 kg, or 77–88 lb) whose present distribution is limited to the east Asian islands of Sumatra and Borneo. Fossil evidence indicates they were once more widely distributed on the east Asian mainland. They normally dwell in trees, where they eat their normal diet of fruit, and when that is unavailable, leaves and bark; they will also eat a variety of insects. Orangs are among the most unsociable of higher primates, with females and one or two young the most common group. Males tend to be solitary.

The family Hominidae is composed of two subfamilies, the Paninae and the Homininae. The panines are the African great apes, the chimpanzee and the gorilla. Both of these primates are confined to the forests and woodlands of central Africa (Figures 5.12 and 6.18). Chimpanzees (*Pan*) have been classified into two species, the common chimp and the pygmy chimp, although there is really little difference in size between them.

FIGURE 5.19. An orangutan. This primate, the only great ape in Asia, is limited to the islands of Sumatra and Borneo. The orangs apparently do not socialize to the extent observed in the African apes, the chimpanzee and the gorilla.

Common chimpanzees spend most of their waking hours on the ground, foraging for their major food, fruit; but other vegetation like tender leaves, nuts, and seeds is also eaten. They also consume insects, sometimes using tools to obtain them, and they have been observed hunting and killing a variety of small mammals. When on the ground, chimps move via a form of locomotion known as *knuckle-walking,* a quadrupedal movement in which the long front limbs support the body on the knuckles of the hands instead of on the palms, flat down. At dusk, chimps move into trees, where, lacking the calosities of the monkeys, they bend tree branches under them to form a sleeping nest. Common chimpanzees are organized into local communities of forty to sixty animals who usually form temporary, similar sex foraging groups of three to five animals.

The other panine, the gorilla (*Gorilla*) is the largest living primate (males 135–160 kg, or 300 to 350 lb; females are about half the male body size) (Figure 5.20).

FIGURE 5.20.   A gorilla social group, including, on the left, a silver-backed adult male.

Saddled with a fearsome, and undeserved, reputation, gorillas are herbivorous primates who must spend their days eating enough of the abundant but low nutritive, green-leafed plants that make up their diet to support their bulk.

Like chimps, gorillas are knuckle-walkers, but unlike chimps, who move into the trees at night to escape predators, gorillas lack any serious nonhuman predator and sleep on the ground. Gorillas are organized into small social groups of several females and their young and an adult male.

The hominine subfamily of the hominids is composed of humans and our immediate ancestors. Living hominines, furless, bipedal creatures with big brains and small, nonprojecting canines, have developed social systems and complex behaviors as the core of their adaptation.

Molecular Anthropology

Most of the taxonomic relationships we have just discussed are based on anatomical comparisons between living animals. Clearly, the assumption in all such taxonomic statements is that the closer two animals are in the classification, the closer their evolutionary history has been. But just how close is close? Are there any techniques that can establish quantifiable levels of comparison? Recent developments in molecular biology offer the possibility of estimating living primate relationships more directly and providing additional insight into the patterns of primate evolution.

Using the techniques of molecular biology, not only can we establish the relationships between living species more firmly, we can also analyze better the organization of the genes in these species and the processes that result in genetic alterations. With recombinant DNA methods, we can now directly determine the base sequence of specific genes in different species for comparison. Many anthropologists feel that this closer scrutiny enables them to understand living primate relationships more fully, to reconstruct our order's evolutionary history more accurately, and to comprehend better the operation of some genetic and evolutionary forces.

An underlying assumption of evolution is that as genetic differences between living species increase, so does the time since the species last had a common ancestor. Thus, if we can estimate the genetic "distance" between species, we can estimate the time of divergence. Even if the divergence time cannot be expressed in terms of numbers of years before the present, it can be put in relative terms: x and y had a more recent common ancestor than x and z. Here is one area where molecular studies offer a significant advantage over more traditional studies. Although the anatomist can document the ways in which the dental systems of several species differ and might be able to explain the functional or dietary significance of the differences, they cannot at this time estimate the amount of underlying genetic difference. To reconstruct the path of evolution, however, it is necessary to be able to measure the amount of genetic divergence. This is perfectly feasible at a molecular level.

Molecules performing similar functions in different species may be given the same name yet can differ in composition. If these molecules are derived from a common evolutionary ancestor, they are said to be *homologous*. A variety of techniques are available to measure amounts of similarity among homologous molecules in different species. Some of these, including the first attempts, involve the use of immunology to estimate crudely the level of similarity between comparable protein molecules in different species. These techniques are not terribly accurate, but they can quickly estimate the amount of physical similarity between related proteins. In the early 1900s, for instance, G. H. F. Nuttall was the first to see that it might be possible to measure molecular differences. His techniques were crude by today's standards, but his insight was highly sophisticated. When foreign molecules are introduced into an animal, the animal's defense system may react by producing molecules called antibodies in an attempt to neutralize these invading substances. Nuttall noticed that antibodies produced against the proteins found in the fluid portion of the blood (the serum of the blood) of fowls also reacted, although less strongly, with the serum of pigeons. The reaction made a precipitate, or a solid substance that comes out of a solution. Measuring the amount of precipitate gave Nuttall an estimate of the strength of the reaction. He concluded, correctly, that a strong reaction between an antibody directed against a protein in one species and the homologous protein in a second species indicated a similarity between molecules in the blood of both animals, with the strength of the reaction reflecting the degree of molecular similarity. Extending this research to many vertebrates, he was able to establish degrees of relationship between species by their molecular and (because genes produce the molecules) genetic similarity. Immunologists today have many more elaborate techniques, but Nuttall's data and modern data are strikingly similar.

Most of the techniques used today can be separated into two types: those that use immunological methods such as Nuttall's to measure the strength of the reaction between an antibody and the substance against which the antibody is directed (the *antigen*) and those that measure gene differences more directly. All the procedures come to the same conclusion: Humans, chimpanzees, and gorillas are very close relatives (which agrees with anatomical evidence) and last had a common ancestor no more than 10 million years ago. Most molecular anthropologists believe that humans and apes separated 5 to 10 million years ago. As recently as fifteen years ago, anthropologists who study the fossil evidence had placed this separation much earlier, perhaps 20 million years ago. New fossil finds and the reevaluation of already known specimens now also tend to agree that this split took place sometime between 5 and 10 million years ago.

Immunological approaches to the study of primate evolution are rapid and generally reliable, but they have one big drawback: Antigenic similarity cannot always be equated with genetic similarity. The same protein in two species may look identical immunologically even though its actual amino acid sequence is different in each species. If the amino acid difference is in a part of the molecule that does not function as an antigen, that is, if it is hidden inside a three-dimensional molecule, immunological approaches will underestimate genetic differences.

Comparing the amino acid sequence of homologous proteins in different species is more precise than immunological approaches because the amino acid sequence is directly controlled by the genetic material. Although getting the sequence data is a long and tedious job, many groups of researchers have gathered such information, and we can now compare some sequences directly. Table 5.4 lists comparable regions of hemoglobin from several species.

Comparing Protein Sequences

Minimum Mutation Distance   With a copy of the genetic code (see Table 2.2) we can compute the smallest number of mutations needed to change the hemoglobin of one species into that of another. For instance, for the region shown, human hemoglobin differs from the comparable area in gorilla hemoglobin at position 104, where the gorilla has the amino acid lysine and the human has arginine. The genetic codon for lysine may be either AAA or AAG (shorthand: AAA/G), and arginine may be either AGA or AGG. A change at least in the second base (letter) of the DNA word could account for the difference between the human and gorilla. Only one mutation is necessary to change the human sequence into that of the gorilla (or vice versa).

Humans and the rhesus monkey (a macaque from Asia) differ at position 87 on one hemoglobin chain, among others, humans having threonine and rhesus having glutamine. At this position, at least two mutations are necessary to convert one into the other: Both the first and

TABLE 5.4
Amino Acid Sequences for Part of One of the Hemoglobin Chains in Several Primate Species[a]
(Only the variable positions are shown.)

Species	Position													
	5	6	9	13	21	22	33	50	56	76	80	87	104	125
Human-Chimpanzee	Pro	Glu	Ser	Ala	Asp	Glu	Val	Thr	Gly	Ala	Asn[b]	Thr	Arg	Pro
Gorilla	Pro	Glu	Ser	Ala	Asp	Glu	Val	Thr	Gly	Ala	Asn	Thr	Lys	Pro
Gibbon	Pro	Glu	Ser	Ala	Asp	Glu	Val	Thr	Gly	Ala	Asp	Lys	Arg	Gln[b]
Rhesus monkey (Old World)	Pro	Glu	Asn	Thr	Asp	Glu	Leu	Ser	Gly	Asn	Asn	Gln	Lys	Gln
Squirrel monkey (New World)	Gly	Asp	Ala	Ala	Glu	Asp	Val	Thr	Asn	Thr	Asn	Gln	Arg	Gln

[a]Careful examination of this table in conjunction with a copy of the genetic code (Table 2.2) will indicate that the human-chimpanzee sequence is most similar to that of the gorilla, next most similar to the gibbon, then to the rhesus monkey, and least like that of the squirrel monkey of the New World.
[b]Asn and Gln are alternate abbreviations of AspN and GluN.

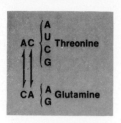

FIGURE 5.21
Diagram of threonine and glutamine codes. Threonine is encoded by ACA, ACU, ACC, or ACG; glutamine is encoded by CAA or CAG.

DNA Hybridization

second bases would have to be changed (Figure 5.21). Adding all the minimum mutations for each position gives a minimum mutation distance (MMD) of 10 between the human and rhesus hemoglobins. Like immunological data, MMDs measure species differences. The MMD-derived measure of relationships has the advantage of greater accuracy.

Primate Relationships Based on Protein Sequences   Using this line of reasoning and data on several proteins, especially hemoglobins, M. Goodman and colleagues at Wayne State University have generated trees such as that in Figure 5.22. The "best trees" are those that require the fewest number of mutations to unite all of the protein sequences. We see that humans, chimps, and gorillas form a very tight-knit cluster, while the orang is more distant and the gibbon more distant still. Based on this result, Goodman has suggested a taxonomic revision that would class the humans, chimps, and gorillas together and separate the orang and gibbon groups. The Old World monkeys form a cluster next closest to us, while the New World monkeys are significantly more distant. As we saw, the tarsier has been at times classified in the prosimian category, while the Strepsirhine/Haplorhine classification places it close to the higher primates. Amino acid comparisons class tarsiers with the anthropoids (higher primates); they do not appear to be prosimian. Within the primates, the lemurs and lorises are our most distant relatives. The tree shrew, which at one time was considered a primate, is outside the primates by amino acid sequence criteria; however, the tree shrew and rabbit do look to be the closest mammalian relatives of the primates.

The next molecular technique we will consider, developed in the 1960s by a group at the Carnegie Institute, is known as DNA hybridization. The actual procedure can take several forms, but the essence of the technique is based on the complementarity of DNA. In all versions of the technique one constructs double-stranded DNA molecules in which each strand is from a different species. In the time since the two species started to evolve separately, differences have accumulated in the exact sequence of DNA bases. If we can measure the degree to which there are mismatches between the homologous complementary strands of DNA, we will have a measure of how genetically different the species are.

The version of the technique described here is called liquid hybridization. In this test, the double-stranded DNA from a species, say human, is heated to separate the molecules into single strands. Other single-stranded human DNA can be made radioactive and the radioactive and nonradioactive forms then mixed together. If this mixture is left to incubate under the proper conditions, a large number of the radioactive pieces will find and bind to their nonradioactive complements (hybridization). Ideally, in this reaction all the DNA could find its perfect matching complement, but because of a variety of factors this will never really

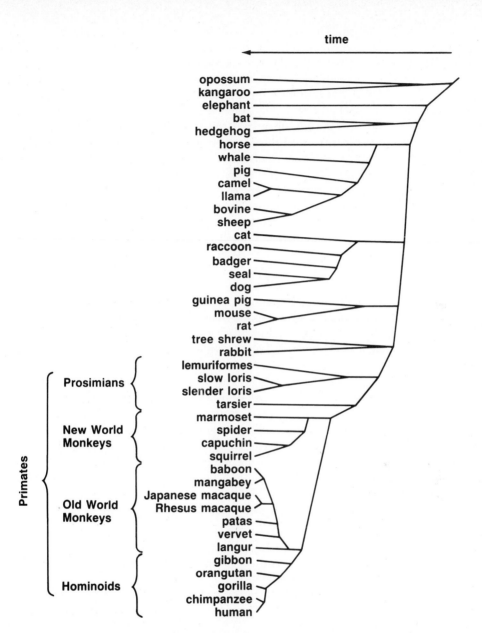

FIGURE 5.22.   A computer-generated evolutionary tree of some mammals, with special emphasis on the primates. The tree is based on sequences of several proteins, including hemoglobins. Note that the primates group along taxonomic lines.

happen. The degree of hybridization can be measured by heating the double-stranded DNA and measuring the temperature at which the molecules separate back into single-stranded form. This is called dissociation, or melting. One can plot the melting curve for double-stranded DNA and find the temperature at which half the double-stranded DNA has melted into single-stranded DNA. This value is called the T_m. The DNA does not all melt at the same temperature because some of the molecules formed during the incubation are not perfectly matched; this weakens the bonds between the strands and they melt at a lower temperature. Generally for every 1 percent of mismatched bases, the T_m temperature is lowered 1 degree Celsius.

Carrying out this test using radioactive and nonradioactive DNA from humans sets the base line: It tells us the T_m for a human-human reaction. What happens to the value if we hybridize human DNA with chimp or gorilla DNA? What happens when the hybridization involves reactions between even more distant relatives, such as humans and Old World monkeys? Charles Sibley and Jon Ahlquist[5] have conducted a large number of such comparisons. Again, the genetic materials of humans and chimps are found to be extremely similar, even more alike than those of chimps and gorillas or humans and gorillas. The gorilla is the next most similar to human, while orangutans are much further removed and gibbons even more dissimilar (Table 5.5). Other data shows the Old World monkey-human reaction to have an even lower T_m, indicating that we and they are less similar genetically. Data of this sort can be used to create trees of genetic similarity that will usually reflect evolutionary relationships (Figure 5.23). Some even feel justified in computing the length of time necessary to evolve a certain degree of genetic difference by using a proportionality. For instance, Sibley and Ahlquist say that it takes 4.3 million years of separate evolution for the DNA of two higher primates to lower the T_m by 1 degree Celsius. Thus, the human-chimp value of 1.8 corresponds to a divergence time of roughly 7.7 million years.

TABLE 5.5
Reduction in Melting Temperatures (Delta T_m) for Hybrid DNA Formed Between Various Hominoids

	Hs	Pt	Gg	Pp
Pt	1.8			
Gg	2.4	2.1		
Pp	3.6	3.7	3.8	
Hl	5.2	5.1	5.4	5.1

Key: Hs = *Homo sapiens* (human)
    Pt = *Pan troglodytes* (common chimpanzee)
    Gg = *Gorilla gorilla* (gorilla)
    Pp = *Pongo pygmaeus* (orangutan)
    Hl = *Hylobates lar* (gibbon)

Source: Adapted from C. G. Sibley and J. E. Ahlquist 1984. "The Phylogeny of the Hominoid Primates, as Indicated by DNA-DNA Hybridization." *J. Molec. Evol.* 20: 9.

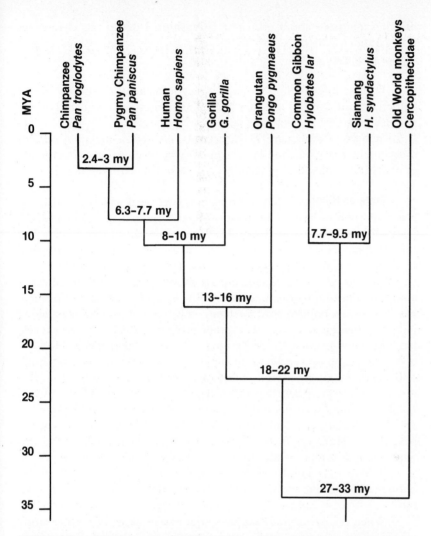

FIGURE 5.23. Phylogeny of hominoids and their relationship to the cercopithecoids based on DNA hybridization. Assuming that a change in the T_m (delta T_m) of 1.0 corresponds to 4.3 million years, the times of divergence are as shown on the left-hand scale. The numbers at the nodes are the delta T_m values.

Recently Jon Marks of Yale and Vincent Sarich of the University of California have raised questions about the best way to measure and interpret DNA hybridization data. In the opinion of Marks and Sarich, the original data do not compellingly support all of Sibley and Ahlquist's conclusions, particularly that regarding the proposed close relationship of humans and chimpanzees (Figure 5.23). Considering gorilla, chimpanzee, and human, Marks and Sarich feel that the data to date cannot decide which two are most closely related. Regardless of the outcome of this debate, DNA hybridization is capable of helping to answer a number of other questions about primate relationships. Later in this chapter we will consider various views of the evolutionary relationships among higher primates.

Nucleic Acid Sequence
Comparisons

Further information about the genetic makeup of species can be gathered via use of the enzymes known as restriction endonucleases and recombinant DNA techniques (Chapter 2). If a gene or cluster of genes is isolated by recombinant DNA methods, restriction enzymes can provide a preliminary measure of the similarity between comparable stretches of DNA, while other procedures can provide even more details.

More on Globins   Here again globins have been widely studied, and it is important to know a little more about their structure. The protein, hemoglobin, in human red blood cells is composed of two units called the α (alpha) and β (beta) chains. The production of each is controlled by a separate gene; the α on chromosome 16, β on chromosome 11. The chains produced by these genes are assembled in units of four, so that a complete adult human hemoglobin (Hb) molecule, that is, the protein, has 2 α chains bonded to 2 β chains: $\alpha_2\beta_2$. Analysis of human blood indicates that adults also have a minor protein called HbA_2, which also has 2 α chains but, instead of 2 β chains, has 2 δ (delta) chains: $HbA_2 = \alpha_2\delta_2$. The amino acid sequence of δ chains shows them to be very similar to β chains. Fetal hemoglobin, the hemoglobin we make from about two months after conception to roughly the time of birth, is called HbF and is composed of 2 α chains and 2 γ (gamma) chains. The first hemoglobin we make during development is called embryonic hemoglobin and can have the structure $\alpha_2\varepsilon_2$ (ε = epsilon). Looking at the makeup of the protein subunits, studies of the amino acid sequences have shown that ε, δ, γ, and β form a family of related molecules. These are collectively known as the β-like globin family. (In fact, there is an α chain family, too.)

When recombinant DNA techniques were used for further study of this group of genes, several new features were uncovered. As noted in Chapter 2, the genes were seen to be interrupted. The sequence of bases coding for each chain was not continuous, as had always been supposed, but was broken into parts called exons and introns.

Additionally, the γ gene of humans was found to be present twice on each chromosome. That is, the gene has been duplicated and the two copies are arranged back to back on the chromosome. The copy on the 5' side is called $^G\gamma$ as it causes the amino acid glycine to be inserted at position 136 of the γ subunit. The 3' gene is called $^A\gamma$, for it puts alanine, a different amino acid, at this position.

Surprisingly, it was also determined that the "gene" to the 3' side of $^A\gamma$ was not a functional gene at all. At this position, people have a pseudogene, originally called ψβ1 (ψ = psi, and stands for *pseudo* or *false*). This is a sequence of DNA that bears an obvious relationship to the other β-like genes. Upon looking at its complete DNA sequence, however, it is apparent that it possesses mutations that make it incapable of directing the production of a protein subunit (see pages 40–43 on mutation). This gene has recently been renamed the η (eta) gene in species in which it is functional. Since it is a pseudogene in humans, it is called ψη.[6] Remembering that the DNA has a 5′ end (written to the left) and a 3′ end, the organization of the human β-like globin genes is as a cluster about 40,000 bases long (40 KB, where KB = kilobase, or 1,000 bases). The sequential arrangement of genes is:

$$5′\ ε-{}^{G}γ-{}^{A}γ-ψη-δ-β\ 3′$$

β-like globin clusters of other species have been plotted. Those of the chimp and gorilla have exactly the same organization; the genes that are expressed early in development are 5′ (to the right) to the ones expressed later. The Old World monkeys, typified by the baboon in Figure 5.24, are slightly different in that the δ gene, although present, is a pseudogene, incapable of being expressed. Moving further from humans, the New World monkeys have a shorter cluster with fewer genes. Old World higher primates all seem to have two γ genes, while those of the Americas have one. As prosimians too have only one γ gene, it seems reasonable to conclude that the γ gene duplicated in the Old World after the divergence of New and Old World higher primates. It is a shared derived trait of Old World higher primates.

The prosimians have a yet smaller β-like gene cluster, being only about 20 KB long. The lemurs have the cluster organization:

$$5′\ ε-γ-ψη-β\ 3′$$

FIGURE 5.24. The size, arrangement, and evolution of β-like globin gene clusters in the primates.

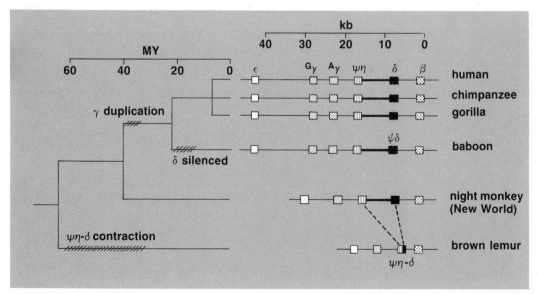

The ψη gene of the lemur is in fact a hybrid gene. As shown in Figure 5.24, it was produced by the loss of part of ψη, part of δ, and all the DNA in between. All this information, together with other data, suggests the tree of evolution for this gene family as pictured in Figure 5.25.

Restriction Enzyme
Maps

The size and organization of the cluster are not the only useful indices of similarities between species. In Chapter 2, we noted that many known enzymes can recognize specific sequences of DNA. These are called restriction enzymes. After the gene clusters (or parts of them) are isolated, a next reasonable step is to use a battery of these enzymes to approximate the similarities between comparable stretches of DNA in different species. For instance, if the β-globin genes of a baboon, gorilla, and human are treated with Bam HI, we see that identical six-base sequences (GGATCC) are recognized near the exon 1–intron 1 boundary in all three species. The enzyme Hind III cuts human and gorilla DNA at a site (AAGCTT) 5′ to the gene. The DNA sequence of the baboon is different in this region, and Hind III cuts the DNA at a different site and "restriction maps" can be produced (Figure 5.25). Certainly the enzymes are sampling only a small percentage of the total DNA for any of these genes. One can argue, however, that the number of identical restriction sites approximates the overall similarity between the genes of different species.

Using such approaches Paul Barrie of Leicester University in England found a small amount of divergence between the restriction enzyme maps of the gorilla, human, and baboon. As noted, the brown lemur gene cluster is quite short and remarkably similar to that of the rabbit (see also Goodman's protein tree, Figure 5.22).

FIGURE 5.25. β-globin genes of human, gorilla, and baboon. B indicates sites cut by Bam H, Hind III; E, Eco RI. This is a very abridged restriction map of this region. The dark boxed regions are exons; the light boxed areas are introns.

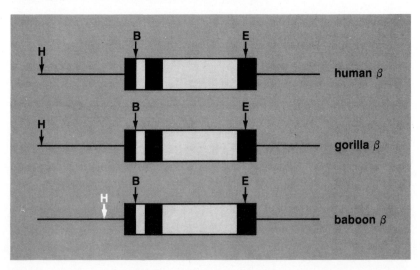

We can couple the ability to isolate specific genes from particular organisms with rapid techniques for the determination of the base sequence of a gene. We no longer need to estimate gene similarities via immunological or biochemical approaches; we can actually compare, base by base, the makeup of genes in different species. Several such techniques now exist that can tell us the makeup of any piece of isolated DNA in the matter of a few days.

If we isolate and sequence homologous genes from different species, we can accurately total the number of similar or different bases between all such sequenced genes. Just as with data derived from the preceding techniques, the numbers expressing the differences between all the compared sequences can be arranged into a matrix—or chart—that shows the number of genetic differences between each pair of sequences. For instance, looking at Figure 5.26, we see that the difference between comparable parts of the β-globin sequence of human and rabbit is one substitution, while rabbit and goat differ by six, and human and goat by seven.

This technique has great potential, but there is a danger of drowning in the data. The β gene alone is over a thousand bases long. To compare large amounts of data many computer programs have been developed. Based on somewhat different assumptions, these programs can be used to generate trees that reflect the amount of similarity or difference between species. For instance, in the small amount of data shown, the human/rabbit pair shows the least difference. These then are linked most closely in the tree. The computer then can generate a *likely* sequence for the human/rabbit ancestor. The modern human and rabbit sequences are discarded; the matrix is reformed (now including the presumed ancestral gene sequence) and scanned, and the two most similar genes are united. In this clustering fashion, all sequences are paired and built into a "tree" that is often a reasonable reflection of genetic relationships.

Why isn't this matrix a perfect reflection of evolution? For one, we are here looking at a very small component of an organism. The β-globin gene is one out of the thousands of genes each of us has. If the amount of difference between two homologous sequences was only the result of random neutral mutations undergoing drift (Chapter 3), then even one

FIGURE 5.26. First nine bases of exon, one of the β-globin genes in human, goat, and rabbit. Vertical lines indicate differences between adjacent sequences. Underlined bases in the goat sequence indicate differences from the human sequence.

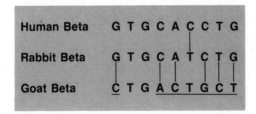

gene might provide a perfect record of evolutionary relationships. But we know that other factors are involved; for example, natural selection might be making the structure of some sequences more similar and causing others to diverge.

When comparing very distantly related genes, we run into other problems. For instance, the β-globins of humans and chickens have been evolving independently for about 300 million years or more (that is, roughly since the separation of the ancestors of mammals and birds). The β-globin gene has been undergoing independent mutations on both lines. We can be certain that at least some mutations on one line by chance also happened on the other line (Figure 5.27a and d). When comparing the sequences of the living species, we will underestimate the number of mutations which occurred on each lineage. Likewise, again by chance, some base positions will have changed more than once in a gene's history (Figure 5.27a, b, and c). A particular base in a gene of humans and chickens may appear identical today, but the actual route may resemble the paths shown in parts a, c, or d of Figure 5.27. This would also lead us to underestimate the amount of genetic change. We can minimize the misleading effects of these features by statistical methods, but the comparison of gene sequences is not without pitfalls.

At this time, the most intensively studied set of genes are those for the β-globin chains. Sequences are known for a sizable variety of these genes in a cross-section of different mammals, although our knowledge is still much more wide-ranging at the amino acid sequence level.

Molecules and Hominoid Relationships

The various data gathered at the molecular level yield one very consistent observation: Humans are genetically very similar to chimpanzees and gorillas. Whether one looks at the sequences of genes or proteins, the immunological properties of various molecules, or the hybridizing ability of DNA from these species, they are very much alike. Orangutans have generally been considered close relatives of the African apes, yet orangs are not as much like them as we are. We and the African apes shared a common evolutionary history for some time after the orangutan diverged.

Determining the relationships within this triumvirate of species is not very easy. The differences between the groups are very small, and in some ways chimps and gorillas appear a bit more alike, while in other ways we and chimps are a bit closer. The hybridization data of Sibley and Ahlquist support the relationships shown in Figure 5.28a, as does much of the nucleic acid sequence data. Restriction maps and sequencing of the DNA found within the mitochondria (see page 31), not the nuclear DNA, marginally favors a closer tie between chimps and gorillas (Figure 5.28b). More will be said about the mitochondrial DNA in Chapter 14. Evidence does not support the option shown in Figure 5.28c, and there is virtually no evidence to support a particularly close relationship between the African apes and the orangutans. Likewise, the little comparable data on the gibbon clearly indicates that it is least similar to the other hominoids.

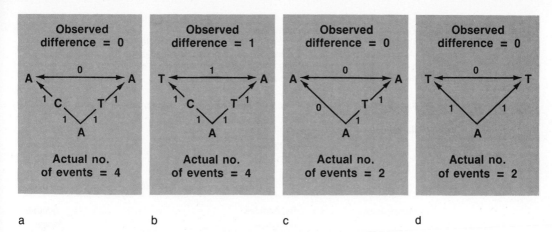

FIGURE 5.27. Various routes by which amounts of change can be underestimated. (a) Multiple independent mutations to identical bases; (b) multiple independent mutations along different lines of evolution, producing one observable difference; (c) multiple mutations along one line of evolution yet producing observed identity; (d) independent single mutations leading to observed identity.

Such findings have led some to propose a revision of the traditional taxonomy so as to more accurately reflect evolutionary relationships. In Table 5.6 we show one possible realignment, originally proposed by Morris Goodman, that puts humans, chimps, and gorillas in the same family. In fact, some have already proposed an even more extreme revision that places all three in the same subfamily. Although this may ultimately come to be the accepted classification, for now we will adhere to the hominoid taxonomy shown in the upper half of Table 5.6.

FIGURE 5.28. Humans and African apes are very close relatives. Probably either (a) or (b) is the true picture of our relationship.

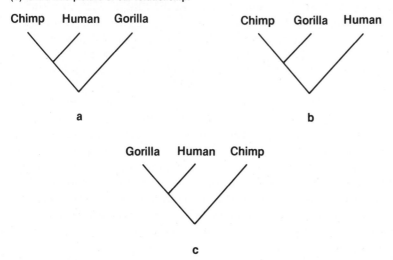

TABLE 5.6
Two Alternative Views of Hominoid Taxonomy
The upper scheme is supported by molecular evidence of a close relationship among chimpanzees, gorillas, and humans. The more traditional scheme, presented in the lower half, groups orangutans, chimpanzees, and gorillas together and creates a wider gulf between the African great apes and humans.

Superfamily	Family	Subfamily	Genus
Hominoidea	Hylobatidae		Hylobates
	Pongidae		Pongo
	Hominidae	Paninae	Pan
			Gorilla
		Homininae	Homo
Hominoidea	Hylobatidae		Hylobates
	Pongidae		Pongo
			Pan
			Gorilla
	Hominidae		Homo

Summary

This chapter introduces the mammal order Primates and briefly identifies and describes its living members. Using comparative anatomical, protein, and genetic studies, primatologists are in general agreement with the composition of the order. However, they continue to debate more specific taxonomic groupings and attempt to place living animals in the overall context of primate evolution by relating them to the rich primate fossil record. A technique known as cladism is becoming a commonly used method of this type of analysis. Cladism undertakes to establish evolutionary relationships by examining biological features to recognize developments that are shared with ancestors or have evolved only in closely related and recently separated evolutionary lines.

Broadly, the order Primates can be divided into two major categories of living animals: the prosimians and anthropoids, or higher primates. Prosimians are restricted today to the Old World continents of Africa (and the nearby island of Madagascar) and Eurasia. Anthropoid primates, mainly diurnal and social, have a broader distribution. New World monkeys, the platyrrhines, have evolved a diversity of arboreal adaptation in the tropical forests of central America southward to northern Argentina.

Old World higher primates, the catarrhine primates, are even more diverse. They are divided into the Old World monkeys, or the Cercopithecoidea, and the apes and human superfamily, or the Hominoidea. The Cercopithecoidea are composed of an enormous array of monkeys inhabiting tropical forests, savannas, grasslands, arid highlands, and temperate woodlands stretching all across Africa and eastward from Afghanistan through Asia and southeast Asia. Hominoid primates include humans and our closest living relatives, the apes. Living apes are confined to narrow zones in central Africa and southeast Asia.

That the primates are closely related to us seems obvious; the proof can be found by dissecting dead animals. This anatomical relationship was known a long time ago. Today molecular anthropologists are classifying primates by comparing them genetically. Comparisons of immunological reactions, amino acid sequences, restriction enzyme maps, and the sequences of the bases of DNA itself give us a measure of the genetic difference between two living species; the greater the difference, the longer the time is assumed to be since the two species had a common ancestor. The molecular evidence extends the anatomical data by showing the very close relationships among chimpanzees, gorillas, and humans.

Molecular studies are used in conjunction with the evidence from anatomy, behavior, and fossils to provide a more accurate picture of the relationships among living primates. Although they also tell us a lot about the biological history of the primate order, molecular studies give us only an indirect picture of primate evolution. To clarify and understand the complete evolutionary development of our order, we must continue to rely on the direct evidence of primate evolution, the fossils.

In the next two chapters, we will consider the behavior and biological history of the nonhuman primates and how this information can help place the biology and behavior of humans in a more understandable perspective.

6

The flexible and highly complex behavioral and anatomical systems of living primates have allowed them to adapt successfully to a wide range of environments.

Primate Behavior

Living primates are very successful animals whose behavior and anatomy have permitted them to adapt to a wide variety of environments throughout much of the tropical Old and New Worlds. In this chapter, we will explore some of the behavioral characteristics common to all social higher primates, and then describe some examples of their social behavior within an environmental context.

A central theme of this book is the relationship between biology and behavior. Scientists generally agree that physical characteristics that are part of the biological equipment of a species are directly related to the successful patterns of behavior an animal employs in coping with the demands of its environment. Some relationships are easily recognized, such as that between tool making and the enlarged areas of the motor cortex in the human brain devoted to hand and finger control; other ties between the biological and the behavioral are not so clear, especially when we try to relate biology to the diverse adaptive patterns of higher primates.

Behavior, Biology, and Adaptation

Many animal behaviorists have become concerned with the relationships between evolutionary biology and behavior and especially the connections between primate behavior and natural selection. This approach is termed *sociobiology,* and its proponents seek to explain why certain primate behaviors have appeared in particular environmental contexts. For example, it is apparent that primate species have evolved behavioral mechanisms permitting them to interact successfully in social groups and to exploit their environment efficiently. But how have these behaviors evolved? What is the relationship between behavior and biology?

Primate Sociobiology

As we have seen in earlier chapters, evolution operates through the mechanism of natural selection, in which individuals who possess traits of greater fitness within a particular environment have a better chance of reaching reproductive maturity and passing on their genes to the next generation. In this interaction, it is successful behavior that accounts for the ability of certain individuals to reach reproductive maturity and produce offspring carrying their genetic materials. But how does one account for the appearance of behaviors, such as acts of *altruism* (self-sacrifice), that seem to act against the survival of an individual and its continued ability to reproduce? In other words, when a female primate defends her infant from a predator and is killed or wounded in the process, how can this act be understood as successful if it results in limiting the female's reproductive potential? It would seem that behaviors of this sort would be weeded out of the behavioral repertoire and that each animal would strive to maximize its own reproductive future.

According to sociobiologists, acts of altruism must be seen in relation not only to the individual but also to the consequences of the act for others who share the genetic material of the individual performing the selfless behavior. In social species like the nonhuman primates, group members are likely to possess many of the same genetic materials. Indeed, a number of studies have demonstrated that a high degree of relatedness exists in many primate social groups. This is partly the result of the very common pattern among higher primates of females remaining in the group they were born in for their whole lives; male primates commonly switch social groups. In a study of the movements of male monkeys after they had left their natal group, which is extremely difficult to observe in most research on wild primates, there appeared to be a tendency for these animals to join a group that already contained an older brother.[1] Therefore, altruistic behavior, while quite possibly resulting in the death or injury of the animal performing the behavior, also causes other animals in the group to increase their reproductive potential and this behavior then ensures that their particular genetic materials will be well represented in succeeding generations. This aspect of natural selection has been called *kin selection* by sociobiologists.

Over the past few years, an increasing number of studies of primates have focused not on the patterns of behavior and adaptation of a particular primate species, which was the major feature of earlier work, but rather on analyses to test possible explanations of how these patterns may have evolved. Several examples of the sociobiological perspective in primate studies have explored behaviors that were difficult to understand in the context of an individual primate's reproductive potential.

A recent study by Sarah Blaffer Hrdy of the langur monkeys of India has revealed a pattern of behavior in male monkeys that seems to maximize their genetic contribution to the next generation. The stable langur social group is composed of females and young, who are joined by one and sometimes more adult males. Although female langurs remain in their natal group for their entire lives, males usually leave (or are forced out of) the group of their birth and join other males in all-male groups. According to Blaffer Hrdy, once every twenty-seven months,

*See pages 617–618 for notes to Chapter 6.

on average, the all-male group in the study area would attack a female-male group, which resulted in the usurping of the resident male by another male from the all-male group. On several occasions, after the take-over, the new male was observed killing the unweaned infants in the group. Female langurs whose infants were killed almost immediately began sexual cycling and had sexual relations with the usurper. Since the new male had only a little more than two years before he himself would be supplanted, Blaffer Hrdy argues that infanticide can be most reasonably understood as an example of individual selection operating to insure that the new male's offspring, and thus his genetic materials, will be represented in the succeeding generation.[2]

A variety of other explanations might account for this behavior, including one offered by Phyllis Dolhinow, a primatologist who also worked with the Indian langurs. According to Dolhinow, the number of observed infanticides is small, and they occurred in areas of high monkey population density. For Dolhinow, a more plausible, although not an adaptive or sociobiological, explanation would ascribe this behavior to a social pathology brought on by overcrowding.[3]

Many problems in primate sociobiology remain, and convincing evolutionary explanations will have to await the collection of more detailed information on primates living under natural conditions. In a recent survey of primate sociobiological research, Alison Richard and S. R. Schulman listed a number of the most important, including long-term (of at least several generations) data on population size and structure, biological relatedness, and use of the environment.[4]

The Environmental Context

Land-dwelling mammals have basically three options for living patterns: They can live on the ground (*terrestrial*), they can live in the trees (*arboreal*), or they can live under the ground (*fossorial*). No living primates have adapted to an underground life in burrows; all inhabit either a ground-dwelling adaptation, a tree-dwelling adaptation, or some combination of the two. In fact, of all living nonhuman primates, only the gorilla is completely terrestrial; some other Old World primates spend considerable time on the ground during their active hours but retreat to the safety of trees or high cliffs to sleep. Many primates are completely arboreal, some never coming to the ground.

Primate Habitats and Distribution

Although the fossil record of past primate habitats indicates that during the early Cenozoic Era primates were more widely distributed, especially in North America and Eurasia, their present distribution is much more limited. With the exception of several macaque species and one langur species (*Rhinopithecus*), all nonhuman primates live within the tropics (Figure 6.1), which in a general sense are the middle latitudes of the planet, bounded by the Tropics of Cancer and Capricorn. This zone is characterized by warm temperatures year-round with a mix of vegetation patterns primarily founded on variations in soil and water.

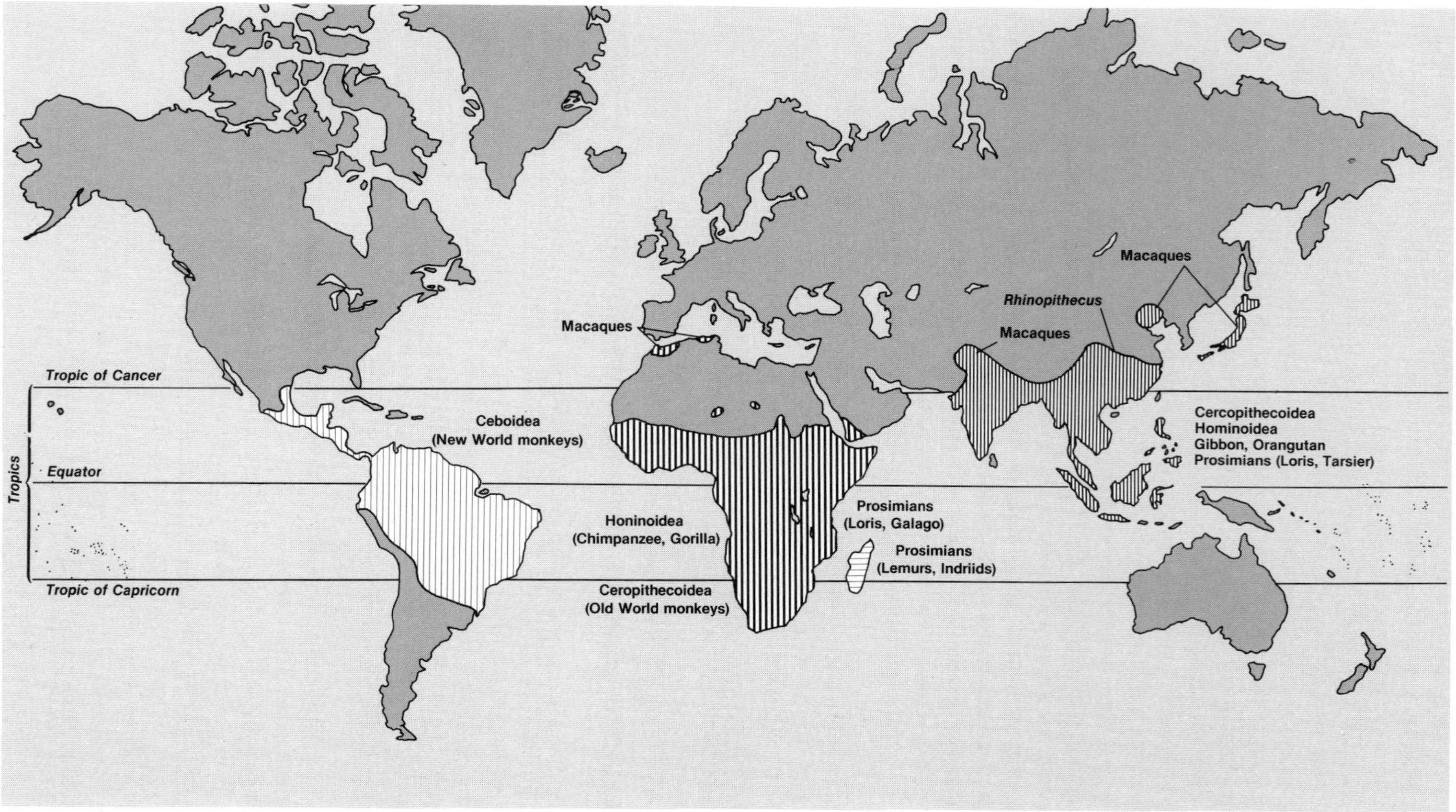

FIGURE 6.1. Worldwide distribution of nonhuman primates, illustrating their tropical adaptation. With the exception of a number of macaque species in Africa and Asia and one langur species, *Rhinopithecus*, the snub-nosed langur, the nonhuman primates are broadly found within the tropics.

Lowlands near to the equator with plentiful rainfall (more than 1,500 mm, or 59 in. a year) are covered with evergreen tropical rain forests with enormous plant diversity—thousands of different species. This vast array of vegetation results in a dense forest, with trees of various kinds forming stratified layers (Figure 6.2). In the upper story, the tallest trees are discontinuous, and an arboreal primate has to be agile enough to span wide, open spaces. It is in the middle and lower stories, where the diversity of vegetation provides almost continuous branch-to-branch contact, that most arboreal primates live. Movement in these layers—the closed canopy—is a matter of following arboreal pathways.

Away from the equator or in areas of lower or more seasonal rainfall (locales with a prolonged dry season, for example), tropical forest is replaced by deciduous forest (where the trees will lose their leaves sometime during the year) and savanna grassland. In these zones, deciduous woodlands may be either continuous or broken into strands separated by open grassland known as savanna-woodlands. Even in these areas, the banks of waterways will be covered by dense vegetation, or the gallery forest.

Primates have adapted to all of these habitats. In the trees, they consume primarily the fruit, flowers, leaves, bark, sap, and gums of the trees as well as the vines (lianas) that use the trees to climb to the sunlight. Primates also eat insects that live in the vegetation and occasionally small vertebrates. Ground-living primates of the savannas, like baboons, eat grasses and herbs, while the largest of the living primates, the gorilla, feeds on a variety of ground-level herbaceous plants.

Primate adaptations to these habitats are very complex and are based on many environmental variables. There are many species of trees in a tropical forest; many are represented by only a small number of

Primate Adaptive Niches

FIGURE 6.2.   A tropical forest in West Africa, showing the stratification of forest layers.

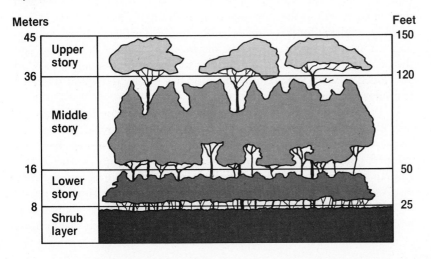

specimens. These individual trees will be scattered throughout a forest. Seasonal changes affect the vegetation in a forest, with the production of fruit, flowers, and leaves varying through the year. Since those primates that eat insects consume mainly herbivorous insect species, seasonal change will also affect this part of their diet.

Nonhuman primates must also consume a balanced diet. Chapter 13 details the nutritive needs of modern humans. Primates require the same range of vitamins, minerals, protein, fats, and carbohydrates as we do, although the precise amounts may vary. Fruit, for example, is a very good source of carbohydrates along with vitamins and minerals. Leaves are good sources of protein, with younger, immature leaves apparently providing more protein than the tougher, harder-to-digest mature leaves.

Finally, it should be noted that trees, in an attempt to limit the damage to their leaves and other essential parts of their structure, have evolved a number of protective systems. Many tree species produce bad-tasting or smelly substances. Others have elements in their cells that limit the digestibility of their leaves or other plant structures. Some plants actually produce toxic chemicals that would kill a primate if they were eaten. These substances often develop during the course of leaf matura-tion, for example, so that some plant foods will be safe and nutritious at one point in their cycle and dangerous at other times.

Primate Adaptive Strategies

The adaptation of many primates, which may appear simple and straightforward, thus is actually extremely complicated and variable. The variations in the distribution of food-producing plants, the seasonal variations in when food is produced by the plants, and the nutritional needs of the animals are among the many variables that are part of the primate adaptive situation. As a consequence primate species have evolved a broad array of strategies for dealing with these factors.

For many primates, the food sources are "patchy," or unequally distributed through the forest and the seasons. Primates have evolved numerous strategies to deal effectively with patchy concentrations of food. Primates, for example, seem to possess "mental maps" of the area they inhabit, and groups are able to move rather directly to where sea-sonably available food resources can be found. Further, the size and or-ganization of the social group, the distance it will cover in one day, and the size of the area lived in and utilized by the group (its range) have all developed in ways to maximize the primates' ability to exploit scattered and unevenly distributed foods.

Primates have likewise evolved strategies to obtain foods that will provide required nutrients. Some of these strategies are social. For ex-ample, chimpanzees, being basically fruit eaters (frugivorous), have de-veloped a social system in which small foraging groups of one to five animals are the normal grouping; this permits the animals to be widely dispersed in their range and maximally exploit available fruit sources.

Some strategies are biological. Old World monkeys of the Colo-binae subfamily, for example, have evolved a large stomach that permits them to consume large quantities of mature leaves. Certain members of this group, the langur monkeys of Asia and colobus monkeys of Africa, utilize this large stomach as part of a long digestive process like that in ruminants, like cows, in which bacteria break down the cellular structure of the leaves and allow nutrients to be digested.[5]

All mammals are social; for a large number of mammals, interaction with adult members of their own species is for specific purposes, like reproduction, and thus is maintained for only a limited time. Many mammals (including all higher primates except the orangutan), however, live in a permanent social grouping. Within the prosimian primates, social living is also a feature of the behavior of several lemur and indriid species on Madagascar. Whether social living evolved in the common ancestor of the higher primates and the Madagascar prosimians is not known, but some fossil evidence (to be described in the next chapter) suggests that it may have been a part of the adaptation of some of the earliest known higher primates, dated to the Oligocene period, about 35 million years ago.

As we would expect, there seems to be a direct relationship between the environment and the size and type of social organization, although the connection is very complicated. For example, a sociobiological model of mammal group size proposed by J. F. Wittenberger suggested that while the size of a primate group will be limited by crucial resources, there will be different evolutionary selection pressures on the number of females and males in a group. This is because it is more important to the species to have an optimal distribution of females, who give birth to and care for the young, throughout the environment, than males, whose contribution to the continuation of the species is more limited.[6]

Population size and social groupings are related not only to the type, range, abundance, and seasonal availability of foods consumed but also probably by the number of sleeping places as well as other environmental factors. For example, T. H. Clutton-Brock and P. H. Harvey showed that within dietary specializations (that is, fruit or leaf eating), the size of the area inhabited by a primate social group and the total weight of the animals in the group are directly related. Further, folivorous (leaf-eating) primates tend to occupy a smaller range per total social group weight than do frugivorous primates. This is probably because fruit is a more scattered, or patchy, resource than are leaves.[7] K. Milton and M. L. May compiled information on many primates that indicates that frugivores move further each day seeking food than do folivores. These scientists also found that frugivorous primates utilize a larger range than do folivores but that ground-dwelling primates move further each day and have larger ranges than either folivorous or frugivorous arboreal primates.[8]

A higher primate is born into a social group, is nurtured by its mother, and plays with its peers; throughout its life the animal functions and interacts with other members of a group. Males of many species often leave the natal group, become solitary, join another social group, or return to the original group. In only a few species have females been observed leaving the group of their birth. Often, within the social context, animals will establish especially close and long-lasting relationships with their mother or siblings. These are variations on the theme of social living; in large measure, the environment determines the characteristics of a particular social system; such as whether there is a dominance network (a rank ordering of adult animals, usually with each sex having a separate ranking); whether there are lasting relationships between the males of the group or nonreproductive relationships between the males and females; and even the group's size and composition, including the ratio of adult males to females.

Higher primates live in groups of many kinds, ranging in size from one adult female orangutan and her offspring, through small groups with an adult male and female and their immature offspring, up to large groups with adult males, adult females, and the young. Within this range there are many types and sizes of social groupings. Despite variation, some behaviors are common to almost all higher primates, although they are modified by each species in response to a specific environment.

The first pattern common in all higher primates but the orangutan is the social group containing at least one male, one female, and their immature offspring. Second is the close mother-offspring relationship of childhood dependency (Figure 6.3). Third is a period of offspring dependency, in which the young primate learns by observing and imitating other animals' behavior, picking up appropriate skills and behaviors in

FIGURE 6.3.   A young chimpanzee nursing. Like most mammals, chimpanzees undergo a prolonged dependency period, but the attachment of the chimpanzee offspring to their mothers is an especially long one. Even in adulthood, they maintain a special relationship with their mothers.

relationships with other members of the group, either in the one-to-one relationship of mother and infant or in interactions with the peer play group. Fourth is communication between animals by vocal and nonvocal signals. Fifth are stereotyped, discrete behaviors, learned during maturation, which are shared by members of the group and ensure its continued existence. Finally, primate groups occupy a *home range,* a specific geographic area from which most female members do not roam. These important primate patterns deserve a more detailed look.

The primate social group has been observed in nature in many shapes and sizes. Social groups are more or less permanent aggregations of animals living in a specific area. The small group (adult male, adult female, and immature young) typical of the human family is found among one of the Asian apes, the gibbon, and several New World monkeys, including the titi monkey (genus *Callicebus*), marmosets (genus *Callithrix*), tamarins (genus *Saguinus*), and the night monkey (genus *Aotus*), the only nocturnal higher primate. These monogamous, pair-bonded groups, however, are extremely rare in Old World monkeys. Tarsier prosimians also live in these groupings.

The pattern that seems most prevalent among Old World higher primates is a multimale group of adult males, adult females, and their offspring; it is found among all the Asian macaques, all the baboons except the hamadryas, some monkeys of Africa (genus *Cercopithecus*), many of the langurs (genus *Presbytis*), and at least some New World howler monkeys (genus *Alouatta*). It has also been observed among several species of lemurs and indriid prosimians on the island of Madagascar.

There is also the single-male group, or harem, with one adult male and one or more adult or young females (the group often includes sexually immature female animals and the young). These harem groups may also be part of a community, coalescing at night to sleep in the same area and separating during the day to forage on their own. A number of Old World monkeys share this type of social system: the hamadryas baboon (genus *Papio*) of Ethiopia, the patas monkey (genus *Erythrocebus*) of the savannas of Central Africa, the gelada (genus *Theropithecus*) of highland East Africa, some arboreal African monkeys, and some langurs, the colobine monkeys of Asia. It is also characteristic of some African *Cercopithecus* monkeys. Although some gorilla groups are multimale units, most are led by one mature male, identifiable by lighter colored fur on the back and called a silver-backed male.

A relatively uncommon type of social organization is a large, rather amorphous group of animals that can be considered a "community." It is not a distinct group; the animals are normally found in smaller, impermanent, foraging subgroups that may occasionally coalesce to form the larger social entity. They may come together at night to sleep or during the day to move on the ground across an especially dangerous

Social Organization

open space. Ordinarily, however, the subgroups will move about more or less independently of one another. These subgroups are generally not stable but reflect a situation in which different individual animals come into and depart from the group at irregular intervals. This pattern is found in one New World monkey, the spider monkey (genus *Ateles*), and one great ape, the chimpanzee.

Social Learning

Higher primates share with other mammals the mother-offspring bond, including a fairly long childhood dependency. Social living, an efficient way of maintaining the species, is also important because it provides the opportunity to pass information from one generation to the next. All higher primates, including humans, have this basic system for learning, which begins with the relationship between mother and offspring (Figure 6.4). By observing the mother, a young animal learns a great deal about its immediate environment, including what food to eat and what not to eat. The mother also gives the offspring a sense of security. In several famous and important experiments, Harry and Margaret Harlow demonstrated that two early relationships are crucial for the growth and development of a normal, functioning social primate: the mother-offspring relationship and the peer associations of the young animal with others of its own age. The Harlows raised young macaque monkeys in isolation, depriving them of these relationships, and found that when the animals reached adulthood they were incapable of normal interaction with other monkeys and even lacked the ability for sexual relations, although the females eventually learned to participate successfully in sexual behavior. The monkeys were asocial, a deadly handicap for an animal that depends on sociality for survival. The early associations, therefore, were vital in the development of healthy, normal adult social animals.[9]

The peer relationship in most primate species takes the form of the play group, young animals close in age who associate informally. There the young primates learn the behaviors they will use as adults. Primate groups do not do any formal teaching; instead, the young watch adult animals behave, imitating and practicing this behavior in play groups. When they become adults they will possess a set of behaviors that permits successful interactions with other adult members of the group. Play takes up more and more of the young primate's waking time after it begins moving away from its mother and until it becomes a fully adult member of the group.

Primate sociality is thus founded on a prolonged early maturation period, during which the young animals learn the behaviors characteristic of their social group and which permits successful behavioral interactions as adults. They learn by observing the behavior of other animals and imitating these actions in the play groups. The biological basis of this ability in the primates is a large brain with a complex cerebrum capable of assimilating a great deal of learned behavior during maturation.

FIGURE 6.4. A baboon mother and infant. The bond between mother and offspring in higher primate social groups is perhaps the most intense relationship within the social unit and may continue into adulthood.

Higher primates, like most other mammals, have vocal and non-vocal communicative signals. Part of the system of behavior that primates learn is discrete vocal signals, fixed in number. Primate vocalizations may be directed toward a single individual, several individuals, or the group as a whole. A male baboon, for example, in an antagonistic encounter with another male, may combine vocal and nonvocal signals directly toward the other male. In other contexts, such as when a predator threatens, an alarm call will be directed toward the whole group.

Communication

FIGURE 6.5
A male baboon making what has been interpreted as a tension canine display.

In nonhuman primates, vocalizations are a closed system; the limited number of sounds are the whole repertoire. The human communication system is open. Human language depends on the speaker and the listener understanding the rules that govern the construction of grammatically correct sentences. Once the human speaker masters these rules and learns the vocabulary, it is possible to generate an infinite number of communications comprehensible to other speakers of that language. The fixed, limited vocalizations of nonhuman primates have no flexibility.

In addition to vocalizations, many interactions between members of a primate group are communicated by nonvocal signals using the body, especially the head and face. Nonvocal gestures are stereotyped and discrete. They communicate feelings from one animal to another, providing for smooth interactions between members of the group. Like vocal behaviors, the young animal learns these signals during socialization, and they thus form part of the behavioral repertoire of the animals in a group. Figure 6.5 illustrates primate nonvocal communication. A male baboon uses the closed eyes, which provide a contrast to his light eyelids surrounded by the darker face, and the yawn, which exposes the large canine teeth, to communicate his state of high tension to others in the group. As with all behaviors that are performed by members of species other than our own, our identification of this behavior, and thus our understanding of its significance, may be incomplete. However, within the context of the baboon social group, the signal is recognized, and other group members can react appropriately.

Most nonhuman primates possess distinctive features of the face and head as well as fine-muscle control of the facial muscles that permit a wide range of facial movement and expressions. In this, modern humans, who also possess this muscle control, reflect the common higher primate evolutionary background.

Nonhuman Primates and Language   Over the past fifteen years, a number of researchers have worked with captive apes, primarily chimpanzees but also gorillas and orangs, in an attempt to teach these primates to communicate by using human-created signaling devices. Apes do not possess the anatomical structures in the throat, the fine-muscle control of the tongue and lips, or the specialized neurological structures in the brain that permit humans to speak. But are these the only differences that prevent chimpanzees from employing an open communication system? Several long-term studies suggest that chimpanzees are capable of learning the meaning of a limited variety of symbols, including symbols for concrete objects such as foods and symbols for actions or verbs. In one experiment David Premack and his associates taught a chimpanzee named Sarah to recognize and identify over two hundred chips whose color and shape stood for different objects and actions. Sarah was able to understand what was "said" when the researcher arranged the chips in a particular order and to respond appropriately. She was also able to request favorite foods or actions (such as to have her back scratched) by arranging the chips to communicate these wishes.[10] A review of these studies has challenged the notion that they demonstrate true language abilities and suggests instead that they reflect the ability of the apes to learn the meaning of particular words but not the rules that govern the correct ordering of words into sentences, and thus are not indicative of the human capacity for language.[11] The question of the language learning abilities of the apes remains an open one with no clear-cut answers.

All the learned behavioral attributes that are basic among the higher primates form a functioning system of social behavior. This system includes not only vocal and nonvocal communicative signals but also features that promote peaceful interactions among members of the group. Grooming is one of these; most primates spend several hours a day at it. Normally two or more animals sit together quietly, one combing and picking through the hair of the other, pulling out dirt, parasites, and insects. After a while they may reverse roles, and the passive animal will begin grooming the other one.

Taken together, behaviors of this sort are essential to the maintenance of the social group, because its existence depends on the primates' ability to live together in their environment. The individuals must be able to interact in a way that is not harmful to the group. During growth and development they learn how to get along with any other member of the social group: male-female, female-infant, male-infant, male-male, female-female, or any other type of interaction will conform to an acceptable and expected pattern. Because the behaviors toward any individual are stereotyped and predictable, the animals know exactly what an action means to them, and they can respond with an appropriate behavior. The word *appropriate* is important, because the continued functioning of the primate group is based on the sharing of a common but limited set of behaviors. This provides for a stable group organization with peaceful interactions between members.

An equally important role of the social group is the transmittal of information about the environment from one generation to the next. A social group lives within a particular environment, an area that is never uniformly rich in foods throughout the year. Effective exploitation of the environment is based on knowledge of where and when foods will be available. Observations indicate that in many monkey species males are much more likely than females to switch social groups and that it is therefore the female members who carry this environmental information (the "mental map" of the group's range), exerting considerable influence in directing group movements in search of food. As a young female primate matures, she travels through the yearly round and learns from the female adults where the group has found sources of food in the past; the adults have acquired this information by traveling with the group when they were maturing. The members of the social unit thus passively transmit vital information about the environment; the "traditions" of the primates that have lived in that area are carried down through the generations.

These mechanisms provide for the continuation of the social group (and the species) in their environment through time. We can think of the social group as an organized entity greater than the sum of its parts—the individual animals. Before an animal is born, an effective structure is already in existence; a primate grows and develops within the social system, learning the actions it needs to be a part of the system and to survive in its environmental context. It becomes an adult and a functioning part of the structure, contributing genes to the next generation of animals. That generation in turn will grow into integrated adulthood by learning the appropriate social behaviors from the present adults.

A primate group's behavior is very conservative, changing little as time passes. This stability is necessary, for if behavior were modified rapidly, the group would not have its limited set of stereotyped behaviors, known by every member of the group. Individual members of the group would find themselves not understanding actions of others, and the group's cohesiveness would ultimately be upset. Because the behaviors are learned, however, they do have the potential for being modified quickly in response to the environment's demands.

An example of how new behaviors can become part of the repertoire of a primate group comes from the study of the macaque monkeys (genus *Macaca*) native to the islands of Japan. These monkeys, which live in multimale groups and spend much of their time on the ground, have been studied extensively over a number of years. To facilitate observations, these animals are provisioned by the Japanese researchers. The macaques continue to forage for food, but they are also given a variety of foods, such as wheat kernels and various fruits and vegetables, including potatoes. During a provisioning of a group of macaques that lived in a particularly open area along the ocean on the island of Koshima, researchers noticed that one adolescent female took a potato and carefully dunked it in a fresh-water stream. Later, the potatoes were washed in fresh or sea water. Over time, scientists noticed that other animals in this social group were also beginning to dunk their potatoes in the water, obviously learning by observing and imitating the young female. However, this behavior did not spread to all members of the group. First to pick it up were the young animals, her peers, and also her close female relatives; later, other young animals picked the behavior up; and after three and a half years, when these animals had grown to adulthood, it had become a behavior typical of most members of this social group. It never became part of the repertoire of most animals older than the female who began the activity. It seems relatively clear that the adult animals, having grown and learned within a social situation that lacked potato-dunking activities, found it difficult to learn an innovative behavior of this sort.[12]

Because of the appearance of innovative behaviors in response to specific environments, social groups of a particular primate species exhibit variations in behavior. Each primate species has a "core" of behaviors common to all members of that species; different parts of the core are stressed in different environments. A good example of this flexibility is the terrestrial monkeys of the subfamily Cercopithecinae, who have been able to exploit successfully wide areas of sub-Saharan Africa (Table 6.1). The adaptation of these monkeys to their environment will provide us with important perspectives in understanding the pattern and evolution of primate behavior.

Monkeys adapted to ground living are found only in the Old World. Baboons, the most widespread and abundant nonhuman primates on the African continent, are found almost everywhere south of the Sahara. Terrestrial monkeys that are generally accepted as baboons include members of the taxonomic genus *Papio* and the mandrills and drills, found in West Africa, which are sometimes placed in the genus *Mandrillus*. The heavily mantled hamadryas baboons (*Papio hamadryas*), once the sacred baboons of dynastic Egypt, live in East Africa and a small portion of the Arabian Peninsula and are considered a different species from the savanna baboons, although they are known to interbreed successfully. The gelada, superficially like the baboons but placed in its own genus, *Theropithecus* (Figure 6.6), lives in the highlands of Ethiopia. The much more gracefully built patas monkeys (genus *Erythrocebus*) of the savannas of East and Central Africa are also adapted to a terrestrial niche, but in a pattern different from that of these other monkeys. The vervet monkeys (genus *Cercopithecus*), widely scattered through sub-Saharan Africa, also spend a good deal of time on the ground (Figure 6.7). They are one species of more than twenty of the genus *Cercopithecus* who inhabit various parts of Africa. The other *Cercopithecus* monkeys are primarily arboreal, which may explain why the more ground-adapted vervets are the most widely distributed of these monkeys.

Biologically and evolutionarily, Africa's ground-dwelling monkeys are a diverse lot; the one factor they share in common is their terrestrial

TABLE 6.1
Terrestrial Monkeys of Sub-Saharan Africa

Monkey	Vegetation Zone	Location
Mandrill and drill	Tropical wet forest	West Africa
Savanna baboon	Tropical wet forest, savanna, and thorn savanna	Sub-Saharan Africa
Vervet	Savanna	South, Central, and East Africa
Patas	Savanna	Central and East Africa
Hamadryas baboon	Thorn savanna	East Africa
Gelada	Thorn savanna	East Africa

FIGURE 6.6
A gelada (*Theropithecus*)
male (left) grooming a
female.

adaptation. Evolutionarily, the members of the genus *Papio* and the drill and mandrill seem closely related. On the other hand, the gelada (*Theropithecus*) has been distinct from the members of *Papio* since the late Miocene or Pliocene. The separate evolutionary development of the patas and vervet is longer, for they are closely related to the arboreal monkeys of Africa.

Other terrestrial monkeys, the macaques (genus *Macaca*), are limited mainly to Asia, although macaques are found also north of the Sahara in northern Africa. The African baboons and the macaques are so similar in behavior and morphology that a number of primatologists have grouped them in a single genus. In Asia, the leaf-eating monkeys, the langurs (genus *Presbytis*), also leave the trees. Two great apes, the chimpanzee and the gorilla, both spend much of their time out of the trees. The gorilla is too heavy to travel in the trees and has little to fear from predators; the chimpanzee makes use of terrestrial pathways. Both of them exploit many ground foods. Orangutans also spend time on the ground. Several daylight-active prosimians spend time on the ground, principally the ring-tailed lemur (*Lemur catta*) of Madagascar; all the African and Asian prosimians and the nocturnal prosimians of the Malagasy Republic are arboreal.

With the notable exception of the gorilla, the terrestrial existence of all these primates lasts only as long as their active hours during the day. At dusk the risk from predators increases, and all ground-living monkeys and the chimpanzees retire to relative safety, spending the night and the dangerous early dawn hours in places high above the ground (Figure 6.8). In forested regions or on the savanna along watercourses, the animals settle in trees for the night. Each night, chimpanzees construct a sleeping nest of branches that have been bent into a supporting structure; monkeys, in contrast, generally rest on their "sleeping pads,"

FIGURE 6.7
A vervet monkey (*Cercopithecus aethiops*). Unlike other *Cercopithecus* monkeys of Africa, the vervets often spend considerable time on the ground.

FIGURE 6.8. A baboon group that has escaped from a lion by moving into a tree. Although baboons spend most of their daylight hours foraging on the ground, they will move into the safety of trees or other high places at dusk or when danger threatens.

the ischial callosities that cover their buttock region. In the Ethiopian home of the gelada, mostly arid, open, bush country at elevations above 2,100 meters, and in other parts of Africa that offer few convenient sleeping trees, the monkeys spend the night on rock faces.

Being so widely distributed, the ground-living monkeys have adapted to a variety of environments, and their behavioral attributes are consequently distinct. The social group's size will depend directly on the environment's ability to support it; baboons, for example, are found in multimale as well as single-male groups. Much of their other behavior is determined by the environment's lushness or sterility. All terrestrial monkeys are basically vegetarians, eating fruits, grass, leaves, tree sap, blossoms, seeds, seedpods, rhizomes, and stems along with occasional insects and bird eggs. Some groups occasionally kill and eat a small mammal or bird. Some species have specialized to exploit particular food sources; for others, diversification ensures survival. Despite seasonal fluctuation, for example, even in the harsh Ethiopian highlands, the variety and amount of their foods allow the geladas and baboons to coexist in the same habitat.

Savanna Baboons

Let us examine the behavioral patterns of the most common of all baboons, the savanna baboon of the genus *Papio*. Although most of these animals are found in savanna areas, they are also adapted to other habitats, including forested regions; high, open, bush country; and combinations of these environments. Savanna baboons live in multimale groups ranging in size from two to almost two hundred, with an average of about forty. They are diurnal, like all Old World higher primates, and spend their days moving across the savanna searching for food: grass, roots, seeds, seedpods, and blossoms. Studies in East Africa by Robert Harding and Shirley Strum have shown that some baboons at least occasionally hunt and kill small animals and birds.[13] They also consume insects if they are available. Grasshoppers are devoured in vast quantities when available; fruit, too, is eaten in season.

At dusk, when predators (leopards, hyenas, and lions) are most active, the baboons move into sleeping trees and settle in for the night, spending the hours of darkness in the trees and returning to the ground soon after daylight to begin their daily rounds. Baboons exploit their environment efficiently. The distance a troop will travel in a day depends on the richness of the environment, the size of the group, and the season of the year; most groups average about five kilometers per day. In the dry season a troop may move as far as ten kilometers a day. But during the rainy season, when fruit ripens (figs are a favorite), the troop may spend days in the same groves of trees, gorging themselves and not moving at all.

In their daily rounds of leaving the sleeping trees, foraging in the forest or savanna, and returning to the trees in the evenings, the baboons move as a group. In fairly open spaces on the savanna, where the grass is low and the animals can see for long distances, the group may be dispersed over several hundred meters. But when they enter heavy undergrowth where observation is difficult or when a predator threatens, the group will close up into a compact mass. During group movements, females with young appear to stay near the large males.

Terrestrial monkeys, especially savanna baboons that spend most of their time in open country away from trees, are much more liable to predator attack than arboreal primates or baboons found in more forested habitats. It may be for this reason that baboons are strongly sexually dimorphic. Many nonhuman primates exhibit marked *sexual dimorphism* in body and canine size; for example, the gorilla male may be a hundred kilograms heavier than the female. Other primates are not as markedly dimorphic; there is only a minor difference in size between male and female chimpanzees. Still other primates, including many arboreal African monkeys and the small ape the gibbon, show no sexual dimorphism at all; body size and canine size are similar in males and females.

Sexual dimorphism may be related to social organization. Those primates like the gibbons and many New World monkeys, who live in family groups of adult female, adult male, and dependent young, show little or no dimorphism. Primates like baboons and gorillas, on the other hand, that are found in multimale or single-male (harem) groups, possess marked dimorphism.

A male savanna baboon weighs between 22 and 30 kilograms, a female between 11 and 15. Males also have very large canine teeth; the female's canines are visibly smaller. The male's big canines are associated with a much larger face, because large roots are needed to secure the teeth in the jaw, requiring an enlarged facial structure to house the roots (Figure 6.9).

Sexual dimorphism in baboons and gorillas appears to be related to differences in roles in the social group and to mating behavior. Male baboons are said to be mean tempered and aggressive; their large bodies and great canines suggest that their role is to defend the group from predators. Several observations of male baboons making threats toward predators seem to provide evidence that the sexually dimorphic differences may be a partial reflection of this protective role. Other observations, however, reveal that when a predator attacks a baboon group, the whole group, including the males, runs for the safety of trees. Many primatologists have seriously questioned the importance of protecting the social group from predation as an explanation for male baboon biology. These scientists emphasize instead the role of body size in male mating success.

FIGURE 6.9. **The skull of a male hamadryas baboon (*Papio hamadryas*). Notice the huge canine teeth, which necessitate very large roots. The female baboons generally possess canine teeth much smaller than the males' (see Figure 7.15 for a female baboon dentition). The large male canine tooth and long root occupy a large portion of the face, as the root outline shows.**

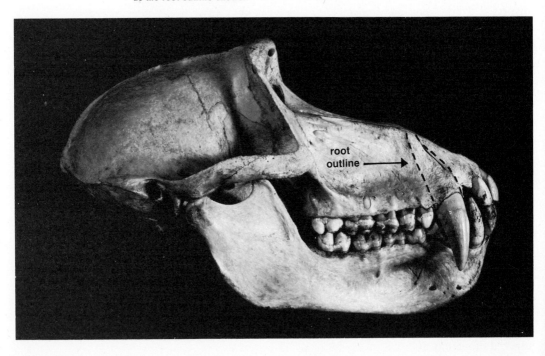

In savanna baboon groups, adult males are organized, at least some-times, into dominance hierarchies, with a number one (alpha) male, a number two (beta) male, a number three (gamma) male, and so on down to the lowliest male. The hierarchy provides some stability in the rela-tionships between males, and it is maintained by occasional fights and threat gestures (Figure 6.10). Part of the behavioral repertoire is a system of stereotyped threat and response gestures known and understood by all members of the group. These predictable and limited behaviors give the individual a number of appropriate actions to use in interacting with those both above and below it in the hierarchy. Although the dominance hierarchy enables the larger, highly aggressive, well-equipped adult males to interact without continuous fights and injuries, the arrangement is neither permanent nor stable, but appears to reflect changing patterns of behavior within the group and the fact that male baboons tend not to be permanent members of a group. This has led to the development of a sociobiological model that suggests that a male baboon high in the dominance hierarchy will have greater access to limited resources such as food or sexually receptive females.

Baboons' sexual relations are promiscuous, but male-female con-sort pairs may be formed when the female is going through the *estrus cycle*. Estrus, the monthly reproductive cycle a female goes through un-less pregnant or lactating, has both anatomical and behavioral effects (Ta-ble 6.2). Ovulation occurs in the middle of the cycle; it is then that the female is most likely to conceive. Like some other Old World monkeys, the female baboon also goes through other, more obvious anatomical changes that make sexual receptiveness evident to the males. The skin

FIGURE 6.10. Two male baboons fight in a dominance interaction. The baboon males' large canine teeth may be related to their defense against predators; the teeth are also related to the establishment of a strongly marked dominance network among the males. Although fights, as a general rule, seldom cause damage, the huge canines are capable of inflicting deep wounds.

TABLE 6.2
Female Baboon Monthly Reproductive Cycle (Estrus)
Accompanying the anatomical and behavioral changes listed are several physiological changes, including ovulation, or the release of the egg, usually about midway in the cycle.

Days in the Estrus Cycle	Anatomical Change	Behavioral Change
1 to 10	Gradual enlargement of sexual skin and change in coloration	Female initiates sexual behavior by approaching and presenting to males; mates with juveniles and less dominant males; forms permissive associations; becomes more active and excitable
11 to 19	Maximum enlargement of sexual skin, which is bright red	Female forms consort relationship with dominant males; increased tension and excitement in the group
20 to 35	Sexual skin decreases, becomes flabby, wrinkled, and finally flat	Female becomes less active and unresponsive; interacts infrequently with males in the group

around the buttocks and sexual organs swells and becomes deeply pigmented and red (Figure 6.11); the female also secretes odorous substances that are signals. In the first part of estrus the female is receptive to males, and subadult or low-dominance males may mount the female. As the cycle progresses toward ovulation and the time when conception is most likely to occur, the female becomes involved with dominant males and may form a temporary consort relationship, mating and remaining with one male. Sometimes male and female baboons maintain a close relationship for longer periods, occasionally for years. Although high-dominance males do not seem to have greater access to reproductively active females, they are able to concentrate their activities during those times when conception is most likely. The dominant male baboons therefore have the best chance of fathering the next generation; by providing their genetic material, they reinforce and select for the large body size and aggressive behavior that led to their dominance. After ovulation, toward the end of the estrus cycle, the female baboon reduces sexual activity until, at the end of the cycle, it reaches zero. If pregnancy has not resulted, the estrus cycle begins again.

FIGURE 6.11
Sexual swelling of a female baboon during the estrus cycle.

Baboons breed all year, but births may reach a peak at certain times of the year. Some monkeys breed only at one time of the year and have births at only one time of the year; the rest of the time they have no sexual relationships.[14]

In contrast to the unstable dominance network of male baboons, the ranking of females tends to be far more stable, with relationships in the hierarchy lasting for long periods. This stability is related to the crucial roles of the female in the group and to the absence of group switching by these animals in most Old World monkeys. Females are responsible for looking after their offspring and probably also for directing group movement, since adult male baboons are likely to switch social groups, leaving the females to carry on the traditions of the group. Obviously, the female role is more important, since the group's continued successful adaptation depends on the continual birth and socialization of young animals who can pick up the necessary behaviors to survive in that social group in that environment. The importance of the stable female component in most Old World monkeys is reinforced by the recent recognition that one of the basic organizing foundations of a primate social group may well be the fact that most animals in the group are genetically related. Females therefore are usually more numerous in a group, since a smaller number of adult males is adequate to protect the group, fertilize the females, and furnish role models for young males. Also, everything else being equal, a small female uses fewer of the resources in the environment and therefore seems more efficient. In Old World monkeys, females thus maintain the long-term stability of a group within an environment.[15]

Primate dominance systems are exceedingly complex, and even in primates who do show dominance, like the baboons, their intensity and frequency can be quite variable and may also be related to environmental factors. Baboons studied in the forest regions of Uganda by Thelma Rowell showed much less dominance activity than the same species living in the savannas of Kenya studied by Irven DeVore, S. L. Washburn, and K. R. L. Hall.[16] This difference in dominance between forest and savanna baboons may in part be a reflection of the higher level of stress imposed by life on the open savanna. The ground-living macaques of Asia and North Africa seem to have dominance hierarchies like those of the baboons; but some macaques, apparently under fewer population and environmental pressures, exhibit much less dominance than the savanna baboons.

Dominance, and probably aggressive behavior in general, seem to be directly related to environmental circumstances, such as predators, overpopulation, scarce food, and lack of sleeping trees, in addition to mating behavior and other factors we have yet to identify. Several studies have demonstrated this relationship. Charles Southwick and S. D. Singh observed macaque groups living in three Indian environments.[17] One was forest, a "natural" environment for the monkeys. Another was along a road, where the monkeys lived in contact with humans but could also retreat into the woods. The third was the city, where the animals were dependent on humans for food and good treatment. Aggressive interaction, fights, and wounds were much more frequent in the city animals than in the other groups. One explanation is the higher density of macaques per square mile in the city; the larger numbers in a smaller space faced greater competition for resources and sleeping areas. The observers reported that the city animals seemed more tense and more ready to fight. This psychological state was less apparent in the other macaque groups.

Donald Sade has made an interesting study of the macaque's dominance network.[18] Like the baboons, these ground-living monkeys have a strong network, and as one might expect, the dominance varies with the habitat. Sade observed these monkeys on Cayo Santiago Island, off the coast of Puerto Rico in the Caribbean, where they were placed in the 1930s to provide rhesus macaques, who are native to India, for use in medical research. The thirty-seven-acre island is not large enough to support all the rhesus macaques, and they are given food once a day. Over the years they have been observed by many scientists, so we have a fairly complete history of the macaque groups on the island, comparable to the information gathered by Japanese researchers on their native macaques.

On Cayo Santiago all the animals are tattooed with an identifying sign so that they can be recognized by observers. Relying on these identifying marks in studying the dominance networks, Sade concluded that the offspring of high-dominance females are usually of high dominance themselves. That is, a male monkey whose mother was of high dominance in the female hierarchy had a much better chance of being of high dominance in the male hierarchy than an animal whose mother did not rank as high. Similarly, a female will be higher in the dominance network than all those females her mother outranks, and is subordinate to all those who rank higher than her mother.[19] Position in the dominance hierarchy probably results from both biological and behavioral factors. A young monkey, watching and learning the behaviors it will need as an adult, observes the kind of actions its mother takes part in and perhaps learns to be a dominant animal. This pattern of dominance "inheritance" has also been documented in baboons.

A number of observational studies have focused on the terrestrial monkeys of the semiarid highlands of Ethiopia in East Africa. Geladas, hamadryas baboons, savanna baboons, and vervet monkeys all inhabit this region, and although it might seem difficult to conceive of four species of terrestrial monkeys coexisting in the same area, differences in the kinds of foods most often eaten and the specific environments utilized by the various monkeys permit each species to live with the others. There are also differences in social organization that are related to the adaptive needs of the monkeys in different environments.

In areas where geladas, savanna baboons, and vervets are all found, such as the Bole Valley of Ethiopia (Figure 6.12), where the Dunbars observed their behavior, the animals utilized somewhat different parts of the habitat, and exploited slightly different food resources.[20] In this valley both the baboons and the vervets were organized into multimale groups, although the latter has been observed in other parts of Africa in single-male groups. The geladas were formed into single-male foraging groups as in other areas, but in the Bole Valley, these harem groups seldom clustered into larger aggregations, or herds, which John Crook has observed in areas where the environment is richer.[21] In the Bole Valley the vervets preferred the forested zones near the river; the geladas stayed mainly in the open grassland; and the baboons, although found in all the areas, seemed to be more populous in the forested zones.

Geladas in the Bole Valley are almost exclusively grass eaters, while vervets and baboons eat a much wider variety of foods. Geladas proved

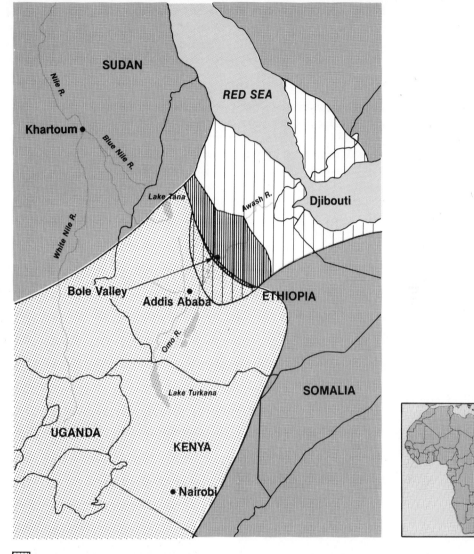

☐ Savanna baboon distribution

☐ Hamadryas baboon distribution

▥ Gelada distribution

FIGURE 6.12.   Distribution of terrestrial monkeys in Ethiopia. Hamadryas baboons, native to the highlands of East Africa, and savanna baboons, with a more extensive distribution through much of sub-Saharan Africa, overlap in this zone. Geladas have a more limited distribution, living primarily along a band through the middle of Ethiopia. Vervet monkeys are the most widespread of the four primates and are found throughout this area.

to be extremely efficient feeders, sitting back on their haunches and using both hands to harvest grass blades and roots. Baboons also feed on grasses but with only one hand, so geladas would appear to be able to eat a greater amount of food in a given time than the baboons. Similarly, vervets and baboons seem to utilize many of the same foods, including fruits, leaves, flowers, and bark, but the smaller vervet monkeys tended to harvest their foods from a higher layer of the trees.

Differences in food choice thus permit coexistence among three species living in the same area. Baboons tend to move a greater distance each day in foraging, which would be expected given their less efficient methods of harvesting grasses and their larger body size. The Dunbars concluded that actual competition between specific social groups of the different species would be minimal in most seasons because the baboons, whose use of the habitat overlapped the other two, moved about twice as far each day as the vervets and geladas, and thus were in contact with the others for only a short time.

In the Awash Valley of Ethiopia, near the Bole Valley, savanna and hamadryas baboons live in the same area but utilize different parts of the environment.[22] Hamadryas baboons (Figure 6.13), like geladas, are organized into single-male groups. Hans Kummer believes that this organization is the result of the need to adapt to an open country habitat not rich enough to support large, multimale groups of vegetarian, foraging baboons. During the day, the single-male hamadryas groups move about

FIGURE 6.13
Two hamadryas baboon females and their offspring.

with their adult females and their young searching for food. In the evening these small groups come together at sleeping cliffs and form large groups, sometimes of several hundred animals. Lack of suitable sleeping trees and cliffs seems to be the reason for these large aggregations. During the night, the single-male groups remain close but do not intermingle. Adult males are very possessive of the females in their groups and forcibly prevent them from interacting with other males or even with other females. The males watch the females closely, asserting their dominance and encouraging them to follow by judicious bites on the neck. Fights between males are rare.

As with the geladas in the Bole Valley, hamadryas baboons in the Awash Valley seem to be more efficient than the multimale savanna baboons in exploiting the resources of the open, semiarid grassland. The single-male group appears to reflect a pattern of adaptation in a harsh environment that limits the number of baboons that can stay together as a group. Whether the single-male group is an evolutionary outgrowth of the savanna baboon multimale organization is disputed. But the important point is that the biological basis of social behavior permits varied responses to different environments. Kummer demonstrated the level of learning flexibility in baboons in a series of experiments. Although female hamadryas and savanna baboons live in different kinds of social groups with different sorts of relationships with males, when female hamadryas and savanna baboons were captured and then released near social groups of the other species, they both learned quickly to interact successfully within the new social circumstances. Hamadryas females soon learned not to follow a particular male and to adopt a more independent life, while the savanna "females learned, within one hour on the average, to follow the one hamadryas male who would threaten and attack them, and to interact with no other male."[23]

The Patas Monkey

The patas monkey has developed a different adaptation to the demands of terrestrial life. Patas monkeys are widely distributed through the savanna, woodlands, and other open country of central and eastern Africa. They are not found in tropical forests. Dietarily, they are like other terrestrial monkeys, eating grasses, fruits, seeds, as well as some insects and small vertebrates. Like the hamadryas baboons and the gelada, patas monkeys live in single-male groups of about twenty. They are also markedly sexually dimorphic; the males are twice as large as the females. Patas monkeys are long-limbed and slender compared with the much heavier, stockier baboons (male patas: 13 kilograms; male baboons: 22–30 kilograms) (Figure 6.14). This body build is well suited to rapid running; the patas are without doubt the swiftest of living primates, running with a bouncing movement like that of the cheetah. Speeds of up to 55 kilometers per hour (35 miles per hour) have been recorded.

Male patas monkeys are distinctively marked, especially around the rump and the rear of the hind legs, where they are conspicuously pure

FIGURE 6.14
Erythrocebus patas, a ground dwelling monkey of Africa. The patas monkey is popularly known as the military monkey because the white moustache and reddish coat give the animal a cavalry officer–like appearance.

white. K. R. L. Hall, who studied the patas on the Uganda savanna, wrote: "The rear view of the adult male in the wild, when he is standing or moving, contrasts very strikingly with that of the other much smaller animals of the group, for the white expanse shows up very vividly against the grass and bare ground. No white is visible in the other animals as they move across country."[24]

Males are often well away from the group, keeping a lookout for predators and leaving group movement and direction to the females. When faced by a predator, the single-male patas group responds very differently from other African terrestrial monkeys. The brown females and young freeze in the grass and blend into the background. The adult male begins a bouncy, very conspicuous run across the savanna, drawing the predator's attention from the rest of the group. With its great speed, the male outdistances the predator, which is led away from the females and young. This pattern permits the patas monkeys to roam farther out onto the savanna than the baboons and thus to utilize environmental zones not open to other monkeys.

The African monkeys adapt to terrestrial life in many ways. All are successful in their habitats and cope with predators and the need for food and sleeping places. The monkeys are successful because the basic higher primate system gives them flexibility in their behavioral repertoire. Thus it is very difficult to generalize about primates: No terrestrial monkey behavior is typical, just as no human behavior is typical; individual groups suit their activities to their environmental requirements by modifying their behaviors. However, it must be kept in mind that these animals are limited biologically in their behaviors; they are not little humans dressed up in monkeys' suits. Like modern humans, part of their success is founded on their ability to use learned behaviors in adapting to the environment; unlike modern humans and many of our immediate extinct ancestors, their behavioral repertoire is limited and not completely flexible.

To place the adaptation of the terrestrial monkeys in perspective, let us examine the South American monkeys.

New World Monkey Behavior

The New World arboreal monkeys' behavior is quite different from that of the African terrestrial monkeys. But they share some attributes that make it clear we are dealing with a higher primate. Fossil evidence suggests that the Old World and New World higher primates have been evolving independently since the Late Eocene or Oligocene, perhaps 40 to 50 million years ago.

Howler monkeys (genus *Alouatta*) are among the most widely distributed New World monkeys (Figure 6.15). There are at least six species

FIGURE 6.15
A howler monkey (*Alouatta*).

scattered from the Yucatan Peninsula in southern Mexico through Central and South America to northern Argentina. They were first studied under natural conditions in 1932 by C. R. Carpenter, the great pioneer in the study of wild primates, on Barro Colorado Island, formed when the Panama Canal was flooded.[25] It is owned by the Smithsonian Institution, which uses it for the study of animal and plant life.

Although there is a difference in body size, the howler monkeys have little sexual dimorphism in canine size. Many such characteristics that are obvious in terrestrially adapted forms are not found at all in the howlers. Their dominance network is very subtle, and the males do little intragroup fighting; instead, intragroup behaviors are mild and placid. Unusual among New World monkeys, juvenile female howler monkeys leave the group of their birth just before reaching maturity and join a new one. It is difficult to explain the adaptive reasons for this behavior within the overall context of howler adaptation.[26]

Unlike the baboons, howler monkeys defend a *territory*. Territoriality is not part of the behavioral system in most primates. The geographic area in which a primate social group lives is called its *home range,* which is not the same as a territory. Different social groups may sometimes have overlapping home ranges, especially at rare but essential places such as fruit trees or waterholes (Figure 6.16). These parts of a

FIGURE 6.16.   A hypothetical map depicting the primate group's core area, home range, and territory.

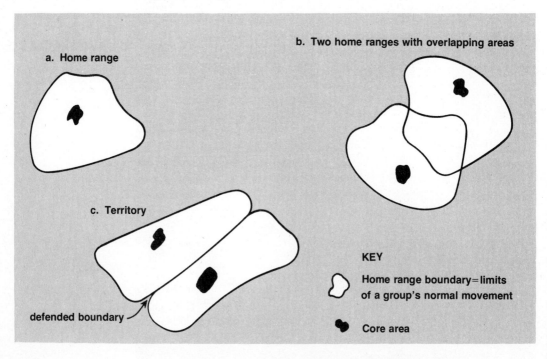

a. Home range

b. Two home ranges with overlapping areas

c. Territory

defended boundary

KEY

Home range boundary=limits of a group's normal movement

Core area

group's home range that—for the richness of resources, presence of sleeping trees, or other factors—are the most heavily exploited and the most frequently occupied are known as the *core area*. A group may occupy a home range of three square kilometers, but the core area may be only about one square kilometer. A territory is a home range that is physically or vocally defended against incursions by members of the same species. Baboons, like most primates, are not territorial. Howlers, along with the gibbons and a number of other monogamous, pair-bonded monkeys including the marmosets, are.

Like other primates, the howler monkey's social group size and pattern are related to the environment. On Barro Colorado Island, howler monkeys live in multimale groups ranging in size from two to thirty-one, with an average of about twenty. Howlers in other areas, however, live in smaller groups, sometimes composed of a single adult male, adult females, and dependent young.

Like the terrestrial monkeys of Africa, the howlers share their environment with other monkeys. Lewis and Dorothy Klein observed the ways by which four different species of monkeys were able to coexist in the same trees in a national park in Colombia, South America.[27] Along with the howler monkeys, they observed groups of spider monkeys (genus *Ateles*), capuchin monkeys (genus *Cebus*), and squirrel monkeys (genus *Saimiri*). The howler monkeys in this area were organized mostly into single-male groups of three to six animals. Their diet was composed of leaves and immature and mature figs along with smaller quantities of other ripe fruit, decaying wood, and leaf stems. Spider monkeys, in contrast, although they ate more than fifty kinds of fruit during the study period, including figs, consumed large quantities of palm fruit, which howler monkeys were never observed eating. Moreover, spider monkeys concentrated on ripe fruit with only a very small amount of unripe fruit in their diet.

The Kleins suggest that this feeding adaptation may be responsible for the specialized social organization of the spider monkeys. These animals are organized into social units whose members interact peacefully with one another. This unit, however, is not a cohesive group but is composed of animals who at times are isolated and at other times are members of subgroups of different sizes and compositions. The subgroups, ranging in size from two to twenty-two spider monkeys, are unstable; they share a home range as part of the larger social unit but travel and forage independently of other subgroups. It appears likely that the spider monkeys' reliance on ripe palm fruit, a relatively abundant but scattered forest resource, requires them to form small foraging groups to exploit this food source efficiently.

Squirrel monkeys are basically insectivores who live in multimale groups ranging in size from twenty-five to more than thirty-five animals. They eat vegetable materials, particularly fruit, and are adapted to capturing and eating insects such as katydids, grasshoppers, caterpillars, spiders (not spider monkeys), and cicadas. The comparatively large size of their groups may be an advantage; their disturbance of the branches and leaves as they move through a tree enables them to flush out and capture their prey.

Capuchin monkeys, like the squirrel monkeys, live in multimale groups, although of a smaller size (from one to twelve; several capuchins were solitary). As feeders, they are the most diversified of the monkeys, eating fruit, nuts, flowers, leaf buds and stems, insects, and small vertebrates. To the extent that capuchin monkeys eat insects and palm fruit, they would appear to compete with both squirrel monkeys and spider monkeys for food. Capuchins, however, specialize in insects that must be dug out of dead bark and branches, an important difference from the squirrel monkeys, and their more diversified diet leaves them out of serious competition with spider monkeys. This diet is probably also the reason capuchin monkeys are not organized into unstable subgroups like those of the spider monkeys.

The behavior of these New World monkeys illustrates the complexity of their adaptation and the difficulties involved in generalizing about the nonhuman primates. Differences in diet permit several species of monkeys to coexist in the same environment and account for differences in the social organization of, for example, spider and howler monkeys. Typical of diurnal higher primates, daily activity for the howlers begins about dawn, when the animals begin moving about in their sleeping trees; once awake but before the group moves, they start howling. Their larynx and *hyoid bone* are massively developed, making a large resonating chamber (Figure 6.17). The howls can be heard for several miles. These vocalizations, which gave the howler its name, are said to be a memorable sound. The morning howling seems to be a spacing mechanism, ensuring that the howlers are aware of the location of other groups. The gibbon, another territorial primate, also uses vocalizations (hoots) to announce the position of the family groups, as does the orangutan.

Occasionally, a howler group moving through the trees may come to the edge of its range and into visual contact with a howler group coming from another direction. Both groups start a territorial display. The males shake branches and howl; the females scream; the juveniles and the young become excited, running up and down branches. Each group remains in its own area, perhaps ten or fifteen meters apart. After ten or fifteen minutes of this, the troops slowly retreat into their own areas, occasionally looking back and giving a parting gesture. These displays rarely lead to physical contact or combat. Behaviors like this and the localizing vocalizations of these and other primates probably evolved as a way to permit the effective spacing of social groups of a species through an environment and thereby ensure that the species could exploit resources throughout a range.

Katharine Milton conducted a study of the ways by which several howler monkey groups on Barro Colorado Island utilized the food resources in their environment. Milton found that the howlers actually

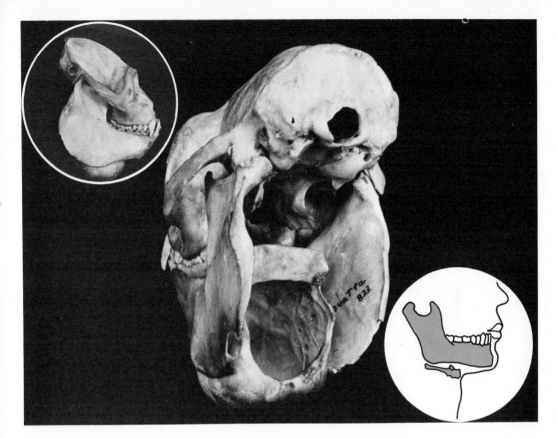

FIGURE 6.17. A howler monkey's skull showing its hyoid bone between the two halves of the lower jaw. In the main picture and the side view, note the inflated, bulbous chamber of the howler hyoid, which provides the resonating chamber that permits the characteristic vocalizations. The lower inset illustrates the much more usual appearance of the hyoid bone beneath the lower jaw of a primate, in this case a modern human.

consumed the leaves, fruit, and flowers of more than one hundred species of tropical forest plants but that many of these were eaten only once during the observational period. Most often eaten were the leaves and fruit of two species of fig. In their foraging activities, howlers usually ate both leaves and fruit each day, using them as complements to supply energy (fruit) and protein (leaves). They concentrated on young, immature leaves, which are easier to digest and higher in nutritional quality.

Howler group movement was almost solely oriented toward obtaining these foods, which are scattered and seasonal (patchy). Movement along arboreal pathways was usually directed to particular trees, which were important food sources and from which the group could then move to other food patches. This deliberate pattern of directed movement indicates the presence of "mental maps" of the environment that permit the howlers to find and exploit patchy food sources efficiently.

Milton discovered that the howlers spent only about a quarter of their day looking for and eating food. Almost two-thirds of the day was spent resting. It is clear from this study that howlers have evolved an effective adaptive strategy involving the knowledge of the location of and efficient movement to seasonal food sources, combined with prolonged periods of rest that reduce the need for additional food.[28]

The howlers, being primarily arboreal, rarely are found on the ground except during the height of the dry season, when their normal diet of leaves, fruit, and other arboreal vegetation is difficult to find. Even minor interruptions in the forest limit their distribution. Species and subspecies limits correspond with geographic barriers, such as rivers. Baboons, being ground-living monkeys, are more widely distributed; geographic barriers do not limit such terrestrial monkeys as tightly as they do an arboreal species.

Howlers almost never venture out of the trees. In the branches, they move cautiously, holding on with their hands and feet. Their distinctive grip is between the thumb and index finger and the other three digits. Their prehensile tail is used as a fifth limb for an added grip on the branch. In some ways, the howler skeletal and muscular system (not including the manipulative tail, which is a specialized, later development) reflects a more primitive quadrupedal pattern than displayed by either of the major Old World higher primate groups. The limb bones of an early higher primate from the Oligocene Fayum (30–35 million years ago; see Chapter 7), *Aegyptopithecus,* share a number of similarities with howler anatomy. This does not imply close evolutionary relations but rather aspects of common primate heritage.

The howler monkeys of the New World and the terrestrial monkeys of the Old are variations on a theme, similar in some features, differing in others. All are based on the adjustments that allow the species to survive within its environment.

The Behavior of the Hominoids

Chimpanzees, like baboons, are limited to Africa, and are distributed in a wide band across the central part of the continent, from Sierra Leone in the west to Uganda and Tanzania in the east (Figure 6.18). They are generally found in forest habitats, although they also live at the edge of the forest and in the adjoining open grassland or savanna. Chimpanzees, like the other members of the superfamily Hominoidea (gorillas, orangutans, gibbons, and humans), differ anatomically from the Old World monkeys. These differences include: distinctive molar cusp patterns, an enlarged brain, no tail, and anatomical specializations in the shoulders and arms that permit greater arm mobility and allow the animals to hang suspended below branches. Both of the African apes, the chimpanzee and gorilla, are mainly terrestrial, although chimpanzees build nests in the trees at night to sleep. The African apes' mode of movement on the ground is termed knuckle-walking: both the front and rear limbs are used for locomotion, and the fingers of the hands are

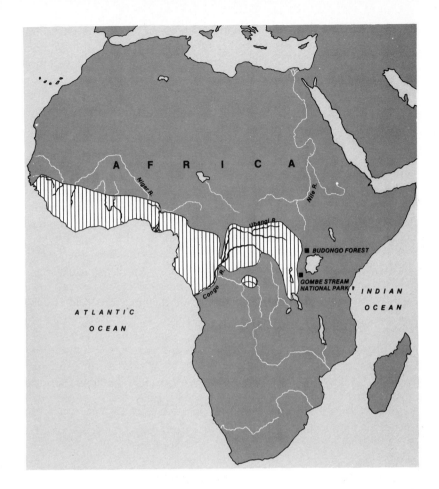

FIGURE 6.18
Distribution of chimpanzees in Africa.

curled or flexed, with the animal's weight resting on the knuckles of the second finger joint (Figure 6.19).

The most famous study of chimpanzees in the wild was conducted by Jane Goodall and her associates in the Gombe National Park, a wild-life preserve on the shores of Lake Tanganyika in Tanzania.[29] These chimpanzees live in a savanna-woodland environment. Chimpanzees have also been observed in a variety of other forest and woodland habitats in Uganda and Tanzania in East Africa and in Guinea in West Africa.[30]

Chimpanzees are organized into bisexual, somewhat amorphous social groups ranging in size from twenty to sixty animals, but these groups are rarely together. Instead, they are normally found in smaller, impermanent bands, with an average size at the Gombe of about 4.2 chimps. They are most commonly composed of either females and their offspring or all males; less common are groups of male and female adults, and these are ordinarily based on the presence of one or more estrus females (Figure 6.20). Membership in these bands fluctuates regularly as the animals move about in their habitat; indeed, Gombe chimps spend

FIGURE 6.19
The steps in the knuckle-walking locomotion in a chimpanzee. Notice that the chimp's weight is resting on the knuckles of the flexed second finger joint in the front limbs.

about one-fifth of their time foraging for food on their own. This social organization is similar to that of the spider monkeys of South America and perhaps occurs for the same reason: to permit maximal exploitation of a scattered food resource.

Chimpanzee social organization is distinct among hominoids. The other African ape, the gorilla, has a social organization that is flexible, but with more group cohesion than that of the chimpanzees. Gorilla groups studied by George Schaller, Dian Fossey, and their associates in the Virunga Volcanos area in Zaire and Rwanda are composed of fully mature (silver-backed) males, females, immature males, and young.[31] Although some groups have two or more silver-backed males, there is usually only one. Group size mostly ranges from about six to sixteen animals. When they reach maturity, male gorillas leave the group in which they were born and become solitary animals. Females, too, have been observed leaving the natal social group. Female gorillas leave their group only to transfer to another; males remain solitary until they form a new social group with emigrant females. Nearly all gorilla females appear to leave the group of their birth, usually before they become mothers. Females who have given birth to living offspring do not leave the groups they are in.

The two Asian apes, the gibbon and the orangutan, also differ fundamentally from the chimp pattern. The gibbon's group consists of an adult male and female and their immature offspring. The gibbon's social group is territorial and will not coalesce with other groups. The social organization of the orangutan (Malay: *orang = man; hutan = forest*) appears to be unique among higher primates and seems to consist of a female and immature offspring. Occasionally they meet with other mother-offspring groups, and the young play together. This gathering is not permanent, and after only a short time, the mothers and their offspring will move apart. Adult male orangs are solitary animals that seem to meet with others only for reproduction. This pattern may be another kind of response to a lack of concentrated food resources that evolved to permit this species to exploit widely scattered foods efficiently.

Like the orang, the chimpanzee's specialized social organization is related to its adaptive niche. Chimpanzees use a very varied diet. Although their primary food source is fruit, they also eat leaves, blossoms, seeds, stems, bark, resin, honey, insects, eggs, and meat. In contrast, the gorilla is a vegetarian, including in its diet leaves, bark, stems, and fruit. Schaller writes that he did not see gorillas eating any animal foods. Chimpanzees have been observed eating a variety of insects, including termites, ants, caterpillars, grubs, and bee larvae. They also hunt larger animals and are known to have caught and eaten some fifteen species of mammals, including young baboons (Figure 6.21). Goodall reports that the chimp group she was observing hunted and killed twenty mammals (as well as birds, eggs, and smaller animals) in one year. She recorded a specific hunting incident involving two adult chimpanzees. A red colobus (a small leaf-eating monkey) was sitting on a branch when the chim-

FIGURE 6.20
Chimpanzee social interactions are normally peaceable and close. Here, a mother and her young offspring sit close together on a branch, feeding.

panzees spotted it. With no obvious communication between them, the two chimpanzees separated, one climbing the tree to the monkey and attracting its attention, and the other, much more quietly, approaching the animal from a different direction. While the first chimp occupied the monkey, the second quickly ran along the branch, grabbed the monkey, and wrung its neck. Both chimpanzees pulled the carcass apart and ate it.

Geza Teleki, who worked for a number of years at the Gombe Stream National Park, is impressed with the variety of the chimpanzee diet, comparing it with the diets of a number of modern human gatherers and hunters (those groups, such as the Australian aborigines and the San, formerly known as the Bushman, of southern Africa who until very recently did not practice agriculture but gathered wild foods and hunted animals).[32] Teleki refers to the pattern of chimpanzee subsistence as that of a collector/predator, emphasizing by this term the wide range of chimpanzee foods. Collector/predators differ from the human gatherer/hunters, according to Teleki, in that humans are able to hunt animals larger than themselves. Although chimpanzees do hunt a variety of animals, including a number of primates, their prey is always smaller than themselves.

Chimpanzee social organization, like that of spider monkeys, apparently evolved to deal with this sort of dietary pattern. Although chimpanzees utilize a wide array of foods and will often at least sample from all the major food categories each day, fruit is a chimpanzee staple and appears to make up more than half of the diet. Fruit is a widely

FIGURE 6.21. Chimpanzees do hunt animals and eat meat. Here a male chimp sits in a tree and eats his prey, a baboon, while another chimp watches.

scattered resource in a forest, and different kinds of fruit mature at different times of the year. The open social organization of the chimpanzees is efficient because it permits them to exploit this scarce resource in small groups. Orangs are also omnivorous in that they consume large numbers of invertebrates (but they have not been observed killing vertebrate animals, as have chimps), and like chimps their main food resource is fruit. One reason why orangs are solitary living animals may be related to the greater distance between clumps of fruit trees in their island habitats.[33]

Chimpanzees have been seen using sticks and their fists to beat on the bases of trees, making loud, hollow sounds that attract chimps from other parts of the forest to an area where food is concentrated. In crossing from one forested region to another, vulnerable to predators, they make similar noises, cross the open area in a group, and disperse on the other side. The large social group apparently serves a limited purpose, at least for the chimpanzees that have been observed, and this large group has never been seen to come together at the Gombe Stream during the thousands of hours of observation on these animals. However, the chimpanzees in the community are generally aware of which animals belong and which do not, and small bands of males often "patrol" the community boundary to ensure that chimpanzees from neighboring communities, male or female, do not intrude into their community area. Several observed episodes of males attacking strange females with infants resulted in the female receiving wounds and being chased from the area as her infant is pulled from her grasp by the males, who then killed the young chimp and partially ate it as they would a prey animal. The carcass was groomed and touched by several chimpanzees, usually not the animals responsible for the killing, as if they were aware of the nature of the creature prior to its death. Although a number of theories have been advanced to account for the adaptive or evolutionary nature of these incidents, they are not compelling, and it remains a difficult behavior to comprehend within the context of primate adaptive systems.[34]

Many years of experiments with caged chimpanzees have demonstrated that with incentives, these animals can perform many tasks, such as building crude shelters, making tools, and solving simple problems to get food or some other reward. Captive monkeys, such as the rhesus and the South American squirrel monkey, can also perform most of these tasks, although they do not usually learn as rapidly.

These experiments were conducted under artificial (man-made) conditions; the one real test of an animal's intelligence is how it performs in its natural environment. It is interesting to find that caged chimpanzees can put two pieces of bamboo pole together, making an implement long enough to reach some bananas suspended from the ceiling. But they would hardly go to such trouble in their natural habitat, where they would simply climb the tree to reach the fruit. Many anthropologists have concluded that humans are the only primate that, in natural conditions, deliberately fabricates and uses tools. Some were therefore more than a little shaken when Goodall and others reported observing chimpanzees making and using a variety of simple tools.

At times the Gombe Park is loaded with insects—termites, ants, caterpillars—and the chimpanzees will eat huge numbers of them. The chimpanzees' really remarkable behavior appears when they gather termites. According to Suzuki and Goodall, when chimpanzees see that termites have pushed open their tunnels on the surface, they will go off to find a suitable termiting tool (Figure 6.22). A foot-long, rather thin, straight twig is best, and it may take quite a while to choose a suitable one; then extraneous side branches and leaves must be carefully stripped off. The ape may even select and prepare several twigs at a time, carrying

FIGURE 6.22. Chimpanzees have been observed making and using tools. This chimpanzee has inserted a grass stem into a termite hole and is withdrawing the stem with the termites clinging to it. Skill is attached to this learned behavior, since it takes careful effort to wiggle the tool into the curved corridors of the termite hill.

them all back to the termiting hill firmly cupped in a closed palm while it knuckle walks. The chimpanzee will lie down on its side, next to the termite hill, and, with skill and care, stick the twig into one of the open tunnels. The animal wiggles the stick, then slowly pulls it out; if the stick has termites adhering to it, the chimp licks them off the tool and does it again. The job may look simple, but it takes skill and practice to maneuver the stick through the twisting termite corridors. This is a complex, learned behavior, based on the manufacture of an implement. The collecting of termites and ants is done primarily by females. This is in contrast to the hunting of vertebrates, which is, in the Gombe study area, a male behavior, although in other areas females have also been observed hunting vertebrates. Orangutans also do a considerable amount of insect collecting, oftentimes on the ground, but this differs from the behaviors seen in chimps in two ways. No tools are used, and both males and females are equally involved in gathering these foods.

Goodall has watched chimpanzees using other objects, modifying some, leaving most others as they are. They chew leaves and cup them in the hand to sponge water for drinking or to sponge out the brains of a hunted baboon.

The emerging picture of chimpanzee life in the natural environment strongly suggests that we may have been overemphasizing the extent of our differences from the rest of the animal world. Chimpanzees make and use tools. Their diet is a diverse one based on vegetable foods but with an appreciable amount of animal foods. In addition, the pattern of their social organization, with small groups existing as parts of a larger social community, has many similarities to the social organization of living human gatherer/hunters. This leaves us with a sticky question: Exactly how do humans differ from other primates? Many traditional ideas about our uniqueness may have to be modified because of the information primatologists are gathering about monkeys and apes in their natural environment.

Summary

Previous chapters have examined the biology, genetic and biochemical similarities, and the taxonomy and distribution of the nonhuman primates. This chapter looks at modern primate behavior, focusing on the social living, higher primates.

Sociobiology, a field concerned with understanding the reasons particular primate behaviors have evolved in specific environmental and social contexts, has become an important research tool in primate behavior studies, and much current research uses this approach to explain primate behavior rather than just observe and record it.

Many aspects of primate behavior are directly related to environmental conditions, especially the availability of food. Tropical forests, home to many higher primates, are rich environments, but the food resources—fruit, leaves, flowers, other plant material, and insects—tend to be scattered in patches and be seasonal in appearance. Primates have evolved a number of strategies to deal with this situation. Social group size and composition as well as movement pattern and range size are among the variables that will be modified in response to environment conditions.

Life in social groups permits primates to accumulate a large repertoire of learned behaviors that in turn gives these animals their indispensable flexibility in responding to environmental demands. The primates' social organization seems to reflect the necessities of their differing environments, and it is not unusual to find different social groups of the same species emphasizing diverse behaviors, although it is sometimes very difficult to comprehend fully all the environmental factors that might influence primate social systems. There is no typical primate behavior or social group. Where resources and other environmental limitations allow large numbers of animals to live together, the social groups will be large. In areas with scattered, specialized, or minimal resources, smaller social groups are the rule.

Field studies of higher primates in the New and Old World have revealed the wide array of dietary resources that these animals consume in the wild as well as the variations in social organization and behavior. Typically, New World monkeys, among whom is found the only nocturnal higher primate, the night monkey, live almost entirely in the trees, with many living in single, pair-bonded male and female groups with their young. However, also found in New World monkeys are larger multimale groupings that are the usual pattern among the terrestrial Old World monkeys, the baboons and macaques. Other Old World monkeys, including terrestrial ones like the patas and hamadryas baboons, live in single-male, multifemale groups, while the numerous arboreal Old World monkeys exhibit a variety of social systems. The pattern common in the New World of a monogamous pair bond is extremely rare among Old World monkeys; it is found in the apes only among the highly arboreal gibbon and siamang, lesser apes.

Among the higher primates the orangutan is unique in being a solitary animal, spending only a very small percentage of its time with other orangs. The African apes, the chimpanzee and gorilla, closely related genetically and anatomically, nevertheless have different behavioral and social systems. The large-bodied gorillas live normally in single-male groups, while chimpanzees have apparently evolved a rather amorphous, communitylike system to deal with the scattered fruit resources that are their major dietary items. Chimpanzees are omnivores in that they consume a variety of invertebrates, mainly ants and termites, collected by the females, and hunted mammal meat, usually killed by the males but sometimes shared with females as well. Chimpanzees have also been observed making and using simple tools, a fact that is often discussed in the context of their close anatomical and genetic relations to those supreme toolmakers, humans.

The study of primate behavior was initially directed at the discovery of behaviors, activities, and adaptations that could be used in further understanding similar patterns in modern humans. Also important was the use of the primate behavior data in reconstructing the behavior and adaptation of our early ancestors. These reconstructions were usually based on ground-dwelling primates such as baboons and chimpanzees. Lately, scientists have recognized that the use of primate behavioral observations in this fashion leads to simplistic and often inaccurate conclusions. Primates and humans, while they share a common evolutionary heritage, are also the products of long, independent lines of their own.

Increasingly, primates are being studied for what they are: a highly successful and diversified mammal order.

Perhaps in the future, when our knowledge of the primates has grown, we will be able to understand more fully the environmental and evolutionary bases for their social organization, distribution, and behavior. We can then use this information with more assurance as the basis for general statements about human evolution and behavior. Certainly, the primates, and especially the chimpanzee and gorilla, are our closest living relatives, and much potential use in understanding humans can result from their study. But these comparisons must be done with great care and with due consideration of the complexity and enormous range of variation in both primates and humans.

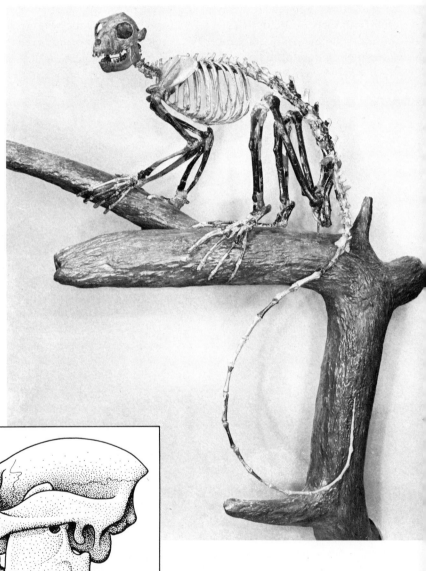

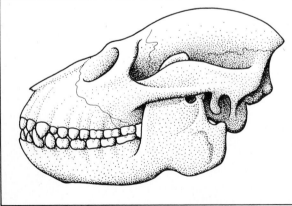

Fossil evidence helps us understand how the primates, one of the oldest living mammal orders, have successfully adapted to their environment throughout their long and rich history.

The Biological History of the Primates

The primates are one of the most ancient of the living mammal orders, with a long and rich biological history that extends over at least the last 65 to 70 million years. In this chapter we will trace this evolutionary record and document its major trends.

To understand fully the biological history of the primates would require a complete collection of fossils from every geological period. We do not have such a collection, and we may never piece together the exact biological path the primates took in their long evolutionary history. Our alternative, and a reasonable one, is to put together a history of the major adaptations, the major trends, and the background for the origin of the major groups of primates, including humans.

We have a variety of materials to work with. The first and most important is the fossil evidence—the remains of once-living animals—which supply the direct data on primate evolution. The fossils give us a framework for reconstructing primate history. But the primate fossil record is very incomplete in many places, especially in the southern hemisphere, and in several epochs, above all the Paleocene, Oligocene, and Pliocene (Table 7.1). Because the fossil evidence is scanty, we fall back on indirect evidence of several types: comparative anatomy, comparative genetics and biochemistry, and comparisons with the behavior of living animals. These are useful because often the fossils are difficult to interpret; different scientists come up with a variety of explanations, even when looking at the same fossil material. This is especially true when we consider ancestor-descendant relationships, such as which earlier primates are the direct ancestors of later forms, and when the later animals split off from an ancestral group. As we have seen in Chapter 5, comparative biochemistry and genetics can be of enormous help in resolving issues of this kind. Fossils, however, remain the foundation of any examination and furnish the only *direct* evidence of primate evolution. Various methods have been developed for analyzing the fossils and extracting information about the animals.

The Primate Fossil Record

TABLE 7.1
Geologic Time Scale of the Mesozoic and Cenozoic Eras, Illustrating the Relative Abundance of the Birds and Mammals
The primate and human lines have been added to illustrate their presence during this time, but they are not drawn to the same scale as the mammal and bird groups, which were much more abundant.

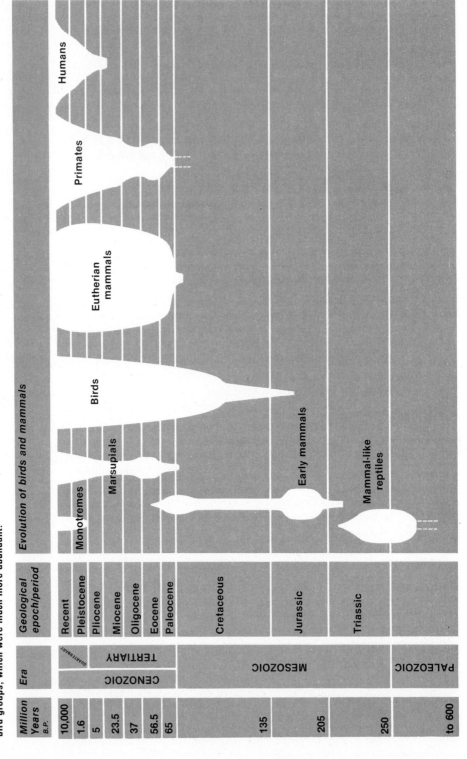

Fossils are the inorganic remains of once-living animals. Fossilization is a process that occurs largely through chemical substitution or change whereby a bone or tooth reaches a state of equilibrium with its environment and no further disintegration occurs. Because fossilization is relatively rare, the fossil record does not contain representatives of all animal species that once lived; it is estimated that we have found representative bones and teeth of less than 1 percent of all the mammals that roamed the earth during the Cenozoic era. After an animal dies, destruction of the body is usually very rapid, and unless the carcass falls into a deposit that quickly covers it and thus removes it from destructive agents such as scavengers and insects, nothing will be left to fossilize. Streams and lakes are good places for fossilization to occur, because an animal falling into the water can be covered with sediment and the bones and teeth thus preserved. Because soft tissue parts are only very rarely preserved, the work of reconstructing the biological history of the primates is overwhelmingly a matter of understanding the significance of bones and (the much more commonly found) teeth. The task is made more difficult because it is unusual to find the complete skeletons of extinct animals and rarer still to find two or more complete skeletons of animals of the same species. Thus reconstructing the primate past involves the minute examination of fragmentary and incomplete fossil bones and teeth. The study of what happens to any animal bone from the time an animal dies to its eventual deposition and fossilization has contributed a great deal of information about the environment the animal lived in (or rather died in) and its possible adaptation. This study, known as taphonomy, is more fully discussed in Chapter 8.

Several kinds of analysis can be applied to fossil remains. Initially, we examine and describe the form of the fossil and compare this description with similar structures in other fossil bones and in living animals. Our comparisons have two important aims at this level. One goal is to relate the fossil remains to other known fossil samples and to living animals to reconstruct the evolutionary relationships of these forms and, in conjunction with comparative anatomical studies and the various molecular techniques discussed in Chapter 5, to determine the biological history of living animal groups. The other aim is to use the structural description of the fossils in a comparison with living animals, when the association between structure and function is known, to draw inferences about the ways biological structures in extinct animals functioned. We can use this extremely important information as a base for the next level of analysis, reconstructing patterns of behavior.

Successful behavior is the key to successful adaptation. We arrive at behavioral inferences about fossil remains by studying and understanding the bones' functions when they were parts of living animals. If, in a fossil-bearing geologic deposit, we find the lower limb bones of a primate, our preliminary examination will be aimed at the structure of the bones, their shape, where the muscles were attached, and their nerve and

**Determining Structure
and Function**

blood supplies. We compare the fossil bones with equivalent bones in living animals, whose function we know. We may learn from these comparisons how the bones worked in the extinct animal.

Our examination will also give us an idea of which other living or extinct animals possessed bones that are most like the fossil limb bones. Except in the unusual circumstance in which two unrelated animals evolve similar structures as a response to adapting to similar environmental needs (a pattern termed by paleontologists a *convergence*), similar structures in two animals imply evolutionary relationships; the more specific the structural similarity, the closer the relationship. Using the cladistic methods described in Chapter 5, making comparisons such as these permits us to construct an evolutionary tree indicating ancestor/descendant relationships. If the fossil limb bones seem to be those of a higher primate and to have much in common with those of the modern apes and humans, we can relate them evolutionarily to these modern hominoids and use them in the comparative anatomical studies. On the level of comparative anatomy, we may thus learn something about the evolutionary relationships of the fossil bones and, using their close living relatives as a comparison, how they worked in the living animal.

Reconstructing Behavior

Reconstructing behavior is the next step in our analysis. If the fossil limb bones come from a hominoid and resemble the lower-limb skeleton of modern humans, we may infer from our functional analysis that this form moved much as we do: as an erect biped, fully supported by the rear limbs, using only the legs in locomotion, with the hands free for other functions. Our behavioral studies will focus on the implications of this locomotor pattern for the successful adaptation of the living forms, as part of a population, in the particular environment in which it lived. A bipedal animal has to be mainly terrestrial, because this kind of movement would not be very adaptive in the trees. Does the geologic evidence from the deposit in which the fossils were found tell us anything about the environment in which these animals lived? Were tools or other evidence of complex behavior found in the deposit? Answers to these questions help us decide if functional and behavioral analyses are correct. If the limb bones belonged to a bipedal hominoid, what do they imply about the adaptation of the species?

Many primates, such as baboons, chimpanzees, and gorillas, have successfully adapted to life on the ground. But these are not bipedal animals, and the fact that our hominoid specimen was bipedal raises significant questions about the importance of this locomotor pattern. Evolutionary selection must have led to its development; one possible explanation (although not the only one) is that the hands were freed for fashioning and using implements. Chimpanzees make and use tools, yet they are not bipedal. Modern humans make and use tools, and this behavior has assumed crucial importance among the hominines.

Current fossil evidence indicates that hominines were bipedal 4 million years ago, but stone tools begin to show up at about 2.5 million years ago. Perhaps hominines used bone, wood, or other perishable substances for tools before they used stone. There may be other, more appropriate explanations for the origin of bipedalism; perhaps the hands were used for transporting food or carrying helpless infants over long distances. Still other explanations can be advanced. But the evidence that hominines evolved bipedalism early in their history provides the starting point for reconstructing their adaptation and behavior.

In the end, the important questions from this analysis are those concerned with how extinct animals realized, through natural selection, a long-term adaptation to their environment. We can answer these questions only by understanding how the animals' anatomy provided a basis for adaptive behavior.

Comparisons of extinct animals with living ones are difficult when few closely related forms are still with us. In these cases we need complete skeletons to understand the total morphological pattern and to reach correct conclusions. Reconstructions can be wildly inaccurate if they are based on only a scrap of information about an extinct form of life. One interesting example of this problem occurred in the nineteenth-century studies of the dinosaurs.

In 1822, Gideon Mantell, an English physician, discovered some bones and teeth of a fossil reptile in the Tilgate Forest. An amateur naturalist, Mantell took his specimens to the Royal College of Surgeons in London to compare them with the collections of living reptile bones. The teeth were remarkably like those of the living iguana, a small, quadrupedal lizard native to the Americas. Their only difference was in size; the fossil teeth were much larger. Nevertheless, Mantell felt justified in using the iguana in his studies. He coined the name *Iguanodon* for his fossil reptile (*iguana = lizard; don = tooth*), and he modeled his reconstruction of the skeleton on the iguana (Figure 7.1). Today we know that his analysis of the skeletal system was fundamentally incorrect. *Iguanodon* was a bipedal reptile, like many other Mesozoic reptiles (Figure 7.2); Mantell treated *Iguanodon* as a quadrupedal animal, however, following the comparisons he had drawn with the living animal.

Problems in Fossil Analysis

FIGURE 7.1. Mantell's reconstruction of *Iguanodon*. The bone on the tip of the nose was placed incorrectly in this reconstruction and is actually that of the clawlike thumb.

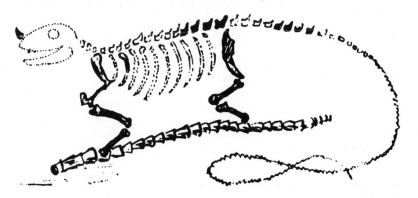

FIGURE 7.2
Modern reconstruction of
***Iguanodon* as a bipedal**
dinosaur (drawn by
Margaret Matthew
Colbert).

Richard Owen, one of Britain's most famous anatomists and paleontologists, introduced the word *Dinosauria* in 1841. No complete skeletons of dinosaurs were found until the 1870s, in Belgian coal deposits. Working many years earlier, Mantell had no clear idea of what a dinosaur was, and he did not know that bipedal reptiles had been commonplace for more than 150 million years. Comparative anatomy has come a long way since the early nineteenth century, making mistakes like Mantell's very unlikely today. Still, through almost the whole primate fossil record, we have only scattered fragments of fossils and few complete skeletons from one individual. The implication is clear: Until we have adequate samples of primate fossil bones on which to base our investigations, many conclusions about earlier primate anatomy and adaptations must remain tentative. Fragmentary evidence also leads to alternative hypotheses in the reconstruction of primate and especially hominine biological history, as will be apparent in the discussions in this and succeeding chapters.

The study of primate evolution has achieved important results in sketching the general course taken by the primates. Many details still have to be worked out, however, with little hope of clear-cut answers from the fossil evidence we now have. The discovery of new fossils and the reevaluation of known material may solve many of these problems. Differences of opinion reflect the continuous nature of the study and demonstrate its vitality.

Primate Beginnings

As we saw in Chapter 4, the mammals evolved at some time in the Mesozoic era, probably in the Triassic period, with the more advanced placental group, to which the primates belong, first appearing in the Cretaceous (Table 7.1). Toward the end of this period (70 to 80 million years ago), an animal that has been identified as a primate lived in a place in Montana called Purgatory Hill. The only evidence of its existence is a single, tiny molar tooth. Named *Purgatorius ceratops* (the species named *ceratops* because bones of the horned dinosaur *Triceratops* were found nearby in the deposit), it has been placed in the same genus as a number of Paleocene epoch teeth found at the same site. The Paleocene *Purgatorius* teeth probably did come from a primate, but the one Cretaceous tooth may not have.[1]* At that time, of course, the differentiation so apparent today in mammalian teeth had not been fully developed. We have, then, very early but also very tentative evidence that the primates appeared during the last days of the dinosaurs. Although some disagree, most primate paleontologists would maintain that the primates did evolve then, but better evidence will be needed before we can be sure.

Early Mammals and the Environment

The primates share more biological characteristics with the mammalian order Insectivora, a group that includes the shrews, moles, and hedgehogs, than with any other animals still alive (Figure 7.3). This suggests that the primates evolved from insectivore-like mammal ancestors.

*See pages 619–620 for notes to Chapter 7.

FIGURE 7.3. Two living insectivores, the common mole (left) and the tree shrew (right). It has been suggested that the primates may have evolved from the Mesozoic ancestors of these living, specialized insectivores.

The insectivores are among the earliest placental mammal groups to have evolved. Until relatively recently there was little agreement among primatologists as to whether the primates sprang from a single ancestral animal or from different ancestral species. It is generally agreed now that the primates are a *monophyletic* order; that is, all primates are ultimately related to a single ancestral species. The numerous primitive vertebrate anatomical features, like the collarbone (*clavicle*), found in all primates but lost in most other later-evolving mammal groups, also suggest that the primates appeared early in mammal evolution.

What was the environment like when these early placental mammals were evolving? In the plant kingdom, the deciduous trees, the flowering plants, and the grasses, all members of the last major vegetative class to evolve (the *angiosperms*), began to expand in number and distribution during the Cretaceous; this had a dramatic effect on the earth's ecological systems. It was during the Cretaceous that the familiar forest, bush, and grassland habitats started to predominate, and the basis was developed for the establishment of the modern food chain, with its dependence on the sun for energy to produce enough angiosperm plants to support a wide array of mammalian, bird, and insect herbivores, which were in turn preyed upon by carnivores.

During the Cretaceous era the continental land masses were arranged somewhat differently than they are today (Figure 4.2d), and they were also apparently far to the south. Because of the northward drift of the continents, the climate changed and temperatures gradually declined during the Cenozoic. During the Paleocene and the early Eocene epochs, for example, tropical forests were widespread in the western United States—in Wyoming, Colorado, Utah, and the Dakotas—with plants like palms and cypress that today are found in the continental United States only in southernmost Florida. The current fossil evidence suggests that the primates probably originated in the Laurasian continental land mass, for the earliest primates have been found only in North America and Europe. Asia was separated from Europe through much of the early Cenozoic by a wide sea, the Turgai Strait.

Early Primate
Adaptations

Lacking fossil evidence of the earliest primates, it has been very difficult for scientists to develop reasonable models of the origin of the primates and the adaptations of the earliest members of the order. One suggestion has been to look at the earliest primates as mammals that were adapting to exploit omnivorous and herbivorous niches. Because they consumed some animal protein and many fruits, berries, leaves, buds, and flowers, the easiest place for them to live was in the trees, where the food was. To exploit these food resources, the primates evolved as arboreal animals.[2] Many Mesozoic mammals seem to have evolved to fill an arboreal, nocturnal, insect-eating niche, and there have been proposals to consider the earliest primates as being adapted to this niche as well.

Matt Cartmill argues that the earliest primates shared a niche with many of the other early mammals, who were also eating insects. With the development of the angiosperms, the number of adaptive niches open to insects would have increased enormously and their numbers risen dramatically. According to Cartmill, many of the primates' biological features, such as manipulative hands and better vision, evolved to provide the earliest primates with the adaptive equipment for becoming efficient nocturnal insect predators; many of the early primate fossils possess teeth with the same sharp cusps as the insectivores'. The primates probably became at least partly arboreal to reach the many insects living on the fruit and flowers of trees and shrubs.[3]

These proposed explanations for the early primates' evolution as arboreal animals, which are educated guesses, appear reasonable and in accord with evolutionary processes. In 1916 the British anatomist Frederick Wood-Jones suggested in his book, *Arboreal Man,* that the modern primates look the way they do because very early in their evolution many became tree dwellers. Wood-Jones called this the *arboreal adaptation.* Many modern primatologists continue to believe that numerous characteristic features of the primates, especially those used by Le Gros Clark in his list of trends (pages 150–154), evolved as a part of an arboreal adaptation.

Trends in
Primate Evolution

An animal that lives in trees, a three-dimensional environment, needs to perceive depth (Figure 7.4). An arboreal creature not only has to move in one plane, like a terrestrial animal, but also has to be aware of the planes above and below. In the course of their evolution, primates thus developed *stereoscopic vision,* or depth perception, by a rotation of their eye orbits from the sides to the front of the skull (Figure 7.5). Safe movement in the trees also calls for acute perception of shades and color, which is probably important as well for recognizing food; many primates are thus equipped with color vision. The abundance of open space in the trees would disperse smells quickly; smell therefore became less important as the primates evolved.

FIGURE 7.4
The arboreal habitat of the howler monkey provides a good illustration of the complex environment through which a tree-dwelling animal, like a primate, must successfully move.

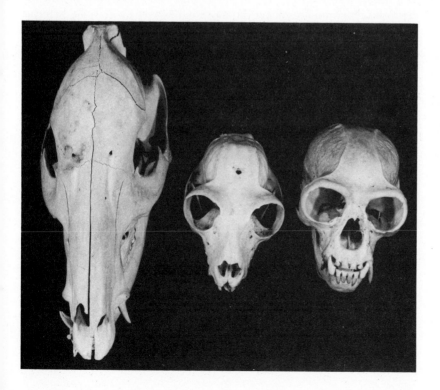

FIGURE 7.5
From the left, the skulls of a mammal (a pig), a modern prosimian (an indriid), and a higher primate (a gibbon). Note the position of the orbits on the side of the skull in the pig and their placement in the two primates. The rotation of the orbits in primate evolution has resulted in the development of depth-perceiving vision.

The system of locomotion must be specially developed, because moving in the trees forces an animal to traverse supports of many different shapes. One branch that has to be grasped may be very small in diameter; another's surface may be as broad and flat as a path on the ground. The flexibility of the locomotor system that this environment demands seems to have been well satisfied by the primates' retention of the primitive vertebrate limb pattern with, in the fore- and hindlimbs, the single upper limb bone, two lower limb bones, the wrist or ankle complex, and the five-digit hand and foot. Most living orders of mammals are thoroughly specialized in their niches and have lost this pattern; the horse, for example, in adapting to life in a terrestrial environment, has evolved a limb pattern with only one of the two lower limb bones and only one of the five digits; the remaining toe is now expanded for use in body support and movement (Figure 7.6).

The primates have kept the general vertebrate pattern of two bones in the lower part of the limb because these elements enable the wrists and ankles to rotate. The outside bone rotates around the fixed inner bone and thus permits the palms of the hand and soles of the feet of primates to be mobile enough to adjust to a wide variety of tree branches (Figure 7.7).

Most primates have a high degree of finger *opposability*, or the ability to touch with the thumb the tip of each of the other fingers. Some primates do without opposable thumbs because they have a hand and foot mobile enough to grasp supports in the trees. The New World spider monkey has no thumb yet can move in the trees by grasping branches between its fingertips and palms; it also has a prehensile tail.

Most of the nonhuman primates, including the apes and the monkeys, are very agile in moving through the trees. They do fall, though, much more often than we might think, hurting and sometimes even killing themselves. A number of gibbons were collected in Sumatra for examination; 30 percent of these apes had long bones that had previously broken and healed.

Locomotion in an arboreal environment requires not only a mobile limb system capable of grasping but also coordination between the limb system and the eyes. For this and perhaps other reasons, the brains of primates, living and extinct, have become much larger in proportion to body size. This enlargement affected many areas of the brain, especially the cerebral cortex and those areas of the cortex that are involved with motor control of the limbs and with vision. In contrast, those areas of the brain devoted to the sense of smell (olfaction) began to decrease in size.

We have described these aspects of primate biology as a consequence of a life in the trees because most primatologists believe that the arboreal adaptation has exerted the greatest adaptive pressure on the evolution of these primate traits. This is not, however, an opinion held by all who study the evolution of the primates. Cartmill, for example, argues that the patterns in the vision and locomotor systems developed as

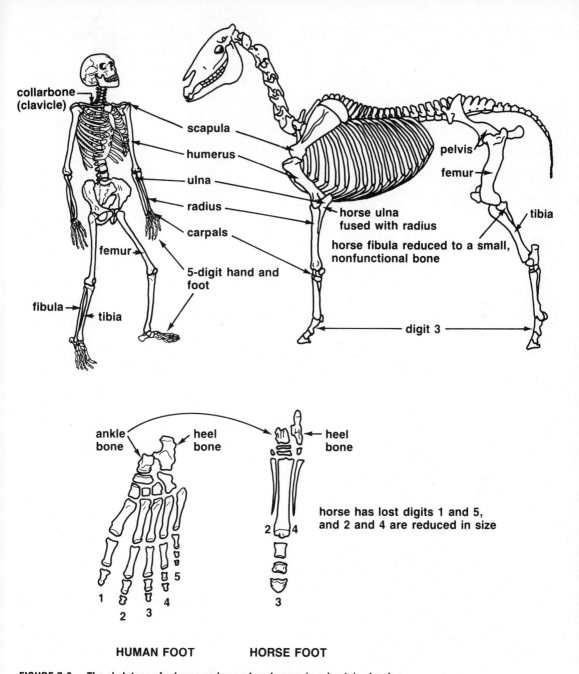

collarbone (clavicle)

scapula

humerus

ulna

radius

carpals

5-digit hand and foot

femur

fibula
tibia

pelvis

femur

tibia

horse ulna fused with radius

horse fibula reduced to a small, nonfunctional bone

digit 3

ankle bone

heel bone

heel bone

horse has lost digits 1 and 5, and 2 and 4 are reduced in size

1 2 3 4 5

2 4

3

HUMAN FOOT   HORSE FOOT

FIGURE 7.6.   The skeletons of a horse and a modern human (a primate), showing the specialized nature of the horse's limbs, which is a response to the needs of the animal in its terrestrial, open-country adaptation. Note that one of the major changes in the limbs of the horse, as in many other ground-dwelling mammals, is the loss of one or more of the digits and the lengthening and modification of the lower parts of the limb system. The human skeleton, like those of all primates, has retained most of the primitive elements of the earliest vertebrates (compare with Figure 4.5), such as all five digits and the collarbone.

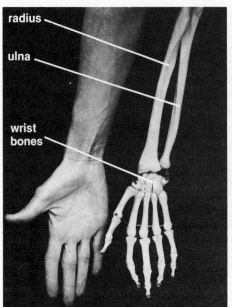
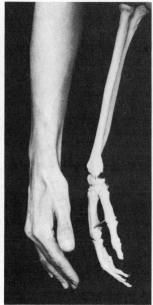
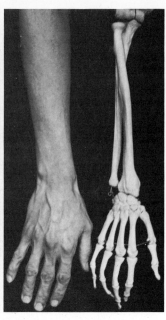

radius

ulna

wrist
bones

FIGURE 7.7. Wrist rotation in humans and apes. In the illustration on the left the two bones of the forearm, the radius and the ulna, are positioned side by side. Note that as the wrist rotates, it is the outside bone, the radius, that rotates around the fixed inner bone, the ulna. In humans and the large-bodied apes, the bones of the wrist are attached primarily to the radius, thus permitting a much greater degree of wrist mobility than in other primates, such as monkeys, where the ulna and radius are involved in the wrist attachment. See Figure 7.13 for a comparison of monkey and ape wrist joints.

a result of the need in early primates to see and grasp insect prey effectively. Regardless of the reasons for their initial evolution, modern primates do not all inhabit arboreal niches, nor, it is certain, were all extinct primates arboreal. As an order, they may have evolved as arboreal animals, but many primates subsequently adapted to life on the ground and developed specialized biological features of those niches. One of the best examples is humans and the evolution of bipedalism.

It is important to keep in mind that the evolution of these traits is brought about by successful behavior in a feedback relationship between behavior and morphology (biological features). *Morphological variability* in any population leaves some animals better able to perform some of their behaviors. An example is the group of Sumatran gibbons that revealed a significant percentage of healed broken bones. This suggests that in using their characteristic locomotion, an under-the-branch swing called brachiation, some gibbons have the physical equipment to make the swing successfully more often than others; they will fall less frequently. Their genetic variation will remain in the population; natural selection preserves the morphological patterns that are responsible for the successful behavior. The range of variation eventually shifts toward the more successful pattern. This shift in turn feeds back to behavior as part of the range of morphological variability in the population, which is reflected in the behavior patterns, and so on. In other words, the changes to be observed in the evolution of the primates, including humans, are founded in the mechanisms of evolution.

Early Primates

Apart from the single *Purgatorius* tooth from the Cretaceous period, the earliest evidence of animals that are recognized as primates comes from the Paleocene epoch, 60–65 million years ago. Classified into more than a dozen species and many genera found at sites in Europe and western North America, these animals did not look like modern primates; they had claws; their eye orbits were on the sides of their skulls and were not protected with a bony bar as in later primates; and they had long snouts that indicate a continued reliance on the sense of smell (Figure 7.8). Because of these differences, these Paleocene animals have been placed in their own major category, the *Plesiadapiformes,* of equal status with the prosimians and anthropoids in the Primate order (pages 157–158). Some primatologists, like Cartmill and R.D.E. MacPhee, have suggested that the Plesiadapiformes have a number of molar tooth similarities with the undoubted primates of the Eocene, but not enough additional features to assign these animals unambiguously to the primates.[4] For these scientists, the first true primates appear in the Eocene. Others identify the Plesiadapiformes as primates because they may possess the characteristic pattern of arteries in the inner ear (pages 150–153) that is currently used by many to define a primate. Further, they were adapted to an arboreal environment. A study of the Paleocene mammal *Plesiadapis* (from whose name the larger taxonomic group derives) by F. S. Szalay and R. L. Decker shows that modifications in the limbs of these animals permitted them to turn their wrists and ankles toward each other so that they could climb a tree. Other Paleocene mammals lack this development; their limbs are directed downward in the posture of a typical four-legged terrestrial animal.[5]

FIGURE 7.8. The skulls (partially restored) of the Paleocene fossil *Plesiadapis* and the Eocene primate *Adapis* (one-half actual size). Although their names suggest a close evolutionary relationship, there is no evidence that the earlier *Plesiadapis* evolved into *Adapis*. Note in the *Plesiadapis* skull the lack of the postorbital bar and the rather rodentlike teeth. *Adapis* is much more primatelike and has many features similar to those of living prosimians.

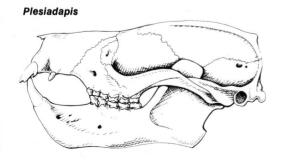

Plesiadapis

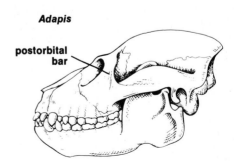

Adapis

postorbital bar

The Plesiadapiformes survived into the early part of the succeeding Eocene. By this time, animals with features similar to those of living prosimians had appeared. No fossils document an evolutionary origin of these prosimianlike animals in the plesiadapiform group, so their ancestral stock remains unknown. Like the Paleocene forms, fossil primate remains from the Eocene turn up in North America and Europe; by late Eocene times, primates are also known from Asia. In many geologic strata they are exceedingly common. In this early Tertiary time the primates appeared in the greatest number of forms. Many Eocene geologic formations in the western United States can be identified by the kinds of primates found in them. Fossil evidence of more than one hundred species of Eocene primates have been identified. No wonder the paleoanthropologist W. W. Howells once referred to the Eocene as "the Golden Age of the Prosimians."[6] Morphologically, primate evolution in the Eocene reveals important developments: Orbits rotate forward to provide the basis for depth perception (see Figure 7.5); the postorbital bar (a piece of bone separating the orbit from the back of the skull) is completed (Figure 7.8); a bony layer begins filling in the back of the orbit; the snout is smaller, possibly reflecting a decreased emphasis on the sense of smell; the dentition has many features found in living prosimians; and claws are replaced by nails. Like modern prosimians, many seem to have been hoppers and leapers. E. L. Simons, a primatologist who accepts the Plesiadapiformes as primates, describes the Eocene as the time when "primates of modern aspect" appear,[7] meaning those with close morphological similarity to living prosimians (Figure 7.9).

Toward the middle and late Eocene, climatic and biological conditions were changing, and the optimal environment for these early primates was disappearing. In the early Eocene and early part of the middle Eocene, primates are most common in geologic formations in Utah, Colorado, the Dakotas, and Wyoming. In late Eocene times the primates disappeared from these areas and were limited to southern parts of North America. Changes in climate caused at least part of this shift in primate distribution. Colorado, Utah, and the Dakotas during the early and middle Eocene were probably rather congenial to prosimian survival with their warm, damp environment. In the late Eocene, as North America drifted northward, the climate became cooler and drier, destroying the primates' best niches. Then, too, other mammals were evolving. The rodents, for example, would have been highly competitive for many primate niches. It seems reasonable that these events in the Eocene also had an important bearing on the adaptation and distribution of the living prosimians, which, apart from the Malagasy primates, are found today only in very specialized, arboreal niches. The modern prosimians—lorises, galagos, lemurs, and tarsiers—all live in the Old World; none survived in the New World. Living prosimians are directly related to the ancestral prosimians of the Eocene, but they are not the same species that lived at that time.

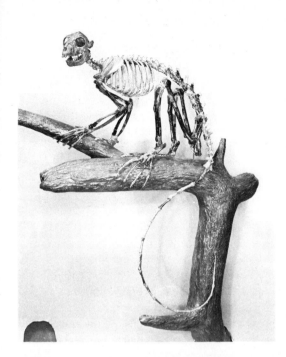

FIGURE 7.9. Skeleton (left) and flesh reconstruction (right) of an Eocene prosimian. Eocene prosimians, like their living descendants, probably exploited a wide range of food sources, including fruit, nectar, gum, and other vegetable foods as well as insects, birds, birds' eggs, and perhaps other smaller vertebrates.

The lorises, the galagos, and the tarsiers that live today in East Asia and Africa are completely arboreal and nocturnal. It is significant that no Old World monkeys are nocturnal. Probably there were primates inhabiting every niche during the Eocene—arboreal, terrestrial, nocturnal, and diurnal—but the only prosimians who survived were the very specialized few who were both nocturnal and arboreal. Their descendants are the living prosimians. The prosimians on the island of Madagascar in the southern Indian Ocean are an exception (see Table 5.3). The island has been separated from mainland Africa since the Mesozoic. Sometime during the Tertiary, the ancestors of the aye-aye, the lemurs, the indriids, and the cheirogaleids must have drifted from Africa across the Mozambique channel to Madagascar on large clumps of riverbank that had broken off and moved down river during the rainy season (zoologically, this pattern is known as *rafting*).

Until the arrival of humans, with our domesticated animals (including rats!), about a thousand years ago, the prosimians on Madagascar were among the only mammals. The diversity of their adaptations and behavior may offer a picture of the primate world before the late Eocene: prosimians living in a variety of adaptive niches, on the ground and in the trees, active at night and during the day.[8]

The Evolution of the Higher Primates

By late Eocene times, signs of primates are few and far between. Some fragmentary evidence suggests that members of the suborder Anthropoidea—the higher primates, including monkeys, apes, and humans—may have begun their evolution at this point. This evidence consists of several fragmentary jaws from late Eocene deposits in Burma. Placed in the genus *Amphipithecus,* these jaw fragments are simply too scanty to make any but the most preliminary identifications, and we are therefore in the dark about the reasons for the evolutionary appearance of the higher primates, or even which Eocene prosimian was the ancestor of the anthropoids.[9]

The climatic changes that shifted the prosimians southward in the latter stages of the Eocene seem to have contributed to the major geographic distinctions found in the higher primates. Until that time the Eurasian continent and the North American continent were connected. Continental drift studies indicate that northeastern North America and the European parts of Eurasia were tied by a bridge of land. Because of the climatic shifts in the late Eocene, probably no primates could live in this cooler, drier northern area, and the faunal connection between the New World and the Old World was broken. Continental drift ultimately completed the break by severing the land bridge. Until the climate changed, very similar primates lived both in Europe and in North America. Several Paleocene and Eocene species are the only primates, besides *Homo sapiens,* known from both the Old and New Worlds. By early in the following geologic period, the Oligocene, there is evidence of a very primitive New World monkey in deposits in Bolivia in South America, and thus the pattern of subsequent separate Old and New World primate evolution was established.

The later Eocene climatic conditions seem to have continued into the Oligocene; primate fossils are completely absent from Europe, and rare in North America. Our knowledge of Old World Oligocene higher primates comes from a fossil-rich area one hundred kilometers outside Cairo, Egypt, called the *Fayum Beds.* There is thus a profound change in the pattern of primate distribution. Early in their evolution, during the Paleocene and Eocene, primates are known only from the Laurasian continents, and this is where the primates probably originated. By the beginning of the Oligocene, however, the focus of primate evolution had shifted southward to the Gondwanaland continents of Africa and South America.

During the Oligocene the Fayum area of North Africa was a lush tropical gallery forest, an ideal environment for arboreal primates. The Fayum primates may very accurately reflect the higher primates' evolution during this time, but keep in mind that this is the only existing fossil evidence of Old World Oligocene primates; this area could also be a "backwater" of primate evolution. Important trends in their evolution may have gone on elsewhere, to places that have as yet given up no evidence.

The Fayum fossils are remains of higher primates related ancestrally to the monkeys, apes, and humans. They are not apes, Old World monkeys, or humans, however, but the primitive ancestors of these living forms, and they are therefore troublesome to characterize taxonomically. Modern apes and monkeys are distinguished by biological features such as the locomotor system and dentition.

The anatomy related to locomotion differs significantly in the monkeys and apes. Old World monkeys of the superfamily Cercopithecoidea (see Table 5.1) are basically quadrupedal in the trees and on the ground. When moving in the trees, they walk on top of the branches, using their grasping hands and feet to hold on, and they jump or leap from branch to branch. On the ground, their palms and soles are flat on the surface. Their skeleton reflects this pattern of movement: The front and back limbs are about equal in length; the rib cage is narrow from side to side, with a relatively small collarbone, or clavicle; and the shoulder blade, or scapula, is on the side of the rib cage, with the shoulder joint itself facing front, or downward, when the animal is in its normal walking position (Figures 7.10 and 5.2). The shoulder joint surface is curved so that the joint can act effectively in quadrupedal movement; this gives monkeys stable but relatively immobile shoulder joints. Old World monkeys have tails, which although not prehensile (only some New World monkeys have prehensile tails), are used for balance in the trees. Old World monkeys also possess ischial callosities, or flattened areas on the buttocks covered by insensitive connective tissue having few nerve or arterial connections. They serve as padding on which the animal can rest or sleep in the trees for long periods without undue discomfort.

The living apes and humans of the superfamily Hominoidea have a much more specialized anatomical system related to locomotion. None of the living hominoids possess tails, and, except for the gibbon, none have an ischial callosity. In all living hominoids, the front limbs and supporting structures have a number of rather distinctive elements. The rib cage is broadened from side to side, which places the shoulder blades on the back of the rib cage, with the shoulder joint facing outward, rather than downward as in monkeys. The collarbone is larger and more strongly developed in the hominoids. The shoulder joint in hominoids is flatter, with less bony contact between the shoulder blade and the ball of the upper arm bone, resulting in a much more mobile but less stable joint. Ape front limbs tend to be longer than the rear limbs, and the hands are equipped with a thumb about human length but with fingers that are very long in proportion to the thumb (Figure 7.11). These anatomical features may have evolved as part of an adaptation in the ancestors of the apes for using the front limbs to hang suspended from underneath branches (Figure 7.12), or they may have developed as part of an adaptation for swiftly climbing vertical tree limbs. Either of these changes would require both a mobile shoulder joint and reinforcement

Locomotion

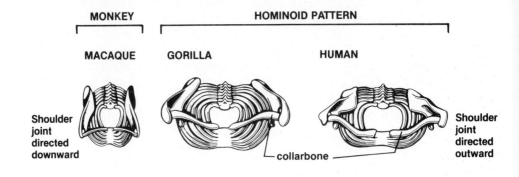

MONKEY

HOMINOID PATTERN

MACAQUE GORILLA HUMAN

Shoulder joint directed downward

collarbone

Shoulder joint directed outward

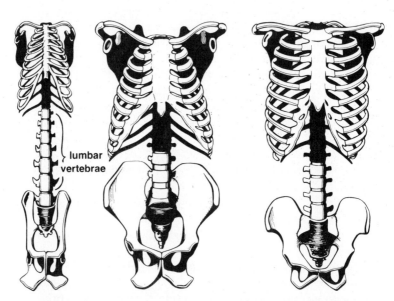

lumbar vertebrae

FIGURE 7.10.   Three major differences in skeletal structure among monkeys, gorillas, and humans are in the shoulder, the lumbar region of the spine, and the pelvis. The shoulder blades of a monkey (here a macaque) are almost parallel to each other on opposite sides of its rib cage, as seen from the drawing of the skeleton (top) as viewed from above. The shoulder blades of a human are on the upper back, and a gorilla's extend up with a large bony collar. Note the enlargement of the clavicle (collarbone) in the gorilla and human skeletons. The transversely enlarged (broad) chest in both humans and gorillas, associated with the large collarbone, is part of the anatomical equipment of an animal with a highly mobile shoulder. Monkeys usually have six or seven lumbar vertebrae (ones with no ribs attached), most apes have three, and humans normally have five. The monkey's tilted pelvis provides an anchor for the leg muscles of the quadrupedal animal. The gorilla pelvis gives anchorage for the muscles that support the animal in its normal quadrupedal knuckle-walking posture. The human pelvis not only supports the upper part of the body but also gives a base for strong walking muscles.

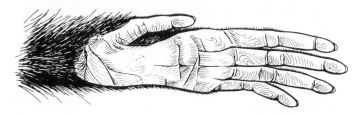

FIGURE 7.11. A gibbon's hand. Notice the elongation of the fingers in proportion to the thumb.

from an enlarged collarbone. Additional strengthening comes from the enlarged hominoid breastbone, or sternum, and additional limb mobility comes from the arrangement of bones in the wrist joint (Figure 7.13).

It has been suggested that this *suspensory hanging or climbing* adaptation may have evolved to permit these hominoid primates to exploit food items efficiently. An animal hanging from a branch by one hand and able to use its grasping feet to provide additional support from other branches would be better able to reach fruit and other foods growing at the ends of branches than a monkey that would have to move quadrupedally along the top of an increasingly thinner and unstable branch to reach the same foods. Or, these features may have evolved to permit more efficient climbing, especially up vertical branches. This anatomical specialization has led to the development in the lesser apes, the gibbon and siamang, of brachiation, an under-the-branch, swinging locomotion (Figure 7.12).

FIGURE 7.12. A brachiating gibbon and a gibbon skeleton. Compare with Figure 5.2. Note the difference in limb proportion, especially the length of the front limbs.

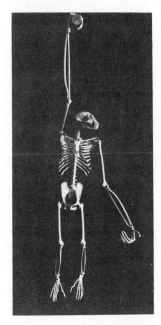

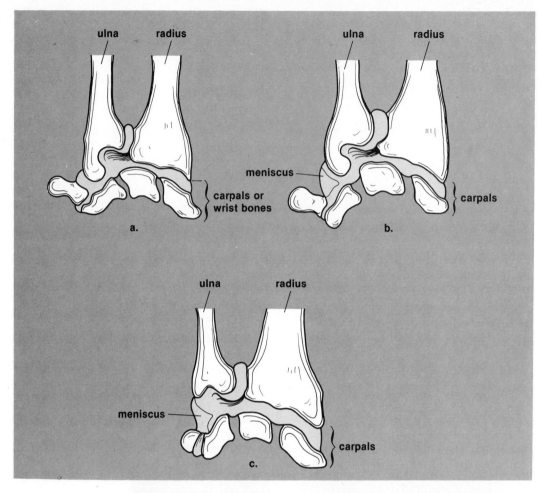

FIGURE 7.13. The wrist joint of (a) *Cercopithecus* (a quadrupedal Old World monkey), (b) a chimpanzee (a knuckle-walker), and (c) a modern human. The suspensory hanging or climbing adaptation of the ancestors of the apes and humans can be seen in certain anatomical features of the wrist joint. In the chimp and human, a disc of cartilage, a meniscus, lies between the ulna (the inside bone of the lower arm) and the carpal or wrist bones. This disc makes for less bone-to-bone contact in the joint and therefore allows a greater degree of rotary movement in the wrist. Figure 7.7 illustrates the pattern of wrist rotation and shows why apes and humans have greater wrist mobility than monkeys, whose wrists, lacking a meniscus, are more restricted in movement.

The great apes—the gorilla, chimpanzee, and orang—are not brachiators, although occasionally younger animals do swing in the trees. Chimpanzees and gorillas spend most of their time on the ground, where they move by knuckle-walking, in which their weight is supported on the knuckles, not the palms of their hands (see Figure 6.19). A number of additional features have evolved in the hands of the knuckle-walkers to permit this kind of locomotion (Figure 7.14).

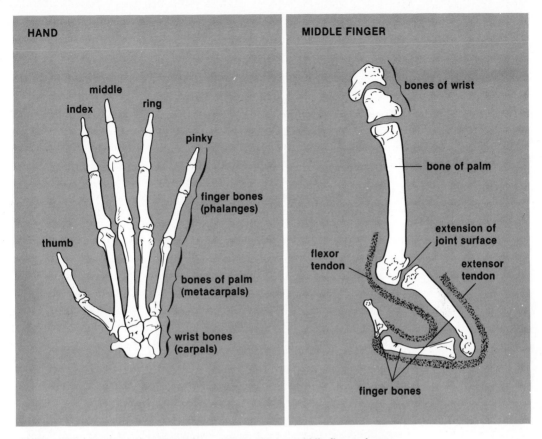

HAND

middle
index
ring
pinky
finger bones
(phalanges)
thumb
bones of palm
(metacarpals)
wrist bones
(carpals)

MIDDLE FINGER

bones of wrist
bone of palm
extension of
joint surface
flexor
tendon
extensor
tendon
finger bones

FIGURE 7.14. The hand of a chimpanzee, with the third or middle finger shown enlarged from the side. Note the backward extension of the joint surface of the end of the palm bone (metacarpal), which permits the finger bones to be bent back considerably farther than is possible in modern humans (try it yourself). This allows the chimpanzee to place its fingers in the typical knuckle-walking posture (see Figure 6.19). The flexor tendons attach to the muscles that close the hand (making a fist), while the extensor tendons attach to muscles that open the hand. Because of the stresses involved in maintaining the hand bones in the knuckle-walking position, the flexor muscles in chimpanzees are prominently developed.

Because many of the anatomical features in the shoulder and front limbs of the apes are also found in modern humans, it is clear that our ancestors shared this suspensory or climbing adaptation. The question is still open as to whether the ancestors of the living great apes and humans were once brachiators like the gibbons, or whether this locomotor behavior is limited to the lesser apes and their ancestors. Fossils do not provide clear evidence either way, but it is likely that it would have been difficult for large-bodied apes like gorillas and orangs to be efficient brachiators. Despite the uncertainties involving a common brachiating ancestor, the significant differences in the anatomy of the monkeys and the apes provide an important basis for distinguishing the two groups in the fossil record.

Dentition   Another major difference between the monkeys and hominoids is their dentition. Mammals' teeth are specialized for several functions, and the number of their teeth depends on the kind of adaptation. We think that the original dental formula for early mammals was 3.1.5.3, or three incisors, one canine, five premolars, and three molars, totaling forty-eight teeth. Most prosimians have a dental formula of 2.1.3.3, as do New World monkeys of the family Cebidae. The New World marmoset family has a formula of 2.1.3.2. Among the higher primates, Old World monkeys, apes, and humans have lost one more premolar, making their formula 2.1.2.3. The molar cusp patterns of Old World monkeys are distinctly different from those of apes and humans (Figure 7.15). The occlusal, or working, surface of an Old World monkey molar is divided roughly into two halves with a deep groove between them. Each part of the tooth has two high cusps with a transverse ridge between them. Each half, with the two cusps, is called a *loph,* giving the pattern its name: *bilophodont* (two-loph tooth). Dentition with bilophodont molars is characteristic of the upper and lower molars of all the Old World monkeys.

The hominoids (apes and humans) have more complicated molar patterns. The upper molars have four cusps, like those of the Old World monkeys, but in a different arrangement. Instead of two sets of two cusps, with transverse ridges connecting them, the cusps on hominoid upper molars have an oblique ridge between the inside front cusp and the back outside one; no deep groove separates front and back halves of the tooth.

Unlike Old World monkeys, whose lower molars are the same as the upper teeth, hominoids have lower molars with different configurations. The basic pattern in apes and humans is five cusps (Figure 7.15).

When we view a lower molar tooth from the tongue side outward, the arrangement of grooves separating the cusps looks like a Y. These molars have five cusps, which is known as the *Y-5 pattern*. This distinctive Y-5 pattern shows up in all living and extinct ape lower molars. But in humans, although the first lower molars usually follow this configuration, evolutionary selection has reduced the size of the second and third molars. This decrease has been accomplished by losing one cusp, so that modern human back molars usually have four cusps, arranged in a simple plus (+) groove pattern.

A number of studies have attempted to provide a functional interpretation of the differences between the molar teeth of monkeys and apes, thus far with only limited success. One suggestion, which appears reasonable, is that the bilophodont molars are a specialized development that evolved to permit the monkeys to chop various kinds of cellulose-based leaves, grasses, and other vegetation into small pieces more effectively and therefore to increase the ability of these animals to exploit herbivorous dietary niches.[10] It is apparent that the hominoid upper and lower molars represent a more generalized mammalian pattern, and it is likely that bilophodont molars evolved from a pattern like that of the hominoids.

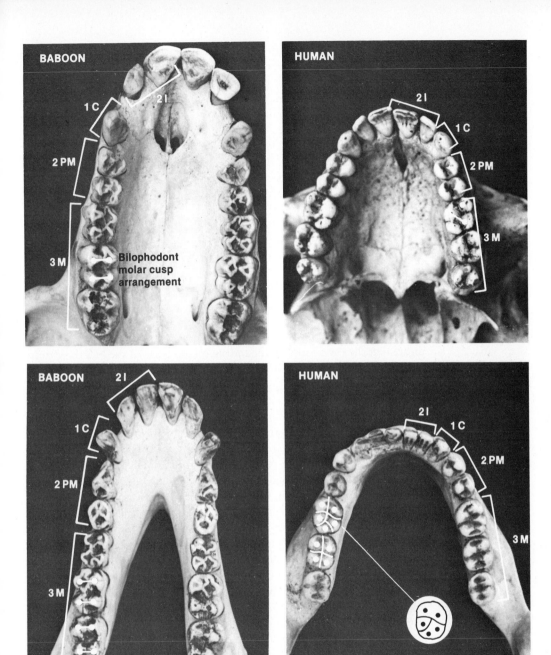

FIGURE 7.15. Upper and lower jaws of a female baboon and a modern human, showing the bilophodont molars found on the upper and lower jaws of Old World monkeys and the molar patterns found in the hominoids: the apes and humans. Note, too, the relatively small size of the canine teeth in the female baboon compared to the much larger canine teeth of the male (Figure 6.9). Human canine teeth are not enlarged, and the wear on these teeth is at the tips rather than along the back edges. The first two lower jaw molars of the baboon possess the standard bilophodont pattern, but the third has an additional (fifth) cusp in the back, which is sometimes found in the larger Old World monkeys.

Primates of the Oligocene

These two major differences in the locomotor system and in the dentition are the basic features distinguishing Old World monkeys and hominoids. The Oligocene fossils discovered in the Fayum Beds possess features that identify them as anthropoid primates, and several of them possess molar patterns similar to those of the hominoids, but they apparently had none of the distinctive locomotor characteristics of the ape superfamily (the Hominoidea).

Although the Fayum Beds have been searched for fossils since early in the century, over the past thirty years Elwyn Simons and his associates have discovered a large number of fossil bones of the skeleton, skull, and jaws along with lots of teeth in this area. These fossils have been placed in at least three genera, all higher primates, but differing in dental and jaw details. Early work on the Fayum fossils had led to the suggestion that these primates represented the direct ancestors of specific living Old World monkeys and apes. The new fossil discoveries have modified this view, and now point to these North African fossils as primitive higher primates who lived before the lines leading to specific monkeys and apes had separated.[11]

The number and variety of higher primates at the Fayum Beds indicate that they were important and successful parts of the North African fauna in the Oligocene. Of all these animals we have found more parts of *Aegyptopithecus,* including skulls, skeletal parts, and numerous jaws and teeth. *Aegytopithecus*'s skull is that of a higher primate, but the snout is more pronounced than in most living anthropoids, suggesting that smell was still important (Figure 7.16). From impressions left on the inside of the brain case, it appears that the sense of smell was emphasized. The eye orbits are filled in with bone like those of later higher primates, but their size is intermediate between the large orbits of nocturnal primates and the smaller ones of daylight-active animals. The dental formula is 2.1.2.3, as in other Old World higher primates, and the upper and lower molars are much like those of the hominoids. The recent discoveries in the Fayum Beds indicate that there was a considerable amount of sexual dimorphism in the canine teeth and perhaps in body size as well.[12] Sexual dimorphism refers to differences in the size of biological features in the males and females of the same species; in sexually dimorphic primate species, it is always the males who will be larger. Larger size of the canine teeth and perhaps body size, too, suggest that *Aegyptopithecus* lived in social groups, since it is rare for solitary-living primates, like many prosimians, to show any difference in size between males and females. Finally, analysis of the skeletal bones reveals a generalized quadrupedal limb system, lacking any of the suspensory hanging or climbing adaptations of the hominoids; it also had a tail. John Fleagle, who studied the skeletal bones, believes that *Aegyptopithecus*'s bones are most similar to those of the South American howler monkey, although lacking that animal's prehensile tail, and thus indicative of a relatively primitive arboreal primate.[13]

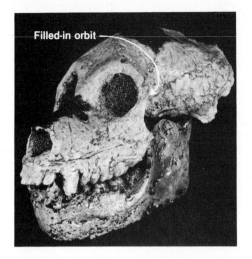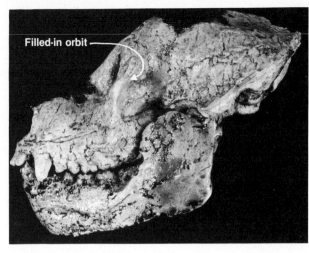

FIGURE 7.16. A partially restored skull of *Aegyptopithecus zeuxis* found in the Fayum Beds. The lower jaw restoration is based on fragments not found with the cranium. The upper incisors are also restorations. *Aegyptopithecus* dates to the Oligocene and is probably ancestral to the apes of the African early Miocene.

The evidence of *Aegyptopithecus,* the most well-known of the North African Oligocene primates, thus tells us that by this time, a social, arboreal higher primate (member of the Anthropoidea) had evolved; whether this early anthropoid was active at night or during the day is not clear from present evidence. The Fayum evidence is representative of primitive higher primates, but none of the Oligocene primates can be identified with living forms, because the lineages leading to living forms were apparently not yet distinct. The evolutionary connections between the Fayum higher primates, like *Aegyptopithecus,* and earlier primates of the Eocene, are unknown. The most reasonable evolutionary connection is that *Aegyptopithecus* evolved into the early Miocene hominoids of Africa.

Miocene Primates

Unlike the Oligocene fossil evidence, which is very limited, fossil primates of the Miocene age are much more abundant and widespread. Fossil evidence of Old World higher primates in the Miocene is known from East Africa, many parts of Europe, the Middle East, China, India, and Pakistan (Figure 7.17). If the Eocene can be called the "Golden Age of Prosimians," the Miocene might be considered the golden age of the hominoids.

We have much Miocene fossil material, several hundred specimens in all—some postcranial (skeletal) bones, some cranial (skull) bones, and a lot of teeth—placed in a number of taxonomic categories.[14] There are fossil teeth possessing bilophodont molars, which indicate that the Old

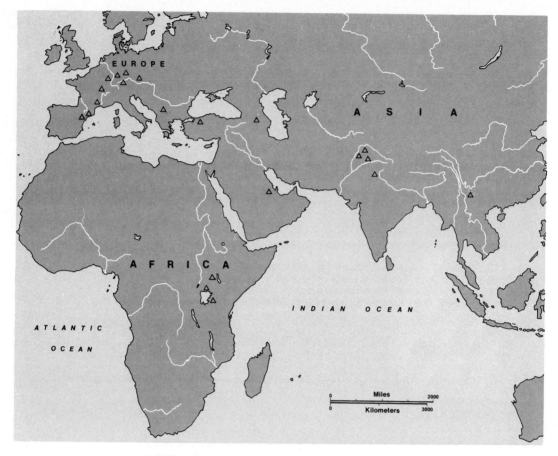

FIGURE 7.17. Fossil bones of Miocene primates have been found in many parts of the Old World, with the first discovered in France in the nineteenth century. The most important and complete collections have come from East Africa, Pakistan, and India.

World monkeys had begun their separate evolutionary history early in the Miocene. All of the other specimens have teeth with the molar pattern first seen in *Aegyptopithecus* and still found in modern apes and humans (see Figure 7.15). There is little evidence, however, of the suspensory hanging or climbing adaptation; primarily, it should be emphasized, because there are so few fossil bones of the skeleton. Studying these collections, paleontologists have come to little agreement about what the fossil evidence means. Comparative biochemistry complicates the issue with evidence of another sort, which does not always agree with the fossil data.

The Miocene is very important for primates: By the end of the period, the human subfamily, the Homininae, had evolved as a distinct lineage, and the major lineages of the modern Old World primates had appeared.

Miocene hominoid fossils have been classified into more than ten genera, based primarily on geographic distribution, dating, size, and general morphology, and, in particular, details of the jaws and dentition. Living hominoids include the large-bodied great apes (chimp, gorilla, and orang) and the small-bodied lesser apes (gibbon and siamang). Miocene hominoid species are also often grouped into large-bodied and small-bodied categories. These characterizations are general descriptive placements and do not imply any particular relationship between the living hominoids and these fossil species. Table 7.2 lists the major large- and small-bodied Miocene genera according to geographic area and time. The earliest material comes from East Africa; later Miocene fossils are more widely distributed. This suggests that the Miocene hominoids had their origins in Africa, presumably evolving from earlier forms such as

TABLE 7.2
Miocene Hominoids, Grouped According to Time and Geographic Area
The small-bodied Miocene hominoids are shown in parentheses.

Millions of Years B.P.	Geological Epoch	East Africa	Europe and Middle East	Asia (China, India, Pakistan)
5	Pliocene			
	Late Miocene			*Sivapithecus* *Gigantopithecus*
10			*(Pliopithecus)* *Sivapithecus* *Dryopithecus*	
	Middle Miocene		*Dryopithecus* *Sivapithecus*	*Sivapithecus*
15		*Kenyapithecus*		
23.5	Early Miocene	*(Limnopithecus)* *(Dendropithecus)* *(Micropithecus)* *Afropithecus* *Turkanapithecus* *Rangwapithecus* *Proconsul*		
	Oligocene			

Aegyptopithecus. A significant geologic event occurred at the beginning of the Miocene. The African continent, which had been independent from Eurasia for much of the Tertiary, collided with Eurasia, forming a closed-ended Mediterranean Sea. Prior to this time, these continents had been separated by a seaway called the Tethys Sea, connecting the Atlantic and Indian Oceans (Figure 7.28). With the early Miocene continental contact between Eurasia and Africa, these hominoids and other African mammals could begin to spread to the Eurasian continent.

The major hominoids of the Miocene now appear to have a long and complicated evolutionary history. First appearing in the early Miocene of East Africa, they later spread to Eurasia; by middle to late Miocene times, they are known from Spain in the west right across Eurasia to South China in the east. Although they appear earliest in Africa, evidence of them virtually disappears from that continent about 14 million years ago. By the end of the Miocene, some 5 million years ago, they totally disappear from the fossil record.

While the fossil evidence is suggestive, it does not answer questions as to when the lines leading to the specific living hominoids diverged, where this occurred, and why this evolution took place. Although recent discoveries have shed light on the Miocene ancestry of the Asian great ape, the orangutan, little or nothing is known of the ancestors of the lesser apes, the gibbon and siamang. The fossil record of the direct line of human evolution, the hominines, is a reasonably rich one, beginning with fossils about 5 million years old (to be described in the next three chapters). The fossil evidence documenting earlier events, however, is virtually unknown, as is the entire fossil history of human's closest living relatives, the African apes—the chimpanzee and gorilla. We will return to these problems and the role comparative genetic and biochemical studies can play in sorting things out after considering the Miocene fossil evidence.

Early Miocene Hominoid Evolution

Proconsul. The first hominoid fossils found in Africa were uncovered by A. T. Hopwood and Louis Leakey in the 1930s and 1940s at Rusinga Island in Lake Victoria. Later finds of similar fossils have been made at a number of sites in western Kenya along the shores of Lake Victoria and in Uganda.

Hopwood, impressed by the resemblances between these African fossils and living apes, coined the name *Proconsul* for them (after Consul, a chimpanzee then performing on the stage in London). A considerable number of *Proconsul* fossil bones have been found, including portions of several skulls (Figures 7.18 and 7.19) and much of the skeleton of a single animal. The age of the East African deposits has been determined by the potassium-argon dating method (K-Ar dating; see Chapter 8), which places them in the early Miocene, some 17 to 21 million years ago, making these the earliest Miocene hominoid fossils.

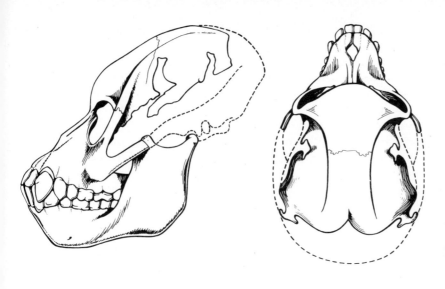

FIGURE 7.18
Side and top views of a reconstructed skull of *Proconsul africanus* (two-thirds actual size).

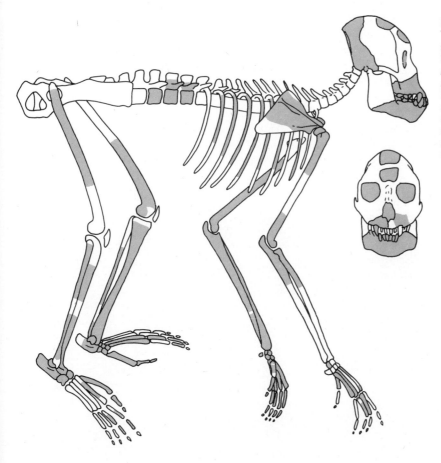

FIGURE 7.19
The reconstructed skeleton of the early Miocene primate, *Proconsul,* from East Africa.
Note the absence of a tail and the generalized skeleton lacking the suspensory hanging or climbing adaptations in the upper trunk.

Examination of the upper and lower molar teeth of *Proconsul* shows the distinctive traits of the hominoids, although they also possess some primitive features found in *Aegyptopithecus*. The skull of *Proconsul* is that of a higher primate, with a brain somewhat smaller and more primitive than that of living nonhuman hominoids, but essentially similar to later forms. Like the bones of *Aegyptopithecus*, *Proconsul*'s skeletal system appears to be that of a generalized, primitive arboreal primate, without a tail and with no adaptations toward suspensory hanging or climbing.[15] The fossil bones and teeth of *Proconsul* have been divided into three species, primarily on the basis of size: a large, a medium, and a small form. Because of the primitive elements in the bones and teeth, it is unlikely that these early Miocene hominoids represent direct lineal ancestors of living apes, and indeed *Proconsul* appears to share as many features with the earlier Oligocene *Aegyptopithecus* as with later Miocene hominoids. It has been suggested that these primitive elements in the skeleton and dentition make it more appropriate to classify *Proconsul* with the higher primates but not to place it more specifically within the hominoid superfamily. The fossil bones of other animals that were found with *Proconsul* suggest that it inhabited a tropical forest environment.

Afropithecus. In 1983, Alan Walker uncovered fragmentary pieces of several hominoid jaws at a locale in Kenya known as *Buluk*. In 1985–86, at a site west of Lake Turkana in northern Kenya known as *Kalodirr*, major portions of a skull, a lower jaw, and many additional fragmentary jaws and teeth were discovered by a team from the National Museums of Kenya (Figure 7.20). These Buluk and Kalodirr fossils have been classified together as *Afropithecus*. Dated to about 16–18 million years B.P., the *Afropithecus* fossils, although still primitive, are in some ways more like living hominoids than is *Proconsul*. With a relatively foreshortened snout and thick layers of enamel on the molar teeth, *Afropithecus* may

FIGURE 7.20. ***Afropithecus*, an early Miocene hominoid from Kenya.**

represent part of the early ancestry of the African apes and humans. We will consider the further implications of *Afropithecus* after describing the other major Miocene hominoid fossils.

Turkanapithecus and Rangwapithecus. *Turkanapithecus* was also discovered at the Kalodirr site with the remains of *Afropithecus.* Known from much of the skull and an assortment of skeletal bones, *Turkanapithecus* has not yet been studied in detail. It is distinct from other living and extinct hominoids, including *Rangwapithecus,* another early Miocene hominoid whose fossil jaws and teeth have been found at sites in western Kenya around the shores of Lake Victoria.

Micropithecus, Limnopithecus, and Dendropithecus. Found at sites in Kenya and Uganda, these small-bodied early Miocene forms are known primarily from fossil jaws and teeth. Identified as hominoids on the basis of upper and lower jaw molar morphology, they possess distinctive structures in the dentition and jaws that distinguish each from the others, and their very small size marks them as a group.

Kenyapithecus wickeri. From the early part of the middle Miocene, and thus somewhat later than the early Miocene fossils just described, are the specimens known as *Kenyapithecus.* Discovered at a place called *Fort Ternan* in western Kenya, they have been dated by the K-Ar technique to about 14.5 million years B.P. Called by Louis Leakey *Kenyapithecus wickeri* (the species name after the owner of the farm where the site is located, Mr. Wicker), they consist of fragments of a lower and upper jaw and some isolated teeth (Figure 7.21). One possibly associated upper arm bone was also discovered. Because the canine is reduced (although still large and projecting by human standards), and the face is

FIGURE 7.21. The fragmentary jaws of *Kenyapithecus* (right), compared with the same area on a chimpanzee. Not enough of *Kenyapithecus* is known to draw any firm conclusions about its evolutionary relationships with living African apes and humans.

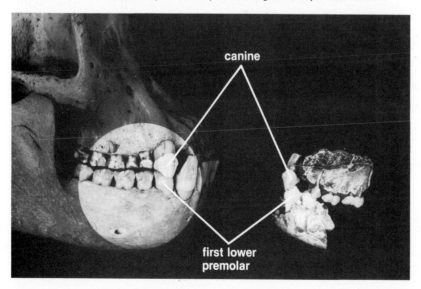

canine

first lower premolar

somewhat foreshortened, they have been suggested by some as possibly representative of the line leading toward the hominine subfamily. The *Kenyapithecus* fossils are, however, much too scrappy to draw any but the most tentative of conclusions. Unlike the early Miocene sites, the Fort Ternan fossil animal remains, like ostrich bones, have suggested that *Kenyapithecus* may have been adapted to more open-country conditions.

The earliest hominoid fossil material has thus been found in Africa and seems to represent a number of hominoid groups. Some time after the beginning of the middle Miocene, which began some 15 million years ago, hominoids begin appearing in Eurasia, apparently having spread there from Africa.

Middle and Late Miocene Eurasian Hominoid Evolution By the middle of the Miocene, fossil evidence of hominoids has become more widespread.

Dryopithecus. In Europe, hominoid fossils dated to the middle and late Miocene have been placed in the genus *Dryopithecus* (*Dryo = forest; pithecus = ape*). *Dryopithecus* fossils are widely distributed in Europe, having been found in France, Spain, Germany, Austria, Hungary, Russia, and perhaps in other countries as well, and they have been divided into a number of species. The teeth of *Dryopithecus* are similar to those of the other hominoids, with four-cusped upper molars with the oblique ridge and lower molars with the Y-shaped grooves between the cusps. The few cranial and jaw specimens of *Dryopithecus* are somewhat different from those of the living apes, while the very few skeletal bones suggest the beginning adaptation for suspensory hanging and climbing.

Sivapithecus and Gigantopithecus. In Asia, Miocene hominoids have been discovered in Turkey, Saudi Arabia, and in parts of south China, but the bulk of the evidence comes from northern India and Pakistan in a range of hills known as the *Siwaliks,* which forms part of the western foothills of the Himalayas. Here, at a number of sites, an imposing array of fossil bones and teeth have been found that seem to represent a number of hominoid species. These specimens, which range in date from about 11 to 12 million years ago to about 7 to 8 million years ago, differ as a group from the bulk of the African fossils and from *Dryopithecus* in several ways;[16] they share some intriguing features with *Afropithecus* and *Kenyapithecus*.

The hominoid fossils from India and Pakistan have been divided into two genera: *Sivapithecus* (after the Indian deity Siva), and *Gigantopithecus* (because of the huge molar teeth and jaws). The distinctive traits of these Asian forms are apparently related to dietary adaptations. *Sivapithecus* and *Gigantopithecus* have molars whose chewing, or occlusal, surfaces are covered with thick layers of enamel. The teeth of *Dryopithecus, Proconsul,* and the living African apes, the chimpanzee and gorilla (but *not* the orang or *Afropithecus* and *Kenyapithecus*), in contrast, have much thinner layers of enamel. Further, there appears to be a tendency in these Asian hominoids to have back chewing teeth that are, in proportion to the front teeth, relatively larger in size (Figure 7.22). The combination

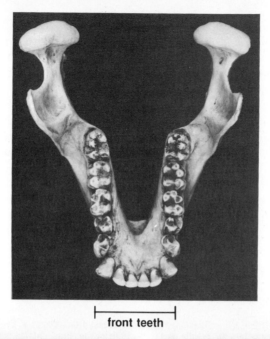

front teeth

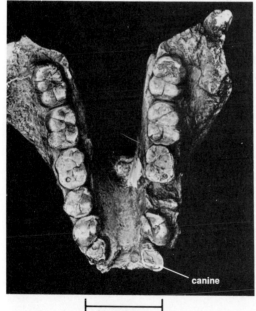

canine

front teeth

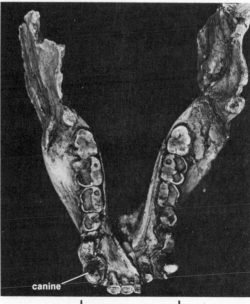

canine

front teeth

FIGURE 7.22. The jaw of a modern ape (a gorilla; top), compared with the casts of the jaws of *Gigantopithecus* (lower left) and *Sivapithecus* (lower right). (This *Sivapithecus* jaw, GSP 15000, is shown from the side in Figure 7.25.) Note the relatively large size of the back teeth compared with the front teeth in the fossil jaws, and the wear on the tips of the canine teeth. The gorilla jaw has different front and back teeth proportions.

of thick enamel on the chewing surfaces of the molar teeth, and the proportionally larger size of the back teeth seems to indicate that *Sivapithecus* and *Gigantopithecus* were adapted to a different niche than other Miocene hominoids; therefore they have been placed in a separate family, the *Sivapithecidae*.[17]

Gigantopithecus was probably the largest hominoid that ever lived (Figure 7.23). In addition to the Indian and Pakistani Miocene specimens, a number of jaws and several hundred teeth of this creature have been discovered in south China. These Chinese specimens are dated to the early Pleistocene, a time when hominine fossils are found in various parts of the Old World.

Sivapithecus was smaller than *Gigantopithecus* and shows sexual dimorphism in tooth size. Into the genus *Sivapithecus* has recently been incorporated the genus *"Ramapithecus,"* which for a considerable time was thought to represent the ancestor of the hominines. Fossils from a part of the Siwaliks in Pakistan known as the Potwar Plateau showed

FIGURE 7.23. *Gigantopithecus*, the largest primate known, lived in Asia from the Miocene into the middle part of the Pleistocene. Only isolated teeth and several broken lower jaws of this creature have been found. This picture shows in the background a reconstruction of the largest of the *Gigantopithecus* jaw fossils, compared with the jaw of a male gorilla whose body size was at least 120 kg (265 lb).

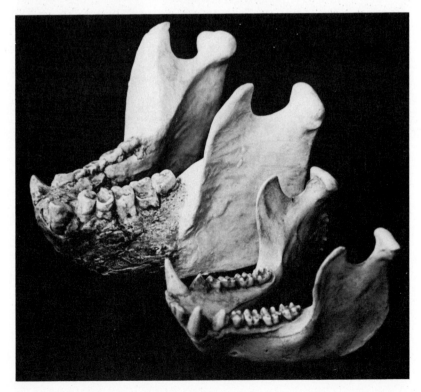

that "Ramapithecus" was a smaller version of *Sivapithecus,* perhaps representing females of a dimorphic species. As it became increasingly difficult to distinguish a large "Ramapithecus" jaw from a small *Sivapithecus* jaw, it was realized that the two groups were in reality parts of a single species.[18]

In addition to the Indian and Pakistani *Sivapithecus* fossils, jaws and teeth belonging to this genus have been uncovered in Miocene deposits in the Middle East, and recently a major portion of skull was found at the site of Lufeng in south China, where a number of jaws had previously been discovered.

Pliopithecus. Fossils of the genus *Pliopithecus* have been found in late Miocene deposits in a number of sites in central and eastern Europe. *Pliopithecus* was a small-size hominoid, and its jaws and teeth look in many ways like the living lesser ape, the gibbon, whose ancestor it may be. However, complicating this evolutionary assignment is the fact that *Pliopithecus* postcranial bones reveal a generalized, quadrupedal anatomy, a tail, and a decided lack of suspensory or climbing specializations.[19]

Miocene Evolution: Biochemical Evidence   Before examining some of the hypotheses about the evolution and adaptation of the Miocene hominoids, the evidence from comparative biochemical and genetic studies must be described. There are two aspects of these comparative studies: They provide evidence for the construction of evolutionary trees—cladograms—that show relationships, and they can be used to calculate when the branching points, or nodes, on these trees occurred (Figure 7.24).

FIGURE 7.24.   A molecular phylogeny of the Hominoidea based on nucleic acid, immunological, and electrophoretic data (Goodman and Cronin, 1982). No molecular data have been conclusive in determining whether any pair of the lineages *Homo, Pan,* and *Gorilla* share a common ancestor to the exclusion of the third species.

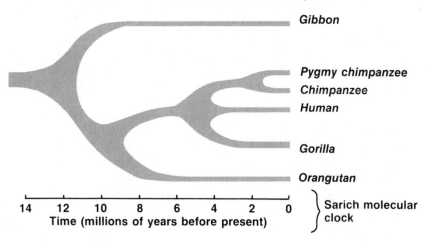

In Chapter 5 we saw how the study of comparative biochemical and genetic traits can help solve problems of primate classification, and therefore provide insight into the evolutionary relationships of living forms. Figure 7.24 graphically summarizes the pattern of hominoid evolutionary divergence as developed by the variety of biochemical and genetic systems discussed in Chapter 5. It shows that modern humans are grouped with the African apes, the chimpanzee, and the gorilla and that it is difficult to determine more precise associations between the three members of this group, since most tests indicate that humans and chimps are more closely related, and several suggest that chimps and gorillas are closest (see Figure 5.28). This human/chimp/gorilla group is separated from its nearest living form, the orangutan, and that animal is in turn separated from the lesser apes, the gibbon and the siamang. This latter group seems to be in some ways intermediate between the human/chimp/gorilla group and the orang on one side and the Old World monkeys on the other.

While these results are in general supported by most scientists working on this question, and the relationships in fact seem to be in basic agreement with comparative anatomical studies, some scientists believe that this data can be carried even further. They suggest that the amount of genetic divergence between species can be used to tell us how long it has been since the species last had a common ancestor. The biochemical and genetic comparisons are thus viewed as having the potential to serve as a "molecular clock" to compute the dates when the ancestors of living species diverged to follow different evolutionary pathways.

Comparison of the genetic material—DNA—of primates has resulted in the amassing of much useful information about living primates. In Chapter 5, we described Sibley and Ahlquist's DNA hybridization experiments and their conclusions concerning the relationships of the living hominoids. By comparing the amount of difference in the DNA of many animals, they were able to determine a rate of DNA change over time, which permitted them to use the results of their hybridization work as a "molecular clock" to calculate divergence times among these animals (Figure 5.23).

Prior to Sibley and Ahlquist, anthropologists such as Vincent Sarich had developed "molecular clocks" using the comparative analysis of blood proteins. Sarich focused his attention on serum albumin. He believed that his data on the evolution of this blood protein showed a constant rate of evolution for this molecule and that a *phylogeny* (evolutionary history) could thus be reconstructed essentially without reference to the fossil record.[20] Assuming the constancy of molecular change in serum albumin in many lines of primates, Sarich compared immunologically a number of living animals and computed the times of divergence of the higher primates (Figure 7.24). Sarich's results from serum albumin agree closely with the results of DNA hybridization. Both conclude that humans, chimps, and gorillas split, evolving their separate ways, between

5 and 10 million years ago. The two results differ in the divergence times of orangs and gibbons, with the Sibley and Ahlquist data showing earlier split-off times.

The times of divergence arrived at by both the DNA hybridization and blood protein studies are founded on the use of fossil evidence to establish a beginning calibration point. For example, Sibley and Ahlquist decided that the split-off time between orangutans and the line eventually leading to chimps, gorillas, and humans was about 16 million years B.P. (see Figure 5.23). At this time animal interchanges between the African and Eurasian continents began, and it is reasonable to assume that the ancestors of the orang spread out of Africa then. All of the other dates of divergence are determined from this base line. If the base line point is changed to either an earlier or later time, all of the other split-off times must also be recalibrated. Similarly, Sarich uses the divergence of the prosimian from the anthropoids at about 60 million years as his calibration point. Note that if 12 million years B.P. is used as the orang/chimp/gorilla/human split, as some primatologists suggest, the protein and DNA hybridization data fit rather well (Figure 7.24).

There have been numerous criticisms of Sarich's results. It is also important to recall that Sibley and Ahlquist's DNA hybridization study has not been totally confirmed by others. Generally, others feel that the DNA hybridization data are not precise enough to resolve the chimpanzee/gorilla/human trichotomy. Likewise, many feel that the data do not conform to a "molecular clock" and thus do not attempt to compute dates of divergence. Until confirmation is achieved, we ought to consider the evolutionary tree depicted in Figure 7.24 as preliminary.

Nevertheless, these studies do provide a framework for us to examine the fossil record, and although "molecular clock" information should be used cautiously, it is a useful place to begin putting the Miocene hominoids into an evolutionary perspective. Can the results of these studies be reconciled with the evidence from the fossil record? In other words, do we have fossils that might be representative of the common ancestors of the different living hominoids and dated in accord with the DNA hybridization and protein evolution data?

Views of Miocene Hominoid Evolution   A number of hypotheses have been developed about the evolution of the Miocene hominoids and their relationships to the origin and evolution of the living hominoids.

By the beginning of the Miocene, biochemical and genetic comparison and fossil evidence suggest that the two major lines of Old World higher primates, the superfamilies Cercopithecoidea (monkeys) and the Hominoidea (apes and humans) had diverged. Earliest fossil evidence for both groups is found in Africa (Table 7.3).

The early Miocene of Africa seems to be a time of major radiation of primitive hominoids. Many genera have been identified, apparently adapted to forestlike conditions. Little can be said about their biology

TABLE 7.3
Views of Miocene Hominoid Evolution
Both schemes place the fossil groups in the same positions. Part A organizes the possible evolutionary relationships of living and extinct hominoids and Old World monkeys on the basis of DNA hybridization. Part B is based on protein comparisons, which place the evolutionary separation of orangs from the African hominids later in time. These schemes are meant to provide a general view of Miocene evolution relating living and extinct forms. Future fossil discoveries and the reevaluation of what is already known will certainly lead to the development of other models.

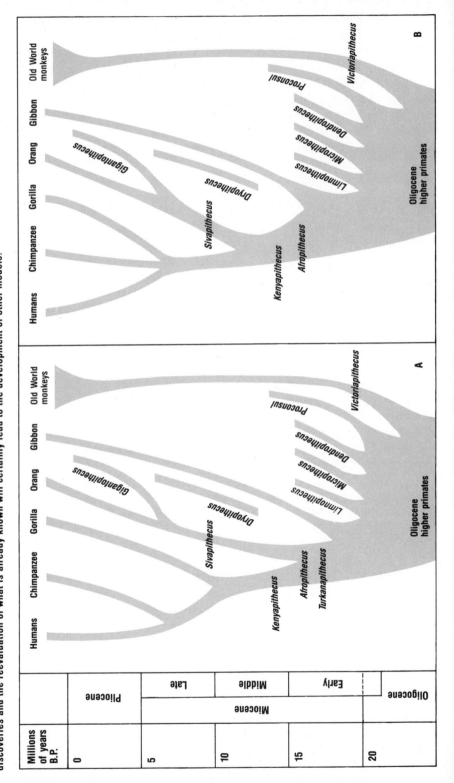

and adaptation, since most are known only from jaws and teeth. Those hominoids, like *Proconsul,* for whom skeletal bones have been recovered, lack the characteristic upper limb and trunk features of the living hominoids. Forms such as *Proconsul, Afropithecus, Turkanapithecus, Rangwapithecus, Micropithecus, Dendropithecus,* and *Limnopithecus* were parts of an extensive array of presumably arboreal hominoids who appeared in the early Miocene of Africa.[21]

Sometime around middle Miocene times, hominoids along with other African animals spread into Eurasia. *Sivapithecus* is found at a number of middle Miocene deposits of Asia and Greece, while *Dryopithecus* has been discovered at widely scattered locales in Europe. Both these forms continue into the late Miocene, with recent finds from Pakistan indicating *Sivapithecus* may have lasted there virtually to the end of the Miocene, 5 million years ago. *Pliopithecus* appears in the late Miocene of Europe, while *Gigantopithecus* is first found in late Miocene rocks in India.

After the early Miocene radiation of forms in Africa, the middle and late Miocene hominoid record is very limited there, with *Kenyapithecus* the major fossil group.

At the Miocene/Pliocene boundary, 5 million years B.P., virtually all of these Miocene forms have disappeared from the fossil record. Apart from the hominine fossil record, there is a blank in our knowledge between these Miocene hominoids and all living apes. Because of the fragmentary nature of much of this fossil material, its diverse geographical distribution, and its considerable time spread (about 13 million years), it has been very difficult for primatologists to construct phylogenetic trees of hominoid evolution. Table 7.3 illustrates some of the suggestions that have been made. These models place the Asian hominoid *Sivapithecus* in the ancestry of the orangutan.

David Pilbeam and his associates have been responsible for many of the recent discoveries in Pakistan. One of Pilbeam's findings in late Miocene deposits in Pakistan's Potwar Plateau was truly spectacular. Known by its catalog number, *GSP 15000,* it is one of the most complete late Miocene fossils ever found, parts of the jaws and face of a *Sivapithecus* (Figure 7.25). The jaws and teeth identify it as *Sivapithecus,* but the upper part of the face, until now completely unknown, shows a remarkable similarity to the distinctive facial regions of the living orangutan (Figure 7.25). Orangs, alone among the great apes, have thick layers of enamel on the chewing surfaces of their teeth, which is one of the distinctive features of *Sivapithecus.* The similarity of facial structures between the orang and this late Miocene *Sivapithecus* argues for its placement as the direct ancestor of the living orang. The fact that it is from Pakistan in south Asia and near to the modern orang distribution makes the case even stronger. Thus, it appears likely that *Sivapithecus* represents the direct ancestor of the orang.[22]

The recognition of the evolutionary connections of *Sivapithecus* and the established patterns of relationship within the living Hominoidea

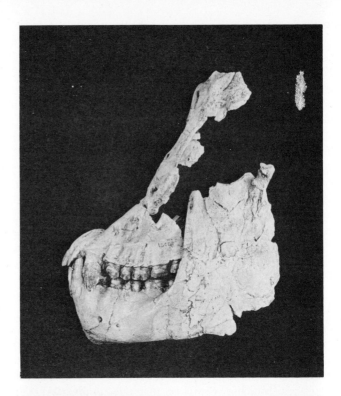

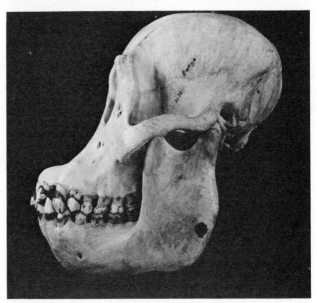

FIGURE 7.25. A cast of the late Miocene GSP 15000 *Sivapithecus* face (top) from the Potwar Plateau compared with the skull of a modern orangutan (bottom). Note the similarities in the shape and orientation of the facial region.

linking chimp, gorilla, and human argue that the ancestors of these animals have to be sought elsewhere. Since chimpanzees, gorillas, and the earliest of our hominine ancestors are all from Africa, it is logical to think of the common ancestor of this group as living in Africa.

After Africa's continental collision with Eurasia, faunal interchanges between Africa and Eurasia begin to appear in the fossil record about 16 million years ago. Perhaps this is the correct date of divergence between the orang and African ape/human groups (and it was taken as the base line calibration point by Sibley and Ahlquist in the DNA hybridization-based "molecular clock").

Of all the early Miocene forms currently known, *Afropithecus* would make the most reasonable African ancestor for the later *Sivapithecus*. It shares with *Sivapithecus* the thick layers of enamel on the chewing surface of the teeth and a number of details of the snout, brow region, and front teeth. Dated at 16–18 million years B.P., it would also make a reasonable early Miocene ancestor for the line leading to the African apes and humans. Keep in mind that no skeletal bones of *Afropithecus* have yet been found, and for this fossil hominoid to be considered as an ancestor, it must possess the anatomical features of the trunk and shoulder related to suspensory hanging or climbing. Without exception, all living hominoids have these structures. It is unreasonable to believe these structures evolved independently in different lines and thus that the anatomical features associated with suspensory hanging or climbing evolved in the common ancestor of hominoids before any of the lines leading to living forms had diverged.

Because of the absence of fossil bones of the *Afropithecus* skeleton and the other uncertainties involved in the establishment of ancestor/descendant relationships, the attribution of *Afropithecus* as the common ancestor of the great apes should be considered tentative.

The early–middle Miocene *Kenyapithecus* also appears to possess thick layers of enamel. Of the known fossil material, perhaps the best current candidate for placement as an ancestor to the Hominidae (chimpanzees, gorillas, and humans) are the *Kenyapithecus wickeri* fossils from Fort Ternan.[23] Composed of dental and fragmentary jaw bones, they share many features with the *Sivapithecus* fossils from Asia and with *Afropithecus,* but they also have traits that might relate them to the hominids. Until more fossil material of this creature is discovered, however, it is very premature to make any but the most tentative suggestions about its evolutionary relationships.

Miocene Hominoid Evolution and Living Hominoids Where then does this leave all of the questions we posed earlier that relate the Miocene hominoids to living forms? Perhaps the most reasonable way to deal with these questions is to examine each of the major living hominoids in the context of Miocene evolution.

Gibbon and Siamang. It is apparent that the lesser apes (gibbon and siamang) diverged from the main hominoid line early, certainly before the split between African and Asian great apes. There are no recognizable gibbon fossils that early, and in any case, accepting even the late Miocene *Pliopithecus* as an ancestral gibbon raises significant problems, the most important being the anatomy of suspensory hanging or climbing. A close, direct ancestor of any living hominoid must possess the anatomical traits of suspensory hanging or climbing, and *Pliopithecus,* with its generalized skeleton, does not qualify. Evidence from other Miocene hominoids would suggest that the line leading to the lesser apes has had a long separate evolutionary existence, but at present there are no acceptable fossils documenting this development.

Orangutan. As we have seen, the fossil history of the orang is the best-documented line in the nonhuman hominoids. The few pieces of skeletal bones of *Sivapithecus,* which have been discovered primarily in Pakistan, have suggested to Michael Rose, who has studied them, an agile arboreal climber and suspensory hanger.[24]

The Family Hominidae (African apes and humans). Comparative biochemical and genetic studies (see Figures 5.23 and 7.24) indicate that after the divergence of the line leading to the orangutan, the hominid line continued and, sometime between 5 and 10 million years ago, separated into the lineages of humans, chimpanzees, and gorillas. The comparative studies do not yet provide conclusive evidence of the exact pattern of divergence of these animals (see Figure 5.28), and there is no fossil evidence. Indeed, one of the major problems in evaluating hominid evolution is the lack of any fossil evidence of the African apes. Until this gap is filled, it is very difficult to place these animals in the context of primate evolution.

We know somewhat more about the human line in this context because we have a fossil record of hominine evolution beginning some 5 million years ago. Dentally, these early hominines possess traits—thick occlusal enamel and large back teeth—that are also found among the members of *Sivapithecus* and *Kenyapithecus*. It is this dental similarity that provided the basis for the suggestion that *Kenyapithecus* was on the line leading to the hominids (Table 7.3).

However, this raises a problem in our evolutionary relationships with the African apes. Both the chimp and the gorilla differ in these dental details, possessing thin layers of dental enamel and back teeth that are relatively small in relation to the large front teeth (Figure 7.26), whereas the orang seems closest to us with its thick enamel. Jeffrey Schwartz has suggested that this dental similarity and a number of other very subtle, shared biological traits may indicate that, in spite of all the other comparisons, humans may be evolutionarily more closely related to orangs than to chimps and gorillas.[25] Most primatologists have rejected this notion, pointing out that it is much more reasonable that hominines and orangs have retained the thick enamel on their molars' chewing

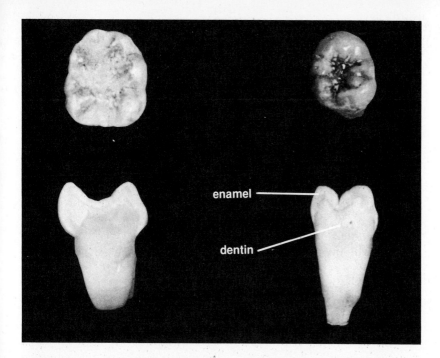

FIGURE 7.26. The lower jaw third molars of a chimpanzee (left) and a modern human (right). The illustrations on the top show the teeth from the chewing surface, and the lower illustrations show the same teeth sectioned (cut) through the front cusps. Note that the enamel is thicker in the human molar. Thick molar enamel also characterizes orang teeth, whereas gorillas, like chimps, have teeth with thin enamel. The functional reasons for these differences are unclear.

surfaces from their common ancestor, while chimps and gorillas, becoming more specialized, have developed thinner layers (Figure 7.26).

The functional reasons for the evolution of thick or thin layers of enamel on the molar teeth are unclear. Dental enamel is a very complicated hard tissue, and there are subtle differences in the patterns of deposition and structure of enamel even in primate species whose molars have the same relative enamel thickness. Richard Kay has shown that modern monkeys who possess thick layers of molar enamel have a diet of tough-shelled seeds and other coarse vegetation.[26] Perhaps this was the reason thick enamel evolved in some early Miocene hominoids like *Afropithecus* and was retained in *Sivapithecus,* the orangs, and the hominines.

Chimpanzees and gorillas are quadrupedal knuckle-walkers, spending most of their time on the ground foraging for food. Orangs are much more arboreal than either of the African apes. The early hominines, to be described in Chapter 9, were like us, their descendants, in being adapted to two-legged walking (bipedalism), although the earliest of them may also have used other forms of locomotion. We might speculate that sometime after the split between the ancestors of the orang and those leading to the hominids, the latter evolved a terrestrial adaptation. What the specific locomotion of this ancestor was we have no idea; it was almost certainly not bipedalism, but whether it used knuckle-walking, like the living African apes, or a more generalized quadrupedalism, which gave it the ability to climb vertical tree trunks swiftly, is unknown. Perhaps, as Pilbeam has suggested, the ancestor of the hominids routinely used a number of locomotor behaviors, including quadrupedalism, suspensory hanging, vertical climbing, and some bipedalism.[27] It would be simplistic for us to characterize its locomotion as one thing or another. In this matter, however, speculation is all that can be presented at the moment; between the earliest hominine fossils at about 5 million years and a possible hominid ancestor at 14 million years (*Kenyapithecus*), there are only the merest scraps of undiagnostic fossil bone and teeth from Africa.

Fossil-bearing rocks of this crucial middle and late Miocene time have been located in the hills of western Kenya, and in the next few years finds from this area or some other locale will illuminate the evolutionary history of the immediate forerunners of the human subfamily.

Old World Monkey Evolution in the Miocene

Comparative protein and genetic studies suggest that the ancestors of the Old World monkeys diverged from those of the hominoids late in Oligocene or very early in Miocene times. At the early Miocene site of Napak in Uganda, a tooth and a fragment of a skull were discovered. The tooth, a bilophodont molar, documents the first fossil appearance of this distinctive molar cusp pattern of the Old World monkeys. The Napak fossils demonstrate the presence of Old World monkeys in the African early Miocene.[28] Numbers of fossil teeth from the middle Miocene, including bilophodont molars, have been found in Kenya (Figure 7.27). The late G. H. R. von Koenigswald, who placed these teeth in the genus *Victoriapithecus,* has noted that the bilophodont molars look as if they had evolved from the hominoid molar pattern.[29]

FIGURE 7.27. The last upper and lower molars (one and one-third actual size) of the fossil *Victoriapithecus,* an Old World monkey of Miocene East Africa, compared with the last upper and lower bilophodont molars of a living monkey (about one-half actual size).

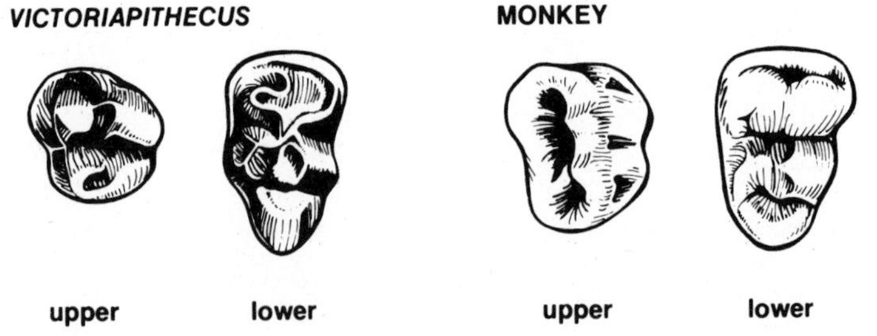

VICTORIAPITHECUS   MONKEY

upper   lower   upper   lower

From this time on, increasing numbers of Old World monkeys are found in the fossil record, and by the late Miocene it appears that the two major groups of Old World monkeys, the cercopithecines and colobines, had diverged (pages 170–174). Eric Delson, who has studied these fossils in detail, suggests that the reason for this evolutionary development was that, in a deciduous forest environment, the eating of leaves as well as fruits would prolong the time during which food was plentiful. Early Old World monkeys, then, became increasingly specialized, with the colobines emphasizing leaves and the cercopithecines fruit and more open-country foods.[30]

Also by the late Miocene, Old World monkeys had expanded their distribution to include northern India and Pakistan and many parts of Europe.

It is interesting that the monkeys become more numerous in the fossil record at about the time the hominoids are becoming less common, and it may be that increasing competition from the highly successful Old World monkeys played an important role in the extinction of many of the Miocene hominoids.

Evolution in the New World

The prosimian primates of the Eocene were widely distributed in the northern hemisphere of both the Old and New Worlds. Toward the end of the Eocene epoch, they became scarce in the northern parts of North America, and in the succeeding Oligocene they were rarer still. These Eocene primates were not morphologically New World monkeys, and one major problem in understanding primate evolution in the New World has been to document the evolutionary transition from the prosimian primates of the Eocene and early Oligocene to the New World monkeys, which first make their appearance in the fossil record in early Oligocene strata of Bolivia. Termed *Branisella,* this fossil skull shows many distinctive attributes of Platyrrhine (New World) monkeys. No fossil evidence has been found linking Eocene prosimians evolutionarily with early New World monkeys. Lacking such evidence, several views of New World monkey origins have been proposed.

Until very recently, it was thought that after the middle Eocene, Old and New World primates evolved independently. Because of their similar environmental adaptations, the evolution of Old and New World monkeys was often cited as one of the best examples in paleontology of parallel evolution, in which two independent evolutionary lines adapt to similar niches, are selected for similar attributes, and evolve along similar paths. Richard Hoffstetter has suggested an alternative explanation. During the Eocene and Oligocene, South America and Africa were much closer than they are today; South America had yet to join with North America, and Africa did not become connected with Eurasia until the beginning of the Miocene (Figure 7.28). Hoffstetter views the similarities between Old and New World monkeys and some Old and New World rodents as indications that early in the Oligocene evolution of the anthropoids in Africa, some of these primitive higher primates, perhaps

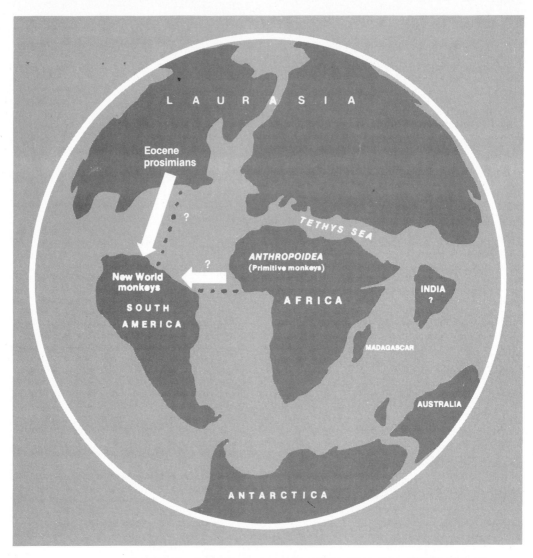

FIGURE 7.28. Hoffstetter's view of the relationship between Old World and New World higher primates, suggesting that during the Oligocene, Africa and South America were closer than they are today and that primitive Old World higher primates rafted from Africa to South America.

related to the Fayum anthropoids, rafted across the narrow ocean barrier between the Old World and the New. There may also have been a number of now-submerged volcanic islands between the two continents, making the proposed ocean crossing a more practical possibility. According to Hoffstetter, Old and New World monkeys are similar in appearance because they have a common higher primate ancestor.[31] Protein and genetic comparisons suggest an Old World–New World divergence in the early Oligocene, providing additional support for this view. Other ideas concerning New World monkey origins suggest that the ancestors of these forms ought to be sought among the widespread and successful Eocene prosimian groups of North America and that it is more reasonable to postulate rafting, also using islands, from North to South America than from Africa to South America.[32]

The fossil record of New World monkey evolution is exceedingly sparse, and little is known regarding their early development and radiation. Whatever their origins turn out to be, the New World monkeys subsequently evolved into two rather different groups of animals, the Cebidae and the Callithricidae. As noted in the last chapter, the New World monkeys never evolved terrestrial forms, like those that appeared in the Old World. They have, however, developed a diverse set of feeding patterns and social organizations, and even one monkey with a nocturnal adaptation. All these live within the Central and South American tropical forests.

The Callithricidae, whose living representatives are the marmosets and tamarins, retain a larger number of primitive characteristics than the Cebidae, whose representatives today are monkeys such as the spider, howler, and capuchin. Marmosets, for example, possess claws on all digits but the big toe, whereas the other New World monkeys, like the Old World variety, have nails. With a dental formula of 2.1.3.2, the Callithricidae are the only higher primates with less than three molars. The cebids' dental formula, 2.1.3.3, is like that of many prosimians.

New World monkeys show a rather wide variety of molar shapes, including in some species a form similar to those of the hominoids, but they do not possess the bilophodont molars distinctive of all Old World monkeys. Many but not all New World monkeys have prehensile tails that can be used as a fifth appendage. No Old World monkey has a prehensile tail; its tail may be used for balance, but not for grasping objects. Finally, Old World monkeys have that very special adaptation, an ischial callosity (see page 170).

Summary

This chapter has reviewed the fossil evidence documenting the evolution of the mammalian order Primates. Fossil bones represent the only direct evidence of the evolution of an animal group, although comparative anatomy, biochemistry, and genetics can also provide important supporting data. The analysis of fossil bones is carried out through a logical series of steps that aim to establish the extinct animal's evolutionary relationships with other animals and to furnish information on how the fossil bones and teeth functioned in the living animal. The final step in a fossil analysis, and the most difficult, is the reconstruction of behavior. This step provides the link between fossil animal bones and the ways by which animals whose parts they were successfully adapted to their environment.

Primates share many biological features with the members of the mammalian order of insectivores, one of the most primitive of living placental mammals. This relationship and the numerous general vertebrate features that are still a part of primate biology but are lost or modified in most other living mammal orders suggest that the primates evolved early in placental mammal history, probably sometime at the end of the age of the dinosaurs, in the Cretaceous period of the Mesozoic era. Fossil evidence of the very earliest primates is extremely scanty, and although the notion that many of the most distinctive primate features evolved because early in their history the primates became tree-dwelling (arboreal) animals continues to be held by many primatologists, there is little direct evidence in support.

Early in the Tertiary, during the Paleocene and early Eocene, primitive primates, members of the suborder Plesiadapiformes, with features in many ways different from later members of the order, were a common part of the then-tropical forests of the western United States and Europe. Later in the Eocene epoch, primates with a biology similar to living prosimians were extremely successful, with large numbers of different species occupying the tropical forest habitats of many parts of the northern hemisphere.

In the latter part of the Eocene, changing climatic and perhaps zoological conditions led to the extinction of most of these early primates. The only members that survived were those adapted to highly specialized niches, mainly arboreal and nocturnal, and those isolated on the island of Madagascar from the great trends in mammalian evolution.

Several fragmentary jaws from Burma offer evidence that at some time in the latter part of the Eocene epoch, the suborder Anthropoidea arose from the prosimians. In the following Oligocene, primates disappeared virtually entirely from Europe and North America, where they were found in such great abundance during the Eocene, and the only fossil information we have for the evolution of Old World primates during this time comes exclusively from the Fayum Beds in Egypt. A number of higher primates have been identified in the Fayum. Although they are recognizable members of the Anthropoidea, they do not have the important distinguishing features of living higher primates: the distinctive molar crown patterns of the Old World monkeys and the anatomical evidence in the shoulders, trunk, and arms of suspensory hanging or climbing, a feature of apes and humans. The fossil evidence for the direct ancestry of modern Old World higher primates is first found in Miocene times, apparently arising from the generalized anthropoid primates of the Oligocene.

The Miocene witnessed the evolutionary development of a number of higher primate groups; in this epoch appears the first evidence of the distinctive molars of the Old World monkeys. Miocene hominoids appeared earliest in Africa; they underwent an extensive radiation with many fossil genera discovered in sites in Kenya and Uganda. They spread to Eurasia by the middle Miocene, undergoing further evolutionary diversification. By the end of the Miocene, evidence of hominoids becomes very rare, although it is clear from subsequent fossil evidence and comparative studies that the lines leading to humans and the living apes had diverged earlier and were already in existence when the Pliocene began from 5 million years B.P.

The Miocene fossil evidence, although abundant, is as yet too incomplete to provide any definite information about the evolutionary history of any of the hominoids, except the orang. In the case of this Asian great ape, members of the genus *Sivapithecus* known from the middle and late Miocene of Asia, appear to be the ancestors of orangutans.

The Miocene ancestors of chimps, gorillas, and humans, the family Hominidae, probably evolved in Africa, and although several early and middle Miocene hominoids may represent parts of this lineage, the evidence is too fragmentary for definite statements.

The biological history of the primates provides an essential background for an examination of the fossil evidence for human evolution. The next three chapters will build upon the information presented here and describe in some detail the evolution of the hominines.

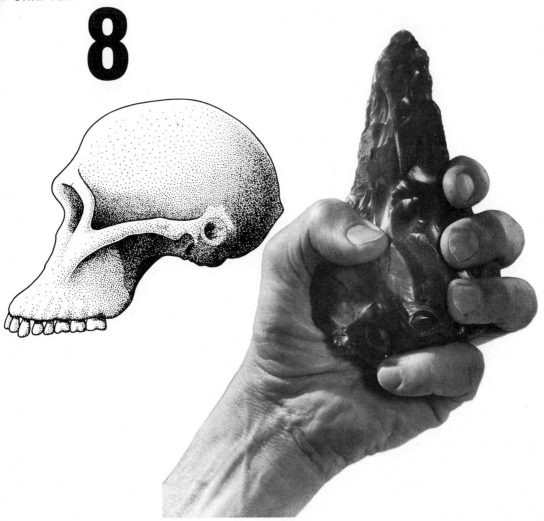

A reconstruction of the lifeways of our hominine ancestors requires an understanding of the environment they inhabited, the foods they ate, and the behaviors they used to adapt successfully to their environment.

The Homininae

The information we have reviewed on the biological history and behavior of the nonhuman primates, including the mechanisms that result in evolutionary change, provides the background necessary to explore the origin of modern humans and the evolutionary development of our immediate ancestors. Ideally, we should treat the biological history of the subfamily Homininae, modern humans and our immediate direct ancestors, as we would that of any other animal group. Unfortunately, in dealing with our own ancestors this proves to be very difficult. The hominines, however, are subject to the same evolutionary mechanisms as other animal groups. As we look at their evolution through time, we see changes in physical features as the genetic characteristics responsible for their appearance increase or decrease in frequency in response to various factors. As in the study of other animal species, the picture of human evolution is in many places foggy and difficult to interpret mainly because the fossil record documenting this biological history is an incomplete one, based on scarce, scattered, and usually broken and distorted fossil bones.

The Study of Human Evolution

The scientific study of human evolution has two major goals: (1) the development of a hominine taxonomy and (2) the identification and reconstruction of our ancestors' patterns of adaptation. These aims are not mutually exclusive but rather employ much of the same evidence, and together will ultimately provide a complete picture of human evolution.

Hominine Taxonomy

One object of human evolutionary studies is to identify the genera and species of our extinct ancestors and place them within the overall context of higher primate evolution. The ultimate goal is to construct a human family tree in which our evolutionary relationships with our living and extinct close relatives are expressed via the concepts and terms of biological classification. This permits us to evaluate our connections with both close and near relatives, and to place in perspective the biological traits that we share with other animals as well as our uniquely human attributes.

A modern taxonomy includes both living and extinct animals. The information used in establishing relationships among living forms includes comparative anatomy, embryology, genetics, and biochemistry. Our close anatomical relationships with the great apes—the chimpanzee, gorilla, and orangutan—have been recognized for over two hundred years. Genetic and biochemical comparisons, reviewed in the chapters on primates (pages 188–190), confirm that these apes are our closest living relatives. Until recently, this relationship had been expressed in taxonomy in the placement of humans and apes in the same superfamily, the Hominoidea, but in separate families, the Hominidae for humans and the Pongidae for the apes. This organization was, in a sense, a reflection of a view of ourselves as unique and apart from the rest of the animal world. Over the past ten years, however, numerous studies of ape and human proteins and direct comparisons of their genetic material via DNA hybridization experiments (see pages 177–188) revealed a somewhat different picture. The new findings indicate that humans and the African apes, the chimpanzees and gorillas, are more similar to each other than to any other living form, including the orang. One major result of these studies has been a reordering of the Hominoidea and the inclusion of humans, chimps, and gorillas within the family Hominidae, with the orang remaining in the Pongidae (see Table 5.1). Humans and our close extinct ancestors are placed in the subfamily Homininae.

The relationships among the living great apes and humans are illustrated in Figure 8.1. A complete taxonomy, however, also includes extinct animals and their possible relationships to living forms. In Chapter 7 we examined the apelike fossils from the Miocene of Africa and Eurasia and found that *Sivapithecus* has many features that link it with the orang and that can therefore be reasonably placed on Line 1 of Figure 8.1. There is, however, little compelling evidence for placing any of the Miocene fossils on Line 2 of the figure, which represents the common ancestry of the hominids (that is, the African apes and humans after the

FIGURE 8.1.   **The evolutionary relationships of humans and our closest living relatives.**

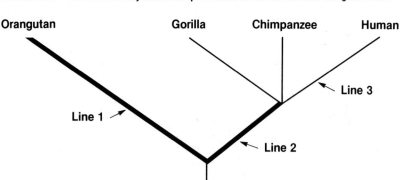

separation of the orang). It is hoped that future fossil finds will fill in the blanks along this line and help us understand this crucial time, which set the stage for human evolution. Line 3 on Figure 8.1 represents the evolution of the hominines from their separation from the apes to the present. This and the next two chapters will focus on the fossil and other evidence that documents this line. Although the line is drawn as a single one leading directly to living humans, the pattern of human evolution may be more complicated, with a number of hominine species evolving at various times and becoming extinct without descendents. This question, as well as many others, can be addressed only by examining the fossils.

Before considering the fossil specimens, we must first consider the problems of how to identify a hominine and what criteria can be used to determine whether the sometimes fragmentary fossils that are unearthed are those of hominines. We recognize a host of features that are unique to modern humans: language, bipedalism, complex toolmaking, large brain, and small, nonprojecting canine teeth. It is not clear, however, when many of these features appeared, so although they are useful in examining modern humans, it is difficult to use them in defining all hominines.

Identifying the Hominines

Modern humans possess physical attributes in the upper trunk region—such as a broadened rib cage and an outwardly directed and very mobile shoulder joint—that suggest that our ancestors at one time shared with the apes particular climbing or suspensory ability. It is in the lower trunk and legs that the unique human form of locomotion is most marked. It has long been thought that the evolution of bipedalism in human evolution was directly related to the need to free the hands for toolmaking, but the fossil evidence (to be related in the next chapter) now indicates that early hominines were bipedal at least 1½ million years before definite signs of toolmaking turn up in the record. It seems likely that the ability to stand erect and walk on the back limbs, whatever the reason for its development, is one of the earliest profound changes to have occurred in human evolution. Evidence for the evolutionary appearance of bipedalism thus appears to be the best marker in identifying a hominine and bipedalism itself the most definitive trait of the subfamily Homininae.

Bipedalism

The jaws and teeth of modern humans differ in a number of ways from those of the African apes. Most apparent are the projecting, tusklike canines of the African apes (Figure 8.2). These large teeth are associated with a first lower premolar that functions by rubbing against the back of the upper canine, maintaining a sharp edge along this border, and with spaces between the teeth (termed a *diastema*) that permit the large canines to slide past each other and the jaws to close. Humans possess small, nonprojecting canines; the first lower premolars do not perform a sharp-

Jaws and Teeth

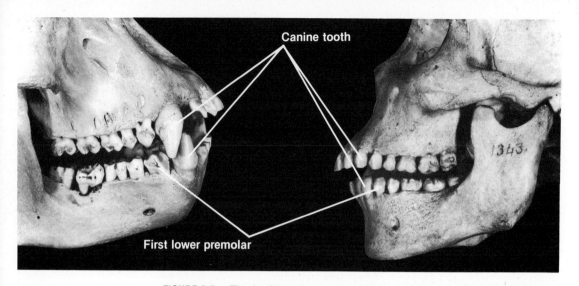

FIGURE 8.2. The dentition of an ape (a gorilla), on the left, compared with that of a modern human. Note the large projecting canines in the ape, and the way the upper canine has worn a deep facet on the front side of the first lower premolar. By rubbing against the canine, this side of the premolar serves to keep the canine's back edge sharp. The human dentition has nonprojecting canine teeth and a first lower premolar that lacks the sloping side that rubs against the canine in the apes.

ening function and there are no spaces between the teeth. Darwin had speculated in *The Descent of Man* that the human line had evolved small canines because of the development of tools, which assumed functions previously performed by the large canines. Fossil evidence, however, suggests that the reduction of the canines occurred early in human evolution, more than a million and a half years before the first tools are recognized in the record.

Another attribute that distinguishes human from African ape teeth is the thickness of the enamel on the teeth (Figure 7.26). The chewing surfaces of human molars are characterized by thick layers of enamel, while the molars of chimpanzees and gorillas possess relatively thin layers. The functional reasons for this difference are unclear. It is not even clear which state—thin or thick layers—represents the primitive (that is, the ancestral) condition. As seen in Chapter 7, thick layers of enamel on molars are found in a number of Miocene hominoids, including *Sivapithecus;* its possible living descendent, the orangutan, also has thick enamel.

Culture

Another uniquely human characteristic often helpful in separating humans from other animals is culture. Cultural anthropology has long studied behavior and habits in modern human societies, but because of the complexity of modern human behavior, there is considerable dis-agreement as to how to define and describe culture. Some early anthro-pologists saw it as the embodiment of all of a society's material goods: tools, pottery, dwellings, boats, clothing, and weapons. Other anthro-pologists thought of culture as the way in which human groups are or-ganized. Many would agree with Ward Goodenough, who has defined culture as the acceptable standards of behavior learned and understood by all members of a society. During socialization, the individual learns these standards of behavior to be able to interact successfully with other members of the society.[1]* These behaviors include learning the spoken language as well as all the subtle gestures and movements that commu-nicate so much to members of the same group and nothing to outsiders. Technological skills and economic pursuits are included in the repertoire of acceptable behaviors; such as how to make and use a tool, and what crops to farm and where to farm them. Modern human groups have complex social organization, and individuals have to master the govern-ing rules and regulations as they learn to be members of their particular society; including whom one may marry; which relatives one can go to for help; who one's close relatives are; and which clan or club one is assigned to or born into. All these behaviors are internalized by the young as they grow to maturity in their society.

This definition of culture is troublesome when we are searching for uniquely hominine attributes, for it is very similar to our way of describ-ing the nonhuman primates' behavior. The higher primates too must learn, while they grow up, standards of behavior appropriate to their social group. Human and nonhuman primate behaviors differ in com-plexity, but the nonhuman higher primates also have a form of cultural behavior.

Toolmaking

One possible way of differentiating human culture from that of other primates has been offered by Ralph Holloway.[2] Emphasizing the crucial relationships between the social group's standards of behavior and their translation into reality, Holloway focuses on the manufacture of a tool. He stresses that a tool does not have to have a particular shape to be effective; rather, its final form is dictated by what the toolmaker thinks its right shape should be when beginning to make the tool. Con-sider the wood saws in Figure 8.3: They perform the same function, yet they look different. This is because the toolmaker, during socialization, has observed adults making and using tools and has learned what the society believes an appropriate tool should look like. This is the image the toolmaker has when beginning the fabrication of the implement. Thus toolmakers from different societies can produce tools of similar function yet different in form. For Holloway, the human ability to trans-late this mental image of a tool onto the raw material represents the foun-

*See pages 621–622 for notes to Chapter 8.

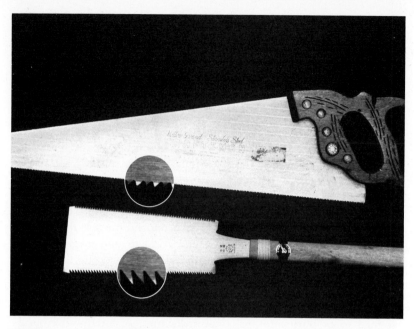

FIGURE 8.3. Japanese (bottom) and American wood saws. The Japanese saw is designed to cut on the pull stroke, while the American saw cuts on the push stroke. Note the orientation of the teeth in each saw. Both tools will cut wood, but they differ in their design, reflecting the ways in which each society visualizes a wood-cutting tool.

dation of uniquely human behavior. In short, social rules governing what constitutes the shape of a tool are internalized by the toolmaker, and this standard of what is appropriate is then the image for the tool that will be made.

Although bipedalism precedes evidence of stone toolmaking in the fossil record by over 1½ million years, it is possible that prior to the use of stone as a raw material, other, more perishable materials, such as wood, were employed in toolmaking. Jane Goodall's discoveries in Tanzania of chimpanzee toolmaking proclivities have shown that these close relatives are also capable of this behavior,[3] but Holloway's views of the nature of toolmaking may represent a pattern unique to the hominines.

Language   Language is one of the most important characteristics of modern humans. Language permits humans to communicate an open-ended series of thoughts, ideas, and concepts. In modern humans, language abilities are founded on a unique set of biological features in the brain, facial and tongue musculature, and voice box. Unfortunately, these attributes are extremely difficult to document on fossil bones. Certainly, with the development of language the hominines would have been able to expand dramatically their ability to share information about environmental resources and dangers.

In identifying a fossil specimen as a hominine, anthropologists examine the state of development of its behavioral and anatomical features, with the former far more difficult to discern. For example, although there is a strong biological basis for human language and although the origin of language would have had crucial import in hominine evolution, there is little agreement among anthropologists about how clearly speech-related anatomical features can be identified on bones. Therefore, the language capability of an extinct hominine cannot be accurately determined. Anatomical traits, on the other hand, are obviously more easily documented because they leave clear structural signs. Of all these features, the anatomical signs for the presence of bipedalism would seem to offer the most accurate basis for the identification of a fossil as a hominine. The reduction in size of the canine teeth can also be important.

Clearly, to establish the pattern of hominine evolution and to comprehend the changes that have affected the teeth, the brain case, or any other structure, it is essential that fossil discoveries be accurately placed within the hominine time continuum. Tracing the evolution of a particular complex necessitates the placement of a series of fossils in chronological order so that we can follow the changes that have taken place over time. A variety of methods and techniques has been developed to place a fossil find precisely or generally in time.

Some fossils can never be dated, either because little attention was paid to their depositional context when they were found; because different dating techniques give different answers; or, most often, because difficulties in understanding the geology and the associated animal bones make dating impossible. We will encounter each of these problems in our discussion of the human fossil record.

For most fossil discoveries, however, some idea of their position in time can be achieved, either in terms of years before the present or by reference to some event in earth history or the evolutionary history of a better known animal group.

One of the most important developments facilitating the study of human evolution is the use of techniques measuring the decay of radioactive isotopes to date geologic deposits and organic remains.[4]

Carbon-14   In the late 1940s Willard Libby studied the decay of the radioactive isotope carbon-14 into the element nitrogen, eventually winning a Nobel Prize for this work. The earth's atmosphere is made up mainly of nitrogen in gaseous form; when it is struck by the sun's radiation, part of this gas is transformed into radioactive *carbon-14* (C^{14}). This naturally occurring conversion takes place continuously in the atmosphere, and C^{14} thus makes up a minute percentage of the planet's air. Every plant, taking in carbon dioxide, also absorbs trace portions of C^{14} into its system. Plants are eaten by animals, which in turn are eaten by

Hominine Features: A Summary

Placing the Hominines in Time

Radiometric Dating Methods

other animals; thus C^{14} is incorporated in small but constant amounts into the bodies of all living things. When a plant or animal dies, C^{14} stops being replenished, and the unstable isotope begins to break down into nitrogen again. Reducing the C^{14} to half its original amount takes about 5,730 years; the other half becomes nitrogen. This reduction is called the *half-life,* and it continues, with a quarter of the original amount left after the next 5,730 years, and so on. A living being has a constant proportion of C^{14} to the common, stable element carbon-12 (C^{12}). By analyzing the changed proportion in organic remains, we get some idea of when an animal or plant died: that is, when it stopped taking in C^{14}. Thus, the C^{14} technique can only be employed on organic remains, such as bone, wood, charcoal, and shell, materials that have had the C^{12}-C^{14} relationship.

This technique is extremely valuable in dating many hominine fossil bones and archaeological deposits, but it has a serious drawback: the time span of its usefulness. If the organic material to be dated is older than about 40,000 years, the amount of C^{14} remaining is so small that it cannot be measured. As much of the human evolutionary record extends far beyond 40,000 years, this procedure currently cannot be used in dating the earlier phases of human evolution. Recent advances in physics promise to increase the time depth of C^{14} dating materially. Highly sophisticated (and expensive!) devices, such as the tandem accelerator, offer the potential of dating remains as ancient as 80,000 to 90,000 years old.[5]

Potassium-Argon Another radiometric dating method, which covers part of the distant time periods beyond the range of C^{14}, is the *potassium-argon* (K-Ar) method. It does not rely on organic material but is applied to rocks that contain the radioactive isotope potassium-40. This unstable element breaks down into the element argon much more slowly than C^{14} breaks down into nitrogen: Its half-life is 1.3 billion years. With sensitive reading instruments, dates earlier than about 200,000 B.P. can be determined. In a rock, the isotope breaks down and the resulting argon accumulates. If the rock is heated to a high temperature, the argon gas will escape; when the rock cools, the argon will begin accumulating again. In many rocks of volcanic origin, such as basalt or obsidian, the proportion of potassium-40 to argon can reveal when the rock was last heated and when the argon began to build up. This technique has been used in dating many primate fossils. It has proven invaluable in placing many of the early hominine fossils in time, especially those from East Africa, where basalts and other volcanic material can be used to date the geologic strata.[6]

It should be remembered that this technique is not performed directly on the fossils but rather on the rocks that contain the datable material. Except for the unusual circumstance of a fossil found directly in a deposit of volcanic origin, a K-Ar date will derive from a level either above or below the fossil and thus give a date that is somewhat younger or older than the fossil.

Carbon-14 and K-Ar are the two most valuable and widely used radiometric dating techniques. Unfortunately, their time spans do not overlap, and there is a gap of over 100,000 years in which neither can provide dates. To overcome this problem, a number of other dating procedures have been used or are under development.

Other Radiometric Dating Methods One of the methods that has the potential of providing dates in the time gap between C^{14} and K-Ar is the *uranium series* technique. This is based on the radioactive decay of uranium into almost a dozen isotopes that are found in shells, some bones and teeth, and a variety of geological sediments. Although its time span covers virtually the entire last million years, contamination of the material to be dated by other sources of environmental uranium remains a serious limitation of this method.

Thermoluminescence has been used extensively by archaeologists to date pottery and ancient bronzes. Applications of this technique are now being extended to burned flints from hominine-bearing deposits. Employing the same physical principles as thermoluminescence is another dating technique, *electron spin resonance* (ESR). Originally developed to test the structural integrity of construction and insulating materials, ESR as a dating technique is based on the behavior of radioactive atoms caught in the calcium carbonate (calcite) crystals found in a variety of substances, including cave deposits, bones, and shell. The potential age range for ESR is from about 75,000 years B.P. to about a million years B.P.

Fission track dating is employed on minerals that contain uranium traces and is based on the counting of the radiation damage tracks left in the mineral crystals. Fission track has a time range encompassing the last 2 million years.

Frequently in the planet's history, the earth's magnetic polarity has completely turned around and remained so for a period of time. During those intervals when the polarity was reversed from the present "normal" magnetism, a compass needle would point south instead of north. When iron-bearing rocks are being formed, the iron atoms in the rock become aligned with the earth's magnetism; with sensitive instruments, these rocks can be "read" to determine the direction of the magnetic polarity (north or south) when they formed.

Paleomagnetism

The reading of the magnetic polarity contained in cores of ocean floor sediments, where continuous deposition has occurred, have permitted geologists to chart the pattern of paleomagnetic reversals over the past several million years. Table 8.1 is a record of the last 5 million years of the earth's paleomagnetic history, calibrated in time by means of K-Ar radiometric determinations on datable rocks in the sediments. Prolonged periods when the earth's magnetism remained stable, either as it is presently (a time of normal magnetism) or reversed, are termed *paleomagnetic epochs*. During these epochs, there have also been shorter inter-

TABLE 8.1
Paleomagnetic History Chart
Here the last 5 million years of the earth's paleomagnetic history are divided into epochs of long duration, with shorter intervals of polarity change within them (events). The Pliocene/Pleistocene boundary is also marked.

Millions of Years B.P.	Paleomagnetic Epochs	Paleomagnetic Events	
	Bruhnes Normal		Late Pleistocene
			Middle Pleistocene
.73	Matuyama Reversed	Jaramillo event (.87–.92)	Early Pleistocene
		Olduvai events (1.6–1.8)	
		Reunion events (1.95–2.1)	
2.47	Gauss Normal	Kaena event (2.8–2.9)	Pliocene
		Mammoth event [2.9 (or 3.0)–3.06 (or 3.08)]	
3.4	Gilbert Reversed	Cochiti event (~3.7–3.8)	
		Nunivak event (~4.0–4.1)	
		C1 (~4.3–4.4)	
		C2 (~4.5–4.7)	
5.2			

vals when the polarity switched again; these are called *paleomagnetic events.* The present epoch of earth polarity, the *Bruhnes Normal epoch,* began, and the preceding *Matuyama Reversed epoch* ended, about 730,000 years ago. Within the Matuyama Reversed epoch, there are a number of shorter episodes of normal polarity, the Jaramillo, Olduvai, and Reunion events.

Paleomagnetism becomes a way of placing fossils in time when a long, continuous series of rock samples are taken from above and below the level in the deposit in which the fossils were found. These samples are analyzed and their magnetic polarity determined. This pattern of reversed and normal polarity determinations is aligned with the established paleomagnetic sequence, permitting the fossil to be located in time.

Stratigraphic Correlation

Under certain circumstances neither radiometric nor paleomagnetic determinations are possible. In such situations, geologic deposits and archaeological sites are given relative ages based on the relationship of the deposits or sites to other geologic contexts or to associated faunal bones; a find could then be said to be older than, younger than, or the same age as another. The relative time at which a geologic deposit was laid down might be identified by the strata above and below it. The stratum might be recognizable as one in a long sequence of geologic deposits laid down over eons. Placing the deposit within the sequence gives some idea of its relative position in time. Similarly, by identifying the fossil bones and relating them to other, closely related fossils found elsewhere, a relative age determination is possible.

Under these conditions, only a very approximate age can be worked out; errors in correlating geologic deposits over wide geographic areas and in cross-referencing fossil bones are common. Nevertheless, because many geologic deposits containing hominine fossil bones cannot be precisely dated, the geologic contexts as well as the faunal correlations retain great importance.

In Chapter 5, the discussions of taxonomy focused on cladistics, the widely used technique for comparing the biological features of different animals and making judgments about their evolutionary relationships, such as how they might be ordered in an evolutionary sequence. This system looks at particular biological features in various fossil and living animal groups and assesses their relative level of development. If a particular biological feature is found in many groups, it is viewed as having evolved long ago and is termed an ancestral, or primitive, feature, while a trait that is found in only a few animals is seen as having evolved recently and is termed a derived, or specialized, feature.

The Subfamily Homininae

Considering bipedalism and the reduction of the projecting canine teeth as derived or specialized features that have developed as part of the hominine line permits us to examine fossil specimens and determine if they belong in the subfamily Homininae. Once a fossil has been identified as a hominine, we can then use the state of development of more detailed or specialized features, along with an understanding of where in time a fossil is placed, to establish a time-ordered sequence of species and construct the hominine evolutionary tree.

Although this may sound relatively straightforward, in practice the establishment of relationships within fossil specimens is unfortunately very difficult. For much of human evolution the fossil evidence consists of broken and fragmentary bits and pieces of bone and teeth. There are only small numbers of complete bones, few associated bones from one individual, and fewer still complete or even relatively complete skeletons. Furthermore, each time we unearth a fossil, we retrieve a slightly different part of the hominine chronology. The specimens often come from different parts of the world and reflect the morphological variation inherent in and among all populations. One of the results of this situation is that it is sometimes very difficult to decide whether two fossil specimens discovered in different places and from somewhat different times are similar enough to be considered members of one species, perhaps a larger male and smaller female of a sexually dimorphic species, or different enough to be parts of two distinct species.

Anthropologists continue to debate questions of hominine species number and distribution, with some suggesting the presence at various times in human evolution of three, four, or more hominine species all living at the same time and perhaps in the same environments. Future fossil discoveries will help in resolving these debates. Most anthropologists today, however, agree that the known hominine fossil evidence can be grouped into two genera, one of them extinct. Table 8.2 lists the most commonly used species names in these genera. The next two chapters will examine the fossil evidence on which this taxonomy is based and consider the evolutionary trees that have been constructed.

The earliest known fossils of the subfamily Homininae are members of the genus *Australopithecus,* whose fossils have been dated from more than 5 million years ago to about 1.5 million years ago. Discovered at a number of sites in East and South Africa, this genus currently represents the first appearance of the hominines in the fossil record. The australopithecines apparently evolved into the surviving genus of the hominine subfamily, *Homo,* about 2 to 1.5 million years ago (Table 8.3).

Reconstructing Hominine Lifeways

The construction of a hominine evolutionary tree is an important aim in the study of human evolution. Another major goal is the reconstruction of the pattern of evolutionary adaptation of our hominine ancestors. We wish to learn about the environments they inhabited, the foods they ate, the social groups they lived in, and the behavior they employed in successfully coping with the demands of their environment.

Behavioral Changes

To reconstruct the behavior of our ancestors, we use the fossil bones themselves and the archaeologist's analyses of the traces that past human activity has left. Usually, the farther back in time we travel, the less we find. There are two reasons for this. First, the recent archaeological record is well supplied with the evidence of our hominine ancestor's

TABLE 8.2
Members of the Human Zoological Subfamily Homininae
All but the last, *Homo sapiens,* are extinct. The locations indicate where fossils and/or other evidence of hominine presence have been found.

The Subfamily Homininae		
Genus	*Species*	*Location*
Australopithecus	*A. afarensis*[a]	Ethiopia, Tanzania
	A. africanus[a]	South Africa, Kenya, Ethiopia
	A. robustus[a]	South Africa
	A. boisei[a]	Tanzania, Kenya, Ethiopia
Homo	*H. habilis*[a]	Tanzania, Kenya, South Africa
	H. erectus	Africa, Asia
	H. sapiens	worldwide

[a]These categories are grouped in this book as the "australopithecines," a purely descriptive term for all hominine fossils dating from 5.0 million to about 1.5 million years B.P.

TABLE 8.3
The Hominines: Dates and Distribution

Date (B.P.)	Geological Epochs	Africa	Asia	Europe	North America and South America
10,000	Recent				
300–400,000		Homo sapiens			
1,600,000	Pleistocene	Homo erectus			
	Pliocene	Australopithecines			
5,000,000					
	Miocene				
23,500,000	Oligocene				

complex behaviors, including tools of stone, bone, wood, and other material (Figure 8.4); bits of skin clothing; evidence of dwellings; and ornaments. Burials yield clues to ideological and social systems; animal bones, plant pollen, and other food debris provide data for reconstructing economic patterns. Further back, before 100,000 years B.P, many of these remains have disintegrated without leaving the slightest trace. The only evidence of the behavior of our ancestors that far back are items hardy enough to survive, such as stone tools and animal bones. Second, the behavioral abilities of our more remote hominine ancestors were much more limited and thus less is left for us to study. This leaves us with sometimes difficult decisions to make regarding the significance of the lack of archaeological evidence: Were the tools and other traces of

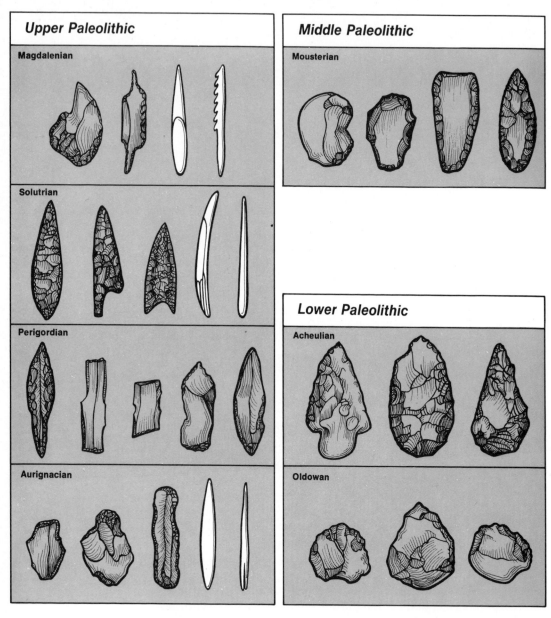

FIGURE 8.4. The evolution of stone and bone tools. These drawings (bone artifacts are in white) show the general changes in tool technology during hominine evolution. Many—but not all—of the same styles of tools, however, are found in more than one culture and time period.

behavioral activities present but destroyed? Or is the lack of any tools or other clear indication of complex behavior a sign that early hominines were incapable of these activities?

The archaeological record of hominine activity shows a pattern of increasing complexity and sophistication over time. However, this trend begins with a very long period when almost no change can be recognized. Later the tempo of increasing complexity speeds up so that by the development of agriculture some 10,000 years ago, cultural change was occurring at a rate many times swifter than at the beginning of the archaeological record some 2.5 million years ago.[7]

This pattern is clearly reflected in the stone tool technology. The earliest evidence is the cobble tools of the australopithecines (*Oldowan*), which are crude and have few marks of delicate workmanship (Figure 8.4). These Oldowan tools appear first about 2.5 million years ago and seem to remain more or less similar for almost a million years. At about 1.5 million years ago, the hand axe traditions (*Acheulian*) evolve, and they exhibit better-made tools in greater variety, suggesting specialization for individual tasks. Both of these early tool industries are known as Lower Paleolithic (*paleo = old; lithic = stone: old stone age*), and can be contrasted with later stone tool traditions of the Middle and Upper Paleolithic, which show the makers' greater skill and the growing complexity of the artifacts. Middle Paleolithic industries, like the *Mousterian* of Europe and the Middle East, first appear after about 125,000 years ago, and these industries are in turn replaced by the more complex and finely made Upper Paleolithic industries about 30,000–40,000 years ago.

The Geologic Background of Hominine Evolution

Our perspective of ancient environments and geologic time is very much the product of recent work. For example, research in the geologic and physical sciences has tended to increase the time depth of the geologic epochs and periods. In 1930 Sir Arthur Keith, a British anatomist, published a major work on the hominine fossils, *New Discoveries Relating to the Antiquity of Man,* that analyzed the fossil record in terms of a length of about 200,000 years for the Pleistocene. Today we continue to recognize the Pleistocene epoch as a crucial time for hominine evolution, yet radiometric dating methods, unknown when Keith wrote, have extended the epoch back to about 1.6 million years, an eightfold increase since 1930.

Darwin speculated in his 1871 book, *The Descent of Man,* that the human subfamily might perhaps extend as far back as the Eocene. We have since limited the possible time span of the hominines to more recent geologic periods, in particular the Miocene, Pliocene, Pleistocene, and into the Holocene, or Recent, epoch (Table 8.3). We are particularly interested in analyzing Eurasian and, especially during the earliest phases of human evolution, African geologic events, because the major phases of hominine evolution took place in the Old World, and the earliest seem to be limited to Africa.

The Miocene

Recent studies of continental drift indicate that the African plate did not make a final land connection with Eurasia until the beginning of the Miocene, more than 20 million years ago. Large interchanges of animals between the two continents probably did not begin until then. The continental collision between the African plate and the Eurasian plate during the Miocene may have created geologic instabilities that caused the beginning of the *Rift Valley system* of East Africa and the Middle East. Stretching today from Mount Carmel in northern Israel down the Jordan River Valley to the Red Sea, the Rift Valley continues south along the East African coast to central Ethiopia, where it turns south and west, cutting through Ethiopia, Kenya, and Tanzania, finally ending in southern Africa. Formation of many of the East African sites, where the earliest hominine fossils have been found, is directly linked with Rift Valley geologic activity.

Another result of this continental collision was the development of the Mediterranean Sea. Prior to Africa's contact with Eurasia, there was an open waterway, called the Tethys Sea, between the Atlantic Ocean on the west and the Indian Ocean on the east (see Figure 7.28). It has been suggested that the closing off of the Tethys at its eastern end and the formation of the Mediterranean resulted in the changing of wind directions and thus rainfall patterns. A variety of analyses of the beginning Miocene epoch suggest that in East Africa, east of the developing Rift Valley system, tropical forests were slowly giving way to a more open country environment.[8] It is possible that climatic changes caused by the geologic changes were responsible for the development of these new habitats; as it has often been suggested that the hominines originated on the open savannas, it may be that these changes were the basis for the appearance of our subfamily. The Miocene period merges without apparent break into the Pliocene about 5 million years ago. During the Pliocene, the patterns established in the Miocene continued, with the extensive East African forests diminishing at the expense of grassland and more mosaic habitats (combinations of grassland, bush, and small stands of forest).

The Pleistocene

About 1.6 million years ago, the transition between the Pliocene and the Pleistocene is marked. This stratigraphic zone has been defined by Southern European deposits in which a number of characteristic mammal fossils were found. Today, although geologists continue to define the Pliocene/Pleistocene boundary by means of deposits in southern Europe, paleomagnetic reversals have taken on an increasingly important role as a practical way to mark this boundary worldwide. The Olduvai events, short-lived periods of normal polarity within the long Matuyama Reversed epoch (see Table 8.1), seem to have occurred about the time the Pliocene/Pleistocene boundary strata were being deposited. Since magnetic reversals occur very quickly (by geologic standards—recent calculations suggest a reversal is completed in about 5,000 years) and simultaneously all over the planet, they represent a very convenient and effective way of correlating geologic activity in different areas. The top of the Olduvai events, at about 1.6 million years ago, is thus used as the beginning of the Pleistocene.

The Pleistocene epoch has been divided into early, middle, and late segments. Because of the difficulties in dating many hominine fossil specimens, it is often not possible to do more than to say that a fossil dates generally to the early, middle, or late Pleistocene. The border between the Matuyama Reversed and the Bruhnes Normal epochs, at about 730,000 years B.P., is used as the border between the early and middle Pleistocene (see Table 8.1). A much more limited marker, the beginning of the last warm period in Europe (the last interglacial period), at about 128,000 years B.P., is used to separate the middle and late Pleistocene.

More than a million and a half years ago the climate changed drastically in the northern hemisphere, breaking the rest of the Pleistocene into alternating *glacial* and *interglacial* periods. During the glacial advances, large parts of the northern hemisphere were covered by very slowly expanding ice sheets. Interglacial times were marked by climatic warming and the retreat of the glaciers. Not including the ice-bound Antarctic continent, Pleistocene glaciers may have occupied an area thirteen times greater than the glaciers of today, most of which are confined to high mountain areas and Greenland. Because so much water was trapped in the glaciers, sea levels dropped, and previously independent land masses came into contact. For example, a land bridge between Siberia and Alaska was formed by the glacier-caused drop in sea level. Hominines crossed this bridge into the New World, but only 20,000 to 30,000 years ago, when they were already fully modern in physical features.

The classic studies of Pleistocene glaciation were carried out on geologic deposits in the central European Alpine region early in this century. This research suggested that there were four glacial advances (from the earliest to the latest): Günz, Mindel, Riss, and Würm, named for the locale where each was identified. Interposed between these glacials were three interglacials, when the climate warmed and the glaciers retreated. Later, a pre-Günz glacial, the Donau, was proposed. It was also recognized that the glacial advances were more complex and that within a glacial, the climate briefly warmed at times; these warm periods are termed *interstadials*. Recent research in Europe has indicated that the pattern of glacial advances and retreats is extremely complicated and that glacial activity cannot be neatly divided into four or five glacial advances; there is now evidence for seventeen climatic fluctuations in central Europe during the Pleistocene, and more than twenty over the last 800,000 years have been identified from the analysis of sea cores.[9] Because of the complexity of these fluctuations and the fact that subsequent glacial advances tend to scour away the marks of previous ice sheets, correlations between glacial systems in different parts of the northern hemisphere, or even within limited areas, have been very difficult. In Europe, two great

The Glaciers

glacial systems have been identified. At its maximum, the Alpine glacial system covered almost all of Switzerland and moved north into southern Germany, west into France, east into eastern and central Europe, and south into much of northern Italy. The other, the Fenno-Scandinavian system, at its maximum covered the areas that are now Scandinavia—Denmark, Norway, Sweden, and Finland—and spread south and east into parts of northern Germany, the Low Countries, and the Baltic regions. Correlations between these two glacial systems have not been completely satisfactory, except for the last glacial advance, called the Weichsel in Scandinavia, which correlated with the Würm (Figure 8.5).

FIGURE 8.5. The extent of the Weichsel and the Würm glacials during the last glacial advance in Eurasia.

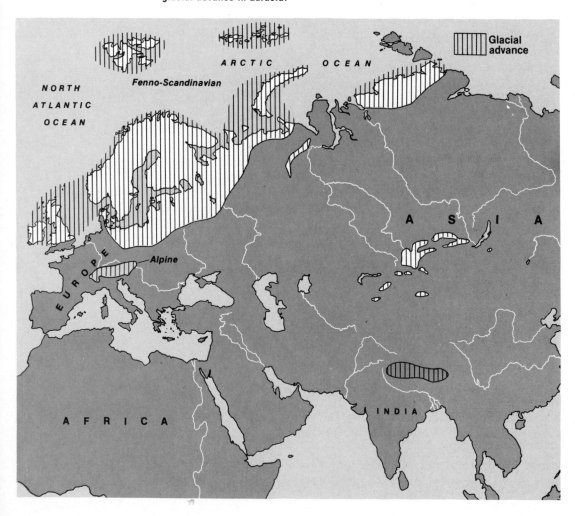

Asia, too, had ice sheets, the most important in the Himalayas, which at their maximum extended to the north, east, west, and south and prevented animals and people from moving between northern and southern Asia and Europe. Other glacials were localized in the Ural Mountains between Asian and European Russia and on many other mountain chains in Europe and Asia.

The glacial–interglacial sequence occurred only in the northern hemisphere. There is some evidence that glacial advances seem to have affected rainfall in the southern hemisphere, giving many areas less rain than they get today. There is also evidence in the southern hemisphere for glacials, but only at very high altitudes. Mount Kilimanjaro in East Africa, at about 7,000 meters, had a glacier, as did the high Andes of western South America. These local phenomena extended only short distances, however, and were nothing like the northern hemisphere's glacial advances, which entombed huge parts of North America and Eurasia.

Glacial advances and retreats profoundly affected the life zones; although hominines did not live on the ice, its spread nevertheless strongly influenced their environments. As the northern latitudes got colder, all fauna and flora were forced southward. Hominines, too, had to shift with the environment, probably moving as the climate changed. In addition, the hominines had to adapt to these severe climatic conditions. Both cultural and biological adaptations were at work to make survival possible in these harsh environments. Modern humans subjected to extremes of temperature have evolved biological ways of dealing with chronic cold (see Chapter 13). These adaptations evolved by natural selection over thousands of years. Growing up in a cold climate can also increase an individual's tolerance to cold; this is a developmental response that can occur rapidly but cannot be passed on across generations. Cultural and behavioral adaptations (such as warm clothing, fire, and ingeniously constructed shelters like the igloo) are a third and much swifter response to environmental changes than strictly genetic adaptations, which must rely mostly on natural selection and chance mutations. Human evolution is much more complex than that of other animals because hominines have employed artifacts and other manifestations of cultural behavior to adapt to inhospitable environments. This interaction of the biological and the cultural, which has made it possible for humans to exploit greatly varied environments, has made humans unique among living creatures.

The cultural complexity or efficiency that enabled hominines to survive in severe cold took several million years to evolve. The biological bases for these cultural behaviors, such as large, complex brains, skill in using the hands, and numberless others, were developed in milder climates before our ancestors eventually spread to all parts of the world. Much of the early history of the Homininae took place in the tropical zones of the Old World, mostly in Africa, and it is only relatively late in

Hominine Evolution in the Pleistocene

human evolution that we find evidence of hominine occupation of the cold areas of central Europe and north Asia.

By convention, the Pleistocene is said to have ended, and the Holocene, or Recent, epoch to have begun, about 10,000 years ago, when the last glaciers retreated and the climate began to warm. However, many geologists believe that we are currently living in an interglacial period and that glacial advances will recur; although modern industrialization and pollution (the "greenhouse effect") may interfere with these climatic changes and prolong or even intensify the current warm period.

Hominine Environments

Hominine presence in Europe and Asia during Pleistocene glacials, when they would have been subjected to severe winters, has been directly documented by archaeologists excavating occupation sites. These sites, which represent actual hominine accumulations, are often found in caves, but open-air locales are also known. Finds at these sites include broken animal bones, stone tools, the waste pieces chipped off in the manufacture of stone tools, fire hearths sometimes still containing charcoal, and occasionally, if the site is after 70,000 years B.P., the buried body of a hominine. At the open-air sites there is often evidence of tent-like or other structures. As archaeologists excavate a site, multiple occupation levels are sometimes discovered, indicating that the hominine group returned to this same spot year after year. The size of the site can offer clues about the size of the social group, and its geographic location provides information about the habitats that were being exploited. The animal bones and other evidence offer data about important attributes of the adaptation and way of life of these hominines, although, as we shall see in the following chapters, much is still uncertain.

These archaeological finds permit reconstruction of the later parts of human biological history. When we attempt to reconstruct the earlier phases of human evolution, however, the evidence becomes much more scanty and difficult to interpret. Between 700,000 and 200,000 years B.P., there are few archaeological sites of the sort that characterize later human evolution; none are earlier than 700,000 years B.P. Traces of early hominines from these remote periods come not from true occupation sites but from accumulations amassed by natural agencies, such as lake sediment deposition. Often what is found at these sites are hundreds, even thousands, of animal bones, sometimes with hominine bones intermingled and occasionally with stone tools mixed in. These collections are not the result of deliberate hominine behaviors such as hunting, but rather represent the slow, gradual accumulation of materials by natural activities.

Taphonomy

Taphonomy, a branch of geology, is the study of how animals are killed and the various processes that operate in the environment after an animal's death to the time its bones are incorporated into a geologic deposit. To illustrate the process of taphonomy, imagine the following scene, which has often been pictured in natural history programs on television. On an African plain at dusk, an antelope comes to the edge of a lake and while drinking is attacked, killed, and partly eaten by lions, who then abandon the carcass after a day or two. Scavengers like jackals, hyenas, and buzzards mob the remains of the antelope, fighting over what is left and dragging pieces away to be safely consumed at a distance. A portion of the lower jaw is accidentally kicked into the lake; the rest of the dead animal is either eaten or eventually trampled by other animals on their way to the lake to drink. In a few weeks, all that is left of the antelope is the piece of the jaw that ended up in the lake.

The lake's current carries the jaw until it reaches a shallow, still backwater, where the bone settles to the lake bottom and is covered by accumulating sediments. Safely removed from the environmental agencies that would have destroyed it, the bone in time may be infused with minerals from the surrounding sediment and become a fossil. In this way, the antelope jawbone and thousands of other bones from many different animals, including early hominines, can end up forming a fossil assemblage in the bottoms of lakes, streams, and rivers as well as caves.

When fossil bone accumulations are discovered, it is essential to understand the processes that created them. Taphonomists use a wide variety of experimental and observational techniques to reconstruct the natural agencies that have contributed to the kinds and range of animal bones in a specific accumulation. One of the questions taphonomists seek to answer is why particular bones, such as lower jaws, are more likely to be represented in some fossil collections than other bones, such as ribs or vertebrae. Alternatively, certain fossil bone collections contain high numbers of lower leg bones but few other bones. A consideration of the shape, hardness, and density of the bones provides a great deal of useful information about this finding.

By experimentally investigating how water currents carry bones of various sizes, taphonomists can reconstruct which animal bones may have been carried a similar distance and thus sort out groupings of animals in a deposit. In this fashion, a large mass of bones, perhaps representing hundreds of different animals, can be divided into a number of groupings, each having originated in a different place and being transported by the water a different distance.

Taphonomy provides a crucial basis for understanding the processes that formed the early hominine deposits. By identifying the animals that are part of the same grouping as the hominines and relating them to their living descendents, for whom the environmental adaptation is known, taphonomists can suggest the sorts of environments in which the early hominines were living (or at least dying). Taphonomy can thus provide the evidence necessary to reconstruct the environment in which early hominine evolution occurred. Although much information has already been amassed (to be described in the next two chapters), a great deal of data remains to be gathered, and many ambiguous details must be more fully investigated.

Diet and Human Evolution

Modern humans, in their worldwide distribution, have survived on an enormous array of diets, from one based predominantly on meat, found among people like the Eskimos living in the far north, to a diet of vegetables and grains, characteristic of numerous human societies. Although most living humans have a diet intermediate between these two extremes, what is virtually universal is the reliance on agriculture (and domesticated animals) to supply the vast range of foods consumed by living peoples. Later chapters will describe the ways by which modern humans have adapted to these dietary resources and their implications for human biology and adaptation. Here we shall explore the history of human dietary patterns.

Today, only a few human societies survive by gathering wild vegetables, insects, and small animals and hunting larger animals. It seems likely, however, that prior to the invention of agriculture (which seems to have occurred in several parts of the world virtually simultaneously, about 12,000 years B.P.), this pattern, termed *gathering and hunting,* was the way of life of our ancestors. But how far back does gathering and hunting extend, and what kinds of foods made up the diets of our ancestors before the development of agriculture?

The main source of evidence for reconstructing the diet of our pre-agricultural hominine ancestors comes from the analysis of remains found at archaeological sites, including animal bones and other food debris, and the identification of objects that might have been used in the preparation of particular foods. Unfortunately, we do not have such evidence for the early phases of human evolution, and even for the later times, when archaeological sites are numerous, preservation problems have made it very difficult to come up with reasonable answers. For example, because animal bones are much better preserved than vegetable residues and insect bodies, the presence and number of animal bones (and the lack of other remains) have often been used to suggest that our ancestors were overwhelmingly meat-eating hunters. We now know that this is a very simplistic view and that we must employ much more sophisticated techniques if we wish to understand the food ways of our ancestors.

Chemical Analysis of Bones

One set of techniques that promises to provide answers to these questions is the chemical analysis of hominine bones. Most of these studies have emphasized the analysis of trace elements in bone, including stable isotopes of common chemical elements and the calculation of strontium/calcium ratios.

Stable Isotope Analysis   This technique relies on the presence in bones of differing amounts of variants (isotopes) of such common elements as oxygen, nitrogen, and carbon. These stable (nonradioactive) isotopic variations can be related to different foods in the diet. Because of the nature of their metabolism, some plants, like peas and beans, contain higher levels of a particular isotope of carbon than do other plants, which contain still another carbon isotope. Because bone will incorporate these differing carbon isotopes into the amino acid chains that make up its fibrous protein structure, analysis of the carbon isotopes in the bone can provide information about the relative amount of different kinds of plant foods in the diet.

Strontium/Calcium Ratios   This analysis may eventually provide information on the relative amounts of meat and vegetables in the diet. Both calcium, an extremely important nutrient for all living things, and strontium are found in soils. As plants grow, they take up calcium to use in their metabolic processes; small amounts of strontium are also incorporated into the plants' tissues. When animals eat the plants, the strontium, which as an element behaves very much like calcium, becomes part of their bones, taking the place of some of the calcium. The more plant material an animal eats, the greater the amount of strontium incorporated into the bones. As a result, plant-eating animals have more strontium in their bones than do meat eaters. By comparing the ratio of strontium to calcium in bones, it may be possible to determine whether an animal was mainly a herbivore (a high amount of strontium in proportion to calcium), a carnivore (a low amount of strontium in proportion to calcium), or an omnivore (strontium/calcium proportion in between). This technique works well on human bones that have not been fossilized. At the present time, scientists are experiencing serious problems in the interpretation of the strontium/calcium ratios found in fossilized hominine and other animal bones. These will have to be worked out before information about hominine diets can be obtained from this technique.

Another sophisticated technique for reconstructing the dietary patterns of our ancestors involves the careful examination of the chewing surface of the back teeth. Chewing even relatively soft foods like fruits leaves distinctive tiny scratch marks or grooves on the occlusal surfaces of teeth. With a scanning electron microscope, these minute scratches on early hominine fossil teeth can be viewed. These scratches, when compared with those on the teeth of living animals, whose diet is known, have revealed a number of interesting similarities. Because this analysis literally identifies the last meals an individual ate before it died, it is unclear just how accurate a picture of the total diet is being preserved by these scratch marks, and research is continuing on their overall significance.

Microscopic Analysis of Teeth

The reconstruction of hominine lifeways, including the environments they inhabited and the foods they ate, is of great importance if we are to understand the evolutionary patterns that eventually led to modern humans. This reconstruction, along with the ordering of a hominine family tree, will form the basis of the next two chapters in which the fossil evidence for human evolution will be presented.

Overview of Hominine Lifeways

The subfamily Homininae includes two genera, the extinct genus *Australopithecus* and our own genus *Homo*. The earliest documented fossil bones identified as members of the Homininae date from about 5 million years ago. In Chapter 7, protein and DNA comparisons of living primates formed the foundation for the development of the "molecular clock" used to estimate times of divergence of major living primate species (pages 271–273). These calculations suggest that the human line diverged from the one leading to the chimpanzees between 5 and 8 million years ago. It is thus possible that our known fossil evidence represents virtually the entire record of hominine evolution. If the evolutionary separation occurred earlier, around 8 million years B.P., there is a gap of about 3 million years between the origin of the hominine line and the earliest fossil evidence. It is hoped that future research will resolve this question and permit us to understand more fully the evolutionary context in which the subfamily Homininae originated. Many speculative models have been developed to explain hominine origins.

Hominine Origins: Some Hypotheses

Tools and Adaptations

For a new line of organisms to evolve, there must first be reproductive isolation. The first step in the divergence of the hominines from their apelike ancestors, then, was the prevention of interbreeding between populations. This isolation could have been realized either by a geographic barrier between the two populations, such as a river or mountain range, or simply by distance. Because the living apes are adapted to the forest or its fringe, the common ancestors of both apes and humans might have been forest forms. During the early Miocene, changes in climate appear to have led to a shrinkage of the extensive East African forests, with an increase of mosaic and open-country habitats between the now-limited forested areas. Populations of these ancestral apes would have been isolated in different forested areas, with the result that interbreeding would be prevented even though the distance between the groups was not great. If, in the now-isolated population that was to lead to the hominines, the usual foods were harder to find, perhaps because of changes in climate, toolmaking, until then of minor importance, might have become more important as a way of gathering new food resources. There is not much difference between the termiting stick used by modern chimpanzees in getting at termites (see Figure 6.22) and the digging stick, a longer, more robust, wooden stick that many modern human groups still use to dig up edible tubers, roots, small burrowing animals, insects, and insect grubs. If this change in the behavioral emphasis occurred and was successful, natural selection would modify the physical features of the population to use the behavior more suitably. One hypothesis for the origin of the hominines thus involves a shift in the food-gathering behavior of an ancestral ape population to one based on tools.[10] The proposal seems reasonable enough, but there is little definite evidence to support it. Furthermore, no one knows how closely this ancestral ape population resembled the modern chimpanzee; modern chimps may have changed as much as the hominines have in the millions of years since the human and ape lines diverged.

A Diet of Seeds

Another suggestion for origins is offered by Clifford Jolly.[11] He is impressed by the morphological resemblances, especially in dentition, between early hominine fossils and the gelada, the baboonlike terrestrial monkey of the Ethiopian highlands. The geladas feed on small objects such as grass, tubers, and seeds. As an adaptation to this kind of feeding, the geladas have hands with great manipulative ability. Jolly suggests that the hominines originated as small-object feeders and that this basic adaptation opened the way for the later development of toolmaking and other hominine morphological and behavioral traits. In this view, tools would have little to do with the origin of the hominines.

The Savanna and Bipedalism

Another hypothesis concerning hominine origins focuses on the importance of the evolution of bipedalism. A number of anthropologists, including G. H. R. von Koenigswald, J. T. Robinson, and Russell Tuttle, suggest that the need of an increasingly savanna-adapted primate for a more efficient type of locomotion was the initial impetus for the appearance of the hominines. In their view, bipedalism evolved as an adaptation to savanna life, and from this later hominine traits, such as tool use, followed.[12]

A Male Foraging Model

Finally, Owen Lovejoy views hominine beginnings as taking place not on the savanna but in the forest. Lovejoy believes that a pattern of decreased time between births was crucial to hominine development because it meant that females spent more time with their dependent offspring. As a result the males were required to forage for food for their mates. This behavior in turn necessitated the development of a pattern of locomotion—bipedalism—that would permit males to carry food back to the females.[13]

Hominine Origins: A Summary

These different views of hominine origins are based on the varieties of habitats and food resources that are thought to have influenced the earliest hominines' pattern of adaptation. The major difficulty, as Jane Lancaster has pointed out, is that the forms representing the evolutionary transition from an ancestral ape population to the earliest hominines are all extinct, as are their lifeways.[14] It is probable that these earliest hominines were unique in many ways, which leaves us with a serious practical problem: Lacking fossil evidence, what living animals and what parts of their total adaptations are we to use as models in reconstructing the adaptive patterns of the earliest hominines? Are we to consider the chimpanzee, whom many believe to be our closest living relative, as the best approximation of what the earliest hominines were like? Or, if the needs of a savanna adaptation were most important to the earliest hominines, perhaps the savanna baboons of the genus *Papio* are the most appropriate model of hominine origins. Or maybe the gelada represents a better model, as Jolly suggests. It has also been suggested that because some aspects of hominine social behavior are similar to those of the social carnivores, such as wolves and African hunting dogs, the hominines' origin and early evolution ought to be viewed in terms of cooperative hunting.

Also to be considered is the adaptation of living humans who do not practice agriculture, the gatherer/hunters, such as the *San* of southern Africa. It is interesting to note that both chimpanzees and the gatherer/hunters that have been studied seem able to exploit a number of different environments by eating a great variety of plant and animal foods. Seen in the context of human evolution, this similarity would suggest that the earliest hominines moved through a variety of habitats in a yearly round and ate a wide variety of seasonally available plant foods as well as some animal foods, including insects and small vertebrates like amphibians, reptiles, birds, and small mammals.

The Pattern of Human Evolution

Future discoveries may invalidate all of these hypotheses, and another explanation, not yet proposed, may well fit the new facts more closely. Whatever the ultimate solution to the problem of hominine origins, examination of the known fossil evidence has revealed a number of morphological and other trends. The major changes in physical appearance from the earliest hominine to living humans are the development of bipedalism, a decrease in size of the face and teeth, and an increase in size of the brain. These changes did not come all at the same time or proceed at the same rate. They are general trends in hominine biological history, spread over millions of years.

Biological and Behavioral Changes

The major changes in the brain, face, teeth, and locomotion in hominine physical evolution are closely interrelated with changes in behavior. Whatever the reason for its initial development, bipedalism frees the hands for using tools and other implements. Perhaps the face and teeth became smaller as tools took over tasks once performed by the teeth, such as holding objects. It is more likely, however, that the interrelationships are far more complex; we are only now beginning to understand the complicated patterns of interaction between different biological systems in a single individual. The hints we currently possess suggest that changes in the size of the brain, for example, which lead to modifications in the shape of the brain case, influence the positioning of the face in relation to the brain case; this in turn may modify the shape and size of the dental arch, leaving less room for the teeth. The ultimate result of all this is that an increase in the size of the brain may also lead to reduction in the size of the teeth through a complex series of steps.

The increasing size of the brain can be related to changes in behavior. If successful behavior is one of the keys to a successful adaptation, and if in the hominines a successful adaptation is based on the use of tools, natural selection will favor individuals who are better able to make and use tools. In a variable population, individuals whose nervous system gives them a stronger basis for this behavior would be better able to survive and reproduce; evolution would select for more complex brains. The changes in the brain would include increasing size and complexity of the motor cortex and other parts of the cerebrum and expansion of the cerebellum. Thus, the hominine brain's organization and complexity would eventually shift toward providing enhanced ability in making and using tools. This shift would also feed back into the behavior, providing for still more complex activities.

We may treat the physical and behavioral complexes as separate, but very clearly the components are strongly entwined. As one system evolves it directly affects the others; for this reason, it is not easy to examine any one system, physical or behavioral, without reference to the others.

The expansion of the geographic areas occupied by our ancestors represents another major trend in human evolution. The earliest fossil evidence comes from East Africa, around 5 million years B.P., with sites about 2 million years later known from South Africa. Since chimpanzees and gorillas, our closest living relatives, are also known only from Africa, it is reasonable to suppose that the hominine subfamily originated in Africa. Hominines apparently are confined to eastern and southern Africa until sometime after a million years ago, when they, along with other African mammals, began to expand into the tropical and subtropical areas of Eurasia. Much later, perhaps 50,000 years ago, hominines were able to cross the water barrier into Australia, and only after the appearance of modern humans, sometime after 30,000 years ago, did peoples move into North and South America.

Expansion of Range

Summary

This chapter deals with a number of general issues related to the study of the evolution of the subfamily Homininae, which includes modern humans and our immediate direct ancestors. Like all animals, the hominines have evolved via the mechanisms of natural selection in response to the demands of the environment. Two important aims of this study, which will form the core of our examination of the fossil evidence in the following chapters, are: (1) the ordering of the fossil material into an evolutionary tree showing the pattern of human evolution, and (2) the reconstruction of the lifeways of our hominine ancestors during the course of their evolutionary history.

The construction of a hominine evolutionary tree involves defining the subfamily as well as those species, living and extinct, who are its members. It also requires an understanding of when these creatures lived. Although there are difficulties in precisely defining the subfamily Homininae, the fossil evidence now suggests that one of the earliest of the important evolutionary changes, the development of bipedalism, is the most appropriate way of defining the subfamily. The fossil bones and teeth identified as hominine have been divided into two genera: *Austral-opithecus,* all of whose members are now extinct, and *Homo*, of which modern humans are the living representatives.

Various methods have been developed to date hominine evolution. An important development is the use of techniques measuring the decay of radioactive elements in geologic deposits and organic remains. The carbon-14 and potassium-argon techniques are the most often employed, but a number of others have been developed and are increasingly being used. Paleomagnetism, or the identification of the periodic reversals in the earth's magnetic polarity, can also be used to determine when a hominine lived. Where these dating techniques cannot be used, a rough approximation of the fossil's age can be determined by the relative position of the site or the remains in the context of geologic strata.

The reconstruction of the lifeways of our hominine ancestors requires an understanding of the environments they lived in, the foods they ate, and the behaviors they used in successfully adapting to their environments.

Hominine evolution has been dated to the Miocene, Pliocene, Pleistocene, and Holocene epochs. The most important stages occurred in the Old World, probably beginning in the Miocene epoch. Recent studies of continental drift suggest that the African and Eurasian continents became joined at the beginning of this epoch. The geologic changes that ensued perhaps caused climatic changes that resulted in the development of a more open, less forested environment in East Africa. Some researchers believe that the hominines originated in such open country, although this is merely an educated guess, since no fossil evidence of the very earliest hominines has been found. The early phases of hominine evolution—when biological changes such as bipedalism developed—occurred in the tropical zones of the Old World, probably in Africa. By the time hominines first appeared in the temperate regions of the Old World, their biological development was sufficiently advanced to permit cultural adaptations to severe climatic conditions.

In the course of hominine evolution, a number of major changes have occurred. These changes did not all happen at once, nor did they proceed at the same rate; morphologically, they include the evolution of bipedalism, expansion of the brain, and decrease in the size of face and teeth. Behaviorally, there were changes in cultural complexity, as seen in the stone tool industries and other archaeological remains. These biological and behavioral trends are probably interrelated: Changes in one have influenced others.

Another important change in human evolution has been the expansion of geographic areas. Initially limited to eastern and southern Africa, the hominines later expand into the tropics of Eurasia and then into the temperature regions of that continent. Only later do hominines cross into Australia, and finally, after the appearance of modern humans, into North and South America.

We can thus now discern the general outline of hominine evolution. Anthropologists have not agreed on when these behavioral and physical trends began; the most reasonable estimates range from 5 to 8 million years B.P. Nor is there any general agreement on the factors responsible for the origin of the hominine family: Changes in the environment, alterations in the diet, and the beginning of toolmaking have all been suggested. Only the discovery of new fossil evidence may eventually solve these problems. Nevertheless, we do know a great deal about hominine evolution through our analysis of the existing fossil material, which will form the topic of discussion in the following two chapters.

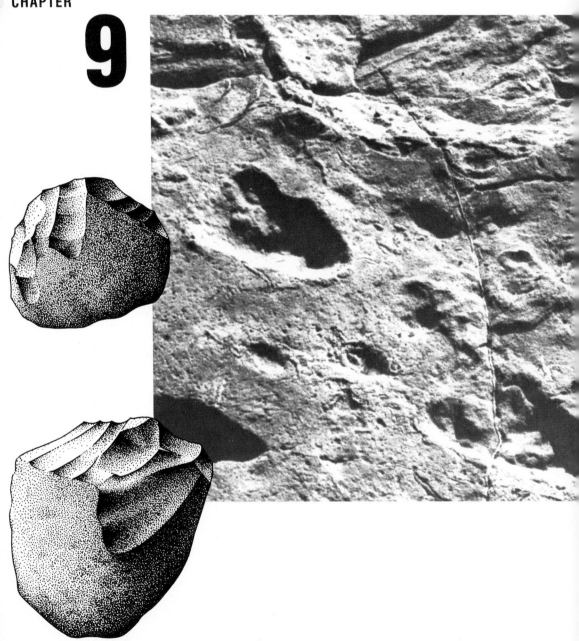

The fossil evidence of the early hominines reflects the evolutionary changes that led up to the appearance of modern humans: bipedal locomotion, decreased size of the face and teeth, and increased size of the brain.

Human Evolution I: The Early Hominines

The fossil specimens discussed in this and the following chapter were unearthed in many areas of the world and outline the general path that our hominine ancestors followed over the past few million years.

As we have seen in earlier chapters, there continues to be much debate about the exact time of the origin of the hominine subfamily and which fossils are its earliest true representatives. Biochemical evidence suggests that the hominines did not become a separately evolving group until about 5 to 8 million years ago. If we accept this date, no hominines could have been around earlier, and our presently known fossil evidence just about reaches back to the beginnings of our line.

Many paleontologists view the Miocene hominoid family Sivapithecidae as sharing important dental and jaw features with the early hominines: less jutting faces, thick layers of enamel on the molar teeth, and relatively large molar teeth. Out of the sivapith group or a closely related group may have evolved the earliest members of the hominine subfamily, perhaps 5 to 10 million years ago. We do not yet have fossil evidence documenting a connection of the hominines with any Miocene apes, but it is often suggested that the sivapiths are representative of the general group from whom the direct hominine ancestor sprang.

Only the discovery of additional fossil material can resolve the issue of the timing of hominine origins and the identity of the group from which they evolved. At present, the fossil evidence of the hominines begins at about 5 million years, with the *australopithecines*.

Australopithecine fossils dated from the end of the Miocene, the Pliocene, and from the early part of the Pleistocene have been found at sites earliest in East Africa and somewhat later in South Africa (Figure 9.1).

In 1924, Raymond Dart, a young South African anatomy professor, was given some fossil bones from a limestone quarry at Taung in the Cape Province (Figure 9.2). It was the skull of a young primate child

The Beginning of the Hominine Line

Discoveries of Australopithecines: South Africa

The Taung Fossil: *Australopithecus africanus*

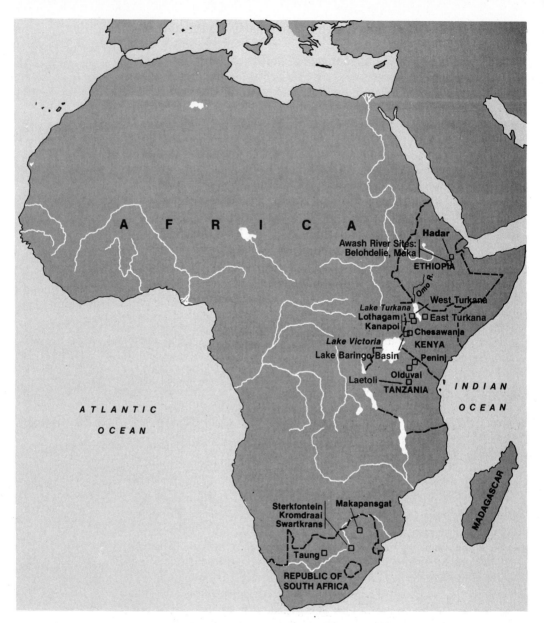

FIGURE 9.1.   Major australopithecine sites.

with the first permanent molars just erupted (in modern human children this would occur at about six years of age). Its molar teeth were larger than modern molars, but the milk canines were small and nonprojecting, the whole dentition had a human shape, and the dental arch was human. Only the size of the brain, comparable to that of a chimpanzee, distinguished it from other hominines. Since the brain of a fossil has long since disintegrated, its measurement is based either on the volume (expressed in milliliters, or ml; for comparison: 1,000 ml = 1 liter = 1.1 quarts) of

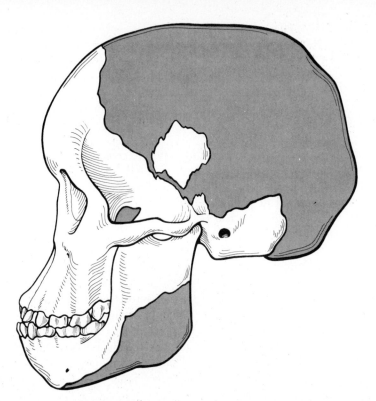

FIGURE 9.2. A drawing of the Taung fossil, the first australopithecine specimen found (four-fifths actual size; right side reversed). The shaded area at the back of the skull delineates the size of the brain case, which can be accurately restored from the cast of the inside of the brain case also found with the fossil.

the inside of the skull or (as with the Taung child) on that of a fossilized cast of the inside of the brain case. Modern human brains vary greatly in size, from about 1,000 to more than 2,000 ml; most, however, are between 1,350 and 1,450 ml. Chimpanzee brains are usually between 350 and 450 ml and gorilla brains about 500 to 600 ml.

The Taung child's brain is about 440 ml. Professor Dart decided it may have been a hominine or perhaps an intermediate step between the apes and humans, gave it a scientific name, and described it in the journal *Nature* in 1925[1]*. Dart called his creature *Australopithecus africanus,* or the southern ape of Africa. Most of Dart's colleagues disagreed vehemently, believing instead that the Taung child was a young anthropoid ape. At the time, they had valid reasons, one of them being the very small sample—the remains of one individual. But there were other reasons for not classifying *Australopithecus* as a hominine or even a near-hominine. It was then believed that the human line had originated in Asia, and not much attention was paid to Africa. Darwin had suggested in *The Descent of Man* (1871) that Africa was the hominine homeland, mainly because the chimpanzee and the gorilla, our closest living relatives, were natives there,

*See pages 622–624 for notes to Chapter 9.

but by 1924 emphasis had shifted from Africa to Asia. Another reason was that a human child and a young chimpanzee look more alike than an adult chimpanzee and an adult human. Many of the features that strongly distinguish chimpanzees from modern humans only develop during adolescent growth. The Taung fossil was that of a young child; Dart's critics suggested that had it grown to maturity, it would have developed clearly apelike features.

The Piltdown Hoax   Perhaps the most important objection to considering *Australopithecus* a hominine was the existence of known fossils whose morphological characteristics contradicted those of the Taung child. *Australopithecus*'s jaws and teeth were homininelike, but its brain was the size of an ape's. Fossils of two individuals had been found in a gravel deposit near the river Thames in Piltdown, Kent County, England, between 1912 and 1915. The features they showed were exactly the reverse of the Taung fossil: The Piltdown fragments had a brain as big as that of a modern human, but the jaws and teeth were those of an ape. The Piltdown story, however, is one of the more interesting, not to say embarrassing, stories in the hundred-year search for the remains of human ancestors.

In 1912 at a meeting of the Royal Geological Society an amateur naturalist named Charles Dawson announced he had discovered parts of a darkly patinated skull and lower jaw, along with flint tools and worked animal bones, in early Pleistocene deposits (Figure 9.3). The fossils were

FIGURE 9.3. Excavation at the Piltdown site. Charles Dawson, the most likely perpetrator of the Piltdown hoax, is seen on the left, holding the screen, while Sir Arthur Smith-Woodward searches for more of the Piltdown "fossils." The workman on the right stands in the pit where Dawson said the original "fossils" were found.

given the scientific name "Eoanthropus dawsoni" (*eo = dawn:* Dawson's dawn man). Their physical features are remarkable from our perspective, but from the point of view of early twentieth-century evolutionary theory there was nothing strange about them. Here was a creature that had a modern human brain case with about the same cranial capacity, 1,400 ml, yet its lower jaw could not be distinguished from those of the living apes except by the modern human wear patterns on the teeth (Figure 9.4). The canine teeth were missing, as was the whole facial portion of the skull. One of the outstanding paleontologists of the time, Sir Arthur Smith-Woodward, tried to reconstruct the important missing canine, building from the size and appearance of the preserved canine tooth socket. His carved chalk model, similar to the canines of chimpanzees, was exhibited at another meeting of the Geological Society. Several months later, further excavation in the Piltdown gravels uncovered the missing canine tooth, almost an exact duplicate of the model Smith-Woodward had carved. No one suspected a connection between the shape of the Piltdown canine and the model Sir Arthur had made. In 1915, pieces of another individual, Piltdown II, were discovered at a gravel pit some distance from the first.

FIGURE 9.4.   Side view of the fraudulent Piltdown skull; the dark areas are the recovered parts. Notice that the knob that attaches the lower jaw to the skull was not found but was reconstructed for this model. (The dashed lines show the break between the part of the jaw that was "found" and the restored part.) The skull mirrored early views of hominine evolution, possessing a modern human brain case and the large jaws and projecting canine teeth of an ape.

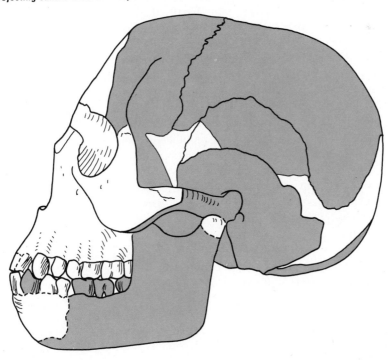

The Piltdown remains, it turned out, were a carefully assembled fraud, perpetrated with full knowledge of the theories and expectations of early twentieth-century evolutionary scientists. At that time it was believed that the enlarged human brain had evolved before the teeth and jaws. A very early hominine, then, should have a modern human-sized brain and ape-sized dentition; the Piltdown fossils had just that. Later a great number of authentic hominine fossils proved that human evolution had not taken that route. Even at the time of discovery some scientists did not believe that the skull, so apparently human, and the jaw, so totally apelike, had ever been together in one animal.

It was not until 1953 that the Piltdown remains were looked at with any suspicion of a deliberate hoax. They had become an enigma that could no longer be shoved aside. A careful look revealed traces of the forger's hand, however. A small hole drilled in the jaw showed that the dark patina was only on the surface; the drill came up with fresh bone. The skull seems to be that of a Roman-age British burial, probably chosen for its unusually thick cranial bones, which helped convince the early investigators of its great antiquity; the jaw belonged to a modern orangutan. The perpetrator of the fraud knew a great deal about anatomy: the jaw would not articulate with the skull if it were left complete, so the articulating knob, or condyle, at the back of the jaw was conveniently broken off; the large ape canines would have prevented the rotary chewing characteristic of modern humans, so the teeth were filed down to simulate a human wear pattern. The site was shrewdly salted with these "human fossils" and with appropriate worked animal bones, unworked animal bones, and flint tools, all probably authentic artifacts except for a club made from an elephant bone. Finally the pieces were stained to give them the dark color typical of some fossil material.

The Piltdown hoax has been the subject of many books in the years since its unmasking. Practically every scientist who was ever associated in any way with the Piltdown material has been identified by one author or another as the guilty party, but most of the evidence appears to point to the original discoverer, Charles Dawson, as the most likely culprit.[2] Dawson died in 1916, well before the truth came out. In 1925, however, Piltdown was still a recognized member of the hominine lineage and proved a stumbling block to the acceptance of *Australopithecus africanus*.

More Finds in South Africa

Sterkfontein   One man not deterred by Piltdown and convinced that Dart's ideas were correct was Robert Broom. Trained as a physician, Broom had a lively interest in the study of extinct life. His earlier paleontological research had resulted in the discovery of the therapsids, the mammal-like reptiles that helped bridge the evolutionary gap between the reptiles and the mammals. Broom was convinced that more fossils, especially those of adults, were needed to bolster Dart's claims for the hominine status of *Australopithecus*. Helped by some of Dart's students, he began looking into limestone quarries in and around Pretoria. On a visit to the Sterkfontein Valley, thirty miles west of Johannesburg in the

Transvaal, he asked the quarry manager if he ever saw fossils, and he was handed some remarkable pieces, several of which he saw immediately might be hominines. Back at the Transvaal Museum in Pretoria, where he worked, Broom felt confident he had discovered adult individuals of an extinct hominine—similar to Dart's *Australopithecus africanus*. Broom eventually named his find "Plesianthropus transvaalensis" (near-man of the Transvaal) because he believed the fossils from Sterkfontein were different enough to be put into a new genus. It was recognized later that the Sterkfontein fossils, as well as those from another site in the northern Transvaal, Makapansgat, were much like the child from Taung, and all are now called *Australopithecus africanus*.

Kromdraai and Swartkrans About a kilometer from the Sterkfontein site, also in the Sterkfontein Valley, Broom discovered another hominine fossil deposit in 1937. This site was Kromdraai, situated atop a small hill east of the limestone quarry of Sterkfontein; here Broom found fossils with interesting differences from those now called *Australopithecus africanus*. The Kromdraai fossils had bigger molars and premolars than *Australopithecus africanus*, as well as more robust faces and chewing muscles. Broom felt justified in naming these finds *Paranthropus robustus* (robust near-man). In 1948, on the other side of the Sterkfontein Valley, quarrying in a small hill on the Swartkrans farm uncovered a third australopithecine fossil site. The finds from Swartkrans are much like those from Kromdraai, and have been placed in *Paranthropus*. Many, but not all, anthropologists today would place the *Paranthropus* fossils in the genus *Australopithecus*, but retained in a separate species: *Australopithecus robustus* (or *A. robustus*). (To save space, scientific convention permits the abbreviation of the genus name after its first use has identified the precise genus being discussed.)

Makapansgat Dart began work in 1948 at the last of the South African early hominine sites, about 320 kilometers north of Johannesburg in the Makapan Valley. The Makapansgat (*gat* = Afrikaans for *valley*: Makapan Valley) hominines were found in a cave in the valley where limestone was being quarried. The five South African sites of Sterkfontein, Kromdraai, Swartkrans, Makapansgat, and Taung have yielded the fragmentary remains of 130 to 150 individuals.

The South African sites Taung, Sterkfontein, and Makapansgat, where *Australopithecus africanus* has been discovered, and Kromdraai and Swartkrans, where *Australopithecus robustus* has been found, are geologically similar (Figure 9.5). They are the remains of caverns deep in the limestone hills. The hominines never lived in these caves but perhaps lived on the surface of the hills, which have long since eroded away. The caverns were connected with the surface by vertical shafts; animal bones, hominine bones, and other debris accumulating on the surface were swept down the shaft and became incorporated into the deposit. The

The Geology of South African Sites

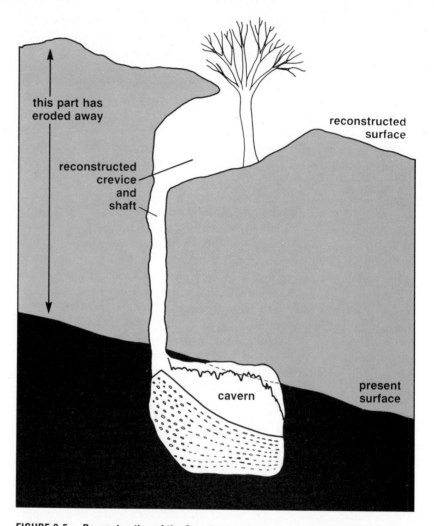

FIGURE 9.5. Reconstruction of the Swartkrans site. Most australopithecine fossils found in South Africa accumulated in caverns. At Swartkrans there was apparently a shaft from the cavern to the surface, down which dirt, bones, and other matter tumbled and eventually became consolidated with limestone to become the rock-hard, fossil-bearing matrix called *breccia*. At the surface, there may have been a crevice or a depression in which trees would probably have been found. This location offered trees shelter from the wind of the open grassland. This situation may provide a clue to why many bones entered the shaft to the cavern: Some predators, such as leopards, eat their prey in trees to escape scavengers, and leftover bones could drop into the crevice and down the shaft. Erosion of the hillside occurred after the cavern filled.

geologic history of these sites is somewhat more complicated because it now seems likely that during their long history, they may have had different vertical shafts connecting them with the surface at different times. This means that each cave had material added to the deposit a number of times; at two of the sites, Sterkfontein and Swartkrans, there is evidence in upper and therefore presumably later cave fillings of a hominine more advanced than *Australopithecus*.

At the present, it is not possible to use radiometric dating methods to determine the precise age of these deposits. However, analysis of animal bones found with the hominine fossils suggests that the two *A. africanus* sites of Sterkfontein and Makapansgat are earlier than the *A. robustus* sites of Kromdraai and Swartkrans, with Makapansgat the earliest at 3 or more million years B.P., Sterkfontein somewhat later, and Kromdraai and Swartkrans perhaps a million or more years later than Makapansgat.

Australopithecines in East Africa

Olduvai Gorge, Tanzania

The dramatist Robert Ardrey, deeply interested in early hominine studies, talked about the three "wild men of Africa" who were responsible for finding much of the early hominine fossil material.[3] These men had strong imaginations and marked fascination with our early ancestors. Dart and Broom are two of these. The third was Louis S. B. Leakey, who concentrated his work in East Africa. Born in Kenya of missionary parents, Leakey went to school at Cambridge, England, and in the late 1920s returned to Kenya to begin a long and renowned career. With his wife, Mary, he explored many areas in East Africa, discovering fossils of the Miocene higher primate, *Proconsul,* at sites on the shores and islands of Lake Victoria. They also explored one of the more interesting geologic formations in East Africa: Olduvai Gorge in northern Tanzania (Figure 9.6).

In 1959, Mary Leakey discovered major parts of a hominine skull in a deposit deep in the gorge, at a site called FLK (Frida Leakey Korongo, named after a relative; *korongo* is Swahili for gully). The skull, when excavated and cleaned, looked very much like the *Australopithecus robustus* specimens Broom had collected from Kromdraai and Swartkrans in South Africa, but possessed back teeth and a face even larger than those forms (Figure 9.7). Louis Leakey decided the fossil was different enough for him to establish a new taxonomic category: "Zinjanthropus boisei" (*Zinj* = an old Arabic word for East Africa; *boisei* commemorated the Boise Fund, which provided funds for Leakey's scientific work). Today, the "Zinj" fossil is usually placed in *Australopithecus,* but retains the species name, becoming *Australopithecus boisei.*[4]

After this discovery, the Leakeys uncovered many other hominine fossils at Olduvai, at different sites up and down the gorge. Some of these fossils, including parts of upper and lower jaws, almost complete skulls, and postcranial bones, seemed to possess features, such as smaller teeth and larger brains, that were more advanced than either the "Zinj" fossil or the South African hominines. These fossils were given the name *Homo habilis* and placed in the same genus as modern humans.[5] Recent excavations in the gorge led by Americans Donald Johanson and Tim White have uncovered a very fragmentary skeleton of a female *Homo habilis.*

Geologically, Olduvai Gorge is an erosion gully, recently carved out by the runoff from two nearby lakes. Since the early hominines lived in the area, there has been a slow accumulation of material so that the

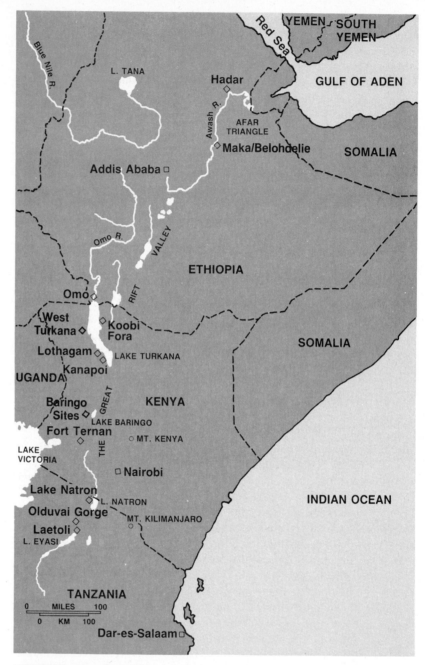

FIGURE 9.6. The distribution of early hominine sites in East Africa, showing their locations in relation to the Rift Valley system.

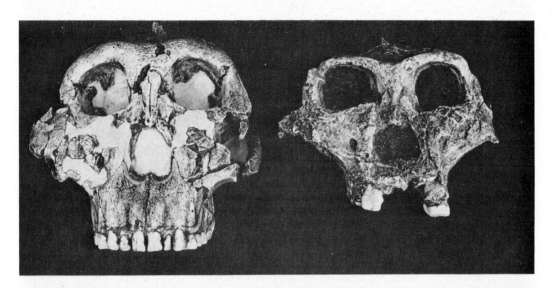

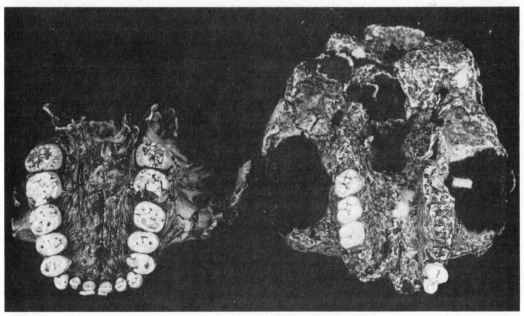

FIGURE 9.7. Casts of the face and upper jaws of *Australopithecus robustus* from Swartkrans (right) and *Australopithecus boisei* ("Zinj") from Olduvai (left). Note that both possess the robust chewing muscle attachment areas of the top and sides of the skull but that the East African specimen has a much larger facial region and that while the South African robust specimen has large back teeth, they are dwarfed by the truly massive premolar and molar teeth of "Zinj."

lower layers containing the hominine fossils have been covered by several hundred feet of deposits. Without erosion of the material above, there would be no way of reaching the fossils or even knowing they were there. The development of the gorge has thus exposed the ancient fossil-bearing strata. The stratigraphy, or layers, through which the gorge cut is divided into four major beds, from I up to IV, with several later beds on top (Table 9.1). Because of past volcanic activity, some of the rocks in Olduvai Gorge can be dated by the potassium-argon (K-Ar) process. The bottom of Bed I is dated to a little more than 1.8 million years ago; the change from Bed I to Bed II occurred about 1.7 million years ago. The "Zinj" fossil (*A. boisei*) was found in Bed I and dated to about 1.75 million years B.P., but other "Zinj"-like fossils and the *H. habilis* fossils have been found scattered from the bottom of Bed I to the middle of Bed II.

Omo River Basin, Ethiopia

At sites along the Omo River, which flows southward through southern Ethiopia, a large number of hominine fossils, mostly teeth but also a few jaws and other bones, have been found in geologic contexts that have been particularly well dated by the potassium-argon (K-Ar) process and confirmed by paleomagnetic determinations. The leaders of the expedition, F. C. Howell and Yves Coppens, have reported at Omo forms similar to the South African *Australopithecus africanus* from contexts between 2 and 3 million years B.P.; forms like *Australopithecus boisei* first appear in the sequence about 2.2 million years B.P.[6] Later-in-time fossils that belong in the genus *Homo* have also been found in deposits along the Omo River. The Omo River flows into Lake Turkana on the Ethiopia-Kenya border; here, along the eastern and western shores of the lake, are hominine fossil sites of incredible richness (Figure 9.8).

TABLE 9.1
Highly Schematic Diagram of Olduvai Gorge and the Fossils Discovered There
After the time of Upper Bed I, volcanism in the Olduvai Gorge area ceased and K-Ar dating cannot be employed. The Bed IV date is extrapolated from a paleomagnetic reversal.

Date (B.P.)	Geological Beds	Hominine Fossils	
	Later beds	Homo sapiens	
c. 400,000–500,000	Bed IV	Homo erectus	
	Bed III	Homo erectus	
	Bed II (Upper)	Homo erectus	
c. 1,700,000	Bed II (Lower)	Homo habilis Homo habilis	Australopithecus boisei
c. 1,800,000	Bed I	Homo habilis Homo habilis	Australopithecus boisei Australopithecus boisei

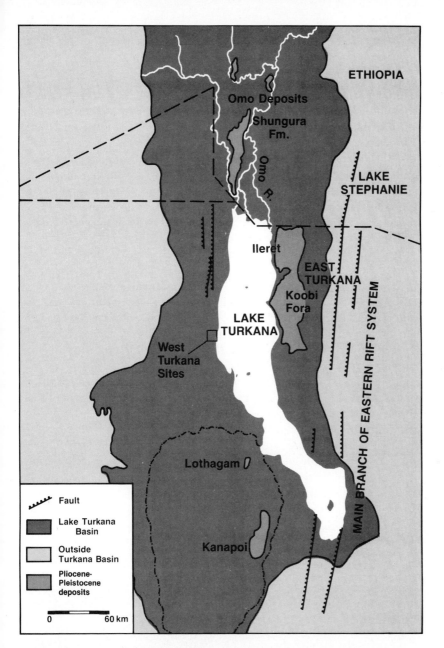

FIGURE 9.8.   The Lake Turkana and Omo River areas, where large numbers of early hominine fossils have been found. In East Turkana, the Koobi Fora peninsula region has been the richest area to date; along the Omo, the Shungura Formation has provided the overwhelming bulk of fossils. To the south and west of the lake are Lothagam and Kanapoi, where only scraps of hominine fossils have been found. Current fossil hunting is focusing on the areas to the west of Lake Turkana, where several fossil discoveries have recently been made.

Richard Leakey, son of Louis and Mary, had been hunting fossils along the Omo River, when on a flight back to Nairobi, Kenya, he passed over the eastern shores of Lake Turkana (then known as Lake Rudolf) and noticed that this wind-eroded and mostly desolate place might prove to be a rich fossil area. In 1968 he visited the area and quickly found a number of animal fossils and, soon after, some hominines. Since then Leakey and his associates have discovered hominine fossils representing well over a hundred individuals.[7] The fossil-bearing locales along the eastern shore of the lake are numerous and contain many hominine skulls, jaws, and skeletal bones. Volcanic activity has resulted in the presence of rocks in the Turkana deposits that can be dated by the K-Ar process, but because these volcanic ashes were laid down in exceedingly complex ways, very careful preparation of the rock samples to be dated is required if consistent dates are to result. A small number of fossils are earlier than 3 million years B.P., but the vast majority of hominine fossil bones from the East Turkana sites are dated between about 2 and about 1.4 million years B.P. The East Turkana hominines possess a wide variety of features, some with attributes similar to *Australopithecus boisei*, a few suggesting *Australopithecus africanus*, several undoubtedly *Homo habilis*, and others very difficult to assign to one or another category. We will consider in detail the morphological features of all these forms after reviewing the fossil sites themselves.

Having explored the eastern shores of Lake Turkana for over fifteen years, Richard Leakey and his associates have increasingly devoted their efforts to examining the deposits on the western shore of the lake, which are similar in age and content to those on the other side. These explorations have been rewarded by several recent discoveries.[8] Among these were an australopithecine skull (Figure 9.9) and a fragmentary lower jaw with many similarities to *A. boisei* but with some quite unique features, like a smaller brain. Dated at a little older than 2.5 million years B.P.,

FIGURE 9.9. A robust australopithecine skull from west of Lake Turkana, northern Kenya. Known by its catalog number, WT 17000, it is dated earlier than other robust australopithecines. It also possesses features such as a projecting face and small brain size, which have led some to propose that it be placed in the species *A. aethiopicus.*

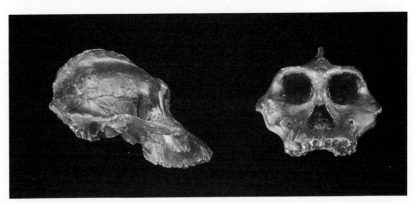

these would be the oldest *A. boisei* specimens yet found, if they are indeed members of that species. Several anthropologists have argued that the skull morphology is different enough to warrant placement into a species called *Australopithecus aethiopicus*. This taxon was originally established for lower jaw fossils discovered along the Omo River but had only been rarely used prior to these West Turkana discoveries. We will return to the place of these new fossils in the scheme of human evolution presently.

At Hadar in the Afar region of north-central Ethiopia, 1,600 kilometers north of Lake Turkana, a joint French-American expedition, headed by Donald Johanson and Maurice Taieb, searched for fossils in the dry, desolate lands along the Awash River. Like the locales around Lake Turkana, Hadar is an extremely rich fossil area that has yielded many hominine and fossil animal bones, including the most complete early hominine skeleton yet found: Approximately 40 percent of the bones were preserved (Figure 9.10). Potassium-argon dating has placed the hominine levels between 2.9 and more than 3.2 million years B.P. The hominine bones from Hadar seem to differ in a number of ways from the others we have so far described; their closest affinities appear to lie with the fossils discovered in Tanzania, at the site of Laetoli.[9]

Hadar, Ethiopia

The Laetoli site was first worked in the late 1930s by the German paleontologist L. Kohl-Larson, who discovered an early hominine fossil there. But it was in 1975 when Mary Leakey and later Tim White re-

Laetoli, Tanzania

FIGURE 9.10. *Australopithecus afarensis* **skeleton found at Hadar, Ethiopia. Approximately 40 percent of this one individual, given the name "Lucy," was preserved.**

turned to the area that significant numbers of fossils were found and the hominine levels dated. Laetoli is important for a number of reasons: Its date, about 3.7 million years B.P., makes it the earliest site with an appreciable number of fossils; the hominines are in some ways similar to those from Hadar; and finally, hominine footprints have been discovered there. The footprints provide direct evidence that hominine bipedalism had evolved at this early date, for they are unquestionably those of an animal that walked much as we do (Figure 9.11).[10]

According to Johanson and White, the hominine fossil specimens from Hadar and Laetoli, dated earlier than other australopithecines, possess a number of distinctive features that led to the establishment of a new taxonomic species: *Australopithecus afarensis*.[11]

Other East African Sites

Just south of the Kenya-Tanzania border lies Lake Natron; near its shore is the site of Peninj, which has yielded a large lower jaw comparable in many ways to *Australopithecus boisei* fossils from Olduvai, Omo, and East Turkana. The Peninj jaw has been dated to about 1.5 million years B.P. In western Kenya, the site of Chesowanja has yielded a broken *A. boisei* skull.

A number of fossils have been found in deposits earlier than those just described, but their fragmentary and incomplete nature do not permit us to place them in a particular early species. At the site of Belohdelie in the Awash Valley, near Hadar, part of the front of an australopithecine skull was discovered, and at the nearby site of Maka a fragment of the

FIGURE 9.11. Footprints of the bipedal hominine *Australopithecus afarensis* found at Laetoli. Note that the big toe is aligned with the other toes and that the footprints in general are characteristically human in shape.

upper part of an immature thighbone was found, both in contexts dated to about 4 million years B.P. The thighbone's inner structure is like that of bipedal hominines and differs from the form found in the apes; this bone is the earliest dated evidence for hominine bipedality. At two sites south and a little west of Lake Turkana, Kenya, early hominine fossil bones were found: at Kanapoi, the elbow joint end of an upper arm bone, dated to about 4.5 million years B.P.; and at Lothagam, a small piece of a hominine lower jaw, in contexts dated to about 5.5 million years B.P. Finally, in the Lake Baringo Basin region of western Kenya a fragmentary australopithecine jaw was found with a date of about 5 million years.

A number of locales in western Kenya in the Lake Baringo Basin area have yielded fragmentary fossils, mostly isolated teeth along with a few bits and pieces of skeletal bone. These specimens are found in deposits dated to between about 5.5 and 10 million years B.P. They thus derive from the general time at which the molecular data suggests the hominine line was originating. Unfortunately, the incomplete nature of these finds has made it very difficult to assess their hominine status; future discoveries from this area will hopefully resolve this issue and permit us to place hominine origins more accurately in time.

The Geology of East Africa Sites

Unlike the South African australopithecine cave sites, the East African fossils are mainly found in open deposits that result from lake or stream action. After an animal or an australopithecine died by the side of a lake or stream, its remains were subjected to the attentions of scavengers, with some body parts being carried off by the waters. When the current slackened, the bones and other waterborne debris would settle to the bottom, forming part of the sediments. Much later, after the lake or stream had dried up, these sediments, now solidified into geologic deposits, were acted upon by a number of geologic forces that tilted them on their side or uplifted them. Finally, the sediments recently begin to erode away, bringing the fossilized bones to the surface.

Active volcanos were common in East Africa during much of the time of the australopithecines. Occasionally, the ash fall from a volcanic eruption will be found as over- or underlying layers to a fossil-bearing deposit, and this volcanic material can be used for a K-Ar radiometric determination.

Summary of Early Hominine Sites

Before discussing the physical features of the early hominine fossils, it is useful to summarize the location and dating of the discoveries as shown in Table 9.2. Of the robust forms, *Australopithecus robustus* is limited to South Africa, while *Australopithecus boisei* is known only from East Africa. *Australopithecus afarensis* is earlier than other fossil groups, while evidence of the genus *Homo* seems restricted to a period later than 2 million years B.P.

The geographic range of early hominine finds in Africa suggests that they were distributed continuously from South Africa north to Ethiopia. Were they also living in other parts of Africa or the Old World?

TABLE 9.2
The Australopithecines, Grouped by Date and Location
Most of these sites have been K-Ar dated, but Lothagam is relatively dated, and the South African sites are only tentatively placed in time.

Millions of Years B.P.	Geological Epoch	African Australopithecines					
		A. afarensis	A. africanus	A. robustus	A. boisei	Homo[b]	Not Further Identified
1	PLEISTOCENE		East Turkana[a]	Kromdraai	Chesowanja Peninj Olduvai Gorge East Turkana	Omo East Turkana Olduvai Gorge ←	
2	PLIOCENE		Omo Sterkfontein Makapansgat →	Swartkrans	Omo West Turkana[c] ←		
3		Hadar Laetoli ←					
4							Maka, Belohdelie
5	MIOCENE						Kanapoi Lake Baringo
6							Lothagam

[a] The presence of A. africanus forms at East Turkana is uncertain.
[b] Includes Homo habilis.
[c] May be a new species: A. aethiopicus.

Drawing conclusions from this kind of evidence, or the lack of it, is very difficult. Other parts of the Old World have been searched for traces of early hominines but with no luck thus far. All that can be said at the present is that the early hominines appear to be limited to eastern and southern Africa, but the question must remain an open one.

The fossil evidence for human evolution from about 5.0 million to about 1.5 million years B.P. has been placed in five taxonomic categories: *A. afarensis, Australopithecus africanus, A. boisei, A. robustus,* and *Homo.* The term "australopithecine" is often used as a descriptive name for all of these early hominines. Because most of these australopithecine fossil specimens are very fragmentary and incomplete, there is continuing debate about the placement of some of the fossil samples in particular groups as well as about the establishment of additional categories such as *A. aethiopicus.* After considering the morphological features of each category we will look at these differing views and how the various australopithecines might be ordered in an evolutionary sequence.

General Australopithecine Morphology

There is considerable variation among the australopithecine fossils in brain size, tooth size, body size, and the development of some muscles, but all of these fossils share a number of morphological features that permit us to place them in the hominine family and to assess their evolutionary position in relation both to later hominines and to each other. These general morphological traits include the skeletal bones relating to bipedalism, the general structure of the teeth, and the size of the brain.

Bipedalism

One of the australopithecine's most important sets of physical characteristics is related to bipedalism. Prior to the discovery at Laetoli of hominine footprints indicating a bipedal animal, postcranial bones indicating bipedalism formed the most convincing evidence for calling the australopithecines hominines. Habitual bipedalism and the anatomical structures responsible for it are unique to hominines. Chimpanzees and other primates occasionally move with their body weight completely on their rear limbs, but this is not their usual method of locomotion. Bipedalism, which frees the hands from the requirements of locomotion, has drastically changed the postcranial skeleton, especially the lower part of the vertebral column, the pelvis, the thighbone, the knee joint, the ankle joint, and the foot. The bone modifications are accompanied by changes in the muscles, in particular those in the lower back, which help hold the trunk upright; in the thigh and buttocks; and in the foot.

In modern humans these skeletal and muscular elements operate together to permit a kind of bipedal locomotion called the *striding gait* (Figure 9.12). In stride, the legs move through alternate phases, *stance* and *swing,* which are basic to solving the built-in problems of bipedal locomotion. First, all the body's weight is transmitted to the ground through the lower limbs, so that the lower back, pelvis, and legs must be stout enough to handle the additional weight even when the individual is running, adding stress from bouncing and jarring footfalls. Second,

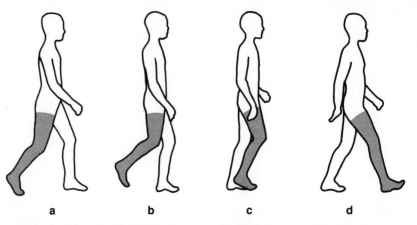

FIGURE 9.12. The human stride. (a) The right leg (shaded) is about to begin the swing phase of the stride, which starts with toe off. (b) The right leg has begun the swing phase, while the left leg, in the stance phase, furnishes support to the body. (c) The right leg's swing phase is at its midpoint and (d) moves toward heel strike and the end of the swing phase. At this stage the left leg is about to begin its swing phase as it moves toward toe off.

movement itself is a problem. In quadrupedal animals, such as dogs, cats, and monkeys, the four limbs work as a unit, usually with at least two limbs on the ground at a time when the animal is walking. If bipedalism is to be efficient, each foot must leave the ground in turn as a step forward is taken; when one of a hominine's feet leaves the ground, only one is left for support, and all the body's weight is transferred to the ground through one limb.

Human beings move forward by alternating the two limbs through stance and swing phases. First, from a stationary position, one leg flexes at the knee and is bent forward, taking the whole foot off the ground. The swing phase begins here for this limb, with the other leg in the stance phase furnishing the sole support for the whole body. The leg in the swing phase is swung ahead of the body, the knee begins to straighten, and the foot regains the ground, the heel touching first with *heel strike*. While this leg is moving forward, the trunk has been carried forward too, and after heel strike, body weight is gradually transferred to this forward foot as the trunk moves over the leg. Heel strike is the end of a leg's swing phase and the start of the stance or support phase. The other leg, which has been in the stance phase, begins the swing phase as body weight is gradually transferred from it, the knee begins to flex, and the foot begins to leave the ground. The last part of the foot to leave the ground is the end of the big toe, which pushes off the ground with some muscular force, giving the leg a propulsive push as it begins its swing phase. *Toe off* marks the end of the stance phase and the beginning of the swing phase.

The skeletal modifications that make this form of locomotion possible contrast obviously with the skeletal parts of the apes, our closest living relatives and quadrupedal animals. In the human vertebral column, the lower bones of the spine form the characteristic *lumbar curve*, which provides a more efficient way of transmitting the upper body's weight to the pelvis (Figure 9.13). The human pelvis is also distinctive. The mammalian pelvis has three bony elements: The two pelvic bones (*innominate bones*) make up the sides of the pelvis and are joined at the front; the *sacrum,* the last major bone of the vertebral column, fits like a keystone between the two pelvic bones at the back of the pelvis (Figure 9.14). On each side of the pelvis is the hip joint socket, where the ball of the thighbone articulates with the pelvis. Many muscles attach to the pelvic bones, some directed downward to the legs, where they assist in movements of the leg; and some directed upward, helping maintain the trunk in an upright position.

The modern human pelvis is shorter from top to bottom than that of the chimpanzee and has a larger area for the attachment of the sacrum (the sacroiliac joint) (Figure 9.14). Human pelvic bones are foreshortened because all of the upper body's weight has to be transmitted to the ground through the pelvis. The shortened human pelvic bones reduce the distance between the sacral-pelvic bone joint, which transmits the upper body's weight, and the hip joint, which transmits it to the legs. The large sacral-pelvic bone joint provides additional strength at a point subject to more weight. The upper parts of the pelvic bones, the blades (the *ilia,* plural of *ilium*) are much broader than in the chimpanzee. This broadening puts several important muscles of the front of the thigh, which attach on the blade, in a more advantageous position for lifting

FIGURE 9.13.   Spinal columns of a gorilla and a modern human. The curves in the human spinal column—especially the lower back, or lumbar, curve—are part of the anatomical system of bipedalism.

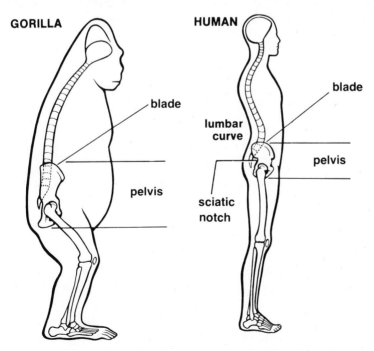

GORILLA

HUMAN

blade

blade

lumbar
curve

pelvis

pelvis

sciatic
notch

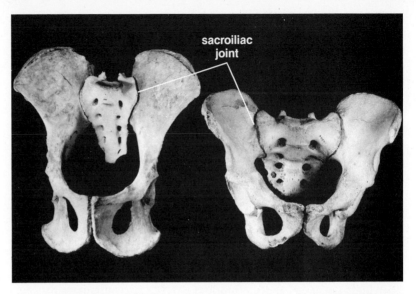

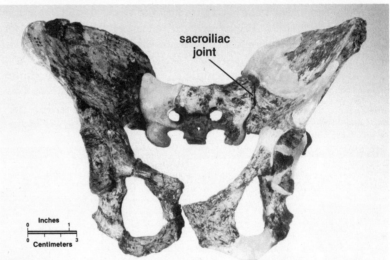

FIGURE 9.14. The pelves of a chimpanzee (top left), a human (top right), and STS-14 (*Australopithecus africanus* from Sterkfontein) (below). Note the similarities between the human and the australopithecine bones, especially in the foreshortening of the pelvis, the size of the sacroiliac joint, and the broadening of the blades. (Not to scale.)

the thigh as the swing phase begins. In addition, the expansion of the pelvic blades has repositioned two muscles (*gluteus medius* and *gluteus minimus*) extremely important for bipedalism to the sides of the hip joint rather than behind, where they are located in the apes (Figure 9.15). These muscles contract when the opposite leg is lifted off the ground during the swing phase; by attaching from the pelvic blade to the top of the thighbone (*femur*), they maintain the stability of the pelvis when the body is being supported by only one leg. This broadening of the blades

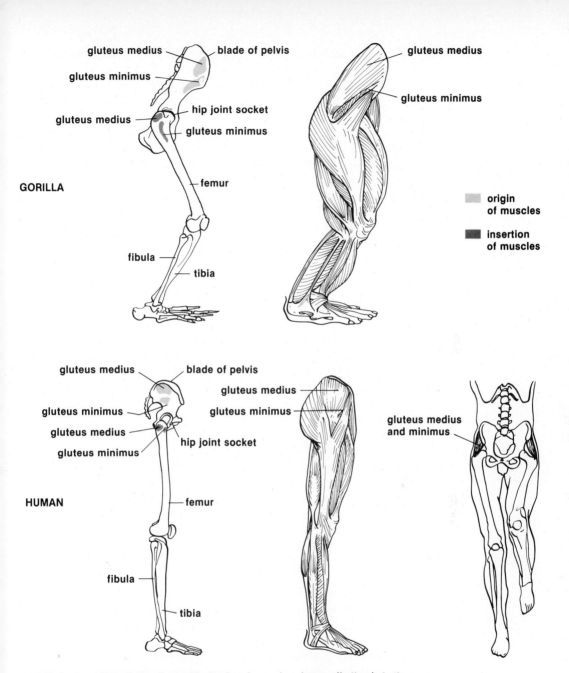

FIGURE 9.15. Lower limbs of a gorilla (top) and a modern human (bottom). In the drawings of the bones, the two attachment areas (the origin and insertion) of each gluteal muscle are indicated. In apes, the *gluteus medius* and *gluteus minimus* lie behind the hip joint socket because the blade of the pelvis does not curve around the animal's side. In humans, the blade of the pelvis has expanded around to the side, and these muscles are outside of the hip joint. Therefore, as the drawing on the lower right illustrates, in humans *gluteus medius* and *gluteus minimus* maintain the stability of the pelvis during stride when the opposing leg is lifted off the ground.

of the pelvis has led to the development of a strongly angulated notch at the back of the pelvis, the *sciatic notch*.

Parts of the pelvis and virtually complete pelves have been recovered from a number of sites in South and East Africa (Figures 9.10 and 9.14); all show that the australopithecine pelvis is remarkably like that of modern humans: The pelvis is foreshortened, the blades are expanded, and it has an enlarged area for the sacral-pelvic bone joint and a marked sciatic notch. The several australopithecine fossils vary in size, and the most complete specimens, from Sterkfontein and Hadar, are smaller than skeletons of most modern humans. The fossils also differ morphologically from modern human bones, but the australopithecine pelvic material is clearly closer to modern humans than to the apes; the vertebral column also seems to have the lower back curve characteristic of humans.

Added to the distinctive bipedal features of the pelvis are important characteristics in the knee, ankle, and foot. The human knee joint is underneath the body, giving maximum support during stride (Figure 9.16); the hip joint is at the side of the pelvis. For the knee joints to be in an efficient position, the thighbone (femur) must angle in from its upper joint at the hip to its lower joint at the knee. Modern humans are thus characterized by thighbones that are directed, not more or less straight down as in the chimpanzee but at an angle, to bring the knee joints much closer together than the hip joints. The knee joint itself, which must be able to transmit body weight to the lower part of the leg, has three bones, with the lower end of the thighbone (femur) and the upper part of the shinbone (tibia) meeting, and the kneecap (patella) sitting in front of the articulation and its muscles and ligaments maintaining the integrity of the front of the joint. The thighbone and shinbone are joined by two concave surfaces on the shinbone, into which fit two condyles, or rounded projections, of the thighbone. If the angle the thighbone makes from the hip to the knee were to be continued down the shinbone, the legs would cross, making bipedal locomotion somewhat difficult if not impossible. To compensate for the thighbone angle, the inside condyle of the thighbone is larger than the outside one, thus allowing the shinbone to drop straight down from the knee to the ankle. The size of the inner condyle at the lower end of fossil thighbones can be examined to determine whether the thighbone angled in and whether the knee joints were beneath the body's weight. We have quite a few fossil australopithecine thighbones, and they show the enlarged inner condyle typical of modern human skeletons. A complete knee joint discovered at Hadar also confirms the bipedal nature of the australopithecine locomotor system. Analyses indicate that the bones of this joint were capable of the same range of movement that is found in modern humans and much greater than that characteristic of apes.

Because the human anklebone (*talus*) must support body weight, it is more robust than in the apes. Australopithecine anklebones differ from those of both modern humans and the chimpanzee, but they are closer to those of the hominines.

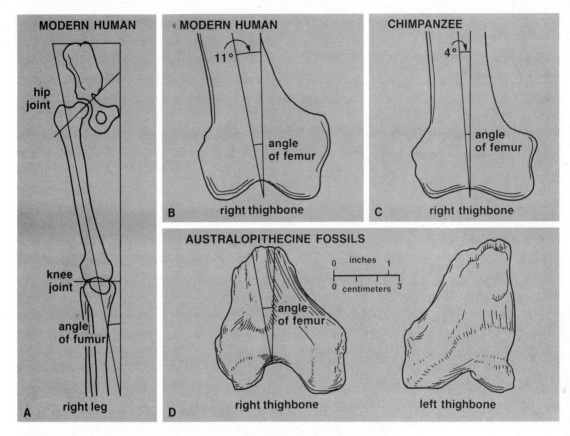

FIGURE 9.16. Because humans need to bring the knee joint directly under their body weight, (a) the shaft of the thighbone (femur) angles in from the hip to the knee joint. This angle is reflected in the relative sizes of the knobs, or condyles, at the ends of the thighbone. (In b, c, and d, the inner condyle is on the right in all but the lower right illustration.) In modern human thighbones (b), the inner condyle is larger than the outer, but the two are more equal in the chimpanzee (c). (d) In two hominine fossils (from different individuals) from the Sterkfontein site in South Africa, the inner condyles are larger than the outer, emphasizing the hominine nature of the australopithecine knee joint.

The modern human foot is specialized for supporting body weight. The foot's complex arch has developed, and the last bone of the big toe is enlarged and flattened to provide the push off at the beginning of the swing phase (Figure 9.17). Unlike the ape's opposable big toe, the modern human digit is set against the other toes and cannot be opposed. Another fortunate find, this time at Olduvai Gorge, was the greater portion of an australopithecine foot. Like all the other structures, there are some differences between these bones and those in modern humans; the fossil foot, nevertheless, is meant to support weight. The big toe is not opposable, and the arch seems to have had some development. At another site at Olduvai Gorge, the last bone of the big toe was found. It shows the flattening and enlargement typical of modern human bones.

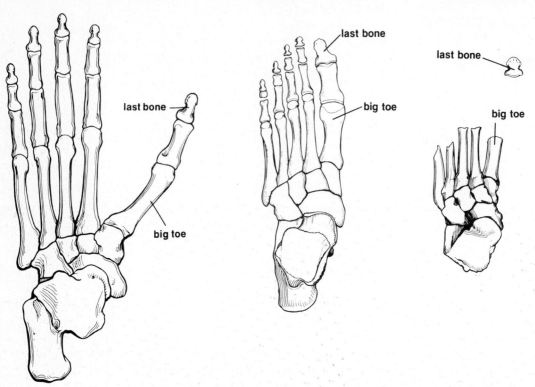

FIGURE 9.17. Human and gorilla foot bones compared with those of an australopithecine from Olduvai Gorge, Bed I. This fossil foot is incomplete, but its big toe was placed up against the other four toes and was not an opposable digit, as is the big toe of the apes. Note the differences between the last bones in the ape and the human big toe. The strongly developed last bone in the modern human big toe is related to the push off in walking. A last bone of the big toe was discovered in Bed I, Olduvai Gorge, but it was not from the same individual as the rest of the foot; this bone is very similar to that in modern humans. (Not to scale.)

Recent examination of australopithecine fossil foot bones by Randall Susman and Jack Stern have focused on the shape of the bones of the toes. While they do not deny that the early hominines were bipedal when on the ground, these authors suggest that the somewhat curved shafts of the toe bones are reminiscent of those of chimpanzees, who habitually flex their toes on tree branches to support themselves. Susman and Stern conclude that these toe bones, along with several other features of the lower limb, indicate that the australopithecines may have spent a considerable amount of time in the trees, perhaps retreating up into the safety of the branches during the dangerous nighttime hours.[12] This assertion of the australopithecines' arborealty has become a hotly debated issue, and at the present, no clear-cut answers to the question are possible.

In reviewing modern human locomotor abilities and the fossil evidence of the australopithecines, we have ignored other structures related to bipedalism and known from the fossils. Human locomotion, too, has been treated in less than full detail. The points raised, however, demonstrate that the australopithecines were bipedal animals.

The discovery in 1976 of australopithecine footprint trails at the Laetoli site in Tanzania (Figure 9.11) confirmed the evidence of the fossil bones. The footprints are those of an animal with a smaller foot and with a shorter distance between footprints; they suggest a hominine of smaller stature, but certainly an animal that moved with the striding gait.

A major morphological difference between the postcranial bones of the australopithecines and those of modern humans is in the upper part of the thighbone, or femur; many australopithecine bones show a longer neck and smaller head (the ball of the hip joint) than are found in modern

FIGURE 9.18. The upper part of a thighbone of a modern human and a fossil thighbone of an australopithecine from Swartkrans. The main difference between the two is the longer, narrower neck and smaller head (which fits into the hip socket) of the australopithecine bone. Other australopithecine thighbones, especially some from East Turkana, are more like those of modern humans.

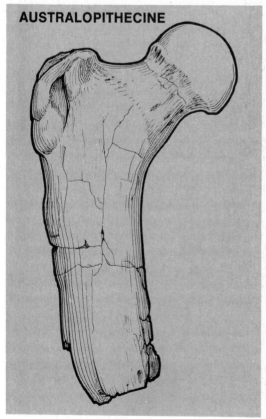

AUSTRALOPITHECINE

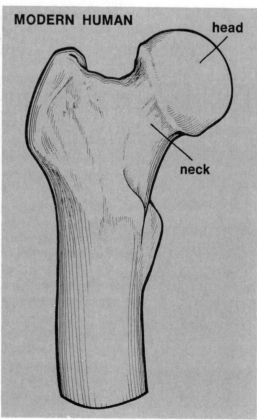

MODERN HUMAN

head

neck

humans (Figure 9.18). The fossil evidence from East Turkana in north Kenya suggests that femurs much like those of modern humans, with larger heads and shorter necks, first appear in the fossil record between about 2 and 1.5 million years B.P., toward the end of australopithecine evolution. Although some have interpreted these differences as an indication that the australopithecines may have moved in a somewhat different fashion than modern humans, Owen Lovejoy has suggested that the differences in the head and neck of the australopithecine femurs are more closely related to brain and body size than to any fundamental differences in their patterns of movement. Lovejoy suggests that during the course of later australopithecine evolution, when brain size was increasing, there was a need to provide a larger birth canal for a larger-brained infant. This created evolutionary pressure to increase the distance between the hip joint sockets (Figure 9.19), resulting in a shorter-necked femur in those australopithecine species with larger brains. Lovejoy points out that these changes in the shape and size of the thighbone neck and pelvis appear in the fossil record at about the same time as hominines with larger brains.[13]

FIGURE 9.19. In an early hominine with a small brain, the distance B–B′ can be smaller because of the small size of the infant brain. Thus distance A–B (and A′–B′) can be greater. In the course of human evolution, as brain size increases, the size of the birth canal also increases, and this results in a greater distance between B and B′. Since the total pelvic breadth (A–A′) must remain the same to permit efficient stride, A–B (and A′–B′) must decrease in length, which is reflected in the shortening of the neck of the femur, or thighbone.

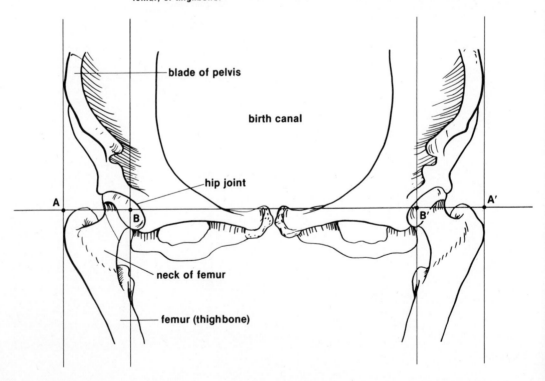

blade of pelvis

birth canal

hip joint

A   A′

B   B′

neck of femur

femur (thighbone)

Complete and nearly complete australopithecine skulls have been found in both East and South Africa. In general the volume of the brain cases ranges from about 400 to almost 800 ml, with those dated earlier tending to be smaller.

Skull   The australopithecine skull differs in its general form from that of modern humans, especially in the relationship of the facial portion to the brain case (Figure 9.20). In the australopithecines, the facial area is large and juts out in front of the brain case; its position is similar to an ape's. In modern humans, the face is smaller relative to the total size of the skull, and the enlarged brain case is positioned above the face. The differences in the australopithecine and modern human skulls reflect the evolutionary changes that occurred between the time of the australopithecines and the emergence of modern humans: the increase in the size of the brain and the decrease in the size of the face and teeth (trends that were discussed in Chapter 8).

FIGURE 9.20.   Skulls of two australopithecines—*A. africanus* and *A. robustus*, both from South Africa—a modern human, and an orangutan. Notice the difference in size between the brain cases of the australopithecines and that of the modern human, as well as the difference in position of the faces in relation to the brain cases.

A. AFRICANUS

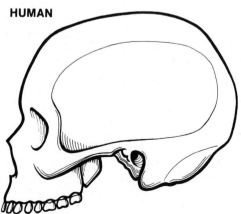

position of cheek

A. ROBUSTUS

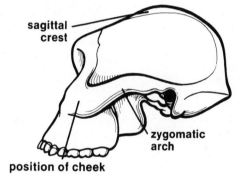

sagittal crest

zygomatic arch

position of cheek

HUMAN

ORANGUTAN

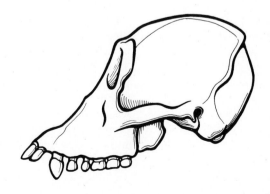

Teeth and Jaws   Because there is a great deal of variation in the teeth of australopithecines, differences in details of dentition are the most important features (along with brain size) used to identify and distinguish the various species of early hominines. The australopithecines, like all hominines, have a dental formula of 2.1.2.3, with the upper and lower molar cusps in an arrangement typical of hominoids. Other features of the australopithecine dentition and its relationships to ape and human jaws and teeth can be better understood from a comparison of a human jaw with an ape jaw (Figure 9.21).

Two of the major changes in human evolution are the reduction of the face and teeth and the enlargement of the brain case. Both have contributed to the differences in the jaws of modern humans and apes. The apes' dental arcade has two long, parallel rows of back teeth, the premolars and molars, with the last molars occasionally converging (Figure 9.21a). The human tooth row is shorter because the teeth are smaller, especially the canines (Figures 9.21b and c). The human dental arch forms a diverging, parabolic shape. The size of the teeth accounts only partially for this difference in shape. The evolutionary expansion of the brain has positioned the human face and jaws beneath the brain case rather than in front of it, as in the apes (Figure 9.22). The position on the base of the skull where the knobs of the lower jaw attach remains constant in apes and humans. The jaw thus changes dimensions: As it becomes shorter, the relationship of width to length changes (compare jaw width to length in Figures 9.21a and b). The relatively shorter and wider human jaws are parabolic in order to remain functional as the brain expands and facial size decreases. One measure of this change is the position of the origin of the cheek (Figure 9.22): In humans, it usually lies above or slightly behind the first molar, reflecting the decreased amount of face and jaw jutting out in front. In contrast, in chimpanzees it is above the third molar and sometimes even behind that.

Ape canines are long and tusklike, projecting above the other teeth; wear is on the sides, not the tips (Figure 9.21d). Human canines are much smaller and do not project beyond the other teeth; they are not pointed or tusklike and the wear is on the tips. Two other features are functionally related to the large canines in the apes. Ape canines are so big that if the upper and lower ones met tip to tip, the rest of the teeth could not occlude, and chewing would be impossible. The canines therefore slide together, with the back of the lower canine rubbing against the front of the upper canine. In addition, the back of the upper canine, which fits between the lower canine and the first lower premolar, rubs against a long shoulder on the latter tooth. The interdigitation of these three teeth provides for honing on the back surfaces of the canines, giving them sharp edges on this border. The space between the teeth, the *diastema,* lets these pointed canines fit together and the jaws close. The first lower premolar with the elongated shoulder is unlike the other lower premolar and the two upper premolars in that it has only one cusp; it is called a

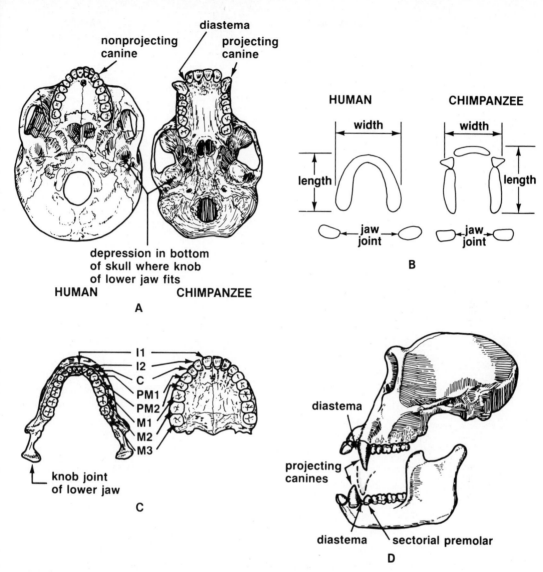

FIGURE 9.21. The jaws and teeth of a modern human and chimpanzee. (a) The bottom of the skulls of a human and chimp, showing the differences in the size and dimensions of the face and teeth; (b) the relative differences in the proportions of human and chimp jaws; and (c) the human upper and lower dentitions. Note the small size of the canine teeth, the wear on their tips, the lack of a diastema, and the first lower premolar's shape and similarity to the second lower premolar. (d) A skull and jaw of a chimpanzee showing the relationships of upper and lower canines and first lower (sectorial) premolar and the resultant wear patterns on the teeth.

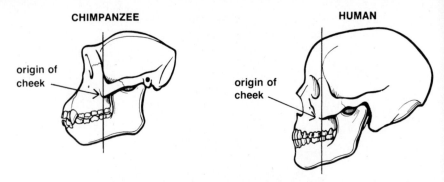

FIGURE 9.22. The skulls of a modern chimpanzee and a modern human. Note the differences in size of the brain cases in relation to the faces. The modern human face is positioned more directly underneath the brain case than the chimpanzee's. The chimp's large canine teeth are also clearly visible.

sectorial premolar. The large canine, diastema, and sectorial premolar form a functional unit found in all the apes. Modern humans lack all three: the large canine, diastema, and sectorial premolar. In humans, the first lower premolar, like the second, has two cusps (*bicuspid*) and none of the functional relationships with the canine that characterize the dentition of the apes.

All australopithecine teeth are larger than those in modern humans, although there is considerable variation among early hominine taxa. With the notable exception of the canines and first lower premolars of some *Australopithecus afarensis* fossil specimens, however, all australopithecine teeth are completely hominine in form.

The jaws of the australopithecines are large, with a thick lower jawbone to house the large teeth securely and an arch shape different from those in both apes and humans (Figure 9.23; see also Figure 9.29). Large muscle attachment areas for large chewing muscles are a feature of all the early hominines, with some species possessing huge jaw-closing muscles.

Although this general description of features can be applied to all australopithecines—bipedal, with small brains and large teeth—there is enough variation among these structures to justify a number of taxonomic categories.

Australopithecine Varieties

Australopithecus robustus and *Australopithecus boisei*

Fossil specimens of *Australopithecus robustus* from the South African sites of Swartkrans and Kromdraai and *Australopithecus boisei* fossils from the East African sites of Olduvai Gorge, East and West Turkana, the Omo, Peninj, and Chesowanja possess features that are more robust and larger than those of other australopithecines (Figures 9.7, 9.20, 9.24, 9.25, and 9.26). The robust specimens have very large premolars and molars; larger facial areas, presumably to house the larger teeth; and larger chewing muscles. As in other hominines, there are two primary sets of chewing muscles, *temporalis* and *masseter*. The *temporalis* muscle is at

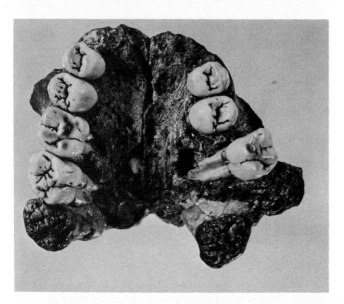

FIGURE 9.23. The upper jaw of a robust australopithecine from the Swartkrans site in South Africa. Note the shape of the dental arcade, which differs from both the chimp and the human upper jaws pictured in 9.21a. During the time between the death of this individual and the preservation of the jaw as a fossil, the left second molar was pushed out of its socket, and the front teeth were lost.

the side of the skull, attaching to the side of the brain case and to the back part of the lower jaw (Figure 9.24). The *masseter* muscle lies outside the *temporalis* and attaches from a bony bridge between the face and side of the skull (the *zygomatic arch*) to the lower part of the back of the jaw. Both muscles are greatly developed in the robust australopithecines; the temporal muscle is so big that a bony ridge or crest, the *sagittal crest,* on the top of the skull, has developed to provide more space for attaching the muscle fibers. Many male gorillas and some male chimpanzees also have such a crest. This development of the muscles and face appears directly related to the large back teeth in a functional complex, perhaps for chewing rough, fibrous foods. The need to place the action of the *masseter* muscle over the back teeth has apparently led, in the robust australopithecines, to the forward projection of the zygomatic arch and its connection to the face in the upper cheek region. In side view, the projecting cheek region completely hides the nasal cavity; note, in the comparison of *A. robustus* with *A. africanus* in Figure 9.20, the position of the zygomatic arch and the projection of the arch and cheek regions in the robust form. It is primarily this complex of features relating to the very large back teeth that separates the robust forms from other australopithecines.

Within the group of robust australopithecines, those from East Africa, *A. boisei,* possess larger teeth and larger and more massive faces and jaws than the *A. robustus* forms from South Africa. Some interpretations

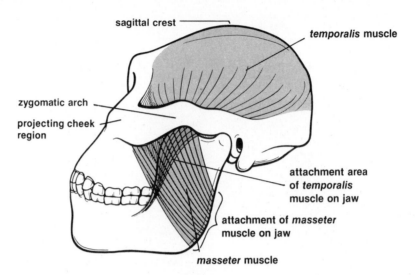

FIGURE 9.24.   A robust australopithecine showing the attachment of the main chewing muscles. *temporalis* and *masseter*. The muscles are drawn on a composite skull and jaw, which are also shown in Figures 9.25 (the skull) and 9.26 (the jaw). These fossils represent two individuals but have been combined here to demonstrate muscle attachments. If they were from the same individual and were not distorted or broken during their long burial, the knob or condyle of the lower jaw would fit into a depression (the *glenoid fossa*) on the base of the skull.

FIGURE 9.25.   A robust australopithecine skull from the Swartkrans site in South Africa. This specimen has been considerably damaged; the back portion of the skull, in addition to bits and pieces on the side and front, is missing. Notice the large zygomatic arch and sagittal crest, along with the projecting face and low forehead.

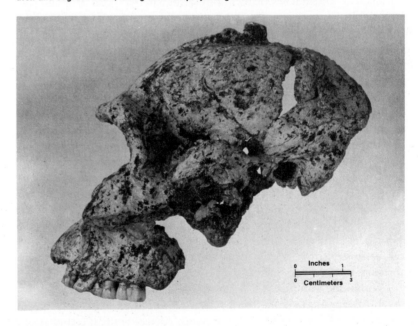

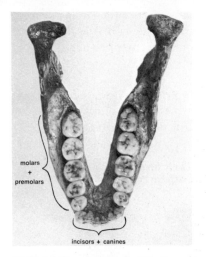

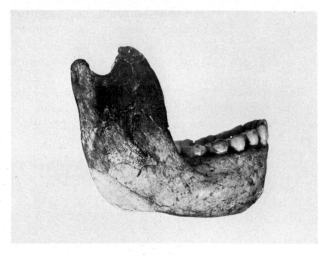

molars
+
premolars

incisors + canines

FIGURE 9.26. Two views of the lower jaw of one of the most complete robust australopithecine jaws found at the Swartkrans site. After the death of the individual, the jaw was broken at the middle and the two halves were pushed together, so that the fossil now has the right and left sides too close together. In life, the jaw would have been wider. Note the larger size of premolars and molars in comparison with the front teeth.

of australopithecine evolution associate the South and East African robust australopithecines together as part of a specialized side branch of human evolution. However, the recent discovery of a robust skull in the deposits on the western side of Lake Turkana, dated at about 2.5 million years B.P., has led many anthropologists to reevaluate these associations. The skull (Figure 9.9), known by its catalog number KNM–WT 17000 (for Kenya National Museum, where the skull is kept, and West Turkana), possesses many traits that ally it with the *A. boisei* skulls from the other side of Lake Turkana, from Olduvai, and from other East African sites. However, it has a brain size of about 400 ml, which is 100 ml or more smaller than other *A. boisei* skulls, as well as distinctive features such as a very large sagittal crest and an angled orientation of the face that is different from that of other robust australopithecine specimens. In spite of these features, most anthropologists would identify this skull as an early example of *A. boisei;* some, however, believe it is different enough to be placed in another category, *Australopithecus aethiopicus.* Whatever the outcome of this debate, this skull clearly represents an early point of the evolutionary line that leads to later *A. boisei* specimens from other parts of East Africa.

The early date for the KNM–WT 17000 skull makes it difficult for anthropologists to continue to support a notion that was widely held prior to its 1985 discovery. It had been suggested that the South African robusts, less extreme in morphology than the East African *A. boisei,* were the ancestor from which the more specialized *A. boisei* evolved. This view can no longer be maintained, and there are now a variety of ideas on how the South and East African robusts can be ordered in an evolutionary sequence. These various views will be described in the context of overall australopithecine evolution after we complete our survey of the various early hominine groups.

Australopithecus africanus

These australopithecines are known primarily from the South African sites of Taung (only one specimen, the original *Australopithecus africanus* child), from Sterkfontein, and from Makapansgat (Figures 9.27

FIGURE 9.27. Two *Australopithecus africanus* skulls from the Sterkfontein site in South Africa. The bottom skull has been damaged, and the front part of the face is missing.

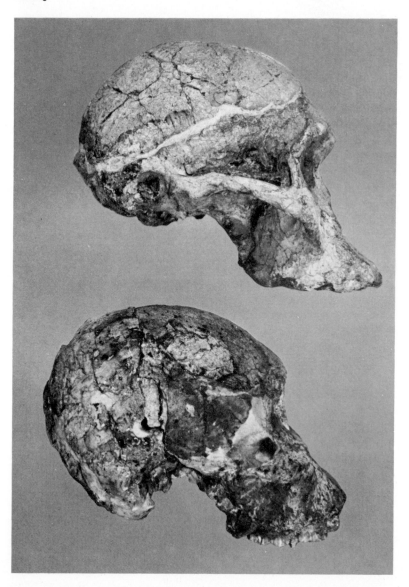

and 9.28). They also may be present at the Omo River, and some anthropologists place several specimens from East Turkana in *A. africanus.*

Their back teeth, the premolars and molars, although large compared with those of the genus *Homo,* tend to be somewhat smaller than those of the South African robust australopithecines (Figure 9.29). As Milford Wolpoff has pointed out, within the range of back tooth sizes of South African robusts and *A. africanus* there is some overlap; some teeth from Sterkfontein, for example, are as large as those from Swartkrans *Australopithecus robustus.*[14] Although the sum of their morphological features makes *A. africanus* look more like later hominines, the size of their teeth has caused debate about their precise position in hominine evolution. In brain size *A. africanus* is similar to the East and South African robust australopithecines: from about 440 ml to a little less than 500 ml.

A. africanus appears to be somewhat smaller in body size than *A. robustus,* but this is based primarily on the fossil bones of one individual, for which we have recovered many of the bones of the spinal column and lower limbs. However, this individual was probably a female, and it is difficult to determine just how different the male was (if there was a sexual dimorphic difference).

The fossils from Hadar and Laetoli have features somewhat different from those of the other australopithecines. These differences and the early dates from these sites—from about 2.9 to 3.2 million years B.P. at Hadar to about 3.7 million years B.P. at Laetoli—led Donald Johanson and Tim White to establish the taxon *Australopithecus afarensis* (named after the Afar region of Ethiopia, where the Hadar site is located) in 1978. Although these fossils are dated earlier than other australopithecines,

Australopithecus afarensis

FIGURE 9.28.   Two views of the broken and distorted lower jaw of *Australopithecus africanus* from the Sterkfontein site in South Africa. Most of the back portion of the left side has been destroyed, and the back part of the right side has been distorted outward. Note, however, that the jaw is smaller than the robust specimen in Figure 9.26 and that the front and back teeth are more in proportion with each other.

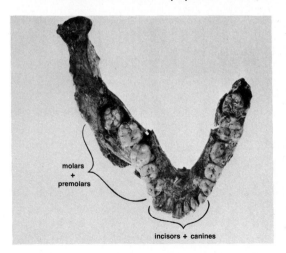
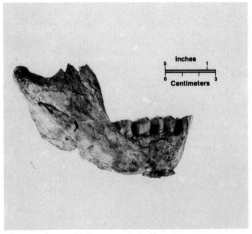

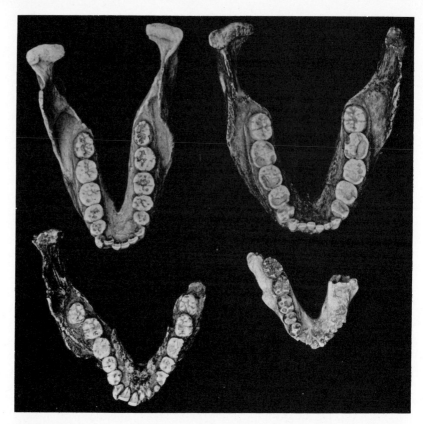

FIGURE 9.29. Four australopithecine lower jaws: *A. robustus* (upper left), *A. boisei* (upper right), *A. africanus* (lower left), and *A. afarensis* (lower right). Note the differences in the size of the jawbones and the back teeth among the four and the relative proportions of back to front teeth in the robust and hyperrobust *A. boisei*. The *A. africanus* jaw has back teeth that are smaller than in the *A. robustus* just above, but the total range of sizes of the two groups do overlap. All of the jaws are typical of most hominine fossils in their being broken and incomplete or distorted. (For example, the two sides of the *A. robustus* jaw have been pushed together.)

their back teeth are generally smaller than in the robust australopithecines and *Australopithecus africanus;* their brains may be smaller, too, with one specimen around 400 ml. The "Lucy" skeleton is virtually the same size as the female *A. africanus* skeleton and has been reconstructed to about 23 kilograms in weight and about 1.1 meters in height. The presence in the Hadar deposits of skeletal bones larger than those of "Lucy" suggests a dimorphic species with larger males, but these bones have also been viewed by some anthropologists as evidence for the presence at Hadar of another hominine species.

What is really distinctive about *A. afarensis* is the size and morphology of some of the canines and first lower premolars (Figures 9.30 and 9.31). First, there seems to be some sexual dimorphism in canine

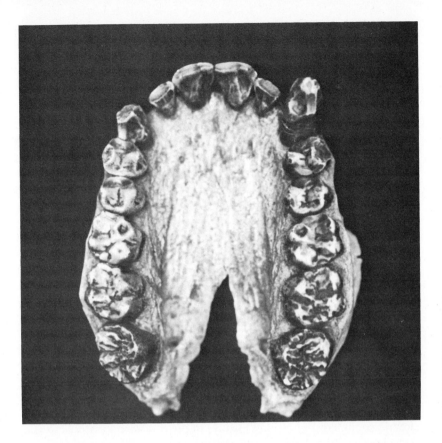

FIGURE 9.30
A cast of an upper jaw of
*Australopithecus
afarensis* from Hadar.
The left canine (on the right
here) has been pushed up
out of its socket, but the
enlarged canine on the
other side is clearly seen.

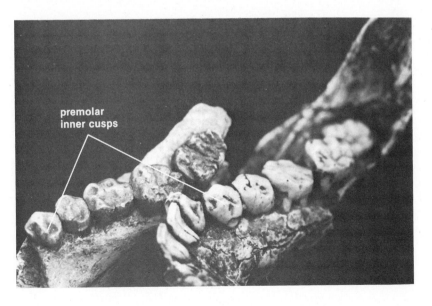

premolar
inner cusps

FIGURE 9.31
Casts of the "Lucy"
*Australopithecus
afarensis* lower jaw (left)
and *A. africanus* from
Sterkfontein.
Note the difference in the
sizes of the first premolar
cusps, with the *A. afarensis*
inner cusp smaller and
those of *A. africanus* more
equal in size.

size. In most apes, male canines are larger and more strongly developed than those of the females. The canines of modern humans and other australopithecines show no sexual dimorphism. The apparently male *A. afarensis* canines are similar in shape to those of the hominines only larger, sticking out slightly above the other teeth, while presumed female canines are somewhat smaller.

Second, in some fossil specimens, the shape of the first lower premolars is different from that of other australopithecines. Figure 9.31 shows the first lower premolars of the famous skeleton from Hadar, "Lucy," and the same tooth from the jaw of a Sterkfontein *A. africanus*. The *A. afarensis* tooth has cusps of unequal size, with the outer cusp being larger and the inside quite a bit smaller. The *A. africanus* tooth, like that of modern humans, has two more or less equal-sized cusps. The "Lucy" premolar is somewhat similar to that in the apes (compare it with the ape premolar in Figure 9.21d), where it serves a honing function against the back of the upper canine. There is evidence that the first lower premolar in *A. afarensis* did serve this function, although to a much more limited extent than in the apes. This canine/premolar complex in *A. afarensis* is associated with a completely bipedal animal, as the skeletal and footprint evidence demonstrate.

Dated early, *A. afarensis* may represent beginning evolutionary trends toward later hominines and is thus representative of the earliest true hominines. However, much debate still focuses on the status of *A. afarensis,* with many arguing that there are valid reasons for doing away with it altogether. For example, Phillip Tobias has suggested that there are not enough distinguishing features of the *A. afarensis* material to warrant its separation from *A. africanus*. According to Tobias, all of the attributes used by Johanson and White to establish *A. afarensis* can be found among the *A. africanus* fossils.[15]

Several European and American anthropologists have separated the *A. afarensis* material into two or more species. Some believe these fossils belong to *A. africanus* and to an early member of the robust group, but others also see a third group, early members of the genus *Homo,* in the sample as well.[16] Finally, there is considerable debate over the lumping of the Hadar (Ethiopia) and Laetoli (Tanzania) fossil evidence into one species. Many anthropologists believe that the significant time difference between the two sites (almost half a million years) argues against their membership in the same species and that the earlier Laetoli fossils show more primitive features than the Hadar fossils. The fragmentary fossil hominines from the sites of Maka and Belohdelie in the Awash Valley near Hadar in Ethiopia, dated to about 4 million years B.P., or from the Baringo Basin of Kenya, dated to about 5 million years B.P., offer the promise of eventually ending this debate. Discovery of additional fossils from these sites will tell us more about the hominines of this early time and allow us to evaluate the features and the justification of *A. afarensis*.

A number of fossils from Bed I and the lower part of Bed II at Olduvai Gorge have cranial capacities ranging from about 600 to 670 ml, larger than in other australopithecines. The teeth, especially the back teeth, are smaller and the dental arcade more similar to those of later hominines (Figure 9.32). Louis Leakey, Phillip Tobias, and John Napier gave these fossils the name *Homo habilis,* suggesting they are more advanced than other australopithecines and deserve to be placed in the genus *Homo.*

This idea did not escape comment. John Robinson suggests that the taxon *H. habilis* ought to be divided into two groups: The earlier fossils, from Bed I, share affinities with other australopithecines, such as *Australopithecus africanus;* those from later deposits, in Bed II, should be placed with members of the later hominine group, *Homo erectus.* According to Robinson, all fossils now assigned to *H. habilis* may be part of the evolutionary transition between the australopithecines and later hominines.[17]

In addition to the *H. habilis* fossils from Olduvai Gorge, a number of other fossils from east of Lake Turkana and the upper part of the Omo sequence have also been placed in the genus *Homo.* There is also a frag-

FIGURE 9.32. Pieces of a skull and jaws from Olduvai Gorge, found in the lower Bed II level. With a brain case larger than those of *Australopithecus africanus* and *A. robustus* and some teeth smaller than in other australopithecines, this specimen and others led Leakey, Tobias, and Napier to propose the term *Homo habilis* for these creatures, suggesting that they are more advanced than the other australopithecines.

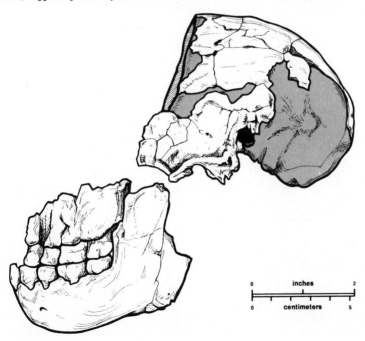

| 0 | inches | 2 |
| 0 | centimeters | 5 |

mentary skull from a deposit above the *A. africanus* levels at Sterkfontein that has been called *Homo*. The most complete and important of these fossils come from East Turkana and date from about 1.5 to 2 million years B.P. They possess several different combinations of features. Some, like the fossil KNM-ER 3733 (*ER* = East Rudolf, the former name of Lake Turkana, the region in which it was found) in Figure 9.33, are unquestionably members of the genus *Homo,* probably *Homo erectus* (see Chapter 10). They have large brains (over 800 ml), small teeth, and morphological features that link them to these later hominines. The fossil dates from about 1.5 to 1.6 million years B.P. Other somewhat earlier East Turkana fossils are not as straightforward. KNM-ER 1470 (Figure 9.34), for example, and another like it, KNM-ER 1590, possess large brains, almost 800 ml, but the teeth are also large, *A. africanus*-sized. Still others, such as KNM-ER 1813 (Figure 9.35), have small brains (this one is about 510 ml) and small *H. erectus*-sized teeth. What criteria can be used to define a fossil as a member of the genus *Homo?* All these creatures were bipedal, so this attribute is not of help. We must focus on the other major trends in hominine evolution: the reduction in size of the face and teeth and the expansion of the brain. Some of the East Turkana fossils possess *Homo*-sized brains and *Australopithecus*-sized teeth, and others the reverse. Depending on which criteria we use, the fossils can be sorted in different ways, and this influences the view of australopithecine evolution. Some anthropologists lump all of these East Turkana specimens into *H. habilis,* but others, who consider brain size of paramount importance, prefer to place only the large-brained skulls in *Homo,* moving KNM-ER 1813, for example, into *A. africanus*.

FIGURE 9.33.   KNM-ER 3733 (left) compared with a cast of KNM-ER 406. The latter, a robust australopithecine with a sagittal crest, flaring cheek region, large chewing muscles, and other attributes of this group, is only slightly older than KNM-ER 3733, which, with its higher forehead, smaller face, smaller chewing muscles, and much larger brain, is clearly a member of the genus *Homo*, perhaps *Homo erectus*.

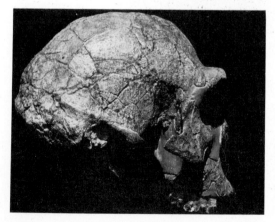 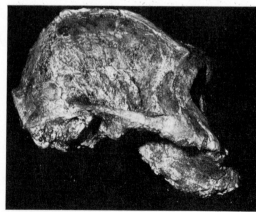

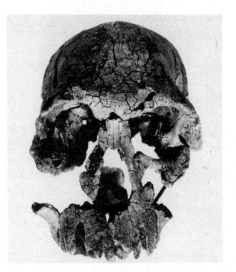
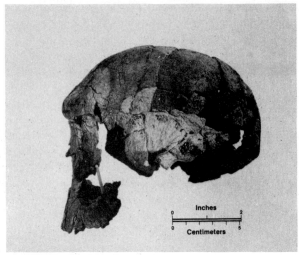

FIGURE 9.34. Two views of KNM-ER 1470, a relatively complete early hominine skull from east of Lake Turkana. The skull was found in many pieces, and there is no good bony connection between the facial portion and the brain case. Since this photograph was taken, a later restoration has moved the face into a more projecting position, giving it more of the appearance of other australopithecines. It does, however, possess a cranial capacity of 775 ml.

FIGURE 9.35. Two views of the skull of KNM-ER 1813, from East Turkana. Note that the forehead rises more steeply than in the *Australopithecus africanus* specimens from Sterkfontein (see Figure 9.27), and in this as well as in the size of the teeth, which are small, this specimen is like members of the genus *Homo*. It does, however, possess a small cranial capacity, just a little over 500 ml.

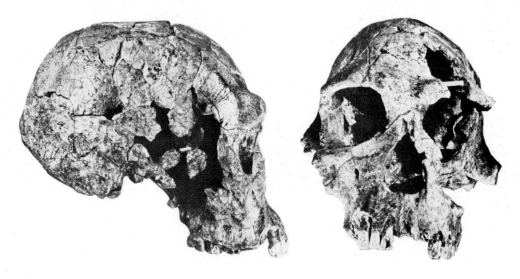

Table 9.3 summarizes the various australopithecine groups, their morphological features, and their placement in time. There is presently no agreement about how all these categories ought to be arranged in an evolutionary sequence or even about whether all the currently recognized species are really necessary or justified.

Several years ago a theory, termed the *"single species hypothesis,"* was proposed that suggested that all early hominines belonged to one variable species and that differences in morphology between the specimens could be accounted for by their separation in time and space as well as by the variability normal in any species. This idea can be rejected on the basis of fossil discoveries. The skull KNM-ER 3733, from 1.5 to 1.6 million years B.P., is a member of *Homo erectus,* for it is similar to specimens in that taxonomic category. At the same level or just a little earlier at East Turkana, however, are *Australopithecus boisei* specimens like the skull KNM-ER 406. The differences between these two skulls are too great to be encompassed within one species (Figure 9.33).

It is thus clear that there were at least two different early hominine species living at the same time. But how many? What are the relationships between the various australopithecines? The available fossil and other evidence permits the construction of a number of possible diagrams linking the australopithecines evolutionarily; all fit the evidence, yet all cannot be correct. In Figure 9.36a, the various australopithecine groups are arranged in a time sequence leading ultimately to modern humans, *Homo sapiens.* The South African forms (*Australopithecus africanus* and *Australopithecus robustus*) are troublesome to place because of the absence of radiometric dates, and their position on this time chart thus represents a reasonable placement. The remainder of Figure 9.36 depicts a variety of current views of australopithecine evolution. Figures 9.36b and 9.36c are similar except in their treatment of the ancestry of the robust australopithecines. These views begin with *Australopithecus afarensis,* which evolves into *A. africanus* sometime after 3 million years B.P. Just after this evolutionary change, the hominine line splits, developing into two branches, one leading to the robust australopithecines and the other eventually to *Homo habilis* and ultimately, ourselves.

After the robusts speciate, *A. africanus* continues, beginning to evolve into members of the genus *Homo* sometime after 2 million years ago. According to this idea, the difficulties in distinguishing members of the genus *Homo* from those of *A. africanus* in the period between 2 and 1.5 million years B.P. arise from the fact that the species at this time contains individuals with features reminiscent of both kinds. Robinson's claim that the *H. habilis* material represents the evolutionary transition between *Australopithecus* and *Homo* meshes with this situation.

Figure 9.36b presents a picture of early hominine evolution favored by Eric Delson and Fred Grine, in which forms similar to KNM-WT 17000, which is the common ancestor of later members of *A. boisei* as well as the South African *A. robustus,* evolve from *A. africanus.*[18] This

TABLE 9.3
Suggested Groupings of East and South African Early Hominines

	Australopithecus afarensis	*Robust Group*	*Australopithecus africanus*	*Homo Group*
Brain size	400–500 ml	400–550 ml	450–500 ml	600–775 ml
Dentition	Back teeth generally smaller than *A. africanus*, larger canines, unequal cusps on first premolar	Very large back teeth, relatively small front teeth	Large front and back teeth	Variable, generally smaller than robust and gracile forms
Species and location	*Australopithecus afarensis* East Africa: Hadar, Ethiopia; Laetoli, Tanzania	*Australopithecus robustus* South Africa: Swartkrans, Kromdraai *Australopithecus boisei*[a] East Africa: Olduvai Gorge, Penini, Lake Turkana, Chesowanja, Omo	*Australopithecus africanus* South Africa: Taung, Sterkfontein, Makapansgat East Africa: Omo, East Turkana	*Homo habilis* East Africa: Olduvai Gorge, East Turkana *Homo* South Africa: Sterkfontein East Africa: Omo
Dating	Hadar: 2.9 to 3.2 million years B.P. Laetoli: 3.7 million years B.P.	East Africa: 2.5 to c. 1.5 million years B.P. South Africa: relative placement = 2 to 1.5 million years B.P.	East Africa: 3 to c. 1.5 million years B.P. South Africa: relative placement = > 3 to 2.5 million years B.P.	East Africa: c. 2 to c. 1.5 million years B.P.

[a]This includes the WT-17000 skull, which is called *A. aethiopicus* by some.

FIGURE 9.36. Theories of early hominine evolution.

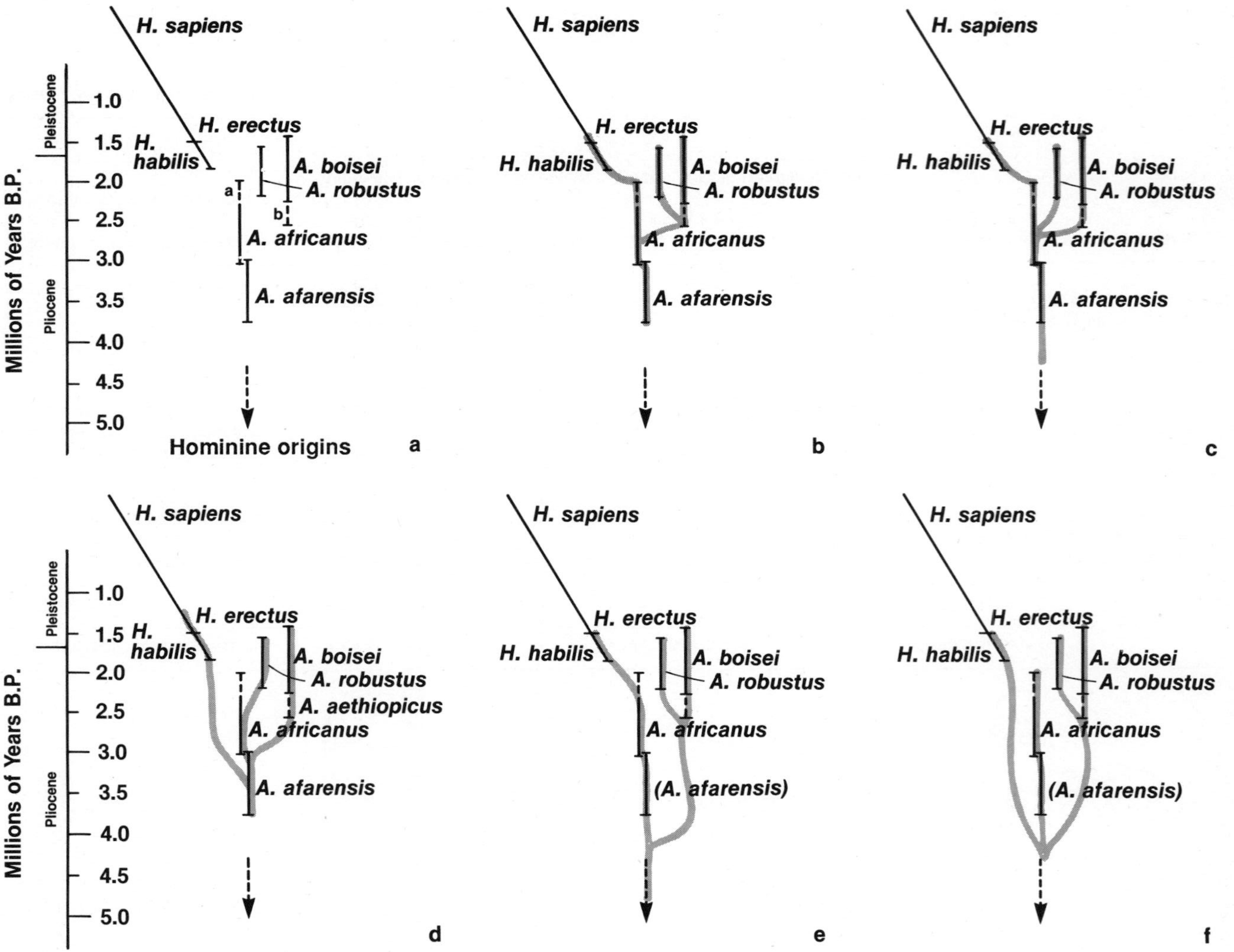

[a]This dashed line refers to the possible existence of *A. africanus* east of Lake Turkana, Kenya.

idea places the earliest robust group, KNM–WT 17000, as the common ancestor of all the later robust forms. Figure 9.36c views the ancestry of the robust forms in a somewhat more complex fashion and suggests that the initial evolutionary divergence of the robust line from the *A. africanus* stock was soon followed by the separation of the South and East African lines into independently evolving groups. This scheme views *A. robustus* as having changed less from the *A. africanus* ancestral form than has *A. boisei*. It also draws from an analysis of the australopithecine face by Yoel Rak, in which he shows that the facial structures and function of both South African forms share many similarities and might most reasonably be seen as being part of an evolutionary sequence.[19]

The evolutionary scheme shown in Figure 9.36d represents a number of differences from those in Figures 9.36b and 9.36c. This idea, proposed by several anthropologists, places *A. afarensis* as the only common ancestor for later hominines. During the time of *A. afarensis*, there was a split, with one line leading to *H. habilis* and modern humans and the other to *A. africanus*. This line, which leads to the robust australopithecines, also later bifurcates, with one branch evolving into *A. robustus* and the other developing into forms like KNM–WT 17000, which is viewed as a separate species, *A. aethiopicus*. This species in turn evolves into later *A. boisei*. This scheme also takes into account Rak's conclusions about the relationships of *A. africanus* and *A. robustus* but is founded on a connection between *A. afarensis* and *H. habilis* that is currently not supported by any fossil evidence.

The evolutionary models in Figures 9.36e and 9.36f are similar in that they reject *A. afarensis* as a valid taxon, preferring instead to place these fossils into two or perhaps three categories. Figure 9.36e, which is the work of Todd Olson, suggests a very early split in hominine evolution between the robust line and that leading to the genus *Homo* and modern humans. In Olson's view, some fossils placed in *A. afarensis* possess specialized traits found only among robust australopithecines. The line leading to *Homo* evolves into *A. africanus* and thus into *Homo,* while the robust line splits, producing the South African robust and East African *A. boisei* species.[20] This idea is founded on the separation of *A. afarensis* into a large-body-size species and a small-body-size species, differences that others prefer to see as evidence for a sexually dimorphic species.

Figure 9.36f also splits *A. afarensis* into different species and thus sees the early differentiation of the various hominine lines. In this case, three early hominine lines are present, one that leads to the robusts, which later diverge into East and South African groups; one that leads to *A. africanus* and later to the small-brained forms from East Turkana like KNM–ER 1813 (Figure 9.35), who subsequently become extinct, and a line that leads to *H. habilis* and ourselves. Like Figure 9.36d, this model also suffers from a lack of fossil evidence supporting a long, separate evolutionary history for the line leading to *Homo*.[21]

Although there are numerous differences in the ways these models view early hominine evolution, they share the idea that the robust australopithecines became extinct without issue sometime after 1.5 million years B.P.

Whether any of these theories or yet another one most adequately describes early hominine evolution will depend on future fossil discoveries. All current theories assume the presence of at least two coexisting hominine lines during the late Pliocene/early Pleistocene. How two hominines were able to coexist is an interesting and important question that requires examination of the evidence for australopithecine adaptation.

Australopithecine Adaptations

Australopithecine Environments

Through the study of plant pollen and the identification of the animal bones found in the early hominine deposits, as well as sophisticated geologic and taphonomic analyses, a general picture of the environments in which the australopithecine sites were located has been developed. This picture is at variance with the traditional notions that early hominine evolution took place in open country and that the australopithecines were savanna-adapted forms. These new investigations reveal a more complicated situation. In East Africa, most of the australopithecine bones come from places that were on the margin of lakes or beside a stream. A variety of habitats were close by: open-country savanna, woodland, and forest. It is not clear whether one or the other australopithecine line was limited to any one of these zones or was able to exploit the resources in all of them seasonally.

At Olduvai Gorge, thanks to the work of the geologist Richard Hay, we have a rather complete picture of the environment during Bed I times when *Australopithecus boisei* and *Homo habilis* lived in the area. According to Hay, beneath the shadow of the then-active volcano of Ngorongoro was a perennial lake that varied in size from season to season. Feeding the lake were a number of streams that ran down from the highlands. Contrasting with the well-watered, forested volcanic highlands were open country and woodland around the lake shore. Early hominine sites are almost always located either by the side of one of the feeder streams or along the lake edge.[22]

In South Africa, the evidence seems to show much the same situation: a variety of habitats in the immediate vicinity of the cave deposits.

The Evidence of Archaeology

The description of a fossil's morphological features is the first step in an analysis. Our goal is to understand the ways by which a population maintained a long-term successful adaptation within its environment. The evidence indicates that the australopithecines were a successful animal group, surviving for about 4 million years, much longer than their modern human descendants have thus far been around. Unfortunately, archaeological materials, which furnish a great deal of information for later periods, are very scarce for this time. The very limited data that have been recovered have proved to be exceedingly difficult to interpret.

The South African australopithecine sites consist of accumulations of debris that fell down a shaft and were incorporated into the deposit. Animal bones, australopithecine bones, and, at one or two of the sites, stone and bone tools are all found. Clearly early hominines were in the vicinity of the caverns, but whether they had any responsibility for the animal bone accumulations is a very difficult question to answer. A detailed assessment of the South African cave fillings by C. K. Brain suggests that most of the animal bones in the deposits are the result of carnivore activity, and this may also apply to the australopithecine bones (Figure 9.37).[23]

FIGURE 9.37.   Evidence indicating that some South African australopithecine fossils were victims of predators' attacks and a hypothetical reconstruction. The photograph shows the back of a young robust australopithecine skull from the Swartkrans site. Notice the two puncture holes. C. K. Brain believes that these holes resulted from a bite by a carnivore's canine teeth, possibly a leopard's. Brain has a fossil leopard jaw whose canines fit these holes exactly and has suggested such a kill in this drawing.

Puncture holes

The East African sites are more rewarding. At one site east of Lake Turkana, known as the Hippo Artifact Site (HAS), the remains of a partially dismembered hippopotamus were found in a dry streambed, with a few stone tools around the carcass. It is not likely that the australopithecines were capable of dispatching a tough creature like a hippo; the context probably reflects the fortunate discovery of a dead or dying animal.

At the site of DK (Douglas Korongo), low in Bed I at Olduvai Gorge, the fragmentary skull of a *Homo habilis* was found with a curious ring of stones (Figure 9.38). First identified by the Leakeys as the remains of a dwelling, it has also been viewed as the remains of a hunting blind, a place near to the lake margin and close to trails used by animals coming down to drink. It remains unclear, however, whether this finding is the result of a natural agency or hominine activity.

Pat Shipman and Rick Potts have shown that under a high-powered microscope, clear and unmistakable signs of hominine scratch marks can be seen on some of the animal bones found at australopithecine sites in East Africa.[24] The identification and meatiness of the bones (often the lower parts of the front and back limbs of antelopes, where edible meat is scanty and difficult to acquire without a scraping tool) have led to suggestions that a major aspect of early hominine adaptation was based on scavenging bones left from carnivore kills.

Reconstructing Behavior

The archaeological and environmental data, along with the australopithecine fossils themselves, do not provide enough information for any firm conclusions to be drawn about australopithecine behavior and adaptation. One point does seem reasonably certain, however: Like all higher primates, the australopithecines lived in social groups. The group size is not known but it could not have been large.

We do not know if the australopithecines hunted any of the animals whose bones we find with them or if scavenging played an important role in their adaptation. The animal bones may have also come from old or sick animals that would be relatively easy for australopithecines to kill. Nothing is left of vegetable or insect foods, so that we have no way of determining how much (if any) of the diet was hunted meat and how much was scavenged remains from predator kills and gathered vegetable foods, insects, insect grubs, birds, birds' eggs, amphibians, small reptiles, and mammals.

Tools and Behavior   The stone tools found at some australopithecine sites are crudely chipped from pebbles, or cobbles, which accounts for the term "cobble tools"; these are called the *Oldowan industry* (Figure 9.39). We cannot reconstruct how the australopithecines used these tools, but they were not suitable for delicate tasks. These stone implements may have been used for digging plants, animals, and insects out of the

Note: The northeast part of
the excavated area
is not shown.

Various Types of Stone
Tools and By-Products
of Their Production

CH   Choppers
P   Polyhedrons
DC   Discoids
SSP Subspheroids
SC   Scrapers
B   Burins
H   Hammerstones
UTH Utilized material, heavy-duty
UTL Utilized material, light-duty
D   Debitage

FIGURE 9.38.   Part of the plan of the site of DK, in Bed I, Olduvai Gorge, prepared by Mary Leakey. The stone ring, some 4 by 5 meters in size, is made up primarily of 10–15 cm (in diameter) lava blocks and is part of a floor littered with stone tools and broken animal bones. It was near the lake and had evidence of nearby game trails. The stone ring is unique in early hominine discoveries. It is unclear whether this is indeed the result of hominine activity or some natural agency.

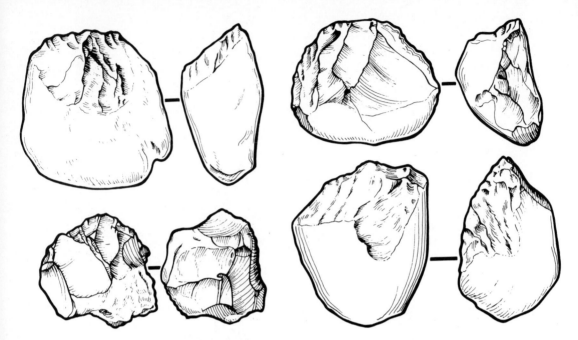

FIGURE 9.39.   Cobble tools of the Oldowan industry from Bed I, Olduvai Gorge, Tanzania (one-third actual size).

ground, for pounding tough vegetable foods, such as tubers, or for cracking open animal bones to reach the marrow cavity inside.

While the earliest stone tools have come from deposits above the *Australopithecus afarensis*-bearing rocks at Hadar in Ethiopia and are dated to about 2.5 million years B.P., stone tools do not become a common element in the hominine record until after 2 million years B.P. It is possible that prior to this, other perishable materials, such as wood, were employed for tools, but the evidence for this is lacking. We do not know if all the early hominines were capable of toolmaking behaviors. The lack of associated tools with *A. afarensis* and *Australopithecus africanus* would argue against viewing them as toolmakers, but were these behaviors limited to the more advanced-appearing australopithecines of the kind represented by the *Homo* group? Or were robust australopithecines also capable of these behaviors? Unfortunately, there have been no discoveries of hominine bones and tools that would demonstrate beyond question that only one line of early hominines were toolmakers.

Body Size and Behavior   The few bones of the skeleton that can be assigned to the robust australopithecines suggest that these early hominines were somewhat larger in body size than the other forms, perhaps 40 kilograms in weight and 1.5 meters tall.[25] The whole issue of australopithecine body size is made difficult by the small number of skeletal bones that have been recovered and by the question of sexual dimorphism: Were there large-bodied males and small-bodied females, similar to the differences seen in baboons and gorillas? And if so, are the skeletal bones we have found those of males or females? Further complicating the issue is that apart from the "Lucy" *Australopithecus afarensis* partial skeleton and one or two other specimens, virtually all of the skeletal bones have been discovered in isolation and not directly associated with skull pieces or teeth.

Nevertheless, there are tantalizing bits of evidence to suggest a significant difference in the male and female body sizes in the *A. afarensis*, *Australopithecus africanus*, and *Australopithecus boisei* samples, and perhaps in the *Homo habilis* collection as well. The fossil bones from "Lucy," the *A. afarensis* partial skeleton, are small, with a reconstructed height of just over a meter. Recall too the small-sized footprints from Laetoli (Figure 9.11). Another Hadar site where a significant number of fragmentary skeletal bones were recovered shows variations in body size ranging from those similar to "Lucy" to those whose reconstructed total body size may be over 1½ meters, which is within the modern human range (Figure 9.10). The *A. africanus* partial skeleton from Sterkfontein, whose pelvis is illustrated in Figure 9.14 is similar in size to "Lucy" and has been identified as a female. Other fragmentary bones from Sterkfontein, like the ends of the thighbones pictured in Figure 9.16, are modern human in size. *A. boisei* skulls from east of Lake Turkana show an interesting range of size variation, with both large- and small-sized specimens that have been interpreted as male and female.

The very fragmentary *H. habilis* skeleton recently discovered at Olduvai Gorge, an adult female, is about 1 meter in height. If the smaller skulls from East Turkana, like KNM-ER 1813 (Figure 9.35), also represent a female *H. habilis,* and if the larger skulls, like KNM-ER 1470 (Figure 9.34) are males, dimorphism may have been strongly marked in early hominines.

This conclusion has important implications for early hominine behavior. In the social-living higher primates, there are few examples of a pair-bonded, monogamous living species that shows significant dimorphism. Virtually all dimorphic primate species are organized into social groups where there are no long-term associations between a male and a female. Clearly, more fossil and other evidence is needed before we can conclude that the early hominines differed from us in such a momentous way.

Before discussing the various adaptive models that have been proposed for the australopithecines, it might be useful to summarize briefly what we do know about these early hominines.

The earliest australopithecines, those belonging to *A. afarensis* and *A. africanus,* have not been found with tools or any other direct evidence of complex behavior. Tools first appear about 2.5 million years ago, unassociated with any hominine. After about 2 million years B.P. stone tools and signs of meat eating appear in East Africa with both the robust *A. boisei* and *H. habilis* fossil bones. There are thus indications that such behavior developed during early hominine evolution.

Given this limited data about the early hominines, it is not surprising that there is little agreement among anthropologists (we know how tired you must be to keep reading that!) in reconstructing the patterns of adaptation of the various australopithecines, with just about every kind of diet and habitat being suggested at one time or another.

Models of Australopithecine Adaptation

One of the most widely accepted models of australopithecine adaptation was offered by J. T. Robinson, who suggested that the robust australopithecines were inhabiting different ecological niches from the others; the robust forms, with larger back teeth, faces, and chewing muscles, were forest-dwelling vegetarians, living on tough, fibrous vegetable materials that require much chewing. The other australopithecines were omnivores more adapted to open country, subsisting on animal tissue as well as plants.[26]

This view of the two early hominine lines being adapted to different habitats and diets has been a favored concept for many because it provides a way to explain how two biologically similar hominine species could coexist in the same area, for example, at Olduvai Gorge. Many models of early hominine adaptation utilize this same basic concept, but modify the diet or the habitats involved.

Raymond Dart proposed that *Australopithecus africanus* and the members of the hominine line leading to *Homo* were adapted to the open savanna and that they were basically predatory hunters. In contrast, others, like Noel Boaz and Charles Peters, view *A. africanus* as essentially opportunistic foragers subsisting mainly on vegetation. Peters has actually gathered edible vegetable materials in the Makapan Valley of South Africa to demonstrate the likelihood of his ideas.[27]

Other suggestions have focused on the kinds of habitats that the early hominines were exploiting, arguing that since social groups of chimps and baboons routinely inhabit a number of environments during the course of their yearly rounds, it is simplistic to believe that the early hominines were not at least as complex. These models must then provide an explanation of how the robust group and the line leading to *Homo* were able to coexist, since this model does away with any environmental limitations on the hominines.

One such model views all australopithecines as adapted to the environment in much the same way, as generalized feeders of plants, insects, and small vertebrate foods. After the robust australopithecines speciate, both lines continue to live in the same environments and to compete for the same resources. Both lines react to this competition biologically but in different ways. The robust group evolves increasingly large back teeth to facilitate more efficient chewing. Large back teeth are an ancient part of the hominine adaptation and perhaps extend back to the hominoid ancestors of the hominine subfamily. The robust group thus elaborates a trait that has been an important part of the basic adaptation of the hominines for a long time, perhaps as a way to increase food processing efficiency in what proved to be a futile change: The robust group disappears from the fossil record after about 1.5 million years B.P. Robust australopithecine brain size changes little; the only development we can note in the robust group is an increase in the size of the back teeth and the supporting structures of muscle and bone.

In the line leading to *Homo,* in contrast, competition leads to more efficient ways of procuring food by more adept toolmaking. This model thus attempts to explain the evolutionary origins of the genus *Homo* in the period from 2 to 1.5 million years B.P. by suggesting that as a result of competition with the robust group there was evolutionary selection for more complex behavior that led to increasing brain sizes in the line leading to *Homo* (Figure 9.40). This is an attractive model because it is able to fit the known fossil information into a pattern that also explains the extinction of the robust australopithecines and the sudden increase in brain size in the line leading to *Homo* as well as the flowering of tool technology. It provides a way of understanding the subsequent evolutionary events that were to lead to the appearance of modern humans and indeed develops a reason for these events. Finally, this model highlights the differences between australopithecines and later hominines.[28]

Attractive though it is, this idea and others like it are unverifiable at present. Excavations are continuing at a number of sites in South Africa and East Africa, and new fossil and archaeological materials are being discovered regularly. We can hope that the additional evidence will help to clarify the still very murky picture of early hominine evolution and its relationships to the appearance of later hominines.

The discovery from East Turkana of KNM-ER 3733 (Figure 9.33) demonstrates that by about 1.5 to 1.6 million years ago, members of the genus *Homo* were present in East Africa. As we have seen, they evolved probably during the period between 2 and 1.5 million years B.P. The next chapter carries on the story of hominine evolution from these early developments to the appearance of modern humans.

Summary

This chapter has examined the fossil evidence for the early phases of hominine evolution. The earliest known members of the subfamily Homininae belong to the genus *Australopithecus,* who are grouped for convenience in this chapter with an early representative of the genus *Homo, Homo habilis,* into the australopithecines. These hominines, from the period from about 5 to 1.5 million years B.P., are known from a number of sites in South and East Africa. They share with later hominines a bipedal mode of locomotion and, except for the earliest australopithecines, possess essentially homininelike although larger dentitions in a large, projecting face. The brain size of these early hominines is generally small, although some general increase in size can be noted from

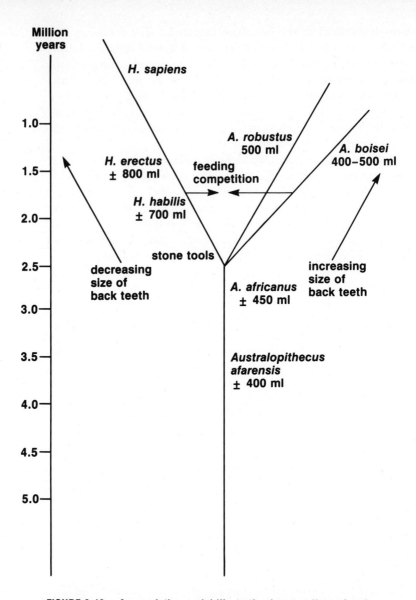

FIGURE 9.40.   A speculative model illustrating how two lines of early hominines, both adapted to the environment in the same way, might have interacted, and the biological and behavioral changes that may have resulted. (Abbreviations: ml, milliliters, a volume measure. 1000 ml = 1 liter.)

the earliest to the latest. On the basis of differences in the teeth, jaws, and skull, five species of australopithecines have been named, including two species of larger, more robust forms that seem to represent an extinct side branch of hominine evolution that disappeared from the fossil record after about 1.5 million years ago. Members of our own genus, *Homo,* seem to appear in the fossil record between 2 and 1.5 million years B.P.

A more elaborate summary including the material covered in this chapter will be found at the end of Chapter 10.

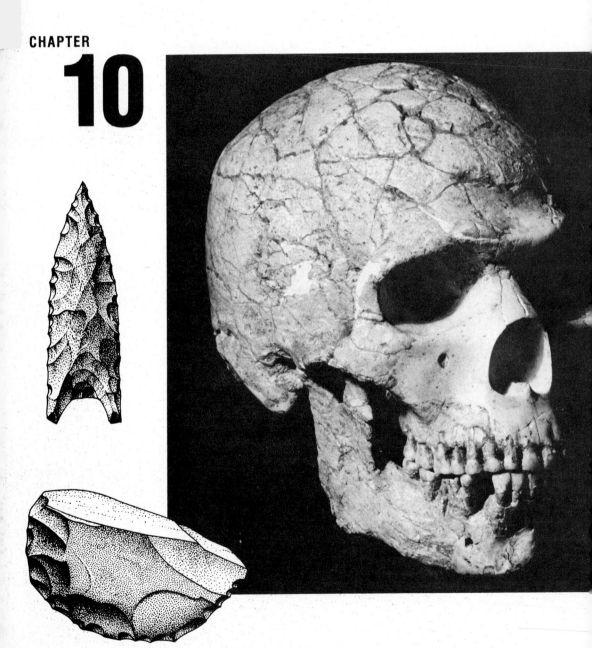

The appearance of modern humans demonstrates the continuing nature of evolution and the action of natural selection in the evolving hominine gene pool.

Human Evolution II: The Emergence of Modern Humans

In the last chapter we traced the development of the subfamily Homininae from its rather shadowy beginnings and described the extensive australopithecine fossil collections from South and East Africa, dated from about 5 million to 1.5 million years ago. By this time, fossil hominines of the category *Homo erectus,* such as KNM-ER 3733 from East Turkana (see Figure 9.33), are on the scene, to remain as the sole hominine until evolving into early members of *Homo sapiens* some 300,000 to 400,000 years B.P. *Homo erectus* is thus the hominine taxon between the earlier australopithecines and later *Homo sapiens* from the early part of the Pleistocene, about 1.5 million years B.P., to the latter stages of the middle Pleistocene, around 300,000 to 400,000 years B.P.

The evolutionary development of *Homo erectus* also coincides with the geographic expansion of the hominines (Figure 10.1). The earliest *H. erectus* appears to have been limited to Africa, and it is only after 1 million years ago, probably closer to about 900,000 years ago, that we find hominines in tropical and subtropical parts of Eurasia, while later *Homo erectus* is found in the colder parts of Asia, like north China, and perhaps the central parts of Europe as well. By the time of the earliest *H. sapiens* fossil evidence, hominines are to be found in most parts of the Old World. Much of the rest of the world, however, remained uncolonized by hominines until very late in human evolution, when anatomically modern peoples moved into Siberia and from there into North and South America; by boat they traveled to Australia; and finally, by means of highly sophisticated navigational systems, they reached and colonized the remote islands of the Pacific.

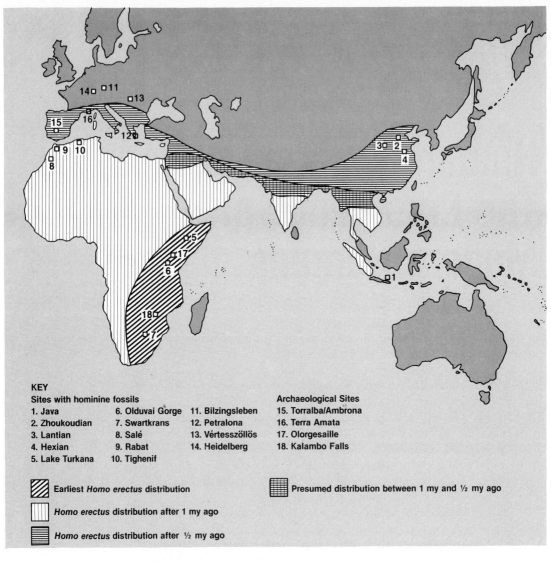

KEY

Sites with hominine fossils

1. Java	6. Olduvai Gorge	11. Bilzingsleben
2. Zhoukoudian	7. Swartkrans	12. Petralona
3. Lantian	8. Salé	13. Vértesszöllös
4. Hexian	9. Rabat	14. Heidelberg
5. Lake Turkana	10. Tighenif	

Archaeological Sites

15. Torralba/Ambrona
16. Terra Amata
17. Olorgesaille
18. Kalambo Falls

Earliest *Homo erectus* distribution

Presumed distribution between 1 my and ½ my ago

Homo erectus distribution after 1 my ago

Homo erectus distribution after ½ my ago

FIGURE 10.1. Distribution of *Homo erectus* fossils and archaelogical sites. The European fossils, Heidelberg, Bilzingsleben, Petralona, and Vértesszöllös, are probably early representatives of *H. sapiens*.

Homo erectus

Discoveries in Java

In the late nineteenth century, more than thirty years before Raymond Dart described *Australopithecus* (see Chapter 9), Eugene Dubois, a Dutch physician, became interested in human evolution. This was a time of great controversy about our origins. Some still hoped that an intermediate form, a "missing link" between humans and the apes, would be found. Dubois, determined to find traces of this creature, joined the colonial service and sailed to the Dutch East Indies in 1887.

In 1891, after several years of fruitless searching, Dubois found a skull cap, a thighbone (femur), and a few other fragments washed out of a riverbank at *Trinil,* on the Solo River, in the central part of the island of Java, now part of the country of Indonesia (Figure 10.2). The skullcap and the thighbone contrasted remarkably. The leg bone was indistinguishable from those of living humans, but the skullcap's forehead was much lower and more sloping than those of living humans (Figure 10.3). The total height of the brain case was significantly lower than those of modern people, and because of this the greatest width across the skull, when viewed from the back, was low on the skull, just behind and above the ear holes. Above the eye orbits were large, projecting brow ridges, and directly behind the orbits was a "waisting," a narrowing or constriction in the brain case not found in modern human skulls because of their larger brain. Dubois' Trinil skull had a cranial volume of about 775 ml, which is larger than almost all australopithecine skulls but smaller than the 1,350 to 1,450 ml capacity normally found in modern human skulls. The Trinil specimen also had very thick bones. Keep in mind, however, that when Dubois was examining his finds, nothing was known of any of the fossils described in Chapter 9.

Dubois decided that these physical features might mean he had found the long-sought missing link. A few years before his discovery, Ernst Haeckel, a German scientist, suggested that if a link between apes and humans were found, it would be logical to call it "Pithecanthropus" (*pithec = ape; anthropos = man: apeman*). Dubois was impressed by the modern human look of the thighbone, which indicated this fossil had in life assumed erect posture, and he gave the Java fossil the taxonomic name "*Pithecanthropus erectus,*" or bipedal apeman. This taxonomic category was changed in the 1960s to *Homo erectus.*

Like many other discoveries of fossil hominines, Dubois' conclusions were strongly criticized by some scientists, who particularly objected to his association of the primitive-looking skull and the modern thighbone. They suggested that the skullcap belonged to an extinct ape, while the thighbone could have belonged to a modern human skeleton accidentally washed into the geologic deposit with the skullcap. The controversy burned on for several decades and was not to be settled until the discovery of new fossil material enabled paleoanthropologists to place Dubois' Trinil finds in perspective.

As we have seen, Dart announced the discovery of *Australopithecus* in 1925. An increased understanding of the implications of australopithecine morphology ended many of the debates over "Pithecanthropus erectus." The australopithecines' morphological characteristics were more primitive than those of Dubois' find, yet they were clearly hominine. In comparison with the australopithecines, "Pithecanthropus erectus," looked more like modern humans. "Pithecanthropus erectus," then, was evolutionarily between modern humans and the australopithecines. Additional hominine fossils, in appearance like that of "Pithecanthropus" and dated to the early and middle Pleistocene, supported this conclusion.

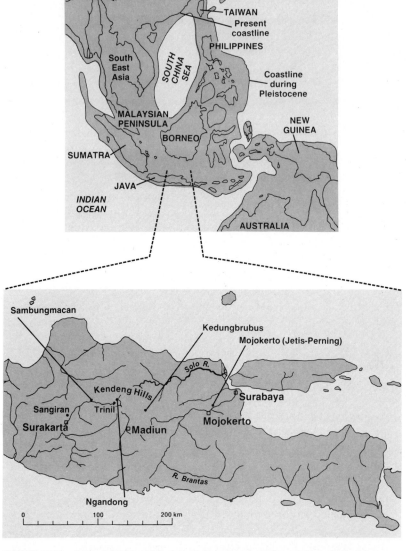

FIGURE 10.2. Map of Southeast Asia and the central portion of the island of Java (now part of the country of Indonesia). Because of the drop in sea levels brought about by the glacials, during much of the Pleistocene, Java and neighboring islands were joined to the mainland of Asia. Thus, at these times, hominines could reach Java without crossing open water.

The closeup of central Java shows the *Homo erectus* sites on the island, including Sangiran, where most of the fossils have been found, and Trinil, where Dubois discovered the first skullcap. Additional *Homo erectus* fossils have been found at Sambungmacan, Kedungbrubus, and Mojokerto, while at Ngandong the so-called Solo skull sample of early *Homo sapiens* or very late *Homo erectus* was uncovered.

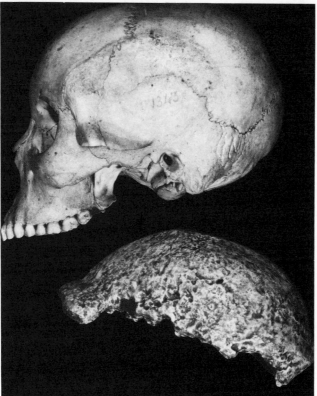

FIGURE 10.3
Cast of the skullcap
Dubois discovered in Java
and a modern human.
In the top picture the Trinil
skullcap (right) shows the
large brow ridges and
marked contriction behind
the brow ridges found on
many members of *Homo
erectus*. The lower
comparison shows the two
skulls from the side,
illustrating the low, sloping
forehead and projecting
brow ridge of *Homo
erectus*.

At a number of sites in central Java, near the original Trinil find, many fossil skull pieces and some jaws and teeth have been found. The richest site is *Sangiran,* where over thirty fossil specimens have been recovered. The hominine-bearing geologic deposits have been examined carefully. Earliest is the *Pucangan Formation,* and lying above this is the *Kabuh Formation,* in which Dubois discovered the original "Pithecanthropus" skullcap (Table 10.1). Fossil skulls similar in many ways to Dubois' original find as well as jaws and teeth have been discovered in the very upper part of the Pucangan Formation and through much of the

TABLE 10.1
The Hominine Deposits on the Island of Java, Indonesia
Most of the specimens listed are from the Sangiran site.

	Geologic Formations	Fission Track Dates: Years B.P.	Hominine Fossils Found
Middle Pleistocene	Ngandang River Terraces		Solo Skulls
	Notopuro Formation	250,000	— — — — — — — — — — — —
Early Pleistocene	Kabuh Formation	750,000	Skull bone ● — — — — — — — — — — — ● Skullcap Skullcap ● Skull ● Skull ● bone (Figure 10.4) Dubois' original skullcap Jaw ● find ● Jaw ●
	Pucangan Formation	1.1 my	Skullcap ● Jaw ● Jaw ● Jaw ● — — — — — — — — — — —

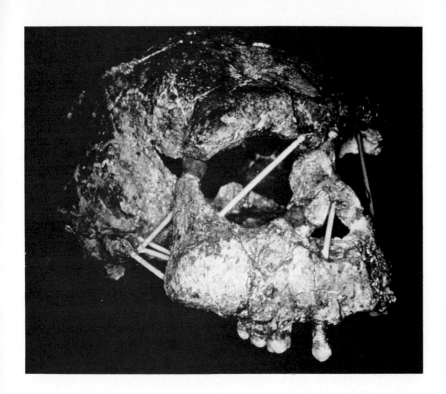

FIGURE 10.4
A *Homo erectus* skull from the Kabuh Beds at Sangiran, Java, one of the few *H. erectus* specimens with a face.

overlying and therefore later Kabuh deposits. Recent age determinations based on the Fission Track technique and paleomagnetism (see page 295) suggest a range from about 1 million years ago for the earliest of the Javan specimens to somewhat later than 700,000 years ago. In the Javan village of *Ngandong* along the Solo River more than ten skulls and some skeletal bones were discovered in ancient riverbank deposits. These fossils, known as the *Solo sample,* appear to be much later, perhaps more than 200,000 years old.

The fossils from both the Pucangan and Kabuh formations have features similar to those in Dubois' original find: strong brow ridges with a waisting behind the orbits; low, sloping foreheads and low, flat brain cases with low maximum width of the brain case; and thick cranial bones. A recently discovered *Homo erectus* skull from relatively high in the Kabuh Formation possesses an exceedingly rare feature for *Homo erectus* fossils: facial bones (Figure 10.4). Except for this specimen and two or three others from Africa, *Homo erectus* fossil skulls are discovered without their faces and usually without the skull bases as well. The *Homo erectus* face was large and jutting, with big eye orbits below the brow ridges, a large nasal structure separating the orbits, and a large and expanded cheek region above the teeth.

The later Solo skull series possesses features, such as larger brain cases, that have made them more difficult to classify; some would identify them as late *Homo erectus,* while others suggest they are early representatives of *Homo sapiens.* The fact that the Ngandong Beds have not been well dated is an added problem. We will return to the complex situation surrounding the evolutionary appearance of *Homo sapiens* presently.

Discoveries in China   Paleontologists had long known that the Chinese believed fossil bones (or "dragon" bones, as they were called) had great curative powers when crushed with other ingredients in many medicines. A tooth bought in a Chinese drugstore that seemed to come from a hominine eventually led, in 1921, to the discovery of a large cave site on a hill, known locally as Dragon Bone Hill, just outside the village of *Zhoukoudian,* 40 kilometers southwest of Beijing. Initiated by a Swedish team, the excavations were continued by a Canadian anatomist, Davidson Black, who was working at the Beijing Union Medical College. In 1927 a clearly hominine tooth was discovered. On this discovery alone, Black established a new fossil taxon: "*Sinanthropus pekinensis,*" meaning the Chinese man of Peking (now Beijing). Work continued at Zhoukoudian almost until World War II under Black and other scientists, including Chinese anthropologist Wu Rukang and German anthropologist Franz Weidenreich.

By 1937 this great cave site had given up the skulls, teeth, and other fossil bones of about forty-five hominine individuals, along with stone tools, bones from thousands of animals, and evidence of fire. At the end of 1941, as World War II began and the Japanese moved on Beijing, it was feared that the fossils might be damaged; they were packed and sent by train to a seaport for shipment to the United States for safekeeping. Sometime after they left Beijing, the fossils disappeared. Although in the years since their loss many theories have been advanced to account for their whereabouts, no trace of these precious bones has been found.[1]* Fortunately, Weidenreich had published a complete description of the bones, and accurate casts, like those in Figures 10.5 and 10.14, were made, so the loss is not total. After the war the People's Republic of China reopened the Zhoukoudian excavation, and several new hominine fossils have been found. The Beijing skulls, with their large brow ridges, low foreheads, low maximum width of the brain case, and other details, do not differ greatly from the Java fossils, except that there is a wide variation in their cranial capacities, with some as great as 1,225 ml. These larger brain cases support the geologic and dating evidence that the Zhoukoudian hominines (now also placed in *Homo erectus*) lived later than the Javanese *Homo erectus* group. Relative dating of these Chinese cave deposits suggests that most of the hominines lived between 400,000 and 600,000 years ago.

Additional fossil material has been uncovered in the People's Republic of China. At *Lantian,* in central China, a hominine skull and lower jaw that look like the Javanese material have been excavated. This fossil material is probably somewhat earlier than the Zhoukoudian fossils, within the time range of the Java specimens, and like the Java fossils, this

*See pages 624–626 for notes to Chapter 10.

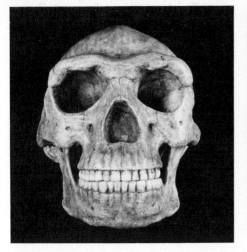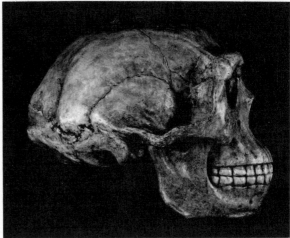

FIGURE 10.5. Two views of the cast of a skull of a Beijing person ("Sinanthropus pekinensis") from Zhoukoudian. Most of the face and the bottom of the skull have been restored.

skull has large, projecting brow ridges; a low forehead; and low brain case height. At *Hexian,* also in central China, another *Homo erectus* skull-cap was excavated in 1982. This fossil is much like the Zhoukoudian skulls in appearance and, like them, seems to be later than Lantian, probably from around 400,000 years ago.[2]

In sum, the *Homo erectus* fossils from China confirm much of what is known from the fossils from the island of Java in Indonesia. By the beginning of the middle Pleistocene, which is marked at about 730,000 years ago by the paleomagnetic change from the Matuyama Reversed epoch to the Bruhnes Normal epoch (see pages 295–296), hominines of the *Homo erectus* grade had spread out of the African homeland, where our subfamily apparently evolved. They had reached the tropical areas of Java and by about half a million years ago were able to expand into the colder areas of north China, where the cave site of Zhoukoudian is located. To follow the earlier phases of *Homo erectus* evolution, we must thus turn our attention to the African fossil evidence.

African Hominines

Hominine fossils similar in appearance to the Asian *Homo erectus* fossils have been found in East, South, and North Africa. At East Turkana in northern Kenya, Richard Leakey's discovery of the KNM-ER 3733 skull (Figure 9.33) confirmed that two separate hominine lines were living at the same time. The KNM-ER 3733 skull shares many features of the brain case with the Asian *Homo erectus,* especially with the much later Zhoukoudian fossils, but its volume of 800 ml also relates it to the somewhat later Java specimens.

In 1984, Kamoya Kimeu, working with Richard Leakey west of Lake Turkana in Kenya in a dried-up stream bed at a place called *Nario-kotome,* discovered the most complete *Homo erectus* specimen ever found.

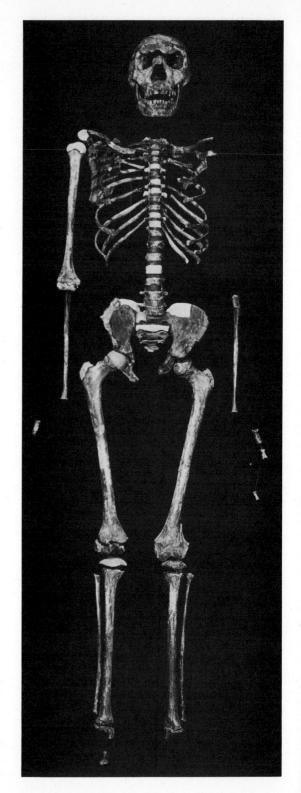

FIGURE 10.6
The skeleton of a boy, perhaps 12 years old when he died, uncovered west of Lake Turkana in northern Kenya. This fossil, known by its catalog number KNM-WT 15000, is the most complete *Homo erectus* ever found.

Dated by the K-Ar technique to about 1.6 million years ago, this specimen, known by its catalog number, KNM-WT 15000 (Figure 10.6), is most of the skeleton of an adolescent boy of about twelve (its age was determined by its state of tooth eruption and its sex by comparison to the much more lightly built and less massive skull KNM-ER 3733, a presumed female). The thighbone is similar in size to those of modern adults, which suggests that the boy, had he grown to adulthood, might have reached a height of 5'4" to 5'6", although with his low skull height, typical of *Homo erectus,* he might have been somewhat shorter.

These fossils from around Lake Turkana, KNM-ER 3733, KNM-WT 15000, and several other more fragmentary specimens, are dated at around 1.6 million years B.P., represent the earliest evidence for the evolution of *Homo erectus,* whose origins probably lie in the still earlier *Homo habilis* group, mainly known from finds from Lake Turkana and Olduvai Gorge in Tanzania.

At Olduvai Gorge, fossils from Bed I and Lower Bed II look somewhat like both the australopithecines and *Homo erectus,* which led to their placement in the transitional taxon, *Homo habilis.* A distinct geologic break divides Lower Bed II from Upper Bed II. In Upper Bed II, at the site of LLK (Louis Leakey Korongo), a large skullcap was found that has many similarities with other *Homo erectus* skulls: a low brain case combined with a low, sloping forehead; large brow ridge; and defined waisting behind the orbits (Figure 10.7); the cranial capacity is about the same as some of the larger Chinese fossils. *Homo erectus* fossils have also been found in Bed IV at Olduvai Gorge, including a piece of the pelvis that, like the boy's skeleton from West Turkana and the thighbone Dubois discovered, confirms that *Homo erectus* was an erect, bipedal hominine. Mary Leakey suggests a date of about 500,000 years for the Olduvai finds. There are other *Homo erectus* fossil materials from Beds III and IV, including a portion of a lower jaw remarkably similar to those found at Zhoukoudian.

FIGURE 10.7.   Views of the restored skullcap of a hominine (OH 9) found at Olduvai Gorge, drawn from a Wenner-Gren Foundation cast.

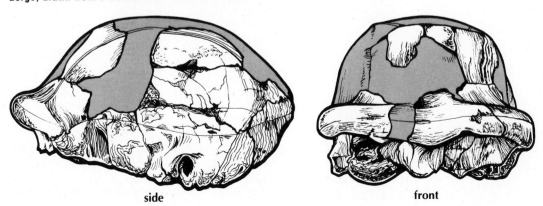

side

front

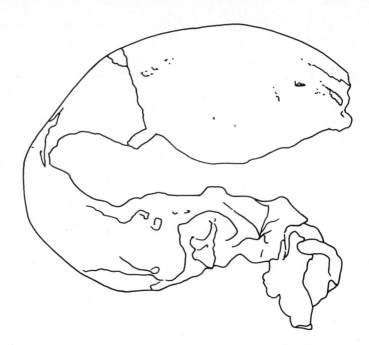

FIGURE 10.8
The partial skull from the
site of Salé in North
Africa.
Dated to the middle
Pleistocene, its features
suggest an archaic *Homo
sapiens.*

The Sterkfontein Valley in South Africa has yielded many austra-lopithecine fossils. At the site of Swartkrans, there is some evidence of *Homo erectus,* a part of the skull and face. The complex geology suggests this fossil was deposited in the Swartkrans breccia considerably after the robust australopithecine specimens were accumulated.

In North Africa, a number of middle Pleistocene fossils have been discovered. Earliest are apparently the three lower jaws and a skull bone discovered by the French paleontologist Camille Arambourg at the site of *Tighenif* (formerly Ternifine), Algeria. Although dating is not conclusive, a suggested date of about 700,000 years B.P. appears reasonable. The jaws share many similarities with those from Zhoukoudian. Dated somewhat later, perhaps about 400,000 years B.P., are the fossil bones from three sites in Morocco. The most complete of these is the partial skull from *Salé* (Figure 10.8), which, according to J. J. Hublin,[3] has features like those on the Solo skull sample, thus linking it to both *Homo erectus* and early *Homo sapiens.* More fragmentary are the finds from *Sidi Abderrahman* and the *Thomas Quarries,* which consist of a small portion of a lower jaw from the former and a part of a lower jaw and very incomplete face from the latter. Like the Salé fossils, these specimens are somewhat difficult to classify.

European Fossils

Some fossil bones found in Europe have been called *Homo erectus,* but, like the Salé skulls from Africa and the Solo skulls from Java, their morphological features are in some ways more advanced than the *H. erectus* fossils from other parts of the Old World. One of these was found in 1907 in a little town called *Mauer,* outside of Heidelberg, Germany. A lower jaw of a mature individual, the Mauer or Heidelberg jaw is difficult to interpret because its massive jawbone, with no chin, is combined with relatively small, modern-looking teeth (Figure 10.9). The geologic and faunal context places the fossil in the middle part of the middle Pleistocene. Opinion is divided as to whether the Heidelberg jaw is a European representative of *Homo erectus* or an early member of *Homo sapiens*.

Like the Mauer or Heidelberg jaw, the back of the skull (occipital bone) found at *Vértesszöllös,* Hungary, in 1965 has inspired differing views. Milford Wolpoff has suggested that the relatively high position of the attachment areas for the neck muscles on the bone identify it as *Homo erectus,* while the Hungarian scientist Andor Thoma believes the bone comes from a skull larger than those usually attributed to *H. erectus* and feels it belongs in the taxon *H. sapiens*.[4]

At *Bilzingsleben* in East Germany, fragments of the front and back of several hominine skulls have been discovered in middle Pleistocene deposits. The front part of the skull has massive brow ridges, and the back part has a large ridge for attachment of the neck muscles. Both *Homo erectus* and early *Homo sapiens* possess such features, however, and the Bilzingsleben fossils are too incomplete to provide a definite answer to the question of their status.

Similarly, the skull found in the *Petralona* cave in Greece in 1960 has been subject to a variety of interpretations (Figure 10.10). The Petralona skull is the most complete of the early European fossils, and probably is about 300,000 to 400,000 years old, somewhat later than the African and Asian *Homo erectus* specimens just described. Christopher Stringer, Clark Howell, and John Melentis have assessed its evolutionary position.[5] They found that the skull height is not as low as the Zhoukoudian or African *H. erectus* fossils and that it possesses a cranial capacity of at least 1200 ml, which is matched only by the largest of the Zhoukoudian skulls. They could not agree whether the Petralona skull was a

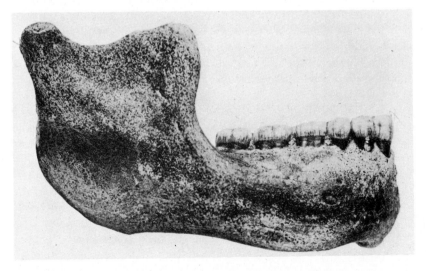

FIGURE 10.9
The Mauer jaw.

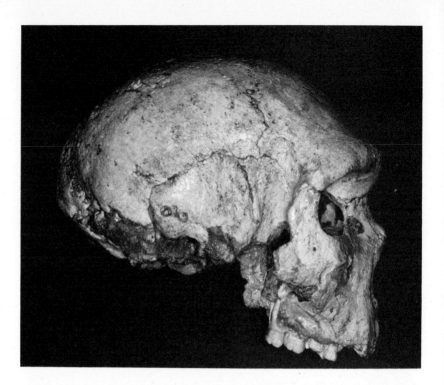

FIGURE 10.10
The Petralona skull.

late *H. erectus* or an early *H. sapiens;* even the most complete of the European fossils thus poses problems of identification, as do the more fragmentary Mauer, Vértesszöllös, and Bilzingsleben bones. Because all the European fossils are difficult to interpret, it remains unclear whether *H. erectus* lived in Europe or whether the earliest hominines to populate this area were *H. sapiens.* This is the same sort of problem that the Salé and Solo skulls presented: How can representatives of *Homo erectus* be distinguished from those of *Homo sapiens?* If the fossils possess features similar to both taxonomic categories, does this not suggest a gradual evolutionary change from *H. erectus* to *H. sapiens,* in contrast to the model of punctuation presented in Chapter 3? These are important questions, crucial to our understanding of human evolution and the emergence of modern humans; they will be dealt with after we have examined more fully the adaptation of *Homo erectus.*

Expansion of Range

During the time of *Homo erectus* hominines expanded out of Africa and into the tropics of the Old World. The earliest *Homo erectus,* like those from the Lake Turkana region and Olduvai Gorge, are from East and South Africa. Later specimens turn up in North Africa and then in places like Java. The still later fossil collection from Zhoukoudian shows that by about half a million years ago, the hominines had spread to the colder regions of north China. The fossil evidence is unclear, however, as to the identity of the earliest inhabitants of Europe: Whether they were *Homo erectus* or their presumed descendents, early *Homo sapiens.*

The reasons for this expansion out of Africa, which marks the beginnings of what will ultimately become the worldwide distribution of modern humans, are still uncertain. At about the same time as the hominines' first appearance in deposits in Eurasia, there is also the first fossil evidence of a number of until-then exclusively African mammals. It has been suggested that this spread out of Africa of *Homo erectus* and other mammals sometime after one million years ago may have been initiated by the disappearance of a geographic barrier in northeast Africa that had been isolating Africa from Eurasia.

The cultural abilities of *Homo erectus* may also have played a role in expansion, permitting these hominines to live in and exploit a broader array of habitats. The behavioral abilities of *Homo erectus* and their similarities to modern humans in this regard are actively debated among anthropologists.

Tool Industries

If fossil bones were the only remnants, we could conclude that *Homo erectus* walked upright, had a brain larger than that of the australopithecines but smaller than that of modern humans, and had a face and teeth larger than those of modern humans. These morphological attributes would help us understand the biology of these fossil hominines and would tell us how *Homo erectus* was related evolutionarily to other hominines. They would not, however, give us an adequate understanding of their behavior. We have luckily found traces of the culture along with the bones of *Homo erectus,* including tools, fire, and cooking debris, which indicate that *Homo erectus* were more sophisticated in their behavior and were capable of producing more complex tools than were the earlier australopithecines. But just how complex were the hominines of the *Homo erectus* grade? The artifacts and other cultural materials give us a glimpse of their behavioral capabilities, but much remains unclear.

The tools found with *H. erectus* fossils belong to the lower Paleolithic. The later australopithecines, too, as we have seen, have been occasionally found with stone tools made from cobbles, the Oldowan industry.

The Oldowan tools are simple and unspecialized. We do not fully understand their use, but they surely were not suitable for delicate tasks. From the Oldowan industry developed a more complex tool tradition, known as the *evolved Oldowan industry*. These tools are better made and perhaps permitted their makers to perform a greater range of tasks. They are found in later deposits at Olduvai Gorge and the Swartkrans site in South Africa. Also found in these deposits at Olduvai, as well as at many other sites in East Africa, in North Africa, and later through much of the Old World, is a stone tool tradition that is rather different from the evolved Oldowan and that is characterized by a distinctive tool, the *hand axe* (Figure 10.11).

In the nineteenth century, the scholars who were to found the science of prehistoric archaeology searched for signs of earlier human activities and in particular the bones of extinct animals associated with stone

**FIGURE 10.11
Acheulian hand axes from Africa.**
These bifacially flaked tools have a pointed end and cutting edges on each side. These hand axes are roughly made with uneven cutting edges; later-in-time hand axes are more finely made.

tools. As part of this search, French archaeologists had investigated a site in a small French village called St. Acheul, where stones of a particular shape came to light. They were large, measuring about 9 centimeters wide by 12 to 15 centimeters long, and were in teardrop form, with one end pointed and the other rounded. The makers of these implements were skilled, for the tools were finely flaked. The tools were called hand axes, but we do not know their actual function. This tool tradition took its name from the village of St. Acheul, and is called the *Acheulian* industry (Figure 10.12). Acheulian hand axes have been found at archaeological sites virtually all over the Old World, from Africa and Europe in the west to Asia in the east.

There are no simple, clear associations between tool types and varieties of fossil hominines. The Acheulian industry lasted for more than a million years and is associated with both *Homo erectus* and the later *Homo sapiens* populations. Cultures, like animals, evolve; the Acheulian industry in the early Pleistocene is different from that found in deposits dated to the end of the middle Pleistocene. Later tools are more competently made in greater variety; they include the stone tools that became part of later prehistoric cultures.

The stone tools and the fossils tell us something about *Homo erectus*. But if we want to learn more about how these hominines successfully adapted to their environment, we must examine archaeological sites that have no hominine fossils associated with them but are dated to the middle Pleistocene. Some of these sites are *Terra Amata* in the city of Nice in southern France, *Torralba* and *Ambrona* in central Spain, and *Kalambo Falls* and *Olorgesailie* in East Africa. Because of the problems in classifying the European fossils, it is difficult to know whether the European sites were occupied by *Homo erectus* or early *Homo sapiens* populations. However, the important point is not the nature of the exact hominine responsible, but rather what these archaeological sites can tell us about hominine adaptations in the middle Pleistocene.

At Zhoukoudian in China, significant archaeological remains were uncovered in addition to the fossil bones of about forty-five *Homo erectus* individuals. Indeed, because of the hominine fossils and the richness of the materials excavated at this cave site, Zhoukoudian has become the cornerstone for our understanding of the nature of *Homo erectus* adaptation. A recent reexamination of the conclusions reached by the original excavators, however, has questioned many of the statements made about the level of adaptive and behavioral complexity of *Homo erectus*.

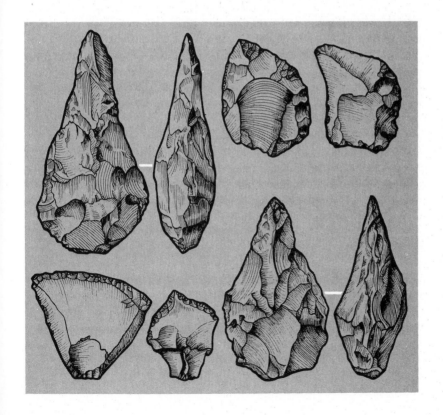

FIGURE 10.12
Acheulian tools (one-half actual size).
The tools in the upper left and lower right are hand axes; the others are mainly scrapers designed to perform a number of tasks.

Terra Amata   Terra Amata is an open-air site in Nice, France, discovered in 1965 when construction workers were digging the foundation of a building.[6] Henry de Lumley, a French archaeologist, had the construction stopped while he and his team excavated the site. According to de Lumley, the site was originally much closer to the Mediterranean shoreline than it is today, and the hominines probably used it for short times as a seasonal camp while they exploited the local plant, animal, and seashore resources. Many animal bones were found, including those of deer, wild boars, elephants, wild oxen, smaller mammals, turtles, and birds. The larger mammals are usually young, probably because they were easier to bring down.

Along with these things and tools of the Acheulian tradition, de Lumley found clear evidence of fire. We think the hominine group that camped at Terra Amata was also erecting shelters (Figure 10.13). In Bed I at Olduvai Gorge, Leakey found a ring of stones (see Figure 9.38) that suggests the australopithecines had built a structure such as a windbreak or hunting blind, but the evidence from Terra Amata is different. At Terra Amata, de Lumley found post holes, that is, the remains of supporting posts, sunk into the ground, that survived after the wooden posts above the ground had completely disintegrated. In an excavation they appear as filled-in circles on the ground, usually of a different color from that of the surrounding soil. The post holes at Terra Amata were so arranged that they must have supported oval structures that were probably covered with interlacing branches. Inside these hutlike dwellings were fire hearths, sunk into the ground or placed on raised stone platforms. The Terra Amata site suggests that our ancestors of middle Pleistocene times may have occupied an environmental niche much like that of modern human gatherers and hunters.

Few human groups today subsist entirely by gathering wild vegetable materials, small animals, and insects, and hunting larger mammals. Most modern human societies practice some agriculture. Before the great changes that marked the introduction of agriculture and the domestication of plants and animals, however, which seem to have taken place independently at several places in the world about 10,000 years ago, all human groups lived by gathering and hunting.

The very few modern human groups still living as gatherers and hunters are found in marginal environments, and it is difficult to reconstruct conditions for gatherers and hunters in richer environments. Early researchers in cultural anthropology overemphasized the importance of hunting to the group's survival, giving the impression that hunting provided most of their food and stressing the male's vital role as hunter. More recently we have found that hunting may not have been that important; for most gatherers and hunters living in tropical and temperate climates, the fruits, vegetables, nuts, birds and birds' eggs, insects and insect grubs, frogs and other small vertebrates, and small mammals gathered were the main part of the diet.[7]

FIGURE 10.13
Reconstruction of the probable appearance of a hut at Terra Amata.

Human societies based on agriculture today are permanently settled in one area, using the land near their village for farming or herding. Gatherers and hunters do not lead a settled existence, because even the richest environments may not be able to support such a group throughout the whole year. Modern groups at this economic level usually move about over a wide area. These movements are not, however, arbitrary, and gatherers and hunters generally do not roam out of known and defined terrain. Over the generations, the group has learned where to find food at different seasons. This lore is part of the group's tradition, as is intimate knowledge about how the plants and animals live in the area.

Gatherers and hunters are superb natural historians; they need to have extensive knowledge of the flora and fauna to be able to exploit all the environment's resources.

The environment limits the group's size. At some times during the year, food and water are plentiful, and then gatherers and hunters may form rather large groups and may even have more or less settled camps. At other times, when food or water is scarce, the group may be small, perhaps no larger than the nuclear family, with a father, mother, and dependent children. Their social organization is not permanent but flexible enough to break apart and reform, depending on the resources. According to pollen studies, it appears that the middle Pleistocene camp at Terra Amata may have been such a seasonal stop during the late spring and early summer, when the group exploited the food available locally for a time and moved on when it was depleted. The group returned to the same site each year for a number of years.

Torralba and Ambrona   Among the other archaeological sites that are helpful in reconstructing more of middle Pleistocene hominine life are Torralba and Ambrona, located about 2 kilometers apart along the margins of a swampy valley with permanent water, some 150 kilometers northeast of Madrid, Spain. F. C. Howell and Leslie Freeman, who excavated the sites, suggest that Torralba and Ambrona were specialized "kill" sites, perhaps along seasonal migration routes of large herd mammals.[8] The remains of many game animals were found at the sites, including deer, horse, aurochs (the wild ancestor of modern domesticated cattle), and elephants. Many of the bones of these animals had been smashed, and a few show slicing marks made by hominines cutting at the carcasses. Many of the skeletal elements, especially the limb bones and feet, are missing, suggesting that these were cut from the carcass and carried off to be eaten elsewhere or, as there is little meat on these parts, simply thrown away. Along with the animal bones were numbers of stone tools and evidence of pieces of wood, some with chisel-shaped or pointed ends. Burnt wood and charcoal are found all over the sites, but there is little evidence of hearths, which may indicate that the middle Pleistocene hominines who hunted in this area used fire as a means of driving their prey into a place where they could be easily dispatched. Although the many dead elephants at Ambrona may mean that the hominines living in this area were, over the years, successful in hunting, records of modern groups suggest that hunting large animals is a consistently chancy business; a hunting group is unlikely to kill an animal each time it sets out. It is much more likely that the hominines returned to the Ambrona site year after year, perhaps when the elephants and other animals were migrating through the area.

Zhoukoudian   The Zhoukoudian deposits outside of Beijing rewarded the researchers with the remains of about forty-five individuals, plus significant archaeological data. Zhoukoudian represents the earliest documented association of fire with hominines, and it is as well one of the most northerly sites of *Homo erectus* times. There may very well be a relationship between the presence of fire and the hominines' ability to survive in an environment that was probably subjected to rather severe winters. Although the site was first excavated in the 1920s, its size is such that excavations continue today, and more material, including hominine fossils, can be expected. This large cave shows evidence of the periodic short-term presence of hominines over perhaps 200,000 years.

All of the hominine skulls lack facial bones, and many were broken open at the bottom (Figure 10.14). It has often been suggested that the skulls were damaged in this way to get at the brain, which is an excellent source of protein. This damage may also indicate that these hominines had an ancestor cult, much in the fashion of some modern New Guinea peoples who place the skulls of deceased relatives in an honored location in their houses. These broken skulls could alternatively represent the attempt by the eater to gain something of the skill, magic, or memories of the dead individual. Perhaps most likely, the breakage may have been the result of the way the bones were incorporated into the deposit. Speculations are all we have, for we know nothing about the ideological patterns of these hominines or even if they had any. There is no evidence of intentional burial of *Homo erectus* individuals; all the fossil evidence comes from the bones that have been incorporated by chance into deposits, like the Zhoukoudian skullcaps.

According to the original excavators, the resources in the Zhoukoudian area during *Homo erectus* times were varied. Huge numbers of the preserved seeds of the oriental hackberry as well as the bones of many animals were found, including those of thousands of deer. Archaeologists

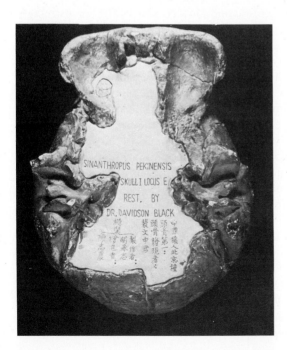

FIGURE 10.14
A *Homo erectus* skull from Zhoukoudian, showing the broken base found on many *H. erectus* and later neandertal skulls.
This is a photograph of one of the original plaster casts made by Chinese technicians under the direction of Franz Weidenreich. The original fossils were lost at the beginning of World War II.

Lewis Binford and Chuan Kun Ho have recently reevaluated the claims of *Homo erectus* behavioral complexity made by the original excavators of the Zhoukoudian site.[9] Binford and Ho point out that the deposit is extremely complicated and that, along with the *Homo erectus* groups, many different animals lived in the cave at one time or another, including several different kinds of carnivores, like hyenas. By carefully examining the animal bones found in the site, they found that the contributions of *Homo erectus* to the bone accumulations may have been quite modest, with the bulk of the animal bones resulting from the activities of carnivores. Similarly, these authors argue that animals may also have been responsible for the hackberry seeds in the deposits. Finally, Binford and Ho note that the evidence of fire in the cave is actually widespread throughout the deposits and is not limited to fire pits or hearths, as it would be if it had been under the control of hominines. While not denying that *Homo erectus* groups used the fire, they suggest that fire may have been the product of the natural combustion of animal guano built up over long periods by animal residents of the cave. Not all archaeologists have accepted this interpretation of the Zhoukoudian site, but there is little general agreement as to exactly what the site represents.

Homo erectus Adaptations

The picture that emerges from the evidence of *Homo erectus* is still shadowy in many details, and the precise nature of this hominine's adaptation and behavior continues to be the focus of active debate. Just how much like later hominines was *Homo erectus*? Although a number of sites provide evidence of their way of life, the archaeological remains from Zhoukoudian have been the major source of data. It was on the basis of these findings that *Homo erectus* was considered to be a gatherer and hunter like modern humans. Binford and Ho's critique of the reconstruction of Zhoukoudian *Homo erectus* activities and their minimizing of these hominines' cultural complexity have resulted in a marked rethinking of the whole issue of *Homo erectus* adaptation.

Binford has gone further to outline a pattern of cultural development that emphasizes the role of scavenging as the central focus throughout much of human evolution.[10] According to Binford, the first evidence of scavenging appears at the end of australopithecine evolution, sometime after 2 million years ago. Scratches on bones at Olduvai Gorge suggest to him that an important source of food for these early hominines was obtained via the removal of the lower portions of the limb bones of predator kills. These bony elements have little edible tissue, and what there is is very difficult for a predator or an animal scavenger to remove. The essential hominine adaptation was to use chipped tools to scrape off these small bits of meat. Binford believes this scavenging adaptation continued for much of human evolution and that only with the origin of modern humans were the hominines able to develop an efficient pattern of big-game hunting. *Homo erectus,* Binford maintains, was a scavenger with a noncomplex set of behaviors and a relatively simple adaptation.

Many archaeologists have rejected this model of hominine and *Homo erectus* adaptation, pointing to other sites, like those in Spain, that appear to indicate a greater reliance on hunting. Other archaeologists argue that even if the course of human evolution were marked by scavenging as an important part of the total adaptation, the hunting and collecting of small animals and insects and the gathering of various plant foods would also be necessary to round out the total diet. Thus even if Binford's reconstruction of earlier hominine adaptation is fundamentally correct, gathering and hunting, although perhaps of a somewhat different sort, would still appear to be a basic adaptation of *Homo erectus* and perhaps of earlier *Homo* as well.

Of course, a total reconstruction of the life-style of *Homo erectus* will never be possible; even with the greatest skill and the most sophisticated techniques, only a small portion of the cultural context can be recovered. Nevertheless, there are tantalizing similarities between *Homo erectus* and modern gatherers and hunters, which can provide some insights into *Homo erectus* behavior.

In all environments, the group's size would have been limited by the resources. The social unit, we assume, never became smaller than the nuclear family. Modern gatherers and hunters, even in the most extreme environments, such as the Eskimos of the North American Arctic and Greenland (during their days as gatherers and hunters, which, for the vast majority of them, are past), did not fragment into units smaller than that. An adult male and female Eskimo made up a complete economic unit; between them, they could manufacture, catch, cook, and build everything they needed for survival. This specialization in roles may have led to pair bonding of women and men during hominine evolution, but this is only one suggestion; the evolutionary development of the long childhood dependency may also have been responsible for this pattern.

Our archaeological evidence is not clear, but *Homo erectus* peoples, like their modern gatherer and hunter equivalents, may have depended for most of their subsistence on the gathering of plants, small animals, and insects, the occasional hunting of large mammals, and perhaps the scavenging of meat from carnivore kills. The similarity between these hominines of the genus *Homo* and modern peoples was one of the major reasons that the genus "Pithecanthropus" was dropped in favor of *Homo*. Because the pithecanthropines appeared to share the same basic environmental adaptation as modern humans, they were placed in the same genus but retained in a separate species.

The Transition to *Homo sapiens*

As we have seen, fossil skulls, such as the Solo group from Java and the Salé skull from North Africa, and European bones, such as the Mauer jaw, the Vértesszöllös occipital, the Bilzingsleben fragments, and the Petralona fossil, all present difficulties in taxonomic identification. There is no generally agreed upon definition of the genus and species *Homo sapiens,* although Stringer, Howell, and Melentis, in their description of the Petralona skull, suggest that changes in skull architecture and shape related to increasing brain size are the most important distinguishing features. In Figure 10.15 a Zhoukoudian *Homo erectus* skull, the Petralona skull, a Solo skullcap, and a *Homo sapiens* (neandertal) skull from

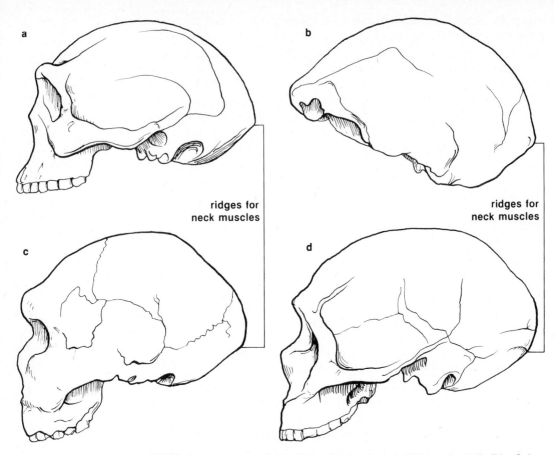

ridges for
neck muscles

ridges for
neck muscles

FIGURE 10.15. Comparisons of (a) a Zhoukoudian skull (reconstructed); (b) a Solo skullcap, (c) the Petralona skull, and (d) a late Pleistocene *Homo sapiens* (neandertal) skull. Note the difference in skull size and shape.

the late Pleistocene are compared. The major differences in these four skulls relate to increasing brain size, which is reflected in the increasing height of the skull and the smaller amount of constriction, or waisting, behind the orbits. Associated with this brain growth are changes in the relative position of the ridges on which the neck muscles attach at the back of the skull. Because of the increased size of the brain, the ridges are lower on the skull in the later hominines. These features, Stringer, Howell, and Melentis suggest, are the main differences between *Homo erectus* and early *Homo sapiens*. The size of the facial area is still large on all the skulls, and the face is positioned relatively in front of the brain case. A decrease in the size of the facial region and its repositioning more underneath the brain case are changes important in the later appearance of anatomically modern humans. It is clear from Figure 10.15 why the Solo skulls and the Petralona skull are so difficult to interpret.

Table 10.2 summarizes the hominine fossil evidence from about 1.5 million years ago to about 125,000 years ago, noting the geographic dis-

TABLE 10.2
Hominines from About 1.5 Million Years Ago to About 125,000 Years B.P.
Some fossils whose time placement is unknown have been omitted, and some that are
included are only very generally placed in time.

Years B.P.	Geological Epoch	European Glacial Sequence	Europe	Africa	Asia
100,000	LATE PLEISTO-CENE	Würm	Neandertals		
125,000		Last interglacial			
200,000		Glacial		Kabwe	Dali Solo
300,000	MIDDLE PLEISTOCENE		Steinheim Swanscombe Arago	↑ ¦ ¦ Bodo	
400,000			Petralona Vértesszöllös Heidelberg	Rabat Salé	Hexian Zhoukoudian
500,000				Olduvai Bed IV	¦ ¦
600,000					¦ ↓
700,000				Tighenif	Lantian
730,000	EARLY PLEISTOCENE			↑ ¦ ¦ ¦ ¦ Swartkrans Olduvai Hominine 9	⊤ ¦ ¦ Java Kabuh ⊥ Pucangan
1.1 MY				¦ ↓	
1.5				Lake Turkana KNM-WT 15000 KNM-ER 3733	
1.6					
1.8	PLIOCENE				

tribution and dating of the *Homo erectus* fossils from Africa and Asia, those from Europe that are difficult to classify, and a number of widely distributed fossils that seem to be early representatives of *Homo sapiens*. Most of these latter fossils are not well dated but can be generally placed in the late middle Pleistocene, from about 275,000 years to about 125,000 years B.P. From Europe, they include the *Swanscombe* skull fragments from England, the *Steinheim* skull from Germany, and the *Arago* fossils from southern France. From Africa, they include the *Kabwe* skull from Zambia, the *Saldanha Bay* skullcap from Elandsfontein in South Africa, and the skull from *Bodo* in the Afar region of north-central Ethiopia. From Asia, they include the Solo skulls from Java and the *Dali* skull from China.

Early Sapiens from Europe

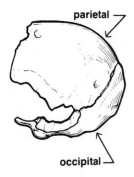

parietal

occipital

FIGURE 10.16
The Swanscombe early
***Homo sapiens* skull**
pieces from southern
England.

Swanscombe   The Swanscombe fossil was discovered in deposits along the River Thames at Swanscombe in southern England in the 1930s, along with tools of the Acheulian tradition. The geologic deposits in which the fossil was found place it in an interglacial of the middle Pleistocene, most probably the next to the last one. Together with a piece of the skull found at the site after World War II, the Swanscombe fossil is composed of three bones of the brain case, the occipital and both parietals (paired bones making up the middle part of the brain case), all belonging to the same individual (Figure 10.16). The frontal bone, with the forehead and brow ridge, and the face were not found. The fossil shows a mixture of physical features. The portions preserved show a rather high, rounded skull characteristic of *Homo sapiens,* and the ridges for the attachment of the neck muscles are rather low on the occipital bone. On the other hand, the cranial capacity, about 1,100 ml, is not as large as that of other early sapiens, but is in the range of the Chinese *Homo erectus* fossils. The skull bone is thick like those of *Homo erectus*. The dating of the Swanscombe fossil and its morphological features suggest that it is a representative of early *Homo sapiens* but somewhat more advanced than the Petralona and Vértesszöllös fossils.

Steinheim   The Steinheim fossil was discovered in 1933 in the village of Steinheim on the River Murr in Germany. It is probably as old as Swanscombe (from the next to the last interglacial), and there are a number of other similarities between the two specimens (Figure 10.17). Steinheim is the more complete fossil, with most of the skull preserved. Unfortunately, it was badly crushed during its long interment in the ground, and its present distorted condition makes it somewhat difficult to assess accurately. The brow ridges are large, but they show the beginnings of separate rounded eminences over each eye orbit, similar to the condition in later *Homo sapiens* and different from the more or less continuous bar of bone that marks the *Homo erectus* brow ridge. The height of the brain case is a little higher than those of *Homo erectus* and the earlier European fossil from Petralona. The face, although large, is smaller than that of *Homo erectus*. The most reasonable interpretation of the Steinheim

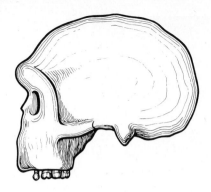

FIGURE 10.17. The Steinheim early *Homo sapiens* skull from Germany (right side reversed). More complete than the Swanscombe fossil, this fossil has been distorted during its long interment, and it is difficult to determine what it looked like before burial.

fossil is that, like the Swanscombe bones, it is representative of early *Homo sapiens*. It has been suggested that the earlier although somewhat larger Petralona fossil and the smaller Steinheim skull can be identified as male and female, respectively, and thus demonstrate the presence of sexual dimorphism in middle Pleistocene Europe.

Arago   The cave of Arago in the village of Tautavel in the Pyrenees Mountains of southern France is being excavated by Henry de Lumley, who also excavated the Terra Amata site. A number of fossil hominines have been recovered at Arago, including the front part of a skull with most of a face (Figure 10.18), several lower jaws, and assorted other bones, including part of a pelvis. The Arago fossils seem to be dated toward the end of the middle Pleistocene, perhaps contemporary with the Swanscombe and Steinheim specimens. Recently, at an international congress held in France, much debate was focused on the identification of the Arago material as either *Homo erectus* or early *Homo sapiens*. There was overwhelming agreement among the assembled scientists that these fossils were representative of early *Homo sapiens* and shared a number of morphological similarities with other early *Homo sapiens* such as Petralona.[11] The two lower jaws from Arago (Figure 10.19) show differences in size which would suggest, like the comparison of the Petralona and Steinheim fossils, that European middle Pleistocene early *Homo sapiens* was sexually dimorphic.

Early sapiens specimens are also known from Africa. The Kabwe skull, from the Broken Hill Mine in Zambia, is more complete than the Saldanha Bay specimen from the west coast of South Africa. The date of these fossils is not clear, but recent evidence suggests the Kabwe skull (Figure 10.20) may be close to 200,000 years old. It has a large face, a low, sloping forehead, and a relatively small cranial capacity, some 1,100 ml. Along with Saldanha Bay it is similar in many ways to both the Petralona fossil from Europe and the Bodo skull from Ethiopia, suggesting either a late *Homo erectus* or more probably an early *Homo sapiens* classification.

Early Sapiens from Africa

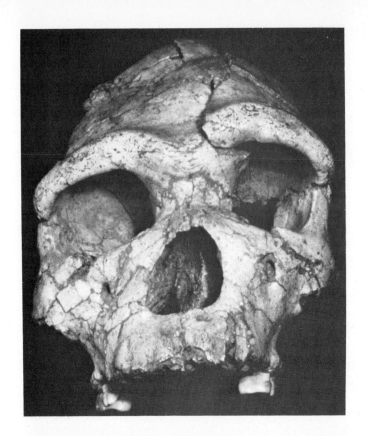

FIGURE 10.18
Front part of the skull
with most of the face of a
fossil hominine from
Arago.

FIGURE 10.19
Casts of two lower jaws of
early *Homo sapiens* from
Arago in southern France.
Note the larger jaw on the
right and its larger teeth.
The different sizes suggest
that this larger jaw
belonged to a male and the
smaller jaw to a female.

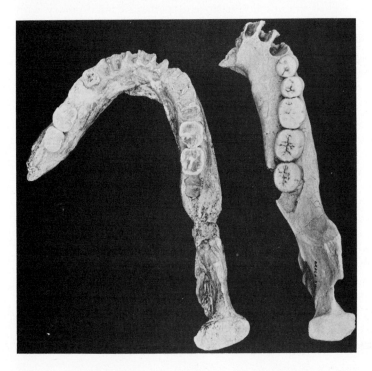

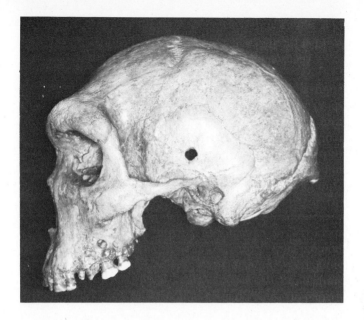

FIGURE 10.20
Skull from Kabwe,
Zambia.

Early Sapiens from Asia

In addition to the skulls from the Solo River in Java, which have been described, a number of other skulls from Asia that may be contemporary with the early *Homo sapiens* from Europe and Africa, including the Dali skull from central China (Figure 10.21). An almost complete skull, it possesses large brow ridges and a large face. Dating this specimen has been difficult, but the general development of its features suggests that it too is an early representative of *Homo sapiens* in China. Unlike many of the other early sapiens we have been considering, the Dali

FIGURE 10.21. Two views of the Dali skull, an archaic sapiens from China. The large face and brow ridges, low forehead and large brain size, among other features, mark this specimen as an early sapiens, but the flatness of the face appears to ally it with later modern humans from Asia, such as that pictured in Figure 10.34.

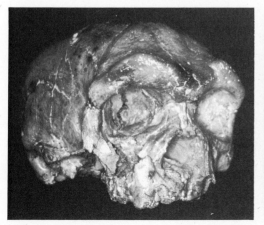
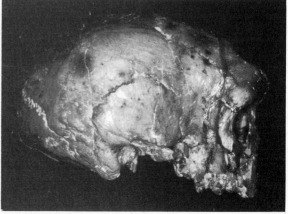

skull has a flat, relatively nonprojecting face, similar to the later living inhabitants of China and suggestive of a pattern of evolutionary continuity from earlier hominines to living humans.

The Evolutionary Appearance of *Homo sapiens*

The fossil evidence from various parts of the Old World (China; Java; North, East, and South Africa; and Europe—from a little earlier than 1.5 million years B.P. to the end of the middle Pleistocene, about 125,000 years B.P.—seems to indicate the continued operation of evolutionary mechanisms on hominine populations. As we have seen in this and the preceding chapter, the fossil record appears to show slow, gradual evolutionary change, and it is difficult to determine exactly when, in the period between 2 and 1.5 million years B.P., the first members of the genus *Homo* appear. It is also difficult to determine accurately which fossils belong in *Homo erectus* and which in *Homo sapiens*. Does this mean that this part of the hominine evolutionary sequence is not marked by periods of relative equilibrium punctuated by short bursts of marked change, a model of evolution suggested in Chapter 3 as an alternative to phyletic gradualism? Although the fossil evidence for this period seems to indicate gradual change, the many problems of dating the fossils precisely indicate that we ought to maintain an open mind on this question until a better understanding of the exact relationships of one fossil group to another have been more fully worked out.

Homo sapiens of the Late Pleistocene

As we have seen, the earliest fossils of *Homo sapiens* are dated to the end of the middle Pleistocene. Although placed in the taxon *H. sapiens,* they are not yet anatomically modern humans. Somewhat later than these middle Pleistocene early *Homo sapiens* but not yet anatomically modern, are the *Homo sapiens* fossils that date to the early part of the late Pleistocene, about 125,000 to about 35,000 to 40,000 years ago. These hominines possess a number of distinctive anatomical features. A variety of names and taxonomic categories have been used to identify this group of fossils, but problems in interpretation have again resulted in rather complicated schemes. One group, limited to a part of the late Pleistocene in Europe and the Middle East, have been called the *neandertals* and have usually been placed in the subspecies *Homo sapiens neanderthalensis* in contrast to modern humans, *Homo sapiens sapiens*. Other groups of late Pleistocene hominines have been placed in their own subspecies. For the early *Homo sapiens* fossils from the end of the middle Pleistocene, such as Steinheim, Swanscombe, Petralona, and Kabwe, however, there is no generally recognized subspecies, and the use of these labels presents problems when fossils from different geographic areas are placed in the same subspecies. Perhaps the most reasonable solution is to call all the *Homo sapiens* fossils dated prior to the appearance of anatomically modern humans about 35,000 to 40,000 years ago *early,* or *archaic, sapiens.* Table 10.3 lists the various fossils from different parts of the Old World who have been grouped into this descriptive category.

TABLE 10.3
Early or Archaic Sapiens
This lists the major finds discussed in the text (and there are numerous additional fossils that could be included), especially in Europe. Many problems in the dating of these finds have yet to be worked out, and therefore the fossils are arranged generally in terms of middle and late Pleistocene.

		Europe	Middle East	Asia	Africa

PLEISTOCENE	LATE	St.-Césaire
		
		Neandertals
		Neandertal
		Monte Circeo
		La Chapelle-
		aux-Saints
			Skhūl*
			Shanidar
			Wadi Amud
			
			Tabūn
			Qafzeh*
				Wadjak
				
				Maba
					Border Cave†
					Klasies River
					  Mouth Cave†
					Omo (Kibish
					  Fm.)
					
					Florisbad

	125,000				
	MIDDLE	Steinheim, Arago Swanscombe Arago Petralona Bilzingsleben Vértesszöllös Heidelberg		Dali Solo	Bodo Kabwe Saldanha Bay

*Skhūl and Qafzeh are considered by many to be anatomically modern humans.
†Border Cave and Klasies River Mouth Cave specimens are difficult to interpret.

Neandertal fossils were the first hominine bones to be discovered. In the seventeenth century, Joachim Neumann, a composer of hymns of some local fame, lived in Düsseldorf. Taking a cue from many individuals of his time, he hellenized his surname to Neander ("new man"). When Neumann/Neander died, a valley where he had spent much of his free time was named the Neander Valley (Neander Tal) in his honor. In 1856, workmen quarrying in a cave in the valley came upon a skullcap and some postcranial bones.

Because this was the first recognized fossil of a "primitive" human, scientists of the day differed as to its identity. Some, like Thomas Henry Huxley, recognized it as an extinct human ancestor; others were not so sure. One anatomist wrote: "It may have been one of those wild men, half-crazed, half-idiotic, cruel and strong, who are always more or less to be found living on the outskirts of barbarous tribes, and who now and then appear in civilized communities to be consigned perhaps to the penitentiary or the gallows, when their murderous propensities manifest themselves."[12] Reasonable anatomical judgment won out, and neandertal took its place in the human lineage.

Since the neandertal discovery, many early sapiens fossils similar in appearance have been found in France, Germany, Belgium, Spain, Yugoslavia, Italy, Gibraltar, Russia, Czechoslovakia, Hungary, Israel, Lebanon, and Iraq (Figure 10.22). As a group, they are called neandertals, *H. sapiens* who inhabited Europe and the Middle East from the beginning

Discoveries of
Neandertals

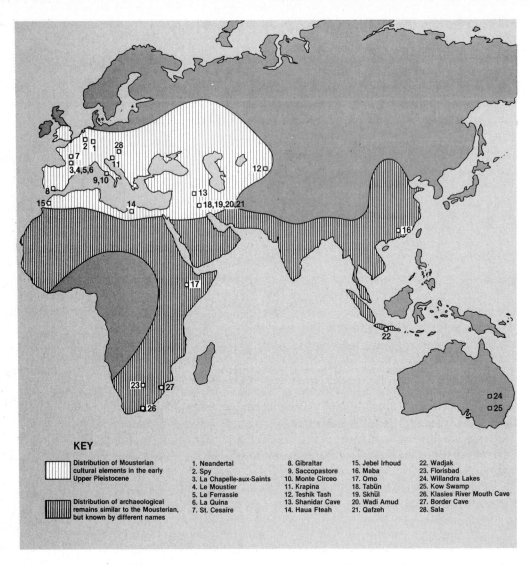

KEY

Distribution of Mousterian cultural elements in the early Upper Pleistocene			

Distribution of archaeological remains similar to the Mousterian, but known by different names			

1. Neandertal	8. Gibraltar	15. Jebel Irhoud	22. Wadjak
2. Spy	9. Saccopastore	16. Maba	23. Florisbad
3. La Chapelle-aux-Saints	10. Monte Circeo	17. Omo	24. Willandra Lakes
4. Le Moustier	11. Krapina	18. Tabūn	25. Kow Swamp
5. Le Ferrassie	12. Teshik Tash	19. Skhūl	26. Klasies River Mouth Cave
6. La Quina	13. Shanidar Cave	20. Wadi Amud	27. Border Cave
7. St. Cesaire	14. Haua Fteah	21. Qafzeh	28. Sala

FIGURE 10.22. Late Pleistocene early sapiens sites where the most complete and/or important specimens have been found.

of the late Pleistocene until the end of the first glacial advance of the Würm, or last glaciation, 30,000 to 40,000 years ago, when they disappear from the fossil record.

Other Late Pleistocene Early sapiens

In addition to the late Pleistocene *Homo sapiens* from Europe and the Middle East—the neandertals—hominines of this period have also been discovered in other parts of the Old World. These specimens possess features generally similar to those of the neandertal group, although there seem to be some distinctive attributes among different geographically limited groups, suggesting that regional evolutionary trends were developing, a point we will return to when we consider the origins of modern human population differences.

The most complete of these late Pleistocene fossils include specimens such as the partial skull from *Maba* in China. From *Wadjak* in Java have come several individuals, including a virtually complete skull. Australia has yielded several groups of fossil specimens from *Kow Swamp* and *Willandra Lakes*. Finally, late Pleistocene discoveries from Africa include the *Florisbad* fossil from South Africa, two skulls from the uppermost beds at Olduvai Gorge in Tanzania, a number of specimens from west of Lake Turkana in Kenya, partial skeletons from the Border Cave site in Swaziland in southern Africa, several fragmentary bones from *Klasies River Mouth Cave* in South Africa, and three individuals from the late Pleistocene *Kibish Formation* in the Omo River Basin of Ethiopia.

Most of these fossil samples from the Old World share certain general physical features: low, flat brain cases with low, sloping foreheads; large brow ridges usually with some curvature over each eye orbit; facial areas that project markedly and are more in front of the brain case than in modern humans; sometimes an inflated cheek area, without the depression just above the canine tooth (called the *canine fossa*) in modern humans; and a weak chin (Figure 10.23). Generally, these late Pleistocene fossils differ from the earlier middle Pleistocene *Homo sapiens* samples (Steinheim and Petralona, for example) by having larger brain cases; in other physical features, they are similar to the earlier *Homo sapiens*. This fossil evidence suggests a trend in early *Homo sapiens* evolution of enlarging brain sizes, which is of course part of the long-term general hominine trend.

Morphological Features of Neandertals   Some morphological features of the early sapiens fossils are more strongly developed in the neandertal sample dated to the early part of the last, or Würm, glacial advance (from about 75,000 to about 40,000 years B.P.). These features include a large brain size, with some over 1,700 ml and most larger than those of modern humans; the average brain size of a large sample of neandertals was recently computed to be about 1,650 ml. The cheek region tends to be inflated and lacks the canine fossa. There are also special features found only in the western European sample. One is a rounded projection on the back of the brain case called the *occipital chignon* or *bun,* which is named for the hair style it resembles. This neandertal group is also characterized by large, robustly developed limb bones with larger-than-usual articular ends. These features, along with limb bones with curved shafts, have been interpreted as indicating that the neandertals habitually used their limbs in very strenuous muscular exertions and were capable of physical feats beyond our abilities.

The European and Middle Eastern neandertal finds are almost always associated with stone tools of a particular kind. This tool tradition has been named the *Mousterian industry* after a village in France, Le Moustier, where an adolescent neandertal skeleton and stone tools were found

The Mousterian Industry

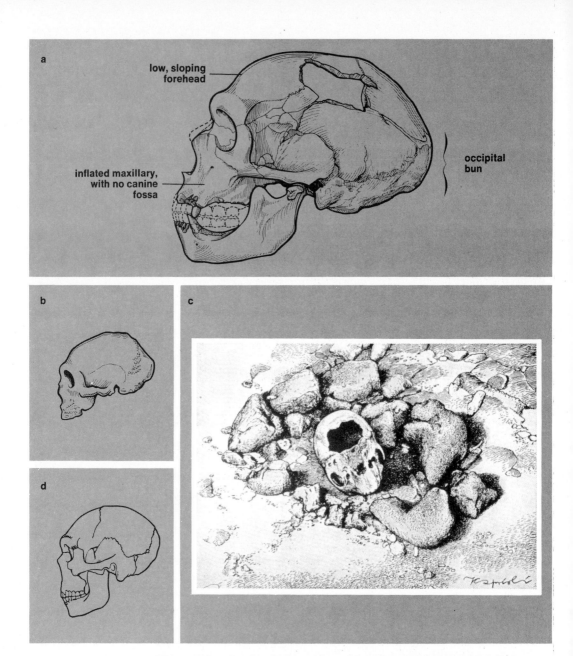

FIGURE 10.23.   Early sapiens fossils from Europe and the Middle East. (a) The neandertal skull from La Chapelle-aux-Saints in France. Before death, this individual had lost almost all his teeth (reconstructed here, as is the upper part of the nasal area). He had a large face, poorly developed chin, and an occipital bun (occipital chignon). (b) A skull from Monte Circeo in Italy, similar to (a). (c) A drawing of the Monte Circeo skull in the position it was said to be in when discovered, lying on the floor of a cave whose entrance had been sealed. The skull was found in a ring of stones, with its mutilated base turned upward. (d) The skull from Wadi Amud in Israel, with features similar to western European forms, but lacking some of their specializations, such as the occipital bun.

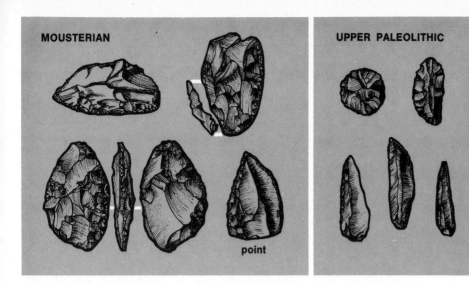

FIGURE 10.24. Stone tools from the Mousterian (Middle Paleolithic, Europe) and Upper Paleolithic (Middle East). The Mousterian point is a typical artifact of the middle paleolithic culture. (All one-half actual size).

(Figure 10.24). The Middle Paleolithic Mousterian industry has been termed a "flake tool" tradition because many of its implements are shaped from flakes of stone chipped off a core. The Lower Paleolithic Acheulian industry is called a "core tool" industry because its characteristic hand axes are made on the cores themselves. Although the Acheulian and Mousterian cultures may be termed either core or flake traditions, respectively, actually there are core and flake tools in both industries. Despite numerous examples of flake tools in the Acheulian tradition, the hand ax has come to represent the most important identifying artifact, or "type fossil," of the Acheulian industry. The Mousterian's typical tools are the point, perhaps to be hafted on to the end of a spear, and a variety of "scrapers," stone tools with a sharp, working edge along the long side ("side scrapers") or at the end of the flake ("end scrapers").

Mousterian Tool Kits   For a long time, archaeologists used the typical artifacts to identify whole stone tool industries. After World War II, these tool industries were recognized as being much more complicated, with each having an assortment of tools that could be found in other traditions, either earlier or later. François Bordes, a French archaeologist, developed a method for identifying a stone tool industry by its total assemblage of tools. Bordes felt that a culture could be identified as Mousterian, even if Acheulian hand axes were found, if the relative percentage of hand axes was low and the relative percentage of Mousterian points and other characteristic Mousterian tools was high. The entire tool kit thus has to be taken into account, and both the number and kind of tools found are important in determining which culture is present.

Bordes found by analyzing the Mousterian collections from a number of sites in France that the Mousterian really consists of numerous subtraditions, all recognizably Mousterian but differing in the percentages of tools.[13] He identified five of these, each with generally the same kinds of tools but in different percentages.

There have been many attempts to understand the reasons for these different Mousterian tool kits. One suggestion linked the various tools to task-related activities. One kind of Mousterian tool would have been used in animal butchery and another for camp maintenance, for example. This idea has been criticized by many archaeologists as not being supported by the data from excavations in Europe. There are now indications that these subtraditions are part of a time sequence; the Mousterian tool kits changed in the percentages of tools over time.

Bordes identified more than sixty kinds of Mousterian tools, an impressive number that suggested complex tool-making patterns among the neandertals and that was often cited by anthropologists as an indication that these hominines displayed behavior similar to that of modern humans. Recently, American archaeologists Arthur Jelinek and Harold Dibble have examined the Mousterian tools in a new light and concluded that this industry may not have been as complicated as Bordes believed.[14]

Dibble has studied the many apparently different kinds of stone scraping tools identified by Bordes as being part of the Mousterian industry. It had been thought that these were specialized tools, each to be used in a particular task. This of course had led to the idea that the neandertals had evolved a highly complex culture requiring many different tools. Dibble discovered, however, that many of these scrapers were actually the same tool in the process of being reduced in size and changed in shape as a result of use (Figure 10.25). A scraping tool was originally flaked to produce a stone implement with a working surface along a particular edge. As the tool was used on bone, skins, or wood, the working surface was worn smooth, losing its cutting edge. The tool user would then reflake the tool to produce a new, sharp working edge. This process would be repeated, with the tool becoming smaller each time until it became too small for efficient use, when it was discarded.

Mousterian and Other Stone Tool Industries One subtradition in the Mousterian, called the Mousterian of Acheulian tradition, has a fairly high percentage of hand axes. Bordes suggested that this subtradition may be the link between the Acheulian industry of the Lower Paleolithic and the Mousterian of the Middle Paleolithic. He believed the Acheulian industry evolved into the Mousterian as typically Acheulian tools were slowly replaced by those of the Mousterian. The transition from Lower Paleolithic Acheulian to the Middle Paleolithic Mousterian seems to have occurred sometime at the end of the middle Pleistocene.

During the final stages of the middle Pleistocene and the early parts of the late Pleistocene, the Mousterian industry continued in Europe and the Middle East. Although the percentages of the various kinds of tools seem to have changed over this period, there was apparently little change

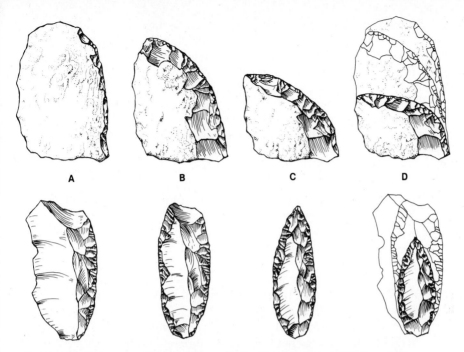

FIGURE 10.25. Mousterian scrapers. According to the work of Harold Dibble, a stone tool can start out as a particular kind of scraper, as illustrated in (A). During use, the working edges lose their sharpness, requiring further chipping to regain a cutting edge. This chipping reduces the size of the tool, into (B) and finally into (C). (D) is a composite, showing the tool as it is reduced in size. These stages in the useful life of a scraping tool were thought to represent distinct tool types.

in the tools themselves; archaeologists note few innovations that resulted in new tool types. About 30,000 to 35,000 years ago, the Mousterian was replaced by a new tradition, the *Perigordian* (named after the district Le Perigord in southwest France, where tools of this industry were first identified), marking the first of many industries of the European and Middle Eastern Upper Paleolithic cultural sequence in which blade tools predominate.

The difference between a blade and a flake is shape: Flakes usually are short and wide; blades are longer and thinner. The blade is also manufactured differently; it too is removed from a core, but the core is longer and usually cylindrical in shape, which means more blades of a similar size can be chipped from the core. A blade is much more efficient for producing a sharp-edged cutting tool, and the blade tools of the Upper Paleolithic possess finer cutting surfaces than do the tools of the Middle Paleolithic. There are a greater variety of Upper Paleolithic tools, they are much more finely made, and their innovation is marked. Throughout the Upper Paleolithic (from about 30,000–35,000 to about 10,000 years ago in the Middle East), tool types change with dramatic speed, one industry replacing another with new kinds of points and other blade tools. Bone tools are also quite common in Upper Paleolithic industries, often showing exquisite skill in their production (Figure 10.26). There are no clear-cut relationships between Middle and Upper Paleolithic industries. In the Middle East, there is evidence that there was a transition from the Middle Paleolithic Mousterian to an early Upper Paleolithic industry, but this changeover is not well marked in Europe, where the Mousterian appears to have been replaced by early Upper Paleolithic industries.

This description of the Middle and Upper Paleolithic has emphasized the European and Middle Eastern stone tool industries because more is known about these cultures than any other. Generally, flake and blade tool industries are known from Africa and Asia, and they are related in much the same way as they are in Europe and the Middle East. What does differ is when the flake tool industries were replaced by blade tool industries. There is some evidence that in Africa this transition may have occurred somewhat earlier.

Archaic Sapiens and Modern Humans

The evolutionary relationships between late Pleistocene hominines and the anatomically modern humans who come after them are extremely complicated. In Europe and the Middle East, Upper Paleolithic industries, like the French Perigordian, are usually (but not always) found with skeletal material not significantly different from that of modern humans. When compared with late Pleistocene archaic *Homo sapiens* skulls, the fossils generally associated with Upper Paleolithic industries possess a skull with greater height, with a maximum width relatively high on the brain case, with a more vertical forehead, generally with no occipital

FIGURE 10.26. Bone tools from the Upper Paleolithic of Europe, including sewing needles, harpoons and a spear point.

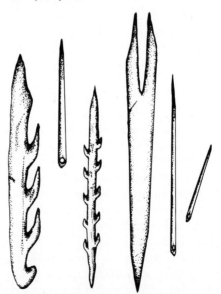

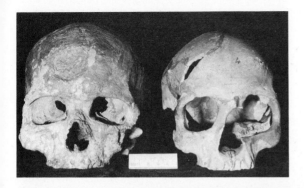

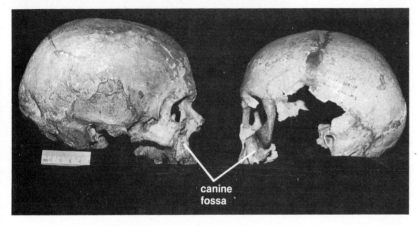

canine
fossa

FIGURE 10.27
Two of the skulls from the Cro-Magnon site in southwest France.
One of the most famous of the early anatomically modern human sites, its name is often used as synonymous for the first modern humans. The male skull on the left and the female skull on the right show such features as the vertical forehead lacking a brow ridge, a face underneath the brain case, and the marked depression on the cheek (canine fossa)—all of which are characteristic of modern *Homo sapiens*.

chignon, and with smaller or no brow ridges (Figure 10.27). The face and nasal cavity are smaller, and the distance between the eye orbits is reduced. The base of the brain case, a plane that separates the facial portion of the skull from the brain portion, shows a flexion (bending) in comparison to early sapiens skulls. This bending is related to the relative positioning of the face more directly underneath the brain case, resulting in changes in the cheek region above the tooth row, where the canine fossa, or depression, has formed above the canine teeth on the cheek (Figure 10.28). The lower jaw has a chin, a specialization that is usually (but not always) lacking on neandertal fossils. These physical features generally appear on fossils discovered in Europe and dated to after about 30,000 years ago, including the Czechoslovakian sites of *Předmosti* and *Mladeč* (pronounced "Mil-ad-ich") and the somewhat later-in-time French cave site of Cro-Magnon (at about 20,000 years ago). A site in Israel, *Qafzeh,* has also produced fossils that appear to be representative of modern humans, but the dating of this Middle Eastern site is appreciatively earlier than the European finds; indeed, at about 92,000 years, it is dated to a time when neandertals were still alive. More tentatively dated than Qafzeh, but possibly of a similar age, are the fossil specimens from Border Cave, on the boundary between South Africa and Swaziland. These latter specimens, along with several others, and the analysis

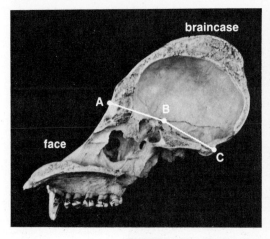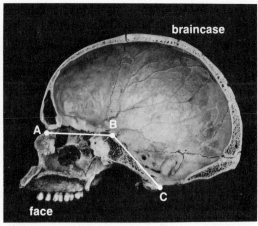

FIGURE 10.28. Skulls of a modern human (right) and orang (left), sectioned down the middle. A line drawn from a point just below the brow ridge (A), to the front of the large opening at the base of the brain case where the spinal cord joins the brain (*foramen magnum*) (C), through the cup for the pituitary gland (B), divides the brain case part of the skull from the face. Note the angle this line makes at (B); in modern humans, this is the flexing of the skull base to accommodate the shifting of the face underneath the brain case. Modern humans have angles that range from 125° to 150° (the orang is closer to 180°), while neandertals are generally at the high end of the human range—from 135° to 150°.

of a particular kind of human DNA have been used in a general scheme that places the origin of modern humans in Africa at a time when neandertals were still around in both Europe and the Middle East.

Theories of Modern Human Origins

How the neandertals and other late Pleistocene early or archaic sapiens fit into the origin and development of anatomically modern humans is a most difficult problem. Stated briefly, the question concerns the relationship of early sapiens populations to the modern human populations that succeeded them in particular geographic areas. Were neandertals and other early sapiens living in different areas the direct ancestors of modern humans, or is there a more complex evolutionary sequence? The question is complicated because the dating of various fossils seems to suggest that anatomically modern humans were already on the scene in some areas when early sapiens were still alive in other places. If, as current evidence suggests, modern humans and early sapiens were contemporaries, how can the relationships between the two groups be satisfactorily worked out?

Further, the question of early sapiens/modern human relationships cannot be examined without also considering the development of living human populations ("races"). Later chapters will look at modern human differences and the adaptive significance of many of these differences. Chapter 14 will specifically deal with human races and their complex nature. In the context of hominine evolution, two alternative views of racial origins have been developed. W. W. Howells has summarized these competing ideas as evolutionist versus migrationist.[15] The migrationist position is that only after the evolution of modern humans did groups spread (or migrate) to all parts of the world and begin evolving distinctive biological features; this view, then, suggests a relatively recent origin of modern human races. In contrast is the evolutionist idea that these differences are of very great antiquity and that from the time of the spread of *Homo erectus* to many parts of the Old World, hominine populations have been adapting to local environmental conditions. This view sees the later phases of hominine evolution as a general continuum, with modern human populations representing the regional evolution of groups in particular environments.

These questions about the antiquity of modern human populations, along with the attempts to describe the place of neandertals and other early sapiens in the context of human evolution, have formed the basis of several theories (Table 10.4).

An American physical anthropologist, Ales Hrdlička, summarized one theory of modern human origins as the *"neandertal phase of man."*[16] He and his supporters give the name neandertal to all hominines throughout the Old World from the appearance of *Homo sapiens* in the middle Pleistocene to the end of the early Würm (last glacial). They call this a *grade,* or *phase,* of evolution between *Homo erectus* and anatomically modern humans. This view emphasizes variability in populations and suggests that all the early sapiens fossils are similar enough to be part of one variable group, distributed both in time and geographically. The early sapiens from Africa and Asia can be integrated into the same theory.[17]

Neandertal Phase of Human Evolution

The neandertal phase hypothesis traces an evolutionary trend from *Homo erectus* through the neandertals and other early sapiens into modern *Homo sapiens sapiens.* This evolutionary sequence would have occurred all over the Old World, including western Europe; in all areas these early sapiens are the immediate ancestors of modern humans.

Several fossil discoveries in eastern Europe and the Middle East have been used to support this hypothesis. Among the most important are the cave finds at *Mount Carmel,* just outside Haifa in Israel (Figure 10.29). At Mount Carmel, Dorothy Garrod, T. D. McCown, and their coworkers uncovered many archaeological levels, from the Acheulian through the Mousterian and into the Upper Paleolithic. Two Mount Carmel caves, *es-Skhūl* (cave of the kids/young goats) and *et-Tabūn* (cave of ovens), yielded fragments and complete skeletons of more than twelve individuals, all associated with Mousterian tools. The two individuals in the Mousterian layers of Tabūn are like other Middle Eastern neandertals in many morphological features. Fossils discovered in *Shanidar Cave* in Iraq and the *Wadi Amud* in Israel are similar to the Tabūn specimens. The ten individuals from Skhūl have varied anatomical characteristics; some appear essentially like modern humans.[18] Unfortunately, the precise dating of many of these fossils is uncertain. Recent estimates place the Tabūn fossils as early as 70,000 years ago, and although the Skhūl fossils are later, just how much later is not certain, although they are probably 35,000 to 40,000 years old. The proponents of the neandertal phase the-

TABLE 10.4
Views of Late Pleistocene Human Evolution

Regional continuity from archaic or early *Homo sapiens* to living humans is illustrated on the left. Note that genetic contact between hominine populations living in different geographic areas is a crucial aspect of this idea. The concept that modern humans originated earliest in Africa and spread from there to other parts of the Old World, replacing the earlier archaic sapiens populations, is pictured on the right. This view of human origins is also supported by mitochondrial DNA research. Human races originate, according to this model, only after the appearance and spread of modern humans out of Africa. Regional continuity, in contrast, visualizes the origin of human races as occurring much earlier, at the time when *Homo erectus* spread out of Africa to other parts of the Old World.

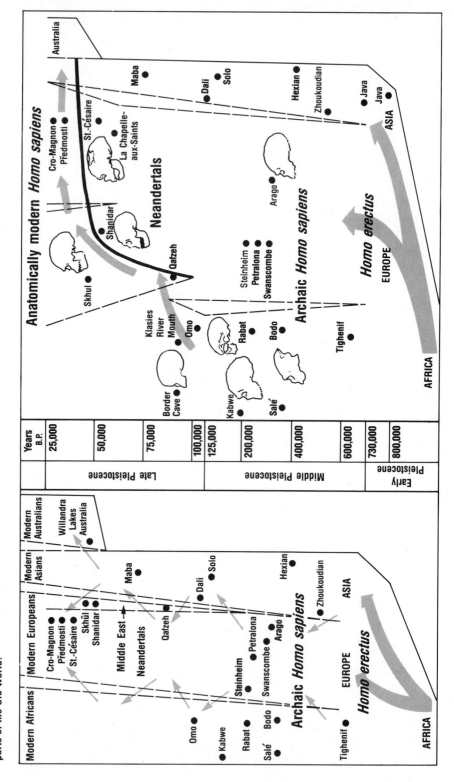

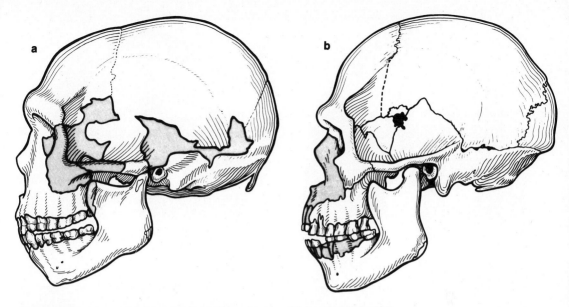

FIGURE 10.29. Two skulls from the Mount Carmel caves, (a) from Tabūn and (b) from Skhūl, one of the more modern-appearing skulls from this cave (right side reversed). Compare to Figures 10.23 and 10.27.

ory suggest that the Middle Eastern fossil evidence may document the evolutionary transition from neandertals like Tabūn, Shanidar Cave, and Wadi Amud to anatomically modern human-appearing forms like those found at Skhūl.

In addition to the fossils from the Middle East, there is a series of fossils from eastern Europe, several of which seem to possess features similar to both the neandertals and modern humans.[19] One of these was dredged out of the Vah River in the town of *Šala* in Czechoslovakia. The Šala fossil (of which only the frontal bone was found; see Figure 10.30) possesses brow ridges, but they are reduced in size, and the forehead is higher than those typical of neandertals. The nature of the discovery, however, precludes precise dating.

The theory of the neandertal phase of humans also emphasizes that early anatomically modern humans, found with Upper Paleolithic tools, sometimes show considerable variability. One group of specimens often used to illustrate this point are the Předmosti skeletons. The site of Předmosti, in what is now Czechoslovakia, was excavated in the nineteenth century. Underneath a covering of limestone slabs and mammoth shoulder blades, the remains of forty-six individuals were discovered in a common grave. All but scraps of this material was destroyed during World War II, but photographs and casts of the fossils reveal an interesting range of variation in the individuals, some with rather large brow ridges and even an occipital chignon, but others with a stronger resemblance to modern humans (Figure 10.31).

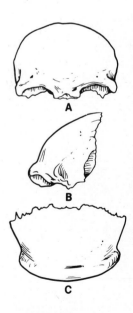

FIGURE 10.30
Three views of the frontal bone from Šala: front (a); side (b), and top (c).

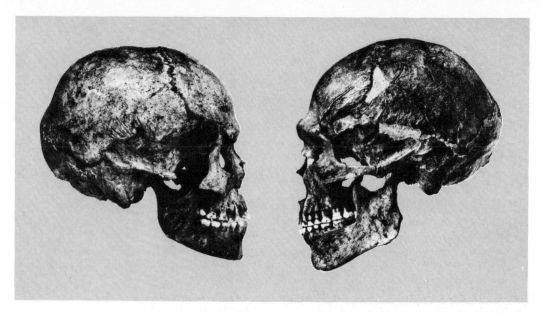

FIGURE 10.31. Two skulls from Předmosti, Czechoslovakia, found with Upper Paleolithic tools at the end of the last century. Note the large brow ridge of the skull on the right and the pronounced areas in the back of both skulls.

Although the neandertal phase of human evolution theory has been widely supported over the past fifty years, several recent developments would seem to destroy its credibility, at least in its present form. First, in 1981, French anthropologist Bernard Vandermeersch excavated a hominine skeleton from the site of *St.-Césaire* in southwest France, close to where many neandertal and early modern human fossils have been discovered in the past one hundred years.[20] The St.-Césaire skeleton was badly crushed, and it has not yet been completely reconstructed. However, much of the front of the skull has been restored (Figure 10.32), and it is clear that this is a neandertal possessing a low forehead; large, projecting face; and other features of this group. What makes the St.-Césaire discovery so important is that this neandertal was found with Châtelperronian tools, a blade tool industry that had previously always been associated with modern human fossils. These tools are not known before about 32,000 years ago, at the earliest.

Second, at Qafzeh, a cave site in Israel in the Galilee, a number of hominine skeletons have been discovered in association with Mousterian artifacts (Figure 10.33). The Qafzeh fossils are similar to the Skhūl fossils and share with these finds higher brain cases; higher, more vertical foreheads; smaller brow ridges; smaller, less projecting faces located more directly underneath the brain case; and a chin. In sum, as F. C. Howell notes, they look "in all respects like a proto-Cro-Magnon"; in other words, like anatomically modern humans. A newly published series of thermoluminescence dates (see page 295) places the Qafzeh fossils at about 92,000 years ago, at the beginning of neandertal times, and 60,000

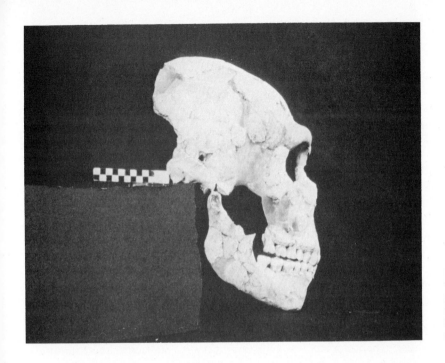

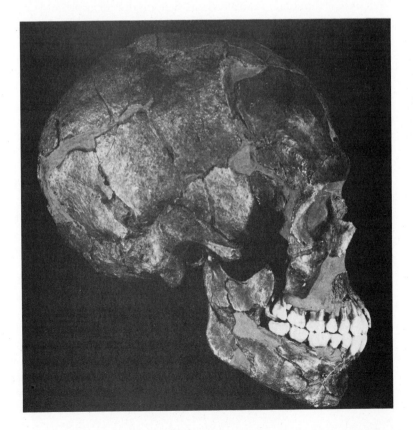

FIGURE 10.32
The partially
reconstructed skull of
the neandertal from
St.-Césaire in
southwest France.

FIGURE 10.33
The skull of one of the
individuals from Qafzeh
cave, Israel.
Note the vertical forehead,
lack of brow ridges,
reduced size of the face
and presence of a chin, all
features indicative of
modern human status.

years earlier than the St.-Césaire neandertal.[21] It is difficult to accept the neandertal phase of human evolution if the humanlike Qafzeh specimens are so much earlier than the St.-Césaire neandertal. The relatively straightforward notion that neandertals are the direct and immediate ancestors of modern humans thus cannot be accepted. There are instead alternative models to account for the origin of modern humans.

The Regional Continuity Model

This model, like the neandertal phase model, is based on the idea that the neandertals and other early sapiens are the ancestors of modern humans. The Australian Alan Thorne, Chinese Wu Xin Zhi, and American Milford Wolpoff have jointly proposed a concept of late Pleistocene hominine evolution that stresses gene flow and morphological variation to explain the relationships between archaic sapiens and modern humans.[22] According to these anthropologists, after the hominines expanded their geographic range during *Homo erectus* times, hominine groups found themselves in a wide variety of environments, some rich and some poor. These *Homo erectus* populations began to evolve biological features to adapt more successfully to the rigors of their particular environments; in doing so, they began the long process of differentiation that has led to modern human populations, or races. These scientists reason that because genetic contact (via gene flow) between and across these hominine groups was always maintained, the hominines remained a single species over time. Hominine populations in rich environments would show a greater amount of variation; groups in poor areas would be under stronger natural selection and thus have less variation.

These authors argue that evolutionary change in the hominines would occur in the areas of greatest morphological variation—in the richer areas, or the "center"—while the "edges," or the poorer environments on the periphery of the hominine distributions, would receive genetic changes from the center. One such center, but only one among numerous rich environments occupied by the hominines during the Pleistocene, was the Middle East.

Thorne, Wu, and Wolpoff suggest the origins of all modern humans can be viewed within this *regional continuity model*. They propose that archaic sapiens evolved into anatomically modern humans in the Middle East, probably sometime after 100,000 years B.P.; the Qafzeh fossils can be viewed as a very early example of these modern humans. Gene flow from this center changed neandertals into modern humans at later and later times as one moves away from the Middle East center. This model explains why hominines at St.-Césaire in western Europe, an edge far removed from the center, lived later than hominines at Skhūl and Qafzeh and still was a neandertal (Table 10.4).

Thorne, Wu, and Wolpoff cite a variety of evidence to support their views. They point out that a number of distinctive features found, for example, in the highest frequency in Asians among modern humans, also appear very often in the earlier hominines of Asia. Modern Asians possess a relatively flat facial skeleton, as viewed from the side (Figure 10.34), a trait often found in earlier Asian hominines but not in other

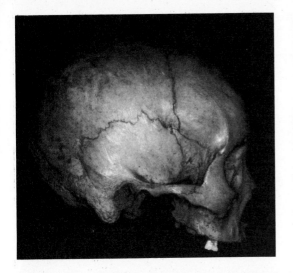 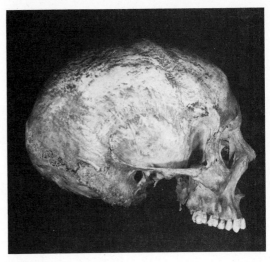

FIGURE 10.34. Skulls of modern humans. On the left, the skull of a Asian, and on the right, a European. Note the relatively flat face of the human from Asia and the more jutting position of the European's face. Lack of facial jutting can also be seen in the archaic sapiens Dali skull from China, illustrated in Figure 10.21. Proponents of the regional continuity model argue that this provides evidence for the evolutionary development of modern humans in Asia from earlier Asian archaic sapiens ancestors.

hominine skeletons. Another example is the *shovel-shaped upper incisors* (Figure 10.35) with their distinctive infolding or reinforcement, which appear most often in modern Asian populations and other closely related modern humans, like Native Americans. Shovel-shaped incisors are often found in earlier Asian hominine specimens, like the *Homo erectus* fossils from Zhoukoudian. These traits, Thorne, Wu, and Wolpoff argue, demonstrate a pattern of regional continuity, with earlier hominines in one geographic area evolving into the later populations of living humans of that area. The regional continuity model thus makes a case for the long-term, in-position evolution of humans from *Homo erectus* times to the present, with genetic contact maintaining a single species. Variable rates of evolutionary change in rich and poor environments have led to a situation in which more archaic populations, like the neandertals, were still alive when modern humans had already evolved elsewhere. Although this is a very attractive concept, several African fossils as well as comparative genetic studies suggest that another model can also fit the known evidence.

Over the past few years, a number of highly sophisticated statistical studies have been performed on the neandertal fossil collections from Europe and the Middle East. Christopher Stringer, whose analysis is the most elaborate, has concluded that although there is some variability in skull and jaw features among the different neandertal fossils, they seem to form a distinct group that can be distinguished both from anatomically

Out of Africa: An Evolutionary Population Model

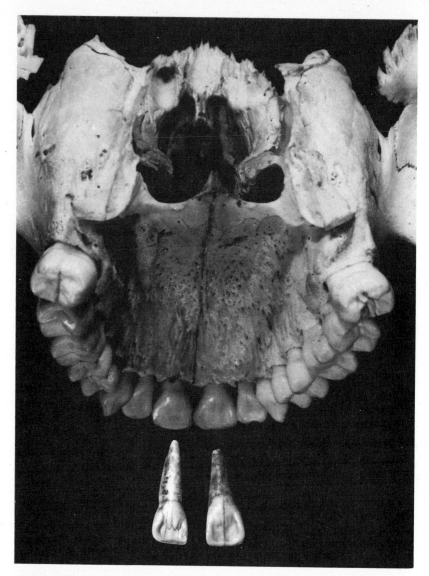

FIGURE 10.35. Top, a view of the upper dentition of a modern human (a European) from the inside of the mouth. The inside surface of the middle incisors is smooth, lacking the characteristic indentations seen in the two isolated middle incisors, pictured below, from the *Homo erectus* site of Zhoukoudian in north China. Termed shovel-shaped incisors because this indentation gives the tooth a shovel-like appearance, these teeth are found more frequently in modern Asian peoples and their close kin, such as Native Americans, than in other human populations. Shovel-shaped incisors are also found with a high frequency in Asian archaic *H. erectus* and *H. sapiens* specimens, suggesting a regional continuity in evolution from Asian *H. erectus* through archaic sapiens to modern Asians.

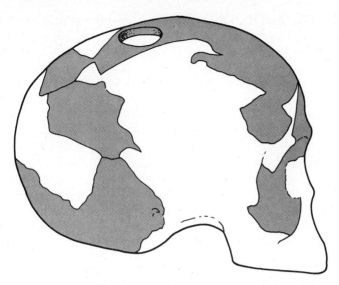

FIGURE 10.36. The reconstructed skull from Border Cave in southern Africa.

modern humans and from fossils such as Skhūl and Qafzeh.[23] This can also be seen in some features of the postcranial skeleton. According to Stringer and other scholars, such as William Howells and Erik Trinkaus, who also support this position, the Skhūl and Qafzeh specimens group with, and should be identified as, anatomically modern humans. Yet both were found with Mousterian tools, and Qafzeh is now dated earlier than most neandertals. Further, several fossil specimens from Africa may, like Qafzeh, be examples of early modern humans. The Border Cave fossil (Figure 10.36) possesses many attributes of a modern human, although it is relatively incomplete. There is also a question of whether the specimen really is associated with the 75,000-year-old deposit in which it was found or represents a much later burial that was dug into the more ancient deposit.[24]

Along the South African coast is the cave site of Klasies River Mouth, which has yielded abundant archaeological remains and thousands of animal bones with a number of rather fragmentary hominine fossils that probably date to more than 70,000 years ago. These appear to possess many modern human features but they are very fragmentary and difficult to assess adequately.[25]

These African fossils seem to share many morphological similarities with modern humans and therefore offer supporting evidence, with Qafzeh, of the early appearance of modern humans. Uncertainty about the circumstances of burial at Border Cave and the fragmentary state of the Klasies River Mouth Cave materials, however, make definite conclusions difficult. Nevertheless, these fossils have provided a framework for the development of a model of modern human origins in Africa that has been significantly strengthened by the results of a study of human DNA.

In addition to the DNA genetic material found in the nucleus of the cell (discussed in Chapter 2), there is another form of DNA in a structure, the mitochondrion, in the cell's cytoplasm. In Chapter 5, a number of techniques were described for using nuclear DNA to assess relationships among living species. *Mitochondrial DNA* (mtDNA) has a number of advantages over nuclear DNA for determining the evolutionary relationships of populations of one species. First, because mitochondria is not present in sperm, an individual receives mitochondria (and the mitochondrial DNA) solely from the mother. Second, in addition to this maternal inheritance of the mtDNA, which eliminates genetic recombination, studies have shown that mtDNA evolves at a much faster rate than does nuclear DNA, which makes it more suitable for intraspecies examinations. A more detailed and elaborate discussion of mtDNA evolution, the techniques used in studying this genetic material, and its potential significance for understanding human population origins will be found at the end of Chapter 14 on the biological history of human populations. In the present context, we will focus on the implications of this study for the evolution of modern humans.

Briefly, Rebecca Cann, Mark Stoneking, and Allan Wilson analyzed the mtDNA of almost 150 people from five different human populations. Using molecular biology techniques, the researchers determined some of the differences and similarities in the mtDNA.[26] By organizing their results into a scheme that reflected the relationships of the members of the various human populations, they concluded that modern humans originated in Africa about 190,000 years ago. From this origin point, humans spread out to Eurasia, displacing or destroying the local early sapiens groups (the mtDNA, according to their work, does not indicate any interbreeding with early sapiens).

Numerous criticisms have been directed at this study, and many geneticists and anthropologists caution that its results ought to be considered preliminary. The mtDNA analysis does, however, support the African and Qafzeh fossil evidence in suggesting an early origin for modern humans. In this scheme, as proposed by Chris Stringer and German anthropologist Günter Bräuer, the origin of modern humans occurred in Africa sometime prior to 100,000 years ago.[27] This evolutionary transition may have occurred very rapidly in a single locale via a punctuation event. This early modern human population gradually expanded out of its original environment, replacing local early sapiens populations. By about 90,000 years ago, modern humans had moved out of Africa and, as indicated by the Qafzeh fossils, had reached the Middle East. Still later, modern humans moved into Europe and Asia, supplanting their indigenous early sapiens groups. In this view, neandertals in Europe could have been contemporary with or even later than modern humans elsewhere. Finally, in this model, the neandertals of western Europe were replaced by modern human populations that had evolved elsewhere (Table 10.4).

Many problems remain to be worked out before a clear picture of the evolutionary appearance of modern humans can be formulated. It does seem clear that some archaic sapiens did evolve into modern humans, but whether all these early sapiens are the direct ancestors of the modern humans who succeeded them is not certain.

Further, the model of the neandertal phase of humans, suggesting continuous evolution between all early sapiens and anatomically modern humans, supports the notion that human races have a great antiquity and that they represent the long-term, in-place evolution of hominine populations in particular environments,[28] a theory also supported by the regional continuity model of Thorne, Wu, and Wolpoff. In contrast, the evolutionary population model, suggesting a rapid development of modern humans from one isolated population, may confirm a more recent origin of human races; modern human population differentiation may have resulted from the spread of anatomically modern humans after their evolutionary appearance in Africa, replacing early sapiens in the other parts of the Old World[29] (Table 10.4). We will deal with this question again in Chapter 14, when we discuss the differences among modern human populations.

A great deal of cultural and other material has been discovered at many early sapiens sites. In spite of this evidence, however, there remain differences of opinion among anthropologists concerning the nature and complexity of early sapiens behavior and adaptation. There are no generally accepted reconstructions of the lifeways of these early *Homo sapiens* peoples. From the archaeological remains, they appear to have utilized a wide range of foods and can be broadly characterized as gatherers and hunters.

Early Sapiens Adaptations

They hunted a variety of animals; the bones of small and medium mammals are especially well represented at their sites. The bones of larger mammals are also often found, but archaeologists differ in their interpretation of these finds. Some view the neandertals and their early sapiens contemporaries as efficient and skilled hunters of big game, especially during the Würm glacial in Europe, when long winters kept them from finding much vegetable food. Other archaeologists, like Lewis Binford, whose views of the limited cultural adaptation of *Homo erectus* were reviewed earlier, believe early sapiens behavior patterns were narrow in comparison to those of modern humans. Binford argues, primarily on the basis of the percentage and identity of the large mammal bones found at the sites, that early sapiens were collectors of vegetable foods and hunters of small animals, obtaining the large animal bones by scavenging them from carnivore kills. Binford suggests that only with the origin of modern humans was a pattern of big-game hunting established.

The archaeological evidence suggests that, like modern gatherers and hunters, early sapiens moved in a seasonal cycle, exploiting one area and then moving on to another. In Europe most neandertal sites are found in caves, probably chosen for their protection from the cold. During the short summer, the neandertals inhabited open-air sites and lived in tentlike dwellings.

At this time, we see what may be the first glimmers of an ideological system. Many neandertals were intentionally buried; occasionally there are grave offerings with the body. As with other aspects of early sapiens lifeways, there are differing interpretations of the meaning and significance of these discoveries. On the southern Russian steppes at *Teshik Tash* in Soviet Uzbekistan, the burial of a neandertal youngster was found. The excavators reported that around the body were the skulls of wild goats, the horns pointing in towards the burial. This burial has been used to document the presence of ritual behavior in neandertals. Other archaeologists have questioned this finding, noting that since numerous additional goat skulls were mixed in with the debris at the site, it is more likely that the skulls were simply discarded bones accidentally thrown in with the burial.

At another site, on the Mediterranean Sea at a place just outside of Rome, called Circe's Mountain (*Monte Circeo*), a neandertal skull was discovered in a large cavern in 1937. According to some reports, the skull was found lying on its top in the middle of a ring of stones. The base of the skull had been broken off, and the skull was partially burned (Figure 10.23). There is no doubt the skull was broken and burned, but the exact position of the skull at the moment of discovery is uncertain. There are differing accounts of its original placement, and no photographs were taken as documentation. How are we to evaluate this find? What is the significance of the partially burnt skull? Does it represent some sort of neandertal ritual, or was the skull burned because it had been lying too close to a fire hearth?

Ralph Solecki discovered nine neandertals in the Mousterian levels in Shanidar Cave in the Zagros Mountains of Iraq.[30] The cave's roof was not stable and periodically fell in, burying the people caught inside. One of the skeletons, Shanidar I, was that of a forty-year-old male who had been crushed and killed by a cave-in. T. D. Stewart found that this individual was crippled, with a malformed right shoulder blade and collarbone and a withered upper right arm bone, and that he had lost the lower part of the right arm just above the elbow joint long before death (Figure 10.37).[31] If the arm was not lost via an accident but was amputated surgically, the techniques and (stone) tools that were used, and how the individual stood the pain, will never be known. The skeleton does reveal that neandertal groups had a strong social bond, capable of supporting a member with a useless arm. In addition, healed scars on the top of the skull testify that prior to being killed by a cave-in, this individual had received several nasty bumps on the head from small pieces of falling cave roof. Many neandertal skulls show similar injuries. Finally, the Shanidar I skull, along with another from the same cave, shows evidence of being artificially deformed. Many modern human societies either accidentally or intentionally deform the skulls of their infants by binding cloths around the head or simply by tightly wrapping an infant on a flat board so that it can be easily carried.

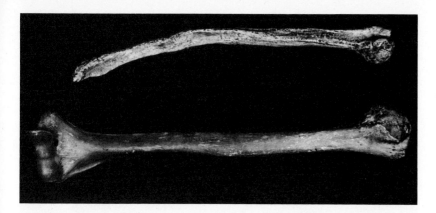

FIGURE 10.37. The withered right arm of the Shanidar I neandertal from Iraq compared with the arm bone of a modern human. That this earlier human had lost his arm just above the elbow joint some time before he died in a cave roof collapse is indicated by the shrinkage and withering of the bone and the ball of the shoulder joint.

These examples indicate that early sapiens, like the neandertals, were capable of complex behavior like the deliberate burial of the dead; certainly their presence in the temperate parts of the world during the last great glacial advance provides strong evidence of their capabilities. The Mousterian and other Middle Paleolithic tool industries are better made and more diverse than the preceding Acheulian. However, Middle Paleolithic stone tools remain rather constant in form and tool type and show little innovation. Further, the work of Jelinek and Dibble discussed previously indicates that the overall complexity and diversity of Mousterian tools are not as great as was thought. In comparison, the blade tool industries of the Upper Paleolithic, which are virtually always associated with anatomically modern humans, show much greater diversity of type, far more sophistication in manufacture, and enormous innovation over a very short time. Associated with this marked technological change between Middle and Upper Paleolithic is the development of artistic expression. Upper Paleolithic Europe is marked by the appearance of the truly remarkable naturalistic art preserved in a number of French and Spanish caves, such as Lascaux (Figure 10.38). In many parts of Europe, the Upper Paleolithic is when plastic art of great significance also first appears in many sites (Figure 10.39). Does this mean that there is a marked difference in the conceptualizing abilities of these early sapiens in contrast to those of modern humans? Dibble and Phillip Chase have suggested that these distinctions between early sapiens and modern humans can be related to a difference in symbolic behavior; the major feature that characterizes modern humans is the ability to use language. The presence of language, a symbol system of enormous flexibility, Dibble and Chase argue, has enabled modern humans to communicate in

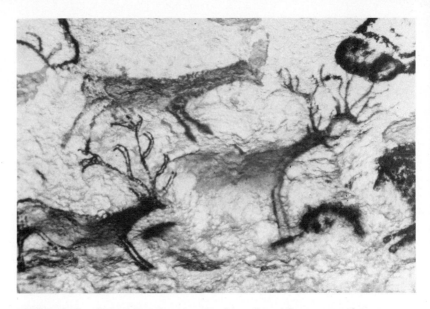

FIGURE 10.38. A scene from Lascaux cave in southwest France, one of many cave paintings known from Upper Paleolithic times in western Europe. Most cave art is concerned with animals, like this one of a reindeer herd, and drawings of people are uncommon. Why these gathering and hunting peoples produced this art is unknown, and many theories have been proposed to explain its presence in these caves. Whatever the reason, the pictures are considered by many as among the greatest naturalistic art ever produced by any human society.

ways that were not available to the earlier hominines. This, they believe, is the foundation for modern human developments in technology and art.[32]

In support of this theory is a study of the base of the neandertal brain case. Based on a number of anatomical attributes, Philip Lieberman and E. S. Crelin reconstructed the entire soft tissue voice tract and concluded that early sapiens were incapable of articulating a full range of modern human language sounds.[33] This idea has not been accepted by many anthropologists, however. One reason is that the neandertals and even *Homo erectus* are associated with archaeological evidence indicating a rather complex technology and environmental adaptation. It is difficult to reconcile these indications of a sophisticated way of life with the notion that these hominines were incapable of speech. Further, although early sapiens' faces and teeth are only slightly smaller than those of *Homo erectus,* their brains are significantly larger. Their average cranial capacity is a little larger than that of modern humans, and the overall structure of their brains, from the limited evidence of endocranial casts, does not appear to differ in any meaningful way from those of modern humans. Finally, there is Ralph Holloway's analysis of the ways by which a hominine neurological system develops a mental image of a tool and then translates this image to the raw material in tool manufacture. Holloway's ideas were presented in Chapter 8 as part of the discussion of the origin

FIGURE 10.39. Upper Paleolithic sculpture. This one of a woman holding a bison horn is from the site of Laussel in southwest France. The sculpture was apparently colored, for there are traces of red ocher on the form.

of hominine toolmaking; Holloway believes that the brain's structures responsible for toolmaking would also serve as the neurological foundation for speech. According to him, then, even early hominines like australopithecines would have been capable of speech.[34]

Except for the difficult-to-interpret fossils such as Border Cave and Klasies, and those from Qafzeh, the earliest documented evidence of anatomically modern humans comes from around 30,000 to 35,000 years ago. Apart from the Qafzeh and Skhūl materials, the fossils are associated with Upper Paleolithic tools and with both open-air and cave sites; the gathering and hunting tradition was continuing. In most respects, Upper

Anatomically Modern Humans

Paleolithic hominines are morphologically similar to modern humans. Some specimens, such as those from Předmosti, possess features similar to the neandertals. However, Upper Paleolithic hominines also differed from modern humans in several features: They were generally taller and, like the neandertals, capable of much more strenuous muscular activity. This greater strength may be related to the need of hominines in a gathering/hunting economic system to be able to deal with the environment more directly than those of us who live in a more sophisticated culture.

Final Expansion of Range   During the Upper Paleolithic the hominines expanded to their current distribution. The evidence suggests that Siberia was first colonized at this time; from there the hominines migrated across the Bering Strait into North America and soon after into South America. The New World was peopled not by a purposeful migration but probably by human groups following herds of large game. The earliest, well documented archaeological evidence in North and South America is about 15,000 years old. The human bones occasionally found with the early evidence reveal a modern human form, with clear physical relationships to northern Asians. By about 10,000 years ago, hominines had spread to all of the Americas.[35]

Recently discovered evidence from the site of Willandra Lakes, near Canberra, Australia, suggests that hominines had developed the sophisticated technology necessary to cross the water barrier between Australia and New Guinea and the islands associated with mainland Asia by 60,000 years ago (Figure 10.40). Only by the use of boats could hominines have reached Australia, and the discoveries at Willandra Lake suggest that this was accomplished much earlier than was previously thought. Much later, humans both from Australia and New Guinea and from mainland Asia began the island-hopping by boat that was to result in the peopling of virtually the entire Pacific island area.

The range of the hominines thus increased, but their basic adaptation—small group, nonsettled, gathering, collecting, and hunting—continued. The tools and the rest of their culture became more complex, with the whole becoming more efficient, capable of providing the basic materials for human groups to exploit almost every environment on the planet successfully. The fundamental pattern, however, remained unchanged.

Agriculture   Sometime around 12,000 years ago, plants were domesticated in both the Old and New Worlds. Shortly after mastering the flora, humans also domesticated animals, two shifts in the economic base that profoundly changed hominine history. Gathering and hunting limits the size of the social group and prevents it from developing a settled life; agriculture and a stable supply of food allow aggregations of large numbers at permanent sites. Only part of the group is needed to raise enough food for all, and roles can be specialized. Biologically, however, hominines are gatherers and hunters; they have passed most of their recent biological history as small-group foragers. Like our primate relatives,

FIGURE 10.40
The most important early hominine sites in Australia.
Evidence from a variety of sources suggests that the first peoples to reach Australia came from New Guinea and landed in the Gulf of Carpentaria area, perhaps as early as 60,000 years ago.

who also live in small groups, the hominines probably evolved many of their attributes in response to the demands of this kind of life. It may be that we are not adapted to life in large social aggregations, a question we will return to in the last chapter.

Summary

The dating and the place of origin of the human zoological subfamily Homininae are still very uncertain (see Table 10.5 for a summary chart). So too is the identity of the immediate hominoid ancestors of the hominines. The earliest documented evidence of hominine evolution is the australopithecines, who appear in the record at the end of the Miocene, about 5 million years ago. The australopithecines have been found in some numbers at various sites in East and South Africa from this time to about 1.5 million years ago. During most of their evolution, they apparently were confined to the African continent—at least we have not found them elsewhere—and there is no evidence of hominines in other parts of the Old World until after 1 million years ago.

The australopithecines are unquestionably hominines; they were bipedal, and later forms are found with tools. There is some dispute concerning the number of australopithecine taxonomic categories living during this period. On the basis of morphological differences, there may have been as many as five or six species of australopithecines.

One, known from sites in Tanzania and Ethiopia in East Africa, is

TABLE 10.5
Summary of the Evidence for Human Evolution

Only the major sites, especially those with reasonable dating, have been included. The chart has not been drawn to scale, but reflects the important times in hominine evolution.

Years B.P.	Geological Epoch	Hominine Groups	Major Hominine Sites Discussed in Text — Africa	Asia	Europe	Some Important Fossils	Brain Size	Evidence of Culture
10,000	HOLOCENE							Agriculture
40,000	LATE (PLEISTOCENE)	Anatomically modern humans		Skhūl	Cro-Magnon Predmosti	St.-Césaire	1350–1450 ml	Upper Paleolithic tools
70,000		Neandertals	Klasies River Mouth	Shanidar Tabūn	Neandertals	Mt. Circeo	1300–1700 ml	Mousterian tools
125,000		H. sapiens	Border Cave	Qafzeh				
.2 MY	MIDDLE	Early sapiens	Kabwe	Dali Solo	Steinheim-Swanscombe Arago Petralona Vértesszöllös Heidelberg		1200–1300 ml	
.3							900–1300 ml	
.4				Zhoukoudian			800–950 ml	
.5			Tighenif					
.6		*Homo* — Transition from *H. erectus* to *H. sapiens*						
730,000	LOWER							
1.0		*H. erectus* / *H. habilis*	Olduvai Lake Turkana	Java		Olduvai Hominid 9	1000 ml	
1.2						KNM-ER 3733, WT 15000, KNM-ER 1813, KNM-ER 1470, 1590	800 ml	
1.5							500–775 ml	Acheulian tools
1.6								
2.0	PLIOCENE	*Australopithecus* — *A. robustus* / *A. boisei* / *A. africanus* / *A. afarensis*	Swartkrans Sterkfontein Makapansgat Laetoli Omo Hadar Maka, Belohdeline Kanapoi Lake Baringo Olduvai			WT 17000	400–500 ml (First evidence of bipedalism)	Oldowan tools First evidence of stone tools
3.0						*A. afarensis* skeleton, jaws, footprints		
4.0								
5			Lothagam					
10	MIOCENE					Lothagam jaw		

Australopithecus afarensis. This species is the earliest of the australopithecines, having been dated to between about 2.9 and 3.7 million years B.P. *A. afarensis* was bipedal; but its front teeth, canines, and first lower premolars were different in some ways from those in the other australopithecines.

Another australopithecine, known from rather large fossil samples from South Africa and perhaps also from East Africa, is *Australopithecus africanus.* Still another, known from large numbers from South Africa, has been termed *Australopithecus robustus,* or the robust australopithecine. In East Africa, fossils similar to the South African robust group are placed in the taxon *Australopithecus boisei.* Although both of the latter groups generally differ from the other australopithecines in having larger back teeth and chewing muscles, the East African sample possessed chewing teeth and musculature that were generally even larger than those characteristic of the South African robust forms. The recently discovered skull from west of Lake Turkana, KNM-WT 17000, resembles the *A. boisei* specimens, but its differences from this group have led some to place it in a species of its own, *Australopithecus aethiopicus.*

Finally, there are fossils known primarily from East Africa that differ in a number of ways from those already described. They possessed larger brains and smaller teeth. First identified at Olduvai Gorge, they were placed in the taxon *Homo habilis,* suggesting they were sufficiently different from other australopithecines to warrant placement in the same genus as modern humans. Discoveries at sites east of Lake Turkana have produced fossil specimens dated to between 1.6 and 2 million years B.P. Some of these, such as the fossil skull KNM-ER 3733, dated to about 1.5 to 1.6 million years B.P., can be placed in *Homo erectus.* Others, dated somewhat earlier, possess a variety of features, some indicative of *Homo* and others of *Australopithecus.*

It seems reasonable that australopithecines evolved during this period into early members of the genus *Homo.* Unresolved is whether *A. africanus,* an evolutionary development from the earlier *A. afarensis,* represents the immediate ancestor of early members of *Homo,* or whether it is already on the separate lineage to robust australopithecines.

The period between 2 and 1.5 million years B.P. provides a reasonable point of transition from some of the australopithecines to *Homo.* Yet at about the same time the skulls and jaws of robust australopithecines are found, demonstrating that the robust australopithecines continued to exist after the evolutionary appearance of *Homo erectus.* The robust australopithecines represent a limited evolutionary specialization from the main hominine line. They apparently became extinct sometime after 1.5 million years B.P., leaving no descendants.

Homo erectus fossils have been discovered in many parts of the Old World, including Java, China, and North, East, and South Africa. Appearing earliest in East Africa, they later spread from the African continent to the tropics of the Eurasian continent. At the end of their evolution, they are found in more temperate environments, like north China. They possessed larger brains and smaller faces and teeth than the australopithecines. Their postcranial skeleton, apart from minor differences, is identical to that of modern humans. *Homo erectus* may be represented in Europe, but the known fossil evidence has features that make it difficult to determine whether these fossils are *Homo erectus* or early *Homo sapiens*.

Sometime in the latter part of the middle Pleistocene, *Homo erectus* evolved into *Homo sapiens*. These early members of *Homo sapiens* differ from the preceding hominine groups in possessing larger brains and related changes in skull form.

Early *Homo sapiens* from the middle Pleistocene generally have smaller brains than the early sapiens fossils of the late Pleistocene. One group of late Pleistocene hominines from Europe and the Middle East are called neandertals. There are also numbers of other late Pleistocene early or archaic sapiens from other parts of the Old World. There are several models to account for the relationship of late Pleistocene early sapiens to anatomically modern humans. These theories differ basically on whether all early sapiens are the immediate ancestors to modern humans, or whether the latter evolved rapidly in one place and then quickly spread, replacing early sapiens populations in various parts of the Old World.

Although most evidence suggests that hominines similar in appearance to modern humans appear on the scene about 30,000 to 40,000 years ago, the recent dates from the Qafzeh cave site in Israel suggest that modern humans may have evolved considerably earlier. Early anatomically modern human finds do not represent humans identical to modern populations, because along with robust skeletons indicative of extraordinary muscular exertion, they display taller stature and other differences. The changes that have characterized the evolution of human populations from then to the present are not as profound as those changes typical of the evolution from the australopithecines to modern humans, yet they illustrate the continuing nature of human evolution and represent the action of natural selection on the evolving hominine gene pool.

During the course of human evolution, the behavior of our ancestors also underwent a pattern of development. We know virtually nothing of the behavior and adaptation of our earliest ancestors, *Australopithecus afarensis*. The first stone tools are known from about 2.5 million years ago. Whether tools made from other materials preceded these is not known. From this time onward, stone tools, initially rather simply made and later showing greater complexity and sophistication, are a part of the hominine pattern. At sites at Olduvai Gorge and East Turkana that are dated between 1.6 and 2 million years ago, animal bones have been found with scratch marks, which indicates that australopithecines of this period were using stone tools to scrape off bits of meat from the bones. Some anthropologists have suggested that this represents the origin of a scavenging adaptation in human evolution. Our ancestors adapted to a diet of various plant material and the small amounts of meat obtainable from bones scavenged from carnivore kills.

Although these discoveries document the presence of humanlike activities in the early hominines, the pace and level of technological change through the later phases of human evolution are questions actively being debated. Fire appears to be present 500,000 years ago in the Zhoukoudian cave in China, although it remains uncertain whether the *Homo erectus* peoples who inhabited the cave actually controlled it. Later, after 100,000 years ago, the first deliberate burials appear in the record. Does this signal the beginnings of ritual and ideological feelings among the early sapiens? The issue remains an open one. Finally, the origins of modern humans are believed by some to mark a major change in behavior. The great naturalistic art of Europe first appears at this time, leading some to view this as the period when symbolic behavior develops, perhaps founded on the origins of language. Again, our knowledge is too meager to make definite statements, and this area too remains a matter of debate.

The detailed catalog of hominine fossils presented in Chapters 9 and 10 provides a basic outline of the evolutionary pathways of our ancestors. Many questions about that evolution are unsolved or clouded by differing interpretations. Only newly uncovered fossil remains will help resolve these problems. More fossils dated from about 5 to 15 million years ago would be extremely important in identifying the time of hominine origins and the physical features of the immediate hominoid ancestors. Additional fossils from East Africa of 2 to 5 million years ago would be of great assistance in unraveling the relationships between the various kinds of australopithecines: How did the robust types speciate? What environmental or other factors led to their speciation? The exact dating of the South African australopithecine fossils would be very useful in sorting out the connections between the South and East African early hominines: Were South and East African *A. africanus* creatures the ancestors of the early *Homo* forms from East Africa? Finally, additional well-dated fossils from 35,000 to 90,000 years ago would be extremely helpful in deciding what happened to the early sapiens and their relationships to the modern humans, who appear on the scene after them.

The last four chapters have traced the evolutionary development of the primates, focusing on those events that led to modern humans. Although the fossil evidence is sufficient to sketch in the broad outlines of human evolution, we are not yet able to recognize all the details. Some of the most crucial details concern those environmental and other factors that are responsible for the emergence of modern humans in their present form and diversity. Modern humans, the living descendants of the animals just described, are diverse in their adaptation and biology. The fossil evidence is not yet rich enough to explain fully the evolutionary context in which this diversity developed, but it is useful and important in examining these biological patterns and attempting to recognize their evolutionary basis. The next four chapters will continue the story of the subfamily Homininae, specifically the biology and adaptation of the living members of this group.

11

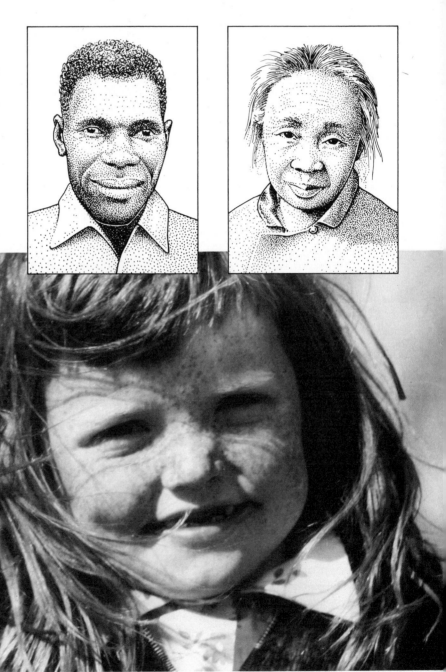

Modern human variability can be studied at a multitude of levels, ranging from the molecular to the organismal, and from the perspective of individuals, populations, or even species.

The Study of Human Variability

The last three chapters have dealt with the fossil record of hominine evolution and the changes witnessed over long periods. Chapter 10 ended with the appearance and spread of modern humans, but this is hardly the end of the story. Physical anthropologists also study the variations seen within our species as well as the commonalities throughout it. Toolmaking, the use of language, and the ability to operate within a cultural setting are all traits that benefit humans wherever they may live and have been selected for throughout our range. We know, however, that there are also variations among humans, and we wonder why they exist. Are they hereditary, or do they develop during a person's lifetime? Can we see evolution operating to produce the variations? If so, what are the forces—natural selection? drift? How do the variations help the people survive in different environments, or is this not their function? In this and the next two chapters, we will apply some of these questions to a variety of human traits and stresses. Some of the variations, such as skin color and body build, are very familiar. Others, such as traits of the blood or DNA, are rather obscure, but each has a story to tell about the causes and patterns of modern human variation. This chapter will set the stage by introducing some key concepts and processes related to variation. It will also discuss the contributions of certain basic aspects of the human growth process to human variability.

The Anthropological Perspective

The word *variation* can have several levels of meaning. One can look at variations that characterize and distinguish whole populations: Sub-Saharan Africans, Asians, and Europeans, on the average, differ in degree of skin pigmentation. Other variations may be encountered in many populations but at different frequencies. Many of the blood groups to be discussed in Chapter 12 fall into this category. Virtually all populations have blood types A and B, but their frequencies may vary widely. Still other variations exist as rare deviations from normal in isolated individuals or families, who are often the focus of medical researchers.

There are thus both a population level and an individual level to variations. Although physical anthropologists and physicians at times overlap in interests, the anthropologist is generally more concerned with the population aspects. Variations that occur in 1 out of 10,000 people are not usually of as much interest as are polymorphic traits. (In Chapter 3 polymorphisms were discussed as genetic traits for which two or more forms [*morph* = *form*] exist at appreciable frequencies within human populations.)

Tied to this interest in the population is the anthropologist's interest in the histories of the traits and the population. Genetically influenced traits are subject to evolution, and it is the population that evolves. Sometimes populations share genetic features. This could result from natural selection favoring the same trait in different places or from migration and a shared biological history of the groups. Anthropologists try to determine the causes of such similarities. Of late, microevolutionists have come to believe that random processes such as genetic drift can also be of great significance in human evolution and variation. For much of our evolution we lived in small groups. Under such circumstances it is not difficult to imagine that accidents and chance could affect the structure of human gene pools.

Because people function as members of cultures with rules regulating mating and reproduction, cultural values too can be particularly important in determining the patterns of variation of traits with social significance. Skin color is an obvious example of a feature that influences the choice of marriage partners in many cultures, including America. Access to economic resources, education, health care, and employment opportunities, which are a few of the cultural factors that affect how well and wisely we eat and exercise, are also major contributors to human variation in Western groups.

Populations and Their Sampling

The study of variation at the population level first assumes that we can define the population. As mentioned in Chapter 2 and as we shall see again in Chapter 14, this is not an easy task. Some human groups are defined by geographic boundaries, but this is not necessarily so. Generally, and especially when evolutionary phenomena are being studied, a population is defined as a community of breeding partners. Breeding behavior of course has a geographic component: We are not going to mate with someone we never meet. Several studies have shown that even in highly mobile, Westernized societies, we are most likely to marry someone who was born near our own birthplace. Nevertheless, membership in a population is more a matter of behavior than strictly of geography.

To describe variation in a population, must we measure every member? The answer, clearly, is no. In testing people, we eventually reach a point of diminishing returns beyond which further testing does not give us enough information to justify spending the time and effort. When we try to tell if a coin is loaded, we know that flipping it two or three times will not accurately assess its fairness. Six heads out of ten tosses likewise does not tell us if the coin favors heads or if the variation from the expected five heads is simply due to chance. One hundred tosses should give us a closer approximation to a 50 : 50 distribution, if it is a fair coin, although 1,000 tosses would give us a still more nearly accurate answer. On the other hand, our assessment of the coin's honesty would not be improved by making 20,000 rather than 10,000 tosses.

When we study human variations, we need a large yet manageable sample of the population. How many people must be tested for a large enough sample without wasting energy by oversampling? The answer depends on the problem and what we want to do with the results, as well as the frequency of the trait being examined. We can sometimes make educated guesses about the size of the sample by examining previous studies. Some statistical tests require larger samples than others to yield valid conclusions. Pilot projects, or test runs for larger projects, use smaller samples. Studying a trait that appears only rarely in a population may require us to look at a greater number of individuals. Biostatisticians can roughly approximate the necessary sample sizes. It is impossible to specify an adequate sample size arbitrarily; the proper size depends on the problem we are considering and such mundane factors as the amount of time and money we have.

Along with the sample's size, we must consider its appropriateness. If we wanted to find the frequencies of normal and sickle-cell hemoglobin alleles in a population, would we use as our sample the people who report to a hospital? The idea is attractive because the hospital would have a list of patients and their blood traits, but our sample would be badly biased if some types are more susceptible to disease than others. Would we want to test only females, cutting our work in half? No, because the genes might be unevenly distributed between the sexes. How about testing everyone on a selected street? Our results would be very different if we chose a street in Fairbanks rather than a street in Manhattan, because the samples would come from two very different biological populations. If we tested members of the same family, we might count the same gene twice, once in the parent and once in the children. A fairer method might be to assign each individual in the population a number, throw the numbers into a hat, mix them well, and draw out a sample of suitable size. This might work well if we could get all the members of the sample to cooperate, willingly or unwillingly, as the Internal Revenue Service does. But this would assume that we know the boundaries of the population we want to study. We also now know that it is often extremely difficult to delimit groups with a biological reality and that at times the sample should cut across biological lines. If we were interested in the hemoglobin types of hospital patients, we might well utilize hospital records.

One of the oldest frameworks for looking at human variation is nature versus nurture. Adherents to this age-old dichotomy ascribe human differences to either genes (nature) or environment (nurture). Usually debates within this approach revolve around socially important traits

Nature Versus Nurture / Nature and Nurture

like intelligence or criminal behavior. Some early anthropologists and psychologists argued that individuals may be fated to act in an antisocial manner because of their heredity. At the other extreme were those who felt that everyone has unbounded potentials that are fettered only by our nurturance. It is not at all unusual to find tinges of racism attached to the discussions.

Over the years it became apparent that this dichotomy is too simplistic. Genes, even those for such a straightforward trait as hemoglobin type (page 57), do not work in a vacuum, nor does the environment shape a geneless organism; genes and the environment interact in complex ways. Each of us has a singular combination of genes functioning in a unique environment that has never existed before and will never exist again. Nature *and* nurture much more accurately describes the causes of human variability than nature *versus* nurture.

Modern Views of Human Variation

Causes of Variation

Why does human variation exist? First, remember that we can answer this question at a multitude of levels. If asked in regard to the genetic processes, we can say that the process of mutation causes new alleles and that these may yield variation. Dominance of one allele over another produces phenotypic variation. When the operation of genes for one trait affects the expression of genes for other traits, we are dealing with a phenomenon called *epistasis,* and this too can cause variation, as we shall see in the next chapter. Much of the genetic difference between people ultimately results from meiosis and sexual reproduction rearranging the genes during the formation of new individuals. Variation from individual to individual is thus largely the outcome of the complex interplay of genetic and environmental factors on human biology.

At the population level, we have considered the ability of the evolutionary forces to affect variation. After mutation produces new alleles, natural selection may increase their frequency if they are adaptive. Migration and admixture may spread alleles from one population to another and hence alter levels of variation. The answer to the question is thus far from simple.

Genes Set Boundaries

The mental disorder known as schizophrenia illustrates the interplay between environment and genetics. We find that genes set certain limits upon possible outcomes and that environment plays a major role in determining our final phenotype. Schizophrenia appears in all human sociocultural settings and populations. Varying extremely in its severity, it shows up as a loss of contact with the environment and a disintegrating personality. By comparing the concordance rate (the frequency with which members of a pair of people suffer from the same disorder) of monozygotic (identical) twins with that of dizygotic (fraternal) twins, many researchers have clarified what causes this disorder. Monozygotic (MZ) twins are genetically identical; dizygotic (DZ) twins and other full siblings share 50 percent of their genes, half-siblings share 25 percent, and so on. If genetics influences the disease, we would expect that the closer the genetic link between individuals, the greater the concordance.

Results indicate that genetics does have something to do with the disease. Imagine picking unrelated people from the general population in groups of two. If the first in a group is schizophrenic, the chances are one in a hundred that the second will also be schizophrenic. But if we are dealing with MZ twinships, not the general population, and we know that one member is schizophrenic, the chance is 80 percent that the twin will also be schizophrenic. For DZ twins and other full sibships, the rate of concordance is only about 14 percent. It seems that the greater the relatedness, the higher the concordance for schizophrenia.

Not all twin pairs, though, are concordant for schizophrenia. They inherit a genetic predisposition to the disorder, not the disease itself. In an environment full of stress and high anxiety, schizophrenia alleles will often express themselves. That MZ twins are not 100 percent concordant proves that environmental factors can modify genetic traits. Even though MZ twins very often dress alike and are treated similarly, their environments are not exactly the same (Figure 11.1). Other diseases, diet, and psychological and physiological stress can all affect them; the same set of genes in two different environments can yield very different outcomes. This fits with the view that schizophrenia is affected by genetically influenced, biochemical differences in the handling of the neurotransmitter dopamine. As diet, disease, and stress alter the dopamine levels, expression of the abnormal behavior may change. Vitamin C, for instance, is involved in the metabolism of dopamine. The amount of vitamin C in the diet and the efficiency with which the body uses it helps determine the mental health of people predisposed to schizophrenia. Concordance studies such as these can be criticized on some grounds, but their overall significance cannot be neglected. Schizophrenia, like most other traits, is not caused by either genes *or* environment, but by genes *and* environment.

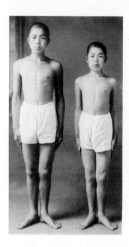

FIGURE 11.1
Genetic identity does not imply that two people will be phenotypically identical. These identical twins, for example, differ in height.

That a strong genetic influence can be environmentally modified is also well demonstrated by a disease known as phenylketonuria, or PKU. This inborn error in the body's biochemical machinery results in the lack of the enzyme needed to convert the amino acid phenylalanine into tyrosine (see page 66), leading to high levels of phenylalanine in the blood. When toxic levels are reached, brain damage and mental retardation result. This trait might be used, incorrectly, to exemplify a purely genetic trait. In fact, by detecting children with this condition shortly after birth and prescribing a phenylalanine-free diet, the phenylalanine build-up can be avoided, and the retardation prevented.

Although schizophrenia and PKU are abnormalities, many non-pathological traits are also subject to both genetic and environmental influences. Stature is one. People do not inherit genes specifying an adult height of 171.653 cm; instead they inherit genes that influence their development. The interaction of their environment—disease, exercise, sunlight, and psychological state—with their genes determines the final phenotype; they inherit a range of possible responses. The maximum adult height in Japanese children born and brought up in Hawaii clearly indicates this range. The males were, on the average, 4.1 cm taller than their parents born in Japan. It is not likely that their genetic constitution differed markedly from that of their parents, but we know that their environment, in terms of diet and medical care, certainly did.

Stature is one of many continuous, or quantitative, traits, for which our genes set broad phenotypic limits but with which the environment interacts quite noticeably. Continuous traits are those in which people differ along a continuum and for which there are no discrete categories. Such traits are largely under the influence of several sets of genes as well as the environment. People also possess discontinuous, or qualitative, traits, for which individuals fall into discrete categories. Every person falls into one or another class for MN blood groups (page 68). No one is a fraction more (or less) type M than someone else. Genetic control of these qualitative traits is usually relatively simple, and the effects of the environment on them may be subtle.

The Environment

Having discussed at some length one part of the variation equation—the genes—it is now time to consider the other part—the environment. The word *environment* conjures up images of climatic conditions and geography, but its application is much broader. It includes the other living things in our area that can affect us—animal, plant, and microbial. Our culture also affects and is part of the environment. As a group's subsistence practices change, resulting changes in diet can affect the people biologically.

There are dental defects that serve as mirrors of environmental stress. Dental hypoplasia (Figure 11.2) is a condition characterized by a deficiency in enamel thickness from which pitting of the teeth and discoloration may result. The study of hypoplasia in early Native American agricultural populations shows them to have been more vulnerable to dietary stress than previous groups with broader-based economies. Researchers have even been able to judge the age of weaning in prehistoric Native American and other populations by noting the age at which hypoplasia reaches its peak frequency.[1*] Anthropologists have not confined their studies to long-past groups. The decreasing incidence of hypoplasia noted by Mahmoud El-Najjar and colleagues in Cleveland may indicate an improving environment for modern, urban Americans.[2]

The effects of disease and malnutrition can show up clearly in longitudinal sections of long bones from human populations (Figure 11.3). The dense transverse areas at the ends of the bone, called *Harris lines,* reflect periods of arrested bone growth during childhood. Had the environment been better, final stature might have been greater. Henry McHenry found that the frequency of Harris lines diminished in California Indians as their subsistence economy expanded from hunting to include fishing and seed and acorn collecting.

We tend to think of the environment in terms of features external to us, such as culture, climate, plants, animals, and available foods. We also have an internal environment, however. Although cells may have

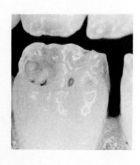

FIGURE 11.2
Dental hypoplasia is more common in groups encountering the stresses of disease and malnutrition.

*See page 627 for notes to Chapter 11.

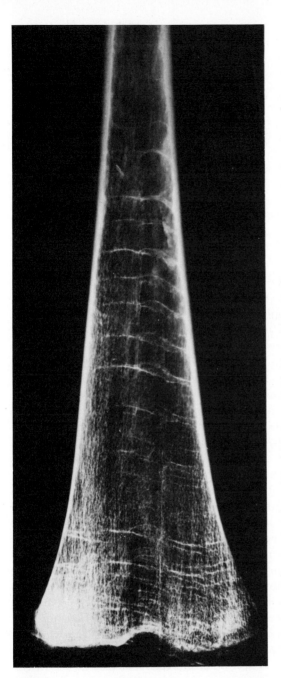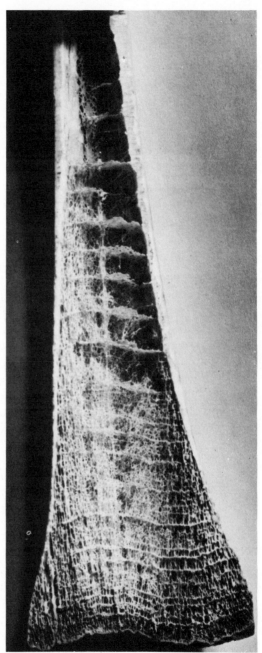

FIGURE 11.3.   An x-ray (left) and a view of the interior of a thighbone from a young California Indian. The horizontal plates of bone, or Harris lines, are clearly visible. These lines are thought to mark periods during which growth slowed down due to environmental causes such as poor diet. Harris lines thus portray how the environment modifies the genes' expression.

the same DNA content, in one tissue some of the DNA may be actively producing protein, but in another the same DNA is "turned off." Different environmental conditions, such as oxygen supply and acid–base balance, in different parts of the body may be partly responsible for this phenomenon.

Genetic factors may also be involved; the environment of one gene can include other genes present in the person. The enzyme deficiency PKU, for example, can significantly affect the expression of other genes that are related to brain function. Interactions between gene products are not uncommon. Environment, then, is not an easily defined nor an easily regulated factor.

Human Plasticity

In contrast to the debunked nature versus nurture hypothesis, we are now seeing a much more complex answer emerging to the question, "What causes variation?" In addition to the interplay between all the aspects of one's genes and environment, there is the added dimension of *human plasticity,* or our ability to mold our functioning to prevailing demands. This is often accomplished through the nongenetic, biological mechanism of our physiology. This does not mean that our physiological functioning is unrelated to our genes but that our physiological alterations are not passed on to our children.

Phenomena related to growth and development are particularly likely to show plasticity. Harris lines reveal that we stop growing when our diet or health are inadequate. When conditions improve, we resume growth and may even exhibit a catch-up period. A. Theodore Steegmann studied the stature of eighteenth-century British soldiers by examining military records. He found that recruits born between 1749 and 1753 were taller (170.5 cm) than those born between 1769 and 1774 (167.3 cm), while soldiers born in the next four years returned to previous norms. These fluctuations in adult height coincide with variations in nutritional adequacy at the time of birth (Figure 11.4). Likewise, his data show that the age at which maximum stature was reached in the eighteenth century (at about 21) was several years later than in modern Europeans with better nutritional conditions (at 18 or 19).[3]

Our responses to environmental problems are sometimes reversible and at other times are not. Suntanning is a reversible response to exposure to sunlight. The extra pigmentation helps to shield the skin cells from the damaging effects of ultraviolet light. Pigment production may go up in the summer and then taper off in the winter. If, however, a problem impinges on a developing child and alters the route of the child's skeletal growth, the effects may be unalterable. The data on the British soldiers suggest that nutritional deprivation around the time of birth will have lifelong consequences for stature. We will consider other examples of developmental responses below. For the moment, realize that the causes of individual variations are very complicated interrelations between our genes, our environment, and our physiological potentials that often involve an adaptive response to environmental challenges.

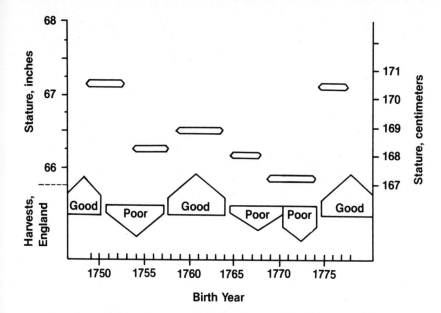

FIGURE 11.4. The lower part of this figure presents a general estimate of food availability in England in the mid to late eighteenth century. The horizontal bars show the average height at maturity of men born in the indicated years.

At the population level we can say that a variable gene pool results from the operation of evolutionary forces. First, there is mutation producing new alleles, with meiosis and recombination reshuffling the alleles every generation. Selection can then operate to produce what Theodsius Dobzhansky has called a "well-adapted gene pool."[4] A gene must not only produce a functioning protein but also work well in its internal and external environments and not interact with the functioning of other gene products in a manner detrimental to the organism. As we shall see later, gene interactions can produce results that would not be predicted from knowledge of the functioning of each separately. These considerations apply not just to the functioning of the gene products but also their timing. As we discussed in Chapter 3, regulation of the timing of genetic events may be a key aspect.

Selection can work against the gene that by itself seems superior in adaptive value but upsets the effects of other genes. As Dobzhansky has said, "A genetic good mixer becomes superior to a genetic rugged individualist."[5]

Dobzhansky places a tremendous emphasis on natural selection as the force of evolution most responsible for the constitution of gene pools. As has been noted, there are now anthropologists and evolutionary theorists who say that people like Dobzhansky are overemphasizing the role of selection. Certainly, they argue, selection can be important,

Population Variation

Population Structure

but it is not vastly more responsible for the genetic organization of to-day's populations than other forces. This challenge to the primacy of selection ascribes much of a group's evolution to its population structure: its mating practices, such as inbreeding (page 101) and assortative mating (see the following paragraph); its size and subdivisions, if any; and its migrations.

As noted in Chapter 2, deviations from random breeding can alter the distribution of genotypes in a population. If people practice inbreed-ing or marry others to whom they are similar for a trait, there will be a decrease in heterozygotes. If type M people always married type M and type N always married N, no heterozygotes would be formed. This is known as *positive assortative mating*. When people who are dissimilar for a genetic trait marry (*negative assortative mating*), the immediate effect is to increase heterozygosity.

If a population is small, the opportunity for genetic drift is clearly enhanced. Drift will cause gene frequencies to change randomly, ulti-mately causing the frequency of an allele to hit either 0 percent or 100 percent. On page 99, it was shown that drift is more likely in small pop-ulations or in large groups that do not randomly breed. India, for in-stance, has a tremendous population, but its complex social rules severely limit some mate choices. The effective size of the subgroups is thus much smaller than one might first imagine.

The size of a population may also vary dramatically over time, which can also allow genetic drift to effect the structure of a gene pool. A large population might be drastically reduced in size due to a calamity such as an epidemic or natural disaster. Although survivors can repopu-late the area, the subsequent generations are all descendants of the few survivors. If survival is purely a result of chance, then the array of genes that goes on through time has been altered by genetic drift. This is known as a *genetic bottleneck*.

Migrations are often affected by cultural and geographic factors. The Greek island of Tinos is subdivided into several local populations. D. F. Roberts and colleagues showed that, to some degree, choice of marriage partners on Tinos was simply a reflection of geographic loca-tion. If two towns were connected by a donkey track, there was a ten-dency to exchange mates. Some potential migration routes were not used, however. Two villages a half-mile apart and connected along a track shared very few mates. Presumably, this lack of migration was the result of some cultural barrier. Among the Yanomama Indians of the Amazon Basin, gene flow may be accomplished by men raiding neigh-boring villages for wives. Family squabbles can lead to the fissioning of a village, as can the exhaustion of local resources. Warfare in state-level societies can likewise be an important cause of migration and gene flow.

While Dobzhansky and many others believe that most of a popu-lation's gene pool is the result of selection and reflects an adaptive solu-tion to some problem, others say that population structure can be equal-ly, if not more, important in molding the gene pool. According to the latter thinking, the allele frequencies reflect the workings of drift, population size (both present and past), nonrandom mating, and migration. This debate is reminiscent of the question, discussed in Chapter 3, of whether all features need be explained in terms of adaptation.

Stress and Adaptation

Stressors

The concepts of stress and adaptation are simultaneously very simple and quite complicated. Simply, a *stress* is something that causes a response, and a *stressor* is anything that causes stress. Before proceeding, however, consider the ramification of this statement: Virtually everything can become a stressor, because not only negative features of an environment elicit a response by humans, although in everyday usage *stress* carries a negative connotation. Feelings of being rushed, under pressure, or overworked are certainly stressful, but so is feeling happy. As we shall see in Chapter 13, there are bodily responses to all of these feelings.

Stress also does not only refer to a psychological state, which is again the common connotation. Forces that have little or nothing to do with one's state of mind also can be stressors. Living in a hot or a cold environment, living at a high altitude, and being over- or underfed are all stressors in that they require that humans adjust their functioning to cope with the prevailing conditions.

One might picture a human body floating, suspended above the earth. The temperature is 37° C. No sound reaches it, no thoughts run through its mind, no energy is expended or required. Outside forces do not disturb its vegetative functioning in this surreal picture; it just ticks along at its basal rate. Anything that can cause a modification in its operation becomes, by definition, a stressor.

Adaptation

Just as human variations can be caused by genetic, physiological, and cultural forces, we can talk of adaptations as being produced by the same factors, although at times such a division can be rather artificial.

What is an adaptation? The answer may seem apparent at first: It is an advantageous change, some alteration that benefits the person or people involved. Often changes are adaptive in that they help maintain an equilibrium. As air temperature rises, we sweat, which cools the body; by changing we try to stay the same. Premature babies need more protein than full-term ones; the milk of mothers who have given birth prematurely has a higher-than-normal protein content, which is an adaptive response to ensure normal growth by the newborn. At a genetic level, the alterations in gene frequencies resulting from selection also are responses to environmental demands in an attempt to survive. Likewise, many cultural adaptations, such as clothing, are attempts to maintain the status quo.

Several qualifications to this definition must be considered. First, genetic adaptations occur over generations; physiological and cultural changes can happen much more rapidly. Some physiological adjustments occur almost instantly; others may take days or weeks. Culture too can change quite quickly, depending on such factors as the effectiveness and social status of the initiator. Second, genetic adaptations often are not as flexible as the other forms. As individuals, we cannot change our genes to adapt to the latest disease in our environment; for better or worse, we have a set of genes from conception to death. But adapting culturally to a new disease is possible. If penicillin will not work, for example, we develop tetracycline—a very flexible response. Exposure to a new disease also triggers physiological alterations that help fight the microbe; an increase in body temperature, or a fever, helps kill off many disease organisms in a comparatively swift response that returns us to a healthy state.

Because adaptation involves change and because all parts of an organism and population are complexly interrelated, we encounter a paradox: Sometimes a response to one stress becomes a stress itself. Sweating, an effective way of dissipating heat, can itself lead to dehydration (water loss) if a replacement water supply is not available. Drinking alcohol may be a culturally acceptable means of tolerating cold, as at a football game, but if too vigorously pursued on too many occasions it may become a problem itself, interfering with proper nutrition and liver function. Alterations may thus be adaptations from one perspective yet quite harmful changes from another.

Because of the interaction of body systems, it is also sometimes difficult to understand how a trait is adaptive at all. Some genetic traits may be common simply because they are linked (page 60) to other, beneficial genes. Sometimes, in fact, an alteration may not be adaptive at all. It would be rather silly to refer to death due to dehydration as an adaptive response to heat. In Chapter 3 we noted that there is a movement away from interpreting all features as necessarily being adaptations. Even when we know a trait is helpful, we do not always fully understand how it helps. The vast number of small blood vessels in the muscles of people living at high altitude may be an adaptation to lower oxygen pressure or lower air temperature. People and populations must deal with more than one stress at a time. Assigning the adaptations to just one of these stresses can be very difficult.

To avoid confusion in discussing genetic, physiological, and cultural responses, we will use the word *adaptation* as a general term to apply to any and all of these three mechanisms. The terms *acclimatization, developmental response,* and *adjustment* are reserved for adaptive physiological alterations made during an individual's lifetime. As we look at a wide range of stresses in this and later chapters, we will consider the ways in which the human body attempts to maintain a steady state by alterations in its functioning. The underlying assumption is that many of the adjustments—whether responses to infections, high altitude, or any other stress—represent an attempt to survive under less than ideal conditions.

Human Form and Its Development

In Chapter 2 we discussed the genetic processes that underlie adaptation at that level, but as we have seen, flexibility is often called upon in the process of adapting. It is thus necessary to consider certain aspects of the role of human growth and developmental factors in this process.

Although psychologists also study growth and development, anthropologists are more interested in the physical changes and associated variability noted throughout the life cycle. Anthropometrists, people who take body measurements, have evolved a series of standardized techniques for gathering data. Stature is one of the most obvious aspects of growth and serves well to illustrate the techniques and information of growth and development studies. Stature is determined with the person standing at attention, heels together; the back is pressed firmly against the vertical measuring rod, as is the head, so that the eyes are aimed straight ahead. The instruments are quite sophisticated to allow for precise and repeatable measurements.

Data can be expressed in terms of the amount of growth: How tall X is, in centimeters, at age A. This is referred to as *distance;* a typical distance curve is shown in Figure 11.5. If we are interested in the dynamics of the growth process, stature and other measures can be expressed in terms of velocity: How much X's stature has increased over a specified time. Velocity is commonly expressed in terms of centimeters per year, as in Figure 11.6.

Gathering data on growth in stature or any of several other anthropometric measurements is a major problem because of the time scale of human growth. It is desirable but often unrealistic to plot the growth of individuals over several decades. The investigator would have a long wait before obtaining the final data, however, and it is very difficult to

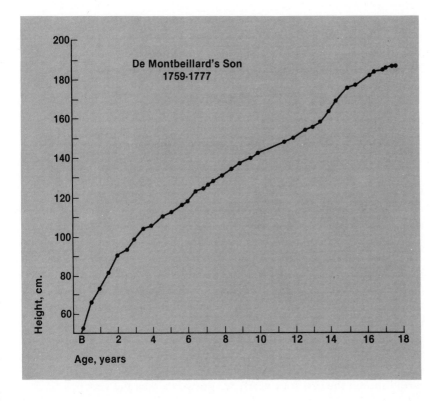

FIGURE 11.5
A distance curve, showing growth in height to age 18.
Count de Montbeillard was the first to do a longitudinal growth study.

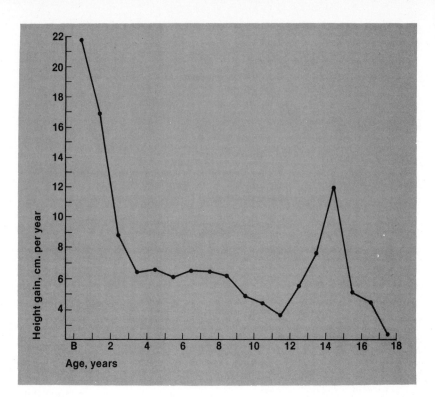

FIGURE 11.6
A velocity curve, showing centimeters grown per year to age 18. The adolescent growth spurt is clearly visible from roughly ages 12 to 15.

enlist subjects' attention and cooperation for years on end. The expense of this sort of study is also prohibitive. Longitudinal studies, ones that remeasure the same individuals at fixed intervals over long periods, are thus rare.

One alternative is a cross-sectional approach; groups of children of different age classes are each measured once, and an average measure is computed for each age group. Although cross-sectional studies need measure the child only once and can be quite useful for some purposes, they are unsuitable for studying rates of growth. Averaging obliterates individual variation; the curve of average increase in stature is a poor reflection of the growth curve of an individual child (Figure 11.7).

A third alternative is a mixed longitudinal study, which, although not a perfect solution, does help ease the problems noted. Children are followed over a period of years, but new subjects may enter and others may leave the sample; some are measured often and some only once. To decrease the number of years required, children may be divided into several overlapping age categories, say 0–6, 5–11, 10–15, and 14–20. By following all groups for five years, estimates of the growth rate can be computed for the entire age range.

From birth through early adulthood children, of course, gain in stature (Figure 11.5); however, the rate of growth is by no means constant (Figure 11.6). The classic description of normal growth is that from birth through the first four years, we grow less than the year before; we grow more slowly. There is then a plateau in growth rate for several years; each year the amount grown is about the same. There follows a further slowing until the adolescent growth spurt, when the rate of growth picks up. Finally, the rate decreases until, at roughly eighteen, we grow very little.

A graph such as Figure 11.6 leaves the impression that growth is a smooth, gradual process. Michelle Lampl and Robert Emde have recently questioned the gradual nature of growth.[6] Growth curves are generated by measuring height (or other anthropometric features) at yearly or twice-yearly intervals. A longitudinal study, for instance, may involve measuring the child on his or her birthday every year. The measurements are plotted on a graph, and a straight line is drawn between the yearly points. Lampl and Emde questioned the appropriateness of this procedure. Why, they asked, assume that during the year growth has occurred on a constant basis? Maybe some days (or weeks or months) a child grows a lot and at other times barely at all. To test this theory, they measured twenty-eight infants once or twice a week for up to a year. What they found was a very uneven rate of infant growth. Infants grow in spurts, a finding that many parents have already realized. In a matter of days an infant may grow a significant amount and then not grow at all for weeks. Others have since produced evidence that the growth of human legs follows this pattern.[7]

Information that better defines normal growth can be quite important for health practitioners as well as academics. There also was evidence in Lampl and Emde's study that the spurts in infant growth (especially

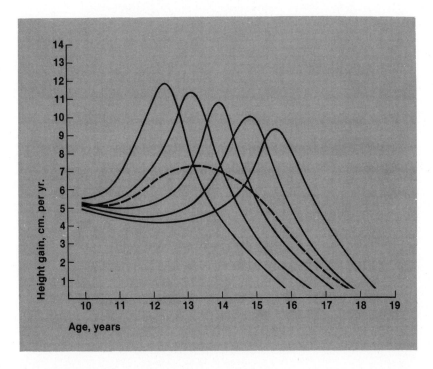

FIGURE 11.7
A curve (broken line) averaging the growth of individual children (solid lines) of the same chronological age does not reflect the growth pattern of any one child.

in the size of the head) correspond with the onset of new behaviors, an observation of great interest to psychologists.

Although many first think of growth in terms of the skeletal system, it is also possible to plot growth curves for other body systems (Figure 11.8). Different systems are under different sets of controls; while stature follows the "general curve," lymphoid tissue, such as tonsils and lymph nodes, grows quite large during adolescence and then decreases in size. The brain attains a large percentage of its maximum growth quite early (80 percent by age five) and then slowly completes its climb to full growth. Evidently the genes, hormones, and other factors controlling the brain's growth rate differ from those controlling the tissue of the immune system. In Chapter 3 we noted that much of the shift from ape to human may have involved alterations in the mechanisms that control the development of different parts of the body.

Size is not the only important aspect of growth; body composition also changes. The layer of fat immediately under the skin, the subcutaneous fat, is one aspect of body composition that changes over time. Subcutaneous fat can be measured in a variety of ways, most simply by measuring skin folds. With skin-fold calipers, the thickness of a double fold of skin and the underlying fat can be ascertained at a number of sites.

FIGURE 11.8. Growth curves for different body parts and tissues. All are distance curves plotted as a percentage of the size of that part or tissue at age 20.

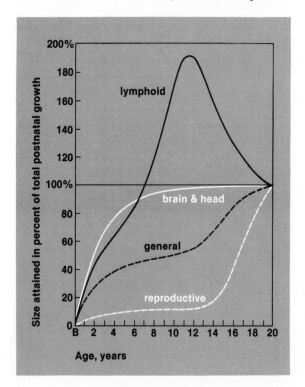

This measure is most commonly taken on the back of the upper arm, at the triceps skin fold. If the circumference of the upper arm is also obtained, the contribution of fat and muscle to limb circumference can be computed by geometric principles. One of the experts on body composition, William Mueller, says it is important to start measuring fat deposits at several points on the body because individuals and populations develop different locations for their fat stores.[8] Being able to subdivide weight gain in a growing child into its component parts, fat and lean body mass, is very important in assessing the child's health (lean body mass + fat = body weight).

Later in life, body composition is important too. It should not be news to anyone that fatness is not healthy. Obesity is often noted as a risk factor in cardiovascular diseases and hypertension (high blood pressure). The situation may not be so straightforward, however. There are indications that it is the *change* in the amount of fat that is the danger. People who as children are relatively thin and become obese adults have a much higher incidence of these disorders than people who have been obese since childhood. Adding to the complexity is the finding of Douglas Crews[9] and others that in some populations, such as American Samoans, elevated body weight and early death are not clearly related.

Women are a particularly interesting group for the study of body composition, as it may well affect their reproductive life. Some researchers have proposed that the end of adolescent growth and the onset of menses are triggered in girls by the accumulation of a threshold amount of fat. Continued menstruation is said to rely on the maintenance of a critical ratio of fat to total mass.

By studying body composition, we can gain some knowledge of the general health of a group. Linda Adair and colleagues studied changes in maternal weight and amounts of body fat in rural Taiwanese women during pregnancy and lactation.[10] Although the number of calories these women take in per day is low enough to qualify them as malnourished, the fact that they increase weight and body fat during pregnancy and lactation argues that they are well adapted.

Variation in stature and other body measurements reflects the outcome of genotype-environment interactions to produce the phenotype. Nutrition is a key environmental factor influencing growth; as the diet's adequacy is altered, children grow accordingly. In 1978, Lampl showed that the addition of protein to the diet of New Guinea children noticeably affected their height, weight, and rate of maturation. Within the limits of this study, growth speeds up in proportion to increasing degrees of protein supplementation.

It appears that we are programmed to follow, at least roughly, a particular growth curve. After periods of deprivation or ill health, we speed up the growth process when conditions permit to get back to where we should be (Figure 11.9). This is called *catch-up growth* and illustrates a phenomenon known as *canalization;* that is, the growth process has a target toward which it will move whenever possible; if prevented from reaching the goal at one time it will try to catch up later.

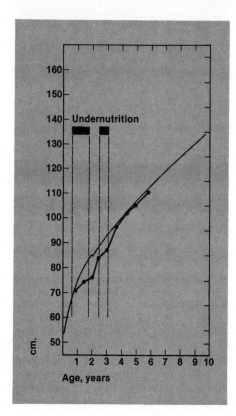

FIGURE 11.9. Catch-up growth in the height of a child who encountered two periods of retarded growth due to undernutrition. The line with dots plots growth of the child to age 7; the solid line is the average for children of the same sex in this population.

Besides nutrition, disease and climatic variables also influence the growth process. These environmental components are in turn strongly affected by political, economic, and other social institutions and cultural variables. Culturally prescribed responses to infection can have significant impact. In the United States many people switch to a bland diet, such as tea and toast, when ill. A normally well-fed American child faced with scant food intake for a few days has large stores of nutrients to fall back upon. Many children, because of poverty and urbanization, do not have these stores, however; at best their growth may be retarded, at worst they may die.

In some parts of the world children account for more than half of all deaths. In the southern Mexican highlands, for example, where Robert Malina and J. Himes found evidence of widespread malnutrition, 59 percent of all deaths occurred before the age of 15; in the United States about 950 of every 1,000 live children born will survive to at least the age of twenty. The Mexican data illustrate a significant opportunity for selection to favor the reproduction of people who are genetically most suited to survive under poor nutritional conditions. If such selection has been occurring, people may well differ in terms of what kind of diet is biologically best for them.

Growth data and anthropometric measures can vividly indicate social inequalities. In Poland, Tadeusz Bielicki and Zygmunt Welon note a clear relationship between the income, occupation, and education of parents and the growth of their children. Individuals with better educated, wealthier parents are taller and grow at a faster rate than less advantaged children.[11]

In the United States, Malina and his colleagues have documented similar trends in the Mexican-American community of San Antonio, Texas.[12] The stature of Mexican-American men and women increases with income. The women are also heavier in the lower class urban ghetto and lighter in the upper income suburbs. Comparison with the Anglos of similar social class indicates that there may be genetic differences in the pattern of fat deposition; that is, people of different ethnic backgrounds may be geared to store fat in different sites on the body. In considering "normal" growth, then, it is important to consider ethnicity as well as other variables.

Stanley Garn has also noted that poor women are generally heavier than the more affluent. Surprisingly, however, he also notes that during childhood, the opposite holds: poor *girls* are leaner than better-off *girls*. As he concludes, "childhood obesity [is] not so closely related to adult fatness as one might expect."[13]

Certainly today there are variations in the social and genetic factors that affect growth in different populations. Over time too society has changed in several ways that affect growth. The nutritious diet, advances of medicine, smaller family size, better sanitation, and child labor laws in Western societies have all contributed to a noticeable increase in both the rate at which we grow and the distance grown at any particular age (Figure 11.10), which is called the *secular trend* (*secular* here refers to time). As a population, our stature (and weight) have increased dramatically. An average fifteen-year-old white American boy in 1960 was more than 12 cm (5 in.) taller and 13 kg (30 lb) heavier than his counterpart in 1880. Our legs in particular have lengthened over the last century, disproportionately contributing to the increase in height. Comparable secular trends are seen in other Westernized countries. During wars, the secular trend can be reversed. It is even suspected that our concern for dieting, when applied to children, and the increasing cost of food may reverse the U.S. secular trend.

Sexual maturation has speeded up too. Girls attain menarche, the onset of menstruation, at about 12.5 years in the United States; in 1900, menarche was at 14. This trend is seen on a worldwide basis. For instance, between 1935 and 1980, the age at menarche dropped almost 1.5 years for Greek girls in Athens. However, data indicate that the secular trend has slowed dramatically in Western countries, if not stopped altogether. This may be for the best, for rapid growth is not necessarily beneficial; there is some evidence, for example, that dysmenorrhea, or incapacitating pain during menstruation, is associated with an early menarche in conjunction with a delayed age of first pregnancy. There are indications too that women who began menstruating very early (under twelve) have a greater rate of spontaneous abortions than women who achieved menarche at twelve to thirteen years of age. It may be that a

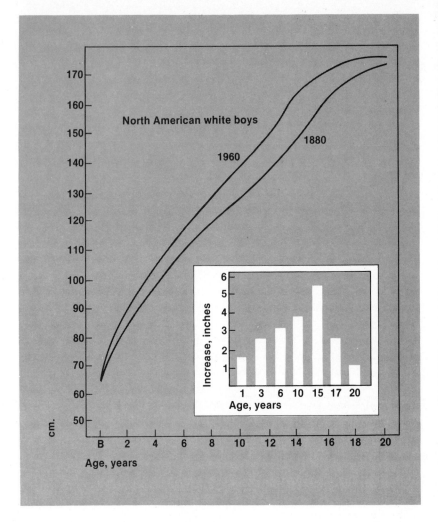

FIGURE 11.10
Curves showing the secular trend for mean height for North American white males in 1880 and 1960.
The insert shows differences between the curves at selected ages.

later maturation age allows a woman to build up a bigger fat store, which serves as an energy reserve during pregnancy.

Skeletal Variability

In Chapter 4 we pointed out that the skeletons of mammals grow in a characteristic fashion. Each bone starts out as cartilage, which over time ossifies, or turns to bone. Each bone has at least one ossification center that appears in the child at a standard stage of development. For long bones, these centers are divided into those that are present in the shaft, or diaphyses, and the terminal ones, or epiphyses. The two are separated by an area of cartilage where growth in length occurs, known as the growth cartilage. Elongation takes place as the cartilage grows at its epiphyseal edge while turning to bone at its diaphyseal border. Ultimately, the whole cartilage turns to bone, at which point growth ceases (Figure 11.11).

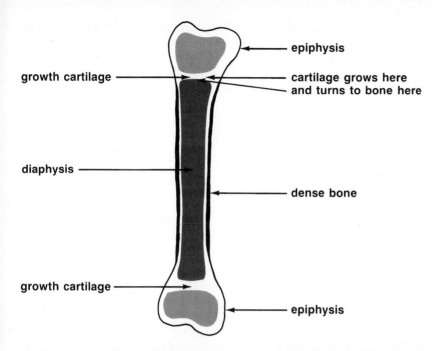

epiphysis

growth cartilage

cartilage grows here
and turns to bone here

diaphysis

dense bone

growth cartilage

epiphysis

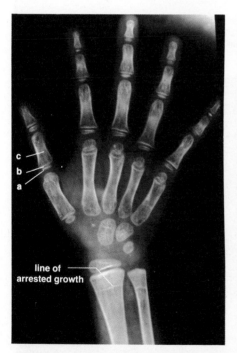

c
b
a

line of
arrested growth

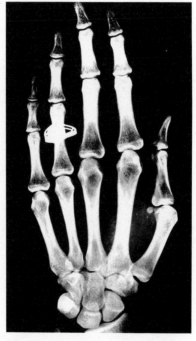

FIGURE 11.11. The epiphyses and diaphyses can be seen quite clearly on radiographs. On this radiograph (left) of the hand of an 8-year-old Japanese boy (a) is an epiphysis, (b) a growth cartilage, and (c) a diaphysis. The line of arrested growth (page 443) seen on the arm bone is attributed to injuries incurred from exposure to the atomic bomb dropped on Hiroshima. Ultimately, the growth cartilage turns to bone and the epiphysis and diaphysis fuse, as seen in the hand of an 18-year-old female (right).

Anthropologists have compiled large amounts of data to uncover the limits of variation in this pattern and the factors affecting human variability. Again, there appear to be individual-to-individual differences, population-to-population differences, and environmental and genetic differences. A person's sex too is a controlling element in skeletal growth.

Information must be gathered for a rather large number of normal children so that we can identify the boundaries of variation within a population. Once in hand, such data can be very useful in many contexts. Populations can be compared and attempts can be made to identify causes of variation.

Growth is a good indicator of health. Many disease states can be detected and monitored by following skeletal maturation via X-rays (Figure 11.12). Nutritional components of health and disease are particularly amenable to such analysis. Skeletal growth can provide a view of the health of a person or whole populations. Measuring the stature of children and comparing the findings to appropriate standards is an efficient and inexpensive way to assess the nutritional status of marginal groups and funnel resources to those in need. Continued measuring can

FIGURE 11.12. Variation in rates of skeletal maturation results from population and individual factors. Disease states also can cause a person to deviate from the norms. This is the hand of a 20-year-old zinc-deficient individual. His skeleton looks to be that of a child of about 11.

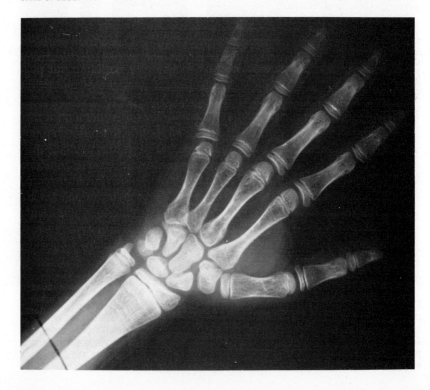

also tell us whether the expected effects are being achieved and, if not, which remedial steps should be taken. This approach to public health assessment has been widely used in the third world (Figure 11.13).

Although any appropriate epiphysis can serve to estimate skeletal age, those of the hand and wrist are quite commonly used on living people. This part of the body can be X-rayed with minimal radiation exposure and contains a number of epiphyses. Since some people mature a bit faster or slower than average, a person's skeletal age—as judged from the skeleton—might not exactly reflect the person's chronological age (Figure 11.14).

Many times archaeological deposits are sufficiently rich to provide information on the demographics of past populations. Aging of skeletal remains can help establish the frequency of infant death, sex differences in age at death, and other aspects of a group's vital statistics.

Then, too, skeletal analysis can have invaluable legal applications. A growing field within physical anthropology, but one with a long history, is called *forensic anthropology (forensic = legal)*. Among its obvious practical applications are solving crimes and identifying remains.

In all these applications, it is important to know that the standards being used are truly applicable to the individual or population in question. American black children, for instance, are born more mature skeletally than American whites, thus requiring different sets of standards.

FIGURE 11.13.   Measurements such as height and weight can be used to assess child health quickly and inexpensively.

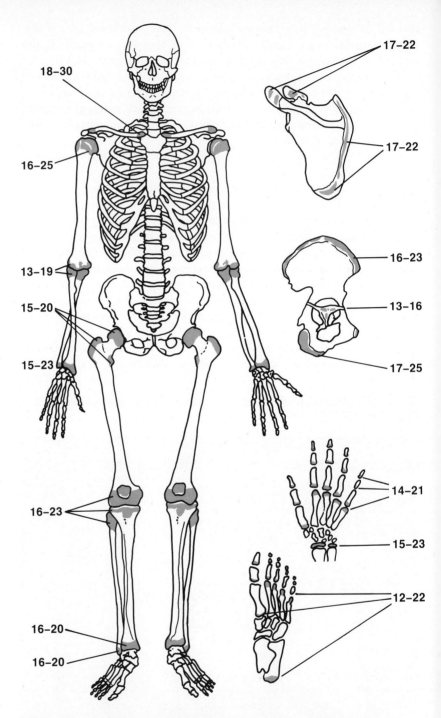

FIGURE 11.14.   Standards have been established for times of appearance and disappearance, through fusion, of epiphyses. Numbers on this chart refer to the ages, in years, when the various epiphyses fuse with the diaphyses.

Generally, children mature in a consistent fashion throughout the growth years. That is, those who are advanced (or retarded) in skeletal maturation at one age will be so at other times. Figure 11.15 shows that girls who attain menarche early are skeletally more mature not only at this time but from seven to seventeen years of age. Conversely, girls who reach menarche later than average also have skeletons that mature more slowly than average throughout the growth period.

For aging skeletal remains, the epiphyseal fusions are quite accurate. As most epiphyses are fused by eighteen years of age or are simply not available for analysis, however, other techniques are utilized. The age at which specific teeth erupt through the gums is quite constant within a population (Figure 11.16), even more so than the epiphyses. Again, children who have one tooth erupt early are likely to have all of their maturation speeded up. Tooth eruption is less affected by nutritional and disease factors than skeletal maturation. Looking at the teeth can help to estimate age in populations that do not keep track of time. For forensic and archaeological purposes, teeth, being very hard, are likely to last in the ground. The drawback is that once all the teeth have erupted, there

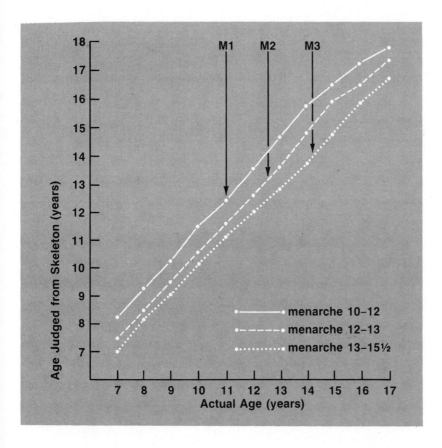

FIGURE 11.15
On the average, girls who show early skeletal maturation also achieve menarche early. Late maturers as judged from the skeleton also achieve menarche late. (M1, M2, and M3 indicate the average age of menarche for the three groups.)

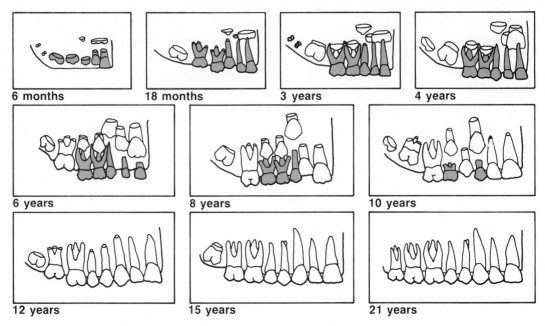

6 months **18 months** **3 years** **4 years**

6 years **8 years** **10 years**

12 years **15 years** **21 years**

FIGURE 11.16. Average pattern of eruption of deciduous (baby) and permanent teeth. Shaded teeth are deciduous.

is little upon which to base an age estimate. All one can say when faced with a fully erupted set of teeth is that the person is more than eighteen years old.

The skeleton can provide information other than age or maturity. In archaeological and forensic contexts, it can be very useful for the sex typing of skeletal materials. A variety of aspects can be looked at in this regard, but the most diagnostic, not surprisingly, are in the pelvis. Most of these features of course relate to the fact that women need a bigger pelvic outlet to allow for births. Hence, on the average, their sciatic notch and pelvic angles are bigger than in men of the same population. The brim of the pelvis is more circular in women as well. A well-trained anthropologist can correctly assign the sex to a pelvis about 95 percent of the time. With a whole skeleton, the right sex can be deduced in about 99 percent of the cases.

Aspects of the skeleton such as its rate of maturation are certainly influenced by both genes and environment. Some environmental components that affect growth have been discussed. Likewise, we know that identical twin sisters reach menarche at very similar ages, while dizygotic twin sisters average ten-month differences in the age of menarche. Skeletal and dental features also mature at very similar times in identical twins. The fact that different populations have somewhat different standards for maturation, even when living in similar environments, argues for the impact of genetic effects.

Anthropometrists have devised many other measures of the human frame. Although originally developed to distinguish "racial types" of people, that is, to establish typologies, many of these measures have new uses today. Human engineers need to make many measurements to fit machinery and clothing to the average person. Automotive companies, for example, use such information to place steering wheels, rear view mirrors, and seat backs in positions that will best suit most potential users.

Measurements may also be used to track variations over time, such as the secular trends noted earlier. The causes of these trends are at least partially due to changes in diet, child labor laws, and health care. They may also have a genetic component, as is seen in the increased growth and earlier maturation resulting from the breakdown of mechanisms that kept earlier populations genetically isolated.

Summary

This chapter provides an introduction to the study of modern human variability. We see that variation can be studied at a multitude of levels, ranging from the molecular to the organismal, and from the perspective of individuals, populations, or even species. Causes of variation are reviewed and found to be in part affected by the level at which we are studying variation. In some senses and examples, evolutionary factors are the cause of variation, but often one can answer the question "Why variation?" within other frameworks. In the case of human beings, environmental factors (and these can be very varied) contribute to differences among people. The environment can include other organisms, internal factors, cultural features and so on, in addition to the physical world.

Much human variability appears to be related to responses to stressors. Long-term stressors can result in built-in solutions in the genes through the operation of natural selection. Much more rapid responses may be made through cultural or nongenetic biological responses. Earlier chapters discussed the genetic aspects of adaptation. In this chapter we investigated growth and developmental responses. We find that variations in response are affected by factors including one's hereditary background, sex, age, diet, and state of health. There are variations too in the ways different parts of the body grow and hence in the ways they can respond to stressors.

The analysis of human variability in general and in growth aspects in particular can have very practical as well as theoretical applications. We can see the boundaries of human physiological plasticity and cultural and genetical adaptability. We can also use the data to assess the health of modern and archaeological populations. There are legal applications in human identification and engineering applications as well.

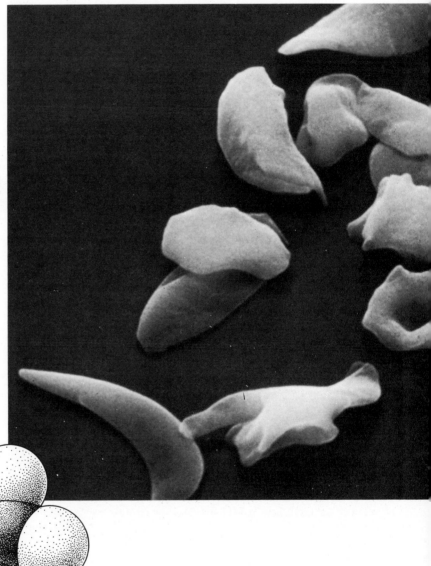

The tremendous variability among people and populations testifies to the wealth of human genetic variation.

Human Polymorphisms

Darwin was not the first to consider the possibility that organisms evolved. Unlike his predecessors, however, he was struck by the importance of variation's role in the evolutionary process. He realized that it was the heritable variations that provided the raw material for natural selection. As we have seen, however, Darwin was not aware of Mendel's work and resultingly was unable to integrate the genetic mechanisms described in Chapter 2 into his theory of evolution by natural selection.

The twentieth century has seen not only the rediscovery of Mendel's work and its application to evolutionary theory in general but also the collection of massive data on human genetic variability. As we have seen, traits that are solely the result of genetic variability are referred to as genetic polymorphisms if there are at least two alleles for the trait and if neither occurs at greater than a 99 percent frequency. As individuals may differ in their allelic composition, these variable traits can be used as *genetic markers* to trace relationships. These traits can be tested for presence or absence in individuals and, by summation, in populations. Although we might not always know their function, they can still be used to describe groups. By aggregation, genetic markers can also be used to trace affinities between whole populations.

The discovery of genetic markers has often been the offshoot of medical research in fields such as immunology and biochemistry. However, information on genetic variability, once discovered can be used to investigate specific anthropological aims. The result is that we now have a tremendous inventory of information on genetically based variability in many populations of our species (and, although not covered here, in our close relatives too).

Anthropologists, as noted in the last chapter, tend to look at this information in an evolutionary framework, asking questions such as: What are the evolutionary causes of similarities and differences between populations? Is there an adaptive explanation for the patterns of variation seen? How have factors such as a group's history or mating practices affected its genetic composition? In this chapter we shall introduce some of the data on a variety of genetic polymorphisms and, to the extent possible, discuss the evolutionary forces underlying modern human variability. There is not only academic or historical interest in telling the story of polymorphisms but also very significant practical applications and lessons to be learned. Differences in resistance to disease, appropriate delivery of health care, control of the spread of new epidemics such as AIDS, and prenatal diagnosis of disorders are all affected by this knowledge, as is much of the tissue transplantation biology. By adopting a somewhat different orientation to such important matters, the anthropologist can help provide a clear and more complete understanding of the issues. There are also legal applications of the anthropologist's knowledge, who can be an expert in human identification. This role may involve the anthropologist in identifying remains of the dead or helping to assign parentage; in either situation knowledge of individual or population molecular and genetic variability can be of great importance.

Blood and Blood Groups

Physical anthropologists have a reputation for having rather sanguine tastes because of the attention they pay to blood. Actually there are some very good reasons for this fascination. For one, several milliliters of blood can be tested for dozens of genetic traits to provide information on variation. Blood is easy to collect; people are much more willing to part with blood than with muscle, although in some cultures there may be strong resistance to allowing blood drawing. For our purposes, the environmental effects on blood type are minimal. If we know a person's phenotype we have a very good indication of his or her genetic composition. This is not true of continuous traits, like height or weight, for which variation falls along a continuum. Knowledge of traits that are almost exclusively affected by genes affords us a greater ability to focus on the causes of evolutionary change.

All the traits referred to as blood group systems deal with classes of molecules on the surface of the red blood cell; they have nothing to do with the molecules inside the red cells. Hemoglobin is not a blood group system. Dozens of blood group systems are known, and each of us has a genotype and phenotype for every system. For MN everyone has M and/or N molecules, depending on the genotype; for Rh, Rh+ and/or Rh−; for ABO, some combination of A, B, and/or O molecules. The surface of red blood cells, or *erythrocytes,* is pictured schematically in Figure 12.1.

Classification or typing of a person according to which molecular forms are present on the red cells depends on antigen–antibody reactions. The antigen and antibody are mutually defining: An antigenic molecule is recognized by an animal's immunological system as a foreign substance, to which it reacts by producing an antibody. Antibodies are the substances produced to counteract antigens.

Although the mechanics of antigen recognition and antibody production are not completely understood or controllable, much research is going on in immunology. In early life the individual's immune system is

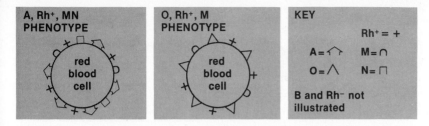

FIGURE 12.1. Two phenotypes of red blood cells. The various blood types result from the attachment of different molecules to the surface of red blood cells. Each of the many blood group systems (ABO, Rh, MN, etc.) represents a series of related molecular forms.

programmed to recognize "self." The substances in the fetus are locked into its immunological memory as "normal." Other substances, such as some bacteria, viruses, and foods, come to be recognized as "not self," and upon exposure to these foreign substances later in life, antibodies are produced to banish them from the body. In MN blood groups, the M and N substances are antigenic: M substance introduced into someone who is not type M will cause anti-M antibodies to be made, and N substance will cause the production of anti-N antibodies in non-N individuals. The isolation and use of these antibodies give us a method for distinguishing among people according to MN type.

When a test tube of blood is revolved at high speed, the denser materials are forced to the outside of the circle of revolution (to the bottom of the tube) and lighter materials move closer to the axis of revolution. Three noticeable layers are formed (Figure 12.2). At the bottom of the tube are the heavy red blood cells. Next are white blood cells, important in preventing disease. Uppermost is the fluid portion, which we can call the *serum.* Floating in the serum are many types of molecules, such as antibodies, hormones, and molecules that transport iron. When we take some serum from a person of known blood type and add it to a drop of blood to be tested, one of two things will happen. The serum may mix freely with the red cells with no noticeable change, or the mixture may *agglutinate,* that is, the red blood cells clump together. If we run this test with serum from a type M person, who is making antibodies to

FIGURE 12.2. After centrifugation, three layers are visible in a tube of blood: the heavy red blood cells, a thinner layer of white blood cells, and the fluid blood serum.

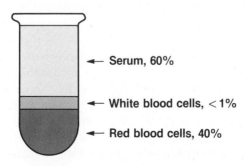

← Serum, 60%

← White blood cells, <1%

← Red blood cells, 40%

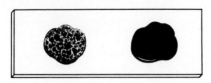

	Reaction with	
Blood type	Anti-M	Anti-N
M	+	−
N	−	+
MN	+	+

FIGURE 12.3. In typing blood for MN blood groups, two drops of a person's blood were placed on a slide. To one drop, antibody to M was added; to the other, anti-N. The anti-M reacted with the blood, causing the clumping or agglutination of the red blood cells (left), while the anti-N did not react with it (right). In other words, the anti-M recognized M substance on these cells, while anti-N did not find any N substance with which to react. Therefore, this person has type M blood.

N (simply called anti-N), and then repeat it using serum from a type N person making anti-M, we can correctly type the blood of any other person for the MN trait. If the sample is agglutinated by anti-M but not by anti-N, it is type M: The molecules on the red blood cells reacted with the anti-M antibodies. Figure 12.3 lists the possible reactions. Tests for other blood group systems may differ slightly because antibodies are a highly heterogenous group of molecules and act in several ways. For example, some, instead of causing agglutination, make the red blood cells break open; others operate best at specific temperatures. Remember, in these tests we are looking for the presence or absence of the antigen on the person's red cells; we are not testing for which antibodies the person has.

Variable characteristics such as blood groups have been used in many studies of human variation because they are easy to test. Furthermore, they are completely genetic, and thus we can explain their variability because it is not compounded by the effects of the environment.

Dozens of blood group systems are known, but we will deal with only a few anthropologically important ones.

The ABO Group

This most widely discussed blood group was discovered in 1900 by Karl Landsteiner, but the precise mode of inheritance was not explained until 1924. This trait is controlled by three alleles A, B, and O, of which each of us has two. The A and B alleles are codominant; that is, they do not mask each other's expression. Because both are dominant over O, there are six genotypes and four phenotypes (Table 12.1).

The ABO alleles produce proteins that result in the attachment of different sugar molecules to a blood group's "core" molecule. What we refer to as A, B, or O substances are not the direct product of the genes (genes produce only proteins), but the result of the gene product's action.

Typing for ABO is a little more complex than for MN, for there are three alleles (A, B, O) but only two antigens (A and B substances) and thus two antibodies. O substance is not antigenic. It is not recognized as a foreign substance by the immune system of anybody, even those who do not have the O allele; hence there is no anti-O. Antibodies to type A substance cause type A cells to clump together. If a blood sample is clumped only by anti-A, the antibody was able to combine with a molecule (A substance) present on the red cells. Having A molecules, the person is type A. Likewise, anti-B clumps type B cells, and AB cells are clumped by either antibody. Type O cells are not affected by either antibody (Figure 12.4). People who are type A will normally have anti-B in their blood as a defense against B substance, which does not belong in them. They will not make anti-A, which would make their own cells clump. The characteristics of the other ABO blood types are set forth in Table 12.2.

At this time, we cannot routinely distinguish AA from AO or BB from BO individuals except possibly by analyzing the blood types of the person's genetic relatives. A person who is AO has just as many A sugar molecules as one who is AA.

One feature in the ABO system may have very important evolutionary implications: Most of us have antibodies against the antigens we lack. ABO antibodies are important not only for their clinical uses but also because their natural occurrence may determine differential susceptibility to disease. If, as some research has indicated, the structure of A substance is like that of a substance found on the syphilis disease organism, people of blood types A and AB cannot produce antibodies to syphilis as readily as type B and O individuals. Moreover, the latter have

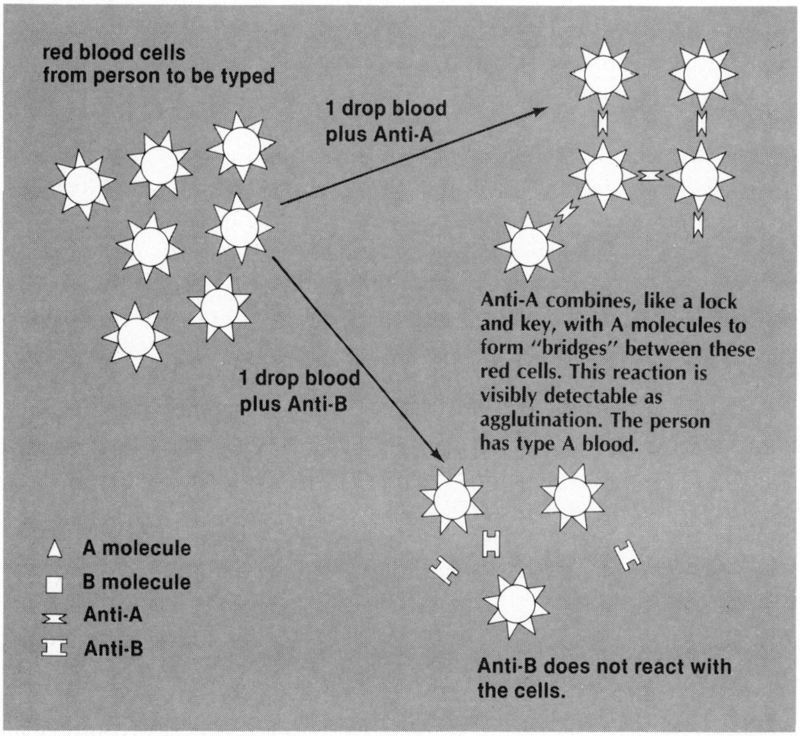

TABLE 12.1
ABO Genotypes and Phenotypes

Genotype	Phenotype
AA ⎫ AO ⎭	A
BB ⎫ BO ⎭	B
AB	AB
OO	O

red blood cells from person to be typed

1 drop blood plus Anti-A

Anti-A combines, like a lock and key, with A molecules to form "bridges" between these red cells. This reaction is visibly detectable as agglutination. The person has type A blood.

1 drop blood plus Anti-B

△ A molecule
☐ B molecule
⚡ Anti-A
⚏ Anti-B

Anti-B does not react with the cells.

FIGURE 12.4
Typing viewed at a molecular level.

TABLE 12.2
ABO Blood Typing
A person's ABO blood type is determined by combining one drop of blood with anti-A and one drop with anti-B. Noting which of the antibodies causes clumping or agglutination (+) and which does not (−) tells us that person's ABO type. The antibodies normally present in the blood stream, as a defense mechanism, are also noted.

Blood Type	Antibody Normally in Blood	Reaction with	
		Anti-A	Anti-B
A	Anti-B	+	−
B	Anti-A	−	+
AB	None	+	+
O	Anti-A Anti-B	−	−

circulating anti-A antibodies that can attack the syphilis microbe almost immediately after exposure. In fact, we all have antibodies to the A or B antigens we lack because we are exposed to A- and B-like substances on bacteria, viruses, and foods we all encounter.

Computing ABO gene frequencies is slightly more complex than for a two-allele trait. We cannot simply count the alleles as we did with the MN system (see page 69). We do have ways of computing the ABO gene frequencies from the phenotype frequencies, however. The frequencies of the alleles are highly variable from population to population around the world, as Figures 12.5–12.7 show. Note that it is not at all uncommon to find neighboring populations with significantly different frequencies. Most Native American populations have very high frequencies of type O blood, low frequencies of A, and almost no B, for example. But the Blackfoot Indians have the world's highest frequency of A, little O, and no B, and Eskimo populations from Alaska to Greenland show frequencies of B ranging from 1 percent to 5 percent. The fact that many unrelated populations have similar frequencies of one or more blood group alleles while related groups differ shows that the frequencies must be affected by a variety of evolutionary forces. Recent common ancestry can, but does not always, result in similar frequencies. Blood group alleles must thus be considered in light of other data when trying to reconstruct population relationships.

The Rh Group

Another blood group system familiar to most people is the Rhesus, or Rh, system. First discovered in 1939, it is one of the most complexly inherited and clinically important blood group systems.

The system was first studied when a woman, after a stillbirth, developed a severe reaction to a transfusion of her husband's ABO-compatible blood. That is, the blood she was receiving contained an antigen against which she had previously produced antibodies. Because she and

(Text continues on page 474)

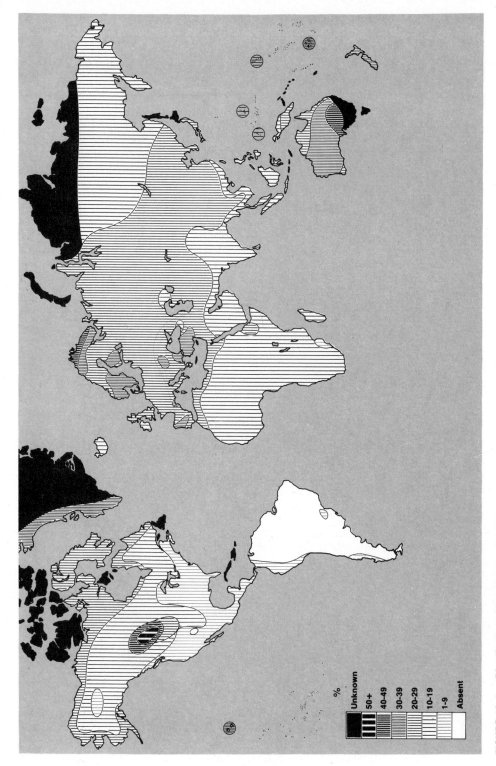

FIGURE 12.5. Distribution of blood group A allele.

FIGURE 12.6. Distribution of blood group B allele.

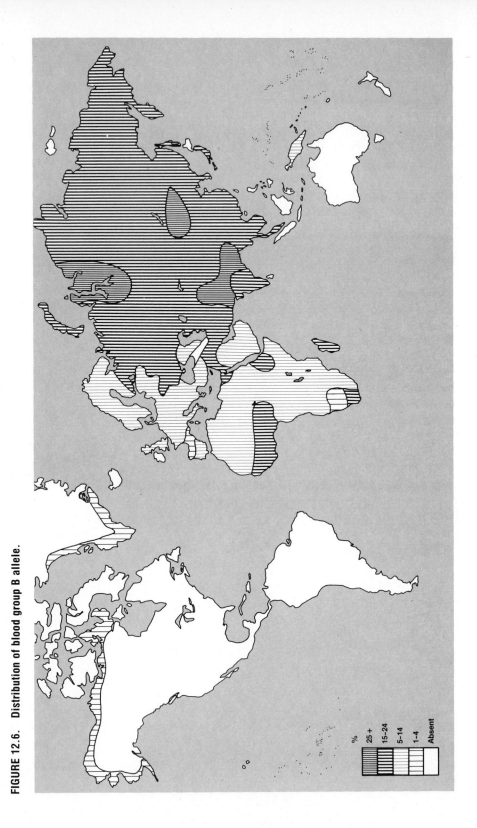

%
25 +
15–24
5–14
1–4
Absent

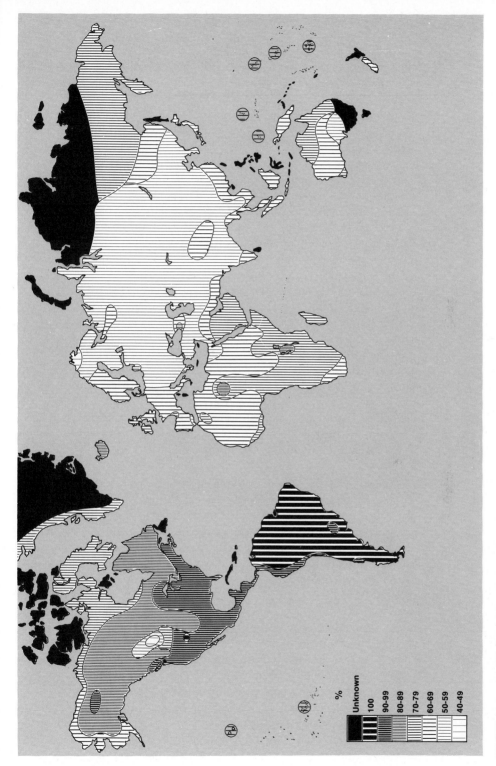

FIGURE 12.7.   Distribution of blood group O allele.

her husband had the same ABO type, she could not have been reacting to the ABO antigens. Her immune system had found some other substance on her husband's red blood cells to be foreign and reacted by producing antibodies against it. Because this agglutination was not correlated with any known blood system, a new blood group system was hypothesized and later named Rh.

Even today we are not certain about the details of the genetics of Rh. One view holds that the Rh antigens are controlled by three closely linked sets of genes, each with two or more alleles. The most common alleles, known as C, c, D, d, E, and e, are inherited as a linkage group such as cde, CDE, and CdE, so that each individual has two such complexes, one maternal and one paternal. The common concept of Rh positive and Rh negative is a function of the D and d alleles only. Those with at least one D allele are Rh+; those who are homozygous recessives, or dd, are Rh−. When blood is referred to as positive or negative, the terms relate to Rh type; as with type O blood, there is no antibody against Rh−.

Unlike ABO, we do not produce antibodies to the Rh antigens we do not possess until we are directly exposed to the antigens by blood transfusion or pregnancy. Evidently, the Rh molecules are much rarer in nature than antigens A and B.

Figures 12.8 and 12.9 show the frequencies of several of the more common chromosome complexes. CDe reaches very high frequencies in Europe and hits its lowest levels in sub-Saharan Africa. It is also very common in Asiatics and Native Americans. The complex cDe reverses the pattern, being most common south of the Sahara and rare elsewhere. The complex cde reaches its highest frequencies in Europe, is uncommon in Africa, and is absent in Asia and the Americas.

The MNS Group

In the examples used for figuring gene frequencies (see page 69), we referred to a seemingly simple system, MN. After the complexities of Rh and ABO, this seems a pleasantly understandable system. Life is not so simple, however. One major modification to the two-allele, codominant situation mentioned is the presence of a second linked trait called S. Here, too, are two alleles, S and s, which are codominant. Thus, instead of two alleles (M and N), there are four complexes, analogous to those of Rh: MS, Ms, NS, Ns. Chemical studies of M and N substances seem to show that they, like ABO, involve sugars bound to amino acids. It also seems that, as with ABO, the difference between M and N antigens results from the attachment of different sugars to a blood group "core." Several chemists have shown that type M cells react weakly with anti-N. Our knowledge of how the MN genes work is thus incomplete.

The worldwide frequencies of M and N are highly variable, making this trait most useful in characterizing peoples from different regions. The frequency of M ranges from less than 30 percent in Australian Aborigines to more than 90 percent in some Native American groups (Figures 12.10 and 12.11).

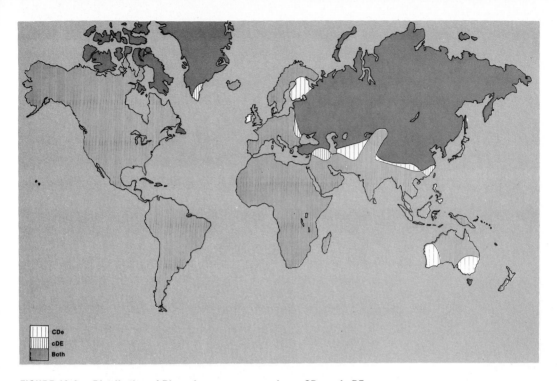

FIGURE 12.8.   Distribution of Rh + chromosome complexes CDe and cDE.

FIGURE 12.9.   Distribution of Rh + chromosome complex cDe and the Rh −
chromosome complex cde.

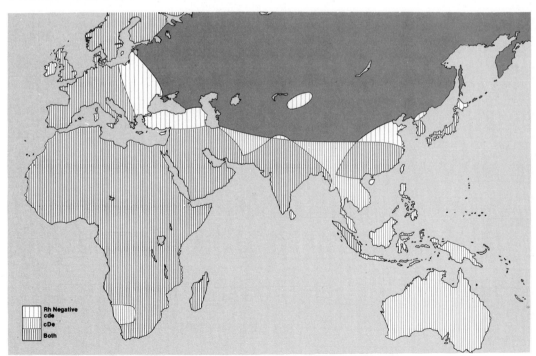

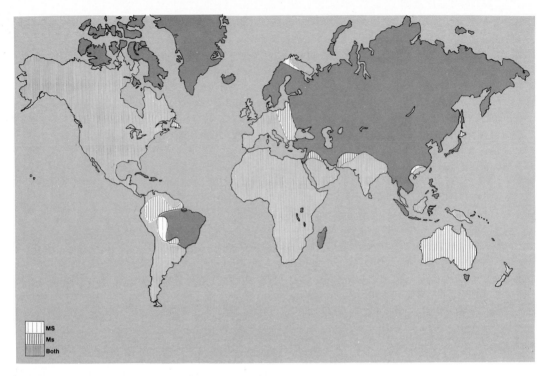

FIGURE 12.10.   Distribution of the MS and Ms complexes.

FIGURE 12.11.   Distribution of the NS and Ns complexes.

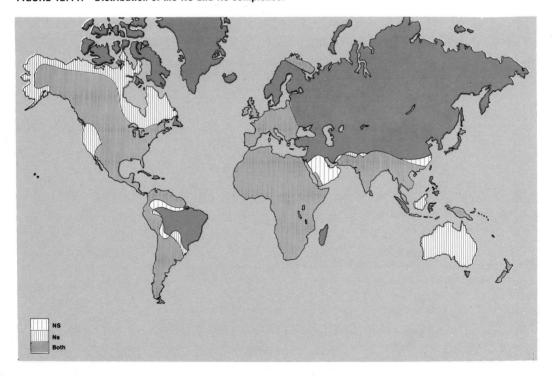

Many other blood groups are known to exist but are not generally considered very important for several reasons. Some are not well understood genetically. Others have been ignored primarily because they have not much medical significance. ABO and Rh are of great clinical importance not only for blood transfusions but also because of their correlations with diseases. Most of the lesser systems are rarely important in transfusions and, as far as we know, are not associated with susceptibility to disease. Many of these blood groups also have a common allele found in most people and are therefore of little use in describing or measuring population characteristics or affinities.

Less Important Groups

The Diego, Sutter, and Duffy Groups The Diego antigen, Di^a, has a unique worldwide distribution: It is found at appreciable frequencies in the blood of native New World inhabitants and Asians. In this way its distribution agrees well with the postulated Asian derivation of Native Americans. Its absence in Eskimos may be due to genetic drift.

The Sutter blood group system also has a unique distribution: the resulting antigen is found mostly in sub-Saharan Africans, especially those from West Africa.

In the Duffy system, the blood of many Africans lacks an antigen that most other populations have. It appears that the absence of this antigen can be helpful, because it keeps certain forms of malarial parasites from successfully invading the host's red blood cells. Such blood group systems can thus not only help illustrate a population's adaptations, but also serve as useful markers to trace migrations and biological relationships between populations.

The Xg Group This is the only blood group system known to be sex-linked in humans. As with hemophilia and color blindness, males have only one Xg allele; whereas females have two. Like many other less-publicized systems, it was first discovered in a person who had received many Rh-, MNS-, and ABO-compatible transfusions yet produced antibodies against something in some units of transfused blood. All known blood groups could be ruled out as the cause of the reaction, leading to a successful search for a new antigen.

The antigen discovered, now called Xg^a, was found to have the complicated distribution of a sex-linked trait: unequal representation in the sexes. The "silent" or, so far as we know, recessive allele of Xg^a is signified as Xg.

Several attempts have been made to locate the blood group traits on specific chromosomes or to determine which other traits they are close to on a chromosome. Those on the X chromosome are the easiest to identify because of their distinctive distribution between the sexes. It is also possible to find the position of Xg in relation to other sex-linked traits, such as hemophilia, color blindness, an enzyme deficiency disorder, and a pigment disorder of the eye. We build linkage maps by seeking *recombinants,* or offspring that show recombinations of traits. We can tell

Linkage Maps

whether the alleles for hemophilia and color blindness are on the same X chromosome or on different members of the pair in the daughter (Figure 12.12). If the father shows both of these disorders, the alleles are on the same chromosome; if he has only one of the abnormal alleles, the other must have been derived from the daughter's mother; therefore, one variant is carried on each X.

Once this information is gathered, we can measure the distance between the two traits by other techniques. If the daughter's genetic structure is like that shown in possibility 1 of Figure 12.12, most of her sons will inherit either the fully normal or the doubly abnormal X. Sometimes, however, a son will exhibit only one of the traits. This change is caused by a breakage of both members of a chromosome pair and a cross-reunion, or cross-over, between the X chromosomes during meiosis in the woman. We expect the frequency of the occurrence of such recombinants to be proportional to the distance separating the traits. The farther from each other two traits are, the more likely it is that the chromosome will break in the intervening space. Chromosomes can be broken and reunited by a variety of factors, including temperature, nutrition, and the age of the parents.

Mapping the nonsex chromosomes is far more difficult. Several linkage groups have been uncovered, however, that involve blood groups. ABO alleles are located on chromosome 9 and are linked to a gene causing an abnormality of the fingernails and kneecaps. Rh alleles are on chromosome 1 and are linked to genes that cause deformed red blood cells.

FIGURE 12.12. The inheritance pattern of two sex-linked traits (hemophilia and color blindness) depends on whether the alleles are on the same member of a pair of chromosomes (left) or different members (right).

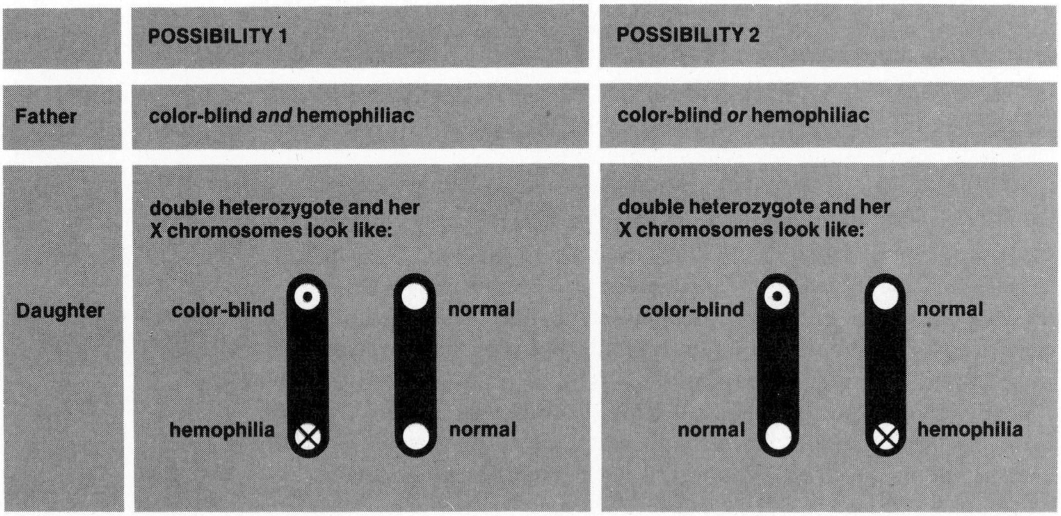

	POSSIBILITY 1	POSSIBILITY 2
Father	color-blind *and* hemophiliac	color-blind *or* hemophiliac
Daughter	double heterozygote and her X chromosomes look like:	double heterozygote and her X chromosomes look like:

Knowing about these linkage groups can be very important clinically. If it is known that the allele for a blood type is on the same chromosome as a harmful allele in a specific mating, the fetus can be blood typed while it is still in the uterus to determine if it too is suffering from the disorder. We cannot always detect fetal defects in this way, but when it is possible, preparation can be made for treatment at birth, or, if the defect is severe, abortion may be chosen. From an anthropological point of view, medical techniques like this one exemplify cultural adaptations to biological problems. Selective mechanisms are culturally modified to reduce the occurrence of genetic defects.

Blood Groups and Evolution

Documenting evolutionary change for the blood group alleles and trying to explain why allele frequencies differ are seemingly unending tasks. Based on the long-held view that all variability is somehow adaptive, many researchers have worked hard to understand why blood group allele frequencies are so variable. While selection is certainly involved to some degree, it is also apparent that population structure has played a role as well. Trying to decide whether the allele frequencies in a population are primarily a reflection of natural selection, other forces, or some combination is exceptionally difficult.

In looking for the operation of selection, scientists have used several approaches. First are the studies that try to show a correlation between a blood group allele, say A, and an increased or decreased susceptibility to a disease, such as smallpox. These studies rely on statistical analysis but are based on laboratory demonstrations of structural similarities between blood group substances and the antigens on disease organisms.

Another technique demonstrates by elaborate statistical analysis that blood group alleles and phenotypes are not randomly distributed according to some variable, such as month of birth, other genetic traits, or birth weight. If the results are significant, the relationship of the variable to the blood group still has to be explained in biological terms.

The third kind of analysis uses a computer to simulate evolution. This requires making some assumptions about the populations and the fitnesses and frequencies of the genotypes.

The associations that have been found in the studies are not always repeatable. Some experts say that all would-be selective forces are invalid except for one well-documented, incompletely understood example. This one universally accepted selective agent is known as Rh maternal-fetal incompatibility.

Rh Incompatibility and Natural Selection

A person can produce high *titer,* or high strength, antibodies against foreign blood group substances. This immunological response is usually desirable, as when bacteria are carrying foreign blood-group-like molecules, but it can have unfortunate consequences when a mother is carrying a fetus of unlike blood type.

Rh incompatibility appears when an Rh− mother (dd) carries an Rh+ (Dd) fetus. The anti-D antibodies of the mother can cross the placental barrier and attack the red blood cells of the fetus, causing a disorder known as erythroblastosis foetalis, or hemolytic anemia of the newborn. This anemia, a reduction in red blood cells, comes about because the mother's antibodies break open the newborn's red blood cells (hemolysis). It can range from a mild to a fatal form; when fatal, it usually kills shortly before or after birth.

Although no blood flows directly between mother and fetus, the placenta provides for a very close apposition of blood supplies; fetal red cells can leak into the mother's system around the time of birth. Assuming the Rh− mother has never received an improper blood transfusion of Rh+ blood, she is initially sensitized at the time her first Rh+ child is born. As it takes some time for the newborn's Rh+ red blood cells to stimulate the mother to produce anti-D antibodies, this first incompatible baby is safe from hemolytic disease; it is out of the uterus by the time the mother is making anti-D. Now the problem has started, for the woman's immune system has learned how to make anti-D, and the antibody will be circulating in her bloodstream. This antibody consists of small molecules that can cross the placenta from mother to fetus. By her second or third incompatible pregnancy, enough antibody is present to cross the placental barrier and harm the fetal red blood cells. This sort of reaction does not occur in the reverse incompatible type (Rh+ mother, Rh− infant), because there does not seem to be an anti-Rh− antibody, or if it does exist it is very weak or cannot cross the placenta.

Every incompatible pregnancy involves a heterozygous fetus. The mother is Rh− and therefore can give only d to the fetus. To be incompatible is to say the fetus is Rh+: It has a D allele from the father. The genotype is Dd. Each time a fetus or a newborn dies, one D and one d allele are thus selected out of the population. The net outcome should eventually be fixation of the allele initially present at the highest frequency at 100 percent and the rarer allele at zero. Because the alleles are being lost in equal numbers, the rarer one disappears first. This result, however, does not seem to have occurred (Figure 12.9). Although before European contact Native American, East Asian, and Oceania populations lacked the Rh− allele, many other populations are maintaining both D and d. We therefore have to ask why our theory does not fit reality. Selection should be reducing the frequency of d to zero in low-d areas such as sub-Saharan Africa, but d is still around. The reply that d is a transient polymorphism that is decreasing but at a very slow rate does not make much sense, for this polymorphism has undoubtedly been with us for a very long time. Are there any factors that would retard the rate at which d is eliminated or support it as part of a balanced polymorphism?

A Selective Interaction:
Rh and ABO

We do have some further tentative clues on the Rh polymorphism, which we owe to the pioneering work of Philip Levine and A. S. Wiener and more recently that of Bernice Cohen. It has been known for some

TABLE 12.3
The Likelihood that Various Maternal-Fetal Incompatibilities Will Result in Fetal Death, Judged from Available Data

Incompatibilities	Likelihood of Fetal Death
Neither ABO nor Rh incompatible	Least likely
Both Rh and ABO incompatible	
ABO incompatible	
Rh incompatible	Most likely

time that a hemolytic anemia can be caused by ABO incompatibility when, for example, a type O mother carries an A fetus. All ABO phenotype combinations are incompatible when the fetus carries an antigen absent in the mother. The causes of the disorder are generally much the same as in Rh incompatibility, except that (1) the mother will usually already be producing antibodies to the antigen she lacks, and (2) ABO incompatibility usually produces abortion early in fetal life. Rh incompatibility, on the other hand, affects developed fetuses and the newborn.

As long ago as 1943, P. Levine postulated that maternal-fetal pairs doubly incompatible for ABO and Rh ran less risk of fetal death than those incompatible for only one system.[1]* Statistical data for some populations support this contention. Due to interactions between the systems, children who are incompatible with the mother for both ABO and Rh have a better chance of surviving than those who are incompatible at just one or the other (Table 12.3).

Such results do not negate the predicted but unfulfilled movement toward fixation for Rh + or Rh − alleles. They do illustrate that selection on this trait is not as simple as we might like to think. More generally it proves that because of epistasis (see page 440) we cannot consider an allele's selective worth in isolation. The benefits of one ABO blood type over another depend at least partly on a person's Rh blood type.

The Rh maternal-fetal incompatibilities that become medically significant appear to be confined to people of European ancestry, while medically noted ABO incompatibilities are more common in Africans. In fact, the protective effect of the double incompatibility we have described does not seem to apply to a population in India recently tested.[2] These phenomena indicate further genetic complications. Far from operating in isolation, gene products interact with one another. The overall reproductive ability of one's alleles can be quite different from what we might expect simply by looking at each set of alleles as an isolated factor.

Besides the well-documented maternal-fetal incompatibilities for both Rh and ABO, little has been definitively proven about blood groups and selection. Several other possibilities relate Rh and disease; these are joined by a huge number of preliminary correlations of ABO types and disease. Many researchers feel that natural selection must be maintaining

Noninfectious Disorders

*See page 628 for notes to Chapter 12.

the ABO allele frequencies in human populations. It is a long jump, though, from intuition to proof.

Several studies have shown that people of different ABO phenotypes are unequally susceptible to noninfectious disorders. Type O people are up to 40 percent more likely to develop duodenal ulcers than other people. They also more commonly have gastric ulcers, at least in the Western societies studied. Type O women taking birth control pills appear less likely to develop blood clots as a side effect than women of other blood types. Group A individuals, on the other hand, seem predisposed to cancer of the stomach and cervix, ovarian tumors, and pernicious anemia. Many of the associations are related to either the gastrointestinal tract or the female reproductive organs; also, large quantities of A or B substances are found in the stomach lining, ovarian cysts, and saliva of some people. The significance of this association is not yet apparent. These disorders seem to have no evolutionary significance, for most of them strike relatively late in life, after the reproductive years.

ABO and Infectious Diseases

The more promising approach seems to be demonstrating antigenic similarities between A or B substances and molecules found on bacteria, viruses, and parasites. In 1959 two doctors at Walter Reed Army Hospital demonstrated that the bacteria *Escherichia coli 086* reacted strongly with anti-B. Anti-B antibodies can kill this bacterium because it has on its surface a sugar molecule very similar to the B sugar molecule. Type B and AB people infected with it cannot make antibodies against this part of the bacterium because they would also destroy their own red blood cells. A and O people, on the other hand, already have or are able to make antibodies against this sugar on the bacterium's surface. Because *E. coli 086* is one of the organisms that cause diarrhea in the newborn, a potentially lethal disease, this selection might favor blood types O and A. But the problem is not that simple. Bacteria do not have just one surface molecule that can stimulate the host's immune system. We have to ask, therefore, whether the ability to produce anti-B affects the newborn's ability to survive diarrhea. Let us assume that this bacterium has ten molecules that a type A person's immune system can recognize and produce antibodies against. Type B and AB people can react to all except the one that is like B substance. How important is it to be able to react to the B antigen? One thing we can do is test the efficiency of antibodies directed against all ten molecules and then compare their ability to kill the bacterium with that of antibodies directed against all but the B-like substance. When this was done, the researchers found that the drop in bactericidal (bacteria-killing) effect was slight but noticeable (Figure 12.13). Type B individuals may be slightly more susceptible to infantile diarrhea, but the ability to react to B-like antigens on *E. coli* is only a small part of a person's ability to kill this bacterium.

A follow-up study was made later at a New York hospital. Instead of looking only for antigenic similarity between *E. coli* and blood group substances, researchers analyzed all young patients with serious infections admitted to the hospital during a one-year period. They blood

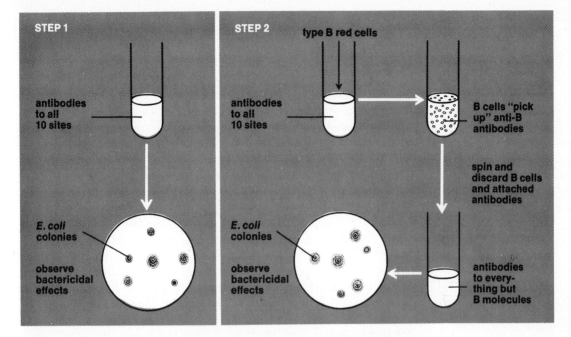

FIGURE 12.13. A method to estimate the bactericidal effects of an ABO antibody. Step 1: The bacteria-killing effects of whole serum from a type A person is observed. Step 2: The bacteria-killing effects of whole serum from a type A person minus anti-B is noted. Anti-B is removed by incubating the whole serum with type B red blood cells. Then the two results are compared.

typed each and cultured the disease organisms for proper identification. They found that the risk of *E. coli* infections among type B and AB individuals really was higher than in type A or O people. Type B and AB people also ran a higher risk of infection with another genus of bacteria that causes typhoid fever and other intestinal disorders. These results must, however, be tempered by the realization that the researchers could identify the causative bacteria in only 36 percent of the patients.

With the worldwide use of effective, inexpensive vaccines, smallpox became the first disease eradicated by humans. Until the vaccine was widely used, however, smallpox was a major killer in many parts of the world. In groups such as the Native Americans, which had never been exposed to the disease before European contact, smallpox killed up to 90 percent of the population at the first exposure. This fact was not lost on early British and American adversaries of the Native Americans. One British lord queried an army officer, "Could it not be contrived to send the small pox among (the) Indians? We must . . . use every stratagem in our power to reduce them."

In 1960 two German researchers claimed they had discovered an A-like antigen on the cowpox virus, a close relative of the agent that causes smallpox. Others tried to extend their results by studying the incidence

Smallpox and ABO

of the disease in people of the various blood groups. One set of data, gathered in India, where smallpox still existed, supports the hypothesized similarity of A antigen and a structure on the smallpox virus. In the rural, unvaccinated Indian population, the researchers found a much higher incidence of smallpox among type A and AB people than in O and B individuals. Not only was the disease more common in the A/AB group, but it was also more often severe or fatal in people with the A antigen. Poor medical care raised the mortality rate in the A/AB group to 50 percent.

More on ABO and Infectious Disease   Other experimenters too have claimed associations between blood group antigens and antigens on pathogens (disease-causing agents). Although none of the associations is unanimously accepted, it is very likely that the ability to produce antibodies directed at A or B molecules has helped determine the world's distribution of ABO alleles. Theoretically it makes sense that populations will have evolved to tolerate diseases in their homeland, and, if antibodies to A and B help determine resistance to a disease, that ABO allele frequencies will in part be affected by indigenous diseases; different populations will have attained different adaptive complexes for ABO alleles.

A complexity introduced several hundred years ago was the rapidity with which humans and their diseases can travel. As the Native Americans found with smallpox, a population may learn to handle its own diseases, only to fall before new evolutionary problems introduced by a foreign disease.

Computer Simulation:
Recapitulating Evolution

When we try to decide on the ABO system's overall evolution, computer simulations are a great help. To re-create a trait's evolution we program the computer with educated guesses about a population's past (the input), including population sizes, fitness values, and admixture rates. The computer races through thousands of years of evolution, reaching the present in short order, and prints out the gene frequencies. The computer's output is then compared with what we see in the real world. If agreement between the two is poor, the evolutionary information is juggled, the computer is turned on, and again the output and the real world are compared. When the two agree, we can conclude that the evolutionary information we fed into the computer is reasonably close to the evolutionary factors that actually prevailed. Computer simulations test possible evolutionary circumstances to see which might account for today's distribution of a trait. One conclusion reached by all computer simulations of ABO is that heterozygote advantage, a balanced polymorphism, must have existed to maintain variability; whether it still exists is another question.

Now we have a problem. If we still have (or ever did have) a heterozygote advantage, is selection operating on the genotype and not the phenotype? Just because we cannot distinguish between AA and AO does not mean that selective agents cannot. Might not some of our problems in associating infectious diseases with ABO blood type be caused by differences in susceptibility of homozygotes (AA, BB) and heterozygotes (AO, BO) necessarily lumped together in the studies?

Alice Brues, trying to determine the relative fitness of the ABO genotypes, used a computer simulation routine. After the computer was given initial gene frequencies, population sizes, and selective pressures related to maternal-fetal incompatibility, it simulated the evolutionary changes that might come about during 500 years (roughly twenty generations). Starting from the populations Brues created, the computer "gave birth" about 100 times a second by picking out gene pairs (newborns) at random from the gene pool, and "threw out" a percentage of the offspring, those who died because they had ABO incompatibilities. The gene frequencies were also subjected to drift by a random component in the computer's way of picking genotypes in each generation. The resulting distribution of frequencies closest to the observed showed that AB was the most fit, followed by AO, BO, OO, AA, and finally BB (Figure 12.14; notice that the smallest populations drifted most).[3]

It is doubtful that we will soon find a final answer on selection and ABO. Anthropologists and serologists have written hundreds of papers on this topic and have designed clever techniques to detect selection, but the problem's inherent complexities have defied a full answer. We may eventually find that bacterial, viral, and parasitic disorders as well as dietary differences, maternal-fetal incompatibility, and interactions with other genes have all helped determine ABO distribution.

Other than disease—both infectious and noninfectious—a variety of possible forms of selection could affect blood group frequencies. Some have been suggested as being involved in the maintenance of the MN polymorphism.

MN Polymorphism

Because people normally do not carry antibodies to the MN antigen they lack, most theories have been built on factors other than selection by infectious disease. Some researchers found that MN heterozygotes were produced more often than would be explained by chance. In MN male × MN female matings, they found, instead of 50 percent MN offspring, about 55 percent. The explanation offered was that the MN genotype was more fit and had a better chance of surviving. If this is true, MN is a balanced polymorphism.

Other hypotheses have tried to account for these results. One theory is that M and N sperm are produced in equal numbers but do not have equal probabilities of fertilizing the egg: In some conditions, the probability of M fertilization is higher; in others, N sperm have a better chance of winning the race. This theory that the sperm compete with each other, has also been used on ABO, and is appealing because cervical mucus can contain antibodies to A or B and thus could select out sperm carrying the unlike antigen. The only problem here is that we are not yet sure if sperm carrying the A or B allele have the corresponding antigen

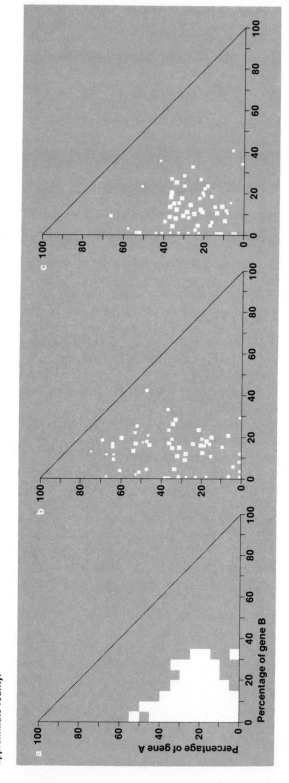

FIGURE 12.14. The actual distribution of ABO allele frequencies and two simulated distributions using different fitness values.

(a) A graphic representation of the worldwide ABO alleles from 350 representative populations. The axes of the graph correspond to the frequencies of A and B; O can be computed by subtracting the A and B frequencies from 100 percent. Most populations are clustered toward the high O, low (10–30%) A, and low (10–20%) B region.

(b) The expected distribution if fitness values for the genotypes were ranked from most fit to least fit as follows: AB > AA = AO = BO > OO > BB.

(c) The expected distribution given another set of fitness values: AB > AO > BO > OO > AA > BB. Based on the comparisons of observed and expected distributions, it seems reasonable that the fitness values in (c) more closely approximate reality.

on the membrane. That we can apply this idea to the MN system is even more uncertain. All these hypotheses are more equivocal than disease associations, and we have very little empirical evidence to support them.

More recently, it has been shown that the parasite that causes a very dangerous form of malaria invades a person's blood cells by first attaching to the MN antigens on the cells' surface. Cells with reduced numbers of MN antigens on their surface are resistant to invasion. Whether this has affected the evolution of the MN trait must be determined.

Other Genetic Traits in Blood

Along with the blood group systems we can find many other genetic traits in the blood. Blood groups result from the attachment of molecules to the surface of the red blood cells, but genetically controlled molecules are also inside the red cells, on the white blood cells, and in the fluid portion of the blood, the serum.

Variant forms of these proteins can often be detected by electrophoresis. This technique relies on the fact that proteins are either positively or negatively charged and will migrate in an electrical field. The greater the negative charge, the farther the protein will move to the positive pole, and vice versa. Differential migration coupled with appropriate use of dyes can yield results such as those seen in Figure 12.15.

The Structure of Hemoglobin

Hemoglobin is the most intensively studied protein inside the red blood cell; it makes up more than 90 percent of the cell's protein content. Briefly reviewing the discussion on pages 184–188, we find that at different times in our life we make different forms of hemoglobin. Most of these forms use the α chains made by the α gene. During embryonic life two α chains combine with two ϵ chains ($\alpha_2 \epsilon_2$) and during fetal life they

FIGURE 12.15. Electrophoresis of monkey serum. These monkeys display a great deal of variation for some serum proteins, particularly transferrin, whereas other proteins, such as albumin, exhibit no variation.

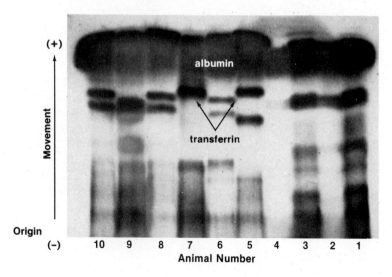

combine with two γ chains ($\alpha_2 \gamma_2$). After birth, we make a major hemoglobin called HbA, with the composition $\alpha_2 \beta_2$, as well as a minor hemoglobin, HbA$_2$ ($\alpha_2 \delta_2$) (see Figure 12.16).

The Sickle-Cell Variant and Malaria

Although most humans make the same forms of hemoglobin, over 400 variants, most of which are rare, have been identified. A few reach polymorphic frequencies, including hemoglobins S, C, and thalassemia. Of these three variants, the one we know most about is hemoglobin S. The allele for this form occurs in high frequencies, up to about 20 percent, in populations from malarial areas in sub-Saharan Africa, and at lower frequencies in Saudi Arabia, India, and parts of the Mediterranean (Figures 12.17 and 12.18). Several explanations have been offered for the high frequencies of this allele in malarial areas. All are based on the observation that people who are heterozygous for the sickle-cell allele are better able to survive and reproduce in such regions.

Malaria is really several diseases caused by different species of parasites of the genus *Plasmodium,* the most dangerous being *Plasmodium falciparum.* The parasite enters the human body through the bite of an

FIGURE 12.16. The oxyhemoglobin (hemoglobin combined with oxygen) molecule, composed of two identical α and two identical β chains. The iron-containing heme groups bind to oxygen for transport to the body's tissues. Hemoglobin A$_2$ contains two types of chains also but has δ chains. In sickle-cell anemia there are again two normal α chains, but the β chains differ from the normal form by one amino acid.

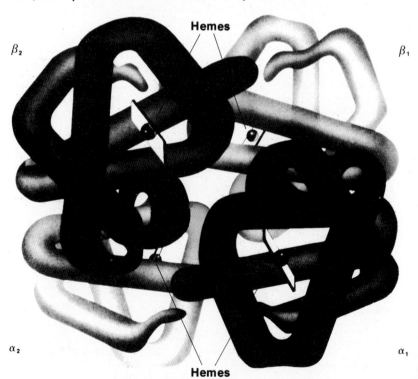

Hemes

β_2 β_1

α_2 α_1

Hemes

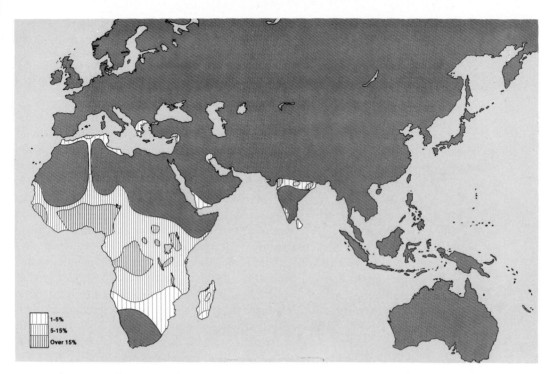

FIGURE 12.17. Distribution of the sickle-cell allele.

FIGURE 12.18. Areas where malaria is common today.

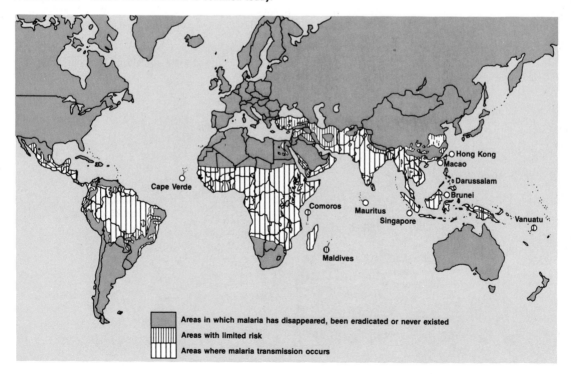

Cape Verde

Hong Kong
Macao

Darussalam

Brunei

Comoros   Mauritus

Singapore

Vanuatu

Maldives

Areas in which malaria has disappeared, been eradicated or never existed

Areas with limited risk

Areas where malaria transmission occurs

Other Genetic Traits in Blood   489

infected mosquito. Once inside, it sets up residence in red blood cells and goes through a development that eventually destroys the red cell (Figure 12.19). In the course of the parasite's life cycle, it can be picked up by another mosquito bite and carried to someone new. If the parasite is able to reproduce easily inside the body, it will infect many red cells; when these cells are destroyed, the malaria victim will die.

Cells containing sickle-cell hemoglobin are not conducive to the parasite's proper development, making heterozygotes for this form of hemoglobin less susceptible to severe malarial infection. Recent research demonstrates that the parasite infects the red cells of heterozygotes but that when the cell sickles, the potassium level drops and the parasite dies. Although the parasite can survive in the heterozygote's nonsickled cells, the resistance provided by sickling is sufficient to allow the person to mobilize other protective mechanisms and survive the disease. Because roughly half the hemoglobin in the heterozygote's red blood cells is normal, many of the red cells do not sickle, and thus these people do not develop sickle-cell anemia. Data from malarial areas show clearly that heterozygosity for normal and sickle-cell β chains does protect against death by malaria. Of 104 malaria-caused deaths considered in one study, only 1 occurred in a sickle-cell heterozygote, although 23 deaths would be expected by chance association. Laboratory data also shows that red cells with sickle-cell hemoglobin provide a very poor environment for the growth of the parasite. As the severity of the malaria is directly related to the number of infected cells, the reduced parasite levels in AS heterozygotes result in lower mortality rates.

Besides greater resistance to malaria, the AS heterozygote may have other advantages in malarial regions. Some research indicates that

FIGURE 12.19.   Uninfected red blood cells and some parasitized by malaria. These parasites eventually destroy the cells.

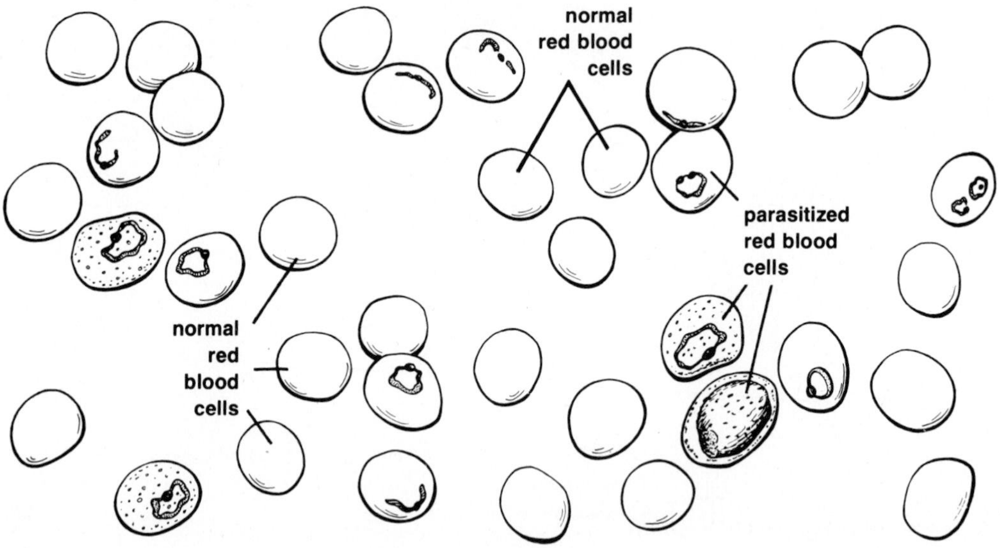

female heterozygotes have greater fertility than AA homozygotes. A possible explanation is that parasite levels in the heterozygote's placenta are lower than in the placenta of AA homozygotes; the fetus therefore is not deprived of oxygen by the parasite. Heterozygous males, too, may have greater fertility in malarial areas. Abnormally high body temperature for a brief period can suppress sperm production for weeks; thus reduced susceptibility to malarial fevers might increase fertility.

For any or all of these reasons, sickle-cell hemoglobin has been maintained as a balanced polymorphism for some time in malarial areas; some have tried to estimate just how long. We can assume that the S allele was not selected for before malaria became a common disease in humans. By observing the malaria-carrying mosquito's ecology we can estimate when that happened.

Before the advent of agriculture in Africa it is unlikely that humans often contracted malaria. But by clearing the land for agriculture, they blundered into playing the host for the *Plasmodium* parasite. The mosquito that carries the parasite has little chance of breeding in a tropical rain forest; although its breeding sites are highly diversified, it cannot reproduce in shaded, salty, or polluted water.

Several scientists demonstrated decades ago that the malaria-carrying mosquito spreads as land is cleared. To establish a rubber plantation in Liberia, the Firestone Company cleared huge swaths of forest. Shortly afterward, scientists found that the malaria mosquito accounted for 46 percent of the mosquito population. Several years later it reached 100 percent. In areas not used for the plantation the jungle cover was restored, removing this form of mosquito almost completely.

Looking at the incidence of malaria in human populations, we find that hunting groups living in rain forests, such as the Pygmies of the Congo, are almost completely free of malaria. Many other peoples of Central Africa depend on agriculture, subsisting on yams, bananas, coconuts, and cereals. To make arable land the natives burn over an area of rain forest, greatly transforming its ecology. The shade cover is removed, and the continued cultivation removes the humus, making the ground impervious to water and establishing stagnant ponds that are perfect breeding grounds for the malarial mosquito.

We conclude, then, that the clearing of land for agriculture brought about the selective advantage for the sickle-cell allele. Some of Frank Livingstone's work, which draws on linguistic, cultural, and archaeological data, indicates that one African mutation of hemoglobin S probably originated in East Africa, in the area of Sudan, and from there spread along with slash-and-burn agriculture.[4] This is an impressive example of our often unwitting disruption of many ecological niches and our propensity for altering the environment, and therefore the course of evolution, in many unforeseen ways.

For some time it was thought that the type of food staple grown also affected the evolution of hemoglobin S. Some research of the 1970s and 1980s purported to show that the effects of sickling would be reduced by the chemical cyanate. In fact, cyanate was even tried as a form of treatment for sickle-cell disease. Moreover, cyanate in the diet was said to prevent the growth of the malarial parasite. Various researchers noted that cassavas, the main carbohydrate source of some African populations, contained cyanate. It was thus suspected that the problems of sickling and malaria should not be as significant in these groups as in people who relied on rice for their carbohydrates because the cassava-eaters should have lowered frequencies of the S allele.[5] Further work and clinical tests, however, have discounted any beneficial role for cyanate in preventing malaria or in helping to prevent the harmful effects of sickling.

More information on the sickle-cell allele has been obtained by use of recombinant DNA techniques (pages 44–45). If one uses the restriction enzyme Hpa I to digest the human β-globin genes of a normal individual, several fragments are produced (Figure 12.20). A fragment 7.6 kb long (kb = kilobase, or 1,000 bases) is the one that contains the β gene. Two scientists at the University of California, San Francisco, noted that the pattern of digestion was somewhat different in many American blacks with the sickle-cell allele. In eleven of fifteen people with sickle-cell anemia (SS), the 7.6 kb fragment was absent, and in its place was a 13 kb fragment. This was interpreted to mean that a mutation had changed the Hpa I site noted in Figure 12.20 so that it no longer could be cut by this enzyme. When treated with Hpa I, the mutated DNA was cut into a 13 kb fragment containing the β gene instead of a 7.6 kb fragment containing this gene. This is called a restriction site polymorphism. (This will be further discussed on page 503.)

Although this change in the Hpa I site has no functional relationship to the mutation that causes the sickle-cell β gene, the two are linked (page 60). Chromosomes with the sickle-cell gene thus coincidentally will often also lack a Hpa I site.

Other scientists wanted to see what other restriction sites were coincidentally linked to the sickle-cell allele. They found that people in

FIGURE 12.20.   1. Sites at which the enzyme Hpa I cuts the DNA in the vicinity of the normal human β gene. 2. Hpa I sites found in association with the sickle-cell hemoglobin gene. The site labeled * is abolished, yielding a 13 kb fragment.

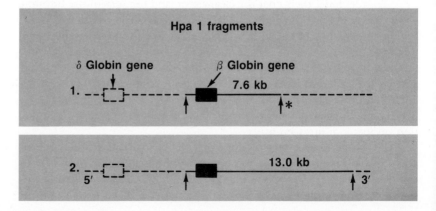

different parts of Africa actually had different constellations of linked characters. From this, many now conclude that the sickle-cell allele arose at least three or four times in different parts of Africa. In each area where falciparum malaria was present, the newly arisen mutation attained significant frequencies because of the advantage it conferred.[6]

Such discoveries illustrate that similar mutations can arise independently in several places. When they are beneficial and become common, they could provide misleading evidence about genetic relationships. If one only knows that the sickle cell is common in two African populations, this does not prove that the groups are closely related or that there was gene flow between them.

It has been mentioned that the sickle-cell allele exists in the Mediterranean, Saudi Arabia, and India, in addition to Africa. Analysis of the DNA around the sickle-cell genes in these populations indicates even more frequent occurrence of the sickling mutation. In these parts of the world too, the disease is not as severe as in Africa, probably a result of other modifier genes.

Direct detection of the sickle-cell allele is now possible in fetal DNA. It is no longer necessary for physicians to look for sites linked to the sickle-cell gene because the enzyme Mst II cuts DNA directly at the mutation site. Mst II recognizes the site CCTNAGG (N means any base). Figure 12.21 compares a short region of DNA surrounding the base pair which differs in normal and sickle-cell DNA. The normal cell has the recognition site for Mst II. The mutation that leads to the altered hemoglobin destroys this site. This phenomenon provides the basis for a test that can directly identify the disease prior to birth.

The C form of hemoglobin is produced by a third hemoglobin allele, so that it too produces an abnormal β chain. People who are homozygous for C suffer from an anemia, but it is not as severe as that suffered by sickle-cell homozygotes. We think some selective advantage must be attached to being genotypically AC; otherwise this allele should not be so common in some populations.

As with the other hemoglobin variant we have considered, this allele's distribution coincides with that of malaria in West Africa (Figure 12.22). There is therefore a sizable overlap in the ranges of C and S alleles, but it seems that the higher the frequency of one of these alleles in

Hemoglobin C versus Hemoglobin S

FIGURE 12.21.   The normal and sickle-cell alleles differ only in one base pair, shown here boxed in the normal DNA sequence. This alteration determines whether Mst II will (normal) or will not (sickle cell) cut the DNA. (The ellipses indicate more of the sequences, the bases of which have nothing to do with this test of the ability to differentiate the alleles.)

Recognition site

Normal allele   . . . A C T C C T G A G G A G G . . .

Sickle-cell allele   . . . A C T C C T G T G G A G G . . .

a population, the lower the frequency of the other: They are alleles of each other and thus are in competition. Because the SC heterozygote has a very low fitness, one of these alleles should drive the other out of the population, which can be proven mathematically.

Some have suggested that the C allele is replacing S where the two overlap; others support the reverse view. Lab studies do not show that C retards parasite growth, which would indicate that it is not as good at defending against malaria. The fitness of AS people is higher than that of AC people, and this may lead to S replacing C where the two are in competition.

Thalassemias

In a number of regions of the Old World, other genetically caused variants are found in sizable frequencies (Figure 12.23). One class of anemias, known as thalassemias (*thalassa = sea; haima = blood*), result in a peculiar hematological picture. While sickle-cell anemia can be traced to an abnormal hemoglobin, thalassemias are characterized by a lack of nor-

FIGURE 12.22 Distribution of hemoglobin C is confined to Africa.

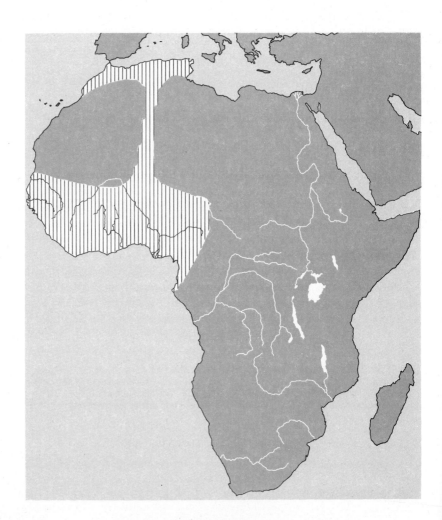

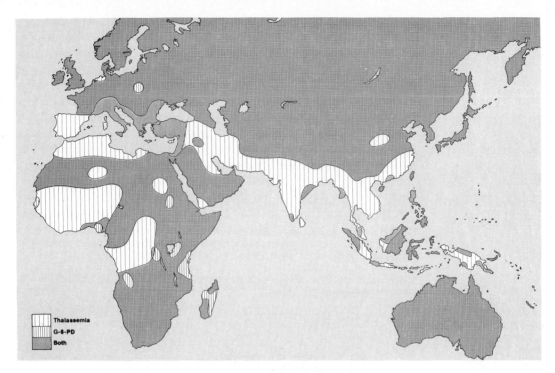

FIGURE 12.23. Distribution of thalassemias and G-6-PD deficiency in the Old World.

mal adult hemoglobin. In some cases, for instance, there is virtually no hemoglobin A coupled with abnormally high levels of fetal hemoglobin and hemoglobin A_2, the normally minor component. No abnormal hemoglobin is present, however. For a long time it was thought that thalassemias were caused by alleles that prevented the production of α or β chains. People thought to be homozygotes for an allele were said to have thalassemia major, with heterozygotes having thalassemia minor.

The disease β-thalassemia manifests itself at birth when β-chain synthesis normally begins. The body compensates for the stress from partial or complete deficiency of adult hemoglobin by continuing to make fetal hemoglobin and also large amounts of hemoglobin A_2. In the homozygote, the body's compensatory action usually is not enough to support life; most thalassemia major victims die before reproductive age. In thalassemia minor cases, normal adult hemoglobin production is enough to support life, and the elevated levels of fetal and minor-component hemoglobin do not appear.

The condition of α-thalassemia is a bit more complicated, as a normal human inherits two copies of the α gene from each parent. Normal people thus have four α alleles, and α-thalassemics can have from zero to three α genes, resulting in varying degrees of hemoglobin deficit.

Again, we find that newer techniques of molecular biology provide insights into the origins of this disorder. To start, we see that thalassemias are in fact a product of many different genetic events. In different parts of the world, they result from one or more mutations. Some cases are due to deletions in which various-sized pieces of DNA encompassing part or all of the β gene are lost. Figure 12.24 shows the normal array of members of the human β-globin gene family and the regions deleted in just a few of the β-thalassemias discovered to date. Other thalassemias come about because of alterations in the switches that are meant to turn the β gene on at the time of birth. Some people with thalassemia have several different defects. As with sickle-cell hemoglobin, it appears that different mutations can cause the same phenotype. Others are caused by

FIGURE 12.24.   Several of the deletions in the β-globin cluster that cause thalassemia. HPFH is a persistence of fetal hemoglobin into adult life that in some compensates for the lack of adult hemoglobin. Note that similar losses of globin chains arise from different deletions in various parts of the world. The black areas are the sections of deleted DNA; the shaded areas reflect uncertainty. The deleted chains are noted parenthetically.

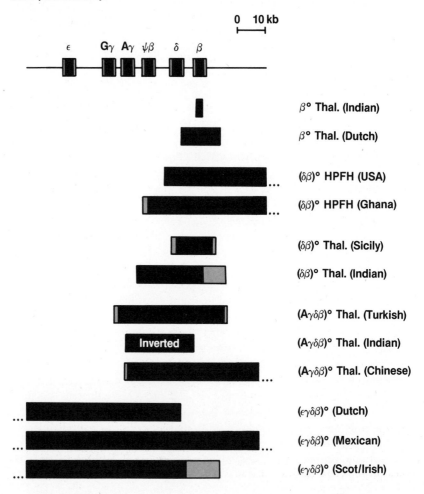

the lack of α chains. As might be expected, α-thalassemias are also highly heterogeneous at the genetic level.

Comparing Figures 12.18 and 12.23 we again see a correspondence between the distributions of a hemoglobin abnormality, thalassemias, and malaria. The high frequencies of α-thalassemia in Melanesia are convincingly associated with endemic malaria.[7] Wherever malaria was common (lowlands and coastal areas), there were high frequencies of α-thalassemia. Similar arguments have been made for β-thalassemia's prevalence in parts of the Mediterranean region, for instance.

Besides the similarities in distribution of thalassemias and malaria, several lines of evidence indicate that the lack of adult hemoglobin can interfere with the growth of the malaria parasite. People who inherit both sickle-cell disease and β-thalassemia are more likely to survive than those with just sickle-cell anemia. As mentioned on page 440, such epistatic interactions can affect the evolution of traits.

Inside the red blood cells are many genetically controlled molecules besides hemoglobin. One class of these is the red cell enzymes, molecules that speed up biochemical reactions. Not nearly as plentiful as hemoglobin, these enzymes are relatively simple to detect, and because there are many, they give us much information about a person's genotype and a population's gene frequencies.

Variation in Red Cell Enzymes: G-6-PD Deficiency

Of the variable red cell enzymes, probably the one that most interests physical anthropologists is glucose-6-phosphate dehydrogenase (G-6-PD), which aids in the reduction of glucose-6-phosphate, a sugar, to another sugar and also produces an energy-rich molecule.

It was found in the early 1950s that primaquine, a drug used in the prevention of malaria, precipitated an anemia in many blacks. Investigators showed that primaquine-sensitive people were deficient in red cell G-6-PD and that their red cells could be broken down by other drugs or foods too. It has also been found that many other populations of the world have an allele that produces G-6-PD deficiency. As is now becoming a common story, the deficiency in southern Europeans is caused by an allele (B−) that is different from the one causing the deficiency in sub-Saharan Africans (A−). In other words, the same phenotype, an enzyme deficiency, is caused by different genotypes. As time goes on, many more alleles causing G-6-PD deficiency have been found. In all cases, however, the genes are inherited as a sex-linked characteristic; males have only one gene for the trait, while females have two.

Plotting the distribution of the variant alleles A− and B−, we see again a large overlap with the distribution of malaria (Figures 12.18 and 12.23). Looking at a more confined locale, the island of Sardinia in the Mediterranean, G-6-PD deficiency is correlated with the presence of malaria. Coastal regions have both the deficiency and the disease; highland regions neither.

We have ample reason to expect a deficiency in this protein to affect the malaria parasite's viability. When the parasite is in a red blood cell, it relies on the cell's biochemical machinery for its energy; if it cannot get energy in this way, it will not develop properly. People affected by the deficiency are usually fully fit, for their cells can produce energy by a route not involving G-6-PD, which the parasite cannot use. Unless anemia is precipitated by food or drugs, those with the enzyme deficiency do not suffer repercussions.

Besides the correspondence in the distributions of G-6-PD deficiencies and malaria, direct support for the malaria hypothesis has come from the laboratory. Researchers have shown that cells with normal levels of G-6-PD are more prone to malaria infection than deficient red cells. This results from the shorter life span of G-6-PD–deficient red blood cells. Normal erythrocytes have a life span of about four months, and the parasite has evolved to develop properly within this time. Because the deficient cells have a quicker turnover, however, the parasite does not have time to grow and multiply. Another suggestion is that it is the female heterozygote alone who is at a selective advantage. These women have enough red cells with G-6-PD to allow for normal oxygen transport, but enough cells are enzyme deficient to prevent large-scale growth of the parasite.

Figure 12.23 shows the frequency of the G-6-PD deficiency alleles in several populations. Only the more common variants are incorporated on this map, although many rare variants are known. It has a wide frequency range from population to population, which can be explained in several ways. In small, isolated populations, the frequency may be distorted from equilibrium because of inbreeding and genetic drift. The fitnesses may also vary depending on the severity and type of malaria. Furthermore, it seems that G-6-PD deficiency interacts with the hemoglobin alleles that provide resistance to malaria. For unknown reasons a female who is heterozygous for G-6-PD and also heterozygous for a thalassemia has greater resistance to the parasite than one would predict simply by multiplying the resistances based on the individual traits. Likewise, at least in Saudi Arabia, people with sickle-cell disease and G-6-PD deficiency are healthier than one would expect. Evidently the G-6-PD variants mix well with the hemoglobin variants, but the hemoglobin alleles do not mix well with each other.

We cannot yet tell how old this enzymatic disorder is, but it is curious that many Greek philosophers and Egyptian priests warned against eating fava beans, one of the agents that cause anemia in deficient individuals. The reason is not clear, but it might have been a cultural adaptation to a biological factor. The widespread occurrence of G-6-PD variants also suggests that this disorder has a long history. Interestingly, fava beans also contain a substance that interferes with the development of falciparum malaria parasites in red blood cells. The interplay of an enzyme, hemoglobin, blood types, and culture is truly complex.

Histocompatibility Antigens

Blood groups and the other blood systems mentioned pertain to the constitution of red blood cells. Over the last thirty years it has become known that white blood cells, or leukocytes, contain on their surface a series of antigens that are markers of our individuality; to a great degree these are the molecules that our immune system learns to recognize as "self." Tissues with a different molecular structure are "not self" and are rejected, as can happen in organ transplants. From this we get the name histocompatibility antigens (*histo* = *tissue*). These antigens are present on most body cells, but as they are most often studied in reference to leukocytes, the system is often referred to as HLA (human leukocyte antigens).

The HLA system is analogous to the Rh system, for both have many alleles occupying closely linked but distinct regions, or *loci* (singular, *locus*). The HLA loci are known to be on chromosome pair 6 and are called A, B, C, and D (the commonality of C and D with Rh is coincidental). The potential variability is remarkable; locus B, for example, has over twenty alleles. Computations show that there are more than 100,000 possible human HLA genotypes based on the known variation, and more alleles are still being identified. This is why it is so difficult to match organ donors and recipients.

Not all the alleles are equally common (Table 12.4), nor are the allele frequencies the same in different populations. Because of the population differences, this system is particularly useful in tracing genetic relationships among populations. The A locus allele W24 is found at frequencies of roughly 35 percent in Oriental populations and about 25 percent in Native Americans, but at less than 3 percent in Afro-Americans and Africans and less than 10 percent in European groups, again indicating the Asian origin of Native Americans.

Because these antigens are so important in separating the self from the foreign, it is not surprising that many alleles appear to be associated with disease susceptibilities. Many of these are with noninfectious disorders, such as arthritic conditions, allergies, diabetes and malignancies. Allele B27, for example, which occurs normally in roughly 5 to 10 percent of American whites, is found in 90 percent of those suffering from a crippling condition of the spine called ankylosing spondylitis. This does not mean that those with B27 will develop the disorder; the vast majority do not, nor do all people with the condition have this allele. The allele does not cause the disease, but it does predispose people to develop ankylosing spondylitis under certain environmental conditions.

The laws of probability state that within any one population the frequencies of various combinations of alleles for the different loci should be predictable—in the absence of evolution. If we know the frequency of, say, an A locus allele and a B locus allele, the frequency with which they appear together should be the frequency of one times the frequency of the other. If, in Europeans, the frequency of A1 is 15 percent and frequency of B8 is 8 percent, we would expect to find them together on the same chromosome with a frequency of 1.2 percent (0.15×0.08). In fact, this combination is found 6.7 percent of the time, evidence that these two alleles are genetically good mixers. This distortion of expectation, known as linkage disequilibrium, along with the known disease associations, is proof that the allele frequencies have been molded by evolutionary forces.

TABLE 12.4
Representative HLA Allele Frequencies for the A, B, C and DR Loci[a]

	Population[b]			
	Europeans	Negroes	Japanese	Native Americans
Locus A				
A1	15	3	<1	2
A2	26	15	25	37
A3	12	7	<1	2
Aw24	10	3	36	24
Aw30	3	15	<1	0
Locus B				
B7	9	9	6	<1
B8	8	3	<1	2
B27	4	2	<1	<1
Bw51	7	1	8	25
Locus C				
Cw1	4	<1	18	11
Cw2	5	12	<1	<1
Cw3	10	9	27	39
Cw6	8	9	<1	2
Locus D				
DR1	7	5	<1	2
DR2	13	15	6	27
DR3	11	17	20	3
DR5	10	13	2	2

[a]Because new, more specific antibodies are still being discovered, these data are only approximate. Not all alleles are included.
[b]The population identities are provided in the source cited below. "Negroes" includes both African and American blacks.

Adapted from M. P. Baur and J. A. Danilovs, "Population Analysis of HLA-A, B, C, DR, and Other Genetic Markers," in Paul Terasaki (ed.), *Histocompatibility Testing 1980: Report of the Eighth International Histocompatibility Workshop Held in Los Angeles, California, USA, 4–10 February 1980* (Los Angeles: UCLA Tissue Typing Laboratory, 1980), pp. 962–963, tables 6–9.

Serum Proteins: Haptoglobin, the Transporter

The serum proteins are the last genetically controlled traits of the blood that we will consider. These proteins have several functions, but the one we will deal with works as a transporting agent, carrying other molecules to the body tissues. Like the enzymes inside the red blood cells, many proteins in the fluid portion of the blood, the serum, are variable from person to person and in frequency from population to population. The reasons for much of this genetic variation are poorly understood, but for the serum protein haptoglobin we do have some hints.

For our purposes, this serum protein is controlled by two common alleles, known as Hp^1 and Hp^2. Most people, then, are either homozygous Hp1–1 or Hp2–2 or heterozygous Hp2–1. The protein is very important as a scavenger, picking up hemoglobin liberated into the serum when a red cell breaks open. It transports the hemoglobin to where the constituent parts of the hemoglobin can be recycled.

It has been shown recently that haptoglobin 1–1 is better able than 2–1 or 2–2 to bind with free hemoglobin and may be advantageous because it conserves this valuable molecule. A team of scientists at the University of Texas has also demonstrated that people who are haptoglobin 2–2 are superior in the ability to survive infection with typhoid bacteria, because they are more effective in producing antibodies against the bacteria. The heterozygous condition Hp2–1 may in time prove to be most helpful in environments containing typhoid and a factor that breaks down red blood cells, such as G-6-PD deficiency. That is, the balance between Hp^1 and Hp^2 alleles may be maintained as a balanced polymorphism.

The distribution of Hp^1 does not coincide well, however, with the distribution of factors that break down red cells (Table 12.5). In Africa, where anemia caused by breakage of red blood cells (from malaria or G-6-PD deficiency for example) is common, the Hp^1 allele is also common. But in Asia, which also has a high rate of anemia, the Hp^2 allele is the most common. The association is not necessarily disproved, however, because other factors may be at work in Asia.

In 1931 a laboratory researcher accidentally dropped a sample of a synthetic compound called phenylthiocarbamide, or PTC. As the cloud of powder spread through the air, some fellow researchers complained about the bitter taste, while others insisted it was completely tasteless.

Other Genetic Variations

Tasters and Nontasters

TABLE 12.5
The Approximate Frequency of the Hp^1 Allele in Some Representative Populations[a]

Population by Country/Tribe/Group	Frequency of Hp^1	Population by Country/Tribe/Group	Frequency of Hp^1
North Africa		**Asia**	
Egypt	.21	North India	.15
Europe		Thailand	.24
England	.41	Japan	.28
Gypsies (Sweden)	.12	Hong Kong (China)	.39
Norway	.36	**North America**	
South Italy	.32	Eskimos (Alaska)	.30
United States		Navajo	.45
(European descent)	.38	**South America**	
(African descent)	.55	Alacaluf (Chile)	.48
West Africa		Quechua (Ecuador)	.78
Liberia	.70	Xavante (Brazil)	.46
Nigeria	.50–.90	**Pacific**	
East Africa		Australia (central)	.20
Kenya	.48	New Guinea	.66
Uganda	.63	Philippines	.39
South Africa		Melanesians	.48
Bushmen	.29	Polynesians	.54
Hottentot	.51		
Zulu	.53		

[a]Arranged to illustrate broadly some genetic relationships.

Adapted from Eloise R. Giblett, *Genetic Markers in Human Blood* (Oxford: Blackwell Scientific Publications, 1969), pp. 94–98, and from Moses R. Schenfield, "HLA and Immunoglobulin Allotypes," in James H. Mielke and Michael H. Crawford (eds.), *Current Developments in Anthropological Genetics*, vol. 1 (New York: Plenum, 1980), pp. 65–85.

Subsequent research proved that the ability to taste PTC (or its close chemical relatives, such as phenylthiourea, that occur in nature) is a genetic trait inherited as a simple dominant Mendelian gene.

As with genetic markers in the blood, many populations have been screened by standardized techniques to find the frequency of tasters (TT and Tt) and nontasters (tt). The percentage of nontasters varies from a high of more than 40 percent in India to a low of less than 5 percent in sub-Saharan Africa, but we have not been able to give a full evolutionary explanation for this polymorphism (Table 12.6). We do have several intriguing leads, however.

Harry Harris and his associates were the first to show that nontasters are more susceptible to a thyroid gland disorder known as nonendemic nodular goiter, which can cause weakness, severe weight loss, and neurological disorders; it could be a selective mechanism. Physiologically this association makes sense, because compounds like PTC that occur in cabbage, brussels sprouts, kale, and other members of the mustard family are known to upset thyroid function and produce goiters. Several researchers have reasoned that those who cannot taste PTC-like chemicals are more likely to ingest the compound and therefore stand a greater chance of developing a thyroid dysfunction. In fact an outbreak of goiter in Tasmania was tied to such an agent in milk from cows fed on kale.

Over the years many other studies have borne out the original findings, but the taster polymorphism appears to be complex. It may well be that the ability to taste PTC is just one part of the biochemical effect of the taster allele. Several anthropologists suggested that the ability to taste PTC may affect body size, because thyroid function is important in regulating growth. Nontasters might be smaller because, theoretically, they ingest more thyroid-depressing foods. On the other hand, it appears that tasters may be more susceptible to another form of goiter, toxic diffuse. Tasters are also more likely to suffer severely from tuberculosis and leprosy.

TABLE 12.6
The Approximate Frequency of the Nontaster (t) Allele in Representative Populations

Population by Country/Group	Frequency of t	Population by Country/Group	Frequency of t
West Africa	.16	Europe	
Asia		Denmark	.57
Japan	.26	Lapland	.25
Malay	.42	Spain	.50
China	.14	South America	
		Indians (Brazil)	.11

Adapted with permission from G. A. Harrison, J. M. Tanner, D. R. Pilbeam, and P. T. Baker, *Human Biology: An Introduction to Human Evolution, Variation, Growth, and Adaptability*, 3rd ed. (Oxford: Oxford University Press, 1988), p. 286.

In Chapter 2 we considered the restriction enzymes, which are produced in nature by species of bacteria. As a class, restriction enzymes recognize specific sequences of bases and cut DNA wherever the particular sequence appears. If two people differ because of a mutation, we may be able to detect that difference if it has either changed a sequence so that now the enzyme cuts at the altered site or, conversely, if the mutation alters what had been an enzyme recognition site to a sequence that is no longer recognized and cut (Figure 12.25). Restriction enzymes thus give us a way to investigate directly variation in DNA structure from person to person.

Technically such research requires that an individual's DNA be purified (this is often done from a blood sample, but as all tissues contain DNA, any tissue will do). After purification, the DNA is digested with one (or more) restriction enzymes, specific pieces are visualized, and their length is measured. The procedure commonly used to determine the fragment length is called Southern hybridization, so named after its developer, Ed Southern (Figure 12.26).

As we saw in Chapters 2 and 5, complementary sequences of DNA can bind to each other, even if the sequences are not exact matches. In this approach, the large number of variously sized DNA fragments are separated on an electrophoresis gel; the DNA is treated to make it single stranded and then transferred to a filter, on which it is immobilized. Briefly, hybridization involves the preparation of the probe, a relatively short piece of radioactive, single-stranded DNA of specific sequence. When the probe and filter are incubated together, the probe seeks out and

DNA Variation

Restriction Fragment Length Polymorphisms

FIGURE 12.25. The action of a restriction enzyme.

The restriction enzyme Bam HI cuts double-stranded DNA at the sequence

```
     ↓
...G G A T C C...
...C C T A G G...
               ↑
```

yielding

```
...G              G A T C C...
...C C T A G   +          G...
```

New sites can be created by mutation. For instance,

```
...A T G C C T G G A C C C G T T...
```

can be changed to

```
...A T G C C T G G A T C C G T T...
```

thus creating a Bam HI site (underlined). Similarly, sites can be destroyed.

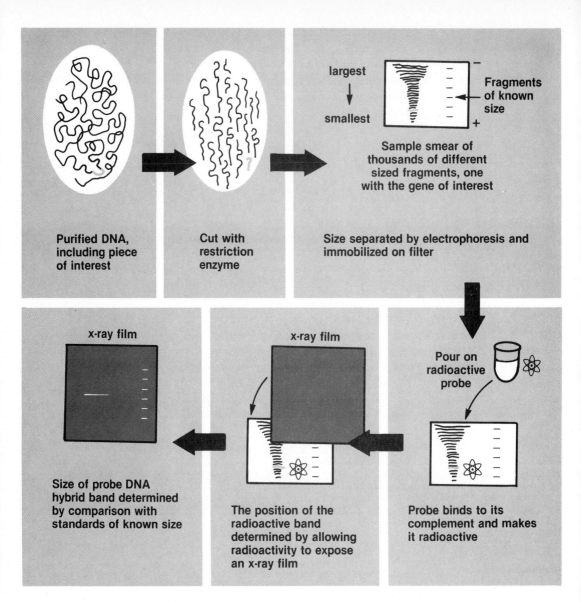

Purified DNA, including piece of interest

Cut with restriction enzyme

largest

smallest

Fragments of known size

Sample smear of thousands of different sized fragments, one with the gene of interest

Size separated by electrophoresis and immobilized on filter

x-ray film

x-ray film

Pour on radioactive probe

Size of probe DNA hybrid band determined by comparison with standards of known size

The position of the radioactive band determined by allowing radioactivity to expose an x-ray film

Probe binds to its complement and makes it radioactive

FIGURE 12.26.   Southern hybridization.

binds to the DNA on the filter to which it is complementary. The location of the now radioactive, double-stranded DNA can be determined easily, and the length of this segment can be determined by comparison with known standards. When DNA digests (DNA digested by use of restriction enzymes) from different individuals are compared, one may find that a probe binds to pieces of different length, which is known as a restriction fragment length polymorphism (RFLP). The variation being detected here is in the length of the piece of DNA containing the specific sequence complementary to the probe in use. For instance, one can study the length of the piece of DNA that contains the β-globin gene after cutting with an enzyme such as Hpa I (see page 492).

The variable Hpa I site associated with the β-globin gene is just one of many instances of this sort of variation. In this case the variation is identified by use of a probe detecting a DNA sequence of known function. Sometimes "anonymous" probes are used: These are sequences known to occur in the DNA but of no known function, since they do not bind to the globin genes or to any other identifiable gene. They do bind, however, to their complementary sequences, and again the complement may occur within different-sized fragments in different people—a RFLP.

Whether anonymous or known, the probe may hybridize to a single, unique fragment or to more than one fragment, each of which contains the complementary sequence. Probes that identify more than one variable fragment can yield that much more information on genetic variability within and between populations. At this point in time more than 1,000 RFLPs have been identified scattered throughout the human DNA. There is certainly more variability here than can potentially be tested in all the blood groups.

Why would anyone want to identify variation in what may be totally nonfunctional DNA? One answer is a very practical one. As in the sickle-cell case, the restriction site may act as an easily detectable marker for the presence or absence of an associated, important gene.

One group, headed by Ray White at the University of Utah, is looking for many RFLPs. These researchers are not particularly concerned with learning anything about these sites except whether they are polymorphic—that is, whether some people have them (either as homozygotes or heterozygotes) and some people do not. White and his colleagues hope to detect a few hundred such polymorphic sites in the human chromosomes.[8] Then one could establish linkages between one or another of these restriction sites and the genes that are involved in producing diseases. For instance, if a site variant was found to be associated with the gene causing a genetic disorder, fetuses could be tested early in a pregnancy for the presence of this very dangerous condition. Parents would then be able to make more informed decisions about continuing the pregnancy. This would be particularly important to couples who had already produced a child with the disorder and were worried about the health of future children. There are many genetic diseases that cannot be tested for directly at the moment. Linkage to a restriction site variant could be a major medical aid.

To establish such associations, White's team is using pedigree records kept by the Mormon Church, which allows the researchers to follow genes through several generations. If they find that a particular site variant (judged by testing the DNA) appears in the same people who inherit a disease, an association is strongly suspected.

RFLPs have been identified that are linked to sickle-cell anemia and other disorders, including PKU, which can cause mental deficiency; cystic fibrosis, which is a fatal respiratory problem; the thalassemias; and a form of muscular dystrophy. Not surprisingly, it was discovered that many of the genetic diseases had multiple origins. The PKU mutation arose several times in different places, as it is associated with different RFLPs in different groups. In fact, even within Northern European populations there were at least two mutations that give rise to the disease. The mutations found within Yemeni Jews, however, are yet different ones. In some populations, the PKU mutations are so common that some wonder whether the mutations might not confer some advantage on heterozygotes.

Finding different RFLPs in different populations illustrates another potential use in anthropology. Restriction polymorphisms can also be used as markers of the genetic relatedness of groups. If two populations share variants for some restriction site, it is a good bet that they have genetic ties. The odds that identical variants would appear independently in separate groups would seem to be very low.

The tremendous amount of variation seen at the DNA sequence level shows that the human gene pool contains far more variation than had previously been imagined. This sort of information has contributed to a reconsideration of the meaning of genetic variability. Not too many years ago it was assumed that most people were carrying basically the same DNA for many traits, with variations being the exception. Now we are seeing that much of the DNA differs from person to person, and although we might not be able to ascribe any functional significance to the variation, we do realize that variation is the rule. The presence of all of these variable DNA sequences in human gene pools probably means that most of them make little difference to a person's fitness; most are probably neutral with respect to one's ability to survive and reproduce. The frequencies of neutral alleles in human populations are governed by genetic drift, thus giving drift a bigger role in producing variation (and selection a smaller one) than had classically been assumed.

Hypervariable DNA

One class of RFLPs is so tremendously variable that they are known as *hypervariable*. Probes that detect these sequences in humans are providing data that have great utility in legal circles. Although they have yet to be tested in an American court of law, the British legal system has already acknowledged that the results based on these related RFLPs constitute a "DNA fingerprint"—an individual-specific picture of a person's genetic makeup. That is, there is so much variation that no two individuals will have exactly the same combination of alleles. Unlike actual fingerprints, though, the "DNA fingerprints" are totally hereditary. They are thus capable of proving parentage, a conclusion already accepted in the British legal system. This is in marked contrast to other genetic markers, which are viewed as being able only to rule out questioned parentage, not to prove it. In the next few years, these hypervariable alleles may come to revolutionize some aspects of the field of human identification.

Summary

The variations covered in this chapter barely scratch the surface of genetically determined human variation. People and populations differ in many other characteristics, such as patterns of hair growth, earlobe shape (Figure 2.18), and ability to role the tongue. Genes even determine whether a person's ear wax is dry or wet and sticky. Many of these are easily determined genetic markers that we can use to judge relationships of populations and to study the operation of the evolutionary forces. Many other such variants may yet be discovered.

In this chapter we have looked at the traits of simple inheritance, ones for which variation within and among populations is determined primarily by alleles. The discussion of the genetics of the various blood group systems was followed by a consideration of the evolutionary forces causing the present-day distribution of the blood group alleles. Various forms of investigation provide clues as to why populations vary with respect to these traits. Laboratory studies have shown similarities between ABO substances and molecules present in disease-producing organisms. Field studies likewise have shown that people of certain blood types are more or less susceptible to various infectious diseases. Correlations have also been found between some noninfectious disorders and specific blood types. Computer simulations have helped clarify which combinations of evolutionary forces might be necessary to produce the observed distribution of blood group alleles. Many studies set out to prove that natural selection is behind much of the observed variability. Sometimes, as with sickle-cell hemoglobin, this is indisputably true and documented. Other cases present hints of the operation of selection, as with ABO, but the ground is shakier. Yet further traits have yielded little if any evidence for an important role for selection and adaptation. Here we can reasonably expect that population structure has been of great significance in molding the distribution of traits seen today.

The discussion also dealt with allelic variation observed for a variety of other traits: hemoglobin, G-6-PD, HLA, and haptoglobin, as well as the ability to taste PTC. Additionally, a new class of variants, directly observable at the DNA level, are starting to assume major importance in anthropological research—restriction fragment length polymorphisms. Studies at the DNA level are proving to be very important for medical applications, and they will prove to be anthropologically useful genetic markers. The tremendous variability already seen testifies to the wealth of genetic variation in human populations.

Several general principles of evolution have been introduced. The ABO-Rh, the G-6-PD deficiency-thalassemias, and the hemoglobin S and C interactions show that the adaptiveness of a genotype depends very much on the other genes present. The Rh group illustrated that selection does not depend on "survival of the fittest" but on reproduction. By considering the known variability in modern humans, and the causes of it, we can better appreciate the ways evolution operates.

Human groups have made a variety of cultural, genetic, and physiological adaptations and adjustments to deal with many kinds of stress, including climate, disease, and diet.

Human Adaptability

Humans can adapt to stress via geographic, physical, and cultural means. In Chapter 11 we considered some generalities about this fact. Additionally, we looked at the development of the human form and the ways factors such as nutrition and health status can affect growth processes. In this chapter we will consider some of the information available about the interactions of various types of stress on both human individuals and populations. We will look at stressors related to the physical environment: heat, cold, and high altitude. We will also consider stressors in which human activity plays a more obvious role in both causing and easing the stresses: nutrition and the transmission of infectious disease. Here we are getting to phenomena that are not confined to exotic peoples in a remote land. While North Americans, for instance, are well buffered against some stressors by virtue of our technology, this same technology or other aspects of our behavior may have definite ramifications that are in themselves stressful. Are the chemicals we use to make for a more pleasant or efficient existence themselves causing health hazards? To what degree do the sources of energy, such as nuclear energy or fossil fuels, become problems themselves? In what ways are aspects of our life-styles themselves harmful? Certainly we know that addictive drugs, alcohol, and cigarettes all carry significant costs, but do life in a city and exposure to artificial lights also entail certain risks?

In this chapter we will survey a number of the stresses that have been analyzed by biologists interested in human adaptation. The coverage is not meant to be exhaustive, nor are all the answers given (or available). However, we see that the human animal is a highly adaptable creature, capable of tolerating a vast range of conditions.

There is a second, pragmatic reason for looking at adaptation. Sometimes the problems faced by a population may mimic the problems caused by disease. High altitude makes the body deal with reduced availability of oxygen. Cystic fibrosis, or CF (see page 59), is a genetic disease affecting the lungs. People with CF also have the problem of reduced oxygen supply to tissues. By understanding the adaptations made by residents in mountainous areas, we may better be able to help CF children. Let us further consider high altitude as a stress.

Altitude Stress

The Quechua Indians of highland Peru have lived at high altitudes for a long time. Their home, the Andean plateau, rises about 2,500 meters (8,200 feet) above sea level, and Indians have also lived farther up in the Andes (Figure 13.1); some Quechua settlements are as high as 5,200 meters (17,000 feet), and some male Quechuas work for short periods as miners at a level of 6,100 meters (20,000 feet). The Incas, the Quechuas' ancestors, also lived on this plateau.

Living at high altitudes causes stresses different from those imposed by lowlands. People have to adjust to lower oxygen pressure in the air they breathe; that is, the percentage of oxygen in the air at 15,000 feet is the same as at sea level, but the pressure, or the force pushing oxygen

FIGURE 13.1
A Quechua town, situated on an eastern slope of the Andes more than 3,000 meters (10,000 feet) above sea level.

across the lung membranes and into the blood vessels, is decreased. Temperatures, too, are lower at high elevations than in lowlands at the same latitude; the natives of the high Andes are thus subject to cold stress as well.

Paul Baker has long investigated the Quechuas' ability to tolerate hypoxia, or oxygen deprivation. One measure of their adjustment to this stress is aerobic capacity, or the body's ability to use available oxygen, which affects a person's capacity for work. Quechuas born and brought up at about 4,000 meters (13,000 feet) have been tested for this capacity, and the results were compared with those of Quechuas who have spent only a month at high altitude. The values for the two groups are quite different: the high-altitude group was much better able to perform work as tested in the laboratory. Because both the highland and lowland Quechuas are drawn from the same or very similar gene pools, the difference in oxygen consumption must not be genetic in origin. Yet if a lowland-born Quechua moves to high altitude, his or her aerobic capacity can eventually approach that of highland Quechuas; the younger the person at the move, the more similar the work capacity as adults. Evidently, a developmental process must be involved. If the oxygen supply is low during the growth years, the chest cavity and possibly the lungs are bigger. Children in a Quechua highland village have larger chests at all ages than do lowlanders. After growth is complete, a lowlander brought to high altitude cannot greatly enlarge the respiratory apparatus and thus can never attain the lung capacity of his or her highland-reared counterpart. The body adjusts itself during development to suit the prevailing oxygen conditions.

The effects of altitude stress are not necessarily the same in different populations. According to Cynthia Beall, the chest dimensions seen in the Quechua are not fully mirrored in Tibetans living at high elevations in Nepal.[1]* The width of the chest starts out smaller in young Quechuas, but by the time growth is complete, the Quechuas have wider chests (Figure 13.2). For chest depth, the Tibetans are smaller through most of the growth period and, at the last moment, catch up to the Quechuas. The Nepalese Sherpas, renowned for their mountaineering skill, have significantly smaller chest circumferences than Tibetan neighbors. Such variation might have a genetic basis, or it may reflect differences in environment such as nutrition and general health.

Many of the adaptations made to high altitude are built into the anatomy during the growth years, and it is not surprising that the growth process is altered at high altitude. As with the chest cavity of the Quechuas, specific parts of the body may grow more or less than in lowlanders. The heart's right ventricle in highlanders, for example, is enlarged to help push blood to the lungs. The timing of the growth process is changed. A. R. Frisancho and P. T. Baker showed that highland Quechuas of both sexes have a longer growth period and a much less marked adolescent growth spurt than sea-level Americans (Figure 13.3).[2]

Other highland populations are also known to grow quite slowly. Brooke Thomas feels that the slower growth and delayed maturation are actually an adaptation to the limitations in food supply encountered by many high-altitude groups.

Ronald Weinstein and Jere Haas looked at the weights of newborns delivered to women who had spent varying lengths of time at high altitudes.[3] Birth weight is a prime indicator of the health of newborns; infants with low birth weights have a much higher risk of death. The reproductive performance of women who moved to Leadville, Colorado

FIGURE 13.2.   Chest dimensions by height in two populations of boys from high altitudes.

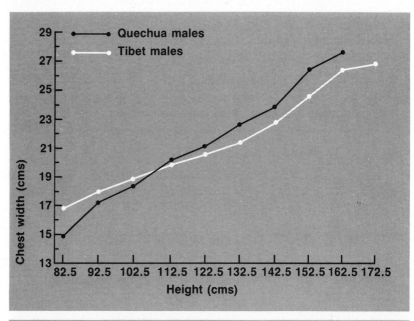

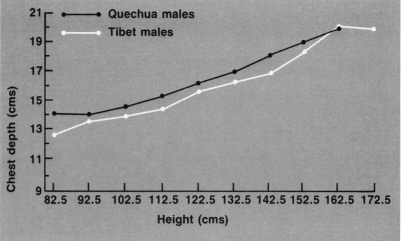

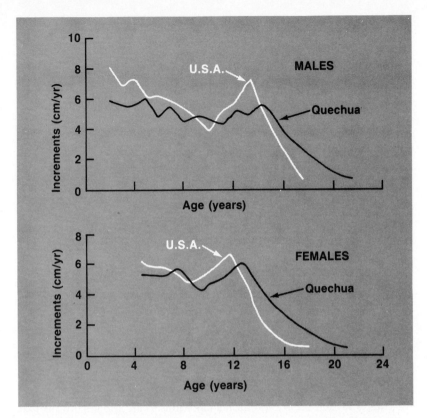

FIGURE 13.3. The time and tempo of growth are different for highland Quechua children and American children reared at sea level.

(altitude: 3,200 meters), before or during puberty was compared to those who moved there after puberty. Newborns of women who had encountered high altitude early weighed more, suggesting that exposure to hypoxia during but not after the critical period of reproductive maturation leads to adaptation. Curiously, a third group, women born and reared at high altitudes, had the smallest newborns. The interpretation of such data is confounded, however, by the need to know if the women all had comparable socioeconomic backgrounds, diets, and prenatal care.

A more recent review of Colorado birth statistics finds that infants with low birth weight are twice as common at higher elevations and that low birth weight does increase mortality risk. The researchers also found, however, that the risk of death involved in low birth weight at high altitude was not as great as at lower elevations in Colorado. In other words, although low birth weight is dangerous, it is relatively more of a danger to infants born at low altitudes. The researchers ascribe this to improved medical care for pregnant women at high altitudes.[4] We can see that the interplay of culture, growth and development, and altitude stress is truly a complex one.

Physiological Adjustments

When an adult is introduced to a stress that had not been encountered during the preadult years, two levels of physical response are generally possible: the initial, immediate response, which is generally not very efficient, and a secondary, more lasting acclimatization. A lowlander at first deals with the stress of hypoxia by increasing respiratory rate, pulse rate, blood pressure, cardiac output, and dilation (expansion) of the arteries. These are all rather inefficient attempts to get more oxygen to the tissues by working the heart harder. Later, secondary responses ease the demands on the heart by producing more red blood cells and hemoglobin; the blood can now carry more oxygen. The lungs also increase slightly in size and surface area, making it easier to get oxygen to and carbon dioxide from the red blood cells. The transfer of gases between blood and muscle is enhanced by expansion of the vascular network in the muscles. Acclimatization is thus a multistage, multifaceted response (Figure 13.4).

Generally the level of acclimatization to a stressor, whether hypoxia, cold, heat, humidity, or any other, is referred to as fitness. This is not the same as genetic fitness. Physiological fitness covers health but not reproductive ability. Fitness at high altitude shows much variability. Some lowlanders feel fine at 3,700 meters (12,000 feet); others faint, are nauseated, and lose peripheral vision; still others may die unless returned within hours to lower elevations. Likewise, Quechuas born and reared at high altitude show a high incidence of respiratory infections, especially tuberculosis, when they move to lower elevations. Dutt and Baker note that this is a result of physiological adaptations to life at high altitude that subsequently become dysfunctional. Lowland Quechuas often are economically deprived, which also adds to disease incidence.

Genetic Adaptations

We have no doubt that much of the Quechuas' ability to live and work in a rarefied atmosphere comes from their physiological acclimatization and plasticity. They may have some genetic adaptations too, but

FIGURE 13.4
The body's fitness for high altitude increases with time.
The inefficient primary responses of a recent arrival do not yield as high a fitness as the secondary responses that are developed after some time at high altitude.

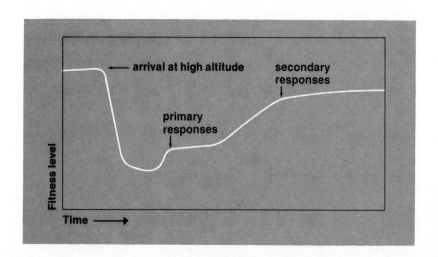

the evidence is debatable. A comparison of two groups of Peruvian students, one Quechua and one "white" (possibly with some Quechua ancestry), both born and reared at about 3,700 meters, showed that, with similar environments, the Quechuas have a higher aerobic capacity and more efficiency in supplying oxygen to the tissues. Similarly, whereas aerobic capacity drops about 20 percent in Europeans brought to high altitudes, Quechuas born and raised close to sea level lose only about 10 percent of their ability to absorb oxygen when moved to high elevations.

This pattern is repeated when children of European ancestry, born and reared above 2,500 meters in Bolivia, are compared to European lowlanders and highland Bolivian Indians. The pulmonary function of highland Europeans is more efficient than that of the lowlanders but not as efficient as that of highland Bolivian Indians matched for body and chest size. Although sufficient data are not yet available for the findings to be conclusive, the existing findings do imply that there is a genetic basis for at least part of the difference in lung function between highland European and Bolivian Indian children.

Tibetan pastoral nomads live at the highest elevations in the world, upward of 5,450 meters (17,500 feet) above sea level. Cynthia Beall and her colleagues tested the blood of 100 of these people for hemoglobin concentration, which is one measure of the blood's ability to carry oxygen.[5] Surprisingly, the results, although higher than what one might see in a typical group of Americans, were not nearly as high as those found in Quechuas living at high altitude. In part, this may reflect the fact that Quechuas often have respiratory diseases, which can also elevate hemoglobin levels. Even Quechuas with no history of disease, however, have notably higher hemoglobin concentrations than highland Tibetans. This would suggest that, while an elevated hemoglobin concentration is an adaptive physiological response found around the world, there are also genetic differences between highland populations in their specific adaptations.

Beall has also noted that the birth weight associated with greatest infant survival, the optimum birth weight, is lower at high altitudes. She suggests that the lower birth weights seen in groups long resident at high elevations in part reflects a genetic adaptation. The genes for lower birth weight are selectively beneficial at high altitudes and hence have become common.

Cultural Adaptations

Along with developmental and physiological adjustments and genetic adaptations, the Quechuas seem to have made some culturally mediated adaptations to life at high altitudes, although the ability to deal with high altitude by behavioral routes is limited. Vast amounts of data indicate that the frequency of miscarriages increases with altitude. Because this is well known to highland dwellers, the richer highlanders, primarily mestizos (hybrids of Europeans and Indians), send their pregnant women to lower elevations to ensure successful gestation. The highland Quechuas also marry at an earlier age and reproduce for a longer time than lowlanders, both cultural factors that maintain population size. Even though the age of menarche is rather late in the highlanders, the average age at first pregnancy is earlier than among lowlanders. The number of childbearing years is thus greater at high altitudes, and among lowlanders fertility drops off markedly after a few years of marriage. Both of these culturally influenced factors help offset the high rate of fetal death brought about by hypoxia.

Cold Stress

Cultural Adaptations: Alcohol and Other Cures

Another important variable at high altitudes is cold stress. In the United States, alcohol is one of the ways people have of trying to keep warm, and it seems to be common among the Quechuas too. Just as the American football game is a socially accepted context for drinking to keep warm, so are Quechua outdoor activities such as weddings, markets, and soccer games. These Indians regularly consume sizable quantities of ethanol in the form of sugarcane alcohol (up to about 85 proof). Beer and sugarcane alcohol account for more than 20 percent of the trading in at least one highland town.

Michael Little conducted some experiments with Quechua males to see if alcohol consumption acclimates the Indians to cold. He gave the subjects fixed quantities of sugarcane alcohol at standardized temperatures while monitoring the Indians' foot temperatures. The foot temperatures were significantly higher when alcohol was ingested, actually an indication of heat loss. For dealing with cold, drinking alcohol is thus a mixed blessing. Alcohol causes greater blood flow to the extremities, which raises skin temperature; the ears, for example, become hot. The increased flow of blood temporarily increases comfort out in the cold, but extending the habit over a long period can be dangerous. In the course of warming the skin, the body throws off heat to the external environment, lowering internal temperature. As Little says, "The consumption of alcohol . . . should give the Indian a thermal advantage during natural exposure to the cold. . . . Over short periods of time, the advantage in terms of comfort should outweigh the disadvantage of [heat loss]."[6]

Quechuas have many other cultural ways of surviving cold stress. The Indians commonly chew coca leaves mixed with lime, which releases several chemicals, one of which is cocaine. Although the narcotic does not appear to alleviate cold stress physically, many said they chewed coca leaves because it made them "feel warm." If nothing else, coca chewing may be giving them a psychological adaptation to cold.

Economics also enters the picture. In the higher reaches of the Andes, economic factors have encouraged many to shift their subsistence activity from agriculture to pastoralism. Because they must constantly move their herds of llama, alpaca, goats, and sheep to new pastures, few bother to build a permanent adobe home. Instead, they build rock-pile huts with straw roofs, which are very poor insulators. At lower (although still high-altitude) elevations, Quechua farmers are more closely tied to the land, for it is privately owned. The homes they build are long-term investments and are better insulators. The farmers are exposed to less cold stress. The thermometer may fall to freezing during the coldest time of the night, but the interior temperature averages 7°C (45° F). The Indians may also sleep in groups to share body heat.

The San Bushmen of the Kalahari Desert in southern Africa use cultural adaptations that, although they may appear crude to us, are very helpful in warding off cold stress. During the winter, night temperatures drop to about freezing. Early in the evening the San split into three groups, each around its own campfire (Figure 13.5). At one are mothers and small children; a second is surrounded by young men and by husbands whose wives are nursing (and therefore taboo). A third group consists of family units in which the mother is not nursing, each family having its own fire. At each fire the people lie with skin cloaks tucked around their bodies and pulled over their heads, and with their feet toward the fire; often they will also huddle together to share their body heat and cloaks. Their feet seem to serve as thermostats, for when the fire dies down, they awaken and add more wood. By using only the cloak and fire, they keep the air next to their bodies at about 18° C (65° F). They do not sleep in their grass huts, but use them as windbreaks, which also reduces cold stress.

One of the most important techniques used to deal with cold is clothing. The Eskimos use a variety of skins for making clothes but prefer those of the caribou. These provide a great degree of insulation that can actually become a problem itself. When exercising strenuously, the Eskimos may become overheated. Their parkas thus have many vents that can be opened and closed with drawstrings to allow more or less ventilation.

FIGURE 13.5.   A San Bushman camp.

Variations in responses to cold, like responses to hypoxia, may be brought about partly by genetically caused physiological differences. Various peoples may be able to generate heat by burning calories with differing efficiency; their bodies may also use the heat differently, and some may be better insulated than others. From the Andes, several researchers have reported tentative results that seem to show a genetic difference between Quechua Indians and whites in reaction to cold.

Paul Baker was able to estimate roughly the relative effects of genetic adaptation and physiological acclimatization to cold by comparing three groups: native Quechua Indians, university students of Quechua ancestry, and Peruvian university students of European ancestry. All three groups lived at about the same altitude, but the two student groups had experienced less than lifelong exposure to cold. When the subjects' fingers were exposed to cold in the laboratory, the two Indian groups reacted in much the same way, which differed from the non-Quechuas' reaction. The fingers of both Indian groups did not cool as much as the non-Quechuas' fingers, and the Indians' fingers rewarmed more rapidly. Baker concluded that "the difference between Indian and white genetic inheritance was of more significance than environmental exposure [and subsequent physiological acclimatization]."[7]

The warmer Quechua extremities appear to be caused by increased blood flow to the limbs, which seems to be adaptive in helping prevent cold stress. Because Quechuas do not wear gloves, this is a vital way of warming themselves. Heat is also needed in the extremities to keep the muscles working properly during physical activity. On the other hand, continuing the heat flow to the limbs for hours on end (as occurs when relying on alcohol) can be a very dangerous way of combating cold. As the warm blood reaches the limbs, the heat it carries warms the tissues but is also radiated away to the environment. This heat loss can cause a drop in internal body temperature. A prolonged drop in internal temperature can kill; therefore, the need for warm extremities and the heat loss that it causes must be balanced. If this balance is upset in either direction, injury or death can result.

To maintain this balance, humans exhibit cyclic constriction and expansion of the blood vessels in the extremities in what is called a *hunting response*. When a hand is exposed to the cold, its vessels close down to help prevent heat loss. After about fifteen minutes, the small vessels open up, allowing the warm blood to reheat the tissues of the hand; then they shut down again. This cycle can be very important to anyone who has to use his hands with dexterity in the cold. Although Eskimos may have very efficient gloves, they cannot tie knots or sew without removing their gloves. As their hands cool, they lose dexterity, but they regain it as a result of the hunting response. All people exhibit this response; however, the rapidity and strength of the response are greater in Eskimos (Figure 13.6).

The Eskimos also seem to deal with cold by burning energy at a very high rate, called their metabolic rate. It is not clear whether this high rate is a result of their diet, which is primarily protein and fat, or

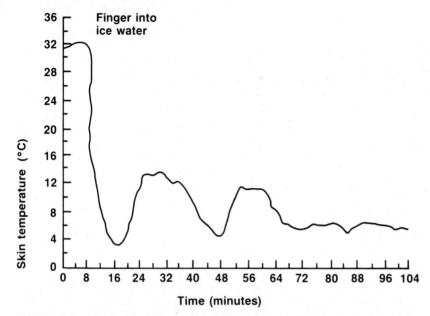

FIGURE 13.6. **The hunting response to cold exposure. The initial large and long skin temperature changes are replaced by smaller, more rapid changes. This is due to changes in the cycle of blood vessel constriction and dilation.**

some other, possibly genetic factor. It is known that when highland and lowland Quechuas and those of European heritage are exposed to overall body cooling, the lowland Quechuas' response is much more similar to that of non-Quechuas, indicating a physiological, nongenetic similarity.

We have presented no more than a very preliminary discussion of responses to cold stress. We have not talked about how the different responses come about nor the relative importance of genes and acclimatization. Other kinds of adaptation may enter the picture, too. Living in an atmosphere deficient in oxygen increases the capillary bed in the muscles and causes greater heart output. The Quechuas' response could be in part anatomical and physiological accompaniments to hypoxic stress. Acclimatization to hypoxia, for example, could be partly responsible for their having warmer extremities. The large lungs of the Quechuas, however, result in a great amount of heat loss via respiration. They thus need to replace this lost heat by burning food at a higher metabolic rate, which then means they need more food. Differences in skin color, age, amount of body fat, and other traits can also affect one's responses to cold.

Heat Stress

Adapting to a hot climate involves interactions as complicated as adapting to cold or hypoxia. But heat by itself is not nearly as important as heat plus humidity, which interact because of one of the body's ways of dissipating heat: evaporation. In a hot but dry environment it is easy for sweat to evaporate from the naked body, thereby removing heat; if the surrounding air is already moist, however, water will not evaporate, and sweating loses its efficiency.

Populations do not seem to differ in the number or distribution of sweat glands: each human being has roughly 2 million. However, different parts of an individual vary in sweat gland density, and a population may also have some person-to-person variability. But some populations do differ in the way their sweat glands work.

As in adapting to cold, in hot conditions the body must reach a compromise between opposing factors, in this case heat loss and water loss. In desert conditions the body can lose up to two liters of water an hour by sweating. If drinking water is scarce, sweating can be very dangerous; water loss that rapid can be fatal in a short time. If the body is not cooled, however, heat stress can bring death. Fortunately, the body has more than one way of cooling itself.

In addition to sweating, the body can also be cooled by radiation, that is, by transferring heat between two objects that are not directly in contact. If we sit by a window in a short-sleeved shirt on a cold day, our arms feel cool because we are radiating body heat to the outside, even though we are not in direct contact with the window. Radiation's efficiency in dispersing body heat is determined partly by the relative size and shape of the extremities and the body trunk.

Two Ecological Rules

Bergmann and Allen, nineteenth-century ecologists who noticed the relationship between the size and shape of extremities and trunk in widely distributed species of mammals, lent their names to two ecological rules.

Bergmann's Rule states that, of two bodies with similar shapes, the larger has less surface area per unit of volume, will hold heat better, and thus is better adapted to the cold. Let us assume that two bodies are spherical (Figure 13.7) and that the radius of one is twice that of the other. Geometry tells us that the surface areas of the spheres are proportional to the radii squared, but that the volumes of the spheres are pro-

FIGURE 13.7. An illustration of Bergmann's Rule: The surface area of a sphere is proportional to the radius squared, and the volume is proportional to the radius cubed. As the radius increases, the ratio of surface area to volume thus decreases, and the body is better suited to retain heat.

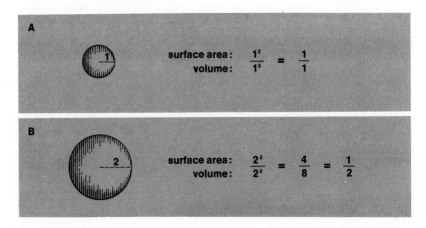

A

surface area: $\dfrac{1^2}{1^3} = \dfrac{1}{1}$
volume:

B

surface area: $\dfrac{2^2}{2^3} = \dfrac{4}{8} = \dfrac{1}{2}$
volume:

portional to the radii cubed. Looking at the ratio of surface area to volume for A and B, we see that as the sphere gets bigger, the ratio of surface area to volume decreases. That is, for every unit of surface area in A there is one unit of volume, but for every unit of surface area in B there are two units of volume. Heat production is related to body volume, but heat loss occurs at the surface and therefore is related to surface area. A has one unit of surface area to radiate away the heat produced by one unit of volume, and B has one unit of surface area to dissipate the heat generated by twice as much volume. A is therefore better adapted for hot conditions because it loses heat more readily, and B is better adapted to conserve heat.

Generally, this rule holds true within a species of mammals. Figure 13.8 shows that the body size of the American puma increases as the temperature of its habitat decreases.

FIGURE 13.8.   The puma is a wide-ranging species that conforms to Bergmann's Rule. This cline of puma body size shows it to be large in cold areas and smaller in warm regions. The map is based on field estimates of E. A. Goldman.

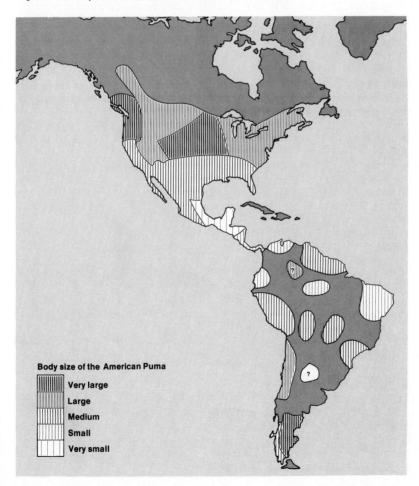

Body size of the American Puma

Very large

Large

Medium

Small

Very small

Several research studies show that human body weight is lower in warmer areas and higher in colder areas. D. F. Roberts, using information on more than one hundred human populations, showed a strong inverse correlation between the average body weight of a population and the average temperature of its environment; that is, as temperature climbs, body weight falls (Figure 13.9).[8] Marshall Newman, working with even more data, confirmed this relationship.[9] However, there was a disagreement as to the causative factor. While Roberts maintained that in cold areas natural selection favored the genes for greater weight, Newman felt that the underlying cause was largely nutritional. The fact that children of Americans living in the Panama Canal Zone were lighter than members of the same gene pool brought up in the colder United States shows that there is room for acclimatization. Undoubtedly, genes too play a role in population differences in body size. Witness Eskimos and Pygmies—no dietary modification could make one look like the other in body build.

In addition to making predictions about body size, Bergmann's Rule states that body shape will vary with temperature. We can again demonstrate geometrically that a circle contains the maximum volume for a fixed surface area. Therefore, the best shape for dissipating heat is a long and slender one, because it has less volume per unit of surface

FIGURE 13.9.   Relationships of body weight to temperature. Although the degree of correlation between body weight and environmental temperature varies from population to population, humans do show a marked conformity to Bergmann's Rule.

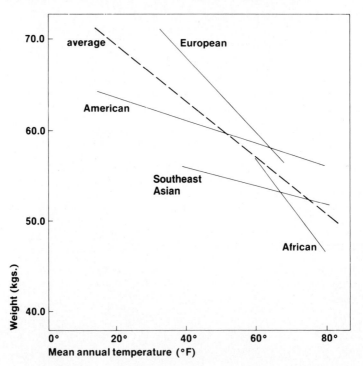

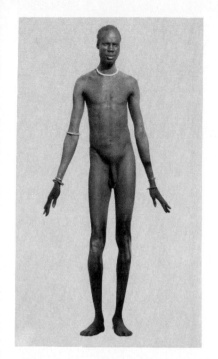
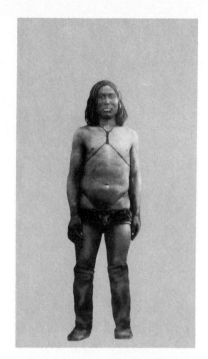

FIGURE 13.10.   A Nilotic black and an Eskimo. Their body shapes conform to Allen's Rule.

area; a compact, spherical body shape is best for conserving heat. Many human populations illustrate this difference: Many sub-Saharan Africans are linear in build, while circumpolar people such as the Eskimos are very compactly built.

Allen's Rule describes regularities of the body's proportions; it states that in hot regions, extremities (in humans, the arms and legs) are long to provide maximum surface area for dissipating heat. In cold regions limbs are short to reduce surface area and therefore heat loss. Most sub-Saharan Africans fit both rules, having long limbs and slender trunks, while Eskimos have large-volume trunks and short limbs (Figure 13.10).

These rules are not the only factors affecting body size and shape, and therefore exceptions exist. Another factor, as we shall see later in this chapter, is diet.

More Physiological Adaptations

Ecological rules also are not the only biological adaptations to heat stress. One very important biological mechanism for throwing off excess heat is an increase in blood flow to the skin of the extremities. Bringing the excess heat to the surface radiates it away. Convection, the transfer of heat between the body and a moving fluid or gas, can also take place. Curiously, it appears that the genetic differences in heat adaptations are quite minimal. All human groups seem to have comparable limits in terms of dealing with heat. Maybe selection for modes of tolerating heat

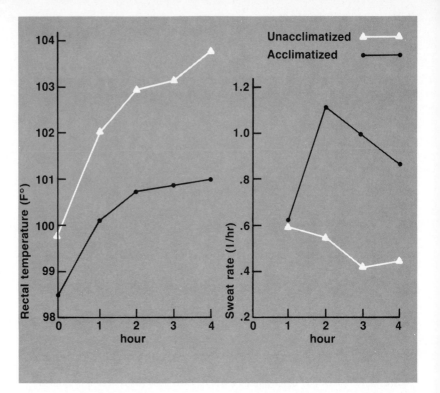

**FIGURE 13.11
Physiological changes
during acclimatization to
heat.**
As the men adapted to
working four hours in a hot,
humid environment,
sweating increased and
body temperature
decreased. The
acclimatized measurements
were taken ten days after
the unacclimatized.

was very strong early in human evolution, when our ancestors lived in the tropics. Current research would indicate that only very minor differences have evolved in varied human populations.

Although there may not be major genetic differences, this is not to say that acclimatization does not occur, for it certainly does. Figure 13.11 shows the changes in sweating rate and body temperature that took place in twelve men as they acclimated to exercising in a hot and humid environment. Before acclimatizing, their sweat rate was very high and very inefficient when they exercised for four hours. Repeating this regime for ten days, they adapted to the heat quite noticeably, and their sweat rate dropped. Likewise, their body temperature when exercising showed a major change over the ten days.

Cultural Adaptations

Depending on the humidity in an area, clothing can serve as a cultural adaptation to heat stress. In hot and dry conditions such as a desert, clothes can be quite helpful. By shielding the skin, clothing reduces the heat increase from solar radiation, much like sitting in the shade. Because less heat is gained, the need to perspire is reduced and the dangers of dehydration are avoided. When working hard and perspiring heavily, loose clothing is best, for it allows for more heat loss by evaporation. In a hot and humid climate, though, clothing is best forgotten—it doesn't help.

Housing can be varied to help tolerate heat. Adobe and stone houses were mentioned as adaptive to life in the cold; they are also good in a hot, dry area. When the sun beats down on these materials, they absorb much of the heat before passing it to the interior, keeping the occupants cool in the day and warming them at night. Using few, well-placed, shaded windows, painting the home a light color, and planting shade trees are other adaptations of people living in hot and dry areas. When the environment is hot and humid, as in a tropical jungle, there is already much shade, but ventilation becomes important. Homes in these areas are made of light, porous materials like thatch. Sometimes the houses are raised off the ground to provide for greater air circulation.

Skin Color and Sunlight

Heat and cold are two aspects of climate that have played a role in the evolution of modern humans. Another is sunlight, and its effects have probably been of most importance in the evolution of a trait that we all note and that has social and political ramifications as well as biological: This trait is skin color.

Until relatively recently the analysis of skin color variation was carried out in a highly stereotypic fashion using very crude measurement techniques. People were categorized according to the perceptions of the researcher. This left a tremendous margin for differences in vision to affect results, to say nothing of the researcher's motivations, preconceptions, and social philosophy. Even with a "scientific" technique there was plenty of room for error or bias. One of these early techniques involved a set of about thirty coded tiles that the investigator could match to a subject's skin. The population could then be described in terms of the number of individuals that matched one or another of these tiles. It is obvious that the acuity of the researcher's color vision is just one of a number of factors that would affect the outcome.

Such techniques have since been replaced by an instrument that measures the amount of light reflected by the skin at different wavelengths compared with a pure white standard. Pure white reflects equally at all wavelengths; skin gets its color by unequally absorbing light because of pigments in the skin. Skin reflectance can then be plotted as in Figure 13.12. These graphs do not give a name to the color, which is a visual phenomenon; they are rather an objective measure of pigmentation.

Measuring skin color in this way is a great advance over previous methods. Because all the older methods required matching some standard with a patch of skin, there was much variation among experimenters due to differences in perceptual abilities and light sources as well as other factors. In addition, skin color is a continuously variable trait, and having to match a person's skin with one or another colored tile is bound to be an inexact process. Reflectometry has resolved many of these problems, although some still remain. It is undeniably more accurate than verbal description.

To make data on skin color gathered by different researchers comparable, techniques have been somewhat standardized. Usually the read-

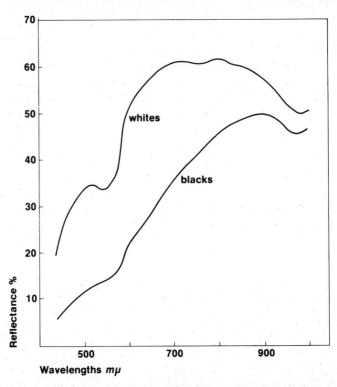

FIGURE 13.12. Developments in instrumentation have led to more accurate ways of describing skin color. The reflectance spectrophotometer measures the amount of light of a specific wavelength reflected by a person's skin. This graph records the percentage of light reflected at each of a number of wavelengths and shows the average reflectance of light for a sample of American whites and blacks. The two plots are similar in shape, except that at each wavelength, light skin reflects more light. The depression in the reflectance curve for whites at about 550 mμ results from the strong absorbance of blue light by the pigment in blood—hemoglobin; darkly pigmented skin prevents the blood from influencing the curve for blacks.

ings are taken on the inside surface of the upper arm to minimize the effects of tanning and hair; the area must be cleaned and the reddening caused by rubbing must be allowed to disappear before readings are taken.

Human skin gets its color mostly from two pigments, melanin and hemoglobin. Melanin is a complex combination of biochemical compounds that have proved very difficult to analyze. In the body it is even more complicated because the melanin is combined with other molecules. We do know that melanin is formed in specialized cells, known as melanocytes, that are in the lower level of the epidermis; each melanocyte has branches or dendrites that extend toward the skin's surface. The dark-colored melanin granules secreted by melanocytes are conveyed into another cell-type, the Malpighian cells, by the dendrites (Figure 13.13). Although melanocytes vary in number in different parts of the body, the average number of melanocytes per unit of skin area does not change for the same body region between sub-Saharan Africans and Eu-

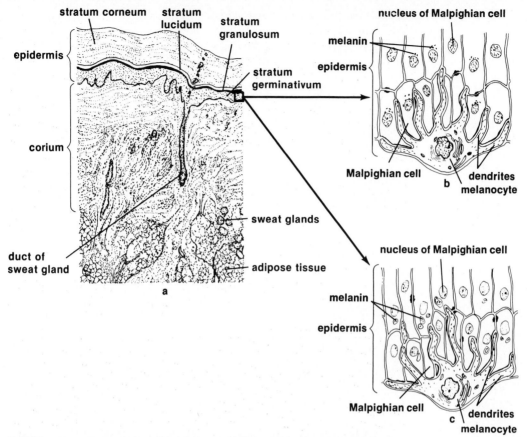

FIGURE 13.13. Human skin has two layers, the outer epidermis and the deeper dermis, or corium. (a) The epidermis is subdivided into several anatomically distinct strata; the dermis is dense connective tissue. Melanin is produced by melanocytes within the lowest stratum of the epidermis. The melanin-producing cell transports the pigment to the Malpighian cells of the stratum germinativum via branches known as dendrites. (b) In sub-Saharan Africans and Native Australians the melanin granules are more plentiful and form a cap over the Malpighian cells' nuclei. (c) In Europeans and Asians the melanin granules form clusters, but not necessarily over the top of the nuclei.

ropeans. The difference in color comes from the varying number and size of granules formed in the melanocytes.

In people who produce little melanin, much of the skin's coloration is produced by reflection from hemoglobin, which gives the skin its pinkish cast. The color can be affected by the number of small blood vessels under the skin as well as by whether the hemoglobin is carrying oxygen.

It is clear that skin color varies gradually, or clinally, in Africa and Europe (Figure 13.14); that is, there is no one place at which darkly pigmented skin abruptly gives way to light pigmentation. Rather, populations progressively farther from the equator average lesser and lesser amounts of melanin.

Skin Color and Selection

What follows is a discussion of several of the ways in which natural selection might have produced the population differences seen today. Virtually all look to sunlight as the ultimate cause of the variation. This idea starts with the fact that the average amount of sunlight, as well as the average amount of melanin, decreases as one moves away from the equator. Some have said that large amounts of melanin protect against sunburn and that in equatorial regions, where the burning rays of the ultraviolet part of the spectrum are strong year-round, dark skin is favored. Away from the equator, seasonal variation is greater; ultraviolet

FIGURE 13.14.   Clinal variation for skin color. Going northward (and to a lesser degree southward) from equatorial Africa, the degree of pigmentation decreases in a relatively even fashion, as shown by the arrow.

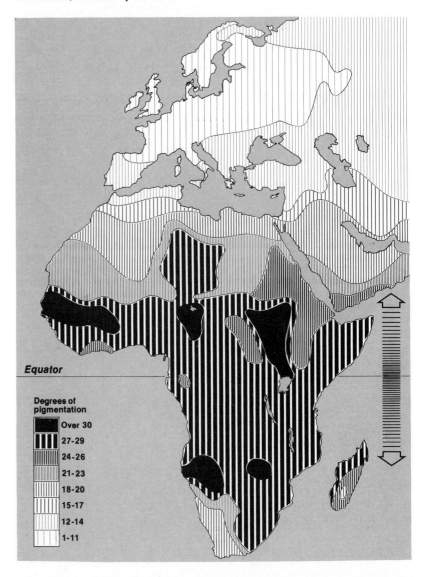

light falls to very low levels in winter and climbs as high as those at the equator in summer. Although the outer layer of dark skin absorbs fewer of the sun's ultraviolet rays, thus avoiding sunburn, one must ask whether susceptibility to sunburn could actually function as a selective agent. People with light skin pigmentation who visit equatorial regions may suffer sunburn, but after a while many of them tan by producing more melanin and become acclimated. Others, however, never tan enough to avoid sunburn; the infections that can appear in badly sunburned areas could reduce reproductive abilities.

Another biological factor that has been discussed is susceptibility to skin cancer. Here, too, ultraviolet light is the troublemaker, for it can precipitate cancerous changes in cells. Skin cancer, though, has a rather low incidence even in Europeans and usually occurs late in or after the reproductive years.

W. F. Loomis, a biochemist, has revived an old theory.[10] Ultraviolet light is important because it stimulates production of vitamin D in the deep layers of the skin. If this vitamin is not plentiful, either because of lack of exposure to sunlight or because dietary intake of the vitamin is low, not enough calcium is absorbed in the intestines. Calcium keeps the nervous system functioning properly and is a structural support for bone. When a calcium deficiency arises, the body ensures proper functioning of the nervous system by drawing the mineral out of the bones. That can cause the symptoms of rickets: deformed legs, spine, and pelvis, and, if it is severe enough, death from a malfunctioning nervous system (Figure 13.15). The changes in pelvic shape can also be dangerous

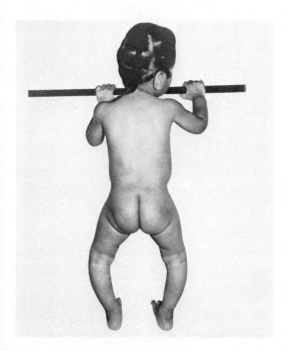

FIGURE 13.15
Rickets can be a severely debilitating disorder, as this child's deformed legs indicate.

for women who have not finished reproducing. Too much vitamin D, on the other hand, causes *hypervitaminosis,* which forms calcium deposits in soft tissues. It can lead to fatal kidney dysfunction.

Loomis contends that proper vitamin D maintenance in the body comes from the skin's ability to accept the right amount of ultraviolet rays. Dark skin evolved in tropical climes to filter out ultraviolet light and prevent hypervitaminosis. When the hominines migrated out of the warm regions, selection favored those with less pigmentation, which would help prevent rickets. Being able to tan helps the European prevent hypervitaminosis during the summer months, when ultraviolet light can be as strong as in the tropics.

However, cultural developments in Europe may have had disadvantageous health effects. By building very narrow streets and polluting the air, Europeans cut down the amount of ultraviolet light reaching the ground; even with pale skin, many eighteenth- and nineteenth-century children and adults were crippled by rickets. Living indoors can powerfully affect the frequency of rickets, as seen in Figure 13.16.

FIGURE 13.16
In India, wealthy Moslems tend to stay indoors more than upper-class Hindus, who in turn are indoors more than poorly fed, lower-class Hindus. Accordingly, the Moslems have the highest frequency of rickets, and the poor Hindus the lowest.

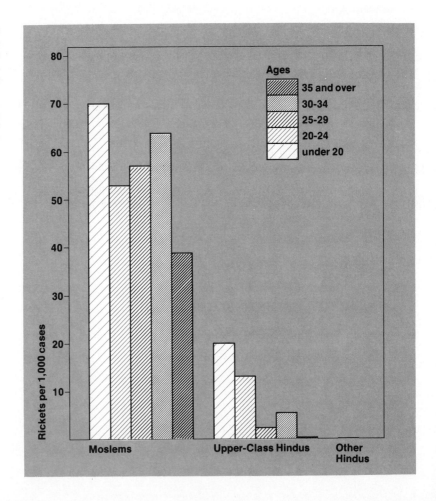

Inviting as this theory is, it remains untested. Many natural situations could be used to test this theory: Do blacks in the northern United States and Canada who have poor diets suffer from rickets more than whites on the same diet? It is probably fair to say that vitamin D synthesis may affect the evolution of skin color, but how great that effect might be is open to question.

Other roles for melanin that are related to diet and light have also been suggested. Folate is one of several vitamins that are light sensitive. Sunlight causes the decomposition of these nutrients, even when the light is filtered through lightly pigmented skin. Richard Branda and John Eaton have shown that blood levels of folate are noticeably lowered in light-skinned people who have been exposed to a lot of ultraviolet light (Figure 13.17).[11] They suggest that heavily melanized skin has evolved to prevent the photodestruction of vitamins in tropical peoples. The selective effect is quite reasonable, for folate deficiency is very dangerous, causing anemia, spontaneous abortions, and infertility, and thus is capable of preventing reproduction by those with little melanin where sunlight is intense. Other nutrients, such as vitamin E and riboflavin, are also known to be damaged by exposure to light. Photodestruction of these substances would add more weight to Branda and Eaton's hypothesis.

Other theories have been tested to relate skin color and the ability to tolerate climatic conditions. Because white skin reflects more light, we would expect it to be better adapted to hot climates than heat-absorbing dark skin. This would bring about a distribution in skin color the reverse of the one we see.

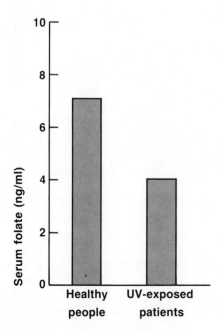

FIGURE 13.17. The concentration of folate in the blood serum of 10 healthy people is compared to that in 10 patients who had been exposed to ultraviolet (UV) light for at least 3 months. The level is significantly lower in those exposed to the UV light.

Many years ago Paul Baker found that a swarthy complexion is best adapted to a hot, dry climate.[12] This medium pigmentation averts severe sunburn and does not absorb the heat that could lead to heat stress and death. It has also been noted by Peter Post and his colleagues that darkly pigmented skin is more susceptible to frostbite, thus partially explaining the presence of light skin colors in cold areas.[13] However, many other factors enter the picture, such as heat loss by sweating, ionizing radiation, amount of body fat, stature, and cultural factors. Although many desert populations have medium pigmentation (San Bushmen and the Papago Indians), wide variation, from Negroes in the southern Sahara to Berbers in North Africa, indicates that skin color is not the only factor providing adaptation for a climatic zone.

It has been suggested that the genes controlling melanin production may have more evolutionary importance for some unknown effect than for pigmentation itself; that is, selection may favor the genes that produce dark pigmentation in equatorial regions not because dark pigmentation is important but because some other effect of the same genes is beneficial there. This would fit with a proposal that heavy pigmentation is a secondary effect of genes that provide increased resistance to disease. As the tropics are conducive to growth of microbes, selection, it is argued, would favor genes that provide resistance to disease. Besides providing for a powerful immune system, these genes also cause production of a lot of melanin.

Infectious Disease

In Chapter 12 we emphasized how genetic variation copes with disease. Humans do, however, adapt to infectious and noninfectious disease by means that are not genetic and rather different.

Physiological Defenses

Our physiological responses to infectious disease agents are multi-faceted, like our ways of adjusting to altitude. The first line of defense is the skin, a strong barrier to microbial penetration. The inside of our respiratory passage is lined with mucous membranes whose sticky secretions trap many foreign particles. The tiny cilia, or hairs, of the cells in the respiratory system beat outward, sweeping foreign materials out of the body (Figure 13.18). We also have a subclass of antibodies, or immunoglobulins (IgA), that appear to be secreted by the cells lining most of our body openings and help keep microorganisms out.

If a microorganism gets through these barriers, several other defenses are set in motion. We start rapidly producing another subclass of antibodies, IgM, somewhat different in structure from IgA, that appear to be effective against comparatively large particles, such as bacteria. IgM acts as an identification tag, attaching to the bacteria and helping the white blood cells identify and destroy the invaders.

Other defenders are the antibodies known as IgG, which counteract infection. They contribute to a reaction known as *immunological memory*. Antibodies specifically produced for an antigen may initially take some time to build; after the antigen disappears, the antibody level drops until it can no longer be detected. Subsequent exposure to the antigen, however, sets off the very rapid production of specific antibodies: The immunological system "remembers" the kinds to produce. Just how our immune system does this we do not know, but it definitely is observable (Figure 13.19). Our cells are geared to start rapid, specific antibody production upon subsequent exposure to an antigen. In this way individuals in a population build immunity to many of the diseases they normally encounter.

Infants get some immunity to disease by acquiring maternal antibodies either by transfer across the placenta or by breast-feeding. The mother's first milk (colostrum) is rich in IgA antibodies. Should infection occur, maternal antibodies help protect the infant until its own immune system becomes effective.

Antibodies are produced by a special type of white blood cells known as B-cells and are an essential part of immunity. There is a second class of white cells, however, known as T-cells, of which there are several types. Some T-cells can directly attack foreign cells, substances, or organisms. These act in cancer surveillance by recognizing and destroying cells that have become cancerous before they are able to produce major health problems. Most of us, it seems, have cancerous cells appearing fairly frequently. Other T-cells help the B-cells make antibodies, and others act to turn off the immune response.

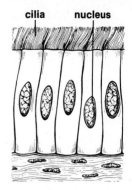

cilia   nucleus

FIGURE 13.18
Cells of the respiratory tract, lined with cilia. These fine, hairlike structures move constantly and help keep the air passage free of foreign substances.

FIGURE 13.19.   The speed and quantity of antibody production upon first and subsequent exposure to an antigen. Upon exposure to a new antigen (at left), antibody production is delayed for a week or more and then rises to moderate levels; the quantity of the antibody subsequently falls off relatively rapidly. Upon subsequent exposure to the same antigen, antibody production is more rapid, and its level rises to greater heights and remains elevated longer.

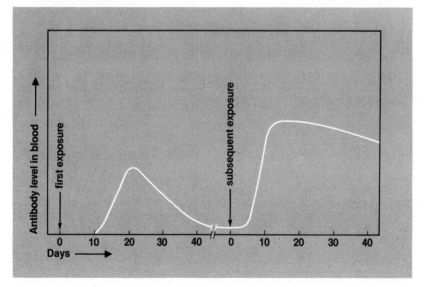

For physiological reasons an infection is often more severe in previously unexposed adults than in children. Cultural practices as well as physiology influence who will and who will not get sick—and sometimes who will be treated and thus who will survive. The natural history of poliomyelitis shows the interdependence of biology and culture. Polio, caused by a virus (see Figure 2.15), was often transmitted from child to child amid poor sanitary conditions, usually because of contact with feces as a result of not washing the hands. In many areas of the world, the polio virus was quite common, but most of the viruses were not too virulent. Usually a childhood infection produced only mild symptoms: headache, slight fever, and respiratory or gastrointestinal problems, followed by complete recovery and the production of antibodies. If a virulent strain came along later, the people rapidly produced effective antibodies and thus avoided paralysis and death. As our culture became more and more antiseptic, many people avoided this early, relatively safe exposure to the virus. When epidemics of highly virulent strains did hit, as in the early and middle 1950s, many young adults were severely crippled because they could not rapidly make antibodies to the virus. In less sanitary areas, the critical cases during an epidemic are mostly those under age five. Table 13.1 shows the attack rates of paralytic polio in a major United States city during several outbreaks.

Disease can strike a previously unexposed population with terrible violence. In 1949, when several Eskimo communities were first hit by polio, 14 percent of the population died and 40 percent were paralyzed. Paralysis rarely occurs in the very young, and here it did not affect any children less than three years old. The disease was spread even faster by the social disorganization and breakdown in nutrition and hygiene that followed the epidemic. Subsequent polio epidemics among the Eskimos have been more comparable to epidemics elsewhere; the Eskimos have adjusted physiologically, psychologically, and socially to the disease.

Social systems can determine the impact of an infectious disease. J. B. S. Haldane has postulated that epidemic diseases did not greatly affect human evolution until agriculture came along and with it large

TABLE 13.1
Paralytic Polio in Detroit, by Age and by Race

Age	1939 White %	1939 White N	1939 Nonwhite %	1939 Nonwhite N	1946 White %	1946 White N	1946 Nonwhite %	1946 Nonwhite N	1952[a] White %	1952[a] White N	1952[a] Nonwhite %	1952[a] Nonwhite N
0–4	23	49	36	19	24	41	64	33	32	144	48	17
5–14	71	147	60	32	47	78	24	12	42	190	46	16
15+	6	13	4	2	29	48	12	6	26	120	6	2
Total cases (N)		209		53		167		51		454		35

[a]The group with poorer sanitation, the nonwhites, usually had both fewer cases and a greater percentage of cases in the 0–4 age bracket, while among whites, the preponderance of cases were in the older age brackets.

After Richard D. Leach, "Socioeconomic Status, Race, and Poliomyelitis in Detroit, Michigan: A Sociological Analysis" (Unpubl. MA thesis, Wayne State University, 1967), p. 73.

population centers. In an epidemic not every susceptible person contracts the disease, nor does every infected individual pass the infection to someone else. In a small, scattered population, the probability that the disease will spread as an epidemic is quite low, but in a large, densely populated city the microorganism has a far easier time finding new hosts. Eventually, even in a large community, the rate of new infections slows down (Figure 13.20). By this time the disease has usually moved to another city, returning to the first city after several years, during which time more susceptible children have been born.

Epidemics need population centers and ways of getting to them. In the Western world today, an infection can easily travel great distances in a short time. Several hundred years ago, with longer travel times and fewer people traveling, epidemics were rather more limited around the world. Epidemics did, of course, scourge people in the past; the waves of bubonic plague that swept through Europe from the 1300s to the 1700s are estimated to have killed more than 25 million people, about a quarter of the European population. Often it was spread as people panicked at its arrival, carrying the disease with them to new areas.

The social subdivision of modern societies also affects disease transmission and incidence. People live in overlapping neighborhoods and contact different subsets of individuals as they move through the day. The effective size of a person's population vis-à-vis disease transmission is not nearly as large as the number of people in the geographic area; the number to which we actually have social links is very important. Lisa Sattenspiel noted this fact in studying epidemics of a liver ailment, hepatitis A, in children attending day-care centers in Albuquerque, New Mexico.[14] For instance, the ways in which children are grouped by age in these centers affects the transmission of the disease.

Socioeconomic status, too, often affects disease patterns; the first polio epidemics were confined almost entirely to the United States, Canada, Scandinavia, and Australia, all comparatively wealthy regions. When polio vaccines were introduced in the 1950s, the incidence of the disease dropped off markedly in the middle and upper classes but not always in the lower classes. In cities that distributed the scarce vaccine via private physicians, the poorest did not receive immunizations, and polio lingered on in that group (Table 13.2).

Noninfectious Disorders

As time goes on infectious disease rapidly shrinks as a cause of human deaths in Western nations, but at the same time deaths from noninfectious disorders rise. This shift is referred to as the *epidemiologic transition,* and its occurrence can be well documented. For instance, three anthropologists were able to use census and burial records to show that the town of Manti, Utah, went through such a transition in the early 1900s. At that time, as the dependence on a contaminated water supply declined and as modern medicine became available, the causes of death changed to degenerative diseases.

Countries like the United States annually suffer hundreds of thousands of deaths from cancer and heart disease, in part because medical

FIGURE 13.20. Schematic view of the spread of an infectious disease. A disease rarely disappears completely, but continues ad infinitum; the final white square in one of the City 1 chains indicates that a few persons will continue to infect others. The final black square in the remaining chains means that the person does not pass on the disease.

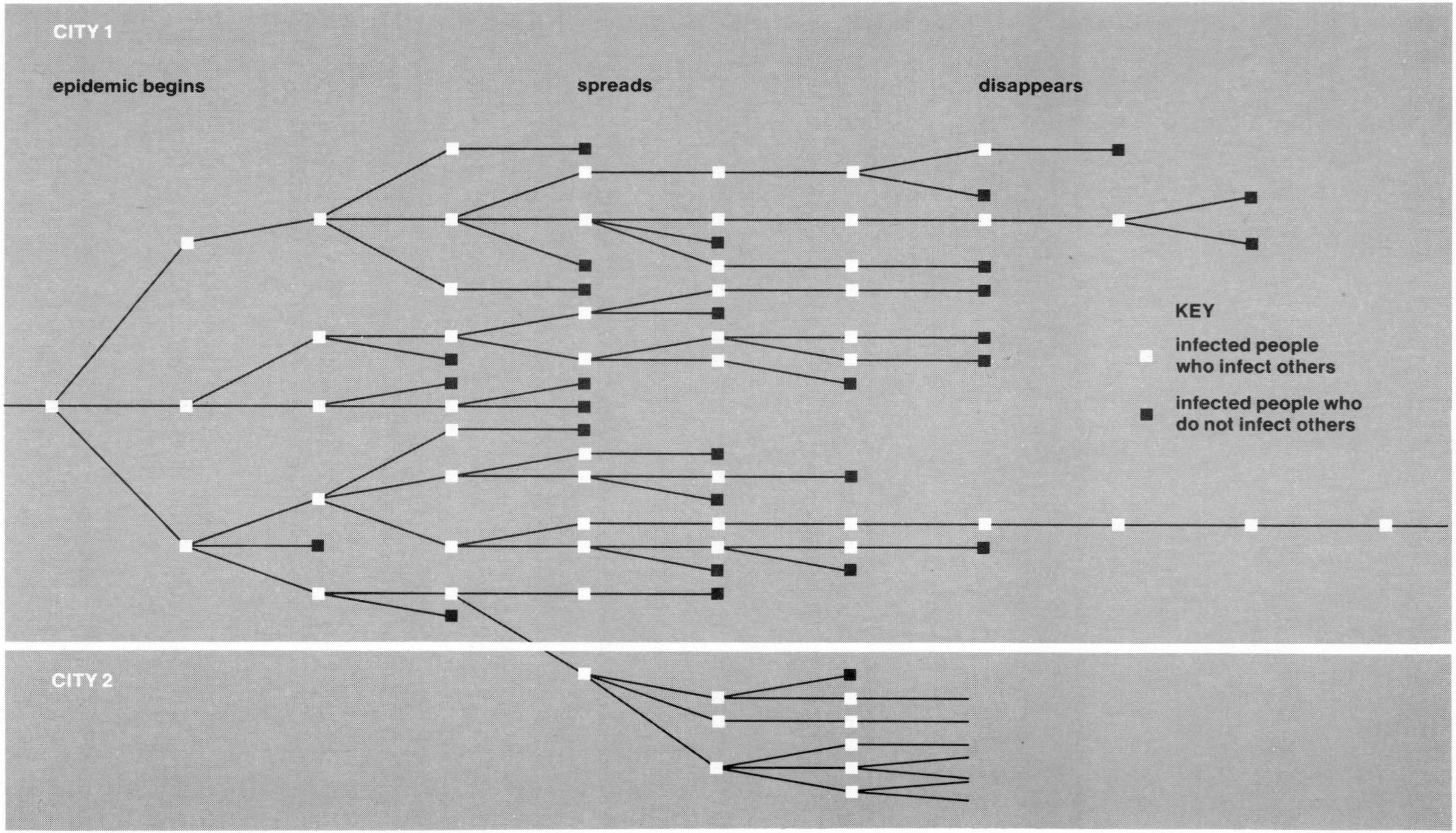

CITY 1

epidemic begins   spreads   disappears

KEY

□ infected people who infect others

■ infected people who do not infect others

CITY 2

TABLE 13.2
Paralytic Polio Rates in Detroit, by Socioeconomic Status and by Race[a]

Socioeconomic Status	1952 White	1952 Nonwhite	1958 White	1958 Nonwhite
Highest	42.5	0.0	1.4	0.0
Upper middle	39.1	10.9	3.7	45.1
Lower middle	17.9	12.5	10.0	52.6
Lowest	24.6	5.9	16.3	51.8

[a]Figures represent the number of cases per 100,000 population. The vaccine was distributed by private physicians during this period.

After Richard D. Leach, "Socioeconomic Status, Race, and Poliomyelitis in Detroit, Michigan: A Sociological Analysis" (Unpubl. MA thesis, Wayne State University, 1967), p. 47.

science is making rapid advances. By not dying of infectious diseases, people can live long enough to develop the noninfectious disorders of adulthood. The average expected life span rose from forty-six years for an American white male born in 1900 to seventy-four years for one born in 1976, reflecting the reduction in contagious diseases. The incidence of the outstanding killers in modern America, cancer and heart disease, is shown in Table 13.3.

We know that many of the noninfectious diseases vary in incidence throughout the world, but the reasons for this variation are complex and poorly understood. The Australian Aborigines in native conditions rarely have cancerous growths or high blood pressure (hypertension). The

TABLE 13.3
Leading Causes of Death in the United States in 1900 and 1983

1900 Cause of Death	Number per 100,000	1983 Cause of Death	Number per 100,000
1. Diseases of the heart and blood vessels	345	1. Diseases of the heart and blood vessels	419
2. Influenza and pneumonia	202	2. Cancer	189
3. Tuberculosis	194	3. Accidents	40
4. Diseases of the stomach and intestines	143	4. Chronic obstructive pulmonary diseases	28
5. Accidents	72	5. Influenza and pneumonia	24
6. Cancer	64	6. Diabetes mellitus	16
7. Diphtheria	40	7. Suicide	12
8. Typhoid and paratyphoid fever	31	8. Cirrhosis of the liver	12
9. Measles	13	9. Homicide	9
10. Cirrhosis of the liver	13	10. Certain diseases of early infancy	8

Data for 1900 from U.S. Bureau of the Census, *Historical Statistics of the United States Colonial Times to 1957*, Statistical Abstract Suppl. (Washington, D.C.: Government Printing Office, 1960), p. 26; and for 1983 from U.S. Bureau of the Census, *Statistical Abstract of the United States 1987*, 107th ed. (Washington, D.C.: Government Printing Office, 1986), p. 75.

low incidence of cancer could be partly genetic, because we do know that cancer tends to run in families. Among whites, anyway, people appear to inherit predispositions to develop some forms of cancer. But the scarcity of cancer-producing agents (cigarettes, pollutants, and others) among the Aborigines may be the major reason for their low cancer rate. Hypertension also may be missing because of environmental differences. Aborigines living in the big cities of Australia show hypertension rates much higher than those of unacculturated Aborigines, which seems to indicate that Western diets and the pressure of life in large cities are most responsible for hypertension. Although genetic factors may affect resistance to noninfectious disorders, environmental factors such as diet, pollution, and crowding are responsible too.

Not surprisingly, the nonlethal effects of noninfectious agents are seen commonly in industrialized settings. People have not evolved genetic adaptations to many of the pollutants, chemicals, and noxious agents to which we are exposed daily; there simply has not been sufficient time. Ironically, many of these substances are the products of technological adaptations to help buffer us from stressors. Love Canal is one of the most infamous examples of human exposure to hazardous wastes. The canal, in Niagara Falls, New York, was the burial site for thousands of tons of solvents, acids, and other dangerous chemicals in the 1940s. Subsequently, the canal was filled and residences were built on the site, which remained occupied until chemical leakage was uncovered in the late 1970s. In 1980 the federal government evacuated all families from the area.

Beverly Paigen and colleagues investigated the health consequences of growing up in a polluted environment by measuring a variety of growth features in hundreds of children from the Love Canal area.[15] Children born and reared there were noticeably shorter than a comparison group, and the pollution-exposed girls appeared to reach menarche later than normal. The exposed children also showed a higher rate of birth defects and chronic health problems; exposure to pollutants can increase the likelihood of contracting infectious illnesses. In many regards, the results in these children parallel those observed in children exposed long-term to other low-level stressors such as cigarette smoke or heavy metal poisoning. The results indicate not only that pollution certainly affects human biology and development but also that as simple a measure as stature is useful in monitoring health in children.

Traces of noninfectious (and infectious) disorders can be seen in the skeletal remains of past groups, as we saw in Chapter 11. Ted Rathbun was able to examine thirty-six skeletons of slaves from a South Carolina plantation from the mid-1800s.[16] In past chapters we have referred to Harris lines and dental hypoplasia as evidence of environmental stress; both are seen frequently in the South Carolina remains. There is also good evidence that these people commonly suffered from anemia, possibly resulting from genetic and environmental causes. Rathbun also noted evidence in many of degenerative changes in hip and shoulder joints, pointing to lives of hard physical labor. Analysis of dozens of post-

Reconstruction skeletons of blacks from Arkansas by Debra Martin, Ann Magennis, and Jerome Rose reveals a continuation of poor health and malnutrition well into the twentieth century.[17]

Stress in Modern Life

The advances of modern civilization have eased the cost of some previous stresses. Our culture allows us to deal quite effectively with heat and cold. Likewise, infectious disease has declined as a cause of human suffering. Unfortunately, as the increase in noninfectious disease implies, we are not without stressors.

Anthropologists have a reputation for being interested in the inhabitants of exotic lands. As Western cultures have expanded and native cultures have disappeared, anthropologists have started to consider all peoples, including Westerners, appropriate for study. In this regard, the anthropological literature now contains information on some of the stresses encountered by the residents of Westernized regions.

Life-style

Up to this point, we have used the word *stress* in a very general sense. In everyday life, however, we tend to give it a more limited meaning that refers to psychological problems encountered in daily living. G. A. Harrison and colleagues at Oxford University have been studying the biology of the people of some Oxfordshire villages for several years.[18] One of the questions they have been exploring is the relationship of life-style to biology.

In situations of stress humans secrete stress hormones, or catecholamines, called epinephrine (also called adrenaline) and norepinephrine (noradrenaline). Very simply stated, catecholamines are secreted into the blood under stressful conditions to gear the body for strenuous activity. This response is called the "fight or flight" reaction; these hormones pass into the urine for excretion. By collecting urine samples it is possible to judge the amount of catecholamines a person has recently produced.

There have been many studies in laboratories of volunteers who are put under stress, but the Oxford group wanted to learn about the hormonal responses of average people going about their daily lives. The basic data on life-style were obtained by questionnaires that asked people about their happiness, boredom, frustration, and similar feelings. Urine samples were gathered and catecholamine levels determined. A number of associations were found in the women and men of Oxfordshire. In the women, high epinephrine levels were related to a feeling of frustration and a general dissatisfaction with life. Cigarette smoking and high coffee consumption were associated with high epinephrine levels in men as well as women. For men, a competitive personality, a need to meet self-established deadlines, and a feeling of being under pressure were also related to high epinephrine levels. High norepinephrine levels went along with a greater amount of physical activity as well. Low levels of catecholamines were found in men who felt bored. It thus seems that subnormal levels of stress hormones can be found in people who are understimulated. The Oxford authors wonder if too little catecholamine might not be as undesirable as too much. Much evidence associates the long-term elevation of catecholamines with coronary heart disease. We have all heard that personality and life-style can be related to heart disease. In light of these results, the authors feel that coffee intake and cigarettes may well be related to coronary heart disease.

One of the aspects of life-style that many view as a behavioral adaptation to the day-to-day stresses of life is cigarette smoking, which is also widely acknowledged to be one of the major, preventable health risks. Not only does smoking increase the risk of developing cancer, it also depresses the immune response and damages the respiratory and cardiovascular systems. There is strong evidence that cigarette smokers not only develop more cases of a variety of cancers but also develop the cancers at an earlier age. Research by Arthur Michalek and K. Michael Cummings indicates that the latter is true even for cancers not shown to be caused by cigarettes. This may be related to the immunosuppressive effects of smoke allowing accelerated tumor growth.[19]

Unemployment

Members of bands or tribes living under aboriginal conditions do not have to worry about unemployment or the need to make money. The members of a band of pygmies cooperate with one another to provide food and shelter. This is not the case in the United States. Sidney Cobb and colleagues undertook a long-term study of men who knew they were about to lose their jobs as a result of a permanent plant shutdown.[20] They collected physiological, social, and psychological data in an attempt to see the interplay among these factors.

The men studied were drawn from six companies: an urban area plant that was about to be closed, a similar plant in a rural area, and two urban and two rural companies (the controls) for which there were no threats of shutdowns. The men were visited five times: just before job loss (the anticipation stage), at termination, and six, twelve, and twenty-four months after job loss. Controls were visited at the same times. The physiological variables that were measured included cholesterol levels and norepinephrine excretion rates.

One of the variables was social support, a measure of the degree to which close relatives and friends would buoy up the unemployed man in part as reflected by the frequency of his social activity outside the home. A second psychosocial variable measured, called psychological defense, was the unemployed man's ability not to blame himself for his situation.

The data show that norepinephrine excretion rates were considerably higher for those whose jobs were abolished, both before and for a year after job loss (Figure 13.21). As mentioned, norepinephrine levels increase to help deal with short-term stress. If the stress—continued unemployment—does not go away, the prolonged norepinephrine elevation can be harmful to one's health. When the terminees are divided along urban-rural lines, it is apparent that social setting affects norepinephrine excretion rates. Rural men seemed much less stressed by unemployment than urban men (Figure 13.22). Those men with high psychological de-

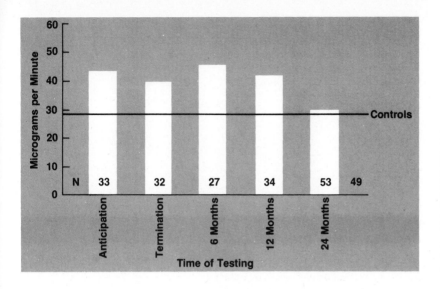

FIGURE 13.21
Norepinephrine excretion rates in micrograms (millionths of a gram) per minute at five different times in the study. The line labeled "controls" indicates the average rate in the unstressed, employed man. Numbers in each bar indicate number of men tested.

fense had significantly lower excretion rates than those who blamed themselves for having lost their jobs (Figure 13.23).

The social and psychological factors also moderate cholesterol and other chemical levels. Those with high social support had noticeably lower serum cholesterol levels than the unemployed with little support. Because cholesterol levels may be related to heart disease, it is entirely possible that those with high social support may live longer.

We see that our biological functioning is thus affected by how we perceive our situation—such as whether we have friends with whom we can share emotions and whether we live in a city—and all these factors

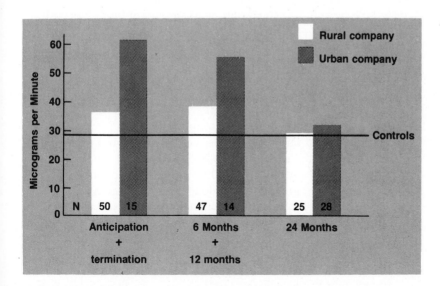

FIGURE 13.22
Norepinephrine excretion rates in micrograms per minute, by location of company and by time.

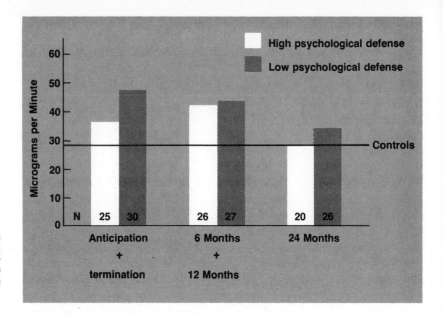

FIGURE 13.23
Norepinephrine excretion rates in micrograms per minute, by time of analysis and by level of psychological defense.

are influenced by the type of society we live in. Comparable socioeconomic effects on health are being documented elsewhere. In Australia, a trend in deaths due to heart disease has been strongly linked to high unemployment and periods of economic recession.

Light

Normally people think of light in terms of the requirements for vision. It was pointed out earlier that different parts of the spectrum can have different effects on us; ultraviolet light, for example, is responsible for sunburn and vitamin D synthesis. When Edison devised the incandescent bulb he was concerned only with amount of light, not with the relative proportions of light of different wavelengths. Figure 13.24 illustrates quite clearly that the spectra of both the incandescent bulb and the cool-white fluorescent lamp are different from that of sunlight. It is not that fluorescent lamps cannot be made to mimic the spectrum of sunlight, but until rather recently no one thought about the biological effects of different kinds of light. Construction of bulbs was based solely on economic and technological considerations.

A study carried out in Boston demonstrated clearly the physiological effects of exposure to different light sources on calcium absorption. In this work a series of elderly, healthy males were divided into two groups, all of whom agreed to stay indoors from the beginning of winter to mid-March. For the first seven weeks all members of both groups stayed inside, where they functioned in light provided by a mixture of incandescent and fluorescent bulbs. At the end of this time, members of both groups were equally poor in ability to absorb calcium through the gut. Although the diet was supplying an adequate amount of calcium, but little vitamin D, the subjects could absorb only about 40 percent of

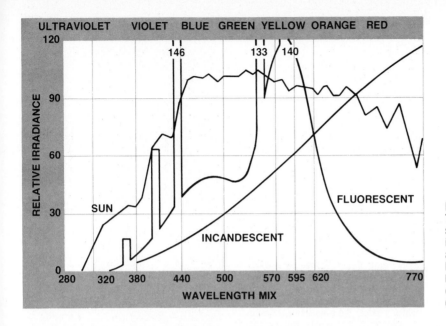

FIGURE 13.24
The spectra of sunlight at sea level, of an incandescent bulb, and of a cool-white fluorescent bulb.
Note that the peak emissions of the curves are quite different.

that present in the food, presumably due to a decreased production of vitamin D. After this initial period both groups continued to stay inside, but one of the groups was exposed to a special lamp designed to mimic the spectrum of sunlight. The amount of ultraviolet light this group received was comparable to what they would receive during a fifteen-minute walk on a sunny, summer day. Calcium absorption was remeasured at the end of this four-week period. The absorption in the unexposed group had dropped to 30 percent, attesting to a deteriorating ability to absorb calcium; the ultraviolet-exposed group increased its absorption of calcium to 50 percent (Figure 13.25). Given that many of us spend little time outdoors during the winter, it is reasonable to postulate that much of the American population, especially the very young and very old, is suffering from some degree of lowered calcium absorption. Low calcium absorption can lead to decalcification of bones and then to fractures. One solution in nursing homes might be to install fluorescent bulbs that have emission spectra similar to the sun's.

Light also is known to affect other biochemical phenomena. Alfred Lewy and his colleagues have been studying people who become depressed during the shortened days of northern winters.[21] They discovered that if these people are exposed to bright lights in the morning to compensate for the reduced amount of sunlight, their depression improved significantly. This is correlated with a change in the timing of the production of a hormone, melatonin, manufactured by the brain. Such results suggest a possible therapy for a large number of people who become depressed during the long winters of temperate regions. Ultimately, this may reflect the fact that humans evolved in the tropics for millions of years and that aspects of biochemistry, at least in some people, have not fully adapted to life in other areas.

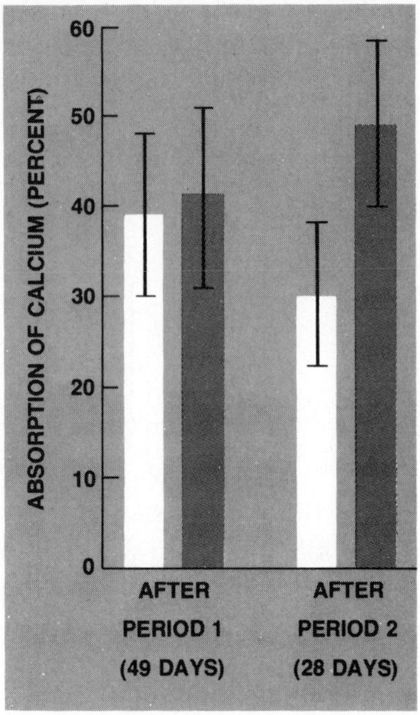

FIGURE 13.25. Effects of light exposure on calcium absorption. The control group (white bars) and experimental group (shaded bars) were initially exposed only to typical indoor lighting for seven weeks. This was continued four more weeks for the controls, while the experimental group was exposed to special fluorescent lamps. The brackets indicate the range of variation within each group.

Noise

One of the side effects of life in a modern society is the increased noise level. It has been well documented that living in a large urban center has a very direct effect on the human auditory equipment itself. Residents of noisy areas and people who must work in noisy places such as factories suffer hearing loss (Figure 13.26).

Noise has, it seems, less obvious effects as well. Noise can be quite disturbing psychologically. People living near a major London airport had a higher rate of admission to psychiatric units than a similar group living in a quieter area. In the laboratory, psychologists have shown that noise that is unpredictable and uncontrollable is very upsetting. If a person believes that he or she can make a bothersome noise stop (whether this is true does not matter), he or she can tolerate the noise much better. Although the psychologists were interested in mental and behavioral adjustments, it would be reasonable to look for biological effects in such experiments also. The frustration of uncontrollable noise could well trigger hormonal shifts, which could then affect a person's health.

A report dealt with pregnant women who lived near a very noisy airport. Looking at more than one hundred such women, Lawrence Schell found that their newborns' weights were lower than expected.[22] This is in accord with other research in Japan, which noted an increased incidence of prematurity and low birth weight in association with maternal exposure to a lot of noise. Some researchers have even found an increase in birth defects in the offspring of women exposed to high noise levels.

FIGURE 13.26.   The noise produced in modern society may have biological effects on us.

There may be harmful effects of too little noise as well. One researcher looked at the offspring of female rats exposed to various noise levels while pregnant. Females exposed to high levels had very small infants, while females exposed to no noise had smaller babies than females exposed to moderate noise levels.

Nutrition

Let us now consider the interrelationship of diet, biology, and behavior. The nutritional content of a group's diet can affect its health, and the existence of vitamin deficiency diseases is well known. People also are more likely to contract or to suffer greater damage from infectious disease when they are undernourished. Often the interdependence of biology and culture as mediated by nutrition is more complex and may have unexpected repercussions.

Diet and Variability

Average dietary requirements have been formulated for the "normal" American living in "normal" environmental conditions (Table 13.4). Variation in age, sex, and body size is allowed for; for example, women need more iron but fewer calories each day than the average male. These figures provide a convenient standard for analyzing and comparing the nutritional status of individuals or populations, although some individuals in any population may need more or less of these nutrients. People with a predisposition to schizophrenia, for instance, may

TABLE 13.4
Recommended Dietary Allowances[a] (RDAs), Revised 1980, for Selected Age Groups

	Age	Weight kg	Weight lbs	Height cm	Height in.	Energy kcal[b]	Protein grams	Fat Soluble Vitamins A μg R.E.[c]	D μg[d]	E mg αT.E.[e]
Children	1–3	13	29	90	35	1,300	23	400	10	5
Girls	11–14	46	101	157	62	2,200	46	800	10	8
Boys	11–14	45	99	157	62	2,700	45	1,000	10	8
Women	23–50	55	120	163	64	2,000	46	800	5	8
Pregnant women						+ 300	+30	+ 200	+5	+2
Men	23–50	70	154	178	70	2,700	56	1,000	5	10

[a]Dietary allowances cover most normal, healthy persons living in the temperate United States.
[b]The number of kilocalories listed for each category refers to people engaged in some physical activity. College professors and other sedentary people need fewer calories. Body size, maturation rate, and climatic conditions can also alter the required number of calories.
[c]Retinol equivalents: 1 retinol equivalent = 1 μg retinol

have an increased vitamin C requirement. It has also been shown recently that these people seem to metabolize the plant protein, gluten, in an abnormal fashion, again indicating individual variation regarding diet.

We do not know if the daily requirements of different populations differ significantly. Because body size partly determines nutritional needs and because this trait exhibits genetically influenced populational differences, some variation probably does exist. We know that many of the world's inhabitants do not approach, for at least part of the year, the levels recommended in the United States. Not all non-Western peoples are malnourished, though; in fact, severe malnutrition usually becomes obvious only as a result of the cultural disruptions produced by industrialization. The Yanomama Indians of the Amazon Basin take in more than adequate amounts of protein per day (75 grams per adult per day). The San Bushmen of the Kalahari Desert evidence some mild undernutrition, but malnutrition is not present. Nor do they seem overly concerned about the source of their next meal. Women, who are the chief suppliers of food (60 to 80 percent), need work only two or three days per week. Men spend about the same amount of time hunting.

Calories, Carbohydrates, Proteins, and Fats: An Adequate Diet

The one requirement most Americans are acutely aware of is caloric intake. A calorie is the unit of heat required to raise the temperature of one gram of water from 15° to 16° Celsius (centigrade); a diet's caloric value reflects its ability to produce energy. The calorie is actually a very small amount of heat, and, for convenience, dieters and nutritionists talk of the large calorie (often with a capital C), or kilocalorie, which equals 1,000 calories. When the caloric intake drops below that needed to perform basic body functions (muscular activity, growth, and maintenance of body temperature), energy reserves, such as fat deposits, are drawn on to make up the deficit.

Water Soluble Vitamins							Minerals					
Ascorbic Acid mg	Folacin μg	Niacin mg	Ribo-flavin mg	Thia-min mg	B_6 mg	B_{12} μg	Calcium mg	Phos-phorus mg	Iodine μg	Iron mg	Magne-sium mg	Zinc mg
45	100	9	0.8	0.7	0.9	2.0	800	800	70	15	150	10
50	400	15	1.3	1.1	1.8	3.0	1,200	1,200	150	18	300	15
50	400	18	1.6	1.4	1.8	3.0	1,200	1,200	150	18	350	15
60	400	13	1.2	1.0	2.0	3.0	800	800	150	18	300	15
+20	+400	+2	+0.3	+0.4	+0.6	+1.0	+400	+400	+25	+12–42	+150	+5
60	400	18	1.6	1.4	2.2	3.0	800	800	150	10	350	15

[d]As cholecalciferol: 10 μg cholecalciferol = 400 I.U. vitamin D
[e]α tocopherol equivalents: 1 mg d-α-tocopherol = 1αT.E.
From *Recommended Dietary Allowances*, 9th rev. ed., 1980, with permission of National Academy Press, Washington, D.C.

The sources of calories vary widely around the world. In poorer agricultural regions the primary source is carbohydrates; hunters get much of their energy from fats and proteins. Beyond the provision of energy, however, the sources fill roles that are not interchangeable. Proteins are the only route by which we can get some amino acids. The eight essential amino acids are the ones we cannot synthesize; they must be present in the food we eat. We then use these amino acids to construct our own proteins (Chapter 2). Synthesizing and repairing tissues, not producing energy, are really the primary functions of proteins. Adequate carbohydrates and fats spare the proteins from having to make energy. We must also eat at least some fat to get fatty acids, which are important in maintaining the structural parts of the tissues and in keeping the sex organs working properly.

The major dietary sources of proteins are animal products: meat, milk, eggs, fish, and some plants, such as nuts. Although all plants have some protein, they are generally poorer in the essential amino acids than are animal sources. Fats too generally come from animal foods, but plants also have them. Carbohydrates are supplied by cereals, fruits, starchy roots, and sugar. Fats are the most concentrated source of calories, providing 9 Calories per gram. Proteins and carbohydrates both provide about 4 Calories per gram.

Equally adequate diets can vary widely in the contribution proteins, carbohydrates, and fats make to the caloric intake. Generally, we see the variation as a reflection of cultural differences. Nevertheless, we have a few indications that a member of one culture cannot always adapt to the diet of another group (Figure 13.27). The high fatty acid content of the Eskimo diet can produce disorders in people not used to such a diet. Most variation, though, is determined by culture and ecology. The Yanomama Indians get some of their protein by eating fried insects and

FIGURE 13.27. A population's sources of nutrition can vary widely from place to place: (left) a wedding feast aboard a Hong Kong junk with a pan of the staple, rice, prominently displayed; (right) children in the Ivory Coast of Africa eating banana fritters.

raw lice. For most of the year, highland Quechua Indians get about 85 percent of their calories from carbohydrates, about 10 percent from protein, and about 5 percent from fats. These proportions reflect their economic dependence on cultivating potatoes and several other plants. Potatoes account for well over half the food consumed daily by inhabitants of at least one Quechua village, meat and fat for less than 10 percent. From this diet, the people take in up to 3,200 Calories per day. Eskimos consume a daily average of about 3,100 Calories. The proportions of protein, fat, and carbohydrates are radically different from those in the Quechua diet, however. Eskimos are primarily hunters and eat a lot of animal fat and protein. These substances provide about 47 percent each of the total calories, with carbohydrates contributing the remaining 6 percent. In Western societies just over half the total calories are, on the average, derived from carbohydrates, about a third from fat, and the rest from protein.

Humans are highly flexible in their ability to tolerate widely varied diets. Culture is generally acknowledged as the source of our great adaptability, but physiologically we are quite flexible too. Many of the other primates are tightly limited in their food sources for physiological and other reasons; humans, on the other hand, can eat and survive on food from many sources. Australian Aborigines get much of their protein by eating insects; Eskimos are almost exclusively carnivores; Hindus are vegetarians. Culture may dictate the choice of foods, but people can eat almost anything.

People do not flourish equally well on all the different diets, however. The large amount of sugar in the American diet (just under 100 pounds per capita per year in the 1970s) does much to decay teeth. Before European contact, gatherers and hunters such as Australian Aborigines rarely had tooth decay, as we see in skeletal remains, and they ate little sugar. Many who live in underdeveloped nations survive on a diet low in animal protein and calories, but they also suffer from disorders known as kwashiorkor (protein deficiency) and marasmus (calorie deficiency).

Protein-Calorie Malnutrition

Although we will consider kwashiorkor and marasmus as protein-calorie malnutrition (PCM), the real picture is often more complex. Some show the swelling (edema) characteristic of a deficiency only in protein, while others, receiving sufficient protein but insufficient calories, show the wasting of marasmus. Many are deficient in both, hence PCM (Figure 13.28). The toll this disorder takes is enormous, being present in between 5 and 45 percent of the children in the developing countries. The Citizen's Board of Inquiry into Hunger and Malnutrition in the United States has also identified it in poor American families; it cuts across ethnic boundaries, being found in poor Hispanics, blacks,

FIGURE 13.28. The effects of protein and calorie malnutrition are obvious in this photograph of a three-year-old child from Upper Volta.

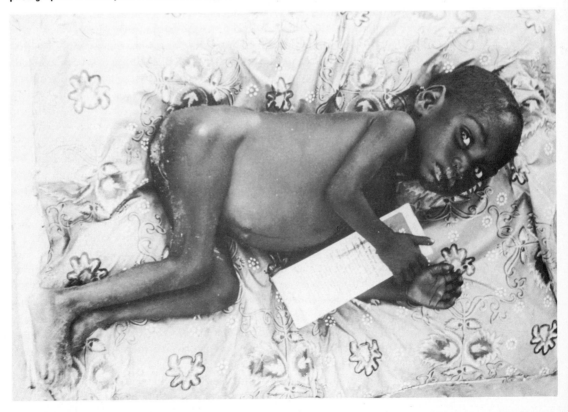

Native Americans, and whites. It may sometimes be caused by child neglect, but its primary direct or indirect cause is poverty, and the poor bear the mental and physical scars of PCM for years.

The joint Food and Agriculture Organization–World Health Organization Expert Committee on Nutrition has described a typical sequence in the development of PCM. The breast-fed child develops normally until about the age of six months. Then the growing child's caloric and protein requirements outstrip the supply in the mother's milk. The mother, because the child is still nursing, fails to see that it is underfed, or else the parents cannot afford to supplement the child's diet. In some societies breast-feeding is continued until the age of three or four. During this time the mother's milk remains high in protein, but the supply dwindles. This postponement of weaning gives the child enough protein to maintain life but not enough to support proper growth; in fact the name *kwashiorkor* is a Ghanian word meaning "the disease affecting the child after it leaves the mother's breast."

Nomadic Turkana pastoralists of northwest Kenya, however, although having a limited food intake, continue on a high protein diet after weaning, for their primary sources of food are milk, blood, and meat.[23] As a result, they continue to grow in stature even when they may be losing weight, a truly unusual situation that once again indicates the need to recognize the cultural behaviors of people in assessing their health. Nonetheless, the short stature of adults in many underdeveloped areas and the greater height of first-generation immigrants to the United States (Chapter 11) are definite reflections of dietary improvement.

In many underdeveloped areas, the food source at weaning is shifted to a cereal gruel or simply water in which cereal has been cooked. Many groups find poor nutrition exacerbated by the cultural disruption that attends urbanization and changing dietary habits. In many urban areas where the mother must work outside the home, breast-feeding is terminated early, and overdiluted cow's milk and thick gruel, which provide a very low protein intake, are the only foods the child receives. The protein supply is now too low to produce enough antibodies to fight off infections successfully, because the child is not getting enough amino acids for the cells to string together to form the proteins. Neither is the youngster receiving antibodies from the mother's milk. The child is now an easy target for many infectious diseases, particularly respiratory disorders. Because of the many related factors, mortality rates for PCM are underestimates; a child who died from pneumonia might well have survived the disease had he or she been well nourished. Table 13.5 shows the results of a study in Guatemala on the interplay of nutrition and infectious disease; the children who had lower weight gains, and thus poorer diets, were sick much longer than those on better diets.

We need not cross the borders of the United States to see evidence of this. The mortality rate for two- to twelve-month-old whites is 5.9 per thousand; in Navajo County, Arizona, it is 40.1 deaths per thousand. The statistic becomes even more striking when broken down by race. White infants die at a rate of 10.5 per thousand in this county, while 58.5

TABLE 13.5
Effect of Infections on Well-Fed and Poorly Fed Children
A comparison of the number of attacks and days of illness per year in six children with greatest weight gain and six children with least weight gain in Santa Maria Caugué, Guatemala, 1964–1966.

Disease	Children with Greatest Weight Gain (6–12 Mos. Old)		Children with Least Weight Gain (6–12 Mos. Old)	
	No. of attacks	Days ill	No. of attacks	Days ill
Diarrhea	12	100	11	170
Upper respiratory infections and conjunctivitis	24	155	23	209
Bronchitis and bronchopneumonia	1	7	2	24
Stomatitis and thrush	3	20	6	39
Totals	40	282	42	442

After L. J. Mata, J. J. Urrutia, and B. Garcia, "Effect of Infection and Diet on Child Growth: Experience in a Guatemalan Village," in G. E. W. Wolstenholme and M. O'Connor (eds.), *Nutrition and Infection: Ciba Foundation Study Group No. 31* (Boston: Little, Brown, 1967), p. 123.

Native American infants per thousand are dying, and PCM has been diagnosed among Native Americans. In Rio Grande County, Colorado, the population is 99.7 percent white but more than 33 percent are poor; here the postneonatal mortality is 36 per thousand.

One of PCM's saddest consequences is the possibility of irreversible tissue damage, including brain damage. Although not completely substantiated, it appears that infants reared on a low-protein diet have retarded tissue growth. If the diet is later supplemented, the child may at least partially catch up with the norm by rapid growth spurts.

For children born to undernourished mothers, the prognosis is not as good. Evidence is growing that chronic protein deficiency in the months before and after birth may cause irrevocable harm, for it is at this time that the brain is growing fastest. Figure 13.29 shows that rats that were undernourished because they were suckled by one female in groups of fifteen have lower brain weights than those suckled in groups of three per female. After weaning at twenty-one days, all rats were given free access to high-protein food. The previously undernourished animals never caught up with the well-nourished animals in brain weight. Because the maximum growth rate for rat brain tissue is achieved just after birth, undernourishment at this time should be comparable with human *in utero* deprivation, for the maximum rate of growth for the brain in humans is reached just before birth. If the model is correct, prenatal protein deficiency in humans should be expected to produce permanent retardation in brain growth. In fact poor fetal nutrition and low birth weight have been linked to later intellectual decrements. One report on white newborns in Boston showed that those weighing more than 6.5 pounds at birth later in life had IQs 13 points higher than those weighing less than 4.5 pounds at birth.

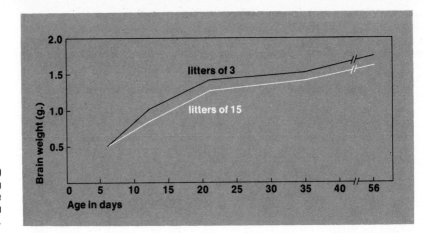

FIGURE 13.29
Malnutrition's effect on the development of the central nervous system in the rat.

Analysis of data on high to low socioeconomic status (SES) Guatemalan children by Francis Johnston and colleagues shows a more complex picture, however.[24] Within the highest SES there is a correlation between nutrition and IQ; the better nourished, the higher the IQ. In the low SES, though, there was no such association; all the children showed low IQ regardless of their nutritional adequacy. It might not be that these children have an organic deficiency but that being poor impairs the learning process.

The consequences of PCM may be long-lived. Many animal studies show the existence of intergenerational effects on normal growth. Poor nutrition during critical growth periods can permanently retard the development of an organ system, such as that for reproduction. Should an affected animal become pregnant, its fetuses are malnourished because the mother's earlier growth problems prevent the formation of a normal placenta, even if she is eating well now. The inadequate placenta in turn starves the fetus, producing a second malnourished generation.

Physiological and Genetic Adaptations   The body can suffer a tremendous toll from malnutrition. What physiological and genetic adaptations might be made to a disorder such as PCM? We know little about them, but one interesting hypothesis states that the body contracts its "metabolic frontiers": Absolutely essential proteins are synthesized at nearly normal rates but at the expense of luxuries such as muscle, skin, and brain. Several studies have shown that animals on a low-protein diet continue to manufacture liver, pancreatic, and intestinal proteins at more or less normal levels but that the output of muscle and skin cells is curtailed. One disadvantage children in poor communities suffer is nutritional dwarfism; as with the brain, body weight and stature are much reduced, presumably to ensure that enough essential materials will be produced. We have many documented examples, even in the United States, of children four or five years old weighing only twenty pounds and of one-year-olds weighing less than they did at birth.

Children born of poorly nourished women also are typically below the normal birth weight. Infants of poor black South African mothers average about 6 ounces less at birth than infants of white South Africans. Offspring of high-income black South Africans average the same weight at birth as South African white infants.

Stanley Garn and other researchers have proposed that small body size, and thus reduced protein and caloric requirements, would be a selective advantage when nutrition is inadequate. They have found that people with a genetic trait known as brachymesophalangia-5 (a short middle section of the little finger) also show a marked reduction in stature compared with unaffected members of the same population or family (Figure 13.30). We know that brachymesophalangia-5, a seemingly unimportant trait, is found at frequencies of 5 percent or more in many populations of Central and South America and Asia. Could it be, Garn asks, that this minor symptom reflects a genetically influenced reduction in body size as an adaptation to chronically inadequate nutrition?

Table 13.6 shows the caloric requirements for a 70 kg (154 lb) man and a 60 kg (132 lb) man. Assuming the smaller man is not suffering from retarded growth but is geared to be small, he can live and work well on a significantly lower number of calories per day. Imagine the reduction in required food resources for a large population, with each member needing hundreds fewer calories every day of the year.

Natural selection may have worked as Garn speculates, but data gathered by Robert Malina and colleagues on two populations of PCM children, one Mexican and one New Guinean, are ambiguous in their

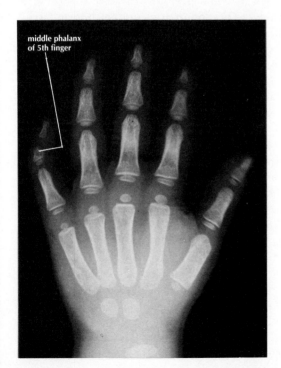

middle phalanx
of 5th finger

FIGURE 13.30
Radiograph of a child with brachymesophalangia-5.

TABLE 13.6
Comparison of Calorie Requirements of a 70 kg U.S. Male with Those of a 60 kg Colombian Male at Similar Activity Levels

	U.S.A.	Colombia
Mean body weight (kg)	70	60
Calorie costs (kcal)		
Resting (8 hrs)	570	480
Very light activity (6 hrs)	630	540
Light labor (8 hrs)	1,624	1,392
Moderate labor (2 hrs)	602	516
Total	3,426	2,928

From William A. Stini, "Human Adaptability to Nutritional Stress," in Paul B. Pearson and Richard Greenwell (eds.), *Nutrition, Food, and Man* (Tucson: University of Arizona Press, 1980), p. 134.

support for this view.[25] Both undernourished groups are shorter, lighter, and weaker than a group of well-nourished children in Philadelphia. When the results are adjusted for differences in body size, the three groups are equally strong; the New Guinea children actually outperform the other two groups in jumping and running. Once again the results are more complex than one might have imagined, possibly resulting from underlying population differences in ability to cope with chronic nutritional deficiencies. There may also be differences related to the particular tasks being performed.

Maybe genes for small body size are best suited to areas where nutritional deprivation is common; maybe not. In any case, we do know that many people in the world would have grown more if they were better fed. This is not simply a question of academic (or humanitarian) interest. Repercussions of suboptimal growth can be seen in very concrete economic terms. The physical work capacity can be measured by the maximum oxygen consumption (VO_2). The maximum amount of oxygen capable of being consumed by a person measures the person's ability to do work. As undernutrition worsens, the maximum oxygen consumption decreases markedly.

The productivity of Colombian sugar-cane cutters was measured in one study by the number of tons of cane they cut each day. The best harvesters cut more than four tons per day, the worst less than three. The best workers weighed more, were taller, and had more muscle and less body fat (Figure 13.31). The best harvesters also had higher VO_2 (Figure 13.32). Healthy people make better workers.

A Cultural Adaptation: Synthetic Foods The social causes of protein-calorie malnutrition are many, although poverty and lack of education are often at the root of the problem. Several foods have been developed that are designed to provide nutritious diets at a very low price. The nutrient content of one, Incaparina, is compared in Table 13.7 with cow's milk and corn gruel, the latter being a common food in areas such as Guatemala. Many of the new foods are mixtures of locally available foods such as soybeans, cottonseed oil, and nut meal.

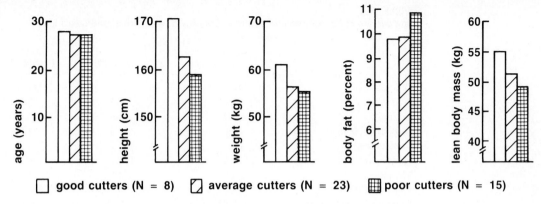

FIGURE 13.31. Physical characteristics of good, average, and poor sugar-cane cutters. The most productive cutters were the healthiest.

Such products have not been a great success. Peruvita, a nutrient-rich soft drink developed in Peru, failed because its taste was unacceptable; Incaparina was a success in Guatemala and Colombia because the people liked the taste. In Ghana, a soybean preparation failed, even though its taste and appearance were not objectionable, because the amount of fuel needed to cook the soybeans was almost as great as the family's total supply. When Pro-nutro, a South African preparation, was first marketed to black South Africans, it was advertised as a special food for poor people. It occurred to no one that the poor would assume it was food no one else wanted and therefore to be avoided. As one expert said, "The poor want . . . the things the non-poor have." In a second campaign Pro-nutro was named "Incumbe," the same as the corn gruel used to feed Zulu children. It was assumed the people would accept and use

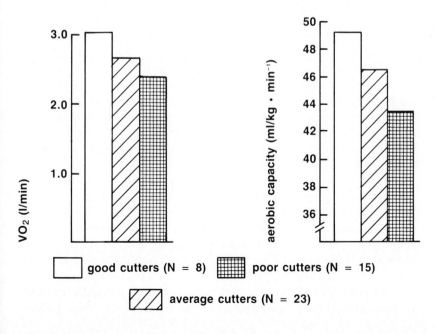

FIGURE 13.32
Maximum oxygen consumption (VO_2 max) in good, average, and poor sugar-cane cutters. The good cutters had a greater biological ability to do work.

TABLE 13.7
Comparison of the Nutritional Content of Corn Gruel, Incaparina, and Cow's Milk[a]

	Corn Gruel[b]	Incaparina[b]	Cow's Milk
Calories	86	138	141
Protein (gm)	1.0	6.9	6.9
Fat (gm)	0.4	1.0	7.6
Carbohydrates (gm)	20.2	25.3	11.3
Calcium (mg)	22.0	164.0	374.0
Phosphorus (mg)	22.0	174.0	168.0
Iron (mg)	0.0	2.1	1.0
Vitamin A (IU)	0	1,125	363
Vitamin B$_1$ (Thiamine; mg)	0.02	0.58	0.08
Vitamin B$_2$ (Riboflavin; mg)	0.0	0.28	0.50
Niacin (mg)	0.19	1.95	0.10

[a]The amount compared was one glass of each.
[b]Prepared with 25 grams of corn *masa*, or Incaparina in one glass of water, boiling and sweetening with 12 grams of sugar.
From *Hunger, U.S.A.: A Report by the Citizen's Board of Inquiry into Hunger and Malnutrition in the United States* (Boston: Beacon Press, 1968), p. 47.

the fortified food because of its familiar name. This tactic also failed, because when mothers brought their malnourished children to the hospital and were asked what they were feeding the children, their answer was "Incumbe." The mothers meant corn gruel, but the doctors thought they meant the new food, giving rise to the mistaken idea that the special food was harmful to children. Some marketing success was finally achieved when Pro-nutro was advertised as a "food of athletes" (which sounds familiar), desirable for people of all socioeconomic levels.

Culture and Malnutrition

In our country, malnutrition may affect poor people who move from one area to another. Many Puerto Ricans in New York are malnourished partly because they continue to eat the tropical foods with which they are familiar (bananas, sweet potatoes, beans) without substituting other nutritious foods for the ones they can no longer get.

Ignorance of simple health standards also perpetuates malnutrition. A child in Brooklyn, for example, was diagnosed as having rickets, which surprised the mother because she thought the child was simply bowlegged.

Old people also suffer from malnutrition, partly because of our social values. Mealtime for the lonely aged is a chore to be finished as soon as possible or completely avoided. It no longer means spending time with the family but makes them remember that they are alone. Restaurants seldom cater to the old because old people take a long time to eat and spend little money; shopping is difficult because it is hard to get around; and many old people live in rooms with no cooking facilities.

The economic sensitivity of the very poorest is particularly pathetic. The 1,000 residents of a tarpaper-shack village near the New Orleans garbage dump had an upsurge in malnutrition when the cost of dumping garbage was raised, causing much of the edible garbage to be dumped elsewhere and depriving the residents of their primary food supply.

In many parts of this country people eat laundry starch or clay to avoid hunger pains. But laundry starch reduces the body's ability to absorb iron from other foods, leading to iron-deficiency anemia. Nutritional anemia in the United States is shockingly common, although its causes vary. More than 40 percent of one-year-old children in low-income families in New York City have abnormally low hemoglobin levels either because of iron-deficiency anemia (iron is one of hemoglobin's building blocks) or insufficient protein to build the hemoglobin chains. In Alabama, 550 of 709 poor children tested had anemia.

Agriculture and Malnutrition   Elsewhere in the world, a changing economic base can result in a marked decline in a group's nutritional status. We can see this in the archaeological record as Harris lines and dental hypoplasias (page 442). Generally, this increase in malnutrition is thought to have occurred when groups shifted to a heavy reliance on agriculture, leading to a decrease in animal protein and a reduced variety of food sources.

In the modern world, other economic phenomena can produce a degenerating state of nutrition and health. One case was beautifully documented by Daniel Gross and Barbara Underwood.[26] The peasants of northeastern Brazil had for some time been self-sufficient subsistence agriculturalists, growing enough beans, corn, and manioc to feed themselves. In the early 1950s the Brazilian government attempted to bring these peasant farmers into a modern cash economy. The government felt that if these farmers grew a crop that could be sold, the peasants would be able to buy more food than they could grow for themselves, and their lives would be improved. The farmers were persuaded to grow sisal, an inedible plant used in the production of rope. This particular choice seemed wise, for sisal was selling for a very high price. By 1966, 300,000 Brazilians were directly dependent on sisal production. When the price dropped as a result of the increased supply of sisal, many people found themselves without homegrown food and without sufficient funds to buy food.

One of the representative families studied by Gross and Underwood showed that malnutrition did not fall equally on all members of the family. To continue working in the fields, the parents took a major share of the purchased food. The children received just over half the requirements for their age group; the three-year-old boy, with a daily requirement of 1,300 Calories, received only about 700 Calories per day. It is not that the parents were greedy and unfeeling; rather, if the father had given the children some of his food, he would have been too weak to continue working, and the family income would have dropped to zero. As a result of this change from growing their own food to working for money, the nutritional health of tens of thousands of Brazilians had suffered.

Food sources can affect health in other ways too. Parasitic diseases like trichinosis may be caused by eating infected foods. A particularly curious example is a disease called *kuru*.

Kuru: Nutrition and Infection   Kuru, found mostly among the 35,000 Fore speakers of New Guinea, causes total incapacitation, inability to swallow, and death by starvation, suffocation, or pneumonia. It affects women and the young of both sexes. Kuru has been known to Western medicine since 1957; from 1957 to 1970 it killed 2,100 people.

Because of its distinctive choice of victims, several research projects were carried out to determine if the disease might be genetically caused. Others thought kuru might be influenced by a cultural variable. At last D. C. Gajdusek found that the cause is a virus passed from person to person by cannibalism, a discovery that helped earn him the Nobel Prize.[27] The virus, which affects the brain, can take years to produce symptoms (Figure 13.33). Women were the primary practitioners of cannibalism before the government stopped the practice in the 1950s. Adult males generally would not use this source of food because they thought it would rob them of vitality or stunt their growth, and under no circumstances would they eat women. Kuru was thus spread among women by their dietary custom. Some young males probably had kuru because the prohibition against cannibalism was not so strictly applied to male chil-

FIGURE 13.33
Kuru is a deadly, progressive viral disease of the nervous system.

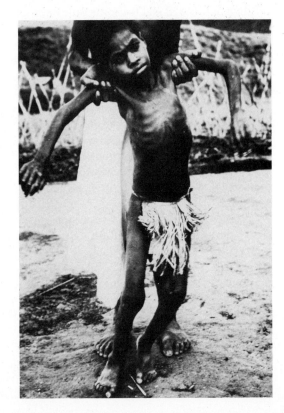

dren. Since the habit was eradicated, kuru has become rarer; no children born after it was banned have developed the disease.

We may yet see that genetic variation has something to do with susceptibility to kuru. The disease was first spotted on the boundary separating the Fore from the Keiagana peoples. It spread poorly through the Keiagana, even though they too were cannibals. Kuru is more likely to appear in people homozygous for an allele that produces the serum protein Gc than in people with a different genotype. The disease is not genetic in origin, but susceptibility to it may be genetically influenced.

Iodine and Social Organization   The people of the South American country of Ecuador are divided into the rich, nonnative peoples (*blancos*) and the poor natives (*indígenas*). Iodine deficiency is quite common among the poor, resulting in a high incidence of thyroid gland malfunction. This can cause an enlargement of the gland, a goiter (see Figure 13.34). People with very severe deficiency also suffer neurological retardation; they have a very low IQ and are often deaf and mute. The people who show such defects due to thyroid malfunction are called cretins. Cretinism is known in many parts of the world. In many areas the normal diet is naturally iodine deficient, so iodine is added to salt to prevent goiter and cretinism. Because of poverty and the uncorrected dietary iodine deficiency, cretinism levels can approach 10 percent in Ecuadorian *indígena* populations.

FIGURE 13.34
People with severe goiters among the Dani people of western New Guinea.
(Plate #DCG59DNGII)

Lawrence Greene has studied several aspects of this situation.[28] First, he tested the mental and motor skills of "normal" *indígenas* and found that about 20 percent are subnormal by our standards. He concluded that for some people iodine deficiency is not severe enough to cause cretinism but may still produce neurological problems. Considering that 25 to 30 percent of an *indígena* population has some degree of defect, it is not surprising that the natives define "normal" as anyone who has more than minimal ability to use language.

A second result of a high frequency of neurologically deficient people in a group is that they are all integrated into the society. Each, including the most deaf-mute cretins, has a functional role, usually in the agricultural sphere. They are not separated from the rest of the society.

Third, the *blancos* see the *indígenas* as being inferior and thus have no qualms about continuing to exploit them as a cheap labor source. The Ecuadorian society continues a pattern of high stratification, with a large number of subnormal people. If it were desired, future cretinism could be cheaply and easily prevented by iodine supplementation.

Elsewhere, cultural definitions of normalcy can include people we would class as defective. In an iodine-deficient area of Java, a Dutch group noted that many "normal" people showed abnormalities of the central nervous system.

Nutrition and the Evolution of Adaptation

A group's nutritional status is the result of interplay between the members' food sources and their culturally determined ways of using them. The amount and type of food in turn determine population size and health standards, and possibly also the individuals' physical shape and size. A group with a hunting economy cannot be large, for example, and dense populations, as we have seen, affect epidemiology.

Body Build

Subsistence patterns may have provided the selective forces that caused some of the morphological differences we see today. Alice Brues suggests that different body builds are suited to using different weapons: "The determining factor in the efficiency of the spear is the velocity with which the weapon leaves the hand, and it is favored by linear build [long and slender]." For a less advanced weapon like the bludgeon, a stocky, powerful build is best: "The archer requires a power leverage in the arm, which is favored by short limb segments and relatively short and thick muscles; the exact opposite of the most favorable structure for throwing a spear. . . . The bow probably developed and spread most rapidly among peoples who were of short stature and relatively mesomorphic [having a strong, muscular build]."[29] As the bow succeeded the spear in a group's cultural evolution, selection favored the archer's body build.

Paul Baker has speculated that "the plainsman of the Argentine stalked and chased his food while the Quechua Indian dug the ground, cultivated, and harvested with a dawn-to-dusk tenacity. In each instance, a different combination of skills and physical characteristics would be favored, suggesting that the subsistence activity may act as a selective force."[30]

Two other researchers, Morton S. Adams and Jerry Niswander, have gathered data that may support a similar hypothesis. Going over Native American birth records for a two-year period in the 1960s, they found greatly varying average birth weights among tribes. This variation correlated closely with variation in adult stature, a trait that has a large genetic component. Both traits also correlate with methods of getting food: The cliff-dwelling agriculturalists are uniformly small, but descendants of the bison hunters are large. Migrating gatherers and hunters, the primitive agriculturalists of the Great Basin and eastern woodland tribes, are between the extremes.

Similarities in the body build of tribes with similar subsistence patterns are not caused by close genetic ties; morphologically similar tribes are known to be linguistically and genetically distinct. Where are the cause and effect here? Are cliff dwellers small because shortness adapts them to their subsistence activities or because their food supply and daily activities result in small offspring? It would seem this variation is adaptive.

Color Blindness

Methods of getting food may also affect the incidence of color blindness. Several researchers, including R. H. Post, have found that color blindness generally is less frequent in the gathering and hunting populations than in agricultural groups.[31] The average frequency of color blindness for males in twelve groups of gatherers and hunters (Eskimos, Australian Aborigines, and North and South Native Americans) is less than 2 percent; the range of variation for groups long removed from a gatherer-hunter existence is from about 5 to 10 percent.

Post has proposed (not without opposition) that agriculturalists have more color blindness because selection against color-blind males is relaxed. A color-blind hunter would be at a disadvantage in getting food because he would have trouble seeing his prey. In primitive groups the trait would thus be kept at low frequency. In an agricultural or industrial society the color-blind male would not be apt to die because of his affliction, and the incidence of the trait could increase.

Enzyme Deficiency

Another example of the interaction of a group's diet and biology involves the inability of most of the world's adults to break down lactose, the sugar found in milk. Until we are about three, our bodies can split lactose into smaller sugars, which we can then absorb through our intestinal wall to obtain their nutritional value. The substance that enables us to digest lactose is an enzyme called lactase.

Whether we continue to produce this enzyme as we enter late childhood or adulthood seems to be settled by alleles. The dominant allele keeps the synthesis of the enzyme going; homozygous recessives stop producing the enzyme at some time during childhood. If a lactase-deficient child or adult ingests any lactose, flatulence, diarrhea, and cramps result, and the calcium, of special importance to growing children, is not efficiently used.

In most of the world's populations adults are lactase deficient, but in several populations most adults are lactase sufficient. The limited data indicate that the populations with many adults who can digest lactose have long depended on dairy herding and drinking fresh milk. Generally, populations with many lactase-deficient adults have not been herders or drinkers of milk. Before dairying began, one hypothesis states, almost all the adults in every population were lactase deficient; when some populations started to herd mammals several thousand years ago, they introduced lactose into their adult diet. Selection then worked toward the rare individual who was best able to use this new food source. As time went on, lactase sufficiency in adults became more and more common in these populations. Selection, then, in the form of milk use, may have been at work in some human populations to increase the frequency of lactase-sufficient adults, while it has been absent in populations that did not rely on dairy herding.

The evidence seems to support this hypothesis. Lactase-sufficient adults are numerous in many European and white American populations, as well as in some populations in southern and northeastern Africa—the very groups that have long practiced dairying. Among American blacks there are many lactase-deficient adults, because most of the American blacks' African ancestors came from coastal West Africa, which even today has little dairy farming. Modern West African adults also show a high frequency of the deficiency. The hypothesis does not fit all populations, but the results are inviting.

In regard to malaria resistance we have seen that different populations adapted to a similar stress by different routes, including sickle-cell hemoglobin, hemoglobin C, and thalassemias. It is entirely possible that the same phenomenon operated in the evolution of lactase persistence. There may well have been entirely independent mutations in different parts of the world that produced the same net effect. Having originated, the mutations could then spread via migration and admixture.

But why, one could ask, did any human or mammalian females evolve so as to produce milk that contains sizable loads of a complex sugar such as lactose? Why not produce milk that was easier to digest? Intriguingly, it is found that lactose stimulates the absorption of calcium, which growing mammals need. Milk of most mammals has high levels of lactose (although humans have some of the highest levels) and calcium; possibly the lactose is there because it helps in the absorption of the calcium. The complex sugar then requires the production of the enzyme, lactase, for its digestion. In fact, according to Gebhard Flatz the continued presence of lactase in developing northern European children may result more from its advantage in calcium absorption than from the population's reliance on dairy consumption.

Even without proof on this trait's evolution, we should use our knowledge of it in dealing with other people. White doctors and government officials have often felt we could help the poor in the United States and other countries by giving them milk. Because milk is good for whites, it is assumed to be good for everyone. This assumption can be very far from the truth, however. One Peace Corps volunteer reported that West Africans felt the powdered milk provided by CARE contained evil spirits, a rumor that could easily have been started by the symptoms they saw when lactase-deficient adults drank the milk. In Colombia, attendance at school was high except just after a shipment of milk came from the United States. As soon as the milk had been disposed of, attendance returned to normal. On the island of Bali, milk is used as a laxative.

An important moral to be learned from the lactase story deals with our concepts of health and disease and normal and abnormal. As the politicians typify, white Americans think that if they can drink milk as adults, this must be the normal condition. If one becomes ill after drinking milk, this is a disease state. Yet on a worldwide basis, the normal state for humanity is not to produce lactase after weaning. Is a condition an "illness" if it is the typical, normal state of being?

Summary

Groups of people react to many kinds of stresses, including climate, disease, and diet. For each we have looked at the adaptations and adjustments a population makes to survive in less than ideal conditions. Cultural adaptation uses behaviors to ease stress; genetic adaptation uses natural selection. Physiological acclimatization changes the body's functioning.

After a general consideration of the concepts of adaptation and physiological fitness, this chapter reviewed a few of the stresses to which humans are subject and the varied adaptations made in one or another setting. The stresses discussed included classic aspects of the physical environment such as heat, cold, and high altitude. Infectious disease and other stresses found in modern, urban environments were also considered. Lastly, nutrition was discussed in terms of the causes and incidence of malnutrition and the genetic, physiological, and cultural adaptations made in response. Of particular note is the realization that food choices are an aspect of culture and as such subject to belief systems and cultural values. Biological variation in metabolic processes can also be of significance in determining the composition of a good diet for different groups of people. A knowledge of anthropology can thus help to assure adequate nutrition.

The specific stresses are not independent; diet influences disease, and climate affects diet and disease. Human beings are integrated organisms that respond to their whole environment, which makes studies of stress very complex. A response to one stress may in turn originate a new problem. Many of the differences we see in people today come from adaptive reactions to stress. Visible traits, such as body build, skin color, and hair form, are probably related to environmental stresses. Blood type, disease resistance, and many other "invisible" characteristics also react to environmental differences. Human variability, then, is the result of dynamic interactions among human biology, culture, and the world around us.

Whether we are studying human variability today or in the past, it is imperative to look at traits as they are actually distributed instead of at stereotypes.

Biological History of Human Populations

Physical anthropology is a historical science. Whether we are looking at the fossil record and the long-term history of our species, the historical reasons why blood group frequencies vary from place to place, or a historical analysis of the forces affecting the growth of a child, we are trying to understand events within a time frame. In the last several chapters, we have concentrated on the recent history of biological traits within populations and how it is affected by genes, development, culture, and evolution.

Until recently, the framework within which physical anthropology studied modern human differences had to do with races; physical anthropology is identified in the public eye as dealing with fossils and races. We have nearly completed the discussion of modern human variability, however, and we have barely used the word *race* at all.

There are two major reasons for the recent shift away from racial analysis. As we will see, while the reconstruction of the history of a group of people is an interesting and valid endeavor, the race concept turns out to be a very poor aid in pursuing this end. Second, to a degree the sorts of questions asked by physical anthropologists have changed over time. As the understanding of evolutionary processes has progressed, we have formulated some questions based on newer information. This is nothing unique to physical anthropology; all spheres of inquiry change as knowledge and assumptions change. Consider fifteenth-century Europe, when it was reasonable and important to ask: "How far west can you sail before falling off the edge of the world?" As the assumed flat earth concept gave way to the globe in the sixteenth century, the important questions changed. A reasonable question of one time and place can be made obsolete by new information. In this way the questions of race, racial purity, and related issues have become the anthropological version of the flat earth theory.

Despite these changes, physical anthropologists remain curious about the relationships between groups and the evolutionary forces that have operated upon them. In this chapter, we shall set forth the reasons for the move away from the race concept and some of the approaches and questions that have taken its place. Certain of the newer techniques are similar to the molecular ones discussed in Chapter 5, but instead of seeking to measure the distance between species, we are trying to fathom the distance between populations. In other cases, the uniquely human ability to leave written records can be exploited to study the biological history of our ancestors.

Definitions and Concepts of Race

The concept of race originated in Western thought several hundred years ago, at roughly the same time as European colonialism, prior to any knowledge of modern evolutionary ideas (Chapter 1). Its origin resulted partly from the need of colonial powers to explain the diversity of people and to rationalize their exploitation. Because the concept has its roots in pre-Darwinian thought, it has proved difficult, if not impossible, to apply to a post-Darwinian view of humanity.

One of the most frequently used biological definitions was proposed by Theodosius Dobzhansky in *Mankind Evolving*: Races are breeding populations that differ from other populations in their frequency of one or more genetic traits. The next step seems easy: listing the human groups within which breeding occurs. But this task is monumentally difficult; many physical anthropologists believe that races are larger aggregates of populations, synonymous with subspecies, as illustrated by units like sub-Saharan Africans and Europeans.

Most people think of race as large groups composed of many smaller subgroups. Few people off the street would call one population a race. If we were asked, "On what do you base a decision about someone's race?," most of us would say "skin color"; we tend to reduce all the ways in which people differ to one easily noticeable, socially important trait. We confuse sociological races (black, white), which in our society are defined mainly by skin color or other obvious features, with biological races, which at least theoretically are based on breeding patterns. Compounding the problem, the word *race* has also been used to differentiate people in terms of time; the neandertals are designated as a subspecies or race (*Homo sapiens neanderthalensis*) of our species in contrast to all modern humans, who are called *Home sapiens sapiens*. The word means many different things to different people and often to even one person. It covers units from as small as a breeding population to large clusters of such groups; many people even refer to the "human race," implying we all belong to the same race.

For the time being, let us set aside the dimension of time; understanding the problem as it stands today is difficult enough.

Pure Races

The idea of the "pure" race can be laid to rest at once. To meet this condition, humanity would have to consist of long-separated, genetically distinct groups, with each group's members having specific features. The

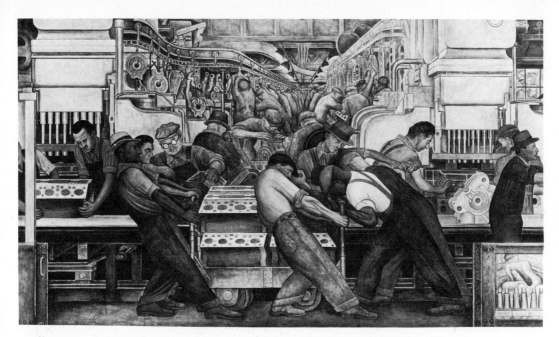

FIGURE 14.1.   People do not look the same—a fact obvious to us all. But do we want to call them members of different races? Mexican artist Diego Rivera sampled the variety of men in his fresco of a V-8 Motor Block Machinery assembly line (a detail of which is shown here from his extensive work, *The Detroit Industry Murals*). Rivera used as his models actual workers from such diverse places as Bulgaria, England, and Mexico.

pure race would not be mixed with the genes of any other race. This kind of treatment of human variation is built on stereotypes and typologies and implies great homogeneity within a group and great differences between groups (Figure 14.1). Descriptions of a "typical" African or a "typical" Asian are based on this approach. No living individual exhibits all the ideal Nordic characteristics, but those who stereotype people explain this as being due to the mixing of pure races in that person's ancestry. In 1923, Jon Mjoen, a Norwegian anthropologist, discussed the "undesirable" consequences of crossing races in his article "Harmonic and Disharmonic Racecrossings." He defined Nordic traits as tall stature; long skull; narrow, high nose; light complexion; heavy beard; blond hair; blue or light brown eyes; "and above all, the Nordic features." Laplanders have short stature; round skull; broad, flat nose; yellow-gray skin; uneven, sparse beard; black, straight hair; and mongoloid features. Having already been unscientifically redundant by defining Nordics as having Nordic features, Mjoen tried to show that crosses between Nordics and Laplanders often resulted in feeblemindedness, drunkenness, and prostitution. After apologetically admitting that light brown eyes are common among Nordics, he attributed the discrepancy to the "mixture between two distant races, the one with blue, the other with black eye color."[1]*

*See pages 631–632 for notes to Chapter 14.

Even if we could ignore the racism in such statements, we should not miss their completely antievolutionary feeling. Because of the ways in which genetics and evolution operate, it would be nearly impossible to have a completely homogeneous group of people. Mjoen considers all variation within a group to be caused by admixture and looks down on all who deviate from the ideal. Interbreeding does produce variability within a group, but it certainly is not the only source. Even if an invariant population were possible, it would have a very poor evolutionary prognosis, for variation allows populations to benefit by continued adaptation. An unmixed race is impossible, because no group has ever gone very long without getting some genes from other populations.

Biological Race/ Sociological Race

The typologist's definition of race has now been rendered obsolete in biological anthropology, but it lingers on in the way most people think of human variation. We tend to think of an American white, black, Arab, or Jew as looking or behaving a certain way. When doing so, we are creating stereotypes. These stereotypes are based in part on biological traits and in part on cultural traits. It should be needless to say that not all Jews are good at business dealings and that not all blacks have broad lips. Neither cultural nor biological attributes are invariant. Stereotypes are created for a purpose. By classifying all members of a group as being greedy or brilliant, we generally are supporting some economic or sociopolitical ideology, although we may try to support the stereotype with "science."

Stephen Gould has reported on the sorts of statements that often masquerade as science.[2] One of the nineteenth century's most productive investigators of human variation in cranial capacity was Samuel Morton, a Philadelphia physician. To Morton, the size of a cranial case was a direct correlate of intelligence: Big brain equals smart. Cranial capacity is the internal volume of the brain case and generally approximates brain size. Today, there is no evidence that brain size reflects anything about ability or behavior. Size is more likely to say something about the sex of the skull's owner (women on the average have a smaller cranial capacity) than anything about intelligence. To Morton, however, size was everything, and the aim of his work was to document the natural superiority of Western Europeans. Although Morton was purported to be a careful worker, Gould has uncovered many shoddy details in his research. Morton misreported information when it served him: Small-brained Europeans were "forgotten." Big-brained non-Europeans were either ignored or became the victims of convenient errors in transcription. Because Morton's work supported a social status quo, it was lauded and went unchecked, to be reported over and over by later researchers. Social divisions along racial lines have often been supported by this type of "scientific" data, and the stereotypes we all have heard are no exceptions.

In physical anthropology, we are not dealing with the sociological view of race, based on stereotypes, but rather with a biological interpretation of populations. Biologically, we are interested in variation within as well as between groups; sociologically, only the variation between groups counts.

Biological and sociological ideas about race do not necessarily coincide, as Gabriel Lasker and Bernice Kaplan found in Peru.[3] Racial names are used there to describe differences in class. The three major classifications are white, mestizo (mixed Spanish-Indian), and Indian. The researchers found little correlation between a person's sociological classification and biological ancestry. In the towns they studied, the European forms of a trait, such as wavy hair, seldom show up in people who consider themselves white.

Geographic Race, Local Race, and Microrace

Stanley Garn has tried to alleviate some of the semantic problems by tightening the definition of biological race. He proposed three specific terms: geographic race, local race, and microrace.[4] Geographic, or continental, races are the large groupings we usually think of: sub-Saharan Africans, Australian Aborigines, Native Americans. Local races are much like the breeding populations that Dobzhansky considered; Garn calls the Eskimos, Ainus, Hawaiians, and East Africans local races. Most microraces are found in densely populated areas and are maintained as distinct units by geography or behavior. American blacks in Detroit are genetically different from blacks in Charleston, South Carolina, in spite of the genetic continuity between them. Microraces also refer to groups living in one area but not interbreeding because of cultural differences. This description generally fits blacks and whites in a large city.

Garn's three racial divisions are an appealing simplification, but some groups of people do not fit neatly into any one category. Native Americans are called a geographic race, like Asiatics, Europeans, and sub-Saharan Africans, yet they are genetically much closer to Asiatics than to the other groups. Garn's groupings do not reflect evolutionary relationships, for each geographic race is not equally different from all the other geographic races.

Garn's breakdown proves to be very artificial; similarities and differences between groupings of people do not fit into neat categories or levels of analysis. We can find myriad levels at which to study differences between groups. Garn established small, medium, and large races; we could just as easily set up tiny, small, medium, and large classes, or six classes, or twelve, or, as Dobzhansky did, only one.

The Individual Population—A Race?

In response to definitions that accord to the status of a race a single population, French anthropologist Jean Hiernaux asks, "Will we equate the concept of race with that of the breeding population?," and answers that "one word is enough for one thing."[5] Races to Hiernaux are groupings of populations.

Frank Livingstone partly agrees with Hiernaux. In his article "On the Nonexistence of Human Races," he says it is impossible to divide a single species into meaningful groups larger than populations. Since Livingstone does not consider populations to be races, races thus do not exist. He thinks the word *race* would have validity only if it could be applied to natural clusters of geographically and biologically distinct populations; it is not valid if applied to artificial groupings. As such, races of people do not exist, he believes. He would not call sub-Saharans a race, for instance, because the desert is not an effective barrier to gene flow; sub-Saharan Africans do not constitute a distinct, natural cluster of populations. "An analysis of the populations and/or genes in the Sahara Desert," he says, "certainly indicates that the desert is not a major reproductive barrier," and it was even less so in the past.[6]

Livingstone suggests that if races really exist, the variable traits should vary together: If a population is 10 percent "Negro" in one characteristic, for example, it should be 10 percent "Negro" for all other traits. But Ethiopia, for example, has dark-skinned peoples without kinky hair and lighter-skinned populations with kinky hair. From such examples it is apparent that the concept of race fails to fit biological reality.

Lack of Agreement

More definitions of race or denials of its existence are unnecessary, for our point is clear. Anthropologists agree that people live in populations and that there are variations within as well as among groups. Few anthropologists today would say that the layperson's view of race (Mongoloids, Caucasoids, and so on) has any biological reality. Species are the only true taxa (and even those are sometimes questionable). Theoretically we can decide that two animals are *conspecifics* if they are actively or potentially interbreeding. We have no such hard-and-fast test for determining membership in one or another race.

Racial ideas are a vestige of the typological approach to variation. Instead of studying human variation as ranges of variation and gradual geographic shifting in frequencies of traits, the classic racial approach emphasizes homogeneity within the group and heterogeneity among groups. Even the lay vocabulary (white, black) reflects this emphasis. We tend to see only what our culture teaches us to see (Figures 14.2–14.8). Many talk of sub-Saharan Africans as a race characterized by deeply pigmented skin; yet the skin color of some members of this group (San Bushmen and some Pygmies) is quite different, being yellowish.

The word *race* therefore arouses several objections: (1) Populations are not the same as races; (2) race is a loaded word; (3) races have no biological reality; (4) races are often typological and therefore antievolutionary; and (5) race is a very vague word.

Ethics and Sociological Races

The sociological interpretation of race and the associated phenomenon of racism have exacted a terrible biological cost. The best-known example is the millions of lives lost during Adolf Hitler's rule. But the United States too has frightening, although more subtle, examples of the cost of racial discrimination.

A white child born in the United States in 1985 can expect to live to be about seventy-five; a black child born in the same year can expect to live to be about seventy. Five years do not sound like much unless they happen to be subtracted from *your* life expectancy. Let us look at the statistics another way. In 1985 the United States had about 29 million blacks. On the average each will live five years less than if he or she were white. These people, and American society, will lose 145 million years of human life and productivity to discrimination based on an inaccurate view of human variability. Major contributors to the lower life expectancy are the high fetal, newborn, and infant mortality rates in black Americans. In 1983 the death rate for white newborns was 6.4 per 1,000 live births; for blacks the rate was 12.4. Similar differences are seen for other age groups and other minorities. Culture and biology do interact, sometimes with appalling results.

What alternative to race do we have for looking at human variation? One that has been used quite successfully is the cline. As mentioned in Chapter 3, a cline is gradual variation in a trait over space shown by the alteration in the frequency of one or more traits from population to

The Cline: An Alternative to Race

FIGURE 14.2. A graduating class of Eskimos in Alaska. The photographs in this chapter show not only how different people look in different parts of the world, but also that many visible traits can vary greatly within what is commonly called a race. Look carefully at the faces in group photos and decide for yourself whether a typological approach to human variation fits the real situation: Do all the members of any group look the same? These photographs by no means capture all populational variability; many regions are not represented. Instead, they highlight a small portion of humanity's variability.

FIGURE 14.3.   Three Navajo women from Big Mountain, Arizona.

neighboring population. In Chapter 12 we saw that the frequencies of the ABO alleles form two clines through Europe and Asia: The frequency of A decreases as one travels east, and at the same time the frequency of B rises.

In Chapter 13 we noted that a similar situation exists in Africa and Europe for skin color: There is no one place where dark skin abruptly gives way to lightly pigmented skin. For many other traits, too, anthropologists have shifted from a desire to form typologies to a desire to explain observed variation, and the clinal approach has come to be much more useful than a racial approach.

By noting changing environmental conditions over space (such as the amount of sunlight or the presence of malaria) or by taking into account known population movements, it has proved possible to develop and test hypotheses about the causes of a clinal distribution. The clinal approach to human variation is preferable to a racial analysis in many ways, because it is closer to reality. Intentionally or not, the word *race* stresses similarities within groups and differences between groups. The word *cline*, besides having no connotations, has the advantage of being based on the frequencies of specific traits and implies an acknowledgment that not everyone in a group exhibits a specific form of a trait.

One polymorphism not mentioned in the earlier discussion is that for cerumen, or ear wax. Two phenotypes exist for this trait: wet and sticky cerumen or dry and hard cerumen. The trait is controlled by two

FIGURE 14.4.   Part of the group that was responsible for the discovery of the Zhoukoudian *Homo erectus* fossils (Chapter 10), including Franz Weidenreich (right), a female assistant (middle foreground), and several Chinese men.

FIGURE 14.5.   A group of children in Japan.

FIGURE 14.6.   An Ainu group from Japan at the St. Louis Exposition.

FIGURE 14.7.   Aborigines from the Northern Territory, Australia.

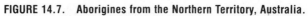

alleles, the one for the wet form being the dominant one. John Mc-Cullough reports that cerumen clines exist among Native Americans, with the wet and sticky phenotype characteristically found in wet climates and the dry and hard cerumen allele characteristically found in dry environments.[7]

The Navajos currently live in the southwestern United States, but archaeological and linguistic evidence tells us that they migrated to the area in the last five hundred years, descending from Athabaskan peoples of western Canada. Thus one would not be surprised to find the cerumen frequencies of Navajos to be similar to those of Canadian Athabaskan-speakers such as the Chilcotin. In western Canada, which is damp and cold, the frequency of the wet phenotype is about 0.67. In fact, however, the Navajo cerumen types fit into the cline of their present Native American neighbors: They have a high frequency of the dry allele (about 0.70). McCullough noted this and, using computer simulations, concludes that the Navajos' conformity to the cline indicates the operation of natural selection. By noting consistencies where we might not expect them to exist, we may be able to clarify further the effects of evolution on human populations.

Studying What Is

The clinal approach can be very useful for understanding the distribution of a trait over space. Anthropologists continue to be interested in the history of the population, however, not just in a trait. While such

FIGURE 14.8
A Kikuyu (Bantu) group in Kenya.

a desire was often seen in racial studies, it was directed toward the end of classifying people according to stereotypes. Now we seek to understand better the genetic and evolutionary forces at work on human groups.

Often such investigations involve looking at not only the frequencies of characteristics in populations but also the demographics of the population (demography is the science of population). The genes and biology of a group are affected by the evolutionary forces: drift, selection, mutation, and admixture. In turn, one or more of these forces are affected by features of the population such as fertility, mating patterns, subdivisions, size, and sex ratio.

Inbreeding, or the mating of genetic relatives, will tend to increase the frequency of homozygosity, for instance. Many societies have a preference for marrying relatives as a way to keep wealth clustered while reinforcing alliances. Well-to-do castes in southern India have very high frequencies of uncle-niece marriage for just these reasons. Some royal families, such as the Ptolemies, even preferred brother-sister marriage. Such behaviors can have noticeable effects on the gene pool and health. P. Govinda Reddy found that inbred higher caste members in India had higher rates of spontaneous abortions and miscarriages than the non-inbred sample.[8]

Biological History of the Yanomama

The unraveling of biological history has come into a new age, as is well exemplified by the research on a South American Indian tribe, the Yanomama (Figure 14.9). A large, multidisciplinary crew of scientists has been trying to document the structure and functioning of this tribe for several decades, not only to understand these people in particular but also to identify the forces that may have shaped the evolution of many earlier human populations. For hundreds of generations the social organization of human groups roughly approximated aspects of life that are still seen in modern, preliterate, preagricultural peoples. In large measure, the work on the Yanomama and other South American tribes is a salvage operation, for there are very few groups still untouched by Western culture. Studies of these people must be conducted now, for soon there will no longer be the opportunity to learn from them.

The Yanomama are living in the Brazil-Venezuela border region. There are about fifty villages, each with a population of 50 to 200 people. Most villages are several days walk from the nearest neighbor. However, there are clusters of villages that regularly interact with each other. About every three to five years, each village must move as the soil becomes infertile or as relationships deteriorate among the inhabitants. Living in an inaccessible tropical rain forest, they were first contacted by Westerners on a continuing basis in the 1950s.

That the Yanomama are isolated genetically can be seen by examining their gene pool and those of neighboring groups like the Guaymi. There are alleles present in the Yanomama gene pool that are lacking in neighboring tribes and vice versa. Evidently, different mutations have appeared in different tribes. The concentration of these relatively newly arisen alleles in different tribes implies that gene flow between tribes is not very great.

Within the tribe, the story is quite different. The general rule is to marry a cousin living in the same village. These marriages are arranged so as to "pay off," much as when a person in our society wants to marry into the "right" family. Because the Yanomama are polygynous—a male may have more than one wife—a complex web of social relations develops. Although marriage usually involves people from the same village, one of the partners may have recently migrated into the community. Villages within a cluster are thus united in part by marriages.

Genetic relatedness between villages also exists because of the manner by which new villages appear. When struggles for leadership or women start to boil, the village splinters, or "fissions." The loser in the power struggle and some of his relatives are forced to pack up and move out, forming a new settlement. Sometimes the offshoot group may rejoin the parent village, a case of village "fusion." A similar sort of group splintering has been documented by James Hurd for a religious isolate, the Amish, living in central Pennsylvania.[9] Here, when tensions rose

FIGURE 14.9. Several Yanomama Indians along with the anthropologist Napoleon Chagnon.

within the group, fissioning took the form of a reorganization of church attendance. The result, the formation of a new group within which people were related, was the same in Pennsylvania and in the Amazon.

The Yanomama are not a particularly peaceable people, and one rather common activity is raiding for women. If a woman is taken from a nearby village, she is apt to be genetically related to her captor, at least to some degree, as a result of past village fissioning. She may later be captured from her new home and moved to yet another village. There is also an appreciable level of raiding for women over long distances. This movement of women has great significance for the effect of migration on the genetic structure of the Yanomama.

Inbreeding is quite high among the Yanomama for several reasons. For starters, the nonrandom nature of village fissioning leads to the formation of new settlements largely composed of genetic relatives. When marriage occurs between these people, inbreeding results (see page 101). Inbreeding is also very high because of the uneven genetic contributions of different men to the next generation. Some powerful men produce many offspring because they have many wives. Those with lesser social standing have fewer wives and children. As much of one generation is sired by a small part of the previous generation, there is an increased likelihood of relatives mating with each other.

It has been speculated that if differences in social power are at all related to genetic differences—for instance, if men with genes for intellectual skills are those who manage to accumulate power and wives—this relationship would provide an opportunity for natural selection to work. Those with genes for intelligence would have more offspring, and the frequency of these genes would increase. Whether this tie between intelligence and reproduction exists, however, is not demonstrated.

This sort of population data on the Yanomama provide a highly detailed view of the biological and cultural features that shaped the genetic structure of the tribe. With this sort of data, we are in a better position to assess the importance of the various evolutionary forces operating on the people. The degree to which cultural features like fissioning have been important in other tribal peoples may never be known. By carefully deciphering the history of the Yanomama, however, we at least get to see the sorts of factors that may have been operating on other human populations and thereby may better understand the origins of variation within and between human populations.

Population Dynamics

The Yanomama are a relatively small, uncomplex, geographically confined society and thus provide a good model for studying the relationship between population structure and evolution. They provide a relatively straightforward natural experiment for looking at population dynamics. Their simplicity has drawbacks, however. For one, they have no written records. The time depth of knowledge about such peoples may only stretch back as far as the oldest person can remember or to the limits of oral history, yet we know that the evolutionary forces operate over long periods. Recently, anthropologists have increasingly looked at the factors that have molded populations familiar to us. As with the Yanomama, we find that demographic factors such as population size and reproductive success are important in shaping modern gene pools. More detailed biological histories of populations are possible, however, when written words are available.

Many studies illustrate the effects of variables such as admixture, long- and short-distance migration, and age at marriage on a population's history. One well-documented example is the history of black American populations. Mid-twentieth-century studies used biological data such as gene frequencies to estimate the relative amounts of African and European ancestry in various black American gene pools. The pioneering work was done by B. Glass and C. C. Li,[10] W. S. Pollitzer,[11] and others. One estimate of admixture can be obtained by the following formula:

$$m = \frac{q_h - q_1}{q_2 - q_1}$$

Here, m is the proportion of genes for some trait that are derived from European ancestors, while the frequencies of an allele in the two ancestral populations are q_1 (West Africans) and q_2 (white Americans). The allele frequency in the hybrid population (here black Americans) is q_h. Using allele frequencies for Gm, a protein found in the blood, m can be estimated. The allele frequency for this protein in West Africans (q_1) is 100 percent; in white Americans (q_2) it is 0 percent; and in black Americans (q_h) it is 73 percent. Hence m is computed as:

$$m = \frac{.73 - 1.0}{0.0 - 1.0} = \frac{27}{100} = .27$$

Of the black American gene pool, 27 percent derived from European ancestors. It became clear, however, that this estimate was not entirely satisfying, because if other allele frequencies were used, the results were not always comparable. In fact different admixture estimates are generated if one uses different estimates for the frequency of an allele or different formulas for estimating admixture.

T. E. Reed used lists from the slaving ships of the seventeenth to nineteenth centuries to carry this research a step further.[12] The early assumption, that the frequency of alleles was equivalent throughout Africa, was clearly wrong. Reed computed that about 50 percent of all slaves came from two areas along the west coast of Africa from Nigeria to Angola. At the other extreme, the peoples of coastal Sierra Leone comprised only about 5 percent of the slaves. Geneticists, however, tended to take virtually any allele frequency from West Africa, and sometimes even from East Africa (which did not even contribute to American populations), to represent the African ancestry. With Reed's more realistic view of the data, m is approximately 22 percent for non–Southern black

American populations. In the South, the proportion of white ancestry was at most half of this value.

More recently, Curtis Wienker has conducted even more specific studies.[13] He documents the social and historical factors that have affected the black population of McNary, Arizona. This small, isolated community has black, white and Apache inhabitants, of whom 40 percent, or about 260 people, are black. There are no intermarriages and a long history of segregation. Using allele frequencies and reflectance spectrophotometric readings as well as historical documents, Wienker finds this small group of blacks to be almost entirely unmixed; their admixture with whites is only about 3 percent. Historical documents show that the majority of blacks of McNary were born in small, isolated lumbering towns in the South. When they migrated to McNary from those towns, they brought along their cultural heritage, so that the economic basis of generations of McNary blacks has been lumbering; people even tend to marry within the community of black lumberers. These marriage patterns have resulted in the formation of a group that is noticeably less admixed than most black American communities.

During both World War II and the 1970s, there were large-scale migrations of blacks from McNary. Such a sudden decrease in population size can create a bottleneck, which in turn can lead to the loss of genetic variation. This is a form of genetic drift. As rare genes are most likely to be lost, whatever European genes that were once present in the black population may have been lost, adding to the development of a minimally admixed modern population.

American blacks are not the only people for whom admixture estimates have been made. The degree of admixture between Jewish populations and their non-Jewish neighbors has been the subject of several studies. Others have estimated the contribution of Norwegians to the present-day Icelandic gene pool. Results are inconclusive in both cases.

Why, one can ask, would one care about such questions? Is it an end in itself, or does the estimation of admixture help us to understand evolution and population biology? Some have suggested that admixture can help us to identify traits that are actively undergoing natural selection. If one computes m using the data in Table 3.4, we find that the sickle-cell allele, Hb^S, yields a much higher value than do alleles for some other traits. This occurs because admixture is not the only force causing the frequency of HbS to drop in black Americans relative to West Africans. In the United States malaria is not a health problem, but sickle-cell anemia certainly is. The selective force that maintains the levels of HbS in Africa is not present in the United States. The modern frequency of the allele in black American populations is a result partly of white admixture and partly of selection ridding the population of HbS via sickle-cell anemia.

A second reason to study admixture relates to the many chronic diseases that appear to have some genetic underpinnings, such as certain forms of hypertension, heart disease, and diabetes. There is no doubt that in all environment plays a role in the appearance of a disease state, but there are questions as to the size of that role, which may be addressed through admixture estimates. Consider two populations with different incidences of a disease. If the two populations have interbred to varying degrees, thus forming a number of hybrid descendants, one can look for a correlation between the contribution of genes from the ancestor in which the disease is common and the disease's frequency in the hybrids. R. Chakraborty and K. M. Weiss looked at the relationship between non-insulin-dependent diabetes and the proportion of Native American genes in various modern groups. A clear relationship exists; as the degree of Native American ancestry increases, so does the prevalence of the disease. This points toward a strong genetic component.[14]

Generalizations about the roles of admixture, population size, and the like on the genetics and health of populations can be enhanced by computer simulations. Frank Livingstone has shown that harmful genes can become quite common due to population bottlenecks and the Founder's Effect, a form of genetic drift that results from the limited variability inherent in a population founded by a small number of individuals.[15]

In the computer Livingstone created small populations composed of twenty to forty normal individuals and one or two heterozygotes for a lethal recessive gene. Having programmed the computer to allow the group to expand in size following certain guidelines, he observed the fate of the harmful allele. Often the allele disappeared entirely, but at other times it reached polymorphic frequencies as a result of chance factors— drift, in other words. Livingstone notes that the harmful alleles that occur at polymorphic frequencies may have achieved these frequencies through such a process. Various European populations for instance, are polymorphic for cystic fibrosis, PKU, and Tay-Sachs disease, a fatal neurological disorder. Livingstone's view contrasts with the assumption made by many that harmful recessive genes must be conferring an advantage in the heterozygote if they are found at appreciable levels. By better understanding the operation of evolutionary forces on human populations, we can gain insights into their health status.

In addition to historical records, genetic data may also be useful in the study of the effects of genetic history on modern groups. One can use simply inherited features like blood groups to trace affinities. Increasingly, however, complex statistical treatments are applied to extract the most information from the data. Some now look at the DNA itself or other molecular data. Others use classical traits in the anatomy. We shall look at some approaches to tracing population affinities.

Population Relations

Anthropologists first used blood group data and later protein allele frequencies to attempt to trace relationships between human populations. Information on a series of populations would be gathered, and by various statistical procedures, the distance between the groups was determined.

Populations with similar frequencies were classed as being more closely related. The study by Newton Morton of the genetic kinship of Jewish populations in different parts of the world illustrates this approach. Morton chose to look at the HLA system (page 498) allele frequencies.[16] As HLA has many different alleles, it can be reasonably assumed that two groups with similar arrays of alleles at similar frequencies share a recent ancestor. It would be quite a coincidence to be very similar by accident.

Morton gathered information on HLA alleles in a variety of Jewish populations scattered around the world. Comparable data also were gathered for non-Jewish neighbors in each area. When the figures were compared, it appeared that Jews in an area are more like their neighbors than they are like Jews elsewhere in the world. This indicates that the Jewish populations have had a significant degree of admixture with their neighbors for many years. Analysis of blood groups and polymorphic proteins points to the same conclusion. Figure 14.10 is a diagram of genetic similarity for four Jewish and four gentile populations. The Ashkenazim (Jews of northern Europe) cluster with North African Jews and European non-Jews. The two groups from Iran are most similar to each other, while the Yemeni Jews and Israeli Arabs are most alike. The genetic data are in accord with nonbiological information such as historical documents.

Although the HLA system is very rich in variation, it is still only one trait out of the thousands coded in the DNA. In judging relation-

FIGURE 14.10.   A statistically derived tree, based on allele frequencies, showing the degrees of genetic similarity between eight populations.

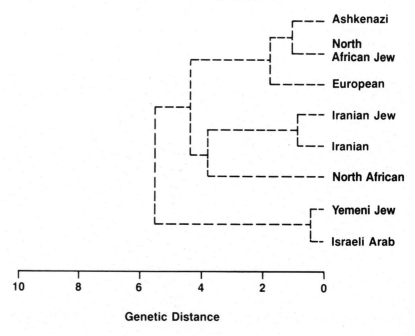

ships one would like to use as many data as are available. A group of statisticians and geneticists headed by Luigi Cavalli-Sforza have used powerful statistical treatments to generate "synthetic variables" that can be mapped in the same manner as gene frequencies (for instance, Figure 12.5).[17] They use a variety of techniques to combine a number of allele frequencies for a population into a single synthetic (as the researchers produce the number) variable. The map can then provide a broad view of population similarities based upon a large amount of genetic data.

One issue that the researchers have considered is the spread of agriculture from the Near East, starting in the Neolithic about 9,000 years ago. Two alternatives have been offered as to how this occurred. According to one, agriculture was spread by cultural diffusion. People borrowed the idea from neighboring groups, but the people themselves did not physically move. In the other view, there was an actual migration of the people as well as the practice. In the former case, the genetic composition of the groups would not be altered by migration and admixture. In the second case, we should expect that gene pools will be altered as farmers move into a region, settle, and start to interbreed with the indigenous peoples. The effects on the gene pool will be tempered by factors such as the relative number of migrants and residents, the rate of population movement, and the fertility levels of the groups, but we do expect that the descendant population will have an altered gene pool. In this model one can also propose that the genetic impact will be related to the distance away from the center of the migration: A cline will be generated as groups near the epicenter will be most affected.

A tentative explanation of the spread of agriculture was developed by looking at data for ten different traits possessing thirty-eight alleles, including ABO, HLA, and Rh. The resulting maps of synthetic variables show clines originating in the Near East and radiating concentrically into Europe, North Africa, the Arabian Peninsula, and India. This is consistent with the spread of people as well as agriculture during the Neolithic. This approach appears capable of providing genetic evidence on long-past population movements and relationships between groups.

DNA and Population Relationships

Not surprisingly, molecular biology and anthropology have lately started to use data on the DNA itself to study population history. A group from Britain headed by J. S. Wainscoat looked at the presence or absence of specific restriction sites in the β-globin gene cluster (page 503) of several hundred people from around the world.[18] Each individual was scored as to whether his or her DNA could be cut at the positions shown in Figure 14.11 by the indicated restriction enzymes. If the DNA cuts at the site, the person is scored as positive (+); if it does not, the person lacks the site and is labeled as negative (−). The results can be assembled into a *haplotype,* or a description (+ or −) of the pattern of restriction sites on a person's chromosomes. For instance, among the sixty-one Africans tested, the most common pattern was − − − − +; that is, a β-

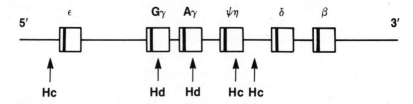

FIGURE 14.11. A map of the human β-globin gene cluster. The arrows show the locations of the sites scored by Wainscoat and his colleagues. Hd is the enzyme Hind III; Hc is Hinc II.

cluster that lacked all except the most 3′-ward site. Having tested a number of groups, including Africans, Melanesians, Polynesians, and Asian Indians, the researchers noted that this most common haplotype in Africans was essentially absent from the other samples. The second most common African haplotype (− + − − +) was also very rare elsewhere. The very common haplotypes in non-Africans were very rare in Africa. Because the work of the Wainscoat group is rather preliminary, it should not be overinterpreted. It does show, however, a closer tie between European and Asian populations than between any of them and the African samples (Figure 14.12).

mtDNA Contained within the cell are organelles, with one sort being known as the mitochondria. These structures are important in generating energy. For some time it has been known that the mitochondria are rather unusual in that they, like the cell nucleus, contain DNA. Mitochondrial DNA (mtDNA) is, however, very unusual in a variety of respects. First, it is very small. Human mtDNA is only about 16,000 base pairs long, while the nuclear DNA is made up of millions of bases. Whereas nuclear DNA directs the production of thousands of proteins, the mtDNA encodes only thirteen. Also, in contrast to the nuclear DNA, we inherit mtDNA maternally. While sperm contains mtDNA,

FIGURE 14.12. A tree showing the degrees of similarity in β-globin restriction sites for samples from eight human populations.

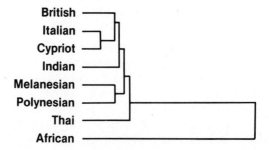

the sperm's mtDNA does not get into the fertilized egg. Barring mutations, we each have the identical mtDNA to that of our mother.

When molecular biologists such as L. Vawter and Wes Brown analyzed the mtDNA of humans and other primates, they found that this component of our DNA evolves much faster than the nuclear DNA—about five to ten times faster.[19] As described in Chapter 10, this feature makes mtDNA quite attractive for studying relationships between recently separated groups such as human populations. The speed of mtDNA evolution means that it will accumulate a significant number of differences in a relatively short period. Nuclear DNA, on the other hand, may change very little or not at all over short periods and thus be of little use in determining degrees of similarity between human populations.

A series of scientists coming out of the laboratory of Allan Wilson have focused their efforts on comparing the mtDNA in a number of human populations to be able to draw evolutionary trees. Most recently, for instance, Rebecca Cann, Mark Stoneking, and Allan Wilson used a battery of twelve restriction enzymes to map the mtDNA from 147 people representing populations from Africa, Asia, Australia, Europe, and New Guinea.[20] The data showed that people can have different patterns of restriction sites. A specific pattern or type was determined by whether a restriction enzyme did or did not cut the mtDNA at specific spots along its length. As with the haplotypes mentioned earlier, a person's mtDNA type can be described with a series of +s and −s. In this sense, the +s and −s described a "superhaplotype" for the mtDNA. One could see that some patterns were quite similar and that others were very different.

The investigators made the reasonable assumption that evolution occurs in a parsimonious fashion. In other words, in the absence of knowledge to the contrary, the most reasonable tree is the one requiring the fewest mutations linking all the mtDNA types. The parsimony view says that in general the patterns that are most similar diverged most recently, while highly divergent sequences have been separated much longer. With this approach, they were able to draw a tree showing similarities between types. Again, the results show that the African populations have the most divergent patterns when compared to the European and Asian groups.

If one assumes that the rate of mtDNA has been approximately constant, one can compute the length of time for which different lineages have been independent. The computations imply that the base of the tree (the common ancestor for all the groups) is at approximately 200,000 years. As the most divergent patterns are found in the African samples and as the Africans are the most variable group among those tested, the indications are that Africa is the home of the ultimate ancestor in the tree of human populations. All human mtDNAs are descendant from an ancient African female.

Such a statement has some startling, major implications regarding the origin of modern humans and our evolutionary relationship with earlier humans, like the neandertals. One interpretation is that there was a "mitochondrial Eve" in Africa about 200,000 years ago, a single female to whom we can all trace our ancestry. This view, described in Chapter 10 as an evolutionary population model, would mean that all modern populations derived from one early or archaic *H. sapiens* population in Africa. The differences we see between modern groups must thus have arisen after the initial humans spread out of Africa and populated the world. We know, however, that for thousands of years, earlier hominines had been living throughout the Old World. The "African origin" theory requires that we explain what happened to these other hominines. Were they exterminated by the expanding new species? If so, what advantage did modern *H. sapiens* have over their contemporaries? If it was a cultural advantage, we would expect to find remains of a rapidly appearing, markedly superior tool kit coinciding with the displacement of one group by the other. This has not been found, however. Perhaps the initial appearance of language can be traced to modern human origins. It has been extremely difficult, however, to document the presence of language in fossil bones.

An alternative hypothesis is that there has been regional evolutionary continuity within geographic areas for long periods. In this view, the genes that are seen today within an area are at least partially, if not largely, those that evolved there. Rather than positing a single origin for modern *H. sapiens* followed by a broad dispersal, this theory suggests that there has been a gradual transition from earlier peoples within areas. Certainly, even if this were true there would have been migration and gene flow between areas, phenomena that would maintain genetic continuity among populations and prevent each from developing into a separate species. But according to this argument, the variations seen across our species today would have a potentially greater time depth. Confounding the issue, the fossil evidence, reviewed in Chapter 10, furnishes support of various sorts for both views.

There may, however, be problems with computing times of separation from mtDNA divergence values. It is by no means proven that the rate of change in DNA is constant, although some feel that it is. If it is not, the dating may be erroneous.

Another question revolves around interpreting similarities in mtDNA. Remember that it is inherited purely through the maternal line. In mainstream American culture, inheritance of a family name is only from the father's side; in each generation the mother's last name dies off. In an analogous fashion, only the maternal mtDNA gets passed on. Because of its unusual inheritance, the date of a last common ancestor for mtDNA types does not necessarily coincide with the time of the last common ancestor of populations or species. It is the nuclear DNA that diverges at the time of speciation, not the mitochondrial.

It may be that there were many different types of mtDNA in human populations for hundreds of thousands of years prior to the hypothetical "Eve." If about 200,000 years ago something caused a bottleneck or constriction in the size of the human population, many mtDNA lines would have died off. This would have effectively reduced the number of mtDNA types that have survived until today (Figure 14.13). Analysis of the surviving mtDNAs could make it erroneously appear as if our species had originated at the later date.

Actually, computer simulations show that even in the absence of bottlenecks, chance alone can result in the loss of many mtDNA types over long periods, making it seem that we all have the same female ancestor. It thus might not be that *H. sapiens* appeared in the late middle Pleistocene in Africa; the mtDNA types may simply create this impression. Looked at another way, even if all current human mtDNA types can be traced to Africa some 200,000 years ago, this does not necessarily mean that our species appeared at that time.

The belief in the African origin of *H. sapiens* at 200,000 B.P. favored by some is a decidedly punctuationalist view of our evolution. Others favor a gradual transition from *H. erectus* to *H. sapiens*. In the gradualist view, the variability we observe in different parts of the world today extends deeply into the past, even possibly predating the appearance of modern humans. The punctuationalist theory places a limit on the time depth of variation, as it could not extend beyond the proposed African population. As the mtDNA data base expands and as we better understand the rates and patterns of its evolution, we will develop a clearer picture of the early evolution of human populations. Additional fossil evidence may also help in resolving this problem.

FIGURE 14.13. The changing number of mtDNA types over time. Each branch represents the appearance of a new mitochondrial type, which may then further change or become extinct. If the population size (indicated by the heavy line) drops precipitously, many types may be lost. All subsequent types will be derived from the few survivors.

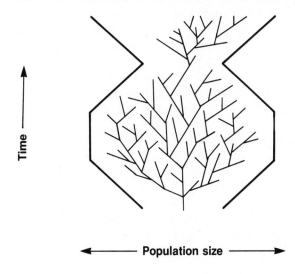

Time →

◄──── **Population size** ────►

Anatomy and Relationships

Like molecules, anatomical traits can be useful for comparing species or populations. Much of hominine evolution is analyzed by looking at teeth, for example. Some prefer to try to judge genetic relations of populations by looking at teeth and the like. The size of teeth has clear adaptive significance, since bigger teeth are important where elaborate food preparation techniques are not present. Big teeth make up for the lack of cultural methods to process food.

C. Loring Brace and Robert Hinton used tooth size to measure the relatedness of people living on islands in the Pacific Ocean.[21] The first people to move into the Pacific were, they say, the big-toothed ancestors of modern, big-toothed native Australians and some New Guineans (see Figure 14.14a). Later, small-toothed peoples moved farther out into the Pacific from Asia, colonizing the islands of Melanesia and Polynesia, whose modern inhabitants have small teeth. Where the two groups met and interbred, people with intermediate-sized teeth appeared. For this intermediate group, the size of the teeth reflects the amount of interbreeding. The map (Figure 14.14b) shows a contemporary cline resulting from degrees of admixture. Small teeth in Melanesia and Polynesia grade into the big teeth of South New Guineans and Australians. The history that Brace and Hinton reconstruct agrees with cultural and linguistic evidence on population affinities in this area. Again, in their work we see an attempt to understand human variation in an evolutionary dynamic framework as opposed to the stereotypic, static view that goes with racial analysis.

Summary

This chapter has dealt with several methods and concepts that are emphasized in trying to uncover biological history. One of the earliest and most debated concepts was race. We have considered some of the anthropological controversy over this issue. As we have seen, anthropologists have offered an assortment of definitions, but there is no unanimity on the validity of any of these postures. Some say a race is a population, others say a race should be a larger grouping. Some say a race is a cluster of populations, others say such groupings have no biological reality. Some say the word is emotionally loaded and propose other terms, but this does not affect the definitional problem. We now feel that biological races simply do not exist and that race is an arbitrary and biologically unrealistic way to consider human variability. It means many different things to different people and can even mean several things to one person. Clouding the biological usage of the word are its sociological connotations. All physical anthropologists agree that (1) there are no pure races and (2) populations of people do vary a lot.

Whether we are studying human variability today or in the past, it is imperative to look at traits as they are actually distributed in the real world instead of at stereotypes that exist only in someone's mind. As Theodosius Dobzhansky has said, "The only way to simplify nature is to study it as it is, not as we would have liked it to be."[22] For this reason,

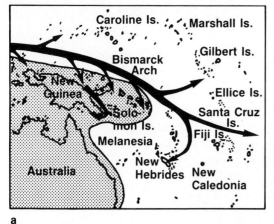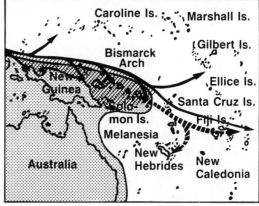

a   b

FIGURE 14.14. (a) The arrows indicate the proposed migration of small-toothed people into Melanesia and Polynesia. The stippled area had been previously populated by large-toothed people. (b) The diagonally shaded region shows a cline for tooth size today. The broken arrow plots the presumed movement of hybrid populations into eastern Melanesia.

the clinal approach has proved to be much more useful than the racial approach in answering questions about human variability.

For questions of relatedness between groups, we can now use rather sophisticated computer programs to generate trees showing genetic similarity from allele data. Analysis of the DNA itself can also be called upon for similar purposes. The mtDNA particularly has raised fascinating questions about the pattern of our evolution and the time depth of human variation. History in such forms as archaeological finds and written documents can also be studied by reference to anatomical data. The detailed knowledge of the evolutionary forces at work in small, isolated groups like the Yanomama also proves invaluable in trying to understand the origins and maintenance of human variability.

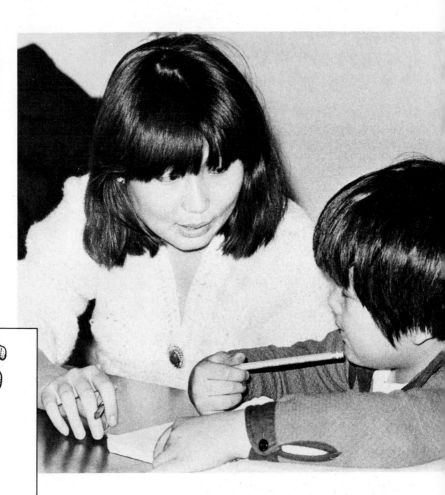

We have reached a time when human beings can affect their environment and in fact their own species in ways never before envisaged. A well-informed public must now make rational decisions about the use of such abilities.

Prospects and Perspectives

This book has been devoted to one task: making human evolutionary history clear. How, why, when, and where did we evolve, and in what ways are we evolving today? These are not purely theoretical questions to be regarded as merely an intellectual exercise. The better we understand our biochemical, anatomical, and behavioral evolution, the better equipped we will be to deal with problems in today's world.

We shall have to appreciate our present cultural and biological variability if we are to run health care and other social services effectively and make new environmental and foreign aid programs work; these must not be done without thorough knowledge of a people's biological and cultural heritage. Constantly coming into contact with people from other cultures or from American subcultures other than our own, we need all the understanding possible about how people function and behave.

Willingness to talk about human variation without assuming that differences imply inferiority or superiority is vital; knowing the facts covered in this book will help. Evolutionary theory tells us that the reasons for variation often can be discerned. Sometimes variation is obviously adaptive; sometimes it is a by-product of nonadaptive change. In either case, views of variation distorted by equating difference with inequality have led to much needless misunderstanding, discrimination, and suffering.

We must be willing to admit too that humans are animals, evolving animals, and that all humans are like one another and like other living things. Not only are we not outside the web of nature, we are very much a part of it. The millions of years of genetic adaptation that lie behind us are the evolutionary legacy that affects how we look and act today. This past has made us able to modify the environment by cultural activity.

Without our large brain, dexterous hands, and bipedalism human cultures would not exist. Although the relationships are exceedingly complex, it was selection for cultural capabilities that produced many of these anatomical traits.

Again, the holistic and biocultural approach of anthropology offers an informative overview of the interactions between cultural and biological aspects of being human. The cultural and biological effects of using tools, for example, evolved in a mutually reinforcing relationship known as a feedback loop. We can say the same about our linguistic abilities, which have both biological and sociocultural attributes. At a microevolutionary level, evidence shows that gene pools are being altered by cultural activities. An example is the appearance of malaria in Africa, which is tied to the development of agriculture. The spread of the disease led to selection for the sickle-cell allele. In turn, a genetic change can produce cultural innovation. When sickle-cell anemia appeared, a search for a medical treatment was begun.

Although the interactions of biology and culture are both longstanding and complex, they are not always recognized. Many people feel that human beings, in particular the technologically sophisticated groups, are not a part of nature. Because we know how to exploit the physical world, some think that we can blithely continue to do so, never paying for the consequences. This is, beyond all doubt, a disastrous way of looking at humans and nature. Animals, including humans, have basic requirements—food, shelter, air, and water—that must not be jeopardized.

Certainly human activities have affected the environment from our beginnings, and however simple or complex a culture's organization, it alters the environment. After all, what we evolved to do best is to modify our surroundings. Complex technological societies undoubtedly affect the world in ways we have not even imagined, yet few of us would be willing to revert to gatherer and hunter economies to stop disrupting the environment. Even if we took such a major step, we would probably not be better off because the human is a biological organism. The return of disease and famine would undoubtedly offset much of the benefit of clean air. Modern medicine, insecticides, and power plants are cultural adaptations designed to make it easier to get along in our environment. Compare the life expectancy in parts of Asia (less than 30 years) with ours (close to 70), and you see that many Western cultural adaptations have their usefulness.

We will surely have to keep producing energy, pest controls, manufactured goods, and the like to retain our standards of living and health. We cannot forget, though, that when fulfillment of these needs opposes our biological requirements, we will need great forbearance and much knowledge and wisdom. Nature will not allow humans to forget that we have biological as well as cultural requirements. In this chapter, as a way of concluding, we shall point to a number of aspects of modern life that can be appreciated more fully by addition of an anthropological perspective.

The biological necessities that modern humans live with, the strong relationships that bind us to the rest of the living world and to the resources of the planet itself, all are clearly visible. In recent years, scholars have looked with great interest back into human evolution to find the reasons for modern human behavior. They have pointed to the small groups that are universal in primate societies, showing how that pattern was carried into hominine evolution and suggesting that it may have deeply marked the ways modern humans learn and socially interact.

All higher primates, except the orang, live in social groups. These aggregations vary greatly in their size and structure, but continual interaction with other members of the species is essential to the higher primates' existence and perhaps to their well-being. Our primate ancestors probably have been organized into social groups for at least 35 million years, long before the origin of the subfamily Homininae. But is group living genetically determined? All we can say is that all human beings known to us live in social groups, and although they are quite variable in composition and size, such groups are certainly a universal of human behavior.

In both nonhuman primate societies and human groups, the young learn how to be social animals in the same way: by watching how adults in their group act (page 202) and by imitating and practicing these behaviors in play groups among the young of similar age and development. These peer play groups are a subgroup within the larger primate social unit, where young animals can practice and perfect their developing muscular coordination and social skills. By learning from the behavior of adult animals, the young are socialized and thus can later successfully interact with other members of the group. Adult primates are rather lenient toward immature animals and will tolerate inappropriate behaviors (such as tail pulling and attempts at fighting) directed at them by young animals. If the youngsters persist, of course, the adult may reach the end of its patience and stop the nonsense by a judicious slap or bite.

In modern human groups there is a tendency for young children to form peer groups, and although the activities of these groups can be greatly varied, including rough-and-tumble play and solitary games, much of the behavior is directed toward developing adult skills and roles. N. G. Blurton Jones, observing nursery school children in Britain, reports that "children in nursery school spend much time simulating adult occupations in their play ('Firemen,' 'Policemen,' 'Shops,' 'Offices,' 'Tea Parties')."[1]* Anthropologists report similar behavior patterns in non-Western societies. They find especially interesting the ways of transmitting important behavior from one generation to the next. As the cultural anthropologist Gladys Reichard points out,

> one reason why it is difficult to study . . . education [in non-Western societies] is that one method used to teach . . . is intangible. It is a method

*See page 633 for notes to Chapter 15.

as old as the life of man but one which our self-conscious analysts often forget: simply that children do not do what adults *tell* them to do, but rather what they see adults *do*. [Non-Western] people do not lay stress on telling. In many languages, the word for "teach" is the same as the word for "show," and the synonymity is literal. One of the things which amuses natives . . . is the habit . . . [anthropologists] have of asking questions: "What are you going to do next?" "What are you doing that for?" The craftsman or hunter always knows what he is going to do next, but he may not be able to give orally the reason for doing it . . . all these things . . . [a] child picks up by constant observation and by imitation.[2]

Human and Primate Learning in Childhood

The human pattern of learning is quite similar to that of the non-human primates. In our complex technological society, many of the skills demanded in many professions are so complicated and known by so few people that we have to have specialists to tell the young how to perform these tasks. Even in modern Western society, however, children continue to learn patterns of behavior—roles, actions used in dealing with other people, standards of moral behavior, clan and family relationships—as well as general tasks like cooking, driving, and speech, by observation and imitation.

The ancient (in the evolutionary sense) primate patterns of learning are continued in modern human groups. They form one foundation holding together the social group: the children's ability to learn the behaviors of the adults in the society and to become fully socialized members of their group who can interact successfully with other members.

An important distinction between the hominines and other higher primates is the length of childhood. Many primates reach adulthood by the fifth or sixth year; it usually takes the hominines twice as long. There is evidence that even early hominines, the australopithecines, went through a long childhood dependency like that of modern human beings. This prolongation of childhood in the hominines may be related to the amount of learned behavior that must be communicated to the younger generation. Hominine evolution is closely related to the development of a wide variety of complex behaviors. Acquiring the skills needed to perform these tasks would take more time, thus extending childhood (Figure 15.1).

The primates' biological basis of learning, involving rates of growth and development of the body, brain, and muscular coordination, is so complex that we cannot tell just how much of it is genetically determined. When we do know the genetic determinants, we will probably find them built into an extremely complex system of genes.

The Small Group in Human Evolution

The hominines may have retained the basic higher primate patterns of learning because they spent much of their evolutionary history in small groups of foragers and collectors. We have just begun to learn how this long history has affected us. It was only 10,000 years ago, after the hominines had spent countless ages gathering and hunting, that this economic system was radically changed by the invention and spread of agriculture and animal domestication. Some biological features may have

FIGURE 15.1. The long human childhood period provides many opportunities for learning.

evolved earlier than agriculture to adapt hominines to a small-group, nonsettled way of living. In a small group of gatherers and hunters, the primate learning system of observation, imitation, and practice would have been efficient. In the nonhuman primates and modern human beings, the young observe adults who are physically close to them; in small groups, every adult comes into visual contact with the young individual, and patterns of behavior of the whole group may thus be observed by the youngster. As an adult, the individual shares with all others in the group the behaviors necessary for getting along in the society. This pattern evolved in the higher primates and continued in hominine evolution because the economic limitations of gathering and hunting kept them from forming larger, more complex aggregations. Agriculture, however, established a new economic base, making way for larger human groups in settled, permanent locations. In larger groups, the young human being continues to learn by observation and imitation but can no longer observe all the adults in the society. The young see only the behaviors of the adults with whom they are in immediate contact.

In most agricultural societies, behavioral differences have developed among the social, economic, religious, and professional subgroups within the larger society. Because a child raised in such a group will not learn the normative behaviors of all segments of the society, as an adult the individual will come into contact with other members of the society with whom patterns of interaction will not be completely successful. Sociologists have said much about the difficulties a person may have in establishing rapport with other members of the same society who have different social, economic, or other backgrounds. Human biologists have seen a pattern like this in the choice of marriage partners in the United States. The chances are high that an American will marry someone with very similar background. Some choices, of course, are made by conscious decisions. Others, however, reflect the fact that individuals with similar backgrounds will be more likely to establish an intimate, meaningful relationship; in a word, they will have more in common. Our evolutionary heritage as primates may influence our behavior even in choosing our marriage partners, and may be the reason for assortative mating (see Chapter 11), which helps maintain genetic diversity among subgroups.

Human Learning and Cultural Diversity

The evolutionary patterns of learning we have been describing also have important implications for understanding why it is sometimes very difficult for peoples of different societies to interact successfully. Rapid transportation and communication have deeply and permanently modified the amount of contact social groups have with one another. More and more, individuals from one society are meeting members of other societies, yet human behavior still differs between and within societies. The difficulty of fully understanding the behaviors of a member of another society leaves many chances for misunderstanding and inappropriate behavior.

Edward Hall, an anthropologist who has been studying the human use of space, reports in *The Hidden Dimension* that people keep distances of varying sizes around them while interacting with others or trying to limit or cut off communication. Many animals, including the nonhuman primates, practice this spacing, which probably has biological foundations in humans. The size of the space around an individual, and the social circumstances in which it may expand or shrink, are learned behaviors that vary from society to society. Hall defines patterns of distance used by middle-class, educated, Eastern seaboard Americans in different social situations. One is social distance, which at its closest is between 4 and 7 feet; this is the distance that separates people in a group at a casual social gathering. These Americans feel uncomfortable when the distance is violated and try to restore the appropriate spacing. Many foreigners visiting the United States have felt rejected and hurt because their own social distance is closer than 4 to 7 feet and, conversing with Americans at a party, think the greater distance is an attempt to minimize communication. This behavior, like many others we use in our interactions, is learned. As Hall points out, however, "concepts such as these are not always easy to grasp, because most of the distance-sensing process occurs outside awareness."[3]

Modern technology has brought us all into close contact, which has often aroused conflicts in people who do not understand the behaviors of other individuals because they are used to doing things differently. Whether we will be able to solve the crucial problems created by these differences, which are based on a pattern of learning that evolved in small groups, may decide whether *Homo sapiens* will survive.

Humans in the Modern World

Knowing now that our ancestors evolved in a very different setting, we can ask whether modern *Homo sapiens* have adapted to the densely populated, specialized, technological environment in which most of us live. Many scientists believe that adaptations to our ancestral condition are inappropriate to our modern world and that stresses may result. We shall outline but a few of the topics to which anthropology can add its unique point of view.

Sex Roles

Why do men and women behave differently? Why, in most societies, do men wield so much more public power than women? Must this state of affairs persist?

Many parallels can be drawn between these questions and the ones raised regarding postulated "racial differences." Some have looked for biological explanations, others have looked at environmental and cultural factors, while still others have considered biocultural phenomena. A complete consideration of the topic would require a book in itself; thus we will have to limit our discussion to but a glimpse of the subtleties involved.

Those who feel that the sex roles are not subject to alteration often look to the "nature" side of the issue. It is argued that if biology accounts for behavioral differences between males and females, nothing can be done to change this natural order. Neither should anything be done, for to do so would be to go against nature. Within this perspective several different lines of evidence have been presented.

As we know, males have an X and a Y chromosome, while women have two Xs. If males are more aggressive, then the genetic underpinnings for their aggression, it is reasoned, are on the Y chromosome. Much of the analysis has focused on men with one X and two Y chromosomes, looking for evidence of "superaggressiveness." To date, the results do not support this line of reasoning, and its proponents are far from proving a chromosomal basis for increased aggressiveness in males.

Another biological argument, which is based on our primate relatives, is more general in approach. Selection, it states, has for millions of years favored sexual dimorphism in anatomy, physiology, and behavior. Males were selected to be larger, better hunters, and more aggressive. Females developed the anatomy and behaviors necessary for motherhood. Any attempt by women to adopt the behaviors normal to men, or vice versa, is thus contrary to our evolution and potentially dangerous. This idea is very tempting to some, but its simplicity is probably an indication of its inaccuracy. Early field studies of primate behavior reinforced this view, however, for the species most commonly studied, baboons, is highly dimorphic. Once other primates were watched we saw the tremendous range of variation within the order (Chapter 6).

Evolutionary hypotheses for differing sex roles abound. Darwin said that males, besides competing for food and shelter, have directly competed for females over the millennia. The most courageous and intelligent won access to the females and thus passed on their genes. Females, in line with Darwin's Victorian worldview, sat on the sidelines waiting for the victors.

Napoleon Chagnon, in analyzing aggression among the Yanomama, finds some support for Darwin's theory.[4] Almost half of the men twenty-five or older had killed or participated in killing someone. Looking at the reproductive history of Yanomama men, he found that those men who had killed had more wives than those who had not killed. If there are genes that predispose a person to violence (a very debatable speculation), then those men who kill may pass on their genes for aggression at a greater rate.

Modern sociobiologists argue for the evolution of many human behaviors. According to one view, human males and females pursue different reproductive strategies. It is more successful for males to have as many children as possible, since their biological investment in each child is rather limited. The male strategy is therefore to attempt to have sexual relations with many different females, in this way insuring that their alleles will be passed on to the succeeding generation. In contrast, females make a much greater biological investment when having children, not only during the prolonged pregnancy but also during the early years of infant dependency. Females thus ensure that their alleles will be represented in the next generation by devoting considerable energy and effort to each offspring. It is accordingly in the best interest of the female to form an attachment with a male to obtain assistance with child care, whereas it is in the best interest of the male to maintain independence and be able to impregnate as many females as possible. In this view, the conflicting interests of male and female reproductive strategies have led to difficulties in male-female relationships and can explain the differing notions about sexual behavior and roles held by men and women in our society.

It is important to keep in mind that there is a great deal of variation in the division of sex roles in cultures other than our own. Until very recently, females in our society were solely responsible for housekeeping and child rearing, a practice that has begun to change very rapidly with more and more women now working full time. However, in other cultures men traditionally have had an important role in both activities.

Proponents of the idea that sex roles are learned behaviors also draw on several sorts of evidence (Figure 15.2). John Money and Anke Ehrhardt describe the rearing, as a female, of a normal male infant who traumatically lost his penis at the age of seven months.[5] As a result of the trauma, it was decided to perform a surgical sex reassignment. This rare

FIGURE 15.2. Sex roles appear to be largely a result of learned behavior.

situation provides both a good control because this infant had a normal male identical twin and important insight into the effects of rearing and learned behavior on the development of sex roles.

At the age of seven there was a tremendous difference in the behaviors of the two children. The little girl liked to be dressed nicely, disliked being dirty, loved to have her hair set, helped with the housework, played with dolls, and wanted to be a doctor or teacher when she grew up. Her brother played in the dirt, helped his father fix things, and wanted to be a policeman or fireman. These children, in spite of having exactly the same genes, conform perfectly to the traditional American sex roles. Learning is evidently of great importance.

Looking at male and female roles in other societies can be even more informative because traumas or pathologies are not involved. We have space to consider only a few general points. In most societies, females do have less control than males over important limited resources, including trade, food, fuel, and political positions. Where they do exert some control or power, it is often in the form of "the power behind the throne" or through kin ties to a male. Indira Gandhi followed her father, Nehru, as prime minister of India, and Juan Perón's wife succeeded him as leader of Argentina.

To some degree adult females may be more tied down than males of comparable age simply because only they can bear children. Because they are somewhat limited by pregnancy, they do not have equal access to the things that mean power, such as control over the distribution of scarce, important resources. Among hunters like the Eskimos, females never have the primary responsibility for catching game. Possibly this is a consequence of the requirement that they carry the children, both during pregnancy and while the child is nursing, which would severely hinder a hunter's ability to track and attack game.

The social position of women may be a cultural adaptation. Females are the limiting factor in the reproduction of a group. Theoretically, because one adult male could father hundreds of offspring, any individual male is expendable. Maintenance of population size depends on the number of females in their reproductive years. Hunting is a dangerous occupation, and females may be too precious a commodity to risk in this way. In any case, female Eskimos have little control over this part of the food supply and in turn do not achieve the power that comes with the distribution of food.

Patricia Draper has reported on the status and roles of another gathering-hunting society, the San Bushmen of the Kalahari Desert in southern Africa.[6] Draper observed two San Bushmen groups, one that was continuing the traditional nonsettled gathering and hunting way of life, and the other that had become settled farmers, herdsmen, and laborers for nearby non-San Africans. Draper found considerable difference in the roles of the San women in the two groups, with relationships between the sexes much more egalitarian in the group continuing the traditional way of life. In this group the women had direct control over the gathered and collected foods, which made up a major part of their diet. Both men and women, because of the importance of their roles in providing food, were about equally absent from the camp, and Draper observed that men frequently performed tasks usually part of the women's work. Draper saw no evidence that women were excluded from sitting around the campfire or any other gathering. In contrast, she reports that the San group that had become settled agriculturalists had modified their social patterns, the result being that the status of the women had declined as their roles came to be viewed as inferior to those of the men. Women were now more confined to the camp, while the work of the men took them outside of the camp. This study suggests that it may have been the introduction of agriculture that resulted in the development of unequal female-male relationships.

Among agriculturalists, control over land becomes very important. As the population grows and new land is needed to grow more food, warfare becomes common. Warfare is again primarily an occupation of males; control of land by conquest gives them control over the food supply and hence control over people.

In industrialized societies, at least until recently, the need to bear children kept women at home or in subservient occupations. To some degree, the advent of relatively safe contraception has freed women of this role and contributed to the feminist movement.

The place of women within society and the behaviors of the sexes thus would appear to rely on many factors. Biology, ecology, and the subsistence pattern of a culture all play a part. Within societies with class structures, one's social status is important. The learning of the group's normative behaviors (Chapter 1) through socialization also certainly plays a part. Once again we see that the old nature-nurture argument is a major and dangerous oversimplification, as is ethnocentrism.

Aging

We take for granted a life cycle that proceeds from infancy to childhood to maturity to old age. Here again reflection indicates that this has not always been the normal progression, however, and that it is not the case in many nonindustrialized areas today.

Studies of the skeletal remains of earlier hominines and even of modern humans show that until very recently, most people were dead by the age of thirty or forty. Although we read and see on television a great deal about the activities of older individuals in classical Rome and Greece and even in seventeenth- and eighteenth-century Europe, these were the fortunate few, usually from the upper class, who had survived until a ripe old age. The life of the vast majority of people was, in comparison to today's Western standards, very short indeed. Keep this in mind when you fantasize about living in the time of Rome during the reign of Caesar, the France of Louis XIV, or even prerevolutionary America.

The lengthening of the human life span is a function of the evolution of human cultural behavior. As our abilities became more sophisticated and complex, so too did the cultural fabric that insulates us from the demands of the environment. Increasingly, we were able to deal successfully with infectious agents, parasites, and other threats to our continued survival as individuals. Even with these developments, however, we do die as the biological complexes that govern our existence break down or slowly wear out.

Although aging is a process that affects all of us, it is very poorly understood. Why do we grow old? What in fact does "growing old" mean in terms of the changes at the cellular and tissue level? We find that, as the years go by, many human biological properties are altered. Our cardiovascular system, recuperative abilities, mental functioning, and responses to stressors are not the same at seventy as they were at twenty. Currently, we do not understand the processes involved in these changes, although many hypotheses have been offered.

As more and more people live longer and longer, the issue of aging assumes ever-increasing social importance. Once again the question of what is "normal" enters the picture. Osteoporosis, a loss in bone density through mineral loss, is a major modern health problem, for the weakened bones of the elderly, especially prevalent in women, are subject to fracture. Although a third of American women sixty-five and over have a fracture resulting from osteoporosis, is this a "normal" aspect of aging? Not necessarily. A number of factors, including diet, exercise, and cigarette smoking, influence the likelihood that the condition will develop as one ages. Modification of these aspects of life-style can significantly alter what is "normal" in aging (Figure 15.3).

We can also question the notion of what is "normal" by looking at the evolution of our species. Perhaps in this context aging is more a matter of changes in one aspect of our biology having interrelated con-

FIGURE 15.3.   As we age our bodies undergo many changes. The degree to which these changes are subject to modification via exercise, diet, and the like is yet to be fully resolved.

sequences for others. As we age, our ability to utilize the calcium we take in via foods decreases. Calcium is an essential mineral for many metabolic processes. As a result, our body begins to draw out calcium from the reserves stored in bones, causing the loss of bone mineral known as osteoporosis. No one knows why our ability to utilize dietary calcium decreases with age, and there is currently no cure for this condition. It may be that osteoporosis is linked with living longer. Earlier humans had few problems with this disorder because only a small minority lived to an age at which it becomes prevalent. Osteoporosis thus becomes a "normal" part of the aging process only when humans have evolved the cultural complexity that permits longer life spans.

An evolutionary perspective also increases our understanding by placing us within the context of other animals, for not all age as we do. Although most mammals exhibit a pattern that is similar to ours, some small marsupials abruptly die after an annual reproduction cycle. Growth processes in rats are not identical to ours; because a rat's epiphyses never fuse, the animal can grow at any age. Some reptiles can and do continue to grow throughout life. Among fishes, the aging process can even involve a change in sex. Groupers and some other perchlike fishes of the family Serranidae are all born as females; those that survive long enough become the males. Certainly, our aging process is not normal for all animals.

Even within our species, "normal" may simply reflect what we find to be common. It need not mean unavoidable nor desirable. By understanding the ways in which stress, life-style, genes, and culture can change the path of the aging process, we can positively alter our definition of "normal."

It is a very rare person indeed who has not heard of acquired immunodeficiency syndrome, or AIDS, now also referred to as HIV disease. This fatal disease, caused by the human immunodeficiency virus I (HIV I), has become epidemic in some American populations as well as in some African groups. The World Health Organization (WHO) documents AIDS in over 130 countries. By 1988 over 80,000 cases had been reported, more than double the number of a year earlier. WHO expects that there will be over 1 million cases worldwide by 1990 and that more than 10 million will have the virus. This disease, like others, has many parameters: its own evolution, the structure and function of the virus, medical effects, social impact, transmission, and variability in susceptibility. In a number of these areas anthropology can help us gain a fuller understanding of the disease and assist in halting its spread.

While Americans and Europeans tend to look at AIDS as being a disease of gay males whose origins may be traced to Africa, Africans think quite the reverse. Christine Obbo notes that in Africa the disease is essentially one of the heterosexual population and that its most noticeable feature is that it makes people thin. As she notes, Europeans are viewed as the ones who are obsessed with looking thin, and thus it is considered to be a European disease.[7]

AIDS

Effective education about prevention of AIDS must take place within the context of a society's own framework. The sexual mores and practices intertwine with the legal, political, and economic systems of a group to affect the structure and success of education programs. Richard Parker has looked at the history and cultural context of the disease in Brazil and found that a more appropriate response could be developed.[8]

The Western medical model makes a clear distinction between heterosexuality and homosexuality, yet this is not how everyone in the world views the choice of sexual partners. While these concepts have been introduced into Brazilian culture, they have been transformed within a larger framework. Brazilians divide sexual behavior along the lines of "activity" and "passivity." Those who are the dominator or penetrator in a relationship are labeled "men," and those who are dominated, passive, or possessed are labeled "women," whether they are biological women or passive, homosexual males. The latter are stigmatized by their culture, but the dominant male is not, for he is still a "man." Neither is this individual necessarily restricted to other men as the objects of his desire, because either a biological woman or a passive male may be an acceptable partner. As a result the disease can be expected to spread quickly out of the strictly homosexual community by virtue of the high frequency of what Americans consider bisexuality. Second, Brazilians regard anal intercourse as a perfectly normal, acceptable form of sexual relation between heterosexual partners. As transmission of the disease appears to be enhanced by anal intercourse, we see another cultural factor that would encourage its spread. Both of these factors lead one to believe that public education focusing on the homosexual community (defined in the Western sense) will be of little help in checking the disease in this society.

An anthropological perspective can assist in many other aspects of the fight against AIDS, including the biological phenomena related to human variability in transmissibility or vulnerability, the evolution of the virus itself, or related aspects of culture and language. Diseases do not affect people in a vacuum; AIDS is a particularly telling example of the interplay of biology and culture.

The Scars of Human Evolution

One of the themes of this book has been the examination of humans not as special creatures, immune from the general laws of nature, but rather as a part of the living world, subject to the same evolutionary mechanisms as other animals. Like other animals, humans possess certain features, like our internal, segmented skeletal system, that we share with other species, and others, like language, that are unique to us. These unique biological and behavioral systems have developed during human evolution, becoming modified from what was already present. Human traits, like those associated with bipedalism, for example, developed from a quadrupedal ancestor. Because of this evolutionary background, human biological systems are not perfect, and our anatomy does not represent the acme of creation. It is rather the product of evolution working by mutation and selection to modify a complex that functioned successfully but differently in our ancestors. When we examine modern human biology, we can discover many features that function imperfectly or break down in the same fashion in many people. W. M. Krogman, a pioneer in the study of human growth and development, termed these sorts of features the "scars of human evolution," meaning that they represent the evolutionary development of systems that have not reached perfection in us.[9]

Lower Back Problems

The orthopedic surgeon René Cailliet has noted that "the human spine of the present-day man must be considered to be still in the evolutionary phase of adaptation of man's body to the forces of gravity."[10] It has been estimated that more than 80 percent of living adults have had back pains that cause discomfort and perhaps missed work, but which usually disappear after a few days of bed rest. These sorts of backaches, probably due to muscle strains or spasms, can be distinguished from the far more serious problems associated with disorders of the bones of the vertebral column.

In Chapter 9 we discussed the evolution of bipedalism and the changes in the muscles and bones of the lower limb that have made this distinctive human locomotor pattern possible. One of the most important is the curve that has developed in the lumbar region of the lower spinal column (Figure 15.4). This lumbar curve positions upper body weight so that it can be carried directly over the hip joint socket. Note the posture of the ape skeleton in Figure 15.4; in four-legged animals, the slightly convex curve of the spinal column, which is important for quadrupedal locomotion, places upper body weight very far forward when the animal stands upright. In the evolution of human posture, the development of the lumbar curve permitted the efficient placement of upper body weight, which in quadrupeds like the ape passes to the ground via the front limbs, right above the hip joints that support it. In sum, the lumbar curve is essential to erect human posture.

Separating each of the bones of the vertebral column is an intervertebral disk. These disks, made of a fibroelastic connective tissue shell surrounding a gellike material in the interior, act as shock absorbers. They permit the spinal column to bend in a variety of directions and absorb the forces of muscle action and gravity that pass through the column. Note, however, that the lower part of the lumbar curve, where the final two vertebrae are located, is very acute and that the disks are at an angle that makes them more liable to breakdown. Disk breakdown, which is known by a variety of terms, such as slipped, herniated, or ruptured disk disease, occurs when the outer fibrous shell tears and either this portion or the inner gel impinges on the nerve roots passing from the spinal cord to various parts of the lower leg (Figure 15.5). About 90 percent of all herniated disks occur in the last two disks of the spinal

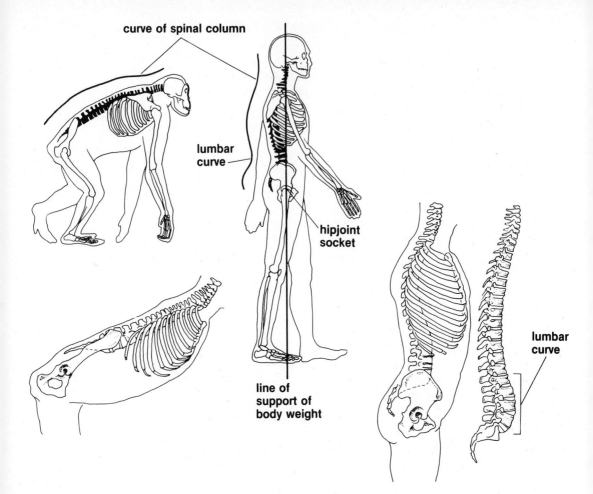

curve of spinal column

lumbar curve

hipjoint socket

line of support of body weight

lumbar curve

FIGURE 15.4. Comparison of the skeleton of a chimpanzee (left) and a modern human. The bend of the lumbar curve permits upper body weight to be positioned over the hip joint socket and the lower limbs, an essential basis for bipedalism.

column, where the lumbar curve is most acute. It has been estimated that about 2 percent of Swedish adults have had back surgery to relieve the pain and loss of muscle control that often accompanies disk breakdown, which represents just a small minority of people with this problem, since most recover without surgical intervention.

Disk disease is a good example of a "scar of human evolution." Clearly, the development of the lumbar curve is crucial to efficient bipedal locomotion, yet it also represents a site where the disks of the spinal column break down with great frequency. Although this condition is an aspect of the biology of modern humans, it is uncertain whether this was also an affliction of earlier hominines. We are far more sedentary than our ancestors, and their better muscle tone may have been sufficient to protect the vertebral column from breakdown. Further, modern humans

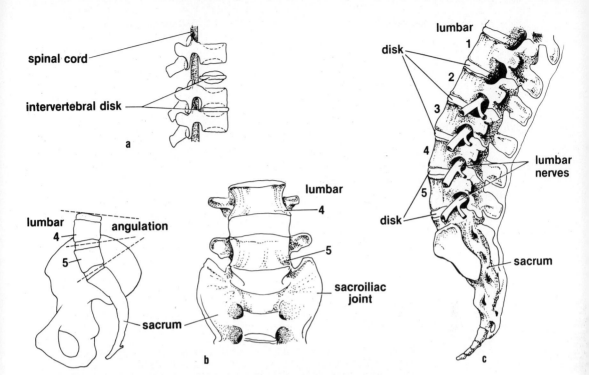

FIGURE 15.5. (a) Segment of a human vertebral column illustrating the placement of the intervertebral disks and the way in which the spinal column surrounds and encloses the spinal cord. (b) Front and side view of the last part of the vertebral column, lumbar vertebrae 4 and 5, and the sacrum, which connects the spinal column with the pelvic bones. Note the angle the last two fibroelastic disks between these bones make in contrast to the upper disk. This angulation is the result of the lumbar curve. Because of their angled position, these two disks are much more likely to break down than other disks higher up on the column. (c) The lumbar vertebrae and sacrum, showing how the nerves to the lower limbs exit the spinal cord via spaces between the bones and disks. Disk breakdowns often lead to impingement of these lumbar nerves, resulting in numbness, pain, and loss of muscle control in the lower limbs.

live longer than our extinct ancestors. The average age of a patient undergoing a disk operation in the United States is forty-two, so perhaps this problem is a function of longer life spans. Whatever will prove to be the answer, this example shows how the study of our evolutionary past can provide insight into the biology of modern humans.

Another biological complex in humans that can be said to be a "scar of human evolution" is associated with the birth process. The discussion of the evolution of bipedalism in Chapter 9 focused on the important changes in the pelvis needed to support the body weight and to orient the muscles used in human walking. Figure 15.6 compares the pelves of a modern human and a chimpanzee. Note the difference in their height: In comparison to chimps and other quadrupeds, humans have pelves that are compressed from top to bottom. The human pelvis is foreshortened

Birth Problems

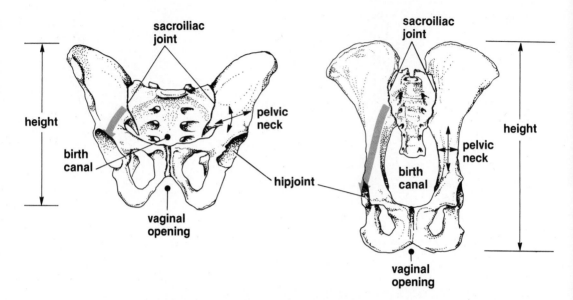

HUMAN

sacroiliac joint

height

pelvic neck

birth canal

hipjoint

vaginal opening

CHIMPANZEE

sacroiliac joint

height

pelvic neck

birth canal

vaginal opening

FIGURE 15.6. Comparison of the pelves of a human and a chimpanzee, showing the shortening of the height of the human pelvis, related to bipedalism and the transmitting of upper body weight from the vertebral column via the sacroiliac joint down the pelvic neck to the hip joint. Note that this decrease of height changes the shape of the birth canal in the human pelvis into a bony ring, making birth more difficult. Arrows indicate the conveying of body weight from the spinal column to the hip joint and then to the ground.

because the joint of the spinal column bones with the pelvis, the sacroiliac, must be positioned to transmit upper body weight to the hip joint efficiently. This has resulted in a marked decrease in the length and a marked increase in the width of the pelvic neck. This change has effectively modified the shape of the bony birth canal and has led to significant difficulties in birth.

Placental mammal infants develop in the uterus and at birth pass through the bony birth canal, exiting via the vaginal opening (Figure 15.7). In modern human birth, because of the ringlike shape of the birth canal, there is often considerable difficulty in the passage of the infant's head and shoulders through the birth canal. Prior to the development of modern medical technology, which has dramatically lessened the danger, childbirth was very dangerous for both mother and infant. Indeed, the death of the mother, and often the child too, was common before medicine provided increased safety. One of these medical techniques being employed with considerable success is the Caesarean section, in which a surgical incision is made to remove the infant directly from the uterus. Although there is currently much debate about the medical necessity of many of the "C" sections now being performed (in the United States in 1986, about 20% of all live births were via Caesarean sections), there is

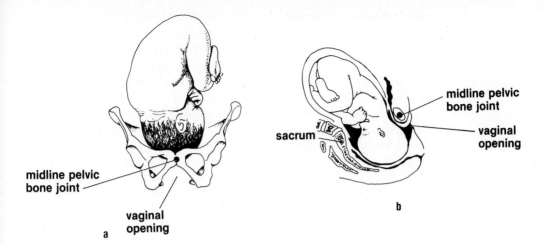

FIGURE 15.7. (a) Front view of a human infant in the uterus just prior to birth.
(b) The infant's body must successfully pass through the bony ring of the birth canal
and exit via the vaginal opening.

little doubt that many women do not have a large enough birth canal to permit the safe passage of the infant.

In this example too we must question how such a situation could have evolved. Did our earlier hominine ancestors also experience birth difficulties of the magnitude found in modern humans, or are there other explanations? One possible suggestion was offered by Owen Lovejoy (see pages 343–344), who observed that our earliest bipedal ancestors possessed small brains. Perhaps during human evolution, as selection favored increasingly larger brains, there was increased difficulty in birth. It may have been during this period that hominine infants began to be born at a less mature state of development than the infants of apes. The helplessness of human infants at birth may be a reflection of the need to be born while the size of the brain is still small enough to pass through the birth canal.

This situation offers an especially good example of the complex interaction between biological and behavioral change. If increasing brain size is the reason for birth difficulties in humans, and if larger, more complex brains are the reason for a greater degree of behavioral complexity, then the larger brains that developed in human evolution are both the cause of and the solution to the problem. Modern medical techniques are one aspect of human culture, which is founded on the evolution of the large brain. The expansion of the brain thus led to birth difficulties, which modern medicine, the result of behavioral complexity that is also the result of expanded brains, has now developed procedures to minimize.

Our Future

What of the future? Biological evolution proceeds by natural selection, responding to environmental demands. No one can predict which direction our future adaptations might take. If we knew that air pollution would continue long into the future, we might evolve biological tolerances for it. But in many Western countries cultural agencies are already being utilized to try to clean the air—in England with notable success. Any speculations about how people might look thousands of years from now are thus just that—speculations based on assumptions about future environments and how we will adapt to these assumed conditions.

Another complication to bear in mind is that, however the environment may change, we can adapt to it through cultural means. Many of the features that we might expect to be important in determining a person's reproductive success can therefore be at least partially removed from the sphere of biological evolution. As technology advances, our biological ability to tolerate heat, cold, disease, and other stressors may well become less and less important.

Some have thought that this cultural "interference" in biological processes has loaded the gene pools of many human populations with harmful alleles. Many people are born each year with genetic defects that in the past would have hampered their reproductive potential. Medical treatment now enables them to survive, reproduce, and pass on the defective genes. Proponents of this view, such as the Nobel Prize-winning geneticist H. J. Muller, see this tampering with selection as a black cloud hanging over our future. Someday, Muller says, all people will be born with one major genetic problem or another, such as diabetes, PKU, or hemophilia.[11]

Muller suggests that we encourage some people to reproduce and discourage others. Is this biological good sense? Reducing human variability might be temporarily beneficial, but if the environment should change (and we can be reasonably certain that it will), we may find ourselves in a bind. We cannot know that traits we select for today because they seem desirable will always be desirable.

Like many biologists, Muller also failed to realize that humans have tremendous potential for cultural change. If we have the cultural ability to prevent human suffering and yet allow for a relatively normal quality of life, why should we not use it? One of the outstanding features of human cultural activity is that societal institutions strive to keep their members alive; culture evolved to fulfill just this end. If we are not going to use our brains and culture to ease the human condition, why did we evolve them? Then too, even if all 245 million Americans had diabetes or bad vision, would we really expend all of our resources and time producing insulin and eyeglasses? It is highly doubtful.

Muller's concerns may now be short-circuited by developments in bioengineering (Figure 15.8). Genetic therapy may be just around the corner, as recombinant DNA technology holds the potential for relief of much human suffering. People with missing or defective genes may be infected with viruses engineered to carry the appropriate replacements. In fact, this has already been attempted in two cases of people with thalassemia. A former researcher at a major American medical school who

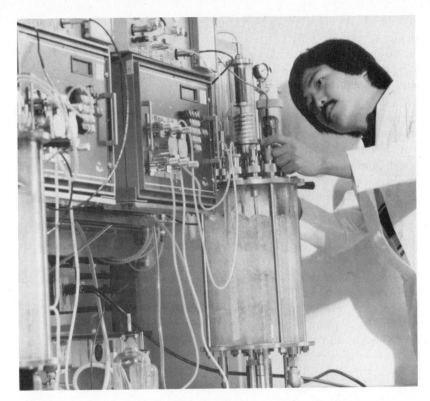

FIGURE 15.8. Cultural advances now allow humans to manufacture biological substances outside their bodies. Such developments in biotechnology will help determine the composition of the human gene pool in the future.

was unable to get clearance to try out the procedure on humans in the United States went to Israel and Italy to perform this genetic surgery. Medically, the results were inconclusive, and ethically the treatment was highly suspect. Although the technique sounds straightforward, in reality it is not so simple. Some work suggests that inserting a new gene into a person's chromosomes can disrupt the function of neighboring genes. Without having a solid understanding of the possible or probable effects, most feel that it is wrong to experiment on humans. This is particularly true for experiments that are "shots in the dark," unlikely to provide information that will increase the success rate of future attempts.

An even more dramatic application of these techniques would be in the cloning of whole individuals. Here the full complement of genes from a cell of one person would be inserted into an enucleated cell (one with the nucleus removed). This newly constituted cell would then be stimulated to start dividing, ultimately to become a genetic carbon copy of the DNA donor. This has already been achieved in mice, and technically it would seem easy enough to replicate in humans. Whether society wants to allow this will be a hotly argued point.

It would even be possible to engineer chimeras, animals that have tissues of two (or more) distinct genetic types. British and German scientists have produced chimeras between two rather dissimilar mammals, a sheep and a goat. These chimeras have some tissues that are purely sheep and others that are purely goat. These are not hybrids, wherein each cell would have some goat and some sheep genes. What reasons other than academic curiosity can justify such research? For one, chimeras are useful in studying immunological phenomena, which can have a wide variety of applications including cancer treatment, organ transplants, and the cure of infertility. Chimeras might even preserve species about to become extinct. Yet again, we must ask if the gains are worth the biological and ethical costs. Mary Shelley's vision of human pride creating a Frankenstein monster is no longer purely fiction.

Recombinant DNA technology also allows us to use bacteria as pharmaceutical factories. If a gene producing a medically important protein such as insulin or growth hormone is inserted into bacteria, the microbes can be tricked into producing vast quantities of the desired product (one geneticist has now rephrased the key sequence of events in biochemical genetics as "DNA makes RNA, RNA makes proteins, and proteins make money"). Although this application would seem to be less questionable ethically, there are ramifications to be considered. Consider the human growth hormone (hGH). This protein is used medically to treat children who do not grow normally. Presently the protein is obtained from the pituitary glands of cadavers and is quite expensive. With increased availability via recombinant DNA, it is reasonable to assume that pressures will be applied to pediatricians to "treat" short children with hGH. Corporations and parents might both apply this pressure, although for different reasons; the corporation for profits and the parents because, in our society, stature is related to status and financial success. Yet if a child is perfectly normal for his or her genes, healthy, and growing at a normal rate, is it good parenting or doctoring to inject hGH? The shots are painful and do not correct a defect. It is one thing to treat a child with a disorder that causes abnormally short stature, and quite another to inject a child whose parents want him to be 6 feet tall, not 5 and a half feet.

We have now reached a time when human beings can affect their own evolution in ways never before envisaged. Such abilities might relieve much pain and suffering, but they could also be misused. Our society must decide on the ethics of genetic manipulation. What would cloning do to our feelings about individuality? Could a copy of Einstein choose his profession, or would he be pushed from birth into becoming a mathematician? From a biological point of view, could we even expect a twin of Einstein to be a genius? The twin would not grow up in the same environment as the original. Then too, who would decide which men and women should be cloned? These questions are crucial, and we have no pat answers. Yet all will require rational decisions by a well-informed public.

Notes and Suggested Readings

Chapter 1 The Perspective of Physical Anthropology

Notes

1. Quoted in Thomas Jefferson, "On the Character and Capacities of the North American Indians," in *The Golden Age of American Anthropology,* ed. Margaret Mead and Ruth Bunzel (New York: George Braziller, 1960), pp. 75–76.
2. David Lack, "Mr. Lawson of Charles," *American Scientist* 51(1963):12–13.
3. David Lack, "Darwin's Finches," *Scientific American* 188(1953):66–72.

Suggested Readings

Burling, Robbins. 1970. *Man's Many Voices.* New York: Holt, Rinehart and Winston.
Eiseley, Loren. 1961. *Darwin's Century.* New York: Doubleday Anchor Books.
Fagan, Brian M. 1988. *In the Beginning: An Introduction to Archaeology,* 6th ed. Glenview, Ill.: Scott, Foresman.
Goerke, Heinz. 1973. *Linnaeus.* New York: Charles Scribner's Sons.
Gould, S. J. 1980. "Wallace's Fatal Flaw." *Natural History* 89:26–40.
Harris, Marvin. 1988. *Culture, People, Nature: An Introduction to General Anthropology,* 5th ed. New York: Harper & Row.
Herbert, Sandra. 1986. "Darwin as a Geologist." *Scientific American* 254:116–123.
Huxley, T. H. 1863. *Evidence as to Man's Place in Nature.* Reprinted as *Man's Place in Nature.* Ann Arbor: University of Michigan Press, 1959.
McElroy, Ann, and Townsend, Patricia K. 1989. *Medical Anthropology in Ecological Perspective.* 2nd ed. Boulder: Westview Press.
Moorehead, Alan. 1969. *Darwin and the Beagle.* New York: Harper & Row.
Savage-Rumbaugh, E. S., Rumbaugh, D. M., and Boysen, S. 1980. "Do Apes Use Language?" *American Scientist* 68:49–61.
Willigen, John Van. 1986. *Applied Anthropology: An Introduction.* South Hadley, Mass.: Bergin and Garvey.

Chapter 2 Genetics: The Study of Heredity

Notes

1. George Gaylord Simpson, "Principles of Classification and a Classification of Mammals," *Bulletin of the American Museum of Natural History* 85(1945):5.
2. John Czelusniak, Morris Goodman, David Hewett-Emmett, Mark L. Weiss, Patrick J. Venta, and Richard E. Tashian, "Phylogenetic Origins and Adaptive Evolution of Avian and Mammalian Haemoglobin Genes," *Nature* 298(1982):297–300.
3. Ernst Mayr, *Animal Species and Evolution* (Cambridge, Mass.: Harvard University Press, Belknap Press, 1963), p. 136.

Suggested Readings

Anderson, W. French, and Diacumakos, Elaine G. 1981. "Genetic Engineering in Mammalian Cells." *Scientific American* 245:106–121.

Castle, W. M. 1977. *Statistics in Small Doses,* 2d ed. Edinburgh: Churchill Livingstone.

Felsenfeld, Gary. 1985. "DNA." *Scientific American* 253:58–67.

Hartl, Daniel L. 1985. *Our Uncertain Heritage: Genetics and Human Diversity.* New York: Harper & Row.

Hassold, Terry J. 1986. "Chromosomal Abnormalities in Human Reproductive Wastage." *Trends in Genetics* 2:105–110.

Lewin, Benjamin. 1987. *Genes,* 3rd ed. New York: John Wiley.

Rosenfeld, Israel, Ziff, Edward, and van Loon, Borin. 1983. *DNA for Beginners.* London: Writers and Readers Publishing Ltd.

Schull, William J., Otake, Masanori, and Neel, James V. 1981. "Genetic Effects of the Atomic Bombs: A Reappraisal." *Science* 213:1220–1229.

Strickberger, Monroe W. 1985. *Genetics,* 3rd ed. New York: Macmillan.

Weatherall, D. J. 1985. *The New Genetics and Clinical Practice,* 2d ed. New York: Oxford University Press.

Chapter 3   Evolution in Action

Notes

1. Sir MacFarlane Burnet and David O. White, *Natural History of Infectious Disease,* 4th ed. (Cambridge: Cambridge University Press, 1972), p. 140.

2. Ernst Mayr, *Principles of Systematic Zoology* (New York: McGraw-Hill, 1969), p. 26.

3. George Gaylord Simpson, *Principles of Animal Taxonomy* (New York: Columbia University Press, 1961), p. 153.

4. Theodosius Dobzhansky, *Genetics of the Evolutionary Process* (New York: Columbia University Press, 1970), p. 207.

5. Harry L. Shapiro, *The Pitcairn Islanders* (New York: Simon and Schuster, 1968).

6. W. J. Schull and J. V. Neel, *The Effect of Inbreeding on Japanese Children* (New York: Harper & Row, 1965).

7. D. F. Roberts, "Migration in the Recent Past: Societies with Records," in *Biological Aspects of Human Migration,* eds. C. G. N. Mascie-Taylor and G. W. Lasker (Cambridge: Cambridge University Press, 1988), pp. 41–69.

8. R. B. Goldschmidt, *The Material Basis of Evolution* (New Haven: Yale University Press, 1940).

9. Steven M. Stanley, *Macroevolution: Pattern and Process* (San Francisco: W. H. Freeman, 1979).

10. S. J. Gould and R. C. Lewontin, "The Spandrels of San Marco and the Panglossian Paradigm: A Critique of the Adaptationist Programme," *Proceedings of the Royal Society of London,* Series B, 205 (1979):581–598.

11. R. L. Holloway, Jr., "Tools and Teeth: Some Speculations Regarding Canine Reduction," *American Anthropologist* 69(1967):63–67.

12. Mary C. King and A. Wilson, "Evolution on Two Levels," *Science* 188(1975):107–116.

Suggested Readings

Bendall, D. S., ed. 1983. *Evolution from Molecules to Men.* Cambridge: Cambridge University Press.

Chakraborty, Ranjit. 1986. "Gene Admixture in Human Populations: Models and Predictions." *Yearbook of Physical Anthropology* 29:1–43.

Dawkins, Richard. 1986. *The Blind Watchmaker.* New York: W. W. Norton.

Gould, Stephen Jay. 1980. *The Panda's Thumb: More Reflections in Natural History.* New York: W. W. Norton.

Godfrey, Laurie Rohde, ed. 1985. *What Darwin Began: Modern Darwinian and Neo-Darwinian Perspectives on Evolution.* Boston: Allyn and Bacon.

King, Mary C., and Wilson, A. 1975. "Evolution on Two Levels," *Science* 188:107–116.

Kitcher, Philip, 1982. *Abusing Science: The Case Against Creationism.* Cambridge, Mass.: MIT Press.

Levinton, Jeffrey. 1988. *Genetics, Paleontology and Macroevolution.* New York: Cambridge University Press.

Michod, Richard E., and Levin, Bruce R., eds. 1988. *The Evolution of Sex: An Examination of Current Ideas.* Sunderland, Mass.: Sinauer Assoc.

Sober, Elliott, ed. 1984. *Conceptual Issues in Evolutionary Biology: An Anthology.* Cambridge, Mass.: MIT Press.

Stanley, Steven M. 1979. *Macroevolution: Pattern and Process.* San Francisco: W. H. Freeman.

Chapter 4   The Evolution of the Vertebrates

Notes

1. D. H. Tarling and M. P. Tarling, *Continental Drift: A Study of the Earth's Moving Surface* (London: Bell, 1971).

2. L. W. Alvarez, Walter Alvarez, Frank Asaro, and H. V. Michel, "Extraterrestrial Cause for the Cretaceous-Tertiary Extinction," *Science* 208 (1980):1095–1108; Walter Alvarez, E. G. Kauffman, Finn Surlyk, L. W. Alvarez, Frank Asaro, and H. V. Michel, "Impact Theory of Mass Extinction and the Invertebrate Fossil Record," *Science* 223(1984):1135–1141.

3. H. J. Jerison, *Evolution of the Brain and Intelligence* (New York: Academic Press, 1973).

Suggested Readings

Bakker, R. T. 1986. *The Dinosaur Heresies.* New York: William Morrow.

Colbert, E. H. 1961. *Evolution of the Vertebrates.* New York: Science Editions.

Desmond, A. J. 1977. *The Hot-Blooded Dinosaurs.* New York: Warner Books.

Halstead, L. B. 1968. *The Pattern of Vertebrate Evolution.* San Francisco: W. H. Freeman.

Miles, A. E. W. 1972. *Teeth and Their Origins.* New York: Oxford Biology Reader.

Miller, R. 1983. *Continents in Collision.* Alexandria, Va.: Time-Life Books.

Olson, E. C. 1971. *Vertebrate Paleozoology.* New York: Wiley-Interscience.

Radinsky, L. B. 1987. *The Evolution of Vertebrate Design.* Chicago: University of Chicago Press.

Romer, A. S. 1966. *Vertebrate Paleontology.* Chicago: University of Chicago Press.

Sullivan, W. 1974. *Continents in Motion: The New Earth Debate.* New York: McGraw-Hill.

Tinbergen, N. 1951. *The Study of Instinct.* London: Oxford University Press.

Van Gelder, R. G. 1969. *Biology of Mammals.* New York: Charles Scribner's Sons.

Wilford, J. N. 1986. *The Riddle of the Dinosaur.* New York: Alfred A. Knopf.

Young, J. Z. 1950. *The Life of Vertebrates.* New York: Oxford University Press.

———. 1957. *The Life of Mammals.* New York: Oxford University Press.

Chapter 5   An Introduction to the Primates

Notes

1. F. S. Szalay, "Phylogeny of Primate Higher Taxa: The Basicranial Evidence," in *Phylogeny of the Primates,* eds. W. P. Luckett and F. S. Szalay (New York: Plenum Press, 1975), pp. 91–125.
2. W. E. Le Gros Clark, *The Antecedents of Man,* 3rd. ed. (Chicago: Quadrangle Books, 1971).
3. J. H. Schwartz, "If *Tarsius* Is Not a Prosimian, Is It a Haplorhine?," in *Recent Advances in Primatology,* Vol. 3, *Evolution,* eds. D. J. Chivers and K. A. Joysey (New York: Academic Press, 1978), pp. 195–204; Morris Goodman, D. Hewett-Emmett, and J. M. Beard, "Molecular Evidence on the Phylogenetic Relationships of *Tarsius,*" in *Recent Advances in Primatology,* Vol. 3, *Evolution,* eds. D. J. Chivers and K. A. Joysey (New York: Academic Press, 1979), pp. 215–225.
4. F. S. Szalay and Eric Delson, *Evolutionary History of the Primates* (New York: Academic Press, 1979).
5. Charles G. Silbey and Jon E. Ahlquist, "DNA Hybridization Evidence of Hominoid Phylogeny: Results from an Expanded Data Set," *Journal of Molecular Evolution* 26(1987):99–121.
6. Stephen Harris, Paul A. Barrie, Mark L. Weiss, and Alec J. Jeffreys, "The Primate Ψβ1 Gene: An Ancient β-Globin Pseudogene," *Journal of Molecular Biology* 180(1984):785–801.

Suggested Readings

Cartmill, Matt. 1982. "Basic Primatology and Prosimian Evolution." In *A History of American Physical Anthropology,* ed. F. Spencer. New York: Academic Press, pp. 147–186.

Clark, W. E. Le Gros. 1963. *History of the Primates,* 4th ed. Chicago: The University of Chicago Press.

Dover, G. A., and Flavell, R. B., eds. 1982. *Genome Evolution.* London: Academic Press.

Fleagle, John G. 1988. *Primate Adaptation and Evolution.* New York: Academic Press.

Ghiglieri, M. P. 1984. *The Chimpanzees of Kibale Forest.* New York: Columbia University Press.

Goodman, Morris, Weiss, Mark L., and Czelusniak, John. 1982. "Molecular Evolution above the Species Level: Branching Pattern, Rates, and Mechanisms." *Systematic Zoology* 31:376–399.

Lewin, Roger. 1988. "Conflict Over DNA Clock Results." *Science* 241:1598–1600, 1756–1758.

Luckett, W. P., and Szalay, F. S., eds. 1975. *Phylogeny of the Primates.* New York: Plenum Press.

Miyamoto, M. M., Slightom, J. L., and Goodman, M., 1987. "Phylogenetic Relations of Humans and African Apes from DNA Sequences in the Pseudo-eta Globin Region." *Science* 238:369–373.

Napier, J. R., and Napier, P. H. 1967. *A Handbook of Living Primates.* New York: Academic Press.

Napier, J. R., and Napier, P. H. 1985. *The Natural History of Primates.* London: British Museum (Natural History).

Schultz, A. H. 1969. *The Life of Primates.* New York: Universe Books.

Sibley, Charles G., and Ahlquist, Jon E. 1987. "DNA Hybridization Evidence of Hominoid Phylogeny: Results from an Expanded Data Set." *Journal of Molecular Evolution* 26:99–121.

Tattersall, I. 1982. *The Primates of Madagascar*. New York: Columbia University Press.

Weiss, Mark L. 1987. "Nucleic Acid Evidence Bearing on Hominoid Relationships." *Yearbook of Physical Anthropology* 30:41–73.

Wilson, Allan. 1985. "The Molecular Basis of Evolution." *Scientific American* 253:164–173.

Chapter 6   Primate Behavior

Notes

1. D. B. Meikle and S. H. Vessey, "Nepotism among Rhesus Monkey Brothers," *Nature* 294(1981):160–161.

2. S. B. Hrdy, "Infanticide among Animals: A Review, Classification, and Examination of the Implications for the Reproductive Strategies of Females," *Ethology and Sociobiology* 1(1979):13–40.

3. P. Dolhinow, "Normal Monkeys?" *American Scientist* 6(1977):266.

4. A. F. Richard and S. P. Schulman, "Sociobiology: Primate Field Studies," *Annual Review of Anthropology* 11(1982):231–255.

5. J. F. Oates, "Food Distribution and Foraging Behavior," in *Primate Societies,* eds. B. B. Smuts, D. L. Cheney, R. M. Seyfarth, R. W. Wrangham, and T. T. Struhsaker (Chicago: University of Chicago Press, 1986), pp. 197–209.

6. J. F. Wittenberger, "Group Size and Polygamy in Social Mammals," *American Naturalist* 115(1980):197–222.

7. T. H. Clutton-Brock and P. H. Harvey, "Primate Ecology and Social Organization," *Journal of Zoology,* London 183(1977):1–39.

8. K. Milton and M. L. May, "Body Weight, Diet, and Home Range Area in Primates," *Nature* 259(1976):459–62.

9. H. F. Harlow, M. K. Harlow, and S. J. Suomi, "From Thought to Therapy: Lessons from a Primate Laboratory," *American Scientist* 59 (1971):538–549.

10. D. Premack, "Language in the Chimpanzee," *Science* 172(1971):808–822.

11. H. S. Terrace, L. A. Petitto, R. J. Sanders, and T. G. Bever, "Can an Ape Create a Sentence?" *Science* 206(1979):891–902.

12. M. Kawai, "Newly Acquired Precultural Behavior of the Natural Troop of Japanese Monkeys on Koshima Islet," *Primates* 6(1965):1–30.

13. R. S. O. Harding and S. C. Strum, "The Predatory Baboons of Kekopey," *Natural History* 85(1976):45–53.

14. J. B. Lancaster and R. B. Lee, "The Annual Reproductive Cycle in Monkeys and Apes," in *Primate Behavior: Field Studies of Monkeys and Apes,* ed. I. DeVore (New York: Holt, Rinehart and Winston, 1965), pp. 486–513.

15. G. Hausfater, "Dominance and Reproduction in Baboons (*Papio cynocephalus*)," *Contributions to Primatology,* vol. 7 (Basel: S. Karger, 1975).

16. T. E. Rowell, "Forest Living Baboons in Uganda," *Journal of Zoology,* London 149(1966):344–364; and S. L. Washburn and I. DeVore, "The Social Life of Baboons," *Scientific American* 204(1961):62–71.

17. S. D. Singh, "Urban Monkeys," *Scientific American* 221 (1969):108–115.

18. D. S. Sade, "Determinants of Dominance in a Group of Free-Ranging Rhesus Monkeys," in *Social Communication among Primates,* ed. S. A. Altmann (Chicago: The University of Chicago Press, 1967), pp. 99–114.

19. E. A. Missakian, "Genealogical and Cross-Genealogical Dominance Relationships in a Group of Free-Ranging Rhesus Monkeys (*Macaca mulatta*) on Cayo Santiago," *Primates* 13(1972):169–180.

20. R. I. M. Dunbar and E. P. Dunbar, "Ecological Relations and Niche Separation between Sympatric Terrestrial Primates in Ethiopia," in *Primate Ecology: Problem-Oriented Field Studies,* ed. R. W. Sussman (New York: John Wiley and Sons, 1979), pp. 187–209.

21. J. H. Crook, "Gelada Baboon Herd Structure and Movement," *Symposium Zoological Society of London* 18(1966):237–258.

22. U. Nagel, "A Comparison of Anubis Baboons, Hamadryas Baboons and their Hybrids at a Species Border in Ethiopia," *Folia Primatologica* 19(1973):104–165.

23. H. Kummer, *Primate Societies: Group Techniques of Ecological Adaptations* (Chicago: Aldine, 1971).

24. K. R. L. Hall, "Behavior and Ecology of the Wild Patas Monkey, *Erythrocebus patas,* in Uganda," *Journal of Zoology* 148(1965):15–87.

25. C. R. Carpenter, "A Field Study of the Behavior and Social Relations of Howling Monkeys (*Alouatta palliata*)," *Comparative Psychology Monographs* 10(1934):1–168.

26. C. B. Jones, "The Functions of Status in the Mantled Howler Monkey, *Alouatta palliata* Gray: Intraspecific Competition for Group Membership in a Folivorous Neotropical Primate," *Primates* 21(1980):389–405.

27. L. L. Klein and D. J. Klein, "Social and Ecological Contrasts between Four Taxa of Neotropical Primates," in *Primate Ecology: Problem-Oriented Field Studies,* ed. R. W. Sussman (New York: John Wiley and Sons, 1979), pp. 107–131.

28. K. Milton, *The Foraging Strategy of Howler Monkeys* (New York: Columbia University Press, 1980).

29. J. van Lawick-Goodall, *In the Shadow of Man* (Boston: Houghton Mifflin, 1971); and The Behavior of Free-Living Chimpanzees in the Gombe Stream Area, *Animal Behavior Monograph,* no. 1, eds. J. M. Cullen and C. G. Beer (London: Bailliérs, Tindall, and Cassell, 1968).

30. J. Itani and A. Suzuki, "The Social Unit of Chimpanzees," *Primates* 8(1967):355–381; T. Nishida, "The Social Structure of Chimpanzees of the Mahale Mountains," in *Perspectives on Human Evolution. Vol. 5: The Great Apes,* eds. D. A. Hamburg and E. R. McCown (Menlo Park, Calif.: Benjamin/Cummings, 1979), pp. 73–121; V. Reynolds and F. Reynolds, "Chimpanzees of the Budongo Forest," in *Primate Behavior: Field Studies of Monkeys and Apes,* ed. I. DeVore (New York: Holt, Rinehart and Winston, 1965), pp. 368–424; and Y. Sugiyama, "Social Organization of Chimpanzees in the Budongo Forest, Uganda," *Primates* 9(1968):225–258.

31. G. B. Schaller, *The Mountain Gorilla: Ecology and Behavior* (Chicago: The University of Chicago Press, 1963); and D. Fossey, "Observations on the Home Range of One Group of Mountain Gorilla," *Animal Behavior* 22(1974):568–581.

32. G. Teleki, "Primate Subsistence Patterns: Collector-Predators and Gatherer-Hunters," *Journal of Human Evolution* 4(1975):125–184.

33. B. M. F. Galdikas and G. Teleki, "Variations in Subsistence Activities of Female and Male Pongids: New Perspectives on the Origins of Hominid Labor Division," *Current Anthropology* 22(1981):241–256.

34. J. Goodall, "Infant Killing and Cannibalism in Free-Living Chimpanzees," *Folia Primatologica* 28(1977):259–282; J. D. Bygott, "Agonistic Behavior, Dominance, and Social Structure in Wild Chimpanzees of the Gombe National Park," in *Perspectives on Human Evolution. Vol. 5: The Great Apes,* eds. D. A. Hamburg and E. R. McCown (Menlo Park, Calif.: Benjamin/Cummings, 1979), pp. 405–427.

Suggested Readings

Altmann, S. A., ed. 1967. *Social Communication among Primates.* Chicago: The University of Chicago Press.

Chalmers, N. 1980. *Social Behaviour of Primates.* Baltimore: University Park Press.

Hamburg, D. A., and McCown, E. R., eds. 1979. *Perspectives on Human Evolution.* Menlo Park, Calif.: Benjamin/Cummings.

Jolly, A. 1985. *The Evolution of Primate Behavior.* 2nd ed. New York: Macmillan.

Kummer, H. 1971. *Primate Societies: Group Techniques of Ecological Adaptation.* Chicago: Aldine.

Michael, R. P., and Crook, J. H., eds. 1973. *Comparative Ecology and Behaviour of Primates.* New York: Academic Press.

Smuts, B. B., Cheney, D. L., Seyfarth, R. M., Wrangham, R. W., and Struhsaker, T. T., eds. 1986. *Primate Societies*. Chicago: University of Chicago Press.

Sussman, R. W., ed. 1979. *Primate Ecology: Problem-Oriented Field Studies*. New York: John Wiley and Sons.

Chapter 7   The Biological History of the Primates

Notes

1. L. Van Valen and R. E. Sloan, "The Earliest Primates," *Science* 150(1965):743–745; G. G. Simpson, "Concluding Remarks: Mesozoic Mammals Revisited," in *Early Mammals*, eds. D. M. Kermack and K. A. Kermack (New York: Academic Press, 1971), pp. 181–198; and Z. Kielan-Jaworowska, T. M. Bown, and J. A. Lillegraven, "Eutheria," in *Mesozoic Mammals: The First Two-Thirds of Mammalian History*, eds. J. A. Lillegraven, Z. Kielan-Jaworowska, and W. A. Clemens (Berkeley: University of California Press, 1979), pp. 221–258.

2. F. S. Szalay, "The Beginnings of Primates," *Evolution* 22(1968):19–36.

3. M. Cartmill, "Rethinking Primate Origins," *Science* 184(1974):436–443.

4. R. D. E. McPhee and M. Cartmill, "Basicranial Structures and Primate Systematics," in *Comparative Primate Biology*, Vol. 1, *Systematics, Evolution and Anatomy*, eds. D. R. Swindler and J. Irwin (New York: A. R. Liss, 1986), pp. 219–275.

5. F. S. Szalay and R. L. Decker, "Origins, Evolution, and Function of the Tarsus in Late Cretaceous Eutheria and Paleocene Primates," in *Primate Locomotion*, ed. F. A. Jenkins (New York: Academic Press, 1974), pp. 223–259.

6. W. W. Howells, *Mankind in the Making* (New York: Doubleday, 1959).

7. E. L. Simons, *Primate Evolution: An Introduction to Man's Place in Nature* (New York: Macmillan, 1972).

8. I. Tattersall, "Of Lemurs and Men," *Natural History* March (1972):32–43.

9. U. Ba Maw, R. L. Ciochon, and D. E. Savage, "Late Eocene of Burma Yields Earliest Anthropoid Primate, *Pondaungia cotteri*," *Nature* 282(1979):65–67.

10. P. Walker and P. Murray, "An Assessment of Masticatory Efficiency in a Series of Anthropoid Primates with Special Reference to the Colobinae and Cercopithecinae," in *Primate Functional Morphology and Evolution*, ed. R. Tuttle (The Hague: Mouton, 1975), pp. 135–150.

11. T. M. Bown, M. J. Kraus, S. L. Wing, J. G. Fleagle, B. H. Tiffney, E. L. Simons, and C. F. Vondra, "The Fayum Primate Forest Revisited," *Journal of Human Evolution* 11(1982):603–632; R. F. Kay, J. G. Fleagle, and E. L. Simons, "A Revision of the Oligocene Apes of the Fayum Province, Egypt," *American Journal of Physical Anthropology* 55(1981):293–322; and E. Delson and P. Andrews, "Evolution and Interrelationships of the Catarrhine Primates," in *Phylogeny of the Primates*, eds. W. P. Luckett and F. S. Szalay (New York: Plenum Press, 1975), pp. 405–446.

12. J. G. Fleagle, R. F. Kay, and E. L. Simons, "Sexual Dimorphism in Early Anthropoids," *Nature* 287(1980):328–330.

13. J. G. Fleagle, "Locomotor Behavior of the Earliest Anthropoids: A Review of the Current Evidence," *Zeitschrift Für Morphologie und Anthropologie* 71(1980):149–156.

14. P. J. Andrews, *A Revision of the Miocene Hominoidea of East Africa*, Bulletin of the British Museum (Natural History), Geology Series, vol. 10, no. 2 (1978); and R. F. Kay and E. L. Simons, "A Reassessment of the Relationship between Later Miocene and Subsequent Hominoidea," in *New Interpretations of Ape and Human Ancestry*, eds. R. L. Ciochon and R. S. Corruccini (New York: Plenum Press, 1983), pp. 577–624.

15. M. E. Morbeck, "*Dryopithecus africanus* Forelimb," *Journal of Human Evolution* 4(1975):39–46.

16. D. Pilbeam, "Recent Finds and Interpretations of Miocene Hominoids," *Annual Review in Anthropology* 8(1979):333–352.

17. R. F. Kay, "The Nut-Crackers—A New Theory of the Adaptations of the Ramapithecinae," *American Journal of Physical Anthropology* 55(1981):141–151.

18. L. Greenfield, "A Late Divergence Hypothesis," *American Journal of Physical Anthropology* 52(1980):351–366.

19. E. L. Simons and J. Fleagle, "The History of Extinct Gibbon-Like Primates," *Gibbon and Siamang* 2(1973):121–148.

20. V. M. Sarich, "A Molecular Approach to the Question of Human Origins," in *Background for Man,* eds. P. Dolhinow and V. M. Sarich (Boston: Little, Brown, 1971), pp. 60–81; and V. M. Sarich, "Appendix: Retrospective on Hominoid Macromolecular Systematics," in *New Interpretations of Ape and Human Ancestry,* eds. R. L. Ciochon and R. S. Corruccini (New York: Plenum Press, 1983), pp. 137–150.

21. R. E. Leakey and M. G. Leakey, "A New Miocene Hominoid from Kenya," *Nature* 324(1986):143–146; R. E. Leakey and M. G. Leakey, "A Second New Miocene Hominoid from Kenya," *Nature* 324(1986):146–148; and E. Delson, "The Earliest *Sivapithecus,*" *Nature* 318(1985):107–108.

22. D. Pilbeam, "New Hominoid Skull Material from the Miocene of Pakistan," *Nature* 295(1982):232–234; P. Andrews, "Hominoid Evolution," *Nature* 295(1982):185–186; and S. Lipson and D. Pilbeam, "*Ramapithecus* and Hominoid Evolution," *Journal of Human Evolution* 11(1982):545–548.

23. M. H. Wolpoff, "*Ramapithecus* and Hominid Origins," *Current Anthropology* 23(1982):501–522.

24. M. D. Rose, "Miocene Hominoid Postcranial Morphology: Monkey-Like, Ape-Like, or Both?," in *New Interpretations of Ape and Human Ancestry,* eds. R. L. Ciochon and R. S. Corruccini (New York: Plenum Press, 1983), pp. 404–417.

25. J. H. Schwartz, "The Evolutionary Relationships of Man and Orangutan," *Nature* 308(1984):501–505.

26. R. F. Kay, "The Nut-Crackers—A New Theory of the Adaptations of the Ramapithecinae," *American Journal of Physical Anthropology* 55(1981):141–151.

27. D. Pilbeam, "Hominoid Evolution and Hominid Origins," *American Anthropologist* 88(1986):295–312.

28. D. Pilbeam and A. Walker, "Fossil Monkeys from the Miocene of Napak, Northeast Uganda," *Nature* 220(1968):657–660.

29. G. H. R. von Koenigswald, "Miocene Cercopithecoidea and Oreopithecoidea from the Miocene of East Africa," in *Fossil Vertebrates of Africa,* vol. 1, ed. L. S. B. Leakey (New York: Academic Press, 1969), pp. 39–52.

30. E. Delson, "Evolutionary History of the Cercopithecidae," in *Approaches to Primate Paleobiology,* vol. 5, ed. F. S. Szalay (Basel: Karger, 1975), pp. 167–217.

31. R. Hoffstetter, "Relationships, Origins, and History of the Ceboid Monkeys and Caviomorph Rodents: A Modern Reinterpretation," in *Evolutionary Biology,* vol. 6, eds. T. Dobzhansky, M. K. Hecht, and W. C. Steere (New York: Appleton-Century-Crofts, 1972), pp. 323–347; and R. Hoffstetter, "Origin and Deployment of New World Monkeys Emphasizing the Southern Continents Route," in *Evolutionary Biology of the New World Monkeys and Continental Drift,* eds. R. L. Ciochon and A. B. Chiarelli (New York: Plenum Press, 1980), pp. 103–122.

32. P. D. Gingerich, "Eocene Adapidae, Paleobiogeography, and the Origin of South American Platyrrhini," in *Evolutionary Biology of the New World Monkeys and Continental Drift,* eds. R. L. Ciochon and A. B. Chiarelli (New York: Plenum Press, 1980), pp. 123–138; and E. Delson and A. L. Rosenberger, "Phyletic Perspectives on Platyrrhini Origins and Anthropoid Relationships," in *Evolutionary Biology of the New World Monkeys and Continental Drift,* eds. R. L. Ciochon and A. B. Chiarelli (New York: Plenum Press, 1980), pp. 445–458.

Suggested Readings

Chivers, D. J., and Joysey, K. A., eds. 1978. *Recent Advances in Primatology. Vol. 3: Evolution.* New York: Academic Press.

Ciochon, R. L., and Chiarelli, A. B., eds. 1980. *Evolutionary Biology of the New World Monkeys and Continental Drift.* New York: Plenum Press.

Ciochon, R. L., and Corruccini, R. S., eds. 1983. *New Interpretations of Ape and Human Ancestry.* New York: Plenum Press.

Ciochon, R. L., and Fleagle, J. G. 1985. *Primate Evolution and Human Origins.* Menlo Park, Calif.: Benjamin/Cummings.

Fleagle, J. G. 1988. *Primate Adaptation and Evolution.* San Diego: Academic Press.

Fleagle, J. G., and Jungers, W. L. 1982. "Fifty Years of Higher Primate Phylogeny." In *A History of American Physical Anthropology,* ed. F. Spencer. New York: Academic Press, pp. 187–230.

Goodman, M., and Cronin, J. E. 1982. "Molecular Anthropology: Its Development and Current Directions." In *A History of American Physical Anthropology,* ed. F. Spencer. New York: Academic Press, pp. 105–146.

Goodman, M., Tashian, R. E., and Tashian, J. H., eds. 1976. *Molecular Anthropology: Genes and Proteins in the Evolutionary Ascent of the Primates.* New York: Plenum Press.

Le Gros Clark, W. E. 1971. *The Antecedents of Man.* 3rd ed. Edinburgh: The University Press.

Morbeck, M. E., Preuschoft, H., and Gomberg, N., eds. 1979. *Environment, Behavior, and Morphology: Dynamic Interactions in Primates.* New York: Gustav Fischer.

Simons, E. L. 1972. *Primate Evolution.* New York: Macmillan.

Simpson, G. G. 1964. "Organisms and Molecules in Evolution." *Science* 146:1535–1538.

Szalay, F. S., and Delson, E. 1979. *Evolutionary History of the Primates.* New York: Academic Press.

Tuttle, R., ed. 1972. *The Functional and Evolutionary Biology of Primates.* Chicago: Aldine.

Wood, B., Martin, L., and Andrews, P. 1986. *Major Topics in Primate and Human Evolution.* Cambridge: Cambridge University Press.

Chapter 8   The Homininae

Notes

1. W. H. Goodenough, *Culture, Language, and Society,* McCaleb Module in Anthropology (Reading, Mass.: Addison-Wesley, 1971), pp. 1–48.

2. R. L. Holloway, "Culture: A Human Domain," *Current Anthropology* 10(1969):395–412.

3. J. Goodall, *The Chimpanzees of Gombe: Patterns of Behavior* (Cambridge, Mass.: Belknap Press, 1986).

4. G. H. Curtis, "Man's Immediate Forerunners: Establishing a Relevant Time Scale in Anthropological and Archaeological Research," *Philosophical Transactions of the Royal Society of London,* B 292(1981):7–20.

5. R. Hedges, "Radiocarbon Dating with an Accelerator: Review and Preview," *Archaeometry* 23(1981):3–18; W. F. Libby, *Radiocarbon Dating,* 2nd ed. (Chicago: The University of Chicago Press, 1955); and E. Ralph, "Carbon-14 Dating," in *Dating Techniques for the Archaeologist,* eds. H. Michael and E. Ralph (Cambridge, Mass.: MIT Press, 1971).

6. H. Faul, "Potassium-Argon Dating," in *Dating Techniques for the Archaeologist,* eds. H. Michael and E. Ralph (Cambridge, Mass.: MIT Press, 1971), pp. 157–163.

7. G. L. Isaac, "Chronology and the Tempo of Cultural Change During the Pleistocene," in *Calibration of Hominoid Evolution,* eds. W. W. Bishop and J. A. Miller (Edinburgh: Scottish Academic Press, 1972), pp. 381–430.

8. P. Andrews and J. H. Van Couvering, "Paleoenvironments in the East African Miocene," in *Approaches to Primate Paleobiology, Contributions to Primatology,* vol. 5, ed. F. S. Szalay (Basel: Karger, 1975), pp. 62–103; and J. H. Van Couvering and J. A. Van Couvering, "Early Miocene Mammal Fossils from East Africa; Aspects of Geology, Faunistics, and Paleo-Ecology," in *Human Origins: Louis Leakey and the East African Evidence,* eds. G. L. Isaac and E. R. McCown (Menlo Park, Calif.: W. A. Benjamin, 1976), pp. 155–207.

9. J. Fink and G. J. Kukla, "Pleistocene Climates in Central Europe: At Least 17 Interglacials after the Olduvai Event," *Quaternary Research* 7(1977):363–371; and N. J. Shackleton and N. Updyke, "Oxygen Isotope and Palaeomagnetic Stratigraphy of Equatorial Pacific Core V28-238: Oxygen Isotope Temperatures and Ice Volumes on a 10^5 Year and 10^6 Year Scale," *Quaternary Research* 3(1973):39–55.

10. A. E. Mann, "Hominid and Cultural Origins," *Man* N.S. 7(1972):379–386.

11. C. J. Jolly, "The Seed-Eaters: A New Model of Hominid Differentiation Based on a Baboon Analogy," *Man* N.S. 5(1970):5–26.

12. J. T. Robinson, *Early Hominid Posture and Locomotion* (Chicago: The University of Chicago Press, 1972); and R. H. Tuttle, "Parallelism, Brachiation, and Hominoid Phylogeny," in *Phylogeny of the Primates,* eds. W. P. Luckett and F. S. Szalay (New York: Plenum Press, 1975), pp. 447–480.

13. C. O. Lovejoy, "The Origin of Man," *Science* 211(1981):341–350.

14. J. B. Lancaster, "On the Evolution of Tool-Using Behavior," *American Anthropologist* 70(1968):56–66.

Suggested Readings

Behrensmeyer, A. K., and Hill, A. P., eds. 1980. *Fossils in the Making: Vertebrate Taphonomy and Paleoecology.* Chicago: University of Chicago Press.

Campbell, B. G. 1988. *Humankind Emerging.* 5th ed. Boston: Little, Brown.

Cornwall, I. W. 1970. *Ice Ages: Their Nature and Effects.* New York: Humanities Press.

Flint, R. F. 1971. *Glacial and Quaternary Geology.* New York: John Wiley and Sons.

Holloway, R. L. 1983. "Human Paleontological Evidence Relevant to Language Behavior." *Human Neurobiology* 2:105–114.

Washburn, S. L. 1968. *The Study of Human Evolution.* Eugene: Oregon State System of Higher Education. Reprinted in *Background for Man,* eds. P. Dolhinow and V. M. Sarich (Boston: Little, Brown, 1971).

Chapter 9   Human Evolution I: The Early Hominines

Notes

1. R. A. Dart, "*Australophithecus africanus:* The Man-Ape of South Africa," *Nature* 115(1925):195–199.

2. R. Millar, *The Piltdown Men* (New York: St. Martin's Press, 1972); S. J. Gould, "Piltdown in Letters," *Natural History* 90(1981):12–30.

3. R. Ardrey, *African Genesis* (New York: Dell, 1961).

4. P. V. Tobias, *Olduvai Gorge,* Vol. 2, *The Cranium and Maxillary Dentition of Australopithecus (Zinjanthropus) boisei* (Cambridge: Cambridge University Press, 1967).

5. L. S. B. Leakey, P. V. Tobias, and J. R. Napier, "A New Species of the Genus *Homo* from Olduvai Gorge," *Nature* 202(1964):7–9.

6. F. C. Howell and Y. Coppens, "An Overview of Hominidae from the Omo Succession, Ethiopia," in *Earliest Man and Environments in the Lake Rudolf Basin,*

eds. Y. Coppens, F. C. Howell, G. L. Isaac, and R. E. F. Leakey (Chicago: University of Chicago Press, 1976), pp. 522–532.

7. M. G. Leakey and R. E. F. Leakey, eds., *Koobi Fora Research Project,* Vol. 1, *The Fossil Hominids and an Introduction to Their Context, 1968–1974* (Oxford: Oxford University Press, 1978).

8. A. Walker, R. E. Leakey, J. M. Harris and F. H. Brown, "2.5-Myr *Australopithecus boisei* from West of Lake Turkana," *Nature* 322(1986):517–522; and J. M. Harris, F. H. Brown, M. G. Leakey, A. C. Walker, and R. E. Leakey, "Pliocene and Pleistocene Hominid-Bearing Sites from West of Lake Turkana, Kenya," *Science* 239(1988):27–33.

9. D. C. Johanson and M. Edey, *Lucy: The Beginnings of Humankind* (New York: Simon and Schuster, 1981).

10. M. H. Day and E. H. Wickens, "Laetoli Pliocene Hominid Footprints and Bipedalism," *Nature* 286(1980):385–387.

11. D. C. Johanson and T. D. White, "A Systematic Assessment of Early African Hominids," *Science* 202(1979):321–330.

12. J. T. Stern and R. L. Susman, "The Locomotor Anatomy of *Australopithecus afarensis,*" *American Journal of Physical Anthropology* 60(1983):279–318.

13. C. O. Lovejoy, "The Gait of *Australopithecus,*" *Yearbook of Physical Anthropology* 17(1973):147–161.

14. M. H. Wolpoff, "'Telanthropus' and the Single Species Hypothesis," *American Anthropologist* 70(1968):447–493.

15. P. V. Tobias, "'Australopithecus afarensis' and *A. africanus:* Critique and an Alternative Hypothesis," *Palaeontologia Africana* 23(1980):1–17.

16. T. R. Olson, "Basicranial Morphology of the Extant Hominoids and Pliocene Hominids: The New Material from the Hadar Formation, Ethiopia, and Its Significance in Early Human Evolution," in *Aspects of Human Evolution,* ed. C. B. Stringer (London: Taylor & Francis, 1981), pp. 99–128; Y. Coppens, *Le Singe, l'Afrique et l'homme* (Paris: Fayard, 1983).

17. J. T. Robinson, "Variation and the Taxonomy of the Early Hominids," in *Evolutionary Biology,* Vol. 1, eds. T. Dobzhansky, M. K. Hecht, and W. C. Steere (New York: Appleton-Century-Crofts, 1967), pp. 69–100.

18. E. Delson, "Human Phylogeny Revised Again," *Nature* 322(1986):496–497; F. E. Grine, "Australopithecine Evolution: The Deciduous Dental Evidence," in *Ancestors: The Hard Evidence,* ed. E. Delson (New York: Alan R. Liss, 1985), pp. 153–167.

19. Y. Rak, *The Australopithecine Face* (New York: Academic Press, 1983).

20. T. R. Olson, "Cranial Morphology and Systematics of the Hadar Formation Hominids and 'Australopithecus' africanus," in *Ancestors: The Hard Evidence,* ed. E. Delson (New York: Alan R. Liss, 1985), pp. 102–119.

21. P. Shipman, "Baffling Limb on the Family Tree," *Discover* Sept.(1986):87–93.

22. R. L. Hay, *Geology of the Olduvai Gorge* (Berkeley: University of California Press, 1976).

23. C. K. Brain, "New Finds at the Swartkrans Australopithecine Site," *Nature* 225(1970):1112–1119.

24. R. Potts and P. Shipman, "Cutmarks Made by Stone Tools on Bones from Olduvai Gorge, Tanzania," *Nature* 291(1981):577–580; R. Potts, "Foraging for Faunal Resources by Early Hominids at Olduvai Gorge, Tanzania," in *Animals and Archaeology: Hunters and Their Prey,* British Archaeological Reports, No. 163, eds. J. Clutton-Brock and C. Grigson (Oxford: 1983), pp. 51–62.

25. H. M. McHenry, "The Pattern of Human Evolution: Studies in Bipedalism, Mastication and Encephalization," *Annual Review of Anthropology* 11(1982):151–173.

26. G. L. Isaac, "The Food-Sharing Behavior of Protohuman Hominids," *Scientific American* 238(1978):90–108.

27. C. R. Peters and E. M. O'Brien, "The Early Hominid Plant-Food Niche: Insights

from an Analysis of Plant Exploitation by *Homo, Pan,* and *Papio* in Eastern and Southern Africa," *Current Anthropology* 22(1981):127–140; R. Dart, "The Predatory Transition from Ape to Man," *International Anthropological and Linguistic Review* 1(1953):201–218.

28. A. E. Mann, "Diet and Human Evolution," in *Omnivorous Primates: Gathering and Hunting in Human Evolution,* eds. R. S. O. Harding and G. Teleki (New York: Columbia University Press, 1981), pp. 10–36.

Suggested Readings

Brain, C. K. 1981. *The Hunters or the Hunted: An Introduction to African Cave Taphonomy.* New York: Alan R. Liss.

Campbell, B. G. 1988. *Humankind Emerging,* 5th ed. Boston: Little, Brown.

Ciochon, R. L., and Corruccini, R. S., eds. 1983. *New Interpretations of Ape and Human Ancestry.* New York: Plenum Press.

Day, M. H. 1986. *Guide to Fossil Man,* 4th ed. Chicago: University of Chicago Press.

Foley, R., ed. 1984. *Hominid Evolution and Community Ecology.* New York: Academic Press.

Grine, F., ed. 1988. *The Evolutionary History of the Robust Australopithecines.* Chicago: Aldine.

Lambert, D., and the Diagram Group. 1987. *The Field Guide to Early Man.* New York: Facts on File.

Leakey, M. D., and Harris, J. M., eds. 1987. *Laetoli: A Pliocene Site in Northern Tanzania.* London: Clarendon.

Lewin, R. 1987. *Bones of Contention: Controversies in the Search for Human Origins.* New York: Simon and Schuster.

Tobias, P. V., ed. 1985. *Hominid Evolution: Past, Present and Future. Proceedings of the Taung Diamond Jubilee International Symposium.* New York: Alan R. Liss.

———. 1989. *Olduvai Gorge.* Vol. 4, *Homo habilis.* Cambridge: Cambridge University Press.

Wolpoff, M. H. 1980. *Paleoanthropology.* New York: Alfred A. Knopf.

Wood, B., Martin, L., and Andrews, P., eds. 1986. *Major Trends in Primate and Human Evolution.* Cambridge: Cambridge University Press.

Chapter 10   Human Evolution II: The Emergence of Modern Humans

Notes

1. H. L. Shapiro, *Peking Man: The Discovery, Disappearance and Mystery of a Priceless Scientific Treasure* (New York: Simon and Schuster, 1974).

2. Xia Ming, "Uranium-Series Dating of Fossil Bones from Peking Man Cave–Mixing Model," *Acta Anthropologica Sinica* 1(1982):196.

3. J. J. Hublin, "Human Fossils from the North African Middle Pleistocene and the Origin of *Homo sapiens,*" in *Ancestors: The Hard Evidence,* ed. E. Delson (New York: Alan R. Liss, 1985), pp. 283–288.

4. A. Thoma, "L'Occipital de l'homme mindelien de Vértesszöllös," *L'Anthropologie* 70(1966):495–534; M. H. Wolpoff, "Is Vértesszöllös II an Occipital of European *Homo erectus?,*" *Nature* 232(1971):567–568.

5. C. B. Stringer, F. C. Howell, and J. K. Melentis, "The Significance of the Fossil Hominid Skull from Petralona, Greece," *Journal of Archaeological Science* 6(1979):235–253.

6. H. de Lumley, "A Paleolithic Camp at Nice," *Scientific American* 220(1969):42–50.

7. R. B. Lee and I. DeVore, eds., *Man the Hunter* (Chicago: Aldine, 1968).

8. L. G. Freeman, "The Fat of the Land: Notes on Paleolithic Diet in Iberia," in *Omnivorous Primates: Gathering and Hunting in Human Evolution,* eds. R. S. O. Harding and G. Teleki (New York: Columbia University Press, 1981), pp. 104–165.

9. L. R. Binford and Chuan Kun Ho, "Taphonomy at a Distance: Zhoukoudian, 'The Cave Home of Beijing Man'?," *Current Anthropology* 26(1985):413–442.

10. L. R. Binford, *Bones: Ancient Men and Modern Myths* (New York: Academic Press, 1981).

11. *L'Homo erectus et la place de l'homme de Tautavel parmi les hominides fossiles,* Congrès International de Paleontologie Humaine, 1er Congrès (Nice: Union Internationale des Sciences Préhistoriques et Protohistoriques, 1982).

12. J. W. Dawson, quoted in Loren Eiseley, *Darwin's Century* (New York: Doubleday, 1958), p. 274.

13. F. Bordes, "Mousterian Cultures in France," *Science* 134(1961):803–810.

14. H. L. Dibble, "Reduction Sequences in the Manufacture of Mousterian Implements of France," in *The Pleistocene Old World: Regional Perspectives,* ed. O. Soffer (New York: Plenum Press, 1987), pp. 33–46.

15. W. W. Howells, "Explaining Modern Man: Evolutionists vs. Migrationists," *Journal of Human Evolution* 5(1976):477–495.

16. A. Hrdlička, "The Neanderthal Phase of Man," *Journal of the Royal Anthropological Institute* 57(1927):249–274.

17. M. H. Wolpoff, J. N. Spuhler, F. H. Smith, J. Radovčić, G. Pope, D. W. Frayer, R. Eckhardt, and G. Clark, "Modern Human Origins," *Science* 241(1988):772–773.

18. F. C. Howell, "The Evolutionary Significance of Variation and Varieties of 'Neanderthal' Man," *Quarterly Review of Biology* 32(1957):330–347.

19. J. Jelínek, "Neanderthal Man and *Homo sapiens* in Central and Eastern Europe," *Current Anthropology* 10(1969):475–503; F. H. Smith, "Upper Pleistocene Hominid Evolution in South-Central Europe: A Review of the Evidence and Analysis of Trends," *Current Anthropology* 23(1982):667–703.

20. A. M. ApSimon, "The Last Neanderthal in France," *Nature* 287(1980):271–272; M. H. Wolpoff, C. B. Stringer, R. G. Kruszynski, R. M. Macobi, and A. M. ApSimon, "Matters Arising—Allez Neanderthal," *Nature* 289(1981):823–824.

21. H. Valladas, J. L. Reyss, J. L. Joron, G. Valladas, O. BarYosef, and B. Vandermeersch, "Thermoluminescence Dating of Mousterian 'Proto-Cro-Magnon' Remains from Israel and the Origin of Modern Man," *Nature* 331(1988):614–616.

22. M. H. Wolpoff, Wu Xin Zhi, and A. G. Thorne, "Modern *Homo sapiens* Origins: A General Theory of Hominid Evolution Involving the Fossil Evidence from East Asia," in *The Origins of Modern Humans: A World Survey of the Fossil Evidence,* eds. F. H. Smith and F. Spencer (New York: Alan R. Liss, 1984).

23. C. B. Stringer, "Population Relationships of Later Pleistocene Hominids: A Multivariate Study of Available Crania," *Journal of Archaeological Science* 1(1974):317–342; E. Trinkaus, "The Morphology of European and Southwest Asian Neanderthal Pubic Bones" *American Journal of Physical Anthropology* 44(1976):95–103; and E. Trinkaus and W. W. Howells, "The Neanderthals," *Scientific American* 241(1979):118–133.

24. G. P. Rightmire, "Implications of the Border Cave Skeletal Remains for Later Pleistocene Human Evolution," *Current Anthropology* 20(1979):23–35.

25. R. Singer and J. Wymer, *The Middle Stone Age at Klasies River Mouth in South Africa* (Chicago: University of Chicago Press, 1982).

26. R. L. Cann, M. Stoneking, and A. C. Wilson, "Mitochondrial DNA and Human Evolution," *Nature* 325(1987):31–36; R. L. Cann, M. Stoneking, and A. C. Wilson, "Disputed African Origin of Human Populations," *Nature* 329(1987):111–112.

27. G. Bräuer, "A Craniological Approach to the Origin of Anatomically Modern *Homo sapiens* in Africa and Implications for the Appearance of Modern Europeans," in *The Origins of Modern Humans: A World Survey of the Fossil Evidence,* eds. F. H. Smith and F. Spencer (New York: Alan R. Liss, 1984), pp. 327–410; C. B. Stringer and P. Andrews, "Genetic and Fossil Evidence for the Origin of Modern Humans," *Science* 239(1988):1263–1268; C. B. Stringer, "The Dates of Eden," *Nature* 331(1988):565–566; R. Lewin, "Africa: Cradle of Modern Humans," *Science* 237(1987):1292–1295; R. Lewin, "The Unmasking of Mitochondrial Eve," *Science* 238(1987):24–26.

28. C. S. Coon, *The Origin of Races* (New York: Alfred A. Knopf, 1962).

29. L. L. Cavalli-Sforza, "The Genetics of Human Populations," *Scientific American* 231(1974):80–89.

30. R. S. Solecki, *Shanidar: The First Flower People* (New York: Alfred A. Knopf, 1971).

31. T. D. Stewart, "The Neanderthal Skeletal Remains from Shanidar Cave, Iraq: A Summary of Findings to Date," *Proceedings of the American Philosophical Society* 121(1977):121–165; E. Trinkaus, *The Shanidar Neandertals* (New York: Academic Press, 1983).

32. P. G. Chase and H. L. Dibble, "Middle Paleolithic Symbolism: A Review of the Evidence and Interpretations," *Journal of Anthropological Archaeology* 6(1987):263–296.

33. P. Leiberman, E. S. Crelin, and D. H. Klatt, "Phonetic Ability and Related Anatomy of the Newborn and Adult Human, Neanderthal Man, and the Chimpanzee," *American Anthropologist* 74(1972):287–307.

34. R. L. Holloway, "Human Paleontological Evidence Relevant to Language Behavior," *Human Neurobiology* 2(1983):105–114.

35. A. B. Harper and W. S. Laughlin, "Inquiries into the Peopling of the New World: Development of Ideas and Recent Advances," in *A History of American Physical Anthropology: 1930–1980,* ed. F. Spencer (New York: Academic Press, 1982), pp. 281–304.

Suggested Readings

L'Homo erectus et la place de l'homme de Tautavel parmi les hominides fossiles, Congrès International de Paleontologie Humaine, 1ᵉʳ Congrès. 1982. Nice: Union Internationale des Sciences Préhistoriques et Protohistoriques.

Howells, W. W., eds. 1962. *Ideas on Human Evolution: Selected Essays, 1949–1961.* Cambridge, Mass.: Harvard University Press.

———. 1973. *Evolution of the Genus* Homo. Reading, Mass.: Addison-Wesley.

Mellars, P., and Stringer, C. B., eds. *The Origins and Dispersal of Modern Humans: Behavioral and Biological Perspectives.* Edinburgh: University of Edinburgh Press.

Novotný, V. V., and Mizerová, A., eds. 1986. *Fossil Man: New Facts, New Ideas. Papers in Honor of Jan Jelínek's Life Anniversary.* Vol. 23, *Anthropos* (Brno).

Oakley, K. P., Campbell, B. G., and Molleson, T. I. 1971. *Catalogue of Fossil Hominids.* Pt. 2, *Europe.* London: British Museum (Natural History).

———. 1975. *Catalogue of Fossil Hominids.* Pt 3, *Americas, Asia and Australia.* London: British Museum (Natural History).

———. 1977. *Catalogue of Fossil Hominids.* Pt. 1, *Africa.* Rev. ed. London: British Museum (Natural History).

Smith, F. H., and Spencer, F., eds. 1984. *The Origins of Modern Humans: A World Survey of the Fossil Evidence.* New York: Alan F. Liss.

Soffer, O., ed. 1987. *The Pleistocene Old World: Regional Perspectives.* New York: Plenum Press.

Spenser, F., ed. 1982. *A History of American Physical Anthropology.* New York: Academic Press.

Weidenreich, F. 1949. *Anthropological Papers of Franz Weidenreich, 1939–1948.* Compiled by S. L. Washburn and D. Wolffson. New York: Viking Fund.

Wolpoff, M. H. 1980. *Paleoanthropology.* New York: Alfred A. Knopf.

Chapter 11   The Study of Human Variability

Notes

1. Alan H. Goodman, George J. Armelagos, and Jerome C. Rose, "The Chronological Distribution of Enamel Hypoplasia from Prehistoric Dickson Mounds Populations," *American Journal of Physical Anthropology* 65(1984):259–266.

2. Mahmoud Y. El-Najjar, Mike V. DeSanti, and Leon Ozebek, "Prevalence and Possible Etiology of Dental Enamel Hypoplasia," *American Journal of Physical Anthropology* 48(1978):185–192.

3. A. Theodore Steegmann, Jr., "Eighteenth-Century British Military Stature: Growth Cessation, Selective Recruiting, Secular Trends, Nutrition at Birth, Cold and Occupation," *Human Biology* 57(1985):77–95.

4. Theodosius Dobzhansky, *Evolution, Genetics, and Man* (New York: John Wiley, 1955), p. 177.

5. Ibid.

6. Michelle Lampl and Robert Emde, "Episodic Growth in Infancy: A Preliminary Report on Length, Head Circumference, and Behavior," in *Levels and Transitions in Children's Development, New Definitions for Child Development* #21, ed. K. W. Fischer (San Francisco: Jossey-Bass, 1983).

7. Michael Hermanussen, Karin Geiger-Benoit, Jens Burmeister, and Wolfgang G. Sippell, "Periodical Changes of Short-Term Growth Velocity ('Mini Growth Spurts') in Human Growth," *Annals of Human Biology* 15(1988):103–109.

8. William H. Mueller, "The Genetics of Human Fatness," *Yearbook of Physical Anthropology* 26(1983):215–230.

9. Douglas Crews, "Body Weight, Blood Pressure and the Risk of Total and Cardiovascular Mortality in an Obese Population," *Human Biology* 60(1988):417–433.

10. Linda Adair, Ernesto Pollitt, and William H. Mueller, "Maternal Anthropometric Changes During Pregnancy and Lactation in a Rural Taiwanese Population," *Human Biology* 55(1983):771–788.

11. Tadeusz Bielicki and Zygmunt Welon, "Growth Data as Indicators of Social Inequalities: The case of Poland," *Yearbook of Physical Anthropology* 25(1982):153–167.

12. Robert M. Malina, Bertis B. Little, Michael P. Stern, Sharon P. Gaskill, and Helen P. Hazuda, "Ethnic and Social Class Differences in Selected Anthropometric Characteristics of Mexican-American and Anglo Adults: The San Antonio Heart Study," *Human Biology* 55(1983):867–883.

13. Stanley M. Garn, "Human Growth," *Annual Review of Anthropology* 9(1980):275–292.

Suggested Readings

Bogin, Barry. 1988. *Patterns of Human Growth.* New York: Cambridge University Press.

Corruccini, Robert S., Handler, Jerome S., and Jacobi, Keith P. 1985. "Chronological Distribution of Enamel Hypoplasias and Weaning in a Caribbean Slave Population." *Human Biology* 57:699–711.

Futuyma, Douglas J. 1986. *Evolutionary Biology,* 2d ed. Sunderland, Mass.: Sinauer Assoc.

Garn, Stanley M. 1980. "Human Growth." *Annual Review of Anthropology* 9:275–292.

Harrison, G. A., Tanner, J. M., Pilbeam, D. R., and Baker, P. T. 1988. *Human Biology,* 3rd ed. New York: Oxford University Press.

Mayr, Ernst. 1982. *The Growth of Biological Thought: Diversity, Evolution, and Inheritance.* Cambridge, Mass.: Belknap Press.

Morse, Dan, Duncan, Jack, and Stoutmire, James, eds. 1983. *Handbook of Forensic Archaeology and Anthropology.* Tallahassee, Fla.: Flordia State University Foundation, Inc.

Weiss, Kenneth M. 1988. "In Search of Times Past: Gene Flow and Invasion in the Generation of Human Diversity." In *Biological Aspects of Human Migration*, eds. C. G. N. Mascie-Taylor and G. W. Lasker. New York: Cambridge University Press.

Chapter 12   Human Polymorphisms

Notes

1. P. Levine, "Serological Factors as Possible Causes in Spontaneous Abortions," *Journal of Heredity* 34(1943):71–80.
2. C. R. Srikumari, J. Rajanikumari, and T. Venkateswara Rao, "Acuity of Selective Mechanisms Operating on ABO, Rh, and MN Blood Groups," *American Journal of Physical Anthropology* 72(1987):117–122.
3. Alice Brues, "Stochastic Tests of Selection in the A-B-O Blood Groups," *American Journal of Physical Anthropology* 21(1963):287–299.
4. Frank B. Livingstone, "Hemoglobin History in West Africa," *Human Biology* 48(1976):487–500.
5. Linda C. Jackson, "Sociocultural and Ethnohistorical Influences on Genetic Diversity in Liberia," *American Anthropology* 88(1985):825–842.
6. S. E. Antonarakis, C. D. Boehm, G. R. Serjeant, C. E. Theisen, G. J. Dover, and H. H. Kazazian, Jr., "Origin of the β^s-Globin Gene in Blacks: The Contribution of Recurrent Mutation or Gene Conversion or Both," *Proceedings of the National Academy of Sciences, USA* 81(1984):853–856.
7. J. Flint, A. V. S. Hill, D. K. Bowden, S. J. Oppenheimer, P. R. Sill, S. W. Serjeantson, J. Bana-Koiri, K. Bhatia, M. P. Alpers, A. J. Boyce, D. J. Weatherall, and J. B. Clegg, "High Frequencies of α-Thalassaemia Are the Result of Natural Selection by Malaria," *Nature* 321(1986):744–750.
8. R. White and J. M. Lalouel, "Investigation of Genetic Linkage in Human Families," in *Advances in Human Genetics,* vol. 16, ed. Harry Harris and Kurt Hirschhorn (New York: Plenum Press, 1987), pp. 121–228.

Suggested Readings

Caskey, C. Thomas. 1987. "Disease Diagnosis by Recombinant DNA Methods." *Science* 236:1223–1229.

Cohen, Bernice H. 1970. "ABO and Rh Incompatibility I. Fetal and Neonatal Mortality with ABO and Rh Incompatibility: Some New Interpretations," *American Journal of Human Genetics* 22:412–440.

Edelstein, Stuart J. 1986. *The Sickled Cell: From Myths to Molecules.* Cambridge, Mass. Harvard University Press.

Flint, J., Hill, A. V. S., Bowden, D. K., Oppenheimer, S. J., Sill, P. R., Serjeantson, S. W., Bana-Koiri, J., Alpers, M. P., Boyce, A. J., Weatherall, D. J., Clegg, J. B. 1986. "High Frequencies of α-Thalassemia are the Result of Natural Selection by Malaria." *Nature* 321:744–750.

Jeffreys, Alec J. 1987. "Highly Variable Minisatellites and DNA Fingerprints." *Biochemical Society Transactions* 15:309–317.

Kan, Y. W., and Dozy, A. M. 1980. "Evolution of the Hemoglobin S and C Genes in World Populations." *Science* 209:388–391.

Mielke, James H., and Crawford, Michael H., eds. 1980. *Current Developments in Anthropological Genetics.* Vol. 1. New York: Plenum Press.

Mourant, A. E., Kopec, Ada C., and Domaniewska-Sobczak, Kazimiera. 1978. *Blood Groups and Diseases: A Study of Associations of Diseases with Blood Groups and Other Polymorphisms.* Oxford: Oxford University Press.

Pagnier, Josée, Mears, J. Gregory, Dunda-Belkhodja, Olga, Schaeffer-Rego, Kim E., Beldjord, Cherif, Nagel, Ronald L., and Labie, Dominque. 1984. "Evidence for the Multicentric Origin of the Sickle-Cell Hemoglobin Gene in Africa," *Proceeding of the National Academy of Sciences, USA* 81:1771–1773.

Roberts, D. F. and De Stefano, G. F., eds. 1986. *Genetic Variation and Its Maintenance.* New York: Cambridge University Press.

Schell, Lawrence M., and Blumberg, Baruch S. 1988. "Alloalbuminemia and the Migrations of Native Americans." *Yearbook of Physical Anthropology* 31:1–13.

Williams, R. C. 1982. "HLA." *Yearbook of Physical Anthropology* 25:91–112.

Wyman, Arlene R., and White, Ray. 1980. "A Highly Polymorphic Locus in Human DNA." *Proceeding of the National Academy of Sciences, USA* 77:6754–6758.

Chapter 13 Human Adaptability

Notes

1. Cynthia M. Beall, "A Comparison of Chest Morphology in High-Altitude Asian and Andean Populations," *Human Biology* 54(1982):145–163.
2. A. R. Frisancho and P. T. Baker, "Altitude and Growth: A Study of the Patterns of Physical Growth of a High-Altitude Peruvian Quechua Population," *American Journal of Physical Anthropology* 32(1970):279–292.
3. Ronald S. Weinstein and Jere D. Haas, "Early Stress and Later Reproductive Performance Under Conditions of Malnutrition and High-Altitude Hypoxia," *Medical Anthropology* 1(1977):25–54.
4. Cynthia Unger, Janet K. Weiser, Robert E. McCullogh, Sharon Keefer, and Lorna Grindlay Moore, "Altitude, Low Birth Weight, and Infant Mortality in Colorado," *Journal of the American Medical Association* 259 (1988):3427–3432.
5. Cynthia M. Beall, Melvyn C. Goldstein, and the Tibetan Academy of Social Sciences, "Hemoglobin Concentration of Pastoral Nomads Permanently Resident at 4,850–5,450 Meters in Tibet," *American Journal of Physical Anthropology* 73(1987):433–438.
6. Michael A. Little, "Effects of Alcohol and Coca on Foot Temperature Responses of Highland Peruvians During a Localized Cold Exposure," *American Journal of Physical Anthropology* 32(1970):239.
7. Paul T. Baker, "Ecological and Physiological Adaptation in Indigenous South Americans," in *The Biology of Human Adaptability,* eds. Paul T. Baker and J. S. Weiner (Oxford: Clarendon Press, 1966), p. 291.
8. D. F. Roberts, "Body Weight, Race, and Climate," *American Journal of Physical Anthropology* 11(1953):533–558.
9. Marshall T. Newman, "Adaptations in the Physique of American Aborigines to Nutritional Factors," *Human Biology* 32(1960):288–313.
10. W. F. Loomis, "Skin Pigment Regulation of Vitamin-D Biosynthesis in Man," *Science* 157(1967):501–506.
11. Richard F. Branda and John W. Eaton, "Skin Color and Nutrient Photolysis: An Evolutionary Hypothesis," *Science* 201(1978):625–626.
12. Paul T. Baker, "Racial Differences in Heat Tolerance," *American Journal of Physical Anthropology* 16(1958):287–305.
13. P. W. Post, F. Daniels, Jr., and R. T. Binford, "Cold Injury and the Evolution of 'White' Skin," *Human Biology* 47(1975):65–80.
14. Lisa Sattenspiel, "Population Structure and the Spread of Disease," *Human Biology* 59(1987):411–438.

15. Beverly Paigen, Lynn R. Goldman, Mary M. Magnant, Joseph H. Highland, and A. T. Steegmann, Jr., "Growth of Children Living Near the Hazardous Waste Site, Love Canal," *Human Biology* 59(1987):489–508.
16. Ted A. Rathbun, "Health and Disease at a South Carolina Plantation, 1840–1870," *American Journal of Physical Anthropology* 74(1987):239–253.
17. Debra L. Martin, Ann L. Magennis, and Jerome C. Rose, "Cortical Bone Maintenance in an Historic Afro-American Cemetery Sample from Cedar Grove, Arkansas," *American Journal of Physical Anthropology* 74(1987):255–264.
18. G. A. Harrison, C. D. Palmer, D. Jenner, and V. Reynolds, "Associations Between Rates of Urinary Catecholamine Excretion and Aspects of Lifestyle Among Adult Women in Some Oxfordshire Villages," *Human Biology* 53(1981):617–633.
19. Arthur M. Michalek and K. Michael Cummings, "The Association Between Cigarette Smoking and Age of Cancer Diagnosis," *Human Biology* 59(1987):631–639.
20. Sidney Cobb, "Physiological Changes in Men Whose Jobs Were Abolished," *Journal of Psychosomatic Research* 18(1974):245–258.
21. Alfred J. Lewy, Robert L. Sack, L. Stephen Miller, and Tana M. Hoban, "Antidepressant and Circadian Phase-Shifting Effects of Light," *Science* 235(1987):352–354.
22. Lawrence Schell, "Environmental Noise and Human Prenatal Growth," *American Journal of Physical Anthropology* 56(1981):63–67.
23. Michael A. Little and Brooke R. Johnson, Jr., Mixed-Longitudinal Growth of Nomadic Turkana Pastoralists," *Human Biology* 59(1987):695–707.
24. Francis E. Johnston, Setha M. Low, Yetilude Baessa, and Robert B. MacVean, "Interaction of Nutritional and Socioeconomic Status as Determinants of Cognitive Development in Disadvantaged Urban Guatemalan Children," *American Journal of Physical Anthropology* 73(1987):501–506.
25. Robert M. Malina, Bertis B. Little, Richard F. Shoup, and Peter H. Buschang, "Adaptive Significance of Small Body Size: Strength and Motor Performance of School Children in Mexico and Papua New Guinea," *American Journal of Physical Anthropology* 73(1987):489–499.
26. Daniel Z. Gross and Barbara A. Underwood, "Technological Change and Caloric Costs: Sisal Agriculture in Northeastern Brazil," *American Anthropologist* 73(1971):725–740.
27. D. C. Gajdusek, "Unconventional Viruses and the Origin and Disappearance of Kuru," *Science* 197(1977):943–960.
28. Lawrence S. Greene, "Hyperendemic Goiter, Cretinism and Social Organization in Highland Ecuador," in *Malnutrition, Behavior, and Social Organization*, ed. Lawrence S. Greene (New York: Academic Press, 1977), pp. 54–94.
29. Alice Brues, "The Spearman and the Archer: An Essay on Selection in Body Build," *American Anthropologist* 61(1959):465.
30. Paul Baker, "Ecological and Physiological Adaptation," p. 279.
31. R. H. Post, "Population Differences in Red and Green Color Vision Deficiency: A Review, and a Query on Selection Relaxation," *Eugenics Quarterly* 9(1962):131–146.
32. Gebhard Flatz, "Genetics of Lactose Digestion in Humans," in *Advances in Human Genetics*, vol. 16, eds. Harry Harris and Kurt Hirschhorn (New York: Plenum Press, 1987), pp. 1–77.

Suggested Readings

Baker, P. T. 1978. *The Biology of High-Altitude Peoples*. New York: Cambridge University Press.
Baker, P. T., Hanna, J. M., and Baker, T. S. eds. 1986. *The Changing Samoans: Behavior and Health in Transition*. New York: Oxford University Press.
Beall, Cynthia M. 1982. "A Comparison of Chest Morphology in High Altitude Asian and Andean Populations." *Human Biology* 54:145–163.

Branda, Richard F., and Eaton, John W. 1978. "Skin Color and Nutrient Photolysis: An Evolutionary Hypothesis." *Science* 201:625–626.

Byard, Pamela J. 1981. "Quantitative Genetics of Human Skin Color." *Yearbook of Physical Anthropology* 24:123–138.

Collins, K. J., and Roberts, D. F. eds. 1988. *The Capacity for Work in the Tropics.* New York: Cambridge University Press.

Flatz, Gebhard. 1987. "Genetics of Lactose Digestion in Humans." In *Advances in Human Genetics,* vol. 16, eds. Harry Harris and Kurt Hirschhorn. New York: Plenum Press, pp. 1–77.

Garruto, Ralph M., 1981. "Disease Patterns of Isolated Groups." In *Biocultural Aspects of Disease,* ed. Henry R. Rothschild. New York: Academic Press, pp. 557–597.

Goodman, Alan H., Thomas, R. Brooke, Swedlund, Alan C., and Armelagos, George J. 1988. "Biocultural Perspectives on Stress in Prehistoric, Historical, and Contemporary Population Research." *Yearbook of Physical Anthropology* 31:169–202.

Hanna, Joel, M., and Brown, Daniel E. 1983. "Human Heat Tolerance: An Anthropological Perspective." *Annual Review Anthropology* 12:259–284.

Harrison, G. A., Palmer, C. D., Jenner, D., and Reynolds, V. 1981. "Associations between Rates of Urinary Catecholamine Excretion and Aspects of Lifestyle among Adult Women in Some Oxfordshire Villages." *Human Biology* 53:617–633.

Jerome, Norge W., Kandel, Randy F., Pelto, and Gretal H., eds. 1980. *Nutritional Anthropology: Contemporary Approaches to Diet and Culture.* Pleasantville, N.Y.: Redgrave Publishing.

Little, Michael A. and Baker, Paul T. 1988. "Migration and Adaptation." In *Biological Aspects of Human Migration,* eds. C. G. N. Mascie-Taylor and G. W. Lasker. New York: Cambridge University Press, pp. 167–215.

Malina, Robert M., Little, Bertis B., Stern, Michael P., Gaskill, Sharon P., and Hazuda, Helen P. 1983. "Ethnic and Social Class Differences in Selected Anthropometric Characteristics of Mexican American and Anglo Adults: The San Antonio Heart Study." *Human Biology* 55:867–883.

Moore, Lorna Grindlay, and Regensteiner, Judith G. 1983. "Adaptation to High Altitude." *Annual Review of Anthropology* 12:285–304.

Pearson, Paul B., and Greenwell, Richard J., eds. 1980. *Nutrition, Food, and Man: An Interdisciplinary Perspective.* Tucson: University of Arizona Press.

Schell, Lawrence M. 1981. "Environmental Noise and Human Prenatal Growth." *American Journal of Physical Anthropology* 56:63–70.

Chapter 14   Biological History of Human Populations

Notes

1. Jon Alfred Mjoen, "Harmonic and Disharmonic Racecrossings," in *Eugenics in Race and State,* vol. 2, Scientific Papers of the Second International Congress of Eugenics (Baltimore: Williams and Wilkins, 1923), p. 46.

2. Stephen Jay Gould, *The Mismeasure of Man* (New York: W. W. Norton & Co., 1981).

3. Gabriel W. Lasker and Bernice Kaplan, "The Relation of Anthroposcopic Traits to the Ascription of Racial Designation in Peru," in *Homenaje a Juan Comas en su 65 Anniversario,* vol. 2 (Mexico City: Instituto Indigenista Interamericano, 1965), pp. 189–220.

4. Stanley M. Garn, *Human Races,* 3rd ed. (Springfield, Ill.: C. C. Thomas, 1971).

5. Jean Hiernaux, "The Concept of Race and the Taxonomy of Mankind," in *The Concept of Race,* ed. M. F. Ashley Montagu (New York: Free Press, 1964), pp. 32–33.

6. Frank B. Livingstone, "On the Nonexistence of Human Races," *Current Anthropology* 3(1962):279.
7. John M. McCullough, "Estimation of Minimal Selection Pressure in a Recessive Trait from Migration Across Climatic Clines," *Journal of Human Evolution* 14(1985):579–586.
8. P. Govinda Reddy, "Effects of Inbreeding on Mortality: A Study Among Three South Indian Communities," *Human Biology* 57(1985):47–59.
9. James P. Hurd, "Kin Relatedness and Church Fissioning in the 'Nebraska' Amish," *Social Biology* 30(1983):59–66.
10. B. Glass and C. C. Li, "The Dynamics of Racial Intermixture—An Analysis Based on the American Negro," *American Journal of Human Genetics* 5(1953):1–20.
11. W. S. Pollitzer, "The Negroes of Charleston (S.C.): A Study of Hemoglobin Types, Serology, and Morphology," *American Journal of Physical Anthropology* 16(1958):241–263.
12. T. Edward Reed, "Caucasian Genes in American Negroes," *Science* 165(1969):762–768.
13. Curtis Wienker, "Admixture in a Biologically African Caste of Black Americans," *American Journal of Physical Anthropology* 74(1987):265–273.
14. R. Chakraborty and K. M. Weiss, "The Frequency of Complex Diseases in Hybrid Populations," *American Journal of Physical Anthropology* 70(1986):489–503.
15. Frank B. Livingstone, "Simulation of the Founder Effect and Its Role in the Determination of the Polymorphic Frequencies of Deleterious Genes in Human Populations," *Human Biology* 59(1987):59–75.
16. N. E. Morton, R. Kennett, S. Yee, and R. Lew, "Bioassay of Kinship in Populations of Middle Eastern Origin and Controls," *Current Anthropology* 23(1982):157–167.
17. P. Menozzi, A. Piazza, and L. L. Cavalli-Sforza, "Synthetic Maps of Human Gene Frequencies in Europeans," *Science* 201(1978):786–792.
18. J. S. Wainscoat, A. V. S. Hill, A. L. Boyce, J. Flint, M. Hernandez, S. L. Thein, J. M. Old, J. R. Lynch, A. G. Falusi, D. J. Weatherall, and J. B. Clegg, "Evolutionary Relationships of Human Populations from an Analysis of Nuclear DNA Polymorphisms," *Nature* 319(1986):491–493.
19. L. Vawter and Wesley M. Brown, "Nuclear and Mitochondrial DNA Comparisons Reveal Extreme Rate Variation in the Molecular Clock," *Science* 234(1986):94–96.
20. Rebecca L. Cann, Mark Stoneking, and Allan C. Wilson, "Mitochondrial DNA and Human Evolution," *Nature* 325(1987):31–36.
21. C. Loring Brace and Robert J. Hinton, "Oceanic Tooth-Size Variation as a Reflection of Biological and Cultural Mixing," *Current Anthropology* 22(1981):549–569.
22. Theodosius Dobzhansky, "Genetics and the Races of Man," in *Sexual Selection and the Descent of Man*, ed. Bernard Campbell (Chicago: Aldine, 1972), p. 67.

Suggested Readings

Brace, C. L., Brace, M. L., and Leonard, W. R. 1989. "Reflections on the Face of Japan: A Multivariate Craniofacial and Odontometric Perspective." *American Journal of Anthropology,* 78:93–113.
Brace, C., Loring, and Hinton, Robert J. 1981. "Oceanic Tooth-size Variation as a Reflection of Biological and Cultural Mixing." *Current Anthropology* 22:549–569.
Crawford, M. H., and Mielke, J. H., eds. 1982. *Current Developments in Anthropological Genetics,* Vol. 2; *Ecology and Population Structure.* New York: Plenum Press.
Gould, Stephen J. 1978. "Morton's Ranking of Races by Cranial Capacity." *Science* 200:503–509.
Morton, N. E., Kennett, R., Yee, S., and Lew, R. 1982. "Bioassay of Kinship in Populations of Middle Eastern Origin and Controls," *Current Anthropology* 23:157–167.

Neel, James V. 1978. "The Population Structure of an Amerindian Tribe, The Yanomama," *Annual Review of Genetics* 12:365–413.

Roberts, D. F. 1988. "Migration and Genetic Change." *Human Biology* 60:521–539.

Spuhler, J. N. 1988. Evolution of Mitochondrial DNA in Monkeys, Apes and Humans." *Yearbook of Physical Anthropology* 31:15–48.

Chapter 15   Prospects and Perspectives

Notes

1. N. G. Blurton Jones, "An Ethological Study of Some Aspects of Social Behavior of Children in Nursery School," in *Primate Ethology,* ed. Desmond Morris (Chicago: Aldine, 1967), p. 365.

2. G. A. Reichard, "Social Life," in *General Anthropology,* ed. Franz Boas (New York: D. C. Heath, 1938), pp. 471–472.

3. E. T. Hall, *The Hidden Dimension* (New York: Doubleday and Company, 1966), p. 115.

4. Napoleon A. Chagnon, "Life Histories, Blood Revenge, and Warfare in a Tribal Population," *Science* 239(1988):985–992.

5. John Money and Anke A. Ehrhardt, *Man & Woman, Boy & Girl* (Baltimore: Johns Hopkins University Press, 1972).

6. Patricia Draper, "!Kung Women: Contrasts in Sexual Egalitarianism in Foraging and Sedentary Contexts," in *Toward an Anthropology of Women,* ed. R. R. Reiter (New York: Monthly Review Press, 1975).

7. Christine Obbo, "Is AIDS Just Another Disease?" in *AIDS,* ed. Ruth Kulstad (Washington, D.C.: American Association for the Advancement of Science, in press).

8. Richard Parker, "Acquired Immunodeficiency Syndrome in Urban Brazil," *Medical Anthropology Quarterly* 1(1987):155–175.

9. Wilton M. Krogman, "The Scars of Human Evolution," *Scientific American* 185(1951):54–57.

10. Rene Cailliet, *Low Back Pain Syndrome,* 2nd ed. (Philadelphia: F. A. Davis, 1968).

11. H. J. Muller, "Our Load of Mutations," *American Journal of Human Genetics* 2(1950):111–176.

Suggested Readings

Chagnon, Napoleon A. 1988. "Life Histories, Blood Revenge, and Warfare in a Tribal Population." *Science* 239:985–992.

Fedigan, Linda Marie. 1986. "The Changing Role of Women in Models of Human Evolution." *Annual Review of Anthropology* 15:25–66.

Goldsmith, Marsha F. 1988. "AIDS Around the World: Analyzing Complex Patterns." *Journal of the American Medical Association* 259:1917–1919.

Kirkwood, Thomas B. L. 1985. "Comparative and Evolutionary Aspects of Longevity." In *Handbook of the Biology of Aging,* 2d ed., ed. Caleb E. Finch and Edward L. Schneider. New York: Van Nostrand Reinhold, pp. 27–44.

O'Kelly, Charlotte, G., and Carney, Larry S. 1986. *Women and Men in Society,* 2d ed. Belmont, Calif.: Wadsworth.

Parker, Richard. 1987. "Acquired Immunodeficiency Syndrome in Urban Brazil." *Medical Anthropology Quarterly* 1:155–175.

Rowe, John W., and Kahn, Robert L. 1987. "Human Aging: Usual and Successful." *Science* 237:143–149.

"What Science Knows About AIDS." *Scientific American* 259(1988) (entire issue).

Glossary

ABO blood group: a blood group system based on red blood cell surface molecules. Its inheritance is controlled by three alleles—A, B, and O. There are six genotypes and four phenotypes. A, B, and O molecules can be found on cells other than red cells.

Acclimatization: adaptive physiological alteration.

Acheulian: a stone tool industry of the Lower Paleolithic, characterized by the presence of hand axes.

Acquired Immunodeficiency Syndrome (AIDS): an often fatal viral disease caused by the human immunodeficiency virus (HIV).

Adaptive radiation: the rapid increase in number of related species following entry into new environments that lack competitors.

Adjustment: a shift in functioning to adapt to stress.

Admixture: the mixing of genes of two or more populations. Often, admixture follows the migration of peoples.

Admixture coefficient: an estimate of the relative contributions of two (or more) parental populations to the gene pool of a hybrid population. The gene pool of the hybrid group, and hence the admixture coefficient, can also be affected by natural selection.

Adrenal cortex: glandular tissue that produces many steroid hormones. Located above each kidney.

Aegyptopithecus: best known of a number of fossil higher primates found in Oligocene deposits in the Fayum area of Egypt. The skull still retains many primitive attributes, although features like the filled-in orbits demonstrate its higher primate status.

Aerobic capacity: a physiological measurement of ability to work.

Afropithecus: an East African Miocene hominoid perhaps closely related to the ancestry of the great apes.

Agenesis: a failure of a biological structure to develop.

Agnatha: a class of primitive vertebrates that lack both jaws and teeth; the major living representative is the lamprey.

Allantois: a structure in the eggs of reptiles and birds and a part of the mammalian placenta that provides for the removal of embryological wastes.

Alleles: variant forms of a gene that occupies the same relative position on members of a pair of chromosomes and affects the same trait but in different ways.

Allen's Rule: the observed tendency of mammals living in cold regions to have shorter extremities than members of the same species living in warm regions.

Altruism: selflessness in the broad sense; in sociobiology, normally referring to acts of selfless or self-sacrificing behavior.

Ambrona: a middle Pleistocene archaeological site in Spain near Torralba.

Amino acids: compounds that are joined in specific sequences under the direction of DNA to form the many proteins found in an organism. There are twenty common amino acids.

Amphipithecus: a fossil primate, represented by fragmentary jaws and teeth, from the late Eocene of Burma. It may be the earliest known appearance of anthropoid primates.

Anagenesis: one form of speciation in which a species evolves through time into a new species. Anagenesis is contrasted with cladogenesis.

Anatomically modern humans: *Homo sapiens* that are identical in appearance to living humans. Often placed in their own subspecies, *Homo sapiens sapiens,* to distinguish them from fossil forms of *Homo sapiens* like *H.s. neanderthalensis.*

Anemia: a deficiency of the oxygen-carrying ability of the blood. It may be produced by a variety of causes, including genetic, as in thalassemia or sickle-cell anemia, or environmental, as in iron-deficiency anemia, infections, or immune reactions.

Angiosperm: a major grouping of advanced plants, including the deciduous trees (those that lose their leaves in the winter), the fruiting and flowering trees, and all the grasses. The last of the major plant groups to evolve, the angiosperms proliferated during the Cretaceous period, profoundly altering the earth's ecology.

Anthropoid: a higher primate. In schemes that divide the order Primates into the prosimian and anthropoid categories, the Anthropoidea are the New World monkeys, the Old World monkeys, the apes, and humans.

Anthropometry: the measurement of living humans.

Antibody: a substance produced as a result of exposure to a foreign substance (an antigen). Through various mechanisms antibodies help eliminate antigens from the body.

Antigen: a substance that the body recognizes as foreign and, as a result, causes the production of an antibody.

Arago: a cave site in southern France with hominine fossils whose morphological features place them in the early or archaic *Homo sapiens* category.

Arboreal: adapted to life in the trees.

Articulation: the joint or point of junction between bones of the skeleton.

Assortative mating, negative: mating with someone who differs from you for a trait.

Assortative mating, positive: mating with someone who resembles you for a trait.

Auditory bulla: paired bulbous bony chambers on each side of the bottom of the mammal skull that house the inner ear structures.

Australopithecine: a descriptive rather than a taxonomic term used in this book to designate the early hominines: all members of *Australopithecus* and *Homo habilis*.

Australopithecus aethiopicus: a proposed species of robust australopithecine possibly including the skull specimen KNM-WT 17000. The validity of this species is still being debated.

Australopithecus afarensis: a fossil hominine species found at the sites of Hadar in Ethiopia and Laetoli in Tanzania and dated from about 2.9 to 3.6 million years B.P. These are the first known, undoubted members of the hominine subfamily. They are fully bipedal, have certain distinctive features in their dentition, and have small brain sizes.

Australopithecus africanus: a fossil hominine species found at sites in East and South Africa and dated from perhaps more than 3 to 1.5 million years B.P.

Australopithecus boisei: an australopithecine found in East Africa from about 2 to sometime after 1.5 million years B.P., when they disappear from the record. It may extend further back in time if the early skull, KNM-WT 17000, is included in this species and not placed in a new category, *A. aethiopicus*. *A. boisei* is noted for the massive size of its teeth, jaws, and face.

Australopithecus robustus: a fossil hominine found at the South African sites of Swartkrans and Kromdraai and relatively dated from about 2 to sometime after 1.5 million years B.P. Because of their similar large teeth and jaws, *A. robustus* and *A. boisei* are sometimes related evolutionarily.

Bacteria: any of a wide variety of one-celled organisms. Many, although not all, cause disease.

Balanced polymorphism: the maintenance of two or more alleles as a result of selection favoring the heterozygote.

Bases: the building blocks of DNA and RNA. The four bases found in DNA are adenine, guanine, cytosine, and thymine. In RNA, thymine is replaced by uracil. The specificity of the genetic material rests on the fact that adenine always pairs with thymine (or uracil) and guanine always pairs with cytosine.

B-cells: the class of white blood cells that produce antibodies.

Bergmann's Rule: the observed tendency for mammals living in cold regions to be heavier and rounder in shape than members of the same species living in warm regions.

Bicuspid: premolar, grinding teeth found in the jaw just behind the canines and in front of the molars.

Bilateral symmetry: the pattern of symmetry found among vertebrates in which the right and left halves of the animal are almost identical.

Bilophodont: characteristic molar teeth of all Old World monkeys, with four cusps, the front two connected by a transverse ridge (one "loph") but separated from the back loph by a deep groove.

Bilzingsleben: a hominine fossil site in East Germany. The fragmentary skull bones found there have some features similar to those of *Homo erectus* and a number relating them to early *Homo sapiens*; they are usually assigned to the latter category.

Binomial: the two-part name given to every living and extinct form. It is made up of the genus and species names.

Biocultural: the interplay between biological and cultural phenomena.

Biological species: a group of breeding populations that are reproductively isolated from all other such groups.

Bipedalism: a special form of locomotion on two feet. Characteristic of all known living and extinct members of the subfamily Homininae.

Blade tools: stone tools, characteristic of the Upper Paleolithic, whose long, relatively thin blades are struck off a core and further worked into projectile points, scrapers, etc.

Blood groups: classes of sugar molecules discernible on the membranes of blood cells and detected by the use of appropriate antibodies. Within each blood group system are two or more alternative types; for example, within the ABO system are types A, B, O, and AB. At times, blood group substances are found on cells and in fluids other than the blood.

Bodo: a fossil hominine skull from the Afar region of Ethiopia. It is similar in many of its features to the early or archaic *Homo sapiens* fossils from Kabwe, Zambia, and Saldanha Bay, South Africa.

Border Cave: a cave site on the border between South Africa and the small kingdom of Swaziland at which several fragmentary *Homo sapiens* skeletons have been found in a context dated to more than 75,000 years ago. Although these findings are often cited as fossil documentation of the early appearance of modern humans in Africa, it remains uncertain whether they are really that ancient or rather more recent intrusive burials into an older deposit.

B.P.: (years) before present.

Brachiation: the specialized method of movement by gibbons through the trees in which the body hangs suspended from the tree limb underneath the arms and swings like a pendulum.

Branching evolution: see cladogenesis.

Breccia: rock and bone cemented together by calcium carbonate (lime).

Breeding population (or Mendelian population): a group of animals of the same species living in the same environment, all of which have an equal chance of breeding with any other member of the group of the opposite sex. The breeding population is the level on which evolution operates.

Bruhnes Normal: the current paleomagnetic time. Earth magnetic polarity reversed to the current orientation about 730,000 years B.P., marking the beginning of the Bruhnes Normal Epoch, and the end of the previous period, the Matuyama Reversed Epoch.

Buluk: a site in western Kenya, East Africa, where jaws of the early Miocene hominoid *Afropithecus* were found.

Calorie: a unit of heat; the amount of heat needed to raise the temperature of one gram of water from 15 degrees C to 16 degrees C. The unit is used to measure the amount of energy in food and the amount of energy required to perform work. When written with a capital C, it refers to a kilocalorie which is one thousand times as large.

Canalization: the propensity for some biological phenomena to return to a predetermined developmental pattern in spite of environmental perturbations or upsets.

Canine fossa: a depression above the canine tooth on the cheek of modern humans resulting from the reduction in the size of the face.

Carbon-14: dating method used on organic remains and based on the knowledge that all living things maintain a constant ratio of the unstable isotope C^{14} to the stable common element C^{12}, which begins to change after the living form dies and the C^{14} breaks down.

Carnivorous animal: an animal that subsists on a diet of meat.

Catarrhini: an Old World higher primate. The catarrhines include the Old World monkeys, the apes, and humans, and are distinguished from the platyrrhines, or the New World monkeys, by a number of biological features.

Catastrophism: a view expressed by some nineteenth-century natural historians that held that the earth and the living things on it were largely shaped by recurrent catastrophes such as earthquakes, floods, and fires (see also uniformitarianism).

Catch-up growth: accelerated growth following a period of subnormal growth.

Cerebellum: the part of the hindbrain that, along with the cerebrum (part of the forebrain), became elaborated and convoluted in the evolution of the mammals due to its role in coordinating muscular activity.

Cerebrum (cerebral cortex): the part of the forebrain that becomes elaborated and convoluted in mammals, especially in humans.

Cerumen: ear wax.

Chesowanja: a site in western Kenya where an *Australopithecus boisei* skull was discovered.

Chopping tool tradition: a Lower Paleolithic stone tool industry that apparently evolved from the Oldowan and is found at various sites throughout the Old World, including Zhoukoudian, China.

Choukoutien: older term, no longer used, for the large cave site now called Zhoukoudian outside of Beijing (formerly Peking) in northern China, (see Zhoukoudian).

Chromosomes: paired bodies present within the nucleus of the cell. They are composed primarily of DNA.

Chronospecies: a series of ancestor-descendant populations with its own evolutionary trends; characterized primarily on the basis of anatomy.

Cilia: microscopic hairlike processes that beat rhythmically; found in the human respiratory tract and elsewhere.

Cladistics: a method for determining the evolutionary relationships among animal groups by comparing shared morphological features. These relationships are usually depicted in a cladogram.

Cladogenesis: one form of speciation in which one species evolves through time into two or more descendant species. Cladogenesis is contrasted with anagenesis.

Cladogram: the result of a cladistic analysis. It is the graphic depiction of the relationships of three or more taxa based on a comparison of their shared morphological features, not of the times at which the animals lived.

Clavicle: the collarbone, which connects the breastbone (sternum) with the shoulder blade (scapula).

Cline: a continuous gradation over space in the form or frequency of a trait.

Clone: a group of genetically identical cells.

Coadapted gene complex: a series of genes, governing different traits, that work well together.

Cobble tool: a stone tool that uses a cobble or pebble as its core. (A cobble or pebble is a stone worn smooth by the action of water or sand.)

Codominance: a condition in which neither of two alleles for a trait masks the presence of the other in a heterozygote.

Codon: a group of three bases that specifies a particular amino acid. Part of the genetic code, it is stated in terms of mRNA sequence.

Collagen: a protein (made up of amino acids) that is the organic component of bone.

Colostrum: the first milk from a mother's breast.

Concordance rate: the frequency with which pairs of people, often genetic relatives, exhibit the same form of a trait or disorder. Used to estimate the genetic contribution to the trait.

Conspecifics: members of the same species.

Continental drift: the phenomenon by which the major land masses of the planet, set on a series of plates, have, over the course of earth's history, moved extensively in relation to one another.

Continuous traits: traits, such as weight, for which variation falls along a continuum.

Convergent evolution: the evolution of similar adaptations in distantly related groups.

Core area: in the study of primates in the wild, the area within home range where a group spends most of its time.

Core tool: a stone tool manufactured from a core rather than from a flake or blade taken off the core. Acheulian hand axes are core tools.

Corneum: the horny stratum of the epidermis, or outer skin layer.

Cranial capacity: the volume of the brain case, expressed in milliliters (ml), from which a rough estimate of brain size can be derived.

Crepuscular: referring to activity during the twilight hours.

Cro-Magnon: a cave site in southern France where anatomically modern humans and Upper Paleolithic tools were found.

Crossover: the exchange of genetic material between members of a pair of chromosomes during meiosis.

Cultural adaptation: the adjustment to enviromental changes through the medium of culture, such as dietary or technological changes.

Cultural relativism: the concept that all cultures are basically equal and cannot be evaluated according to one set of values or morals.

Culture: the learned traditions, customs, and thought patterns of a group.

Cusps: pointed or rounded bumps on the occlusal or chewing surface of a tooth.

Dali: an early *Homo sapiens* skull from China.

Deciduous teeth: the baby teeth, or the first of the two sets characteristic of mammals to erupt in the jaws. They are smaller in size and fewer in number than the adult set.

Dendropithecus: one of a number of small-bodied early Miocene hominoids known from East Africa.

Dental formula: a formula for expressing the number of kinds of teeth (incisors, canines, premolars, and molars) characteristic of a particular mammalian species. Humans, apes, and the Old World monkeys have the formula 2.1.2.3.

Dentin: a bonelike material that forms the core of vertebrate teeth.

Dentition: the complete set of upper and lower teeth of an animal.

Developmental responses: alterations in biological development to suit prevailing environmental conditions.

Diastema: a space between teeth, such as the space in monkey and ape jaws between the enlarged lower canine and the premolar, and into which the upper canine fits, thus allowing the jaws to close.

Discontinuous traits: traits for which variation falls into discrete categories; e.g., blood groups.

Diurnal: referring to activity during the daylight hours.

Divergent evolution: the accumulation of genetic differences in reproductively isolated groups.

Dizygotic (DZ) twins: fraternal twins who are no more similar genetically than any other sibling pair.

DNA: the genetic material deoxyribonucleic acid. Its base sequence directs the production of proteins.

DNA hybridization: a molecular technique using the double helical structure of DNA to determine the relationship of living species to each other and thus to shed some light on evolutionary relationships.

Dominance: the ability of one allele for a trait to mask the presence of another allele. The latter allele is said to be recessive to the former.

Dominance hierarchy: a system of organization seen among some groups of primates in which the males, through the use of predictable behavioral interactions, are sorted into a hierarchy from the alpha, or top-ranking, male to the lowest male. Females are also sometimes formed into hierarchies, which tend to be more stable than those of the males.

Down's syndrome: a genetic defect in which a person has three rather than two copies of the twenty-first chromosome.

Dryopithecus: a genus of extinct hominoids from the middle to late Miocene of Europe. They appear to share features with the early Miocene fossil hominoid, *Proconsul,* from whom they may have descended.

Dysmenorrhea: painful menstruation.

Early or archaic sapiens: a general term used to identify all *Homo sapiens* fossils from their first appearance at the end of the middle Pleistocene to the appearance of anatomically modern humans.

East Turkana: early hominine fossil-bearing deposits along the shores of Lake Turkana in north Kenya. First searched by Richard Leakey in 1968, this area has yielded the remains of over 100 individuals of the genera *Australopithecus* and *Homo* dated from about 2 to 1.3 million years B.P.

Ehringsdorf: a late Pleistocene hominine site in East Germany.

Electron spin resonance: a dating method used on cave deposits of shell and bone. It is based on the same physical principles as thermoluminescence.

Electrophoresis: a technique used to separate proteins or other molecules based on differences in molecular size and/or electrical charge.

Endogamy: marrying within one's group (see also exogamy).

Enzyme: a protein that speeds up a biochemical reaction.

Epicanthic fold: a fold in the skin of the eyelid that produces the "almond-shaped" eyes found primarily in Oriental and Native American populations.

Epistasis: the interaction between genes that are not alleles of each other.

Erythroblastosis foetalis: destruction of fetal/newborn red blood cells by the mother's antibodies to Rh + blood.

Erythrocytes: red blood cells.

Estrus: the reproductive cycle in female nonhuman primates, which is accompanied by physiological, anatomical, and behavioral changes.

Ethnocentrism: the view that the cultural values and practices of one's own society are superior to all others.

Ethnography: the description of modern cultures.

Ethnology: the comparison of cultures.

Ethology: the study of animal behavior.

Eucaryote: an organism whose cells contain a nucleus.

Eugenics: methods of improving the species by controlled breeding.

Evolution: genetic change in a population.

Evolutionary species: see chronospecies.

Evolved Oldowan industry: an early Pleistocene African stone tool industry with more complex tools than the Oldowan.

Exogamy: choosing a mate from another group (see also endogamy).

Exon: the sections of a gene that code for protein (see also intron).

Fauna: animals, especially those of a particular region.

Fayum: a fossil-rich locale near Cairo, Egypt, from which an extensive series of Oligocene primate fossils have been recovered.

Femur: the thighbone.

Fibula: the bone lateral to (outside) the shinbone in the lower leg.

Fission track dating: a technique used to date uranium-containing deposits that is based on counting the tracks left in crystals by radioactive breakdown.

Fixed action pattern: a stereotyped behavior, which is usually biologically based (not learned), that is often the response to a very specific stimulus (a sign stimulus).

Flake tool: a stone tool made from a flake chipped off a core; flakes are generally not as long as blades.

Flora: plants (see also fauna).

Florisbad: a late Pleistocene fossil hominine site in South Africa.

Forebrain: the most forward of the three swellings at the head end of the nerve cord. In the early vertebrates, this area dealt solely with olfaction (smell), but later development of this part of the brain into the cerebrum led to its increasing importance in mediating and initiating behavior.

Fort Ternan: a middle Miocene site in western Kenya where *Kenyapithecus wickeri* fossils have been uncovered.

Fossorial: an animal adaptation based on burrowing or digging.

Founder's effect: one form of genetic drift that results when the founders of a new population do not carry all the alleles present in the original population.

Frugivorous: subsisting on a diet of fruit.

Gathering/hunting: the adaptation of nonagricultural humans that is founded on the gathering of eatable wild vegetation, insects, and small animals and the hunting of larger animals. Gathering and hunting characterized all humans prior to the invention of agriculture, although how far back in time a modern, humanlike gathering/hunting way of life extends beyond that is a matter of debate.

Gauss Normal: a long period of normal earth magnetic polarity that ranged from about 3.3 to about 2.4 million years B.P. Preceding the Gauss Normal Epoch was the Gilbert Reversed Epoch and following it was the Matuyama Reversed Epoch.

Gene: the sequence of DNA that results in the production of a functioning protein or a subunit of a protein.

Gene flow: the movement of genes from one population into another; an evolutionary force.

Gene frequency: the frequency of a gene or an allele in a population.

Gene pool: all the genes possessed by members of a population.

Genetic drift: fluctuations in the frequency of an allele due to chance; an evolutionary force.

Genetic fitness: a measure of the reproductive capability of a genotype.

Genetic markers: detectable genetic variations that can be traced across generations and population boundaries.

Genetic polymorphism: the existence of more than one allele for a trait (see also balanced polymorphism and transient polymorphism).

Genotype: the alleles that one possesses for a particular trait (see also phenotype).

Genus: a category of the taxonomic system above species but below subfamily. Scientific convention requires that valid genus names be written in italics.

Geographic isolation: the division of one species into two or more subgroups by a geographic barrier that prevents breeding. A prerequisite for cladogenesis. Allows for the evolution of behaviorally and/or biologically based reproductive isolation.

Gibraltar: the site at which several neandertal fossils, including a child's bones, have been discovered.

Gigantopithecus: an extinct hominoid characterized by the huge size of its chewing teeth. Known from deposits in India and south China, and extending in time from the late Miocene to the early Pleistocene, *Gigantopithecus* has often been placed with *Sivapithecus* in the family Sivapithecidae because of similarities in their teeth.

Glacial: over the last two million or so years, changes in planetary climate have led to the periodic advance and retreat of glaciers or ice sheets in many parts of the northern hemisphere. Those times when the climate cooled and glaciers advanced are known as glacial times, while the intervening times of warming and retreat are termed interglacials.

Globins: a family of proteins, the manufacture of which is directed by a family of genes related through evolution. Humans produce different globins at different stages of ontogeny.

Gluteus medius: one of three gluteal muscles of the human buttocks region, which with *Gluteus minimus,* begins on the pelvic blade and runs downward, passing to the outside of the hip joint socket and attaching to the top of the thighbone. In bipedalism, these muscles function to stabilize the pelvis when one leg leaves the ground during stride.

Gluteus minimus: see *gluteus medius*.

Goiter: an enlargement of the thyroid, a gland important in regulating metabolism. Goiters can be caused by several different factors, such as too much PTC or too little iodine.

Gondwanaland: the imaginative name used to describe the continents of South America, Africa, Australia, Antarctica, and the South Asian subcontinent during the late Paleozoic and Mesozoic, when they were part of one large connected land mass.

Grade: a level of organization based on the presence of common biological features and used in assessing different evolutionary lines of animals.

Grooming claw: the clawed index toe on the feet of many prosimians, whose remaining fingers and toes are all equipped with nails.

Group selection: in sociobiology, a model of evolution in which natural selection operates on a number of animals as a group, rather than on the features of an individual, which is the traditional Darwinian level upon which natural selection is thought to operate.

Growth distance: the amount of growth up to a point in time.

Growth velocity: the rate of growth.

GSP 15000: a late Miocene *Sivapithecus* face and dentition found in the Potwar Plateau of Pakistan. Its features show many resemblances to the orangutan.

Hadar: an area of rich early hominine fossil-bearing deposits in the Afar region of north-central Ethiopia and ranging in time from 2.9 to greater than 3.2 million years B.P. Hominines found at this site, along with those from Laetoli, have been placed in the taxonomic category *Australopithecus afarensis*.

Half-life: the time it takes for half of a radioactive isotope to decay to its byproduct; for example, for Carbon-14 to decay to nitrogen.

Hand ax: a teardrop-shaped stone tool found in archaeological sites through most of the Old World. Characteristic of the Acheulian industry.

Haplotypes: combinations of genetic traits that can be inherited as a block due to their presence on the same chromosome.

Hard palate: the structure separating the oral and nasal cavities; composed of bone in mammals.

Hardy-Weinberg equilibrium: an idealization of the behavior of alleles in a population. This model predicts the frequency of the various phenotypes and genotypes in the absence of selection, mutation, drift, and admixture.

Harris lines: dense transverse areas or lines appearing in the bones of people who have encountered periods of arrested growth.

Haua Fteah: a late Pleistocene fossil hominine site in Libya in North Africa.

Heel strike: in human walking, a stride is taken and distance is covered when the foot swings forward and leaves the ground at toe off. The defined end of the swing phase, when the foot regains the ground, is marked by the heel touching first, thus, heel strike.

Helix: a spiral. DNA occurs as a double helix—two spirals twisting around each other.

Hemoglobin: the most abundant protein inside the red blood cell; it serves to transport oxygen. Hemoglobin is composed of globin protein plus iron (heme).

Hemolysis: the destruction of red blood cells.

Hemolytic anemia: reduced oxygen-carrying ability of the blood due to destruction of red blood cells.

Herbivorous: subsisting on a diet of vegetable material.

Heritability: the ratio of genetically caused variation in a trait to the total amount of variation observed for that trait in a particular population at a particular time. It is abbreviated h^2.

Heterodont: a dentition composed of specialized kinds of teeth that serve a variety of functions. In most mammals, incisors, canines, premolars, and molars can be distinguished.

Heterozygote: an individual who has two different alleles for a given trait; for example, a person who has one A and one O allele for the ABO blood group (see also homozygote).

Hexian: a middle Pleistocene *Homo erectus* site in central China.

Hindbrain: the most posterior (nearest the nerve cord) of the three swellings that mark the beginnings of the vertebrate brain. Originally, the hindbrain dealt with hearing, balance, and muscular coordination.

Histocompatibility antigens: proteins that are markers of immunological individuality; important in tissue transplantation.

HLA: see histocompatibility antigens.

Holism: the anthropological perspective emphasizing the importance of the whole and the interaction of biological and/or cultural factors in human phenomena.

Home range: the geographical area occupied by a group of animals.

Hominidae: a primate family that includes two subfamilies; the Paninae (chimpanzees and gorillas) and the Homininae (humans and our extinct bipedal ancestors). This use of the family Hominidae is a relatively recent development in physical anthropology, and other textbooks and much of the scholarly literature still refer to the Hominidae as the family of humans and our bipedal ancestors.

Homininae: the taxonomic subfamily within the order Primates that includes modern humans and our extinct close ancestors.

Hominine: the descriptive term for a member of the primate subfamily Homininae, composed of modern humans and our extinct bipedal ancestors.

Hominoidea: a taxonomic superfamily within the order Primates, composed of the lesser and greater apes and humans. Members of this superfamily are called hominoids.

Homodont: a dentition having teeth of only one type; characteristic of lower vertebrates.

Homo erectus: the fossil hominine group that occupied much of the temperate and tropical Old World, except perhaps Europe, from about 1.5 million to 3–400,000 years B.P.

Homo habilis: the taxonomic name for a number of hominine fossils found mainly at Olduvai Gorge in Tanzania and East Turkana in Kenya, and dated from about 2 to 1.5 million years B.P. They are distinguished from members of the genus *Australopithecus* by a larger brain size, a smaller-sized posterior dentition, and a dental arcade more similar to that of later hominines.

Homologous chromosomes: the members of a chromosome pair, i.e., chromosomes having the same gene loci.

Homologous genes or proteins: molecules, found in different species, that are descended from a common ancestor. Homologous molecules usually evidence a degree of similarity in structure and/or function.

Homo sapiens: literally "sapient man," or "wise humans," it is the genus and species of modern humans. Members of *Homo sapiens* first appear in the fossil record between 300,000 and 400,000 years ago B.P.

Homo sapiens neanderthalensis: an extinct subspecies of *Homo sapiens* composed of those early or archaic sapiens, known as neandertals, who lived in Europe and the Middle East from before 100,000 years ago to about 30,000 years ago. Note that in this taxonomic term, the now obsolete spelling of neandertal with an *h* must be retained, since this was the spelling when the category *neanderthalensis* was first established more than 130 years ago.

Homo sapiens sapiens: the subspecies of living humans, as distinguished from now extinct *Homo sapiens* subspecies such as *Homo sapiens neanderthalensis*.

Homozygote: an individual who has two identical alleles for a given trait; for example, a person who has two O alleles for the ABO blood group (see also heterozygote).

Humerus: the bone of the upper arm.

Hyoid: a horseshoe-shaped bone suspended from the base of the skull and forming part of the system of ligaments and muscles that control tongue movement.

Hypoplasia, dental: improper tooth development resulting in the pitting and discoloration of the enamel.

Hypoxia: oxygen starvation; often encountered when first arriving at high altitudes.

Ileret: fossil-rich deposits north of the Koobi Fora Peninsula east of Lake Turkana in northern Kenya, where a number of early hominine fossils have been found.

Ilium: the blade of the pelvis.

Immunoglobins: classes of antibodies.

Immunological memory: the ability of the immune system to remember how to produce a specific antibody.

Inbreeding: breeding between genetic relatives, which results in a decrease in heterozygosity.

Initiation codon: a three-base sequence found at the start of every gene.

Innate releasing mechanism: a term used by animal behaviorists to describe the way a specific sensory perception (sign stimulus) unvaryingly leads to a stereotyped behavior (fixed action pattern).

Innominate: the pelvis is made up of three bones, the right and left innominate and the sacrum, which fits between the two innominate bones at the back.

Insectivorous: subsisting on a diet of insects.

Intelligence: a term used both to indicate differences in reasoning ability and mental processing of modern humans and to describe the characteristic flexibility in the behavior of mammals based on their ability to construct a perceptual model of reality during the prolonged period of infant dependency.

Intergenic: between the genes. Long sequences of DNA separate the genes in most eucaryotes.

Interglacial: the time between glacial periods when the climate warmed and the glaciers retreated.

Interstadial: a relatively brief interval of warming within a major glaciation.

Intron: a sequence of bases that interrupts the coding portions of a gene. Also called intervening sequence or IVS (see also exon).

Ischial callosity: an area on the buttocks of Old World monkeys that is covered by an insensitive layer of connective tissue that allows the animal to sit for long periods without discomfort and without limiting blood supply to the lower limb.

Isolate: a genetically isolated group; one evidencing little interbreeding with other groups.

Jebel Irhoud: a late Pleistocene fossil hominine site in Morocco.

Kabuh Formation: an early/middle Pleistocene geologic deposit on the island of Java, Indonesia, in which a number of *Homo erectus* fossils have been found.

Kabwe: a fossil hominine skull from Zambia, southern Africa, which may date to 200,000 years B.P. Along with the Bodo and Saldhanha Bay specimens, it can be considered an African representative of early *Homo sapiens*. It was formerly known as the Broken Hill skull.

Kalambo Falls: a middle Pleistocene site in southern Africa.

Kalodirr: an early Miocene locale west of Lake Turkana, northern Kenya, where *Afropithecus* and *Turkanapithecus* fossils have been found.

Kanapoi: a site in western Kenya where a hominine arm bone was found and dated to about 4.5 million years B.P.

Karyotype: an illustration of the chromosomes of a cell.

Kenyapithecus wickeri: the fragmentary jaws and teeth of a hominoid primate from the site of Fort Ternan in western Kenya. Dated to the middle Miocene, it may represent the hominoid ancestor of the hominids.

Kibish Formation: a geological formation along the Omo River in southern Ethiopia in which a number of fragmentary archaic *Homo sapiens* fossils have been found.

Kin selection: a concept suggested by sociobiologists to account for behaviors that might otherwise be unexplainable. It suggests that acts of altruism or other self-sacrificing behaviors can be understood not by considering the perspective of the individual who performs the action but rather by examining the genetic benefits to the relatives of the actor.

Klasies River Mouth Cave: a late Pleistocene archaeological site on the Indian Ocean in South Africa with fragmentary hominine fossils that are difficult to interpret.

KNM-ER 406: a fossil hominine skull from east of Lake Turkana, Kenya, dated to about 1.5 to 1.6 million years B.P. It is a member of the species *Australopithecus boisei*.

KNM-ER 1470: a fossil hominine skull from east of Lake Turkana, Kenya, probably dated at about 1.8 million years B.P. It possesses a large brain but also apparently large teeth.

KNM-ER 1590: a fossil hominine skull from east of Lake Turkana, Kenya; enigmatic because of the combination of a large brain with large teeth.

KNM-ER 1813: a fossil hominine skull from east of Lake Turkana, Kenya; enigmatic because of the combination of a small brain with small teeth.

KNM-ER 3733: a fossil hominine skull from east of Lake Turkana, Kenya, dated at about 1.5 to 1.6 million years B.P. It is an early *Homo erectus* specimen.

KNM-WT 15000: the almost complete skeleton of a *Homo erectus* youth discovered west of Lake Turkana, Kenya.

KNM-WT 17000: a robust australopithecine skull from west of Lake Turkana, Kenya. Because it is dated earlier than other robust australopithecines, opinion is divided as to whether it should be placed in *A. boisei* or in its own species, *A. aethiopicus*.

Knuckle-walking: the distinctive terrestrial movement pattern of chimpanzees and gorillas in which the front limbs rest on the second knuckles of the hand.

Koobi Fora: a peninsula east of Lake Turkana in northern Kenya on which a large number of important early hominine fossils, including KNM-ER 1470, KNM-ER 1590, and KNM-ER 1813, have been uncovered.

Kow Swamp: a late Pleistocene site in Australia.

Krapina: a late Pleistocene neandertal site in Yugoslavia.

Kromdraai: one of the early hominine sites in the Sterkfontein Valley, South Africa, from which robust australopithecines have been recovered.

Kuru: a fatal viral disease transmitted by cannibalism.

Kwashiorkor: protein deficiency disease.

La Chapelle-aux-Saints: neandertal site in France.

Laetoli: an early hominine fossil site in Tanzania dated to about 3.6 million years B.P. Hominines from this site are grouped with those from Hadar and placed in the taxonomic category *Australopithecus afarensis*.

La Ferassie: a rock shelter in France that yielded a number of neandertal fossils.

Lake Turkana: a large lake, fed by the Omo River, with its northern shores on the border between Ethiopia and Kenya. Its eastern and western shores are a treasure house of fossil-rich deposits that range in age from less than 1 million years ago to more than 15 million years ago.

Lantian: a *Homo erectus* site in central China.

La Quina: a neandertal site in France.

Laurasia: the name given to the continents of North America and Eurasia when, from the late Paleozoic through the early Cenozoic, they were part of one large continental mass connected across northeastern North America and western Europe.

Law of independent assortment: the Mendelian principle that different, segregating (unlinked) gene pairs are independent in their movement into sex cells during meiosis.

Law of segregation: the Mendelian principle that members of a pair of homologous chromosomes enter separate cells during meiosis.

Le Moustier: a neandertal site in southern France. The site has given its name to the Middle Paleolithic Mousterian industry.

Leukocyte: white blood cells, important in immune response.

Limnopithecus: one of a number of small-bodied early Miocene hominoids from East Africa.

Linkage: the close assocation of two or more genes for different traits on the same chromosome.

Linkage disequilibrium: greater or less than random occurrence of a particular combination of linked genes.

Living floor: the remains of a surface where hominines lived at some point in the past and that is excavated by archaeologists.

Lobe-fins: bony fishes of the order Crossopterygii with modifications of the lateral fins for support during bottom-feeding and locomotion. The ancestral group from which the land vertebrates probably evolved.

Locus (plural: loci): the position on a chromosome occupied by a particular gene.

Loph: the ridge that connects two cusps on the surface of a molar. See bilophodont.

Lothagam Hill: a fossil locale in western Kenya where a small fragment of an australopithecine lower jaw was found in a context dated to 5.5 million years B.P.

"Lucy": the name given by its discoverer, Donald Johanson, to the most complete australopithecine fossil skeleton yet found. An adult female, it is better known to scientists by its catalogue number: AL-288. "Lucy" has been placed in *Australopithecus afarensis.*

Lufeng: a fossil site in south China where some rather complete, although smashed, fossil bones of *Sivapithecus* have been uncovered.

Lumbar curve: an acute curve, characteristic of bipeds, in the lower part of the back where the bones of the spinal column join the pelvis.

Maba: a late Pleistocene, early *Homo sapiens* site in China.

Macromutations: hypothetical mutations that are capable of changing one species into another very rapidly.

Maka: an early hominine site in north-central Ethiopia where a fragmentary hominine thighbone have been found and dated to about 4.0 million years B.P.

Makapansgat: an australopithecine site in the northern Transvaal, South Africa.

Maramus: calorie deficiency.

Marsupial: pouched mammals.

Masseter: one of the major chewing muscles, which runs from the arch (zygomatic arch) on the side of the skull to the bottom outside edge of the lower jaw.

Matuyama Reversed Epoch: a long epoch of reversed planetary magnetic polarity that began about 2.4 million years ago and ended about 730,000 years ago with the beginning of the current period of normal polarity, the Bruhnes Normal Epoch. The Matuyama/Bruhnes boundary is often used as a marker to separate the early and middle Pleistocene.

Mauer: the Mauer or Heidelberg jaw, representing either a European *Homo erectus* or, more probably, an early *H. sapiens,* that was found at Mauer near Heidelberg, Germany.

Meiosis: the process that results in the formation of sex cells. During meiosis, members of the chromosome pairs separate and enter different sex cells; therefore, each sex cell has one-half the number of chromosomes found in other cells.

Melanin: a dark pigment present in many human cells, including skin, hair, and eyes.

Melanocyte: a cell that produces melanin.

Menarche: the onset of menstruation.

Microevolution: small-scale evolutionary changes, often the changes in the frequency of a gene resulting from natural selection, genetic drift, mutation, and/or admixture.

Micropithecus: one of a number of small-bodied early Miocene hominoids from East Africa.

Midbrain: the second swelling at the head end of the nerve cord. In the midbrain of early vertebrates, motor responses were initiated and sensory information terminated. In mammals the midbrain is largely bypassed.

Mitochondrial DNA (mtDNA): the genetic material (DNA) that is found in the mitochondrion of the cell and not in the cell nucleus; this DNA is inherited only from one's mother. The rate of change of mtDNA is much faster than that of nuclear DNA, which makes it more suitable for analyses of recent evolutionary developments.

Mitochondrion: the structure within a cell in which energy is produced.

Mitosis: the process by which chromosomes replicate in the cell before division, thus retaining the number of chromosomes in each new cell.

Mladeč: a site in Czechoslovakia where the earliest modern human remains from Europe have been discovered.

Molecular clock: the dating technique based on the belief that if a molecule evolves at a constant rate, then the degree of molecular divergence between living species can be used as a clock to date past evolutionary events. Not all agree to the existence of such a clock.

Monophyletic: the evolutionary development of a group of animals from a single ancestral species.

Monotreme: an egg-laying mammal.

Monozygotic (MZ) twins: genetically identical twins.

Monte Circeo: Italian name for Circe's Mountain, where a cave was found with a neandertal skull in the center of a stone ring.

Morphological variability: the variation in biological features in all sexually reproducing animals, ranging from the obvious, such as height, weight, and hair color; to the not-so-obvious, such as expression of molar cusp differences; to the invisible-to-the-eye, such as ABO blood groups and nerve cells in the brain. It is on this variation that natural selection operates.

Mount Carmel: the site of two neighboring caves, Skhūl and Tabūn, outside of Haifa in northern Israel, where a series of important late Pleistocene hominine fossils associated with Mousterian tools have been found.

Mousterian: a Middle Paleolithic flake-tool industry, usually, but not always, associated with neandertal fossils.

Mutagen: anything that can cause mutations.

Mutation: a change in the genetic material; an evolutionary force. Mutations are usually very small alterations involving the change of only one DNA base.

Mutationism: the disproved theory that major evolutionary changes represent single, major mutations.

Napak: an early Miocene site in Uganda yielding a fragment of a fossil primate skull and a tooth. The tooth is bilophodont like the molars of Old World monkeys, and may represent the earliest documented appearance of these primates.

Nariokotome: a locale on the west side of Lake Turkana in Kenya, where the almost complete skeleton of a *Homo erectus* youth (KNM-WT 15000) was found.

Natural selection: the differential reproduction of genotypes; the mechanism proposed by Darwin and Wallace to underlie much evolutionary change; often misstated as "survival of the fittest" rather than "reproduction of the fittest."

Neandertal: a descriptive term given to archaic *Homo sapiens* who lived during the later part of the last interglacial and the early part of the last glacial (Würm) in eastern and western Europe and in the Middle East. They may or may not have been the direct ancestors of living Europeans.

Neandertal phase of man: a theory suggesting an evolutionary trend all over the Old World, from *Homo erectus* to modern *Homo sapiens,* which includes a neandertal phase.

Neander Valley: the cave site in Germany where a skeleton was discovered in 1856 and that gave its name to the neandertal fossil group.

Neotony: the retention of infantile characteristics into adulthood.

Ngandong: a village on the Solo River in eastern Java in Indonesia near where a number of fossil hominines, known as the Solo sample, were found. It is also the name given to deposits that overlie and are therefore younger than both the Pucangan and Kabuh Formations.

Nocturnal: referring to activity during the night.

Nuclear family: a social unit composed of an adult male, adult female, and dependent young. This unit is characteristic of modern humans and some nonhuman primates, such as the gibbon.

Nucleic acids: DNA and RNA.

Nucleotides: the building blocks of nucleic acids made of carbon, nitrogen, a sugar, and phosphate. DNA is composed of the nucleotides adenine, thymine, cytosine, and guanine. In RNA uracil substitutes for thymine.

Nucleus: the structure inside an eucaryotic cell that contains the chromosomes.

Objective: based on observable phenomena and uninfluenced by personal prejudice and emotion.

Occipital chignon: the bony occipital protuberance found on some European neandertals.

Occlusion: the precise interdigitation between the teeth in the upper jaw and lower jaw.

OH-9: *Homo erectus* skull cap from Upper Bed II, Olduvai Gorge, Tanzania.

Oldowan: a cobble-tool industry, known from a number of sites in East Africa and representative of the earliest stone tools manufactured by hominines.

Olduvai events: several short-lived periods of normal earth magnetic polarity within the long Matuyama Epoch of reversed polarity. Occurring at about 1.6 million years B.P., these events are used as the marker between the Pliocene and succeeding Pleistocene.

Olduvai Gorge: a deep gorge in northern Tanzania, East Africa, where Mary and Louis Leakey have excavated a number of early hominine fossils, stone tools, and living floors. Very recently, Donald Johanson and Tim White have uncovered a fragmentary *Homo habilis* skeleton there.

Olorgesailie: a large series of Acheulian sites near Nairobi, Kenya.

Omnivorous: subsisting on a diet of both animal and vegetable materials.

Omo: a river basin in southern Ethiopia where a number of australopithecine fossils have been discovered in particularly well-dated deposits. Also found along the Omo River but in layers of much more recent date, are the remains of three archaic *Homo sapiens*.

Ontogeny: the course of development of an individual from conception to death (see also phylogeny).

Opposability: the ability of most primates to bring the thumb into contact with the tips of the other fingers on the same hand in order to grasp objects.

Paleoanthropology: the study of human evolution.

Paleolithic: the stone age, which is usually divided into three units, the Lower, Middle, and Upper.

Paleomagnetic epoch: long intervals of time when the polarity of the earth remains mostly in one orientation (see Bruhnes Normal and Matuyama Reversed Epoch).

Paleomagnetic events: short-lived periods of polarity change within a longer period of opposite magnetic polarity (see Olduvai events).

Paleomagnetic reversals: times when the earth's magnetic polarity shifts 180 degrees. During times of normal polarity, a compass needle points to magnetic north, while at times of reversed polarity, the needle would be directed to magnetic south.

Paleomagnetism: the determination of the changes of orientation of the earth's magnetic polarity over time. Periodically in the earth's history, the planet's magnetic polarity has reversed and has remained so for varying lengths of time. These paleomagnetic episodes are the basis for a technique often employed in dating early hominine sites.

Paleontology: the study of extinct life.

Paleopathology: the study of ancient diseases, as found in fossil bones or mummies.

Paleospecies: see chronospecies.

Paninae: the taxonomic subfamily within the order Primates that includes chimpanzees, gorillas, and their close ancestors.

Paranthropus robustus: the term first applied by Robert Broom to the robust australopithecine fossils found at the sites of Kromdraai and Swartkrans in South Africa. Although most anthropologists now place these fossils in the genus *Australopithecus* with the separate species name *robustus,* several scientists continue to maintain that *Paranthropus* is a more appropriate placement for these fossils.

Pebble tool: a stone tool that uses a pebble or cobble as its core. (A pebble or cobble is a stone worn smooth by the action of water or sand.)

Pedomorphism: in ontogeny, the retention of a juvenile feature into adulthood.

Peninj: a fossil site at Lake Natron, northern Tanzania, where a robust australopithecine jaw was discovered.

Perigordian: an upper Paleolithic tool industry characterized by a high frequency of blade tools, which seems to have evolved form the Mousterian industry about 35,000 to 40,000 years B.P.

Petralona: a middle Pleistocene fossil hominine skull from Greece. Although the skull has a number of features relating it to both late *Homo erectus* and early *Homo sapiens,* it is usually placed in the latter category.

Phenotype: the observable or testable appearance of an organism for a particular trait. If dominance is not present for the alleles controlling the trait and if the trait is genetically controlled, the phenotype is the same as the genotype. If the alleles do exhibit dominance, the homozygous dominant and the heterozygote have the same phenotype but different genotypes. The homozygous recessive exhibits a different phenotype.

Phosphate bond: the chemical bond found in the DNA backbone.

Phyletic gradualism: Darwin's view of the action of evolution as a slow but constant change in biological features generation after generation.

Phylogeny: the evolutionary development of a species.

Physiological fitness: a person's state of health, particularly in reference to a stress such as heat, cold, high altitude, or overcrowding.

Piltdown hoax: a carefully assembled fossil fraud. The fossil, a cranium of a modern human with a lower jaw of an orangutan with typical humanlike tooth wear patterns, was not totally dismissed as fraudulent until 1953, about 40 years after its "discovery."

"Pithecanthropus erectus": "erect apeman." Name given to hominine fossils discovered by Eugene Dubois on the island of Java; later this name was changed to *Homo erectus.*

Pituitary gland: the gland under the brain that is important in the regulation of many body processes.

Placenta: the organ providing for the exchange of material between mother and fetus.

Placoderms: an extinct class of primitive vertebrates characterized by heavy armor plating at the head end and a movable jaw.

Plasmodium: a genus of parasites that cause various types of malaria.

Plasticity: the ability to produce a variable phenotype in different environments.

Platyrrhini: the New World higher primates; the platyrrhines are the monkeys of Central and South America, and include the spider, howler, and night monkeys as well as the marmosets.

Pleiotropy: the ability of one gene to influence more than one trait.

Plesiadapiformes: a major suborder of wholly extinct Primates that includes the primitive early members of this order from the Cretaceous and Paleocene periods.

Plesiadapis: a primitive mammal of the Paleocene with biological structures of the limbs adapting it for life in the trees. It is thought by many to be a very primitive member of the primate order.

"Plesianthropus transvaalensis": taxonomic term originally given by Robert Broom to the fossil hominines from the Sterkfontein site in South Africa. These fossils are now placed in the category *Australopithecus africanus.*

Pliopithecus: a small-sized Miocene fossil hominoid that bears some resemblances to the gibbon but whose skeletal features, like a tail, make it difficult to relate it as the direct ancestor of the living lesser apes.

Polygenic trait: a characteristic influenced by more than one set of alleles.

Polymorphism: genetic variability for a trait.

Population: ideally, those members of a species that share a common gene pool.

Post-orbital bar: a rim of bone around the outside of the eye orbit that provides a measure of protection to the eyes. It is commonly found in the prosimians, while anthropoid primates possess not only bars but also totally enclosed bony orbits.

Potassium-argon (K-Ar dating): dating method applied to rocks that contain the radioactive isotope K^{40}, which decays slowly to its byproduct argon. Since the half-life of K^{40} is much greater than that of C^{14}, this method can be used to date deposits at much older fossil sites.

Precipitate: to cause to come out of a solution; a solid that comes out of a solution during a chemical reaction.

Predators: animals, especially carnivores, that prey on other animals.

Předmostí: a fossil hominine site in Czechoslovakia yielding the remains of 46 individuals buried in a common grave. These early anatomically modern humans, found with Upper Paleolithic tools, show a great deal of morphological variability.

Prehensile tail: a tail that can grasp objects like a fifth limb. It is a unique characteristic of some New World monkeys.

Primatology: the study of primates.

Probe: a radioactively labeled piece of single-stranded DNA of known structure that can be used to isolate its complementary strand.

Procaryote: an organism that lacks nuclei.

Proconsul: an early Miocene fossil hominoid from East Africa. Possessing a number of primitive features of the skull and teeth, *Proconsul* may be the descendant of the earlier *Aegyptopithecus* of the North African Oligocene.

Prognathism: having jaws that project in front of the braincase.

Prosimians: with the anthropoids, one of the subdivisions of the primates. The living prosimians are the lemurs, indriids, and aye-aye, all on the island of Madagascar; the loris group, including the bush babies of Africa and Asia and the cheirogalids of Madagascar; and the tarsiers of southeast Asia.

Protein: a molecule composed of long chains of amino acids. The function of the genetic material is to direct the production of proteins.

Pseudogene: a gene that contains one or more defects that prevents it from producing a protein.

Pucangan Formation: an early Pleistocene geologic deposit on the island of Java, Indonesia. Several *Homo erectus* fossil specimens (underlying, and thus older than the Kabuh deposits), have been discovered in the upper parts of the formation and dated to about 1 million years B.P.

Punctuated equilibria: a view of evolution that contrasts with traditional Darwinian concepts of gradual change. It pictures the evolution of animals as long periods of little or no change (statis) punctuated by very short intervals of rapid change resulting in new species.

Purgatorius: a fossil mammal from Cretaceous and Paleocene deposits in Montana; thought to be the earliest evidence of the evolution of the primates.

Qafzeh: a cave site in the Galilee in Israel with fossil hominines whose attributes are much like those of modern humans and are dated at about 90,000 years B.P. The fossils are associated with Mousterian tools.

Qualitative traits: see discontinuous traits.

Quantitative traits: see continuous traits.

Rabat: a *Homo erectus* site in Morocco, North Africa.

Radius: a bone of the lower arm (on the thumb side).

Rafting: a term used in evolutionary studies to describe the accidental spread of an animal species from one land mass across a body of water to another land mass. Rafting is used descriptively only and does not imply a deliberate, planned movement by a species.

"Ramapithecus": a fossil hominoid from middle and late Miocene deposits of the Siwalik Hills of north India and Pakistan. At one time "Ramapithecus" was thought to be an early member of the human subfamily Homininae, but additional fossil discoveries have now shown that it is a small form of the Miocene genus *Sivapithecus*, into which "Ramapithecus" has been incorporated.

Rangwapithecus: one of a number of early Miocene hominoids from East Africa.

Recessive: the masking of one allele for a trait by the presence of another allele. The latter allele is said to be dominant to the former.

Recombinant DNA: DNA that is constructed in a laboratory so as to be part viral and part from a species under study, e.g., human.

Recombination: the formation of new combinations of genes at separate loci on a chromosome as a result of crossing over.

Red blood cells: those cells that carry oxygen through the bloodstream. The red color comes from the protein hemoglobin inside the cells. Many other proteins are found within the red cells. The molecules determining one's blood type are found on the outside surface of the cells. Red blood cells are also called erythrocytes.

Reflectance spectrophotometer: a machine that measures the amount of light of a specific wavelength reflected by a surface. It is used in the study of skin and hair color.

Regional continuity: a model of late Pleistocene human evolution that views modern human populations as originating from the archaic *Homo sapiens* that immediately preceded them in time. This theory stresses local continuity between earlier hominines and modern humans.

Regulatory gene: a gene that regulates the functioning of another gene by turning it on or off.

Reproductive isolation: the inability of members of two species to mate and produce viable offspring for biological or behaviorial reasons.

Reproductive strategy: a strategy for maintaining adult population numbers adopted by different groups of animals. For example, the strategy among many mammals is to limit the number of offspring produced but at the same time to insure survival of these offspring to reproductive maturity by providing postnatal (after birth) nurturing.

Restriction endonuclease: an enzyme, such as Eco RI, that cuts DNA wherever a particular base sequence occurs; also called restriction enzymes.

Restriction enzyme map: a chart showing the distribution of various restriction enzyme sites within a piece of DNA.

Restriction Fragment Length Polymorphism (RFLP): a variable genetic trait resulting from the presence or absence of a restriction site.

Retrodiction: a form of prediction; making a statement about the outcome of a past event but about which information is currently unavailable.

Rift Valley System: a geological feature beginning in the Middle East and stretching southward through East Africa.

RNA: ribonucleic acid, a chemical similar in structure to DNA. The two types of RNA considered are messenger RNA, which transcribes the genetic information from the DNA and carries it to the site of protein manufacture; and transfer RNA, which incorporates amino acids into their proper position in a protein.

Saccopastore: a late Pleistocene archaic *Homo sapiens* site in Italy.

Sacrum: a bone of the pelvis that fits in the back between the two innominate bones.

Sagittal crest: a bony crest or ridge on the top of the skull of some apes and the robust australopithecines, to which the large *temporalis* chewing muscles attach.

Šala: a fossil hominine frontal bone found in Czechoslovakia. It possesses features reminiscent of both neandertals and anatomically modern humans.

Saldanha Bay: a hominine skullcap from the west coast of South Africa. Along with the Kabwe and Bodo fossils, it can be considered an African representative of early *Homo sapiens*.

Salé: a partial skull from the site of Salé in Morocco, North Africa. Dated to the middle Pleistocene, it appears to be a representative of early *Homo sapiens*.

San: the correct name for the living human groups of gatherer/hunters of the Kalahari Desert of southern Africa. Formerly called "Bushmen."

Sangiran: a fossil locale on the island of Java, Indonesia, from which a large number of *Homo erectus* fossils have been recovered.

Scapula: the shoulder blade.

Sciatic notch: a strongly angulated sciatic notch is characteristic of the pelvis of bipeds; it is the result of the shortening and broadening of the pelvis.

Secretor: a genetically determined trait that determines whether water soluble forms of one's ABO molecules are found in body fluids as well as on the surface of red blood cells.

Sectorial premolar: the first lower premolar of monkeys and apes, which has only one cusp (pointed and caninelike) and thus differs from the first lower premolar of modern humans, which has two fairly flat cusps.

Secular trend: a trend over time; often applied to growth and development phenomena.

Semi-species: populations that are in the process of becoming separate biological species.

Sex linkage: genes that are carried on the sex chromosomes.

Sexual dimorphism: the differences between males and females of the same species.

Shanidar: a cave site in Iraq from which nine neandertals have been recovered.

Shovel-shaped incisors: upper incisor teeth reinforced with extra enamel at their edges on the tongue side.

Sickle-cell anemia: an inability of the blood to carry sufficient oxygen because of homozygosity for the sickle-cell allele.

Sickle cells: red blood cells that have "collapsed" and assumed a sicklelike appearance. This phenomenon occurs most markedly in people homozygous for the sickle-cell allele for hemoglobin type.

Side chain: a variable region in the chemical structure of amino acids. Each amino acid has a different side chain.

Sidi Abderrahman: see Rabat.

Sign stimulus: an action, sign, or other sensory stimulus that, when received by an animal, results in a characteristically stereotyped behavior (fixed action pattern).

"Sinanthropus pekinensis: a category established for the hominine fossils found at the cave site of Zhoukoudian in China. These fossils are now placed in *Homo erectus*.

Single species hypothesis: a disproved notion that all the australopithecines were members of a single species; morphological differences among the various fossils were ascribed to sexual dimorphism as well as to geographic and temporal differences.

Sivapithecidae: a family of Miocene hominoids that includes the genera *Sivapithecus* and *Gigantopithecus*.

Sivapithecus: Miocene hominoids known from discoveries in north India, Pakistan, south China, and perhaps Europe. "Ramapithecus" is now included within this genus. *Sivapithecus* shares a number of characteristics of the jaws and teeth with *Gigantopithecus*. It seems likely that *Sivapithecus* is the direct ancestor of the orangutan.

Siwaliks: the western foothills of the Himalayas in northern India and Pakistan. Large numbers of Miocene hominoids have been discovered in the Siwaliks.

Skhūl: a cave site at Mount Carmel in Israel. Hominine fossil remains, associated with the Mousterian industry, of at least ten individuals that were excavated there show a great deal of morphological variability, some of which is reminiscent of neandertals and some of which is characteristic of anatomically modern humans.

Socialization: the process of learning the normative behaviors of a group or society.

Sociobiology: a perspective within the study of animal behavior that seeks explanations for various patterns of animal behavior and adaptation within the context of the processes of natural selection.

Solo sample: eleven skulls and two shinbones found along the Solo River near the village of Ngandong. The age of these bones is unclear and morphologically they can either be early sapiens or late *Homo erectus;* they are usually placed in the former category.

Southern blot: a means to immobilize DNA on a filter to allow further analysis. Named after its inventor, E. Southern.

Species: the smallest working unit in taxonomy (see also biological species and chrono-species).

Spy: A neandertal site in Belgium.

Stable isotope analysis: a method of dietary reconstruction based on the identification of various isotopes of elements such as oxygen, nitrogen, and carbon. These isotopes are present in varying amounts in different plants, and their identification in an animal bone can reveal details about the animal's diet.

St. Acheul: a French village that lends its name to the Lower Paleolithic stone tool industry, the Acheulian, which is characterized by a high frequency of hand axes.

Stance phase: in the human bipedal stride, the leg that remains on the ground, supporting the body, is said to be in stance phase.

St.-Césaire: a site in southern France with a neandertal in association with Upper Paleolithic tools of the Châtelperronian industry.

Steatopygia: a genetically influenced increased deposition of fat in the buttocks.

Steinheim: a badly crushed hominine skull from the village of Steinheim in Germany. Dating to the latter part of the middle Pleistocene, it is probably an early representative of *Homo sapiens*.

Stereoscopic vision: the depth-perceiving vision that enables the eyes to look forward and focus together on an object.

Sterkfontein: an australopithecine site in the Sterkfontein Valley, Transvaal, South Africa.

Sternum: the breastbone, to which the ribs and the collarbone (clavicle) attach at the front of the ribcage.

Sticky ends: short segments of single-strand DNA often produced after DNA is treated with a restriction endonuclease.

Straight-line evolution: see anagenesis.

Stressor: an agent that disrupts the body's state of equilibrium; anything that causes stress.

Striding gait: the characteristic bipedal mode of movement of known living and extinct hominines, composed of alternating stance and swing phases.

Strontium/calcium ratio: the ratio of these two elements in an animal bone, used to determine whether the animal was carnivorous (meat eating), herbivorous (plant eating), or both (omnivorous).

Structural gene: a gene that directs the structure of a protein.

Subcutaneous fat: fat deposits lying just under the skin.

Subjective: influenced by the experiencer's experience and emotions.

Suspensory hanging and climbing: a pattern of arboreal adaptation suggested for the early hominoids in which major biological changes developed in the upper trunk and arms as a result of hanging and climbing by the arms while suspended in the trees.

Swanscombe: a middle Pleistocene fossil site along the River Thames in southern England where bones of the back of the skull of an early sapiens have been found.

Swartkrans: a robust australopithecine site that has also yielded some later fragments of *Homo erectus;* located in the Sterkfontein Valley, Transvaal, South Africa.

Swing phase: in the hominine bipedal stride, the leg that leaves the ground and swings forward is said to be in swing phase.

Synthetic theory of evolution: the modern view of evolution based on an amalgamation of genetic and evolutionary thought.

Tabūn: cave site at Mount Carmel in Israel. The hominine fossils associated with the Mousterian industry share many morphological features with neandertals. Estimates place these fossils perhaps as early as 70,000 years B.P.

Talus: the ankle bone of the foot.

Tapetum: a reflective surface on the back of the eyeball that enhances night vision in noctural animals.

Taphonomy: the investigation of the various natural activities that act on an animal bone from the death of the creature to the incorporation of the bone into a geological deposit.

Taung: the fossil site in Cape Province, South Africa, from which the first australopithecine fossil was recovered in 1924.

Taxonomy: the classification of plants and animals into categories based on common biological features.

T-cells: white blood cells that are important in immunological reactions. It is a type of T-cell that is negatively affected in the disease AIDS.

Temporalis: one of the major chewing muscles, it attaches from the side of the braincase (at the temporal line, or in robust australopithecines and some apes, from the sagittal crest) and runs down the skull, inside of the arch (zygomatic arch), ending on the top back of the lower jaw.

Ternifine: see Tighenif.

Terra Amata: a middle Pleistocene open-air site in France where stone tools of the Acheulian industry and evidence of fire but no hominine remains were unearthed.

Terrestrial: adapted to life on the ground.

Territory: a home range that is defended from other members of the same species outside the group.

Teshik Tash: a Mousterian site in southern U.S.S.R. where a deliberately buried neandertal youngster was uncovered.

Testosterone: hormone found in greater amounts in males; the "male hormone."

Thalassemia: a class of genetic anemias resulting in a deficiency in adult hemoglobin. These anemias may help to prevent serious malarial infections.

Therapsids: the order of mammal-like reptiles of the Mesozoic that represents the transition between reptiles and mammals.

Thermoluminescence: a dating technique based on the same physical principles as the electron spin resonance process, thermoluminescence is currently being used to date burned stones from hominine sites such as Qafzeh.

Thomas Quarries: a middle Pleistocene site in Morocco from which a fragmentary lower jaw and face were recovered.

Tibia: the shinbone of the lower leg.

Tighenif (formerly Ternifine): a middle Pleistocene site in Algeria, where several *Homo erectus* jaws and pieces of skullcap have been found in association with Acheulian tools.

Titer: a measure of the strength of an antibody.

Toe-off: at the time in bipedalism when the swing phase begins, the foot is pushed off from the ground with some muscular force; the last element to leave the ground is the big toe, hence the term toe-off.

Tooth comb: the name applied to the lower incisors of many prosimians, which are oriented horizontally instead of vertically in the jaw and are used to obtain tree gums as well as to comb through their fur looking for dirt and parasites.

Topography: the description of a surface; in this context, surfaces depicting the genetic fitness of populations as propounded by Sewall Wright.

Torralba: see Ambrona.

Transient polymorphism: a polymorphism that is in the process of disappearing as a result of some evolutionary force; that is, one allele is disappearing.

Trinil: a locale along the Solo River in Java, Indonesia, where Dubois discovered the first *Homo erectus* fossil.

Turkanapithecus: an East African Miocene hominoid.

Typology: the study of idealized types; sociological assignments as to race are highly typological.

Ulna: a bone of the lower arm (on the little finger side).

Uniformitarianism: a theory elaborated by Charles Lyell that holds that the appearance of the earth today represents the action of natural forces like wind, rain, and temperature changes operating slowly and constantly over very long periods of time (see also catastrophism).

Uranium series: a dating method based on the decay of a number of isotopes of uranium.

Vértesszöllös: an archaeological site along the Danube River in Hungary where a hominine occipital bone was discovered. Although it possesses some features reminiscent of *Homo erectus*, it is usually considered an early representative of *Homo sapiens*.

Vertical clinging and leaping: a specialized form of movement of some prosimians in which the animal clings to a vertical tree branch with its elongated rear limbs tightly flexed onto its body. The animal leaps to another branch by a powerful leaping movement created by the uncoiling of the flexed legs.

Victoriapithecus: a middle Miocene fossil primate from Kenya. This genus possesses teeth showing the bilophodont character of Old World monkey molars.

Virus: any of various very small microorganisms that consist of a protein shell and a core of nucleic acid.

Wadi Amud: a late Pleistocene cave site in northern Israel, with hominine specimens similar to both the Tabūn and Shanidar fossils.

Wadjak: a late Pleistocene hominine site in Java.

Wallace's line: the imaginary line marking the boundary between the fauna of Europe/Asia and Australia/New Guinea.

White blood cells: see leukocyte.

Willandra Lakes: a late Pleistocene site in southern Australia with early evidence of modern human occupation of the Australian continent.

Y-5 molars: lower molars characteristic of the hominoids, apes, and humans that have five cusps so arranged that the grooves separating the inner cusps look like the letter Y when viewed from the tongue side of the tooth.

"Zinjanthropus boisei": the taxonomic category for a fossil hominine found in Bed I, Olduvai Gorge. The fossil is now considered *Australopithecus* but with the separate species name *boisei*.

Zhoukoudian: a cave site in the village of Zhoukoudian, just outside of Beijing, People's Republic of China, where a large sample of *Homo erectus* fossils was discovered prior to World War II. The village was formerly known as Choukoutien.

Zygomatic arch: the arch of bone on the side of the skull that is the origin of the *masseter* muscle, a major muscle of mastication.

Credits

Figures

Chapter 1: Page 19: Courtesy of Robert Harding Picture Library/Rainbird Ltd. **Chapter 2:** Page 29, *bottom:* From *Modern Genetics,* 2d ed., by Francisco J. Ayala and John A. Kiger, Jr. (Menlo Park, Calif.: Benjamin/Cummings, 1984), p. 301, by permission of the publisher. Page 44, *left;* Redrawn from *Genetics,* 2d ed., by Irwin H. Herskowitz (Boston: Little, Brown, 1965), p. 339. Page 64: Courtesy of the Gernsheim Collection, Harry Ransom Humanities Research Center, University of Texas at Austin. **Chapter 3:** Page 86: Adapted from "Selection, Gene Migration, and Polymorphic Stability in a U.S. White and Negro Population," by P. L. Workman, B. S. Blumburg, and A. J. Cooper, *American Jounral of Human Genetics,* Vol. 15, Issue 4 (1963), pp. 429–437, by permission of the University of Chicago Press. © 1963 by the American Society of Human Genetics. All rights reserved. Page 90: From E. Peter Volpe, *Understanding Evolution,* 5th ed., p. 152, fig. 11.7. Copyright © 1985 Wm. C. Brown Publishers, Dubuque, Iowa. All Rights Reserved. Reprinted by permission. Page 91: Figure from *Introduction to Evolution* by P. A. Moody. Copyright © 1953 by Harper & Row, Publishers, Inc. Reprinted by permission of the Publisher. Page 103: From "The Development of Inbreeding in an Island Population" by D. F. Roberts, *Ciência e Cultura* (Rev. Soc. Brasil. Progr. Ciência), Vol. 19 (1967), pp. 78–84, by permission of the author and the publisher. Page 112: From *Macroevolution: Pattern and Process* by S. Stanley (New York: W. H. Freeman, 1979), by permission of the publisher. Page 115: From *The Life of Primates* by A. H. Schultz (New York: Universe Books, 1969), © Adolph H. Schultz; and from Life Nature Library, *Evolution* (adapted from drawings by Ed Kasper), © 1964 Time-Life Books Inc. Used by permission. Page 116: © Adolph H. Schultz, *The Life of Primates.* New York: Universe Books, 1969. Used by permission of the publisher. **Chapter 4:** Page 125: Adapted with permission from Kent C. Condie, *Plate Tectonics and Crustal Evolution,* p. 214, Copyright 1976, Pergamon Press PLC. Page 126: Redrawn from *Life of the Vertebrates* by J. Z. Young (Oxford: Oxford University Press, 1950), fig. 48, by permission of the publisher. Page 127: Redrawn from Figure 13 by Lois M. Darling in *Evolution of the Vertebrates,* 3d ed., by Edwin H. Colbert (New York: Wiley, 1980). Page 130: Courtesy of the American Museum of Natural History. Page 135: Redrawn from *The Antecedents of Man* by W. E. Le Gros Clark, copyright © 1959, 1962, 1971 by Quadrangle/The New York Times Book Co., by permission of Edinburgh University Press. Page 139, *top:* Redrawn from *Osteology of the Reptiles* by Alfred Sherwood Romer, by permission of the University of Chicago Press. © 1956 by The University of Chicago. All rights reserved. Page 139, *bottom:* Redrawn after L. B. Arey, *Developmental Anatomy,* 7th ed. (revised), p. 403, W. B. Saunders Co., Philadelphia, Pa., 1974. Page 142: From *The Study of Instinct* by N. Tinbergen (Oxford: Oxford University Press, 1951), by permission of the publisher. Page 145: Adapted with permission from Dyna-Vue, Ward's Natural Science. Page 146: From "Specializations of the Human Brain" by Norman Geschwind. Copyright © September 1979 by Scientific American, Inc. All rights reserved. **Chapter 5:** Page 153 (a): Courtesy of the American Museum of Natural History. Page 153 (b and c): From "Phylogeny of Primate Higher Taxa: The Basicranial Evidence" by F. S. Szalay in *Phylogeny of the Primates: A Multidisciplinary Approach,* Luckett and Szalay (eds.) (New York: Plenum, 1975). Page 154: Redrawn from *The Antecedents of Man* by W. E. Le Gros Clark, copyright © 1959, 1962, 1971 by Quadrangle/The New York Times Book Co., by permission of Edinburgh University Press. Page 183: After "The Phylogeny of the Hominoid Primates, as Indicated by DNA-DNA Hybridization" by C. G. Sibley and J. E. Ahlquist, *Journal of Molecular Evolution,* Vol. 20, p. 12, fig. 6, by permission of Springer-Verlag and Charles G. Sibley.

Chapter 6: Page 197: After *The Natural History of the Primates* by J. R. Napier and P. H. Napier (London: British Museum of Natural History, 1985). © J. R. and P. H. Napier, 1985. Reprinted by permission of the MIT Press, Cambridge, Massachusetts, and London, England. Page 222: Reprinted with permission of Macmillan Publishing Company from *The Evolution of Primate Behavior* by Alison Jolly. Copyright © 1972, 1985 by Alison Jolly. Page 227: Redrawn from "Chimpanzees of the Budongo Forest" by Vernon Reynolds and Frances Reynolds in *Primate Behavior: Field Studies of Monkeys and Apes,* Irven DeVore (ed.). Copyright © 1965 by Holt, Rinehart and Winston, Inc. Originally published in *Chimpanzees: A Laboratory Colony* by R. M. Yerkes (New Haven: Yale University Press, 1943). Used by permission of Yale University Press. Page 228: From "Knuckle-Walking and the Problem of Human Origins" by R. H. Tuttle, *Science,* Vol. 166 (November 1969), pp. 953–961. Copyright 1969 by the AAAS. **Chapter 7:** Pages 241, 242: From *Men and Dinosaurs* by Edwin H. Colbert (New York: E. P. Dutton, 1968). Copyright © 1968 by Edwin H. Colbert. Reprinted by permission of the author. Page 245, *top:* From "The Functional Anatomy of the Lower Limb of the Howler Monkey (*Alouatta curaya*)" by T. I. Grand, *American Journal of Physical Anthropology,* Vol. 28, p. 163, by permission of the Wistar Institute of Anatomy and Biology. Page 249, *left:* Redrawn with permission from *a la Recherche du Primate, Ancêtre, de L'Homme* by E. Genet-Varcin, Boubée et Cie, Editions N, France. Page 249, *right:* Redrawn from *History of the Primates* by W. E. Le Gros Clark, The University of Chicago Press, Fourth Phoenix Books Editions, published 1963, fig. 4.24, by permission of the University of Chicago Press. © 1949, 1965 by The Trustees of the British Museum (Natural History). All rights reserved. Page 256: From "Evolution of the Hominoid Wrist" by O. L. Lewis in *The Functional and Evolutionary Biology of the Primates,* Russell Tuttle (ed.) (New York: Cambridge University Press, 1972), by permission of the publisher. Page 257, *left:* From *An Atlas of Primate Gross Anatomy: Baboon, Chimpanzee, and Man* by D. R. Swindler and C. D. Wood (Seattle: University of Washington Press, 1973), by permission of the publisher. Page 257: *right:* "Knuckle-Walking and the Problem of Human Origins" by R. H. Tuttle, *Science,* Vol. 166 (November 1969), pp. 953–961. Copyright 1969 by the AAAS. Page 265, *top:* Redrawn from *The Miocene Hominoidea of East Africa* by W. E. Le Gros Clark and L.S.B. Leakey, figs. 213 and 216 (1951), British Museum (Natural History) Fossil Mammals of Africa, by courtesy of the British Museum (Natural History). Page 265, *bottom:* From "The Hunt for *Proconsul*" by Alan Walker and Mark Teaford. Copyright © January 1989 by Scientific American, Inc. All rights reserved. Page 271: From "Molecular Anthropology: Its Development and Current Directions" by M. Goodman and J. E. Cronin in *A History of American Physical Anthropology,* Frank Spencer (ed.) (Orlando: Academic Press, 1982), by permission of the publisher. Page 280: Redrawn from L.S.B. Leakey, *Fossil Vertebrates of Africa,* Vol. I, Plate I, 1969. Published with the permission of the National Museums of Kenya. Page 282: Redrawn from Theodosius Dobzhansky et al., *Evolutionary Biology,* Vol. 6, fig. 5, "Relationships, Origins, History of the Ceboid Monkeys and Caviomorph Rodents: A Modern Reinterpretation," Plenum Publishing Corporation. **Chapter 8:** Page 304: Redrawn from *Le Quaternaire* by Jean Chaline, Doin Editeurs, Paris, 1972, by permission of the publisher. **Chapter 9:** Page 319: Redrawn from Ashley Montagu, *Introduction to Physical Anthropology,* 3d ed., 1960. Courtesy of Charles C Thomas, Publisher (Springfield, Illinois), and the author. Page 324: Redrawn by permission after "New Finds at the Swartkrans Australopithecine Site" by C. K. Brain, *Nature,* Vol. 225 (March 21, 1970), fig. 1. Copyright © 1970 Macmillan Magazines Ltd. Page 329: Redrawn from "Plio-Pleistocene Sequences in the Northern Lake Turkana Basin" by A. K. Behrensmeyer in *Geological Background to Fossil Man,* W. W. Bishop (ed.), by permission of Scottish Academic Press and the University of Toronto Press. Pages 339, *top;* 342, *right:* From "The Antiquity of Human Walking" by J. R. Napier. Copyright © April 1967 by Scientific American, Inc. All rights reserved. Used with permission of the publisher and P. H. Napier. Page 339, *bottom:* From "A Biochemical Interpretation of *Australopithecus*" by A. L. Zihlman and W. S. Hunter, *Folia Primatologica,* Vol. 18, pp. 1–19, by permission of S. Karger AG, Basel. Page 342, *left:* From *The Anatomy of the Gorilla* by W. K. Gregory. Copyright © 1950 Columbia University Press. Used by permission. Page 345: Redrawn from *Early Hominid Posture and Locomotion* by John T. Robinson, by permission of the University of Chicago Press. © 1972 by John T. Robinson. All rights reserved. Page 348: Redrawn from *The Antecedents of Man* by W. E. Le Gros Clark, copyright © 1959, 1962, 1971 by Quadrangle/The New York Times Book Co., by permission of Edinburgh University Press. Page 350, *top*: Redrawn from "Swartkrans Ape-Man, *Paranthropus crassidens*," by R. Broom and J. T. Robinson, Transvaal Museum Memoirs, No. 6 (1952), Pretoria, South Africa. Page 357: Redrawn by permission from "Recent Discoveries of Fossil Hominids in Tanganyika at Olduvai and Near Lake Natron" by L.S.B. Leakey and Mary Leakey, *Nature,* Vol. 202 (1964), pp. 5–7. Copyright © 1964 Macmillan Magazines Ltd. Page 367: From *Olduvai Gorge: Excavations in Beds 1 and 2, 1960– 1963* (volume 3 in the Olduvai Gorge series) by Mary Leakey (New York: Cambridge University Press, 1971), by permission of the publisher. Page 368: Reprinted by permission of Faber and Faber Ltd from *The Archaeology of Early Man* by J. M. Coles and E. S. Higgs. **Chapter 10:** Pages 376, 406: Figures from pages 46 and 71 in *Atlas of Fossil Man* by C. Loring Brace, Harry Nelson, and Noel Korn, copyright © 1971 by Holt, Rinehart and Winston, Inc., reprinted by permission of the publisher. Pages 391, 409, *left*: Reprinted by permission of Faber and Faber Ltd from *The Archaeology of Early Man* by J. M. Coles and E. S. Higgs. Page 393: Redrawn from *The Emergence of Man* by John Pfeiffer (New York: Harper and Row, 1972), p. 143. Used with permission of Henry de Lumley, Université de Provence. Pages 401, 408: Redrawn from *Le Quaternaire* by Jean Chaline, Doin Editeurs, Paris, 1972, by permission of the publisher. Page 409, *right*: Figure from *A Tale of Two Caves* by François Bordes. Copyright © 1972 by François Bordes. Reprinted by permission of Harper & Row, Publishers, Inc. Page 417, *bottom*: Redrawn from "Neanderthal Man and *Homo sapiens* in Central and Eastern Europe" by Jan Jelineck, *Current Anthropology,* Vol. 10 (December 1969), pp. 475–503, by permission of the University of Chicago Press. © December 1969 by the Wenner-Gren Foundation for Anthropological Research. All rights reserved. **Chapter 11:** Page 445: Reprinted from "18th Century British Military Stature: Growth Cessation, Selective Recruiting, Secular Trends, Nutrition at Birth, Cold and Occupation" by A. Theodore Steegmann, Jr., *Human Biology,* Vol. 57, No. 1 (February 1985), p. 87, fig. 3, by permission of the Wayne State University Press and the author. Copyright © Wayne State University Press, 1985. Page 449: From *Foetus into Man: Physical Growth from Conception to Maturity* by J. M. Tanner (Cambridge, Mass.: Harvard University Press, 1978), p. 7. Published originally in *Growth at Adolescence,* 2d ed., by J. M. Tanner (Oxford: Blackwell Scientific Publications, 1962). Page 450: From *Foetus into Man: Physical Growth from Conception to Maturity* by J. M. Tanner (Cambridge, Mass.: Harvard University Press, 1978), p. 7, fig. 1. Published originally in *Growth at Adolescence,* 2d ed., by J. M. Tanner (Oxford: Blackwell Scientific Publications, 1962). Page 451: From *Foetus into Man: Physical Growth from Conception to Maturity* by J. M. Tanner (Cambridge, Mass.: Harvard University Press, 1978), p. 12, fig. 3. Published originally in "Standards from Birth to Maturity for Height, Weight, Height Velocity, and Weight Velocity: British Children, 1965" by J. M. Tanner, R. H. Whitehouse, and M. Takaishi, *Archives of Diseases in Childhood,* Vol. 41 (1966), pp. 454–471, 613–635. Page 452: From *Foetus into Man: Physical Growth from Conception to Maturity* by J. M. Tanner (Cambridge, Mass.: Harvard University Press, 1978), p. 16, fig. 6. Published originally in *Growth at Adolescence,* 2d ed., by J. M. Tanner (Oxford: Blackwell Scientific Publications, 1962). Page 454: From *Foetus into Man: Physical Growth from Conception to Maturity* by J. M. Tanner (Cambridge, Mass.: Harvard University Press, 1978), p. 155, fig. 50. Published originally in "Catch-Up Growth Following Illness or Starvation" by A. Prader, J. M. Tanner, and G. A. von Harnack, *Journal of Pediatrics,* Vol. 62 (1963), pp. 646–659. Reprinted by permission of The C. V. Mosby Company. Page 456: After *Growth and Development: The First Twenty Years* by Robert M. Malina (Minneapolis: Burgess, 1975), p. 50, fig. 14. Page 460: From *Digging Up Bones: The Excavation, Treatment and Study of Human Skeletal Remains* by Don R. Brothwell, by courtesy of the British Museum (Natural History). Page 461: From *Human Biology,* 2d ed., by G. A. Harrison, J. S. Weiner, J. M. Tanner, and N. A. Barnicot, Oxford University Press. Published originally in *Growth at Adolescence,* 2d ed., by J. M. Tanner (Oxford: Blackwell, 1962). Reprinted by permission of Blackwell Scientific Publications Ltd. Page 462: Redrawn from Don R. Brothwell, *Digging Up Bones,* after I. Schour and M. Massler, "The Development of the Human Dentition," *Journal of the American Dental Association,* Vol. 28, pp. 1153–1160. Used by permission of the American Dental Association. **Chapter 12:** Pages 471; 472; 473; 475, *top and bottom;* 476, *top and bottom;* 439, *top:* Adapted from *The Human Species: An Introduction to Physical Anthropology,* 2d ed., by Frederick S. Hulse (New York: Random House, 1971). Copyright © 1971 by Frederick S. Hulse. Copyright © 1963, 1971 by Random House, Inc. Page 486: Redrawn from "Selection and Polymorphism in the A-B-O Blood Groups" by Alice Brues, *American Journal of Physical Anthropology,* Vol. 21, pp. 297, 295, by permission of the author and the Wistar Institute of Anatomy and Biology. Page 488: From *The Structure and Action of Proteins* by R. E. Dickerson and I. Geis (Menlo Park, Calif.: W. A. Benjamin, 1969). Copyright © 1969 by Dickerson and Geis. Page 489, *bottom:* Adapted from map "Epidemiological Assessment of the Status of Malaria, 1987," © World Health Organization, 1989, courtesy of Malaria Action Programme, World Health Organization, Geneva. Page 492: Adapted from "Evolution of the Hemoglobin S and C Genes in World Population" by Yuet Wai Kan and A. M. Dozy, *Science,* Vol. 209 (July 18, 1980), pp. 388–390, copyright 1980 by the AAAS. Used by permission of the publisher and Yuet Wai Kan. Page 494: Adapted from *Evolution,* Vol. 18, 1964. Page 495: Adapted from *Evolution,* Vol. 18, 1964, and from *The Human Species: An Introduction to Physical Anthropology,* 2d ed., by Frederick S. Hulse (New York: Random House, 1971), © 1971 by Frederick S. Hulse, © 1963, 1971 by Random House, Inc. Page 496: Adapted from *The New Genetics and Clinical Practice,* 2d ed., by D. J. Weatherall (Oxford: Oxford University Press, 1985), p. 85, fig. 33, by permission of the publisher. **Chapter 13:** Page 512: Reprinted from "A Comparison of Chest Morphology in High Altitude Asian and Andean Populations" by Cynthia M. Beall, *Human Biology,* Vol. 54, No. 1 (February 1982), p. 153, fig. 2, by permission of the Wayne State University Press and the author. Copyright © Wayne State University Press, 1982. Page 513: Modified from A. R. Frisancho and P. T. Baker, *American Journal of Physical Anthropology,* Vol. 32 (1970), pp. 279–292. Reproduced by permission from A. Roberto Frisancho, *Human Adaptation: A Functional Interpretation,* St. Louis, The C. V. Mosby Co., 1979, p. 142, fig. 10–3. Page 519: Modified from T. Lewis, *Heart,* Vol. 15 (1930), pp. 177–181. Reproduced by permission from A. Roberto Frisancho, *Human Adaptation: A Functional Interpretation,* St. Louis, The C. V. Mosby Co., 1979, p. 45, fig. 4–4. Page 521: Reprinted by permission of the American Anthropological Association from *American Anthropologist,* Vol. 55, No. 3 (1953). Page 524: Reproduced, with permission, from "Human Heat Tolerance: An Anthropological Perspective" by Joel M. Hanna and Daniel E. Brown, *Annual Review of Anthropology,* Vol. 12, pp. 259–284, © 1983 by Annual Reviews Inc. Page 526: Redrawn from "Human Pigmentation" by N. A. Barnicot, *Man* (old series), 57-5, by permission of the Royal Anthropological Institute of Great Britain and Ireland. Page 527 (a): Redrawn from *Essentials of Histology,* 6th ed., by Gerrit Bevelander and Judith A. Ramaley (St. Louis: C. V. Mosby, 1970), p. 140, by permission of Judith A. Ramaley. Page 527 (b) and (c): Redrawn by permission from Fitzpatrick Miyamoto, and Ishikawa, *The Evolution of Concepts of Melanin Biology in Advances in Biology of Skin,* Vol. 8, *The Pigmentary Skin* (1966), Plenum Publishing Corporation. Page 528: From *The Living Races of Man* by Carleton S. Coon, with Edward E. Hunt, Jr. Copyright © 1965 by Carleton S. Coon. Reprinted by permission of Alfred A. Knopf, Inc. Page 530: Adapted from "Rickets" by W. F. Loomis. Copyright © December 1970 by Scientific American, Inc. All rights reserved. Page 536: Adapted from *Natural History of Infectious Disease,* 4th ed., by Sir Macfarlane Burnet and David O. White, by permission of Cambridge University Press, New York. Pages 541, *top and bottom;* 542: Reprinted with permission from *Journal of Psychosomatic Research,* Vol. 18, Sydney Cobb, "Psychological Changes in Men Whose Jobs Were Abolished," Copyright 1974, Pergamon Press PLC. Pages 543, 544: From "The Effects of Light on the Human Body" by Richard J. Wurtman. Copyright © July 1975 by Scientific American, Inc. All rights reserved. Page 552: After *Calorie Deficiencies and Protein Deficiencies* by R. A. McCance and W. M. Widdowson, (London: J. & A. Churchill, 1968), by permission of Churchill Livingstone, Edinburgh. Page 555, *top and bottom*: From "Childhood Undernutrition: Implications for Adult Work Capacity and Productivity" by G. B. Spurr, M. Barac-Nieto, and M. G. Maksud in *Environmental Stress* (proceedings of a symposium held at the University of California, Santa Barbara, Aug. 31–Sept. 3, 1977), Lawrence J. Folinsbee et al. (eds.) (Orlando: Academic Press, 1978). Published originally in "Productivity and Maximum Oxygen Consumption in Sugarcane Cutters" by G. B. Spurr et al., *American Journal of Clinical Nutrition,* Vol. 30 (1977), pp. 316–321. **Chapter 14:** Page 582: From "Bioassay of Kinship in Populations of Middle Eastern Origin and Controls" by N. E. Morton, R. Kennett, S. Yee, and R. Lew, *Current Anthropology,* Vol. 23 (1982), pp. 157–167, by permission of the University of Chicago Press. © 1982 by the Wenner-Gren Foundation for Anthropological Research. All rights reserved. Page 584, *top and bottom*: Adapted from "Evolutionary Relationships of Human Populations from an Analysis of Nuclear DNA Polymorphisms" by J. S. Wainscoat et al., *Nature,* Vol. 319 (February 6, 1986), pp. 491, 493. Copyright © 1986 Macmillan Magazines Ltd. Page 589: From "Oceanic Tooth-Size Variation" by C. Loring Brace and Robert J. Hinton, *Current Anthropology,* Vol. 22 (1981), pp. 549–569, by permission of the University of Chicago Press. © 1981 by the Wenner-Gren Foundation for Anthropological Research. All rights reserved. Page 606, *top left, top right*: Redrawn from *A Field Guide to Early Man* by D. Lambert (New York: Facts on File Publications, 1987), p. 21. Page 606, *bottom left, bottom middle*: Redrawn from *The Life of Primates* by Adolph H. Schultz (New York: Universe Books, 1969), p. 71. Used by permission of the publisher. Pages 606, *bottom right;* 607 (a): Redrawn by permission from *The Dyna-Vue Transparencies,* Ward's Natural Science, 1965. Page 607 (b), *left*: Redrawn from *Low Back Pain Syndrome,* 2nd ed., by R. Cailliet (Philadelphia: F. A. Davis, 1968), p. 34, by permission of the publisher. Page 607 (b), *right*: Redrawn from Chairot Yokochi, *Photographic Anatomy of the Human Body* (Baltimore: University Park Press, 1971), p. 10. Page 607 (c): Redrawn from *The CIBA Collection of Medical Illustrations,* Vol. 8, *Musco-Skeletal Systems,* Part 1, illustrated by Frank Netter (West Caldwell, N.J.: CIBA Med., 1987). Page 608: Redrawn from *An Atlas of Primate Growth Anatomy* by D. R. Swindler and C. D. Wood (Seattle: University of Washington Press, 1973), p. 45, by permission of the publisher. Page 609 (a): Redrawn from *Grundriss zum Studium der Geburtshilfe* by E. Bumm (Munich: Bergmann, 1922). Page 609 (b): Redrawn from *Obstetrical Practice,* 6th ed., by A. C. Beck and A. H. Rosenthal (Baltimore: Williams & Wilkins, 1955), by permission of the publisher.

Photographs

Unless otherwise acknowledged, all photos are the property of Scott, Foresman or the author.

Chapter 1: Opposite page 1: Ellis Herwig/Stock Boston. Page 2: The Granger Collection, New York. Page 4: Rene Burri/Magnum Photos. Page 5: David R. Frazier Photolibrary. Page 7: Anthro-Photo. Page 9: Anthro-Photo. Page 10: Courtesy Department Library Services/American Museum of Natural History. Page 11: Academy, Venice. Page 12: Peter Veit/DRK Photo. Page 16: Brown Brothers. Page 18: Robert Harding Picture Library Ltd., London. Page 19: Robert Harding Picture Library Ltd., London. Page 21: Dr. I. Eibl-Eibesfeldt. Page 23, *top*: BBC Hulton/The Bettmann Archive; *bottom left*: Robert Harding Picture Library Ltd., London; *bottom right*: Courtesy Department Library Services/American Museum of Natural History. Page 24: Culver Pictures. **Chapter 2:** Page 26: Museum of Science, Boston. Page 31, *bottom*: Porter, K. R. and Bonneville, M. A.: *Fine Structure of Cells and Tissues,* 4th. ed., Lea & Febiger, Philadelphia, 1973. Page 41, *bottom left and right*: Dr. Marion I. Barnhart, Wayne State University. Page 44, *right*: Courtesy of Harold W. Fisher and Robley C. Williams. Page 47, *top*: Brown Brothers. Page 49, *left*: Courtesy of Harold W. Fisher and Robley C. Williams; *right*: M. J. Murawka. Page 52, *left*: From J. W. Bianchine, *Noonan Syndrome and Trisomy*

21 in Sibs. In D. Bergsma (ed): Part XV. "The Cardiovascular System." Published for the National Foundation–March of Dimes by Williams & Wilkins, Baltimore. BD:OAS 247, 1972. viii (5); *right*: In D. Bergsma (ed), 1973. *Birth Defects: Atlas & Compendium.* Published for the National Foundation–March of Dimes by Williams & Wilkins, Baltimore. Page 59: AP/Wide World. Page 63: The Gernsheim Collection/Harry Ransom Humanities Research Center, University of Texas at Austin. Page 65, *bottom*: In D. Bergsma (ed), 1973: *Birth Defects: Atlas & Compendium.* Published for the National Foundation–March of Dimes by Williams & Wilkins, Baltimore. **Chapter 3:** Page 76: Courtesy Department Library Services/American Museum of Natural History. Page 81: Gabriel Benzur © 1945 Life Magazine, Time Inc. Page 84: *Country Life Newspaper,* Australia. Page 100: Courtesy Department Library Services/American Museum of Natural History. Page 113: Scala/Art Resource, NY. **Chapter 4:** Page 118: George Laycock/ Photo Researchers. **Chapter 5:** Page 148: Russ Kinne/Photo Researchers. Page 161, *left*: Courtesy Department Library Services/American Museum of Natural History; *right*: Sarah Blaffer Hrdy/Anthro-Photo. Page 163: Norman Myers/Bruce Coleman Inc. Page 165: Michael Dick/*Animals Animals.* Page 167: Michael Lyster/Zoological Society of London. Page 168: Bruce Coleman Inc. Page 169: Nina Leen. Page 171: Courtesy of Norris M. Durham. Page 172: Sarah Blaffer Hrdy/Anthro-Photo. Page 173: Joseph Van Wormer/Bruce Coleman Inc. Page 175: Courtesy Department Library Services/American Museum of Natural History. Page 176: A. H. Harlart/Anthro-Photo. **Chapter 6:** Page 192: Jim Moore/Anthro-Photo. Page 200: Courtesy of Geza Teleki. Page 203: Irven DeVore/Anthro-Photo. Page 204: Irven DeVore/Anthro-Photo. Page 208: Zoological Society of San Diego. Page 209: Irven DeVore/Anthro-Photo. Page 210: Courtesy of Dr. Sherwood L. Washburn, University of California, Berkeley. Page 212: Courtesy Department Library Services/American Museum of Natural History. Page 213: Irven DeVore/Anthro-Photo. Page 218: Miriam Austerman/*Animals Animals.* Page 220: Lewis Kemper/DRK Photo. Page 221: Wolfgang Bayer/Bruce Coleman Inc. Page 229: Courtesy of Geza Teleki. Page 230: Courtesy of Geza Teleki. Page 232: Courtesy of Geza Teleki. **Chapter 7:** Page 236: Courtesy Department Library Services/American Museum of Natural History. Page 251, *left and right*: Courtesy Department Library Services/American Museum of Natural History. Page 255, *left*: Ralph Morse, Life Magazine © 1965 Time Inc.; *right*: Courtesy Department Library Services/American Museum of Natural History. Page 266: M. H. Wolpoff. **Chapter 8:** Page 286: Hillel Burger, Peabody Museum, Harvard University. Copyright © President & Fellows of Harvard College, 1980. **Chapter 9:** Page 316: National Geographic News Service, February 1978. Page 320: Courtesy Department Library Services/American Museum of Natural History. Page 330: M. H. Wolpoff. Page 331: From D. C. Johnson, "Ethiopia Yields First Family of Early Man," *National Geographic,* Dec. 1976: 802. Page 332: National Geographic News Service, February, 1978. Page 358, *left and right*: Reprinted with permission of the National Museum of Kenya. Copyright reserved. Page 359, *top*: Reprinted with permission of the National Museum of Kenya. Copyright reserved; *bottom*: Courtesy of Clarendon Press. **Chapter 10:** Page 374: Jay Kelley/Anthro-Photo. Page 383, *left and right*: Courtesy Department Library Services/American Museum of Natural History. Page 384: A. Walker, © National Museums of Kenya. Page 403, *top*: From *Paleoanthropology,* by M. H. Wolpoff. Copyright © 1980 by Alfred A. Knopf, Inc. Reprinted by permission of Alfred A. Knopf, Inc. Page 418: From J. Matiegka, *The Fossil Man of Předmosti in Moravia* (Prague: Nákladem České Akademie Věd A Umění, 1934). Page 428: Rene Burri/Magnum Photos. **Chapter 11:** Page 436, *bottom*: P. Thomann/ The Image Bank; *top left*: Peter Turner/The Image Bank; *top right*: A. Seiden/The Image Bank. Page 441: From Komai and Fukuota, *Journal of Heredity,* Vol. 25, p. 425, 1934, American Genetic Association. Page 457, *bottom*: Reprinted from *Radiographic Atlas of Skeletal Development of the Hand and Wrist,* 2nd ed., by William Walter Greulich and S. Idell Pyle, with permission of the publishers, Stanford University Press. Copyright © 1950 and 1959 by the Board of Trustees of the Leland Stanford Junior University. Page 458: Courtesy of Harry Israel, D.D.S., Ph.D., Dir. of Dental Research, 1 Children's Plaza, Children's Medical Center, Dayton, Oh. Assoc. Clinical Prof. of Pediatrics,

Wright State Univ. School of Medicine, Dayton, Oh. and Harold H. Sandstead, M.D., USDA Human Nutrition Research Center on Aging at Tufts University, Boston, Ma. Reprinted from Falkner & Tanner, *Human Growth/2: Postnatal Growth,* Plenum Publishing Corp., New York. Page 459: William Campbell, © Time Inc. **Chapter 12:** Page 464: Ellis Herwig/Stock Boston. **Chapter 13:** Page 509: George Holton/Photo Researchers. Page 510: Courtesy of Norris M. Durham. Page 517: Stanley Washburn. Page 523, *left:* Reproduced by permission of D. F. Roberts from *American Journal of Physical Anthropology; right:* Knutsen. Arktjsk Institut, Denmark ©. Page 529: From Michael C. Latham, Robert B. McGandy, Mary B. McCann, and Frederick J. Stare, 1972. *Scope Manual of Nutrition,* 2nd ed. (Kalamazoo: The Upjohn Company). Courtesy of Dr. Rosa Lee Nemir and Ward C. Morgan Studios. Page 545: Joel Gordon/Design Photographers International. Page 548, *left:* John Dominis/Life Magazine © Time Inc.; *right:* Marc and Evelyne Bernheim/Woodfin Camp & Associates. Page 549: Topham/The Image Works. Page 553: Courtesy of Dr. Alex F. Roche. Reprinted from Falkner & Tanner, *Human Growth/2:* Postnatal Growth, Plenum. Page 558: D. Carleton Gajdusek. Page 559: Plate #DCG59DNGII Reprinted from "Disease Patterns of Isolated Groups" in *Biocultural Aspects of Disease.* **Chapter 14:** Page 564: Peter Menzel/Stock Boston. Page 567: Gift of Edsel B. Ford/From the Collection of The Detroit Institute of Art. Page 571: Neal Menschel. Page 572: Dan Budnik/Woodfin Camp & Associates. Page 573, *top:* Courtesy Department Library Services/American Museum of Natural History; *bottom:* Thomas Hopker/Woodfin Camp & Associates. Page 574, *top:* Courtesy Department Library Services/American Museum of Natural History; *bottom:* Monkmeyer Press Photo Service. Page 575: Courtesy of Napoleon A. Chagnon, from *Yanomamo The Fierce People,* Holt, Rinehart and Winston. Page 577: Courtesy of Napoleon A. Chagnon, from *Yanomamo The Fierce People,* Holt, Rinehart and Winston. **Chapter 15:** Page 590: Bettye Lane/Photo Researchers. Page 595: Rita Freed/Nancy Palmer. Page 599: Olive Pierce/Stock Boston. Page 602: Bob Kalman/The Image Works. Page 611: Dan McCoy/Rainbow.

Poem on page ii: Reprinted with permission of Macmillan Publishing Company from "On Women," *The Poems of W. B. Yeats: A New Edition,* edited by Richard J. Finneren. Copyright 1919 by Macmillan Publishing Company, renewed 1947 by Bertha Georgia Yeats. Also reprinted with permission of A. P. Watt Ltd. on behalf of Michael Yeats and Macmillan London Ltd.

Index

Page numbers in *italics* indicate illustrations.

Capuchin monkeys (genus *Cebus*), 223–224, 283
Carbohydrates, dietary, 547
    sources of, 547
Carbon-14 dating, 293–294, 314
Carnivora, 122
Carnivore kills, and early hominines, 365–366
Carpenter, C. R., 222
Carson, Hampton, 108
Cartmill, Matt, 244, 246, 249
Catarrhines, 164, 190
Catastrophism, 17
Cat-cry syndrome. *See Cri du chat* syndrome
Catecholamines, 539–540
Cavalli-Sforza, Luigi, 583
Cayo Santiago Island, macaques, 216
Cebidae, 168–169, 283
    dental formula of, 258
Ceboidea, 164, 167–170. *See also* Monkeys, New World
Cebus (genus). *See* Capuchin monkey
Cell division. *See* Meiosis
Cell duplication. *See* Mitosis
Cells
    membrane of, 30
    nucleus of, 30, *31*
    structures of, *31*
Cenozoic era, 124, 132–133, 147, 195, 239, 243
    birds and mammals of, *238*
Cercocebus (genus). *See* Mangabeys
Cercopithecinae, 170–171
Cercopithecoidea, 164, 170, 190, 273
    locomotion of, 253
Cercopithecoids, phylogeny of, *183*
Cercopithecus (genus), *173*, 173–174. *See also* Vervet monkeys
Cerebellum, 144–146
Cerebral cortex, 143, 246
    human, 144, *145*
Cerebrum, 143, 144
Chagnon, Napoleon, *577*, 598
Chakraborty, R., 581
Chase, Phillip, 427
Cheirogaleids, 162–163, 251
Cheirogaleus (genus; dwarf lemur), 162
Chesowanja, fossil finds from, 332

Chest, width of, and altitude stress, 511, *512*
Chickens, β-globins of, 188
Childhood
    learning in, 594, *595*
    length of, 594
Childhood dependency, 594
    of primates, 200–202
Chimeras, 612
Chimpanzees (genus *Pan*), 174, *200, 209*
    anatomy of, 226
    common ancestor with other primates, 178
    diet of, 229
    distribution of, in Africa, 226, *227*
    globins of, 185
    hands of, *257*
    language-learning abilities of, 204–205
    pelvis of, 607–608, *608*
    relationship to other primates, 183–184, 188, 272
    skeleton of, *606*
    social organization of, 198, 202, 227–230, 234
    taxonomy of, 180
    tool use by, 231–233, *232*, 292
    wrist joint of, *256*
China
    Homo erectus in, 382–383, 435
    Homo sapiens from, 403–404
Cholesterol levels, and stress, 540–541
Chondrichthyes, 121, 127
Chordata, 123
Chromosomal anomalies, 54, *55*
Chromosomes, 28, *31*, 49. *See also* Sex chromosomes
    cross-over, 61, *62*
    homologous, 53
Chronospecies, *86*
Cigarettes, 539–540
Circe's Mountain (Monte Circeo), 426
Cladism, 155–157, 190
Cladistics, 156, 297
Cladogenesis, *86*, 86–89, 117
Cladograms, 156, *156*, 271
Clavicle, 243
    in hominoids, 253–255
    in primates, *254*
Climate
    developmental response to, 305
    Eocene, 250, 252
    Miocene, 310
    Pleistocene, 303–305

Clinal variation, 104, 571–575
Cloning, 44–45, 611
Clothing, 517, 524
Clutton-Brock, T. H., 199
Coadaptation, 105
Cobb, Sidney, 540
Coca leaves, 516
Codons, 37
Cohen, Bernice, 480
Cold stress
    cultural adaptations to, 516–517
    genetic adaptations to, 518–519
    physiological adjustments to, 518–519
Collarbone. *See* Clavicle
Collector/predators, 229
Colobinae, 170
Colobus monkeys, 170–171, 199
Color blindness, 477–478
    and subsistence patterns, 561
Columbus, Christopher, *2*
Communication
    human, 204
    nonvocal, primate, 204
    primate, 203–205
Community. *See also* Social groups
    primate, 201–202
Comparative anatomy, 242
Comparative sciences, evidence of evolution in, 82
Computer simulation, of ABO evolution, 484–485
Conspecifics, 570
Continental drift, 123, *125*, 243, 252, 264, 302, 314
Convection, 523
Convergence, 240
Coppens, Yves, 328
Core area, *222*, 223
Crab-eating monkeys (genus *Macaca*), 88
Crelin, E. S., 428
Cretaceous period, 132, 242, 243, 249
Cretinism, 559
Crews, Douglas, 453
Cri du chat syndrome, 54
    appearance of child with, *50, 52*
    karyotype in, *50, 52*
Cro-Magnon, 413, 432
Crook, John, 216
Crossopterygii, 129
Cultural relativism, 3–4
Culture
    and behavior, 3–5
    and biology, *4, 13*, 592
    definition of, 291

Eskimos (*continued*)
  hunting response in, 518
  metabolic rate of, 518–519
  polio epidemics among, 534
  sex roles of, 600
Estrus cycle, of female baboon, 213–214, *214*
Ethiopia. *See also* Hadar, Ethiopia; Omo River Basin
  terrestrial monkeys in, 216–218, *217*
Ethnocentrism, 4–5
Ethnography, 6
Ethnology, 6
Ethology, 13
Eucaryotes, genes in, 39
Europe
  early sapiens from, 400–401
  Homo erectus in, 386–388
Evolution, 12–13, 27–28, 70, 74. *See also* Human evolution; Macroevolution; Micro-evolution
  of African apes, 278–280
  of australopithecines, 360–364, 431–433
  branching, 87, 117
  convergent, 89, *91*, 117
  divergent, 88, 117, 177–179
    hominoid, *271*, 272–273
  evidence for, 82–85
  forces of, 79–82, 116
  of gibbon, 278
  grade (or phase) of, 415
  of Hominidae, 278–280
  hominine, 287, 301–306, 312–314, 317–373
    fossil record of, 278–280
  of hominoids, 260–261, 263–277
  of mammals, 132–133, *181*, 242–243
  of Miocene hominoids, and living hominoids, 277–280
  by natural selection, 22
  neo-Darwinian view, 85
  of New World monkeys, 281–283
  observational studies of, 83–85
  of Old World monkeys, 261–262, 280–281
  of plants, 243
  primate
    immunological approaches to study of, 178–179
    study of, 242
    trends in, 244–249
  of *Proconsul,* 264–266
  of *Siamang,* 278

studies of, 78
theory of, 1, 24, 78, 591
  emergence of, 15–25
  pre-Darwinian, 16
  questioning, 105
  of vertebrates, 119–147
Exons, *39,* 39–40, *186, 187*

Face
  australopithecine, 345, 363
  hominine, 312
  Homo, 358
  modern human, 345
Fats, dietary, 547
Fava beans, 498
Fayum Beds, 252–253, 260–261, 284
Femur, 129, 140, 338, 340
  australopithecine, *343,* 343–344
  human, *343*
Fibula, 129
Fight or flight reaction, 539
Finches. *See also* Darwin's finches
  of Galapagos Islands, 20–22, *21*
Finger opposability, 246
Fire, use of by *Homo erectus,* 392, 394–395
Fisher, R. A., 110–111
Fishes
  bony, 127–128
  cartilaginous, 128
  jawless, 126–127
  with jaws, 127–128
  locomotion of, 129
  and sex change with aging, 603
Fission track dating, 295
Fitness
  at high altitude, 514
  physiological, 514, 563
Fixed action pattern, 143
Flakes, 411–412
Flatz, Gebhard, 562
Fleagle, John, 260
Florisbad, fossil finds from, 407
Folate, in blood serum, and exposure to UV light, 531, *531*
Foods, synthetic, 554–556
Foot
  australopithecine, 341–342, *342*
  gorilla, *342*
  human, 340–342, *342*
Footprints
  australopithecine, 343
  hominine, 332, *332*
Foraging, male, 311
Foramen magnum, *414*

Forebrain, 126, 143. *See also* Cerebral cortex; Cerebrum
Forensic anthropology, 459
Forest
  deciduous, 197
  tropical, 197, *197,* 233
Fort Ternan, 267, 277
Fossey, Dian, 228
Fossilization, 239
Fossil record, 83, 106, 109, 127
  analysis of, 239–242
  of australopithecines, 317–325, 335
  of *Australopithecus,* 298
  behavioral inferences about, 239–241
  dating, 293–297
  determining structure and function from, 239–240
  of hominines, 240–241, 278–280, 298, 301, 310, 317, 322–323, 373, 398–400
  of hominoids, 174
  of *Homo* (genus), 328, 373, 404
  of *Homo erectus,* 328, 433
  of human evolution, 264, 297, 335, 435
  Miocene, 261–262, *262,* 284–285
  of New World monkey evolution, 283
  Oligocene, 260
  of primate habitats, 195
  of primates, 149, 190, 237
  stratigraphic correlation of, 296–297
  of vertebrates, 123, 147
Fossorial, 195
Founder's effect, 99, 581
Freeman, Leslie, 394
Frisancho, A. R., 511

Gajdusek, D. C., 558
Galagos, 157, *161,* 161–162, 250–251
Galapagos Islands, 88–89, *90*
  Darwin's voyage to, 20–22
Gametes, 53
Garn, Stanley, 455, 553, 569
Garrod, Dorothy, 415
Gatherer/hunters, 229, 308, 312, 392–394, 396–397, 429–431, 561, 595
  early sapiens, 425
  modern, 397
  sex roles of, 600
Geladas (genus *Theropithecus*), 207, *208,* 208, 210, 311–312

Howler monkeys (genus *Alouatta*), 169, *221*, 221–222, 283
  habitat of, *245*
  skull of, *225*
  social organization of, 201
Hpa I, 505
  sites of, in association with sickle-cell hemoglobin gene, 492, *492*
Hrdlička, Ales, 415
Hublin, J. J., 386
Human evolution, 278–280, 287, 404, 424–425
  and diet, 308–309
  of early hominines, 317–373
  fossil record of, 264, 297, 335, 435
  in late Pleistocene, 432
  neandertal phase of, 415–420
  pattern of, 312–313
  scars of, 604–609
  small group in, 594–597
  study of, 287–289
Human growth hormone, 612
Human immunodeficiency virus I, 603
Human leukocyte antigens. *See* HLA systems
Human plasticity, 444
Human populations, biological history of, 565–589
Humans, 174–177, *177*
  anatomy of, 253
  as animals, 591–592
  β-globin genes of, *186*, *187*, 188
    map of *584*
    restriction enzyme maps of, 186,
  brain size of, relative to body size, *115*
  common ancestor with other primates, 178
  dental formula of, 258
  future of, 609–612
  globins of, 185
  growth and development of, 448–456
  hemoglobin of, 179
  learning in, 593–594
    and cultural diversity, 596–597
  locomotion of, *336*
  modern
    adaptation of, 435
    anatomy of, 429–431, 434
    biology of, 435
    emergence of, 375–435
    evolutionary appearance of, 424–425

origins of, 414–425, 585–586
  skeleton of, *247*
  taxonomy of, 120
  in modern world, 597–604
  pelvis of, 607–608, *608*
  relationship to other primates, 183–184, 188, *189*, 272
  sexual dimorphism of, 597–598
  skeleton of, 254, *606*
  skull of, *345*
  species of, 86
  spinal column of, *337*, 605–607
  taxonomy of, 180
  wrist of, *248*, *256*
Human variability. *See* Variability, human
Humerus, 129, *130*, 140
Hunting. *See also* Gatherer/hunters
  by chimpanzees, 228–229, *230*
  origins of, 425
  and sex roles, 600
Hunting response, 518, *519*
Hurd, James, 577
Hutton, James, 18
Huxley, Thomas Henry, 23, *23*, 149, 405
  caricature of, *23*
Hylobatidae, 174
Hyoid bone
  howler monkey, 224, *225*
  human, *225*
Hypervitaminosis, 530
Hypotheses, scientific, 77
Hypoxia
  acclimatization to, 519
  adjustment to, 511, 514

Iguanodon, *241*, 241–242, *242*
Ilium (plural ilia), 337
Illness, and culture, 8
Immigration, effect of, on genetic makeup of population, 81–82
Immunoglobulin A, 532–533
Immunoglobulin G, 532
Immunoglobulin M, 532
Immunoglobulins, 532
Immunological approaches, to study of primate evolution, 178–179
Immunological memory, 532–533
Immunology, 466–467
Inbreeding, 101–104, 117, 446, 576
  among Yanomama Indians, 578
Incaparina, 554–556
Incisors, 134–135
  upper, shovel-shaped, 421, *422*

Independent assortment, Mendel's law of, 54, 63
India, inbreeding in, 576
Indriids, *160*, 161–164, 251
  skull of, *245*
  social organization of, 201
Infanticide, 195
  by chimpanzees, 231
Infectious disease
  adaptation to, 532–535
  cultural adaptations to, 534–535
  nutrition and, 550–551
  physiological responses to, 532–533
Initiation codon, 39
Inner ear, arteries in, 249
Innominate bones, 129, 337
Insecticides, 84
Insectivores, 132, 133, 242–243, *243*, 283
Intelligence
  definition of, 142
  evolution of, 142, 147
  and reproduction, 578
Intergenic sequences, 40
Internal carotid artery, *153*
Interstadials, 303
Introns, *39*, 40, *186*
Iodine, deficiency of, and social organization, 559–560
Iron-deficiency anemia, 557
Ischial callosities, 170, 209–210, 253, 283
Isolates, 67

Japanese, *573*
  Ainu group of, *574*
  inbreeding among, 102
Java, 432
  hominine deposits on, 380–381
  Homo erectus in, 376–382
Jaws
  ape, 346
  australopithecine, 348, *351*, *353*
  chimpanzee, *347*
  in identifying hominines, 289–290
  modern human, 346, *347*
  of robust australopithecine, *349*
Jelinek, Arthur, 410, 427
Jerison, H. J., 142, 143
Johanson, Donald, 325, 331–332
Johnston, Francis, 552
Jolly, Clifford, 311–312
Juruma Indians, 103

Kabwe, fossil finds from, 400–401, *405*, 432